Foundations of Computer Music

Foundations of Computer Music

edited by
Curtis Roads
John Strawn

The MIT Press
Cambridge, Massachusetts
London, England

Third printing, 1987

First MIT Press paperback edition, 1987

Printed and bound in the United States of America by Edwards Brothers, Inc.

Library of Congress Cataloging in Publication Data
Main entry under title:

Foundations of computer music.

Includes bibliographic references and index.
1. Computer music. I. Roads, Curtis. II. Strawn, John, 1950–
ML1092.F7 1985   789.9   84-10001
ISBN 0-262-181142 hard
        0-262-68051-3 paper

Contents

Foreword

In the past two decades a new kind of musical instrument has been invented. It is so different from its predecessors that musicians may need another two decades to learn to play it. In the future, it will be considered the outstanding musical innovation of the twentieth century.

What is the nature of an intelligent instrument?

• It can synthesize sounds. Theoretically it can make any sound the human ear can hear. It has already achieved sounds of great richness and variety that resemble nothing ever before heard.

• It can sense the intent of the musician. It has a wide variety of sensors, ranging from traditional keys and knobs to microphones, breath-pressure sensors, eye trackers, TV cameras, and even EEG electrodes. Its sensors will seek out the performer's intent.

• It can execute a program. It includes a stored-program computer. Algorithms that can be programmed are a magic box, the contents of which have no limits except those of the programmer's imagination.

• It can remember. It recalls everything from the score of the music to the gestures of the musician to the sound itself. Memory traces can be recorded, recalled, edited, used by the program, and displayed to the musician.

Intelligent instruments already exist. Indeed, this book is primarily an account of them, of how they are made, and of how they have been played. However, so far very little music has been composed for these instruments or played upon them, and their full potential has in no way been explored. Why? The answer is simply that it takes much longer to learn to play a new instrument than to invent it. Being a musician is harder than being an instrument maker. So, we must be patient.

What are some modes in which these instruments have already been used?

• As a composer's tool. In this mode the composer puts every detail of the sound into the instrument's memory, and the instrument plays the score without a performer. Beautiful and precise music has been made in this way, but the music sometimes lacks the excitement of a live performance.

• As a "super organ." The performer controls every aspect of the sound by means of the instrument's sensors, and must make a separate gesture for each note played. Intimate control over the sound is available, but to master it requires a virtuoso. Because of the richness of its timbres, the instrument needs many controls. In this mode it is more demanding than any normal instrument.

● As a computer. The music may be realized in the form of a computer program. The program can compute aspects of the music using its own rules, read other aspects from a score the composer has put into its memory, sense still other aspects from the performer, and combine all this information in limitless numbers of ways to create the music. Truly, this mode of performance has great potential. At present it is circumscribed by the musician's understanding of what programs can and cannot do. I believe that the future belongs to this mode.

Much has already been accomplished in the twenty years computer music has lived. This volume is an excellent statement of the present position of computer music. The articles printed here give the computer musician and the musical engineer a technical foundation for their arts. These articles plus recordings of existing music give the listener a critical understanding of the nature of computer music.

Many instruments have been invented in the course of history. Only a few are used today. An instrument is a vehicle to externalize and communicate the inner feelings and ideas of the musician. Those instruments that communicate powerfully and facilely will survive; the rest will be forgotten.

The intelligent instruments that already exist promise a new age of communication in which the attention of musicians can be on their inner messages. Musicians need not worry as to whether the instrument will be powerful enough to represent the message. They need not worry whether they will be virtuosic enough to play the music. These concerns can be left to the instrument itself.

Max Mathews

Preface

Just two decades ago, computer music was an infant discipline known to only a few practitioners. This volume is evidence that the field has developed considerably since that time.

Fresh interest continues to converge on the art, science, and technology of computer music from people with a wide spectrum of skills and aesthetic visions. It is this growing interest that prompted us to prepare this book. Specifically, this volume satisfies the many requests we have received for articles from the first three volumes of *Computer Music Journal*. Many of those seminal papers were rapidly becoming unobtainable. We welcome the opportunity to make revised and updated versions of these classic papers available in book form.

Many articles in this collection can be read without a great deal of computer music background. For the student, we have also prepared *Computer Music Tutorial* (MIT Press, 1985), which provides the necessary foundation for the more advanced papers assembled here.

Computer music is an intrinsically multidisciplinary activity, as this volume demonstrates. An awareness of both the powers and the limitations of the various subdisciplines within computer music is essential for those studying the field. The composer who does not take the time to understand the underlying technical foundations of computer music will see only the surface of its full potential. Technical experts can be subject to a similar myopia in ignoring new musical developments. Products of software and hardware engineering that rely on archaic or inflexible concepts of music only nullify their own usefulness. Ultimately, musicians will bypass such designs for those that incorporate a broader and deeper sense of the musical experience.

Thus, from the standpoint of the person entering the field, learning several subdisciplines is a reasonable goal. In general, practitioners of computer music acquire detailed knowledge of a few subdisciplines and attain a good understanding and familiarity with most of the others.

We have divided this volume into four parts on the basis of an informal classification of the articles. The parts are entitled Digital Sound-Synthesis Techniques, Synthesizer Hardware and Engineering, Software Systems for Music, and Perception and Digital Signal Processing. The classification of articles into the parts is informal in the sense that many articles overlap several categories. Since it is expected that most readers will orient themselves, skip to the part that covers their immediate interest, and proceed through selected articles thereafter, each part has been made self-contained, with its own overview. The overview sums up the contents of a part, places it in historical perspective, and refers to related articles in other parts.

Part I begins with a look at sound-synthesis techniques. A synthesis technique is essentially a model (often expressed as a formula) for generating sound. Such models are often based on natural sounds, but other models can be used as well. Musical sound synthesis by computer (or computer-controlled digital synthesizers) remains one of the most active areas of research and experimentation.

Every digital process involving sound takes place on some actual machine. As part II demonstrates, knowing the engineering constraints (both the limitations and the capabilities) underlying signal-processing computers can be essential to the effective realization of a musical idea. Synthesizers may also incorporate algorithms for sound analysis and signal processing in their internal architecture. Many issues in real-time computation and musical interaction are directly confronted in the design of a digital synthesizer.

Software systems for music—the subject of part III—integrate all the necessary score- and sound-processing software and hardware into a usable package. Programming a music system is a formidable job, especially when the goals include musical flexibility and ease of use. Programmers must continually balance the often conflicting constraints of computational efficiency and software complexity. The range of implemented software systems for music is broad, including languages for controlling synthesis hardware as well as systems to assist the composer in compositional tasks.

As the articles in part IV make clear, sound analysis by computer (or by a computer-controlled digital signal processor) can lead to useful insights in acoustics and musical perception. This, in turn, can lead to practical applications in the design of more convincing sound-processing effects. Musical composition itself may be influenced by the results of perceptual research as composers learn to manipulate musical structure in perceptual terms.

Within a single volume it would be impossible to do justice to the breadth of computer music activities. This volume concentrates mostly on the technical side of computer music, leaving the artistic side to be covered in other publications and in the music. But even the technical aspects of computer music are too broad to cover fully in a collection of this size. We have limited this book to articles from the first three volumes of *Computer Music Journal*, with the exception of the paper by R. Cann, part of which appeared in issue 4(1). Later issues of *Computer Music Journal* can be obtained from The MIT Press and can be found in many libraries. These issues explore many important topics not covered here.

Acknowledgments

John Snell, the founding editor of *Computer Music Journal*, contributed to the project in the initial stages, sharing his time in numerous planning sessions. Later, he was unfortunately forced to withdraw from the project because of professional commitments, but he had already made an impact on the form and the spirit of the book.

We thank Stephen McAdams, who between doctoral studies in psychoacoustics at Stanford and research at IRCAM managed to prepare many fine technical illustrations for this book.

We are deeply indebted to the Massachusetts Institute of Technology and Stanford University for their support and facilities, with special thanks to the Experimental Music Studio and the Artificial Intelligence Laboratory at MIT and to the Center for Computer Research in Music and Acoustics and the Artificial Intelligence Laboratory at Stanford.

We dedicate this book to our colleagues, the authors whose work created this field and who joined with us in completing this project. Finally, we thank our close friends and our families for their patience and understanding over the long haul.

Curtis Roads
John Strawn

Foundations of Computer Music

I DIGITAL SOUND-SYNTHESIS TECHNIQUES

Overview

JOHN STRAWN

Synthesis techniques are central to the idea of digitally generated sound. The computer or other digital synthesis hardware must be instructed in some fashion to produce the sound. A synthesis technique is a set of rules for ordering and controlling those instructions.

It is a popular assumption that the computer can create any sound. While this may be theoretically possible, the difficulty lies in specifying the sound with sufficient accuracy without getting bogged down in minute details. Part of the training of the computer musician consists of learning the "handles" provided by synthesis techniques and learning how to manipulate them to achieve the desired musical ends, whether at the level of part of a note or at the level of an entire concert.

The last few years have brought the development of a wide variety of digital synthesis techniques, many of them discussed in this part. The emphasis on *digital* is important here. Many of these techniques have been known in one form or another for decades or even centuries, but, for the most part, their application in the realm of audio synthesis became feasible only with the development of digital technology.

Some of these techniques are motivated by the desire to replicate the sounds of traditional instruments; the precision attainable with the digital computer makes such a possibility attractive indeed. Other synthesis techniques offer ease of implementation, or the capability of producing more sounds (or more complex sounds) with a given amount of hardware. Some techniques have been derived from particularly elegant mathematical gymnastics. Inevitably, compositional issues enter into the formulation of a synthesis technique; the possibility of composing the microstructure of sound along with the rest of the musical work provided part of the motivation for the founding of electronic music studios in Europe after World War II (Stockhausen 1953). This same concern can be found in some of the work presented here.

In this brief overview, it will be impossible to do justice to the history or the scope of synthesis techniques. A more technical discussion can be found in Moorer 1977. However, I will at least mention each of the synthesis techniques represented in this part, and in many cases I will provide pointers to related work in the field (see also Chamberlin 1980).

The most straightforward way of instructing a computer to synthesize a sound is to record the sound into the computer and then play the sound back. Once the sound is recorded, it can be manipulated by the computer in a manner analogous to musique concrète. Many composers have explored these possibilities in the digital domain. A similar approach, which might be called wavetable lookup synthesis, has been used successfully at the Institut de Recherche et Coordination Acoustique/Musique (Barlow 1980).

Historically, additive synthesis is the most important and influential synthesis technique. A technical overview is given in Moorer 1977. This technique often serves as a standard against which other synthesis techniques are measured. Briefly, additive synthesis can be explained by analogy to light. Light can be broken down into its constituent spectral components by passing it through a prism; every shade of light has its own characteristic mixture of spectral components. In the same way, sound can be passed through the equivalent of a prism in order to break it down into its spectrum. Usually these spectral components look like the sine or cosine curves (sinusoids) of trigonometry. Of course, the individual spectral components of light are not ordinarily visible, except in rainbows. Likewise, we do not ordinarily hear the separate spectral components of a sound. However, it is possible to replicate a given sound to a high degree of accuracy by adding together the proper audio spectral components; hence the name additive synthesis. A next step, then, is to add together some arbitrary set of spectral components in order to make previously unheard sounds. The theory for this synthesis technique is closely tied to models of sound and auditory perception that date back to the ancient Greeks. Thus, this technique has dominated thinking about synthesis for a considerable amount of time. Risset's early *Catalogue* (1968), for example, included several additive-synthesis instruments. Many of the synthesizers currently available on the commercial keyboard market and many of the other synthesizers discussed in part II are built around this technique.

In spite of its prominent position, additive synthesis has some drawbacks. One of these is the immense amount of data needed to accurately specify the spectral components. As Rolnick shows in article 25, handling this much data can bring a synthesis system to its knees.

Frequency modulation (FM) is well known to lovers of high-quality radio. It turns out that the same formulas that form the basis for FM radio transmission can also be used to generate musical sound. Like additive synthesis, FM permits control of the audio spectrum with enough precision so that the composer has adequate control of the resulting sounds.

In many cases FM turns out to be more economical in terms of the hardware required to produce a given sound and the amount of data needed to specify a sound. FM is introduced here with the classic paper (article 1) of Chowning, who developed the technique and provided early compositional examples, such as his work *Turenas* (1972). Morrill (article 2) and Schottstaedt (article 4) offer applications of FM to the replication of sounds of traditional instruments, such as the trumpet tones used in Morrill's *Six Dark Questions* (1978–79). Chowning (1980) has also extended FM to the realistic simulation of vocal tones, as in his work *Phōnē* (1981). LeBrun (article 5) and Schottstaedt present an extension of FM theory beyond that given by Chowning in article 1. The variant of triangle FM developed by Saunders (included here, in a corrected and expanded version, as article 3) offers implementational advantages, especially for small computers. Finally, Truax (article 6) presents an approach to compositional structure based on some inherent properties of FM. Since this article first appeared, Truax has continued to explore this area, as shown by his composition *Arras* (Truax 1982). Some other compositional applications derived from this technique are discussed in Holtzman 1981.

A corresponding synthesis technique, amplitude modulation (AM), although widely exploited in analog studios, has not yet found widespread use in digital studios. Dashow (1980) has explored some compositional applications.

Pioneering studies of waveshaping were conducted by LeBrun (1979) and Arfib (1979). Roads offers a less technical, less mathematically demanding introduction in article 7. In article 8, Beauchamp presents the results of his work attempting to emulate the sounds of traditional instruments, in this case the cornet. Beauchamp's approach is practically indistinguishable from waveshaping as a synthesis technique, although his work was done independent of LeBrun and Arfib.

A related set of techniques known as summation formulas are discussed in Moorer 1976 and Moorer 1977.

A considerable amount of work has been devoted to modeling the behavior of the physical parts of a musical instrument with mathematical formulas (see, for example, Hiller and Ruiz 1971 and Smith 1983). However, this approach has not yet found widespread use in synthesis for composition.

Another large class of synthesis techniques is subsumed under the term *subtractive synthesis.* Rather than adding together a selected number of spectral components, as in additive synthesis, the subtractive approach starts with an easily generated signal rich in spectral components (such as noise or a pulse train) and attempts to produce the desired result through a series of filtering operations. In article 9, Cann offers an introduction to linear prediction, which can be used as a kind of time-varying subtractive synthesis. Linear prediction has been used in a variety of compositions, such as those by Charles Dodge and Paul Lansky. A variant of linear prediction called cross synthesis (Petersen 1975, 1976) allows the composer to cross one instrument or sound with another, producing talking orchestras and other unusual effects.

Synthesis by instruction is a technique that has not yet been widely adopted at the majority of studios, perhaps because it is difficult to relate this technique to the sounds produced by traditional instruments. However, as Berg discusses in article 11, this is a technique that is truly wedded to the computer. Berg's article includes part of a composition realized with this technique.

The theory of granular synthesis, on the other hand, was developed before digital audio synthesis became popular. Roads discusses its history and theory and provides a useful introduction in article 10.

References

Arfib, D. 1979. "Digital synthesis of complex spectra by means of multiplication of non-linear distorted sine waves." *Journal of the Audio Engineering Society* 27: 757–768.

Barlow, C. 1980. "Bus journey to Parametron." *Feedback Papers* 21–23.

Chamberlin, H. 1980. *Musical Applications of Microprocessors*. Rochelle Park, N.J.: Hayden.

Chowning, J. 1980. "Computer synthesis of the singing voice." In *Sound Generation in Winds, Strings, Computers*, compiled by Johan Sundberg. Stockholm: Royal Institute of Technology.

Dashow, J. 1980. "Spectra as chords." *Computer Music Journal* 4(1): 43–52.

Hiller, L., and P. Ruiz. 1971. "Synthesizing musical sounds by solving the wave equation for vibrating objects. Part 1." *Journal of the Audio Engineering Society* 19: 463–470.

Holtzman, S. R. 1981. "Using generative grammars for music composition." *Computer Music Journal* 5(1): 51–64.

LeBrun, M. 1979. "Digital waveshaping synthesis." *Journal of the Audio Engineering Society* 27(4): 250–266.

Moorer, J. A. 1976. "The synthesis of complex audio spectra by means of discrete summation formulae." *Journal of the Audio Engineering Society* 24: 717–727.

Moorer, J. A. 1977. "Signal processing aspects of computer music—A survey." *Proceedings of the IEEE* 65(8): 1108–1137.

Petersen, T. L. 1975. "Vocal tract modulation of instrumental sounds by digital filtering." In J. Beauchamp and J. Melby, eds., *Proceedings of the Second Annual Music Computation Conference*, part 1: Synthesis Techniques. Urbana: Office of Continuing Education, University of Illinois, 1975.

Petersen, T. L. 1976. Composing with Cross-Synthesis. Presented at 1976 International Computer Music Conference, Massachussetts Institute of Technology.

Risset, J.-C. 1968. *An Introductory Catalogue of Computer Synthesized Sounds*. Murray Hill, N.J.: Bell Telephone Laboratories.

Smith, J. O. 1983. Techniques for Digital Filter Design and System Identification with Application to the Violin. Ph.D. diss., Department of Electrical Engineering, Stanford University.

Stockhausen, K. 1953. "Arbeitsbericht 1953: Die Entstehung der elektronischen Musik." In *Texte zur elektronischen und instrumentalen Musik*, Vol. 1. Cologne: DuMont, 1963.

Truax, B. 1980. "Timbral construction as a stochastic process." In *Proceedings of the 1980 International Computer Music Conference*. San Francisco: Computer Music Association.

Truax, B. 1982. "Timbral construction in *Arras* as a stochastic process." *Computer Music Journal* 6(3): 72–77.

1 The Synthesis of Complex Audio Spectra by Means of Frequency Modulation

JOHN M. CHOWNING

Of interest in both acoustical research and electronic music is the synthesis of natural sound. For the researcher, it is the ultimate test of acoustical theory, while for the composer of electronic music it is an extraordinarily rich point of departure in the domain of timbre, or tone quality. The synthesis of natural sounds has been elusive; however, recent research in computer analysis and synthesis of some tones of musical instruments (Risset and Mathews 1969) has yielded an insight which may prove to have general relevance in all natural sounds: The character of the temporal evolution of the spectral components is of critical importance in the determination of timbre.

In natural sounds the amplitudes of the frequency components of the spectrum are time-variant, or dynamic. The energy of the components often evolves in complicated ways, in particular during the attack and decay portions of the sound. The temporal evolution of the spectrum is in some cases easily followed, as with bells, whereas in other cases it is not, because the evolution occurs in a very short time period, but it is nevertheless perceived and is an important cue in the recognition of timbre. Many natural sounds seem to have characteristic spectral evolutions which, in addition to providing their "signature," are largely responsible for what we judge to be their lively quality. In contrast, it is largely the fixed proportion spectrum of most synthesized sounds that so readily imparts to the listener the electronic cue and the lifeless quality.

The special application of the equation for frequency modulation, described below, allows the production of complex spectra with very great simplicity. The fact that the temporal evolution of the frequency components of the spectrum can be easily controlled is perhaps the most striking attribute of the technique, for dynamic spectra are achieved only with considerable difficulty using current techniques of synthesis. At the end of this chapter some simulations of brass, woodwind, and percussive sounds are given. The importance of these simulations is as much in their elegance and simplicity as it is in their accuracy. This frequency modulation technique, although not a physical model for natural sound, is shown to be a very powerful perceptual model for at least some.

Frequency Modulation

Frequency modulation (FM) is well understood as applied in radio transmission, but the relevant equations have not been applied in any significant way to the generation of audio spectra where both the carrier and the modulating frequencies are in the audio band and the side frequencies form the spectrum directly.

In FM, the instantaneous frequency of a carrier wave is varied according to a modulating wave, such that the rate at which the carrier varies is the frequency of the modulating wave, or modulating frequency. The amount the carrier varies around its average, or the peak frequency deviation, is proportional to the amplitude of the modulating wave. The parameters of a frequency-modulated signal are c (carrier frequency or average frequency), m (modulating frequency), and d (peak deviation). The equation for a frequency-modulated wave of peak amplitude A where both the carrier and modulating waves are sinusoids is

$$e = A \sin(\alpha t + I \sin \beta t) \tag{1}$$

where e = the instantaneous amplitude of the modulated carrier, α = the carrier frequency in rad/sec, β = the modulating frequency in rad/sec, and $I = d/m$ = the modulation index (the ratio of the peak deviation to the modulating frequency). It is obvious that when $I = 0$ the frequency deviation must also be 0 and there is no modulation. When I is greater than 0, however, frequencies occur above and below the carrier frequency at intervals of the modulating frequency. The number of side frequencies which occur is related to the modulation index in such a way that as I increases from 0, energy is "stolen" from the carrier and distributed among an increasing number of side frequencies. This increasing bandwidth as I increases is shown in figure 1.1, with a constant modulating frequency.

The amplitudes of the carrier and sideband components are determined by Bessel functions of the first kind and the nth order, $J_n(I)$, the argument to which is the modulation index. The first six Bessel functions, J_0 through J_5, are shown in figure 1.2. The zeroth-order Bessel function and index I, $J_0(I)$, yields an amplitude scaling coefficient for the carrier frequency; the first-order, $J_1(I)$, yields a scaling coefficient for the first upper- and lower-side frequencies; the second-order, $J_2(I)$, for the second upper- and lower-side frequencies; and so forth. The higher the order of the side frequency the larger the index must be for that side frequency to have significant

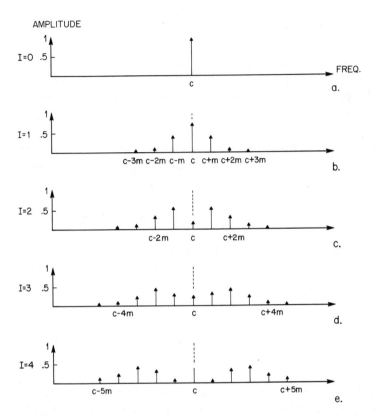

Figure 1.1
Example to show increasing bandwidth with increasing modulation index *I*. The upper and lower side frequencies are at intervals of the modulating frequency *m* and are symmetrical around the carrier *c*.

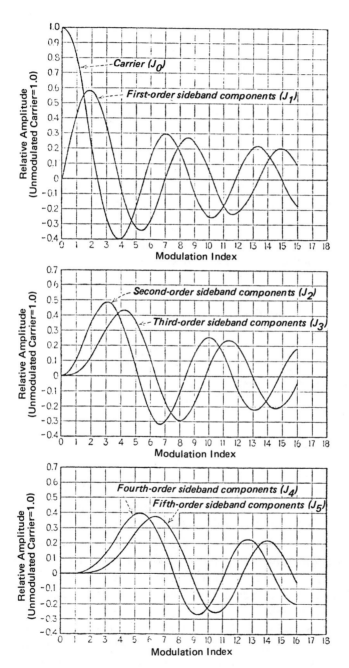

Figure 1.2
Bessel functions determining the amplitudes of the sideband components.

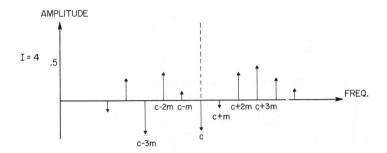

Figure 1.3
Plot of figure 1.1e with phase information included (the modulation index is 4). The bars extending downward represent spectral components whose phases differ by 180°.

amplitude. The total bandwidth is approximately equal to twice the sum of the frequency deviation and the modulating frequency, or

$$BW \approx 2(d + m).$$

All of the above relationships are expressed in the following trigonometric expansion:

$$
\begin{aligned}
e = A\{J_0(I)\sin\alpha t \\
+ J_1(I)[\sin(\alpha + \beta)t - \sin(\alpha - \beta)t] \\
+ J_2(I)[\sin(\alpha + 2\beta)t + \sin(\alpha - 2\beta)t] \\
+ J_3(I)[\sin(\alpha + 3\beta)t - \sin(\alpha - 3\beta)t] \\
+ \cdots\}.
\end{aligned}
\tag{2}
$$

It can be seen in equation 2 that the odd-order lower-side frequencies, $\sin(\alpha - \beta)$, $\sin(\alpha - 3\beta)$, etc., are preceded by a negative sign, and that for an index greater than 2.5 the Bessel functions (figure 1.2) will yield a negative scaling coefficient for some components. Ordinarily, these negative signs are ignored in plotting spectra, as in figure 1.1, since they simply indicate a phase inversion of the frequency component, $-\sin(\theta) = \sin(-\theta)$. In the application of FM described below, this phase information is significant and must be considered in plotting spectra.

By way of demonstration, figure 1.1e is plotted, but with the phase information included, in figure 1.3. The carrier and the first upper-side frequency are plotted with a downward bar representing the phase inversion resulting from the negative Bessel coefficients. The importance of noting the phase inversions will be seen in the following section.

Reflected Side Frequencies

The special richness of this FM technique lies in the fact that there are ratios of the carrier and modulating frequencies and values of the index that will produce sideband components that fall in the negative frequency domain of the spectrum. These negative components reflect around 0 Hz and "mix" with the components in the positive domain. The variety of frequency relations that result from this mix is vast and includes both harmonic and inharmonic spectra.

A simple but very useful example of reflected side frequencies occurs if the ratio of the carrier to modulating frequencies is unity. A spectrum for the values $c = 100$ Hz, $m = 100$ Hz, and $I = 4$ is plotted in figure 1.4a. The component at 0 Hz represents a constant in the wave. The remaining lower-side frequencies are reflected into the positive frequency domain with a change of sign (inversion of phase) and add algebraically to the components which are already there as shown in figure 1.4b. For example, the second lower-side frequency will add to the carrier with like signs, therefore increasing the energy at 100 Hz, while the third lower-side frequency will add to the first upper-side frequency with unlike signs, decreasing the energy at 200 Hz. The spectrum, adjusted for the reflected frequency components and with the bars all up to reveal the spectral envelope, is shown in figure 1.4c.

Harmonic and Inharmonic Spectra

The significance of the case above, where the ratio of the carrier to the modulating frequencies is 1/1, is that it is a member of the class of ratios of integers (rational numbers); thus,

$$c/m = N_1/N_2$$

and N_1 and N_2 are integers. These ratios result in harmonic spectra. If, in addition, all common factors have been divided out of N_1 and N_2, then the fundamental frequency of the modulated wave will be

$$f_0 = c/N_1 = m/N_2.$$

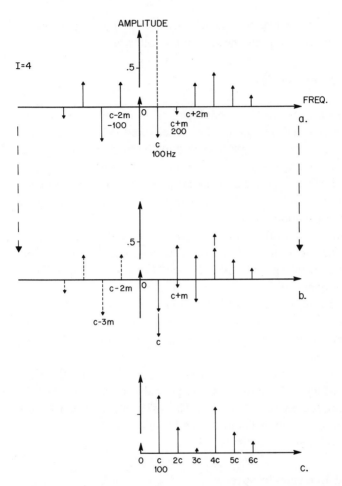

Figure 1.4
(a) Spectrum with components lying in the negative frequency domain. (b) Plot from part a in which the frequencies in the negative domain are reflected around 0 Hz with an inversion of phase and added to the components in the positive domain. (c) Plot of the magnitude of the components of b.

The position of the side frequencies in the harmonic series can be determined from

$$k = N_1 \pm nN_2, \qquad n = 0, 1, 2, 3, \ldots$$

where k is the harmonic number and n is the order side frequency. Except for $n = 0$, the carrier, there are two values for k for each order, corresponding to the upper and lower side frequencies.

Some useful generalizations can be made in regard to simple ratios:

• The carrier is always the N_1th harmonic in the series.
• If $N_2 = 1$, the spectrum contains all harmonics and the fundamental is at the modulating frequency, e.g., 1/1, 2/1.
• When N_2 is an even number, the spectrum contains only odd-numbered harmonics, e.g., 1/2, 1/4, 3/2, 3/4, 5/2.
• If $N_2 = 3$, every third harmonic is missing from the series, e.g., 1/3, 2/3, 4/3, 5/3.

As noted before, the actual number of harmonics that will have significant amplitude is dependent on the modulation index. For small indices and ratios where $N_1 \neq 1$, the fundamental may not be present in the spectrum. This can be seen in the spectra plotted in figure 1.5, where $c/m = 4/1$. Adjusted for the reflected side frequencies, the spectra show the filling out of the harmonics with an increasing index. The fundamental becomes significant only when the index is greater than 2.

Inharmonic spectra will result from ratios of irrational numbers, e.g., $c/m = 1/\sqrt{2}$, $\pi/\sqrt{3}$, $1/e$. In this case, the reflected side frequencies will fall between the positive components, thus forming a spectrum whose components are not in a relation of simple ratios. Figure 1.6 shows an adjusted spectrum where $c/m \cong 1/\sqrt{2}$ and the index is 5.

In summary, the ratio of the carrier and modulating frequencies (c/m) determines the position of the components in the spectrum when there are reflected side frequencies, while the modulation index (d/m) determines the number of components that will have significant amplitude.

Dynamic Spectra

As demonstrated above, the equation for FM has an inherent and, as will be shown, most useful characteristic: The complexity of the spectrum is related to the modulation index in such a way that, as the index in-

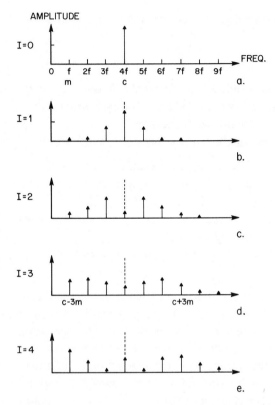

Figure 1.5
Plot of spectrum where $c/m = 4/1$. As the index increases, the reflected lower-side
frequencies begin to affect the spectrum where $I = 3$, where the fundamental, $c - 3m$, is
noticeably greater than the seventh harmonic, $c + 3m$. In part e, the symmetry around the
carrier is no longer apparent.

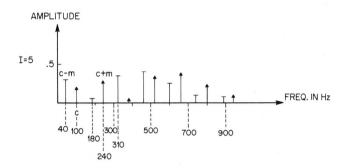

Figure 1.6
Inharmonic spectrum where $c/m \cong 1/\sqrt{2}$ and the modulation index is 5. The reflected components, represented here with the bar at the top, fall between the other components.

creases, the bandwidth of the spectrum also increases (see figure 1.5). If, then, the modulation index were made to be a function of time, the evolution of the bandwidth of the spectrum could be generally described by the shape of the function. The evolution of each of the components of the spectrum, however, is determined by the shape of the Bessel functions. Therefore, if the index increases with time, the overall bandwidth will also increase, but a given component will either increase or decrease in amplitude depending on the slope of the Bessel function at that index range. Figure 1.7 is a three-dimensional representation of a dynamic FM spectrum where $c/m = 1/1$ and the modulation index increases in time from 0 to 4. If the index sweeps over a very large range, for example from 2 to 10, the amplitudes of the components will oscillate around 0 amplitude as the bandwidth of the spectrum increases.

The presence of reflected side frequencies in a dynamic spectrum enormously complicates the evolution of the individual components, to the extent that it is difficult to visualize the amplitude functions with any precision. It is possible to gain an intuitive feeling for their tendency of change, which in the research presented here has proved to be largely sufficient. (A dynamic computer display program was very helpful in visualizing the spectra which result from a changing index and reflected side frequencies. Given a ratio of carrier to modulating frequencies and an initial and terminal index, the program plots the changing spectrum.)

Certainly the complexity in the evolution of each of the components of the spectrum makes an important contribution to the lively quality of FM sounds. Because this complexity is a function of the laws of the

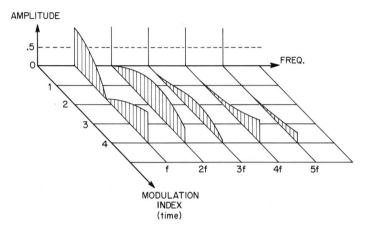

Figure 1.7
Dynamic spectrum where $c/m = 1/1$ and the modulation index increases from 0 to 4 continuously. The increasing bandwidth is easily seen, but because the spectrum includes the reflected side frequencies the evolution of the individual components is not always intuitively clear.

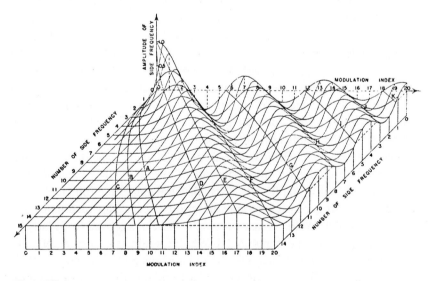

Figure 1.8
Bessel functions J_0 through J_{15} and indices 0 through 20. This representation allows a rapid determination of the bandwidth resulting from a given index.

equation, it is surprising that while the evolution of the components is rigidly determined they can still produce such rich and varied subjective impressions.

In visualizing the effect of sweeping the modulation index, a careful study of figure 1.8 is helpful. This is a three-dimensional representation of the orders J_0 through J_{15} for an index range of 0 through 20 and is a sufficient range of orders and indexes for many useful dynamic spectra. Contour lines A, B, and C represent constant values of the functions at $J_n(I) = 0.01, 0.001$, and 0.0001 respectively. Line A, then, indicates which order side frequency is just significant at a given index. Line D represents the order of the function which is equal to the argument, or $J_n(I)$ where $n = I$. This relation shows that any orders of side frequencies greater than the value of the index decrease rapidly in importance. Line E is the absolute maximum amplitude for each order. Lines F, G, H, I, J, and K show the zero crossings of the functions and, therefore, values of the index that will produce a null or zero amplitude for various orders of side frequencies.

Implementation

The research described here was done using a Digital Equipment Corporation PDP-10 computer for which there is a special sound-synthesis program designed to make optimum use of the time-sharing capability of the machine. Implementation of this research, however, will be described for Music V, a sound-synthesis program that is both well documented and generally available (Mathews 1969).

Music V is a program that generates samples or a numerical representation of a sound pressure wave according to data that specify the physical characteristics of the sound. The samples are stored on a memory device as they are computed. On completion of the computation, the samples are passed at a fixed sampling rate (typically 10,000–30,000 samples/sec) to a digital-to-analog converter, which generates a sequence of voltage pulses whose amplitudes are proportional to the samples. The pulses are smoothed by a low-pass filter and passed to an audio system.

The program is designed so that the computation of the samples is done by program blocks called unit generators. A typical unit generator is an oscillator with two inputs, an output, and a stored waveshape function. The first input specifies the amplitude of the output, the second

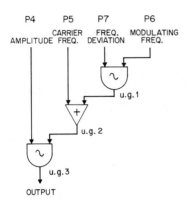

Figure 1.9
Simple FM circuit as represented in Music V notation.

input the frequency of the output, and the function determines the shape of the output. The value of an input can be specified by the user or can be the output from another unit generator, thereby allowing multilevel operations on waveforms. A collection of interconnected unit generators is called an instrument, which is supplied data through a set of parameters, $P_1, \ldots, P_n$, set by the user. P_1 and P_3 are reserved for beginning time and duration of the note the instrument is to play, and P_2 is reserved for the instrument number. The remaining parameters are assigned their function by the user.

Figure 1.9 is an instrument diagram showing three unit generators, two oscillators and an adder. The function for each oscillator is defined to be a sinusoid. This instrument is capable of producing complex FM spectra such as the one in figure 1.4 where the following values are now assigned to parameters:

$P_4 = 1,000 =$ Amplitude of modulated carrier (arbitrary scaling),

$P_5 = 100$ Hz $=$ Carrier frequency,

$P_6 = 100$ Hz $=$ Modulating frequency,

$P_7 = 400$ Hz $=$ Frequency deviation, for $I = 4$.

Since $I = d/m$, then $d = Im$ and for $I = 4$ the peak deviation is 400 Hz. Oscillator 1 produces a sinusoidal output whose amplitude is scaled by P_7 to be 400 Hz at a frequency of 100 Hz given by P_6.

In the case above, which is typical of this application of FM, the instantaneous frequency of the modulated carrier becomes negative at times. That is, from equation 1, the sum of αt (a ramp function) and $I\sin\beta t$ (a sinusoid with amplitude I) can produce a curve that has a negative slope at certain points and, therefore, a phase angle that decreases with time! This condition occurs when either the ratio of the carrier to the modulating frequency is very small or the modulation index is very large. The oscillator (u.g. 3 in figure 1.9) must be able to produce a wave that results from taking the sine of an angle that decreases as well as increases with time. The change in code to the oscillator in Music V to allow for a decreasing angle is the following: For

```
290  IF(SUM-XNFUN) 288, 287, 287
287  SUM=SUM-XNFUN
```

substitute

```
290  IF(SUM.GE.XNFUN) GO TO 287
     IF(SUM.LT. 0.0) GO TO 289
```

and for

```
     GO TO 293
292  J6=L1+J3-1
```

substitute

```
     GO TO 293
287  SUM=SUM-XNFUN
     GO TO 288
289  SUM=SUM+XNFUN
     GO TO 288
292  J6=L1+J3-1.
```

In order to specify the modulation index as a function of time and control the attack and decay of the modulated carrier, it is necessary to alter the instrument shown in figure 1.9 by adding three more unit generators. In figure 1.10, u.g. 4 and u.g. 5 are time-domain function generators (oscillators or envelope generators in Music V). U.g. 4 imposes an amplitude envelope on the modulated carrier, and u.g. 5 and u.g. 6 together allow dynamic control of the modulation index. The parameters for this instrument will have the following functions:

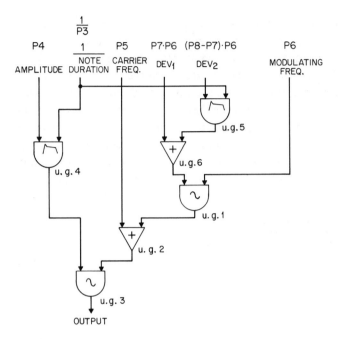

Figure 1.10
FM circuit to produce dynamic spectra. Two function generators, u.g. 4 and u.g. 5, are added to produce an amplitude envelope and a modulation index envelope that will cause the bandwidth to vary.

P_1 = Begin time of instrument,

P_2 = Instrument number,

P_3 = Duration of "note,"

P_4 = Amplitude of output wave,

P_5 = Carrier frequency,

P_6 = Modulating frequency,

P_7 = Modulation index 1, I_1,

P_8 = Modulation index 2, I_2.

Since the bandwidth is related directly to the modulation index (and only indirectly to the deviation), a special routine can be used to produce the

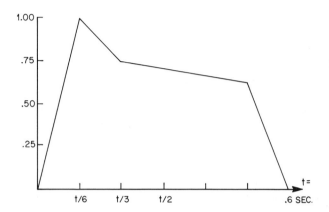

Figure 1.11
Envelope function for brasslike tones.

required deviation, $P_7 \times P_6$ or $(P_8 - P_7) \times P_6$. The same routine can also generate the frequency inputs for u.g. 4 and u.g. 5, such that $P_9 = 1/P_3$ where the relation 1/(note duration) causes the functions associated with these generators to be sampled at a rate so that one period is completed in the duration P_3. The oscillator and the adder, u.g. 5 and u.g. 6, are related in such a way that P_7 becomes the value of the modulation index when the output of u.g. 5 is 0 and P_8 is the modulation index when the output of u.g. 5 is 1. For example, if figure 1.11 represents the function for the oscillator u.g. 5 and

$P_3 = 0.6$ sec,

$P_6 = 100$ Hz,

$P_7 = 2$,

$P_8 = 8$,

first, P_7 and $P_8 - P_7$ are multiplied by P_6 to convert to deviation, then the function is scaled by 600 and added to the constant input to the adder of 200. The output of the adder, then, is a deviation increasing from 200 to 800 in the first 1/6 sec, decreasing from 800 to 650 in the next 1/6 sec, etc. If the values of P_7 and P_8 are reversed, the function is inverted but between the same limits. Having this capability of scaling the deviation in direct or inverse proportion to the function and between any two values for I_1 and I_2 is useful in generating various dynamic spectra.

Simulations of Instrument Tones

In this section, techniques for simulating three classes of instrument tones will be defined using the computer instrument shown in figure 1.10.

Brasslike Tones

Risset demonstrated in his revealing analysis of trumpet tones a fundamental characteristic of this class of timbres: The amount of energy in the spectrum is distributed over an increasing band in approximate proportion to the increase of intensity (Risset and Mathews 1969). A simulation of this class of timbres is developed around the following premises:

• The frequencies in the spectrum are in the harmonic series.
• Both odd- and even-numbered harmonics are at some times present.
• The higher harmonics increase in significance with intensity.
• The rise time of the amplitude is rapid for a typical attack and may "overshoot" the steady state.

Oscillators u.g. 4 and u.g. 5 in figure 1.10 control the amplitude and modulation index (deviation indirectly), and both use the time-domain function shown in figure 1.11. The parameter values for a brasslike tone can be

$P_3 = 0.6,$

$P_4 = 1,000$ (amplitude scaling),

$P_5 = 440$ Hz,

$P_6 = 440$ Hz ($c/m = 1/1$),

$P_7 = 0,$

$P_8 = 5.$

The modulation index (therefore deviation) changes in direct proportion to the amplitude of the modulated carrier wave, the result being an increase or a decrease in significance of the side frequencies in proportion

Figure 1.12
Envelope function for woodwindlike tones.

to the amplitude envelope function. The ratio $c/m = 1/1$ produces components that fall in the harmonic series. By changing the values of the indices by small amounts and the shape of the function, a large number of variations can be achieved.

Woodwindlike Tones

It is sometimes the case with woodwinds and organ pipes that the first frequencies to become prominent during the attack are the higher harmonics, which then decrease in prominence as the lower harmonics increase during the steady state. This type of spectral evolution can be achieved in several ways—for example, by setting the carrier frequency to be an integral multiple of the modulating frequency, or by making the index function inversely proportional to the amplitude function. A simulation of this class of timbres is developed around the following premises:

• The frequencies in the spectrum are in the harmonic series and for some woodwind tones are predominantly odd-numbered harmonics.
• The higher harmonics may decrease in significance with the attack.

In the first example, the carrier frequency is three times the modulating frequency, or $c/m = 3/1$, and the amplitude and index function is shown in figure 1.12. Since during the attack the index increases from 0 to 2, the carrier (third harmonic) will be apparent at the onset of the tone and then quickly decrease as the side frequencies fill out the spectrum. The parameters are

$P_5 = 900$ Hz,

$P_6 = 300$ Hz,

$P_7 = 0$,

$P_8 = 2$.

A ratio of $c/m = 5/1$ will produce a bassoonlike timbre in the lower octaves. The functions remain as above and the parameters are

$P_5 = 500$ Hz,

$P_6 = 100$ Hz,

$P_7 = 0$,

$P_8 = 1.5$.

Another reed quality can be produced by choosing a ratio of c/m that yields the odd harmonics. The parameters

$P_5 = 900$ Hz,

$P_6 = 600$ Hz,

$P_7 = 4$,

$P_8 = 2$

will produce a clarinetlike timbre where 300 Hz is the fundamental and the index is inversely proportional to the amplitude function. The band-width of the spectrum will decrease as the amplitude increases during the attack.

In all of the above examples, small alterations can make the sounds more interesting and/or realistic. A particularly useful alteration is the addition of a small constant to the modulating frequency. If the value 0.5 Hz were added, for example, the reflected lower-side frequencies would not fall exactly on the upper-side frequencies, producing a beat frequency or tremulant of 1 Hz. The realism can be further improved by making the function controlling the index the same as the amplitude function only through the attack and the steady state and thereafter remaining constant. If figure 1.12 is the shape of the amplitude function, then figure 1.13 is the shape of the index function. The evolution of the spectrum during the attack is apparently not always reversed during the decay.

Percussive Sounds

A general characteristic of percussive sounds is that the decay shape of the envelope is roughly exponential, as shown in figure 1.14. A simulation of this class of timbres would be developed around the premises that the

Figure 1.13
Special envelope function for modulation index to achieve a better approximation to a woodwind timbre.

Figure 1.14
Exponential decaying envelope for bell-like timbres.

spectral components are not usually in the harmonic series and the evolution of the spectrum is from the complex to the simple.

Bell-like sounds can be produced by making the change of the index directly proportional to the amplitude envelope. Figure 1.14, then, is the function for the amplitude and the index. The parameters can be the following:

$P_3 = 15$ sec,

$P_4 = 1,000$,

$P_5 = 200$ Hz,

$P_6 = 280$ Hz,

$P_7 = 0$,

$P_8 = 10$.

The ratio $c/m = 1/1.4$ results in an inharmonic relation of the frequency components. With the large initial index the spectrum is dense. As the amplitude decreases the spectrum gradually becomes simple. As the amplitude approaches 0, the predominant frequency is the carrier at 200 Hz. By changing the amplitude function to that shown in figure 1.15, and with the parameters

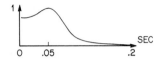

Figure 1.15
Modification of exponential envelope to obtain drumlike sound.

Figure 1.16
Envelope for wood-drum sound.

$P_3 = 0.2,$

$P_5 = 200 \text{ Hz},$

$P_6 = 280 \text{ Hz},$

$P_7 = 0,$

$P_8 = 2,$

a drumlike sound can be produced. The principal difference from the bell sound, in addition to the short duration, is the vastly reduced initial bandwidth of the spectrum.

A wood-drum sound is produced by keeping the previous amplitude function but modulating the index according to the function shown in figure 1.16. The parameters are

$P_3 = 0.2,$

$P_5 = 80 \text{ Hz},$

$P_6 = 55 \text{ Hz},$

$P_7 = 0,$

$P_8 = 25.$

The change of the index causes a burst of energy distributed over a wide frequency band at the onset, followed by rapid decrease of the bandwidth

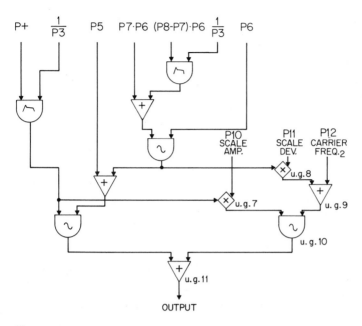

Figure 1.17
FM circuit allowing greater control over the spectrum. The additional carrier wave uses the same modulating wave, but the deviation can be scaled up or down by the multiplier. A formant peak can be placed at an arbitrary point in the spectrum.

to a sinusoid, which has the perceptual effect of a strong resonance. It should be noted that a complex amplitude modulation also occurs in this case. Because the Bessel functions are quasi-periodic around 0, the components undergo an asynchronous modulation due to the rapid sweep of the index over the wide range.

The above examples are intended to give some feeling for the power and economy of means in FM synthesis, although they by no means exhaust the potential of this instrument. With an additional five unit generators, as shown in figure 1.17, further control can be gained over the spectrum. U.g. 10 provides another carrier wave but uses the same modulating oscillator. The frequency deviation (proportional to the index) can be scaled up or down by the multiplier, u.g. 8. Since the second-carrier frequency, P_{12}, is independent, it can be set to be a multiple of the first-carrier frequency and therefore add components in another region of the spectrum. The proportion of the two modulated carriers is determined

by the multiplier, u.g. 7, which scales the amplitude before it is applied
to the second carrier. The outputs are mixed by the adder, u.g. 11. With
the parameters

$P_5 = 300$ Hz,

$P_6 = 300$ Hz,

$P_7 = 1$,

$P_8 = 3$,

$P_{10} = 0.2$,

$P_{11} = 0.5$,

$P_{12} = 2,100$ Hz,

the second carrier will add components centered around the seventh
harmonic ($c_2/m = 7/1$), where the index ranges between 0.5 and 1.5
and at an amplitude ratio of 5/1. The effect is that of a formant region
added to the spectrum.

Conclusion

The technique of FM synthesis provides a very simple temporal control
over the bandwidth of spectra whose component frequencies can have
a variety of relationships. Because "nature" is doing most of the "work,"
the technique is far simpler than additive or subtractive synthesis techniques, which can produce similar spectra. Perhaps the most surprising
aspect of the FM technique is that the seemingly limited control imposed
by "nature" over the evolution of the individual spectral components
proves to be no limitation at all as far as subjective impression is concerned. This suggests that the precise amplitude curve for each frequency
component in a complex dynamic spectrum is not nearly as important,
perceptually, as the general character of evolution of the components
as a group.

Full understanding and comprehensive application of the FM technique
will certainly take a number of years. The applications are surely more
numerous in the unknown timbral space than they are in the known.
There is, however, great informative value in first limiting oneself to

the simulation of natural timbres, since we have such well-formed perceptual images against which we can measure success. What can be learned in this process are those subtle attributes of natural spectra which so distinctively separate them from most synthesized spectra and which can then be applied to the unknown, "composed" timbral space with the result of a vastly enriched domain in which the composer can work.

Acknowledgments

I wish to express my appreciation to George Gucker for the initial insight into reflected side frequencies and to Max Mathews, David Poole, Gary Goodman, Martin Bresnick, John Grey, Loren Rush, and Andy Moorer for their help in this research.

References

Mathews, M. V., with J. E. Miller, F. R. Moore, J. R. Pierce, and J.-C. Risset. 1969. *The Technology of Computer Music*. Cambridge, Mass.: MIT Press.

Risset, J.-C., and M. V. Mathews. 1969. "Analysis of musical instrument tones." *Physics Today* 22(2): 23–40.

2 Trumpet Algorithms for Computer Composition

DEXTER MORRILL

It is interesting that composers began asking pianists to pick up the lid of the piano and fiddle around inside at about the same time as the start of the modern audio age. So much recent music concerns itself with what the instruments can do that it makes you wonder if there is not some kind of link between the seemingly remote worlds of live instrumental performance and digital sound synthesis.

Certainly it will be a while before digital synthesizers and computer music systems are so complete with marvelous programs that the composer/user can ignore the lower levels of computer programming and focus instead on musical problems. Even then it may be important for composers to remain in touch with some of these lower levels unless they are willing at any point to accept a whole computer package as a musical instrument with at least some limitations.

In the early days of computer music the decision to use an orchestra-score, or instrument-note, convention in designing programs was very useful because it helped everyone, musicians in particular, to deal with a large amount of new information and develop new skills. At present, some people feel that such a convention will lead only to a conventional music and that there is no need to divide the computing task in this way. My estimation is that we are still not very far along in a new musical medium and much has been left undiscovered about the acoustics of musical instruments. For the near future, at least, we will need to concern ourselves with sound production and the basic matters of sound synthesis. Moreover, the computer itself may say something about how we use it. Since the computer can make any kind of sound, one gets very involved with just exactly what kind of sound it is going to make.

For now an instrument-algorithm approach with large general-purpose compiler programs seems attractive and has many uses. It enables us to relate what we know about the acoustics of instruments to a potential world of many new sounds. Also, it makes the enormous task of handling data for sound synthesis manageable.

My own interest in designing a computer trumpet algorithm was awakened at the prospect of composing a piece for trumpet and tape. I especially wanted to have a good brasslike tone for use in the piece,

Originally published in *Computer Music Journal* 1(1): 46–52, 1977.

entitled *Studies for Trumpet & Computer*. As my work progressed, the idea of having a timbre resembling that of the trumpet and the idea of a dynamic or changing timbre became very important to me.

This article describes two versions of the trumpet algorithm. In writing and testing the algorithm, an effort was made to achieve a basic trumpet tone. I felt that, while the testing and subsequent judgements about the tones were necessarily limited, the algorithm might have a wide range of sounds for composition programs. Work on this instrument design was carried out on a Digital Equipment Corporation PDP-10 computer, with a 12-bit digital-analog converter designed and built by Joseph Zingheim. This system is located at the Colgate University Computer Center. Programs for sound generation were written by David Poole, John Chowning, Leland Smith, and others at Stanford University's Center for Computer Research in Music and Acoustics. The main music program is a compiler written in assembly language which generates 12-bit samples for storage and conversion to a standard audio system. The Stanford compiler is a descendant of the Music IV program and closely resembles the unit generator concept of Music V. Since all of the manipulations are done at the program level, no external analog equipment is needed to realize the trumpet tones.

Studies of Trumpet Tones

Two well-known techniques of simulating real instrument tones with computer sound-generation programs are frequency modulation (FM) synthesis and additive synthesis using multiple sine waves. The algorithms described in this chapter are built around a powerful technique using FM synthesis developed by Chowning (1973).

During the 1960s, important work on real-tone analysis and synthesis was carried out at the Bell Laboratories by Max Mathews, Jean-Claude Risset, and others. A study by Risset on trumpet tones revealed a nearly harmonic frequency spectrum, a 20–25-millisecond rise time of the amplitude envelope (with higher-order partials building up more slowly), a small quasi-random frequency fluctuation, and a formant peak in the frequency spectrum in the region of 1,500 Hz.

Risset analyzed data on trumpet tones that were recorded and passed through an analog-to-digital converter. He also constructed test tones in digital form using the additive synthesis technique and converted these tones through a digital-to-analog converter. Each partial (seven or more) of the test tone was produced by a separate oscillator and independently controlled. This technique is somewhat cumbersome and requires a large amount of computer time, as 15 or more unit-generator building blocks may be required. Other studies on trumpet tones were made by Luce (1963), Freedman (1968), and Strong and Clark (1967) at about this time.

Chowning's technique is much more economical than the additive synthesis approach. His technique simulates a dynamic spectrum rather than reproducing it faithfully. This simulation has proved to be sufficient, especially if care is taken to represent other characteristics of the instrument tone.

In simulating a trumpet tone, at least five basic things must be controlled: rise and decay times in the amplitude envelope function; vibrato; random high-frequency fluctuations (noise); the principal FM indices, with control of the formant peak in the frequency spectrum; and center-frequency deviation. The first of these items can be dealt with by means of amplitude modulation and the other four by means of frequency modulation.

The Music Program

Like other digital sound-generation programs, the Stanford Mus10 program is a package of programs that create note lists, define functions, create 12-bit samples, and "play" these samples in real time through the converter. In order to work with the programs, the user must carefully define instruments and waveforms that are to be read by the instruments. A compiler, written in assembly language, accepts a series of instrument definitions. A next step involves creating a series of "notes" which these instruments will use to generate the audio waveforms. Notes processed by the compiler program must conform in data structure to these instrument definitions. During the sampling process (20 kHz is a typical sampling rate), audio waveforms are generated for eventual conversion.

Much like the Music V program, the Stanford compiler uses unit generators as building blocks for instrument design. Several types of unit generators exist. Each unit generator produces a series of numbers, which become components of a waveform or a control in the instrument's circuit. The inputs to these generators may be constants or outputs of other unit generators. The ADD and MULTIPLY unit generators of

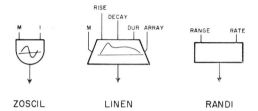

Figure 2.1
Three unit generators from the Stanford Mus10 compiler. ZOSCIL is an oscillator with FM capability; the amplitude of its output is given as a multiplier M, and the frequency is expressed as the increment I. LINEN is especially designed for envelope functions; the input M gives the maximum value of the output function, DUR is the duration of the entire note (with RISE and DECAY specified separately), and ARRAY is the number of the function read by LINEN. RANDI is a pseudo-random-number generator, with the output updated every 1/RATE second within a given RANGE.

Music V are eliminated. The increment of each unit generator is scaled by a variable called MAG (for "magic number"), equal to 512/(sampling rate) for arrays that are 512 words in length.

The three unit generators found in the design discussed below are ZOSCIL, LINEN, and RANDI (figure 2.1). ZOSCIL generates a waveform by reading from an array of numbers defining a function. LINEN is constructed to read through its array once per note; however, it may increment through portions of the array at different rates, depending upon the durations found in its attack and decay parameters. This unit generator is valuable for envelope control, for which it is important to vary the attack and decay times. RANDI produces a series of pseudo-random numbers at a specified rate and within a specified range.

Single-Carrier Instrument

Figure 2.2 shows the design for a single-carrier FM instrument. OUTA is a storage location where sequential 12-bit numbers are stored for later conversion. A percentage of the instrument's signal is sent to the reverberator and then added to OUTA. The parameters, with some typical values, are given in table 2.1.

Unit generator (u.g.) 1 controls the amplitude envelope. The principal FM control creating the dynamic spectrum is caused by u.g. 6 with its own envelope controller, u.g. 4. U.g. 2 provides a small but significant change

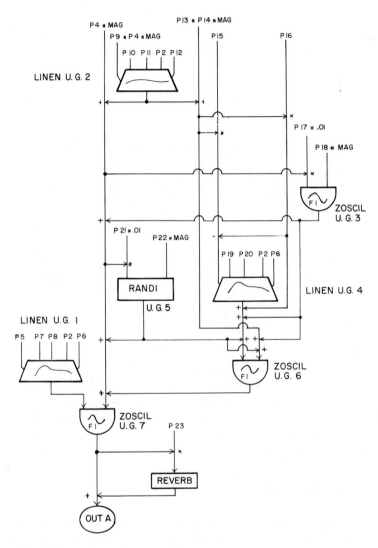

Figure 2.2
Single-carrier FM instrument for producing trumpet tones. The parameters are explained
in table 2.1 and in the text.

Table 2.1
Parameters for the single-carrier FM instrument shown in figure 2.2.

Parameter	Typical value	
P2	1	Duration of note (sec)
P3	1,500	Dummy parameter—resonant peak (see text)
P4	440	Center frequency (Hz)
P5	500	Peak amplitude—scale of 0–2,048
P6	F2	Amplitude envelope function
P7	0.02	Rise time of amplitude envelope
P8	0.15	Decay time of amplitude envelope
P9	0.033	Range of deviation about center frequency
P10	0.06	Rise time for center-frequency deviation function
P11	0.06	Decay time for center-frequency deviation function
P12	F3	Center-frequency deviation function
P13	440	Modulation frequency
P14	1	Modulation frequency multiplier
P15	3.523	Modulation index II
P16	0	Modulation index I
P17	0.33	Peak deviation of vibrato in percent of center frequency
P18	7	Rate of vibrato (Hz)
P19	0.02	Rise time of principal FM index function
P20	0.01	Decay time of principal FM index function
P21	0.5	Peak deviation of random frequency in percent of center frequency
P22	P4/4	Rate of random frequency deviation
P23	0.04	Percentage of direct signal to be reverberated

Figure 2.3
Amplitude envelope for the LINEN unit generator (u.g. 1) in the instrument illustrated in figure 2.2.

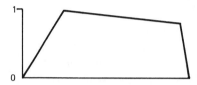

Figure 2.4
Index function for the LINEN unit generator (u.g. 4) in the instrument illustrated in figure 2.2. This function is derived from the function shown in figure 2.3 by simply setting the decay time for the index function (P20) to be quite short.

in the center frequency (P4). U.g. 3 allows for independent vibrato control. U.g. 5 provides a small random FM of center frequency. Finally, the main signal is generated by u.g. 7. All five of the basic controls are independent of each other, with their own parameters and functions. This modular concept is especially valuable when the instrument is used to create unusual and varied sounds.

Figure 2.3 shows the function used by LINEN (u.g. 1) for amplitude envelope control. LINEN enables the programmer to vary the rise time to the peak of the amplitude. A random series of rise times (P7) between 0.02 and 0.025 sec can be used effectively to slightly vary the attack quality of the trumpet sound in passages with many notes. Likewise, a random decay (P8) of about 0.15 sec helps to create a lifelike quality. U.g. 4 together with u.g. 6 provides the principal FM for the instrument. The output of u.g. 6 is added to the center frequency (P4) at each sampling. The function for u.g. 4 can be the same as that found in u.g. 1. However, it does seem best to shorten the decay (P20) of the function in u.g. 4 (figure 2.4). A slow rise or decay of a modulation index function produces a characteristic FM sound that is very unlike the decay of a brass sound. The sweep of the frequency modulation index matching the rise of the amplitude envelope is important because the higher-order partials increase more slowly in real trumpet tones. Thus the dynamic modulation roughly matches the amplitude envelope in shape. Basic to this FM technique is control of the modulation frequency and proper modulation indices to simulate a resonant peak of the instrument. The modulating frequency could be represented here by P4 (center frequency), since only the harmonic partials are desired. However, a slight deviation of the ratio of the modulation frequency to the carrier frequency produces pleasant beats, which may be like a slight tremolo effect. A ratio of 440/439 Hz is quite noticeable. P14 is an extra parameter used to scale the modulation frequency (P13) at the input program level.

Modulation Index

The parameters shown in figure 2.2 can vary only once per note. Thus, if the instrument "plays" or compiles a note of 1 sec, 20,000 samples will be generated (if the sampling rate equals 20,000 samples/sec) and the values placed in these various parameters will remain the same for that note's duration.

In order to obtain an appropriate timbre throughout the trumpet range it is necessary to use proper values in P15. Risset (1966) states that there is a small resonant peak at 1,500 Hz in the trumpet frequency spectrum. This formant peak exaggerates the amplitude of any of the partials close to the peak, regardless of their order. A table of Bessel functions gives the proper index for each pitch. David Hoffman has written a Fortran IV subroutine that is loaded together with Leland Smith's Score program (Smith 1972). Score produces note lists for the compiler, with appropriate parameter values for each note. This program serves as a front end to the compiler, and many operations can occur at this stage. P3 has been saved as a dummy parameter in the instrument design. Here the programmer using Score may place a number for each note, which will represent the desired formant peak in hertz. As the Score program is working to produce its note list, the subroutine loaded with it will look up the values in P3 and P4 and will use them to calculate the modulation index to be placed in P15. The subroutine contains a table of the maximum values of the different orders of Bessel functions. By looking up the center frequency in P4, the subroutine decides which order Bessel function is appropriate for calculating the value for modulation index II.

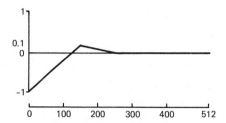

Figure 2.5
Typical function read by u.g. 2 in figure 2.2, used for creating slight variations in the
center frequency of the note.

Vibrato and Center-Frequency Control

Unit generator 3 provides a separate control for vibrato. The output of
this ZOSCIL is added to the center frequency (P4) at each sample. The
frequency of this vibrato (P18*MAG) has been set to about 7 Hz and can
be varied for each note. The peak deviation (P17) of the vibrato can be
selected as desired, but is scaled by center frequency itself. It is necessary
to have the vibrato signal also modulate the frequency and amplitude inputs to the main FM ZOSCIL (u.g. 6). An exaggerated modulation index
occurs if the vibrato signal modulates only the center frequency and not
the modulation frequency. This means that the vibrato control (u.g. 3)
affects all of the frequency terms except for the initial setting of center-
frequency deviation (u.g. 2).

At least some vibrato is needed to make a natural trumpet sound.
Likewise, a slight deviation in center frequency is desirable during the
course of each note. A player would often seem to start below the center
frequency at the beginning of a tone. If single test tones are heard, the
center-frequency deviation may not be important. But in a longer musical
phrase the lack of a deviation in the center frequency results in unnatural
accuracy. Unit generator 2 modulates the center frequency slightly by its
gently sloped function (figure 2.5). Most of the functions used for this
purpose begin slightly below the center frequency and may go above it
during the course of the note. This function is generated once per note. A
variety of similar functions have been used here, mostly to avoid constant
repetition.

I have used slightly modified parameter values when the synthesized
trumpet plays many notes. Likewise, several small changes can easily be
made in the functions used for the amplitude envelope. A small overshoot

at the peak of the envelope is often used, and other small irregularities in the entire shape can be added to these simple envelopes. Much of this change is done without substantial experimental information to support the modifications. Future testing with analog-to-digital conversion systems may provide useful information about the dynamics of natural musical passages.

Double-Carrier Instrument

The single-carrier algorithm described above appears to have some limitations that result in a somewhat less characteristic trumpet tone in the lower register. This unnatural quality is especially noticeable in the lowest seven or eight notes. One can speculate that as the whole frequency spectrum is lowered the ear becomes more critical of what it hears. Data gathered by Benade (1973) show that the spectral envelope changes greatly from the high to the low extreme of the trumpet register. A fairly large modulation index is needed to produce ten upper sidebands. While one can predict what frequencies are produced with a given index, the relative amplitude of those partials cannot be controlled with much accuracy as the index increases above 3. In short, there is no way to shape a spectral envelope that has ten or more partials using a single-carrier FM algorithm.

Figure 2.6 shows an expanded design for a trumpet algorithm using two carriers rather than one. Chowning originally proposed this idea as a way of overcoming the limitations of a one-carrier FM algorithm. The design can be divided into three parts. Unit generators 5–8 form the first carrier system, with main oscillator (U8), amplitude envelope (U7), and frequency modulation (U5 and U6). A second carrier system of four unit generators is needed for the three additional FM functions. These are vibrato (U3) with its own envelope control (U1), random noise (U2), and portamento (U4). The output of these four unit generators, defined as AA in figure 2.6, is used in both the first and second carrier systems. The double-carrier instrument, then, is expanded by five more unit generators, although the vibrato envelope control might also have been included in the smaller instrument. The parameters, with some typical values, are listed in table 2.2.

Some small differences can be noted in the way the two algorithms are written. The double-carrier algorithm does not have the left-side inputs to the vibrato and random-noise generators scaled by center frequency, as in

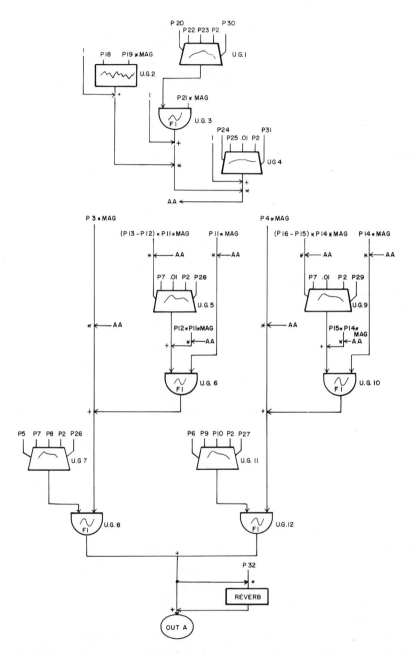

Figure 2.6
Double-carrier FM instrument for producing trumpet tones. The parameters are listed in table 2.2.

Table 2.2
Parameters for the double-carrier FM instrument shown in figure 2.6.

Parameter	Typical value	
P2	1	Duration of note (sec)
P3	250	Carrier 1 center frequency
P4	1,500	Carrier 2 center frequency
P5	1,000	Peak amplitude, carrier 1
P6	200	Peak amplitude, carrier 2
P7	0.03	Rise time of amplitude envelope, carrier 1
P8	0.15	Decay time of amplitude envelope, carrier 1
P9	0.03	Rise time of amplitude envelope, carrier 2
P10	0.3	Decay time of amplitude envelope, carrier 2
P11	250	Modulation frequency, carrier 1
P12	0	Modulation index I, carrier 1
P13	2.66	Modulation index II, carrier 1
P14	250	Modulation frequency, carrier 2
P15	0	Modulation index I, carrier 2
P16	1.8	Modulation index II, carrier 2
P17		Dummy parameter
P18	0.007	Range of random frequency deviation
P19	125	Rate of random frequency deviation
P20	0.007	Range of vibrato
P21	7	Rate of vibrato
P22	0.6	Rise time of vibrato envelope
P23	0.2	Decay time of vibrato envelope
P24	0.03	Range of deviation about center frequency
P25	0.06	Rise time for center-frequency deviation function
P26	F2	Amplitude envelope function, carrier 1
P27	F2	Amplitude envelope function, carrier 2
P28	F2	Modulation index function, carrier 1
P29	F2	Modulation index function, carrier 2
P30	F3	Center-frequency deviation function
P31	F4	Vibrato envelope function
P32	0.04	Percentage of reverberation

the single-carrier algorithm. This could mean that some scaling of the values found in P20 and P18 is required as a function of the center frequency P3 if a linear vibrato and random frequency are sought throughout the register.

There seem to be two ways to use the two independent FM systems. One would be to set both carriers (P3 and P4) to the same frequency and modulate both of them with the same frequency (P11 and P14). These two systems would produce a composite spectrum. In this way a fairly good "fit" of a desired spectral envelope might be obtained by carefully adjusting the index and amplitude of each carrier system. A graphics display capability is almost a requirement in matching and adjusting the two spectra.

Perhaps a better way to use the two FM systems is to have each system produce frequencies for different parts of the desired spectrum. Here, carrier system 1 could produce the fundamental frequency and five or six partials above. Carrier system 2 could produce only the upper partials for the fundamental tone, say five or seven partials. Thus, if carrier frequency 1 (P3) is set to 250 Hz, or the fundamental frequency, carrier frequency 2 (P4) might typically be set to 1,500 Hz, or six times the fundamental frequency. If both carriers are modulated by the same frequency of 250 Hz, then both systems will produce matching sidebands. The lower sidebands of the upper system will not be reflected around 0 Hz if the modulation index of this system is kept sufficiently small. It is important to note that each system has its own amplitude envelope, which will be used to adjust the relative amplitudes in the composite spectrum. Figure 2.7 shows the two FM spectra and the composite spectrum.

When two modulated carrier signals are added together, it is difficult to predict the amplitude of the resulting waveform. Small changes in the two modulation indices, the relative amplitudes of the carriers, and the ratio of the center frequencies would all contribute to the resulting amplitude of the composite waveform. I have attempted only a rough scaling device in the Score program to adjust the amplitudes (P5 and P6) for each note in the trumpet scale.

One reason for having separate FM carrier systems is to set different decay times for the two amplitude envelopes. Data published by Grey (1975) and Beauchamp (1975, 1979) show that the upper partials of a trumpet tone decay in amplitude more rapidly than the lower ones. By increasing the decay time in P10 this effect can be roughly simulated. Several researchers have pointed out that the amplitudes of higher partials

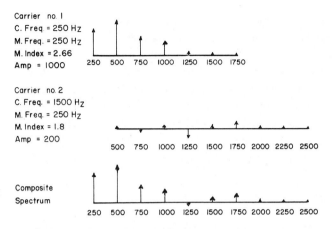

Figure 2.7
Composite spectrum resulting from the double-carrier instrument illustrated in figure 2.6.

increase with louder tones. Again, a double-carrier system makes this kind of control possible. The double-carrier algorithm represents a significant increase in computation over the smaller instrument, and in some ways begins to approach an additive synthesis technique in computational complexity.

Summary

An enormous number of unusual sounds can be produced with both algorithms by changing almost any of the parameter values and functions. The idea of a dynamic instrument with a good natural trumpet sound at the center was most attractive to me. The designs also seem to serve fairly well as general-purpose brass instruments, although no serious attempt has been made to synthesize French horn, trombone, or tuba tones. It is remarkable how a change in center frequency and a slower attack time produces a tubalike sound. Something resembling a flute can be gotten with a small modulation index of 1 or 1.5, and many drumlike sounds are easy to produce.

There is ample reason to want to be able to produce high-quality synthetic instrument tones. What has been poorly understood is the relationship between the study and synthesis of natural sounds and the development of new, or what might better be described as unnatural, sounds. Already experience has shown us that simple electronic sounds with fixed spectra become uninteresting once the ear is acquainted with them. Electronic sounds that once seemed fresh and intriguing may now seem pale and too familiar. As our understanding of acoustics grows, we should be able to apply something of what we know to the development of new sounds. A basic assumption of this chapter is that dynamic time-changing spectra, vibrato, portamento, and some degree of random noise are desirable in many types of unnatural synthetic sounds. This seems to be a fair assumption, especially if one is interested in an interpolation scheme for various sounds, as suggested by Wessel (1979) and Grey (1975).

Acknowledgments

I am deeply indebted to John Chowning for both the basis and the inspiration for this work. John Grey also gave me a great deal of help in understanding digital synthesis and psychoacoustics. Jean-Claude Risset and Jack Dodd provided some helpful insights. Max Mathews's encouragement and suggestions are deeply appreciated.

References

Benade, A. H. 1973. "The physics of brasses." *Scientific American* 229(1): 24–35.

Beauchamp, J. 1975. "Analysis and synthesis of cornet tones using nonlinear inter-harmonic relationships." *Journal of the Audio Engineering Society* 23: 778–795.

Beauchamp, J. 1979. "Brass tone synthesis by spectrum evolution matching with nonlinear functions." *Computer Music Journal* 3(2): 35–43. Article 8 in this volume.

Chowning, J. 1973. "The synthesis of complex audio spectra by means of frequency modulation." *Journal of the Audio Engineering Society* 21(7): 526–534, 1973. Article 1 in this volume.

Freedman, M. D. 1968. "A method for analysing musical tones." *Journal of the Audio Engineering Society* 16: 419–425.

Grey, J. M. 1975. An Exploration of Musical Timbre. Ph.D. diss., Department of Psychology, Stanford University. Department of Music report STAN-M-2.

Luce, D. A. 1963. Physical Correlates of Nonpercussive Musical Instrument Tones. Ph.D. diss., Massachusetts Institute of Technology.

Risset, J.-C. 1966. *Computer Study of Trumpet Tones*. Murray Hill, N.J.: Bell Telephone Laboratories.

Smith, L. 1972. "Score: A musician's approach to computer music." *Journal of the Audio Engineering Society* 20: 7–14.

Strong, W., and M. Clark. 1967. "Synthesis of wind-instrument tones." *Journal of the Audio Engineering Society* 41: 39–52.

Wessel, D. 1979. "Timbre space as a musical control structure." *Computer Music Journal* 3(2): 45–52. Article 35 in this volume.

3 Improved FM Audio Synthesis Methods for Real-Time Digital Music Generation

STEVE SAUNDERS

"The computer as a musical instrument" has been a popular theme and goal for some years now—and rightly so, for the versatility under control of the digital computer is unsurpassed by that of any other man-made device. From the early days of singing line printers and square waves to Music V (Mathews 1969) and more recent systems, great effort has gone into realizing the musical potential of our mathematical engines. Only recently, however, has it become feasible to consider the computer as a performing instrument, with immediate feedback to the performing musician (along with recording, editing, and mixing capabilities, of course). Recent minicomputers are just powerful enough to do the necessary interaction and computation and just cheap enough to be competitive with more traditional methods of sound generation.

Chowning FM

In 1972, John Chowning invented a new method of synthesizing musical sounds that is both extremely simple and exceedingly versatile (Chowning 1973). Chowning's method consists of frequency modulation of a sine-wave carrier (at the desired fundamental frequency) by a sine-wave signal at the same or a closely related frequency. The resulting spectrum contains components whose amplitudes are given by Bessel functions of the first kind, $J_n(I)$, where n denotes the nth harmonic and I is the modulation index (the ratio of the peak frequency deviation to the modulating signal frequency: a dimensionless parameter).

Where the carrier and the signal have the same frequency, the upper side frequencies lie in the harmonic sequence, as one would expect, but the lower sideband "reflects" about zero (DC) and overlaps the same harmonic sequence. So a harmonic spectrum is indeed produced.

Now what is the effect of the parameter I, the modulation index? Consulting any standard book of tables, we see that for $I = 0$ only $J_0(I)$ is nonzero (in other words, only the fundamental occurs). As I increases, the first few harmonics become non-negligible and the fundamental decreases. That is, the spectrum "spreads out," acquiring contributions from ever-higher harmonics of the fundamental. Notice that when $I > 1$ the instan-

Originally published in *Computer Music Journal* 1(1): 53–55, 1977.

taneous frequency is sometimes negative. This poses no difficulty for digital generation, though.

So by varying one parameter, modulation index, we can obtain an entire family of tone colors—from a pure sine wave to a "nasal" or "brassy" spectrally top-heavy sound. But that's not by any means the only advantage of FM. Any of these spectra can be produced by conventional methods—for example, by computing and storing one cycle and playing samples from it at a pitch-determined rate. But these sampling methods always sound "electronic," or lifeless, because the spectrum they produce almost never varies. With FM, on the other hand, one can get tones that evolve in time, the way a trombone goes "blaaaatt" or a big bell gradually settles down to a dim, pure tone. This spectral evolution through time apparently provides much of the signature information by which we recognize various instruments and judge timbre; it is surely an important ability for any device trying to be a universal musical instrument.

Details of FM Synthesis

The process of generating an FM tone digitally can be better understood from the following viewpoint: The instantaneous frequency is just the rate of change of phase. Phase is represented by an index into a sine-wave look-up table or an argument to a sine function; the rate of change is the increment added to this index between samples. If we now recompute the index step (instantaneous frequency) for each sample, we have the capability for FM.

In Chowning 1973, the modulating signal is a sine wave. The resulting signal can be expressed by

$$x(t) = \sin[\theta(t)]$$

with the phase, θ, given by

$$\theta(t) = 2\pi f_c t + I\sin(2\pi f_m t),$$

where f_c is the carrier frequency, f_m is the modulating frequency, and I is the modulation index. The instantaneous frequency is given by

$$f(t) = \frac{d\theta}{dt} = 2\pi f_c + 2\pi I f_m \cos(2\pi f_m t),$$

i.e., a sine wave at the modulating frequency plus a constant for the carrier frequency (Lathi 1965, pp. 490–492). This expression justifies the term "sine FM."

The sinusoidal character of both carrier and modulation allows the analysis of the spectrum in terms of Bessel functions given by Chowning (1973) and van der Pol (1930):

$$\sin[2\pi f_c t + I\sin(2\pi f_m t)]$$

$$= J_0(I)\sin(2\pi f_c t)$$

$$+ J_1(I)\sin(2\pi f_c t + 2\pi f_m t) - J_1(I)\sin(2\pi f_c t - 2\pi f_m t)$$

$$+ J_2(I)\sin(2\pi f_c t + 2\cdot 2\pi f_m t) + J_2(I)\sin(2\pi f_c t - 2\cdot 2\pi f_m t)$$

$$+ J_3(I)\sin(2\pi f_c t + 3\cdot 2\pi f_m t) - J_3(I)\sin(2\pi f_c t - 3\cdot 2\pi f_m t)\cdots.$$

Triangle FM

However, it appears that the exact composition of the spectrum is not nearly as important as the overall character and the time evolution of the tone. Examples abound of uncannily real "trumpet" and "trombone" sounds produced via FM, but the wave shapes and detailed spectra are not at all trumpetlike; only the sensation is.

If we are willing to give up the simple mathematical analysis of our spectra, while retaining the single-parameter control over its extent and general character, a much easier form of FM presents itself. Note in the sine-by-sine modulation step that at least one multiplication seems to be required to implement the effect of the modulation index on the signal. Most microprogrammable minicomputers do not execute multiplications at the requisite rate for real-time generation of several voices with time out for control (that is, reading the input keyboard to see which notes to play).

Suppose, now, that we use for the modulating signal a triangle wave instead of a sine. That is, we let the instantaneous frequency be

$$f(t) = \frac{d\theta}{dt} = 2\pi f_c + 2\pi I f_m \,\mathrm{tri}(2\pi f_m t).$$

(Here the triangle-wave function tri has range $[-1, +1]$ and period 2π, just as with a sine wave.)

For digital synthesis, this function (and all time functions) will be represented by a sequence of values at time intervals T, the sampling period:

$$f(nT) = 2\pi f_c + 2\pi I f_m \operatorname{tri}(2\pi f_m nT).$$

Now we can compute this sequence incrementally by observing that, as long as the step at the present time doesn't cross a (positive or negative) peak of the triangle,

$$f((n+1)T) = f(nT) + ST,$$

where S is the (positive or negative) slope of our modulating triangle wave,

$$S = \frac{d}{dt}[2\pi f_c + 2\pi I f_m \operatorname{tri}(2\pi f_m t)]$$

$$= 2\pi I f_m \frac{d}{dt}[\operatorname{tri}(2\pi f_m t)]$$

$$= 2\pi I f_m \cdot 4 f_m \operatorname{sqr}(2\pi f_m t)$$

$$= 8\pi I f_m^2 \operatorname{sqr}(2\pi f_m t),$$

where $\operatorname{sqr}(t)$ is the square-wave function. That is, $S = \pm 8\pi I f_m^2$, with the sign changing at intervals of $T/2 f_m$ (twice per cycle). Thus, the inner-loop computation can consist of a simple accumulation with limit tests.

When a time step does pass a peak of the triangle wave, we begin to use the opposite slope for future steps. We must also correct for not having used this slope during the part of this step after the peak. The triangle sample just computed will be outside the limits of the true triangle wave; by symmetry, it should be just as far inside the limit as we find it outside. This makes it easy to fix.

A more precise specification of my FM synthesis method is given in the following, hereafter referred to as code listing 1:

```
procedure triFM (fc, fm, I, T, numSamples);
            real   fc,    {carrier frequency}
                   fm,    {modulation frequency}
                   I,     {modulation index}
                   T;     {sample interval, = 1/(sample rate)}
            integer numSamples;
      begin
            real   increment,   {step along triangle,
                                 = ST (See text)}
                   freq,        {instantaneous frequency}
```

```
                    upperlimit,    {maximum-frequency peak of triangle}
                    lowerlimit,    {minimum- . . . }
                    theta;         {phase of output}
            integer N;

            increment := 8 * pi * fm * fm * I * T;
            upperlimit := fc + fm * I;
            lowerlimit := fc − fm * I;
            freq := fc;
            theta := 0;
            for N := 1 step 1 until numSamples do
            begin
                    freq := freq + increment;
                    if freq > upperlimit then begin
                        increment := − increment;
                        freq := 2 * upperlimit − freq; end
                    else if freq < lowerlimit then begin
                        increment := − increment;
                        freq := 2 * lowerlimit − freq; end
                    theta := (theta + freq) mod twopi;
                    enqueue (sin (theta))
            end
        end;
```

This procedure assumes another procedure, "enqueue (sample)," which puts the given sample into the buffer for the DAC process. Of course, a microcoded version of this procedure would use carefully scaled integers instead of floating-point reals.

The exact analysis of the spectrum produced by triangle-wave modulation is rather more difficult than the sine-wave case. There are sidebands produced by each component of the triangle wave. In addition, there are sidebands produced by integer multiples of each component of the triangle wave. In many cases, these sidebands overlap, even for lower-order sidebands. In the formula given at the end of LeBrun's 1977 article, i_n is the modulation index corresponding to the nth harmonic of the triangle wave,

$$i_n = \frac{8}{\pi^2} * \frac{I}{n^3}, \qquad n = 1, 3, 5, 7, \ldots.$$

The θ_n in LeBrun's formula are derived from the expansion

$$\text{tri}(2\pi f_m t) = \frac{8}{\pi^2} [\sin(2\pi f_m t) - \tfrac{1}{9} \sin(3 \cdot 2\pi f_m t) + \tfrac{1}{25} \sin(5 \cdot 2\pi f_m t) \cdots]$$

$$= \frac{8}{\pi^2} \sum_{n=1}^{\infty} \frac{(-1)^{(n-1)/2}}{n^2} \sin(2\pi n f_m).$$

The extra factor of $1/n$ in the formula for x_n comes from the fact that the frequency of the nth harmonic is nf_m.

Noting that $J_n(0) = 0$ for $n > 0$, and that $J_n(x)$ becomes significant about when $x = n - 1$, we see that the triangle-FM spectrum behaves as required: With $I = 0$ a pure sine wave results; with $I \neq 0$ the spectrum is harmonic (it contains components at each sum and difference of the carrier and multiples of components of the signal); as I increases the spectrum must generally spread out, with more energy going into higher harmonics; and the individual spectral components change and grow in complex ways.

Crosby (1938) remarks that FM with a multitone or "program" modulator produces smaller out-of-band components than pure-sine modulation with the same overall modulation index; he refers to band-limited signals, however. In our experience, using triangle waves instead of sines has an effect similar to that of using a modulation index 1.5–2 times larger with a sine modulator.

Advantages

The advantage of triangle FM synthesis over sine-wave FM is simply speed resulting from computational simplicity. Of course, fast multiplication hardware would eradicate this edge completely. Its advantages over other methods of musical sound synthesis for computers are precisely those of sine-sine FM as described by Chowning and mentioned above.

Volume Control

It may be objected at this point that all this FM trickery would still make quite dull sounds because it does not incorporate dynamic (loudness) variations as well as spectral modulation, especially in the critical attack portion of a note's lifetime, and that this seems to require a multiplication per sample after all. The solution, suggested by Purcell (1975), is to note that

$$\sin(x + d) + \sin(x - d) = 2\cos(d)\sin(x).$$

So if instead of fetching just one sine sample at the end of the procedure given above we fetch two, displaced from the computed phase by an amount that is a parameter of the procedure, we can have any amplitude of FM waveform we like, at a net cost of two additions for addressing and one more memory cycle. The required phase-displacement parameter is given by

$$d = \arccos(A/2)$$

for an amplitude of A relative to the stored sine wave. The necessary modifications to the program in code listing 1 should be clear.

Another FM Method

We can, it seems, apply this same trick to computing the modulating signal for the FM computation, eliminating those hard-to-analyze triangle waves. A procedure for doing so follows.

```
procedure newFM (fc, fm, I, A, T, numSamples);
        real   fc,    {carrier frequency}
               fm,    {modulation frequency}
               I,     {modulation index, as a fraction of Imax}
               A,     {amplitude of the generated signal}
               T;     {sample interval}
        integer numSamples;
    begin
        real   carIncr,     {phase step due to carrier frequency}
               modPhase,    {phase of the modulator}
               modIncr,     {step due to modulation}
               modOffset,   {phase offset for scaling modulator}
               theta,       {phase of output}
               ampOffset;   {phase offset for scaling output}
        integer N;

        carIncr := twopi * fc * T;
        modIncr := twopi * fm * T;
        modOffset :=2 * arccos (I);
        ampOffset :=2 * arccos (A);
        theta := 0;   modPhase := 0;
        for N := 1 step 1 until numSamples do
        begin
            modPhase := modPhase + modIncr;
            theta := (theta + carIncr
                        + sin2 (modPhase + modOffset)
                        + sin2 (modPhase - modOffset))
                    mod twopi;
            enqueue (sin (theta + ampOffset)
                        + sin (theta - ampOffset));
        end
    end;
```

This procedure assumes a function sin2 whose values are scaled in amplitude by the maximum modulation index we wish to generate.

As everyone who has programmed real-time digital synthesis will have already realized, much of the formal messiness of the algorithms as presented here disappears with proper choices of data representation. Factors of 2π evaporate, **mod** operations become bit masks, and so on. When done properly, the **for** loops of the two procedures given above involve only integer adds, subtracts, compares, and array accesses.

Implementation

With currently available microcomputers, apparently the only way to get the speed necessary for FM synthesis (10,000 or more samples per second), even with this simplified approach, is through the use of microcode to do the innermost loop. Speed can also be gained by keeping the intermediate stages in high-speed registers through several samples of the wave. This can best be done by making a single entry to the microcode (i.e., through a machine-language "macro-instruction") cause the generation of many samples.

The computer cannot spend all its time in this inner loop, however, since it must respond to control inputs from the performer (e.g., key pressed/released, stop pulled in the case of an organ console) within 10–20 msec.

One solution that has been tried with some success is to run the control and setup code on a 60 Hz interrupt basis. This code checks for changed control inputs, sets up the necessary parameters for the FM microcode, calls that microcode, and quits. The FM microcode, when called, produces enough samples to fill 1/60 sec, places them in a buffer queue, and returns.

A separate parallel process (e.g., a DMA device) reads samples from the queue to a digital-to-analog converter at a constant sampling rate.

This separation has the advantage that low-priority processing, changes of global state, TTY I/O, debuggers, and the like can make free use of any time not required by music generation—typically a small part of the machine. Such "background" actions might include turning music on or off (by disabling the 60 Hz interrupt, for example), reassigning meanings to the control inputs, reading in a block of "compiled" or "recorded" control information to play a specified tune, or running a general-purpose language interpreter in which any or all of the above can be accomplished by typed commands. The separation into parallel, separately clocked processes allows music generation to proceed undisturbed by other, possibly totally unrelated processing.

Experimental Results

The method given in code listing 1 has been programmed on an inexpensive minicomputer and incorporated in a fully interactive music system, with facilities for playing on an organ keyboard, recording, editing, overdubbing, displaying, and printing music. The performance of our system can be summarized as follows.

5 real-time FM voices
12-bit samples at 13.7 kHz rate
60-Hz updating of all FM parameters: carrier and signal frequencies, modulation index, and volume
Arbitrary parameter envelopes with an attack transient, a repeated sustain, and a decay section
Very conventional, cheap, general-purpose, microprogrammed minicomputer
No music-specific hardware but the digital-analog converter.

References

Chowning, J. 1973. "The synthesis of complex audio spectra by means of frequency modulation." *Journal of the Audio Engineering Society* 21(7): 526–534. Article 1 in this volume.

Crosby, M. G. 1938. "Carrier and side-frequency relations with multi-tone frequency or phase modulation." *RCA Review* 3: 103–106.

Lathi, B. P. 1965. *Signals, Systems and Communication.* New York: Wiley.

Mathews, M. V., with J. E. Miller, F. R. Moore, J. R. Pierce, and J.-C. Risset. 1969. *The Technology of Computer Music.* Cambridge, Mass.: MIT Press.

Purcell, S. 1975. FM Audio Synthesis Algorithms: Notes and Suggestions for Improvement. Unpublished manuscript.

Van der Pol, B. 1930. "Frequency modulation." *Proceedings of the IRE* 18: 1194–1205.

4 The Simulation of Natural Instrument Tones Using Frequency Modulation with a Complex Modulating Wave

BILL SCHOTTSTAEDT

The frequency-modulation technique of producing musically interesting audio spectra can be extended in several useful ways. In the basic case (Chowning 1973), a carrier wave is modulated by one modulating wave where both waves are simple sinusoids and both are in the audio band. The modulated carrier then becomes the audio signal. By changing the modulation index and the ratio of the carrier frequency to the modulating frequency, one can easily create many complex audio spectra.

Certain timbres, however, seem to be elusive. Over the last several years at Stanford University's Center for Computer Research in Music and Acoustics, we have been doing extensive work with complex modulating waves. We have found this process to be very useful in, for example, the simulation of string and piano tones. The simulations described below use a complex modulating wave made up of two or three sinusoids, each of whose modulation indices is pitch-dependent. Separate modulating oscillators are used to allow independent control of the modulation indices, thus giving more precise control over the spectra produced. Analysis of actual piano and string tones served as the basis for the choice of the indices and of the ratios between carrier and modulating frequencies.

Frequency Modulation with a Complex Modulating Wave

When a sinusoidal wave is simultaneously frequency-modulated by two modulating sinusoids, sidebands are created at all frequencies of the form

$$f_c \pm if_{m1} \pm kf_{m2}$$

where i and k are integers and f_{m1} and f_{m2} are the modulating frequencies. It is as though each of the sidebands produced by one of the modulating signals were modulated as a carrier by the other modulating signal. The equation of the resultant wave is

$$e = A \sin(\omega_c t + I_1 \sin\omega_1 t + I_2 \sin\omega_2 t) \qquad (1)$$

where e is the instantaneous amplitude, A is the amplitude of the carrier, ω_c is $2\pi f_c$, ω_1 is $2\pi f_{m1}$, and ω_2 is $2\pi f_{m2}$. The amplitude of the sideband $f_c \pm if_{m1} \pm kf_{m2}$ is given (LeBrun 1977) by

Originally published in *Computer Music Journal* 1(4): 46–50, 1977.

Table 4.1

Frequency	Amplitude
f_c, carrier	$J_0(I_1) \times J_0(I_2)$
$f_c \pm if_{m1}$, simple sidebands for f_{m1}	$J_i(I_1) \times J_0(I_2)$
$f_c \pm kf_{m2}$, simple sidebands for f_{m2}	$J_0(I_1) \times J_k(I_2)$
$f_c \pm if_{m1} \pm kf_{m2}$, combination frequencies	$J_i(I_1) \times J_k(I_2)$

$$J_i(I_1) \times J_k(I_2)$$

where I_1 and I_2 are the respective modulating indices of f_{m1} and f_{m2}, and J is the Bessel function of the first kind and ith (or kth) order. For example, the amplitude of the carrier is $J_0(I_1) \times J_0(I_2)$.

It can be shown (LeBrun 1977) that

$$e = \sum_i \sum_k J_i(I_1) J_k(I_2) \sin(\omega_c t + i\omega_1 t + k\omega_2 t). \tag{2}$$

As an illustration of this process, take the simple case of a sine wave modulated simultaneously by two sine waves. The ratios of modulating frequency to carrier frequency will be $1:1$ and $4:1$, with modulation indices of 1 and 0.2, respectively (as is approximately the case at a frequency of 400 Hz in the FM piano described below). In general, the amplitudes of the components would be as shown in table 4.1. If $k = 0$, then only the lower $(1:1)$ modulating frequency would be present and the relative sideband amplitudes would be

$$J_0(I_1) = J_0(1) = 0.77,$$

$$J_1(I_1) = J_1(1) = 0.44,$$

$$J_2(I_1) = J_2(1) = 0.12,$$

$$J_3(I_1) = J_3(1) = 0.02.$$

If $i = 0$, then only the higher $(4:1)$ modulating frequency would be present and the harmonics would have the following relative amplitudes:

$$J_0(I_2) = J_0(0.2) = 0.98,$$

$$J_1(I_2) = J_1(0.2) = 0.10,$$

$$J_2(I_2) = J_2(0.2) = 0.005.$$

However, when both modulating frequencies are present, they interact to produce the following sideband amplitudes:

$J_0(I_1) \times J_0(I_2) = 0.77 \times 0.98 = 0.75$
$\qquad$ (carrier, f_c),

$J_1(I_1) \times J_0(I_2) = 0.44 \times 0.98 = 0.43$
$\qquad$ (first-order sidebands, $f_c \pm f_{m1}$),

$J_2(I_1) \times J_0(I_2) = 0.12 \times 0.98 = 0.12$
$\qquad$ (second-order sidebands, $f_c \pm 2f_{m1}$),

$J_3(I_1) \times J_0(I_2) = 0.02 \times 0.98 = 0.02$
$\qquad$ (third-order sidebands, $f_c \pm 3f_{m1}$),

$J_0(I_1) \times J_1(I_2) = 0.77 \times 0.10 = 0.08$
$\qquad$ (first-order sidebands, $f_c \pm f_{m2}$),

$J_1(I_1) \times J_1(I_2) = 0.44 \times 0.10 = 0.04$
$\qquad$ ($f_c \pm f_{m1} \pm f_{m2}$, combination frequencies
$\qquad$ where $i = 1$, $k = 1$),

$J_2(I_1) \times J_1(I_2) = 0.12 \times 0.10 = 0.01$
$\qquad$ ($f_c \pm 2f_{m1} \pm f_{m2}$, combination frequencies
$\qquad$ where $i = 2$, $k = 1$).

The amplitudes of higher-order sidebands are insignificant.

The process by which these sidebands interact to form a spectrum is shown in figure 4.1. The solid bars in parts a–d represent sidebands with amplitudes as derived above. Some of these components are drawn below the horizontal axis, representing a 180° phase shift that results (LeBrun 1977) from the relation

$$J_{-n} = (-1)^n J_n.$$

Thus, the sign for the sideband $f_c - 2f_{m1} - f_{m2}$ (at $-5f_c$ in figure 4.1d) is given by

$$J_{-2}(I_1) \times J_{-1}(I_2) = (-1)^2 J_2(I_1) \times (-1) J_1(I_2)$$

$$= -J_2(I_1) \times J_1(I_2),$$

whereas the sign for the sideband $f_c - f_{m1} - f_{m2}$ (at $-4f_c$ in figure 4.1c) is given by

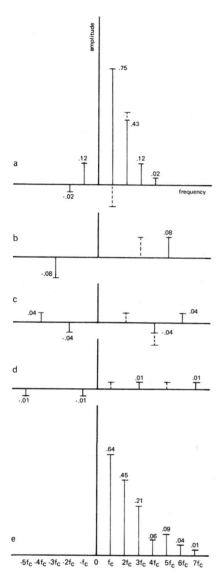

Figure 4.1
Plot of the spectrum with $f_{m1} : f_c = 1 : 1$ and $f_{m2} : f_c = 4 : 1$ (not drawn to scale). "Negative-frequency" components in parts a–d are shown where they theoretically occur (solid lines) as well as "wrapped around" 0 Hz and phase-shifted 180° (dashed lines). The component at 0 Hz is omitted here. (a) Spectral components resulting from f_c and f_{m1}. (b) Spectral components resulting from f_{m2} and f_c (c) Combination components for $i = 1, k = 1$ (see equation 2). (d) Combination components for $i = 2, k = 1$. (e) Plot of the magnitudes in the final spectrum obtained by adding the components shown in parts a–d.

$$J_{-1}(I_1) \times J_{-1}(I_2) = (-1)J_1(I_1) \times (-1)J_1(I_2)$$

$$= +J_1(I_1) \times J_1(I_2).$$

As was explained by Chowning (1973), the phase of a sideband with frequency less than 0 Hz is also changed because it "wraps around" 0 Hz by means of the relation $\sin(-\theta) = -\sin(\theta)$. In other words, the bar representing each "negative-frequency" sideband changes direction as it "wraps around" 0 Hz. Thus, the combination component in figure 4.1a that occurs at $-f_c$ occurs in reality at $+f_c$ (represented by a dashed bar at f_c), but undergoes a 180° phase shift. As a result, energy is in effect subtracted from the 0.75 component present at the fundamental (f_c in figure 4.1a). Adding from top to bottom in figure 4.1, the final energy of the fundamental is derived from components given by ($i = 0, k = 0$) in figure 4.1a, ($i = -2, k = 0$) in figure 4.1a, and ($i = 2, k = -1$) in figure 4.1d. The resultant energy contributions to the carrier are $+0.75$, -0.12, and $-(-0.01)$, adding up to $+0.64$, as shown in figure 4.1e. This procedure is repeated to derive the following spectrum (figure 4.1e).

1 (fundamental)	$0.75 - 0.12 - (-0.01) =$	0.64
2	$0.43 - (-0.02) - 0.04 =$	0.41
3	$0.12 - (-0.08) + 0.01 =$	0.21
4	$0.02 - 0.04 - 0.04 \quad = (-)$	0.06
5	$0.08 - (-0.01) \qquad =$	0.09
6		0.04
7		0.01

In this case, the contribution of the combination frequencies is relatively unimportant. As the index increases, however, higher and higher values of i and k need to be taken into account, causing the contribution of the combination frequencies to become more important.

By modulating the modulating wave itself, one can create a modulating wave with a (theoretically) infinite number of sinusoidal components. The instantaneous amplitude (e) would then be given by

$$e = A \sin[\omega_c t + I_1 \sin(\omega_1 t + I_2 \sin\omega_2 t)]. \tag{3}$$

Here I_2 determines the number of significant components in the modulating signal and I_1 determines the number of significant components in the output signal. The ratio ω_1/ω_c determines the placement of the carrier's sidebands, each of which has sidebands of its own at intervals determined by ω_2/ω_1. Each sideband is both modulated and modulator; the derivation of an equation analogous to equation 2 is rather complicated.

A Piano Simulation

To simulate piano tones it was found best to use a modulating wave made up of two sinusoidal components, one at approximately the carrier frequency and one at approximately four times the carrier frequency. By using two modulating oscillators (one for each component), the amplitude of each component can be handled independently. The amplitudes of the components of the modulating wave (the modulating indices) are made frequency-dependent according to the following formulas:

$$I_1 = 17(8 - \log_e f_c)/(\log_e f_c)^2,$$
$$I_2 = 20(8 - \log_e f_c)/f_c. \tag{4}$$

These formulas produce a spectrum that is rich and complex in the lower register, but gets steadily simpler as the pitch rises. The resulting evolution of the spectrum gives a good piano simulation over its entire range and avoids foldover.

The component frequencies of the modulating wave are slightly larger than integral multiples of the carrier frequency. A small constant, S, with a value of 0.5% of the carrier frequency, is added to the modulating frequencies to simulate the characteristic "stretched" or sharp partials of the piano. The resulting inharmonicity is less than that of a traditional piano (Young 1954), but larger values for S create noticeable beats. A truly harmonic spectrum invariably produces the timbre of an electric piano. Thus, for piano simulation,

$$e = A(t) \sin\left[2\pi f_c t + I_1 \sin 2\pi (f_{m1} + S)t + I_2 \sin 2\pi (f_{m2} + S)t\right] \tag{5}$$

where

$$f_c : f_{m1} : f_{m2} = 1:1:4,$$

$$S = f_c/200$$

with I_1 and I_2 as given in equation 4 and $A(t)$ an amplitude function as shown in figure 4.2.

Another characteristic of piano tones is that the decay time of a given

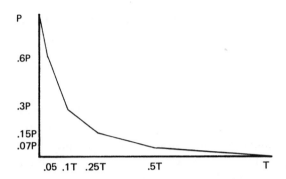

Figure 4.2
Decay function for piano tone. T is given by equation 6; P is the peak amplitude of the tone.

note is dependent on the frequency and peak amplitude of that note. The lower the frequency or the higher the peak amplitude, the longer the note takes to decay if the damper is kept raised. "$A(t)$" in equation 5 is therefore a function of the undamped decay characteristics of a given note that is interrupted by the fall of the damper. This can be easily simulated with two unit generators controlling the note's amplitude— one as the damper (its envelope time set in the play file) and the other as the fixed exponential decay (its envelope time dependent only upon the note's frequency and amplitude).

The decay function that sounds best is not truly exponential. It was found that an exponential amplitude envelope could give either a good attack to the note or a good "ring," but not both. The function used here (figure 4.2) has a rather sharp attack followed by a long, slow decay. Its decay time (which is independent of the note length) is given by

$$T = 10(\sqrt{P})/\sqrt{f_c} \tag{6}$$

where P is the peak amplitude on an arbitrary linear scale of 0–2,000, f_c is the fundamental frequency, and T is the resulting fixed decay length of the amplitude envelope. This formula was obtained by timing the decay times of several notes at several different amplitudes and fitting the results to a simple curve. It, like the tuning formula given below, is only a working approximation of the characteristics of a traditional piano. At middle C, the decay time ranges from 4 sec for a very soft note to 25 sec for a very loud one. At an amplitude of 400 (rather loud), the

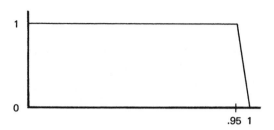

Figure 4.3
Damping envelope for piano tone. The value 1 on the horizontal axis represents the length of the tone.

decay times range from 40 sec in the extreme low register to 4 sec at the highest C of the piano.

The output of the envelope generator containing the fixed decay envelope is then multiplied by the output of an envelope generator containing the damping envelope (see figure 4.3). Its value is 1 until the note is to be cut off, when it falls rapidly to 0.

If equal-tempered tuning is employed throughout, the inharmonicity of the resultant partials seems to fool the ear into thinking that the bass notes are sharp and the treble notes flat. A slight retuning was employed in some of the synthesized pianos, along the lines of traditional piano tunings, by using code similar to the following:

IF $f_c < G/2$ THEN $f_c \leftarrow f_c - (10/f_c)$

IF $f_c > G \times 2$ THEN $f_c \leftarrow f_c + (f_c/200)$

where G is G above middle C.

A better simulation, especially in the higher register, is produced by using two additional outputs (three carriers in all) to mimic the piano's use of several strings for each note. They are slightly mistuned to give a simple chorus effect. The amplitude of each output is controlled by a scaler which removes two of the "strings" in the lower register, as in traditional pianos.

Pedaling can be rather crudely simulated by overlapping the notes being "pedaled" while adding a significant amount of reverberation.

There is no need to change the modulation indices over the course of a note, or to simulate the various noises produced by a piano's action.

String Simulation

String tones can also be synthesized using a complex modulating wave. In the case of the violin, ratios of modulating frequency to carrier frequency of $1:1$, $3:1$, and $4:1$ were found to be most convincing. Once again, frequency-dependent index formulas were used; the following work well in all ranges:

$$I_{1:1} = 7.5/\log_e f_c,$$

$$I_{3:1} = (8.5 - \log_e f_c)/[3 + (f_c/1,000)],$$

$$I_{4:1} = 1.25/\sqrt{f_c},$$

$$I_{3:1} = 10(8.5 - \log_e f_c)/f_c.$$

These formulas can be multiplied by as much as 2 or 3 to produce a more strident timbre. Even higher indices will give a primitive *sul ponticello* effect. Simpler formulas can also be used, and either the second or the third component of the modulating wave can be dispensed with if necessary. Of course, the index formulas will have to be changed in the latter case. The following formulas, for example, also work well in the cello range:

$$I_{1:1} = 7.5/\log_e f_c,$$

$$I_{3:1} = 15/\sqrt{f_c}.$$

To simulate the attack noise of a string instrument, with its frequency skew, chiff, and so forth, a random-number generator is used with a frequency of 2,000 Hz and a bandwidth of 20% of the carrier frequency. This, combined with sharply higher indices in the first 0.2 sec of the note, gives an adequate simulation of the string attack. The index function and noise bandwidth function are shown in figures 4.4 and 4.5, respectively. Figure 4.6 shows the overall amplitude function of the strings. The rise and decay times are fixed at around 0.2 sec. The steady state then takes whatever time is left over.

One can simulate the decay of a detached note by causing the indices to go to 0 with the amplitude during the note's decay. An overlap of 0.2 sec with a short decay time gives a good *legato*.

An oscillator is used to create a 5–6 Hz vibrato. In order to avoid

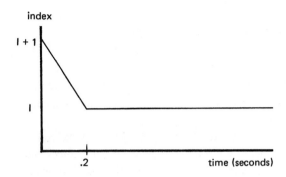

Figure 4.4
Index function for string tone.

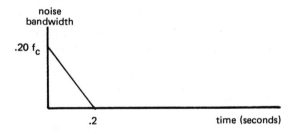

Figure 4.5
Function for controlling noise during attack portion of string tone.

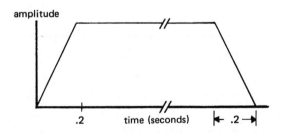

Figure 4.6
Amplitude function for string tone. The length of the "steady state" is determined by the length of the note.

monotony, another random-number generator with a frequency of about 10–20 Hz causes a random fluctuation in the vibrato.

Special Effects

Switches can be added in the instrument definition, allowing one to choose between *arco* and *pizzicato, vibrato* and *non vibrato, legato* and detached, and so on.

Pizzicato can be produced by using the decay function of the piano, decreasing the decay time to $T = 1,000/f_c$, decreasing the indices and attack noise by 25%, and multiplying the indices by the decay function (causing them to go to 0 as the amplitude does).

A convincing choral effect (the sound of an entire orchestral section) can be simulated by adding a second output (two carriers in all) with its own modulators and vibrato generators. One then adds to the various modulating frequencies a series of small (unequal) constants equivalent to that added to the piano to get the stretched harmonics. These constants should be between 1.5 and 4 Hz.

Conclusion

Many other instrument tones can be synthesized using a complex modulating wave, including those of the various brass and percussion instruments. The examples given above should sufficiently illustrate the workings of a process whose potential is only beginning to be explored.

Acknowledgments

I would like to thank James A. Moorer, Julius Smith, Marc LeBrun, John Strawn, Robert Poor, Michael McNabb, and Robert Harvey for their valuable assistance; and in particular I wish to thank John Chowning, who did much of the work on the synthesis of string tones.

References

Chowning, J. 1973. "The synthesis of complex audio spectra by means of frequency modulation." *Journal of the Audio Engineering Society* 21(7): 526–534, 1973. Article 1 in this volume.

LeBrun, M. 1977. "A derivation of the spectrum of FM with a complex modulating wave." *Computer Music Journal* 1(4): 51–52. Article 5 in this volume.

Young, R. W. 1954. "Inharmonicity of piano strings." *Acustica* 4: 259–262.

5 A Derivation of the Spectrum of FM with a Complex Modulating Wave

MARC LEBRUN

The following is a brief exposition of a derivation of the spectrum that results when frequency modulation is performed using a complex signal as the modulating waveform. The basic expression describing frequency modulation which we wish to expand is

$$\sin(C_1 + I_1 \sin\theta_1)$$

where C_1 may be thought of as the carrier, I_1 as the modulation index, and θ_1 as the instantaneous modulation phase. All these elements are subscripted with 1 because the following development can be extended inductively to handle an arbitrary number of modulating signals. I will show only the first step of this induction, that which takes us from the formula for a single modulator to the formula for a double modulator.

The notation has been deliberately chosen in such a way as to "hide" some of the details usually found in the FM formula (Chowning 1973). This is because the derivation makes use of the fact that the transformations used in obtaining the single-modulator FM spectrum are correct independent of what "meanings" we assign to the different variables in the expression. For instance, in the usual formulas C_1 is written as ωt, where ω is the carrier frequency and t is time. However, in the derivation given here, C_1 can in fact be something quite different, although it doesn't hurt (and may help) to think of it as the carrier in normal FM.

In the single-modulator derivation we begin by separating the C_1 term using the elementary trigonometric expansion of the sine of a sum (Spiegel 1968):

$$\sin(C_1)\cos(I_1 \sin\theta_1) + \cos(C_1)\sin(I_1 \sin\theta_1).$$

The next step is to expand the cos of sin and sin of sin terms. This expansion may be looked up in standard references and involves the (by now) familiar Bessel functions. Unfortunately, the formulas usually given have been folded under, that is, the summations have been rearranged so that the index of summation (the subscript on the Bessel functions, etc.) runs from 0 through $+\infty$. This has the undesirable side effect of causing the expressions to become more complicated. We can "unfold" these sums, thus simplifying them, by using the elementary Bessel function

Originally published in *Computer Music Journal* 1(4): 51–52, 1977.

identity (Abramowitz and Stegun 1966)

$$J_{-n} = (-1)^n J_n.$$

We then allow the index of summation to run from $-\infty$ to $+\infty$. The expansion is therefore

$$\sin(C_1) \sum_{k_1 \text{ even}} J_{k_1}(I_1) \cos k_1 \theta_1 + \cos(C_1) \sum_{k_1 \text{ odd}} J_{k_1}(I_1) \sin k_1 \theta_1$$

for all k_1, positive and negative (with the appropriate parity).

We can simplify the two sums by distributing the carrier parts inside, using the elementary trigonometric expansion of the product of sinusoids, and collecting terms in the two summations by using the Bessel function identity for negative subscripts. This gives

$$\sum_{k_1} J_{k_1}(I_1) \sin(C_1 + k_1 \theta_1),$$

the expansion for single-modulator FM.

We will now form the expansion for the double modulator. To do this we will play some games with the carrier term (changing its name in the process), first splitting it into a new carrier and another modulating signal and then absorbing the $k_1 \theta_1$ term into it. First, the split. Let

$$C_1 = C_2 + I_2 \sin \theta_2.$$

This gives

$$\sum_{k_1} J_{k_1}(I_1) \sin(C_2 + I_2 \sin \theta_2 + k_1 \theta_1).$$

Second, the absorption. Set

$$C_2^* = C_2 + k_1 \theta_1.$$

This produces

$$\sum_{k_1} J_{k_1}(I_1) \sin(C_2^* + I_2 \sin \theta_2).$$

The sine term now contains an expression that has exactly the same form as the usual single-modulator expression (although the variables stand for different things). We may therefore perform the appropriate expansion into Bessel functions as before:

$$\sum_{k_1} J_{k_1}(I_1) \sum_{k_2} J_{k_2}(I_2) \sin(C_2^* + k_2 \theta_2).$$

As a final step, we can distribute the outer summand and replace C_2^* by its value to form the double sum

$$\sum_{k_1} \sum_{k_2} J_{k_1}(I_1) J_{k_2}(I_2) \sin(C_2 + k_1\theta_1 + k_2\theta_2).$$

If we think of C_2 as the carrier expression and θ_1 and θ_2 as the modulating-frequency expressions, we have our formula for double modulation (Schottstaedt 1977). In using this formula it is important to remember the Bessel function identity given above for negative values of the summation indices.

A nice result is that we can include a phase angle in the θ parts. Such a phase-angle term would also be multiplied by the appropriate k index. Finally, we can extend this formula inductively by successive "splits" and "absorptions" of the carrier term. The general formula produced is

$$\sum_{k_1} \sum_{k_2} \cdots \sum_{k_n} J_{k_1}(I_1) J_{k_2}(I_2) \cdots J_{k_n}(I_n) \sin(C_n + k_1\theta_1 + \cdots + k_n\theta_n).$$

This completes the derivation.

Acknowledgments

Thanks are due to James A. Moorer for his earlier derivation, to John Chowning and Bill Schottstaedt for introducing this topic in a musical context, to Ken Shoemake and Julius Smith for helping debug this presentation, and to R. W. Gosper for pointing out to me the useful manipulation of unfolding sums.

References

Abramowitz, M., and I. A. Stegun. 1966. *Handbook of Mathematical Functions.* Washington, D.C.: National Bureau of Standards.

Chowning, J. 1973. "The synthesis of complex audio spectra by means of frequency modulation." *Journal of the Audio Engineering Society* 21(7): 526–534, 1973. Article 1 in this volume.

Schottstaedt, B. 1977. "The simulation of natural instrument tones using frequency modulation with a complex modulating wave." *Computer Music Journal* 1(4): 46–50. Article 4 in this volume.

Spiegel, M. R. 1968. *Mathematical Handbook of Formulas and Tables.* New York: McGraw-Hill.

6 Organizational Techniques for $c:m$ Ratios in Frequency Modulation

BARRY TRUAX

Since the introduction of the frequency modulation technique of timbral synthesis (Chowning 1973), a considerable amount of interest has been expressed in this method and a large amount of work has been done in realizing it in a variety of hardware and software configurations. Little, however, appears to have been published as to the systematic organization of one of the main variables of the technique, namely the ratio between the carrier frequency c and the modulating frequency m, also called simply the $c:m$ ratio. This variable is important because it controls the set of partials (called sidebands) in the resultant spectrum. In general, a wide variety of combinations of harmonic and inharmonic partials may be generated depending on careful choice of the $c:m$ ratio. Although it is probably not possible to generate any arbitrary set of partials with this method (for instance, because the partials are always separated by the same linear frequency difference from each other), any useful method of relating $c:m$ ratios will presumably enhance compositional control over their use. Moreover, since some newer synthesis methods, in particular those of Moorer (1976) and LeBrun (1979), take FM as a model or starting point, the applicability of $c:m$ ratio properties may very well transfer to future techniques.

The basic problem of the organization of partials through the sideband generation method of FM stems from the basic form of the FM spectrum,

$$|c \pm nm|, \qquad n = 0, 1, 2, \ldots.$$

In this form, n represents the sideband pair number, the plus and minus signs represent the upper and lower sidebands, respectively, and the absolute-value signs represent the fact that lower sidebands which become negative are reflected into the positive frequency domain with a phase shift of $180°$. Thus we have a set of symmetrically spaced partials radiating outward from the carrier frequency. The reflected lower sidebands in some sense create a lot of the interest in the spectrum, since these may or may not fall on the same frequencies as some of the upper sidebands. The condition for them to coincide is that the $c:m$ ratio be of the form $N:2$ where N is a positive integer; in all cases of N the spectrum consists

Originally published in *Computer Music Journal* 1(4): 39–45, 1977.

of some subset of the harmonic series. With all other ratios, the lower sidebands do not fall against the upper ones, and a considerably richer spectrum results.

Degree of Harmonicity

One generally distinguishes the type of spectrum produced by a $c:m$ ratio as being more or less harmonic, that is, by how many sidebands are multiples of the fundamental and how many are not. To discuss this properly, we need to clarify the means of expressing the $c:m$ ratio. This ratio is expressed most conveniently as a pair of integers. Real numbers could also be used, but since these can be approximated closely by some integer pair we will keep to integers and use their properties. The most intuitive sense of relating degree of harmonicity to $c:m$ ratio is that the simpler the ratio, the more harmonic the spectrum, and vice versa.

A more precise way of saying the same thing is to say that the lower the least common multiple of the two integers c and m, the greater the incidence of sidebands related harmonically to the fundamental. For instance, the extreme end of harmonicity is the $1:1$ ratio, which produces the entire harmonic spectrum. Likewise, all ratios of the form $N:1$ reproduce this same spectrum, with the carrier simply becoming the Nth harmonic in the harmonic spectrum. Next come ratios such as $2:3$ and $3:2$, where the carrier is above the fundamental and all sidebands are multiples of it. This may be generalized for all ratios of the form $N:N+1$ or $N+1:N$, but although such ratios produce a subset of the harmonic spectrum, as N gets higher one progressively loses the sense of harmonicity, just as with ratios of the form $1:N$.

After these ratios producing harmonic spectra come all other ratios where at least some sidebands are inharmonic. Examples using the smallest integers are the ratios $2:5$ and $3:5$, which produce sidebands in the series 2 3 7 8 12 13 .... This may be compared to the "missing fundamental" case, where the fundamental is "filled in" by the higher-order auditory processing, if it is "suggested" strongly enough by harmonics, such as 2 and 3. Theoretically, since we are using only integers, any ratio produces some set of integer-related sidebands above some absent "fundamental." However, as the brain is forced to rely on higher and higher harmonics to supply a fundamental, the effect breaks down.

It should also be remembered that the nth sideband pair is a multiple of the carrier only when n equals c or is some multiple of it. As c increases from small to large integers, the possibility of hearing harmonic relations of sidebands to carrier frequency falls off proportionally.

Typically, then, ratios such as $5:7$ produce what can be heard as distinctly inharmonic spectra (the sideband series is 2 5 9 12 16 19 23 26 ...), comparing favorably with Chowning's ratio $1:1.414...$, which is used to produce an inharmonic bell-like spectrum. This occurs also in the integer case despite the presence of a 6th and 8th harmonic.

Compositional Ordering of $c:m$ Ratios

Although the above relationships may suggest some kinds of compositional ordering of the spectra of certain $c:m$ ratios according to their degree of harmonicity, the tendency is to use these various properties as "rules of thumb," as opposed to systematic principles. However, we are assuming that it is somehow going to be desirable to use different spectra in the same composition. Constant timbre, on the other hand, can be achieved only through $c:m$ ratios that produce the same spectrum. It is when we wish to organize different spectra in a systematic way that the rest of this article becomes useful.

Two methods of organizing $c:m$ ratios will be presented: predicting the precise interval between the carrier and the actual fundamental and relating that interval to just or tempered scales, and predicting sets of $c:m$ ratios producing unique spectra and those producing exactly the same spectrum (i.e. the same set of sidebands).

These methods arose naturally through the use of my POD6 program (Truax 1976, 1977) for synthesis and composition, because this program has the property of being able to select either the carrier or the modulating frequency independent of the $c:m$ ratio. This seemingly unorthodox approach led to the techniques for keeping a constant carrier frequency and determining fundamentals via $c:m$ ratios and the techniques for keeping the modulating frequency constant and using the set of $c:m$ ratios that produce the same spectrum, in contrast with other sets producing a different spectrum. These two methods, derived from compositional practice, led to the two systems summarized above and elaborated in the rest of this article.

Organizing $c:m$ Ratios by Predicting the Fundamental

As will be clear to anyone who has worked even briefly with the FM synthesis technique, the carrier frequency is not always the fundamental frequency of a complex of sidebands produced with a given $c:m$ ratio. In some compositional instances, one wishes to predict—perhaps even control very precisely—where the fundamental frequency lies for any given $c:m$ ratio. We may first distinguish two kinds of cases:

1. Cases in which the carrier frequency is always the fundamental for a $c:m$ ratio where $m \geqslant 2c$, i.e. for the $c:m$ ratio $1:2$ and for those ratios where $m:c$ is greater than 2.
2. All other cases in which the fundamental is below the carrier and is either (a) the lowest unreflected lower sideband or (b) the first reflected lower sideband.

(Sometimes 2a and 2b are identical, but usually either 2a or 2b will be true; that is, one of the lower sidebands closest to 0 Hz will be the fundamental.)

The only other cases are two special instances of case 2, namely the harmonic ratios $1:1$ and $0:1$, which produce all harmonic sidebands above the carrier and above the first pair of sidebands, respectively. These will be ignored in the following discussion.

To predict $c:m$ ratios that have a given fundamental (as in case 2 above), let the ratio of the carrier to the fundamental be expressed as a/b. This allows both just scale intervallic notation, e.g. 15/8, and equal-tempered notation, e.g. 2/1.887749.

For case 2a, where the lowest reflected sideband is the fundamental,

$$\frac{c}{c - nm} = \frac{a}{b}, \qquad n = 1, 2, 3, \dots. \tag{1}$$

Given a ratio a/b, we can find the appropriate $c:m$ ratio(s) by expressing equation 1 as

$$\frac{c}{m} = \frac{na}{a - b}, \qquad n = 1, 2, 3, \dots. \tag{2}$$

Although the given pitch will be present for all $c:m$ ratios determined in this way, equation 2 does not guarantee that the desired frequency will be the lowest. Only certain values of n in equation 2 will produce the desired fundamental. Since the sidebands are spaced apart by m, the pair around 0 Hz such that one is positive and the other negative will determine which of those two becomes the fundamental. The condition will be that the absolute value of the sideband that is the fundamental will be less than or equal to $m/2$. In the case of this distance being exactly $m/2$, both sidebands will fall on the same frequency and be the fundamental.

The condition just described can be expressed as

$$c - nm \leqslant m/2.$$

Therefore,

$$n \geqslant \frac{c}{m} - \frac{1}{2}.$$

Substituting from equation 2, we get

$$n \geqslant \frac{na}{a-b} - \frac{1}{2}.$$

Solving for n gives

$$n \leqslant \frac{a-b}{2b}. \tag{3}$$

The minimum value of n should be 1. Therefore, $(a - b)/2b$ must be greater than or equal to 1. Solving for a/b, we find that a/b is greater than or equal to 3. This shows that, for this case, only intervals that are greater than or equal to 3/1 downward from the carrier are obtainable for a fundamental.

Following the same approach for case 2b, where the first reflected sideband is the fundamental, we may conclude that, much as in equation 1,

$$\frac{c}{nm - c} = \frac{a}{b}. \tag{4}$$

Therefore,

$$\frac{c}{m} = \frac{na}{a+b}. \tag{5}$$

The condition for the fundamental, again, is

$nm - c \leqslant m/2$.

Therefore,

$$n \leqslant \frac{c}{m} + \frac{1}{2}.$$

Substituting from equation 5, we arrive at

$$n \leqslant \frac{a + b}{2b}. \tag{6}$$

Again, since n is minimally 1, $(a + b)/2b$ must be greater than or equal to 1, and therefore a/b must be greater than or equal to 1. In other words, any fundamental frequency below the carrier is obtainable by a ratio where the reflected sideband produces the required frequency, whereas above in case 2a only frequencies lower than 3/1 below the carrier were possible.

Summary

In all cases where the fundamental is below the carrier and forms a ratio of a/b downward from the carrier, the $c:m$ ratio that produces that fundamental may be found from

$$\frac{c}{m} = \frac{na}{a - b}, \qquad n \leqslant \frac{a - b}{2b}$$

for case 2a and from

$$\frac{c}{m} = \frac{na}{a + b}, \qquad n \leqslant \frac{a + b}{2b}$$

for case 2b.

The value of n gives the number of the lower sideband which becomes the fundamental, or the lowest pitch of the resultant spectrum. In terms of frequency modulation, an approximate rule of thumb is that the modulation index is approximately equal to the number of sideband pairs that have a significant amount of energy in the resultant spectrum. This means that a modulation index of I about equal to n will be necessary in order for this fundamental to be actually heard in the spectrum. In addition, the carrier frequency must be in a sufficiently high range that the fundamental is audible. Naturally, for a fundamental very far below

Table 6.1

$c:m$ ratios producing intervals in just intonation between the carrier and the fundamental. The so-called harmonic seventh interval (7:4) is included for comparison even though it does not appear in the major or minor just scales.

Ascending interval	Descending interval	Note	c:m ratio						
			1st octave below		2nd octave below		3rd octave below		
			Unreflected	Reflected	Unreflected	Reflected	Unreflected	Reflected	
2:1	1:1	C	—	1:2	—	2:3	4:3	4:5	8:5
15:8	16:15	B	—	16:31	—	32:47	64:49	64:79	128:79
9:5	10:9	B♭	—	10:19	—	20:29	40:31	40:49	80:49
7:4	8:7	B♭⁻	—	8:15	—	16:23	32:25	32:29	64:39
5:3	6:5	A	—	6:11	—	12:17	24:19	24:29	48:29
8:5	5:4	A♭	—	5:9	—	5:7	5:4 / 5:2	5:6 / 5:3 / 5:2	
3:2	4:3	G	—	4:7	—	8:11	16:13 / 32:13	16:19 / 32:19 / 48:19	
36:25	25:18	G♭	—	25:43	—	25:34	50:41 / 100:41	50:59 / 100:59 / 150:59	

45:32	64:45	F♯	—	64:109	—	128:173	165:136 165:68	165:194 165:97 199:78
4:3	3:2	F	—	3:5	3:2	3:4 3:2	6:5 12:5	6:7 12:7 18:7
5:4	8:5	E	—	8:13	16:11	16:21 32:21	32:27 64:27	32:37 64:37 96:37
6:5	5:3	E♭	—	5:8	10:7	10:13 20:13	20:17 40:17	20:23 40:23 60:23
9:8	16:9	D	—	16:25	32:23	32:41 64:41	64:55 128:55 192:55	64:73 128:73 192:73 249:71
16:15	15:8	D♭	—	15:23	15:11	15:19 30:19	15:13 30:13 45:13	15:17 30:17 45:17 60:17
1:1	2:1	C	—	2:3	4:3	4:5 8:5	8:7 16:7 24:7	8:9 16:9 8:3 32:9

Table 6.2
c:m ratios producing equal-tempered intervals between carrier and fundamental.

Interval	Note	c:m ratio					
		1st octave below		2nd octave below		3rd octave below	
		Unreflected	Reflected	Unreflected	Reflected	Unreflected	Reflected
1.887749	B	—	107:208	—	89:131	89:68	89:110 89:55
1.781797	B♭/A♯	—	55:104	—	110:159	220:171	202:247 229:140
1.681793	A	—	44:81	—	88:125	176:139	176:213 195:118
1.587401	A♭/G♯	—	63:113	—	63:88	126:101 252:101	126:151 252:151 253:101
1.499307	G	—	4:7	—	179:246	251:204 251:102	203:241 251:149 235:93
1.414214	G♭/F♯	—	140:239	—	99:134	198:163 243:100	198:233 243:143 181:71
1.334840	F	—	3:5	3:2	3:4 3:2	6:5 12:5	6:7 12:7 18:7
1.259921	E	—	127:207	127:87	127:167 254:167	127:107 254:107	127:147 254:147 127:49

1.189207	Eb/D#	—	37:59	37:26	37:48 37:24	74:63 148:63	74:85 148:85 222:85
1.122462	D	—	98:153	196:141	196:251 253:162	221:190 221:95 171:49	221:252 221:126 221:84 221:63
1.059463	Db/C#	—	151:231	185:136	185:234 185:117	219:190 219:95 204:59	219:248 219:124 151:57 219:62
1.000000	C	—	2:3	4:3	4:5 8:5	8:7 16:7 24:7	8:9 16:9 8:3 32:9

the carrier, its presence may be perceived more as a low rumble than as a true fundamental. Therefore, it has been assumed in this argument that the desired fundamental lies in a normal musical range (above 60 Hz).

Computer Calculation

A computer program was written to calculate the $c:m$ ratio that best produced the desired fundamental below the carrier as expressed by the interval a/b. The two cases above were both considered. The fundamentals chosen were those pitches that figure in the major, minor, and chromatic just scales and those from the equal-tempered scale. Six octaves for each pitch were considered—that is, each instance of the desired pitch in the six octaves below the carrier. Although intervals are normally calculated or expressed as being above a given note, e.g. 3/2 being the fifth above, these ratios were simply converted into descending intervals, such as 4/3 for the descending fifth, 8/3 for the descending 12th, and so on.

For many different reasons, $c:m$ ratios are best handled as an integer ratio, and therefore the goal of the program was to find the "best fitting" integer $c:m$ ratio. In addition, the current POD6 limitation that the c and m ratio values must be less than or equal to 255 was observed. In some cases this prevented the most accurate ratio being found, but this only occurred for fundamentals four or more octaves below the carrier. At least one accurate ratio exists for all six octaves, and in most cases a multiplicity of ratios (through the various possible n values) were found that produced the required fundamental within 2–5 cents. In the first three octaves below the carrier, the error was less than 0.5 cents; the results for these three octaves are reported in tables 6.1 and 6.2 for the just and equal-tempered scales, respectively.

Organizing $c:m$ Ratios According to Spectral Identity and Uniqueness

Instead of organizing $c:m$ ratios by predicting a carrier/fundamental interval, we now turn to examining the spectra, or sideband sets, produced by certain $c:m$ ratios. In particular, we wish to know which $c:m$ ratios produce identical spectra, i.e. the same set of sidebands, and which produce spectra that are entirely unique, i.e. nonidentical sets of sidebands.

In the case of identical spectra or sidebands, the answer is readily obtained. For the same sidebands to be generated by two $c:m$ ratios, their m values clearly must be identical. What is then different between the spectra is simply the matter of which partial is the carrier frequency. For any sideband set, a $c:m$ ratio exists where the carrier frequency can become the frequency of any sideband.

To clarify the means of expressing $c:m$ ratios, we will refer to the *normal form* of a $c:m$ ratio, which means the case where the carrier is the fundamental (more precisely, where $m \geqslant 2c$). This is the first case considered in the preceding section. Any $c:m$ ratio may be reduced to its normal form by successively applying the operation $c = |c - m|$ until the ratio falls into the proper range; e.g., $11:5$ becomes $|11 - 5|:5 = 6:5$, and then $|6 - 5|:5 = 1:5$, where $1:5$ is the normal form. Likewise, $4:5$ also has the normal form $|4 - 5|:5 = 1:5$.

Rule 1: Given a $c:m$ ratio in its normal form, the set of $c:m$ ratios producing identical spectra or sideband sets is

$$|c \pm nm|:m, \qquad n = 1, 2, 3, \ldots.$$

All such spectra have the same modulating frequency; however, not all ratios with the same modulating frequency produce the same spectrum (compare $1:5$ and $2:5$). For example, the ratio $2:5$, which is in its normal form, has a spectrum identical to those produced by $3:5, 7:5, 8:5, 12:5, 13:5, 17:5, 18:5, \ldots$ In practice there will be a slight difference in timbre because the amplitude of each partial will be different for a given modulation index, even though the same set of partials is present. When two such spectra lie on the same fundamental, they will completely fuse perceptually.

To organize $c:m$ ratios according to the uniqueness of their spectra, we must turn to the mathematical series known as the Farey series, a conclusion for which the author is indebted to Eric Regener. The Farey series and its properties are succinctly presented by Regener (1973) as follows: "The Farey series of order n is the ascending series of irreducible fractions between 0 and 1 whose denominators do not exceed n. The Farey series of order 7, for example, is

$$\frac{0}{1} \ \frac{1}{7} \ \frac{1}{6} \ \frac{1}{5} \ \frac{1}{4} \ \frac{2}{7} \ \frac{1}{3} \ \frac{2}{5} \ \frac{3}{7} \ \frac{1}{2} \ \frac{4}{7} \ \frac{3}{5} \ \frac{2}{3} \ \frac{5}{7} \ \frac{3}{4} \ \frac{4}{5} \ \frac{5}{6} \ \frac{6}{7} \ \frac{1}{1}.$$

If a_1/b_1 is any term of a Farey series and a_2/b_2 its successor, the series has the property that

$$a_1 b_2 - a_2 b_1 = -1.$$

Table 6.3
The $c:m$ ratio series of order 32.

0:1	1:32	1:31	1:30	1:29	1:28	1:27	1:26
1:25	1:24	1:23	1:22	1:21	1:20	1:19	1:18
1:17	1:16	2:31	1:15	2:29	1:14	2:27	1:13
2:25	1:12	2:23	1:11	3:32	2:21	3:31	1:10
3:29	2:19	3:28	1:9	3:26	2:17	3:25	1:8
4:31	3:23	2:15	3:22	4:29	1:7	4:27	3:20
5:33	2:13	5:32	3:19	4:25	5:31	1:6	5:29
4:23	3:17	5:28	2:11	5:27	3:16	4:21	5:26
6:31	1:5	6:29	5:24	4:19	3:14	5:23	7:32
2:9	7:31	5:22	3:13	7:30	4:17	5:21	6:25
7:29	1:4	8:31	7:27	6:23	5:19	4:15	7:26
3:11	8:29	5:18	7:25	9:32	2:7	9:31	7:24
5:17	8:27	3:10	7:23	4:13	9:29	5:16	6:19
7:22	8:25	9:28	10:31	1:3	11:32	10:29	9:26
8:23	7:20	6:17	11:31	5:14	9:25	4:11	11:30
7:19	10:27	3:8	11:29	8:21	5:13	12:31	7:18
9:23	11:28	2:5	13:32	11:27	9:22	7:17	12:29
5:12	13:31	8:19	11:26	3:7	13:30	10:23	7:16
11:25	4:9	13:29	9:20	14:31	5:11	11:24	6:13
13:28	7:15	15:32	8:17	9:19	10:21	11:23	12:25
13:27	14:29	15:31	1:2				

Moreover, any two fractions having this property are adjacent in the Farey series whose order is the greater of the two denominators." The ratios of the $c:m$ series of order 32 are given in table 6.3.

Although the Farey series is defined over the range from 0 to 1, it is symmetrical about $\frac{1}{2}$, and from the definition given above of normal form we can see that we only need the ratios between 0 and $\frac{1}{2}$ where we equate the $c:m$ ratio to the fractions in the Farey series.

Rule 2: Given $c:m$ ratios in their normal form, those producing unique spectra belong to the fractions of a Farey series from 0 to $\frac{1}{2}$ of order n where n is equal to the largest value of m.

Recalling that the Farey series of order n is that where the denominators of the fractions do not exceed n, we can define analogously a $c:m$ series of order n where the values of m do not exceed n. For instance, the $c:m$ series of order 9 is

$$\frac{1}{9} \ \frac{1}{8} \ \frac{1}{7} \ \frac{1}{6} \ \frac{1}{5} \ \frac{2}{9} \ \frac{1}{4} \ \frac{2}{7} \ \frac{1}{3} \ \frac{3}{8} \ \frac{2}{5} \ \frac{3}{7} \ \frac{4}{9} \ \frac{1}{2}.$$

The beginning of the series at the left could be completed with the harmonic ratio $0:1$ or $1:1$. Hearing this series on a low-pitched fundamental, one hears a progression of spectra from widely spaced partials giving a high-pitched coloration to the sound (the ratio $1:9$), gradually descending to the equally spaced sidebands (all odd harmonics) of the $1:2$ ratio. This series was the structural basis of the tape part of my *Sonic Landscape No. 4* (1977) for organ and tape, where each normal-form $c:m$ ratio and its family of ratios producing identical spectra formed a unique harmonic region in each layer of the piece.

Naturally, the series in this simple order with all the ratios in normal form tends to produce predictable results that would seldom be desirable compositionally. However, the purpose of this method is merely to create an organizational scheme that allows all $c:m$ ratios to find their places. Having achieved that, one may then proceed to choose ratios by whatever means one wishes.

In terms of the above remarks on harmonicity, it should be noted that the above series includes both harmonic spectra of the form $1:N$ and inharmonic spectra characterized by $c \neq 1$. The first inharmonic spectra arise with the $c:m$ series of order 5, namely with the $2:5$ ratio. In the series quoted above of order 9, six ratios are inharmonic and eight are harmonic; however, the inharmonic ones are clustered toward the right end of the set and the harmonic ones toward the left end—a pattern the author found suggestive in the above-mentioned work.

The property of fusion between $c:m$ ratios producing the same spectra can be used to eliminate the problem of always hearing the same spectral development as the modulation index changes in a sound. When two or more sounds with different ratios of the same family of $c:m$ ratios are mixed, if they have the same fundamental the resultant spectral envelope will be complex enough to avoid the "typical FM sound" produced by a simple modulation index envelope. Slight mistunings of the component frequencies add a further richness or "choral effect." I used these techniques in *Androgyny* (1978) and in the accompaniment tape for part II of *Love Songs* for voice and tape. Further work has been done along these lines in relating harmonic and inharmonic $c:m$ ratios based on specific harmonics that both kinds of ratios have in common (e.g., $1:7$ and $2:7$ both include the sixth and the eighth harmonic in their spectra). This technique was also used in *Love Songs*, in *Aerial* (1979) for horn and tape, and in *Arras* (1980) for four-channel tape (Truax 1982).

Conclusion

Frequency modulation is a powerful method for timbral synthesis; however, its usefulness remains limited by one's knowledge of the types of spectra produced by this method. To produce a constant timbre with FM, one simply maintains a single $c:m$ ratio. However, to organize different timbres requires some method of organizing $c:m$ ratios if one wishes to do it systematically. Clearly a wide variety of such methods could be generated. Even more elaborate ways than those presented here are possible, such as organization by interval content or with respect to critical bandwidths. Both of the methods reviewed here have proved compositionally useful in experience with my POD6 program for composition and sound synthesis, and their strength lies in the fact that they are systematizations of empirical methods derived through use of an interactive computer system for composition.

References

Chowning, J. 1973. "The synthesis of complex audio spectra by means of frequency modulation." *Journal of the Audio Engineering Society* 21(7): 526–534. Article 1 in this volume.

LeBrun, M. 1979. "Digital waveshaping synthesis." *Journal of the Audio Engineering Society* 27(4): 250–266.

Moorer, J. A. 1976. "The synthesis of complex audio spectra by means of discrete summation formulae." *Journal of the Audio Engineering Society* 24: 717–727.

Regener, E. 1973. *Pitch Notation and Equal Temperament: A Formal Study*. Occasional Paper no. 6. Berkeley: University of California Press.

Truax, B. 1976. "A communicational approach to computer sound programs." *Journal of Music Theory* 20(2): 227–300.

Truax, B. 1977. "The POD system of interactive composition programs." *Computer Music Journal* 1(3): 30–39.

Truax, B. 1982. "Timbral construction in *Arras* as a stochastic process." *Computer Music Journal* 6(3): 72–77.

7 A Tutorial on Nonlinear Distortion or Waveshaping Synthesis

CURTIS ROADS

Recently there have been a number of references to a technique of sound synthesis termed nonlinear distortion, nonlinear processing, or waveshaping. This technique has surfaced as an economical and flexible method of sound synthesis, capable of generating sounds as rich as those produced through computationally costly additive synthesis techniques. In addition, the technique offers a unified theoretical framework for the understanding of several other nonlinear synthesis methods, notably frequency modulation and discrete summation synthesis.

With the public availability of three major technical papers on the subject (Arfib 1979; Beauchamp 1979; LeBrun 1979), there is now a need for a tutorial. Although a precise and comprehensive formulation of the results of the various forms of nonlinear distortion or waveshaping involves a great deal of calculation, the concepts underlying the technique can be presented in a straightforward, largely nonmathematical form. This brief tutorial is intended particularly as an orientation and a pointer to the more technical papers cited above. A musician unfamiliar with signal-processing tools save for electronic music equipment and a Music V–like (Mathews 1969) graphic "patching" language will be able to understand the basic concepts of this powerful technique through this exposition.

Historical Note

The technique was "in the air" a few years ago, and appears to have been conceived by several people in parallel. According to Arfib (1979), Risset used the technique to simulate clarinet tones in 1969. Indeed, example 150 in Risset's *Catalog of Computer Synthesized Sounds* is a description of an instrument in which a sine wave is "submitted to a nonlinear transfer function" and the amplitude control of the sine wave "determines the amount of distortion performed on the sine wave" (Risset 1969). Schaefer (1970) presented the technique in an analog implementation—a form in which the technique is still viable, if somewhat less easy to control precisely—and introduced with Süen (1970) the foundation of the mathematical techniques that can be used to describe the spectra produced by nonlinear

This is a revised and updated version of a paper that originally appeared in *Computer Music Journal* 3(2): 29–34, 1979.

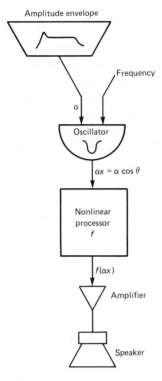

Figure 7.1
A basic waveshaping instrument in a Music V–like graphic notation. The sinusoidal oscillator, whose amplitude is controlled by the amplitude envelope signal α, is fed through the nonlinear processor or waveshaper to produce harmonic spectra.

waveshaping. Hutchins (1976) gave a clear and concise exposition of the theory of nonlinear transfer functions in an analog context. The digital formulation of the technique is an elaboration upon these ideas worked out independently by Arfib and LeBrun.

A Description of the Basic Technique

The classic formulation of the technique starts with a sine or cosine wave, the amplitude of which is controlled by an envelope generator (shown in a Music V–like graphic notation in figure 7.1). (Cosine waves are used for convenience in the mathematical presentations.) This wave is fed into a *nonlinear processing* device, so called because whatever is presented to it as input is "distorted" or transformed by the time it is output. (Hence the term nonlinear distortion.)

The nonlinear processor (or *waveshaper*) may be likened to a distorting amplifier. Various frequencies fed into such an amplifier will be treated unequally; some such frequency components will be suppressed, others will be exaggerated, and a whole new set of spectral components not present in the input signal may be introduced by the nonlinear processor. These new spectral components are called *modulation products*. By turning the volume knob of almost any analog amplifier to maximum, one notices how by saturating the transistors of the amplifier the input signal is subjected to *overmodulation distortion* or *clipping*. In its grossest form this will convert a sine wave sent into such an amplifier into a square wave. For a complex signal, it will introduce so many modulation products that the input signal itself will be blotted out by distortion. In reproducing or recording music, such nonlinear processing is highly undesirable, since distortion of this type can destroy the fidelity of the recording to the original sound source. On the other hand, distortion can be highly useful in analog electronic music synthesis for "enriching" a sound by using preamplifiers with various distortion characteristics as nonlinear processors. For example, amplifiers based on vacuum tubes have different distortion characteristics than amplifiers based on transistors and operational amplifier circuits.

This naturally leads to the question of how one describes the distortion characteristics of various nonlinear processors. One useful method is that of describing the *transfer function* of the nonlinear processor.

The Transfer Function

In papers on the technique of nonlinear distortion or waveshaping, the transfer function (or *shaping function* in LeBrun 1979) is usually represented as a line from the left side of a square to the right side. In order to understand this representation, one might refer back to the amplifier analogy. The transfer function of an ideal amplifier is a straight line; hence, such an amplifier is said to have a *linear* response. The input signal is represented on a normalized scale of values between -1 and $+1$ on the abscissa (x axis); the corresponding output signal is represented on the ordinate (y axis) (see figure 7.2).

A good way to acquaint oneself with the effects of nonlinear distortion

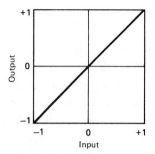

Figure 7.2
Transfer or shaping function F, shown with a linear response. That is, a value of -1 sent into the transfer function will yield -1 at the output, a value of 0 sent in will yield 0 as the output, and so on.

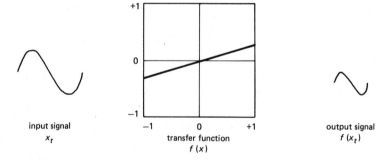

Figure 7.3

or waveshaping is to gain an intuitive visual understanding of the transfer function. Perhaps an easy way to gain this intuitive knowledge would be to play with the image of a transfer-function grid on a visual display device such as a graphics terminal. (For some examples see figures 7.3–7.6.) Given a computer music system with some interactive sound-synthesis capability, one could use some kind of a stylus to draw various transfer functions and then send various sounds through them, playing with their effects in real time.

The effect of a few simple transfer functions can be described in general terms. Figure 7.3–7.6 are examples of transfer functions, showing the effect of each such function on a sinusoidal input signal x_t. If one had drawn the straight line shown in figure 7.3, the effect would be, for any signal input, a signal with identical waveform shape but at a reduced am-

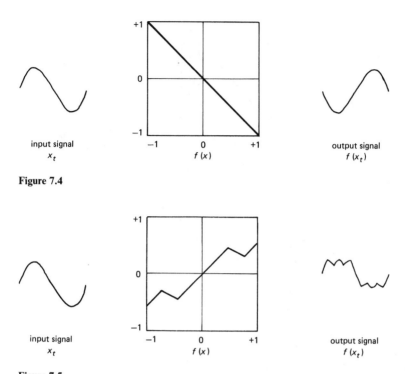

Figure 7.4

Figure 7.5

plitude. Using the line shown in figure 7.4, one sees that for a positive-value input to the transfer function (x axis) a negative value is obtained at the output (y axis). Thus, applying this transfer or shaping function results in phase inversion (or, to be consistent with our terminology, phase distortion). Any bump or irregularity in the transfer function will result in a corresponding distortion applied to the output waveform. See figure 7.5 for an example. As a final example of this type, the amplitude-sensitive nature of the technique can be demonstrated. In figure 7.6, one sees a transfer function characterized by a straight line in the middle (low-amplitude) range of the grid. Such a function will pass a low-amplitude signal through with no distortion. However, when the amplitude of the input signal increases, the extreme ends of the transfer function (acting on the peak and the trough of a high-amplitude sine wave) are subjected to a rather complicated form of distortion. It is easy to see that the most general behavior of a signal passed through such a transfer function is not unlike that of most conventional musical instruments, in that by playing

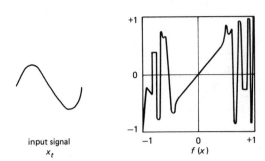

input signal
x_t

Figure 7.6

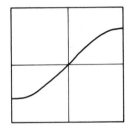

Figure 7.7
An odd function, symmetric about the x axis.

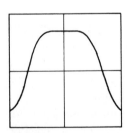

Figure 7.8
An even function, symmetric about the y axis.

"harder" (blowing harder, bowing with more pressure, striking more sharply, etc.) the spectrum of the musical output is enriched. Thus, by passing a signal whose overall amplitude varies over time through the transfer function, one obtains a corresponding *time-varying spectrum* output. This is an important feature of the technique; given a single transfer function, a variety of output waveforms may be obtained simply by varying the amplitude (and/or DC offset) of the input signal in order to apply various regions of the transfer function.

Another convenient property of transfer functions is that any of these functions drawn to be symmetric about the x axis (the definition of an odd function) will generate only odd harmonics (figure 7.7). A transfer function drawn symmetric about the y axis (an even function) will generate only even harmonics of a cosine wave input (figure 7.8).

A More Analytic Approach to Transfer Functions

Drawing transfer or shaping functions intuitively by hand is one way to become acquainted with their effects. However, beyond a certain degree of visual complexity it may become difficult to predict the effects of a given transfer function. Thus, for more predictable results, a more analytic approach is needed.

A well-developed branch of mathematics is the theory of approximation of functions. This theory provides a number of tools for constructing arbitrary curves (e.g. transfer functions) out of elementary functions such as polynomials, trigonometric functions (Moore 1978), and other orthogonal functions. The foundations of approximation theory were laid in the nineteenth century. Weierstrass proved theoretically that any continuous function could be approximated by an algebraic polynomial with any degree of accuracy. Bernoulli proved the theoretical possibility of representing an arbitrary function by trigonometric polynomials with any degree of accuracy. There are several advantages to constructing curves out of these kinds of functions. The main advantage is that, through various mathematical identities (i.e., ways of relating one function to another), some formulas have been derived that, given a mathematical description of an input signal and another mathematical description of a transfer function, make it possible to predict exactly the output spectrum generated by the process of nonlinear distortion or waveshaping. As Arfib

(1979) points out, the first benefit of using a limited-degree polynomial for the transfer function is that the output will be band-limited. This of course makes it possible to predict whether foldover will occur, and thus foldover can be avoided. (Foldover, or aliasing, occurs in digital systems when frequencies above half the sampling rate reflect into the lower range of the spectrum.)

Arfib (1979) and LeBrun (1979) used a particular family of polynomials, the Chebychev polynomials of the first kind, as a tool for specifying shaping or transfer functions. Conveniently, they take on values in the range of the transfer functions $[-1, +1]$. For Chebychev polynomials the following very useful identity holds, making it possible to plug in various formulas for T_k to obtain the kth harmonic:

$$T_k[\cos(\theta)] = \cos(k\theta).$$

The equations for T_0 through T_8 are the following, where $x = \cos(\theta)$:

$$T_0 = 1,$$

$$T_1 = x,$$

$$T_2 = 2x^2 - 1,$$

$$T_3 = 4x^3 - 3x,$$

$$T_4 = 8x^4 - 8x^2 + 1,$$

$$T_5 = 16x^5 - 20x^3 + 5x,$$

$$T_6 = 32x^6 - 48x^4 + 18x^2 - 1,$$

$$T_7 = 64x^7 - 112x^5 + 56x^3 - 7x,$$

$$T_8 = 128x^8 - 256x^6 + 160x^4 - 32x^2 + 1.$$

(For more Chebychev equations, look in any handbook of mathematical functions.) In order to obtain a wide range of harmonics, say, from the ith to the nth harmonics, one simply forms the weighted sum of a set of Chebychev polynomials T_i to T_n according to the formula

$$f(x) = \frac{h_0}{2} + \sum_{k=i}^{n} h_k T_k(x)$$

where $f(x)$ is the transfer or shaping function, $h_0/2$ is a conventional offset, $\sum$ signifies the summing operation for i to n, h_k is the weight (amplitude) of the kth harmonic, and $T_k(x)$ is the Chebychev polynomial that when used as a transfer function will generate the kth harmonic. A major musical implication of this formulation is that it is possible to control even and odd harmonics, upper and lower harmonics, and closely spaced and.widely dispersed harmonics more or less independently. Both Arfib and LeBrun give details on constructing these polynomial transfer functions. In particular, they show how the coefficients of the Chebychev polynomials are related to the amplitudes of the harmonics. Arfib then discusses an implementation in the context of the MUSIC V sound-synthesis program, while LeBrun provides program listings written in an ALGOL variant.

Extensions of the Basic Technique

What has been described so far is a simple instrument that accepts a cosine wave as input and passes it through a transfer or shaping function to produce a steady-state sound whose harmonic spectrum can be determined in advance. Many extensions to this basic configuration are possible. Some of them are discussed informally below.

Obtaining Dynamic Spectra

In the basic configuration it was assumed that the cosine wave sent through the transfer function was of constant amplitude; that is, α in figure 7.1 was equal to some constant. Computation of a steady-state spectrum relies on this steady amplitude. However, if a curved envelope function is used for α, one obtains dynamic spectra as the output of the nonlinear processor. In general, one can expect an overall spectral evolution similar to that of the well-known frequency modulation (FM) technique, in that the greater the amplitude α (functioning similarly to the index in the FM theory) of the input signal, the more harmonics will be generated. Intuitively, this makes sense because as one increases the amplitude of the input, more of the bends and curves of a transfer function such as the one shown in figure 7.6 are being applied to the input, producing ever more complicated distortion and hence a broader band of output sound. Suen (1970) gives a mathematical derivation of the dynamic behavior of a nonlinear processor and points out how the evolution of individual harmonics is not a linear function of the input signal's amplitude α.

Obtaining Inharmonic Spectra

In the basic configuration, the output of the nonlinear processor is always a spectrum with components whose frequencies are simple integer ratios (harmonics). One way to obtain more complex spectra has been suggested by both Arfib and LeBrun. This process involves amplitude-modulating the output of the nonlinear processor $f_{\alpha x}$ with some other frequency f_{am}. The effect of amplitude modulation is to produce a pair of sum and difference frequencies or sidebands symmetric about the frequency f_{am}. If $f_{\alpha x}/f_{am}$ is not a simple integer ratio, inharmonic sum and difference frequencies will be generated.

Normalization or "Post-Compensation" of Amplitude

In generating dynamic spectra, the input envelope or index α is used as a control variable to determine the amount of distortion (and hence the bandwidth) of the sound. An inflexible side effect of using α in this way is that it also lowers or raises the overall amplitude coming out of the nonlinear processor. What if one chooses to sweep over the entire transfer function (to obtain constantly evolving spectra) while maintaining a constant output amplitude? Some kind of *post-compensation* (i.e., after the nonlinear processor) or amplitude normalization is clearly required. The function of this normalization is simply to control the output amplitude independent of the index α. The problem is perhaps not as simple as it would seem at first glance, and various scaling functions may be considered (LeBrun 1979).

Controlling Phase

Controlling the phase of various components in a spectrum can sometimes be useful. One way of controlling the phase of the cosine components x_k produced by waveshaping is to generate an additional signal y that is a sine wave of an amplitude determined by the phase one wishes to obtain. This sine wave y may then be passed through a separate transfer or shaping function U_{n-1} to produce a set of spectral components y_k. Each component y_k corresponds to a component x_k in the original signal, since the transfer functions T and U are related. Indeed, U_{n-1} is a Chebychev polynomial of the second kind obtained by differentiating $T_n(x)$ with respect to x and dividing by n. Summing the two waveforms x_k and y_k effectively shifts the cosine wave to the desired phase.

Other Extensions

For even more flexible (and complicated) types of spectra and spectral evolution, a number of additional extensions can be mentioned. First, one may choose to add a filter to the output of the nonlinear processor, as Beauchamp (1979) has done. There are a number of reasons one might want to do this; suffice it to say here that a filter can add another degree of control (and thus variation) to the evolution of the spectra produced by a nonlinear processor. (See Beauchamp 1979 for more details.)

Another extension to the basic configuration suggested by Arfib (1979) is to multiply two distorted signals x_1 and x_2 by a sine wave modulating at frequency f_{am}. When x_1, x_2, and f_{am} are chosen carefully, rich inharmonic spectra and formant structures may be generated.

A last important extension is to substitute a complex signal for x in figure 7.1, such as a rich electronic sound or a concrète sound like a voice, to obtain a "waveshaped" sound, using various transfer or shaping functions.

Playing with Waveshaping

The analytic approach to waveshaping, using pure cósine waves as input and Chebychev polynomials as transfer functions, is useful in a musical situation wherein precisely defined and controlled harmonic spectra are the desired result. In practice, though, any signal may be sent through any waveshaping function. Until an extensive catalog of interesting wave-shaping sounds is published, trial-and-error use of the technique is the only option. In studio work, the musician who experiments freely with waveshaping faces two technical obstacles: the possibility of foldover with untame transfer functions, and wildly varying amplitude outputs from the waveshaper. Careful tuning and testing is required for even simple deviations from the classical analytic technique.

Conclusions

The technique of nonlinear distortion or waveshaping is a flexible, computationally efficient method of generating a rich and varied collection of sounds. It should be quite feasible to implement the technique in software using the newer microprocessors for real-time or near real-time synthesis of sound. Several digital synthesizer designs incorporate means for realizing the technique in their hardware. It is reasonable to expect that nonlinear distortion or waveshaping will become a widely used technique for both synthesis and processing of musical sound.

Acknowledgments

I would like to thank Leonard Cottrell of Berkeley for his counsel on the subject of this chapter. Thanks also to John Snell and John Strawn for their careful reading and comments on the draft.

References

Arfib, D. 1979. "Digital synthesis of complex spectra by means of multiplication of nonlinear distorted sine waves." *Journal of the Audio Engineering Society* 27(10): 757–768.

Beauchamp, J. 1979. "Brass tone synthesis by spectrum evolution matching with nonlinear functions." *Computer Music Journal* 3(2): 35–43. Article 8 in this volume.

Hutchins, B. 1976. "Project 1—Non-linear transfer functions." *Electronotes* 8(68): 3–8.

LeBrun, M. 1979. "Digital waveshaping synthesis." *Journal of the Audio Engineering Society* 27(4): 250–266.

Mathews, M. V., with J. E. Miller, F. R. Moore, J. R. Pierce, and J.-C. Risset. 1969. *The Technology of Computer Music.* Cambridge, Mass.: MIT Press.

Moore, F. R. 1978. "An introduction to the mathematics of digital signal processing, Part I." *Computer Music Journal* 2(1): 38–47.

Moore, F. R. 1978. "An introduction to the mathematics of digital signal processing, Part II." *Computer Music Journal* 2(2): 38–60.

Risset, J.-C. 1969. *An Introductory Catalog of Computer Synthesized Sounds.* Murray Hill, N.J.: Bell Telephone Laboratories.

Schaefer, R. 1970. "Electronic musical tone production by nonlinear waveshaping." *Journal of the Audio Engineering Society* 18(4): 413–417.

Suen, C. 1970. "Derivation of harmonic equations in nonlinear circuits." *Journal of the Audio Engineering Society* 18(6): 675–676.

8 Brass-Tone Synthesis by Spectrum Evolution Matching with Nonlinear Functions

JAMES BEAUCHAMP

The use of frequency modulation to create sounds resembling those of acoustic instruments has received a great deal of attention in recent years. The popularity of this technique stems primarily from its economy and versatility. Little attention has been focused on attempts to synthetically match specific analyzed characteristics of the sounds of acoustic instruments. A solution to this problem using an economical sound-synthesis model should provide more realistic synthesis, particularly if the acoustic properties of instruments are taken into account. A step in this direction is the use of nonlinear processors and linear filters to synthesize wind-instrument waveforms.

There has been ample evidence from recent analytical studies that the harmonic spectra of brass instruments (and probably those of other wind instruments) are somehow related to spectra that can be produced by the nonlinear distortion of a variable-amplitude sine wave. It is the purpose of this chapter to review this evidence and present some results of attempts to synthesize brass tones using this technique.

Nonlinear Synthesis Model

As shown in figure 8.1, a sine wave of amplitude α is applied to a nonlinear processor with transfer function F. This amplitude α functions like an index in FM terminology, and it is controlled by an envelope generator and therefore varies with time. The nonlinear processor acts to distort the sine wave into a waveform containing several harmonics whose amplitudes depend on the envelope $\alpha(t)$ and the transfer function F. The harmonic amplitudes are further altered by the filter having response $H(f)$. For added flexibility, the output amplitude may be controlled by multiplication by $\beta(t)$, which is produced by a second envelope generator. The entire model is analogous to the acoustic behavior of a wind instrument; the lip-mouthpiece section is simulated by the variable-amplitude sine wave and the nonlinear processor, and the pipe is simulated by the filter.

The essential feature of the nonlinear synthesis model is that as α increases, the evolution of the harmonic spectrum of the output is governed by the form of the function F. If we assume that F is "smooth," it can be

Originally published in *Computer Music Journal* 3(2): 35–43, 1979.

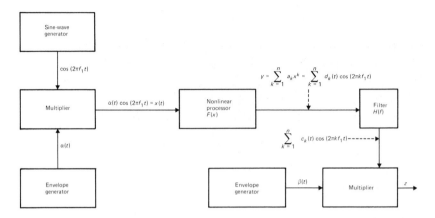

Figure 8.1
Nonlinear synthesis model.

well approximated by an nth-degree polynomial

$$F(x) = a_0 + a_1 x + a_2 x^2 + \cdots + a_n x^n. \tag{1a}$$

x is given by

$$x = \alpha \cos(\theta), \qquad \theta = 2\pi f_1 t, \tag{1b}$$

where α is the amplitude and f_1 is the fundamental frequency. The action of F produces a harmonic series at the nonlinear-processor output:

$$y = \tfrac{1}{2} d_0 + d_1 \cos(\theta) + d_2 \cos(2\theta) + \cdots + d_n \cos(n\theta). \tag{2}$$

The harmonic amplitudes of the nonlinear-processor output are the d_k coefficients, which may be derived directly from the a_k coefficients and the amplitude α according to the formula

$$d_k = 2 \sum_{j=0}^{(n-k)/2} \frac{(k+2j)!}{j!(k+j)!} \left(\frac{\alpha}{2}\right)^{k+2j} a_k + 2j. \tag{3}$$

A detailed derivation of this formula is given by Suen (1970).

The filter acts to selectively modify the harmonic amplitudes according to its response characteristic $H(f)$, which is "sampled" at the frequencies $0, f_1, 2f_1, 3f_1, \ldots$. Thus, the output of the synthesis model, if $H(0) = 0$, is

$$z = \beta[c_1 \cos(\theta) + c_2 \cos(2\theta) + \cdots + c_n(n\theta)] \tag{4a}$$

where

$$c_k = H(kf_1) \cdot d_k \text{ and } \theta = 2\pi f_1 t. \tag{4b}$$

For the purposes of most subsequent discussions we will assume that the output of the second envelope generator is constant, i.e., $\beta = 1$.

The nonlinear processor provides a spectrum that changes with the intensity of the tone and, in fact, is a one-to-one function of the intensity. One way to depict the way such a spectrum evolves is by using nonlinear interharmonic relationships (NIHR). NIHR can be given as a set of plots of spectral components c_k versus c_1 expressed in decibels. (For further discussion of NIHR see Beauchamp 1975.) Define

$$C_k = 20 \log_{10}(c_k), \tag{5a}$$

$$D_k = 20 \log_{10}(d_k), \tag{5b}$$

$$H_{dB} = 20 \log_{10}(H) \tag{5c}$$

as the logarithmic versions of c, d, and H, respectively. Equation 4b may then be converted to

$$C_k = H_{dB}(kf_1) + D_k. \tag{6}$$

The NIHR curves for the output (z in figure 8.1) are plots of C_k versus C_1; at the output of the nonlinear processor (y) they are plots of D_k versus D_1. It may be seen from equation 6 that the shapes of the corresponding NIHR curves for signals z and y are identical; only their relative positions are different.

One important feature of nonlinear processes is exhibited at low amplitudes, i.e., for small values of the envelope function α. In this case equation 3 reduces to

$$d_k \approx 2a_k(\alpha/2)^k \tag{7a}$$

with the special case

$$d_1 \approx a_1 \alpha. \tag{7b}$$

Solving equation 7b for α and substituting the result into equation 7a yields the interharmonic relationship

$$d_k \approx 2a_k \left(\frac{d_1}{2a_1} \right)^k, \tag{8a}$$

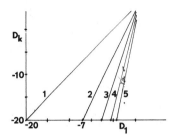

Figure 8.2
Low-level nonlinear interharmonic relationship (NIHR) curves for the function $y = x + x^2 + x^3 + x^4 + x^5$.

with its decibel equivalent

$$D_k \approx kD_1 + 20 \log_{10} \frac{2a_k}{(2a_1)^k}. \tag{8b}$$

An important conclusion to be drawn from equation 8b is that for low amplitudes the slope of the NIHR curve for the kth harmonic is equal to k. Figure 8.2 illustrates the low-amplitude NIHR curves for the case $y = x + x^2 + x^3 + x^4 + x^5$. Note that as the harmonic number increases the curves become steeper and shift to the right. This is a general principle of low-amplitude nonlinear behavior.

The transfer-function polynomial coefficients a_k can be derived from harmonic amplitudes d_k by means of a formula that is the inverse of equation 3. If the d_ks vary with time, one specific d_k vector must be chosen for the calculation. Also, α_o is an arbitrary particular value of α and may be chosen to be equal to 1 without loss of generality. The formula is

$$a_k = \frac{1}{2} \left(\frac{2}{\alpha_o} \right)^k \sum_{j=0} \frac{(-1)^j (k + 2j)(k + j - 1)!}{k!\,j!} d_{k+2j}. \tag{9}$$

Unfortunately, when the signal $y(t)$ is resynthesized from equations 2 and 3 the resulting spectrum d_k is guaranteed to match the original only for the d_k vector used in the calculation of equation 9, i.e., for $\alpha = \alpha_o$. If the synthesized spectrum matches the original for other values of α, either this is a coincidence or the acoustics have dictated such a result.

The NIHR curves can be used to visually estimate the goodness of match between the synthesized spectra and the original ones over a range of α values. It is expected that matching the d_ks at some intermediate intensity would give the best overall match.

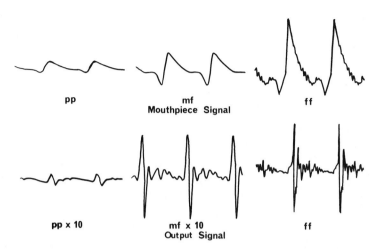

Figure 8.3
Waveforms for three 117-Hz trombone tones. Phase distortion is due to tape recorder.

Results of Brass-Tone Analysis

Backus and Hundley (1971) outlined the mechanism for production of harmonics in trumpet tones. Their analysis was based on measurements of the nonlinear relationship between acoustic impedance and size of the lip opening in the mouthpiece. The derived theory allowed a prediction of the shapes of trumpet mouthpiece pressure waveforms.

I have made simultaneous measurements of some trombone mouthpiece and output signals. Both types of signals for tones played *pp*, *mf*, and *ff* at 117 Hz are shown in figure 8.3. Note that the amplitude range of the output is much greater than that of the mouthpiece. These ranges were measured to be 67–103 dB SPL at the output and 152–169 dB in the mouthpiece for tones played between *pp* and *ff*. This disparity may be explained as follows: The trombone pipe acts as a high-pass filter, severely attenuating the low frequencies while accentuating the frequencies above 800 Hz. As the tone builds up in amplitude, the upper partials of the mouthpiece signal increase in strength much more rapidly than the lower partials. Since the pipe filter responds primarily to these upper partials, the output dynamic range is a magnified version of the input.

Spectra for six waveform cases (*pp*, *mf*, and *ff* at mouthpiece and output) are shown in figure 8.4. The two sets are related via the high-pass characteristic shown in figure 8.5.

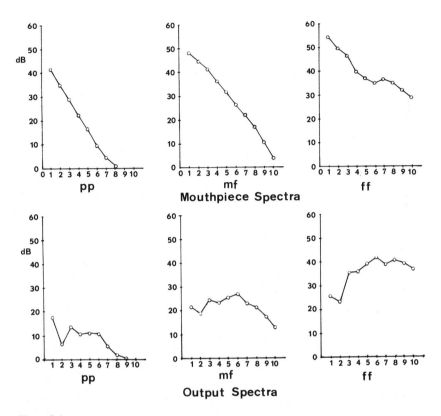

Figure 8.4
Steady-state spectra corresponding to waveforms of figure 8.3.

At this point I would like to make the assumption that the mouthpiece pressure waveform corresponds to the signal y in the synthesis model of figure 8.1 and that the output waveform corresponds to the signal z of the same figure. Arbitrarily taking $\alpha_o = 1$ for the *mf* case, we can compute the polynomial coefficients using the measured d_ks and equation 9 and use equation 1a to plot the nonlinear-processor function shown in figure 8.6. Using this function to distort a sine wave of unit amplitude will produce a spectrum exactly matching the one shown in figure 8.4. The function shape is remarkably similar to a diode I versus V curve.

To be effective the function should also work for the *pp* and *ff* cases. Near-optimum values of α for these two cases were determined by trial and error to be 0.87 and 1.13, and the resulting spectra (together with the

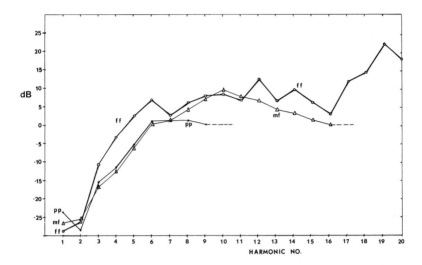

Figure 8.5
Transmission response characteristic for a trombone based on simultaneously recorded mouthpiece and output pressure signals ($f_1 = 119$ Hz) for three dynamic levels: (●) *pp*, (▵) *mf*, and (○) *ff*.

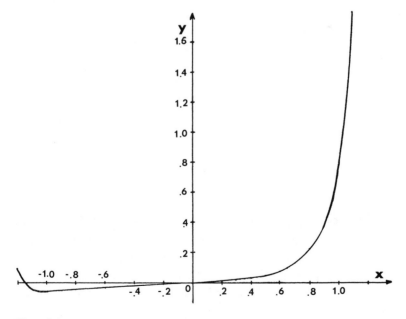

Figure 8.6
Nonlinear-processor transfer function (*y* vs. *x*) for synthesis of trombone tones.

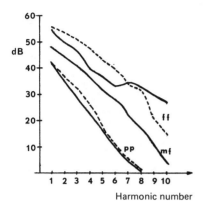

Figure 8.7
Synthesized (dashed lines) and original (solid lines) mouthpiece spectra for trombone
tones.

originals) are plotted in figure 8.7. The computed spectrum of x matches
the original closely for the pp case but not so closely for the ff case.

I have synthesized tones with a computer using this model. The tones
resembled those of a trombone but were somehow lacking in quality. One
problem was that, since the measurements were steady-state, I could only
guess at reasonable envelope functions to use.

Benade (1976, p. 419) measured the spectra of mouthpiece pressures
produced by a professional trumpeter and found them to be very stable.
Benade also gives a transmission characteristic, which can be used to calculate the output spectra (figure 20.14, p. 421) and plots the mouthpiece
spectra in the form of NIHR curves (figure 21.6a, p. 443). The salient
feature of the NIHR curves is that for low levels they obey Worman's Law,
a formula derived by E. W. Worman (1971) which can be written as
follows:

$$D_k = k(D_1 - D_{1o_k}), \qquad D_1 < D_T \text{ dB} \tag{10}$$

where D_{1o_k} is the value of D_1 for which D_k becomes 0 for each k and where
D_T is the maximum value of D_1 for which this equation holds. This is
precisely the form of equation 8b, which is the low-level interharmonic
relationship for the output of a generalized smooth nonlinear transfer
function. From Benade's NIHR curves for a 233-Hz trumpet tone we
conclude that $D_{1o_2} \doteq 18$ dB, $D_{1o_3} \doteq 23$ dB, and $D_{1o_4} \doteq 26$ dB, and $D_T =$
30 dB. (These decibel values are not absolute; they are relative to an

arbitrary reference.) A Bode-plot analysis of Benade's transmission function shows that it can be approximated by

$$H_{dB} = 10 \log_{10} \left(\frac{1 + (300/f)^4}{1 + (1,500/f)^4} \right),$$ (11)

which resembles the frequency response of a treble boost circuit.

The other interesting aspect of the NIHR curves obtained by Benade is that for values of D_1 greater than 36 dB the NIHR curves are approximately parallel, i.e.,

$$D_k \doteq D_1 - 2k, \qquad D_1 > 36 \text{ dB}.$$

In between $D_1 = 30$ and $D_1 = 36$ there is a transition region. It is as if above a certain point the spectrum "freezes" into a certain position and only increases in overall amplitude. This can be effected in the model of figure 8.1 by increasing β while keeping α constant.

Analysis and Synthesis of Cornet Tones

I have measured the time-variant output spectra of several cornet tones using a computer and plotted the resulting NIHR characteristics (Beauchamp 1975). Figure 8.8 shows the harmonic amplitude curves for a single 350-Hz *mf* cornet tone. Figure 8.9 shows the NIHRs for the same tone with the attack portion (the first 0.1 sec) omitted. In 1975 I derived approximate, smooth curves to fit the NIHR characteristics, and the results indicated low-level slopes less than those given by Worman's Law. However, the somewhat murky nature of the original data for $C_k < 15$ dB contributed to an ambiguity of the low-level slopes. The dashed lines in figure 8.8 indicate slopes of $1,2,3,\ldots,9$ for the corresponding harmonics and show that Worman's Law is indeed plausible for $C_1 < 15$ dB. For $C_1 > 30$–40 dB, again the NIHR curves tend to be parallel, as in Benade's trumpet data.

In 1973 I visited Arthur Benade at his laboratory at Case Western Reserve University and obtained from him measurements of the input impedance (mouthpiece pressure p_m divided by mouthpiece velocity v_m) and transmission response (both output pressure divided by mouthpiece pressure, p_o/p_m, and output pressure divided by mouthpiece velocity, p_o/v_m) for the same Conn 80A cornet that was used for the tones analyzed in the 1975 paper. The original graphs of p_o/p_m and p_o/v_m for no valves

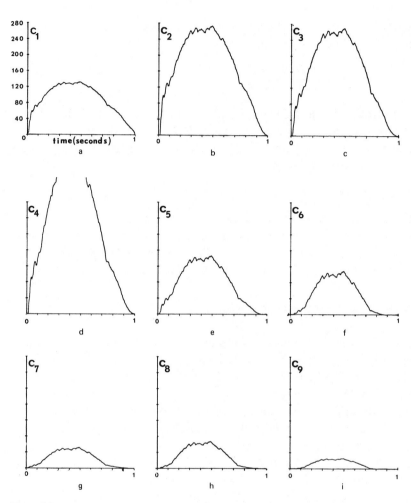

Figure 8.8
Harmonic amplitudes (c_1 through c_9) for original cornet tones, played *mezzoforte* at 350 Hz (F4) with a duration of 1 sec.

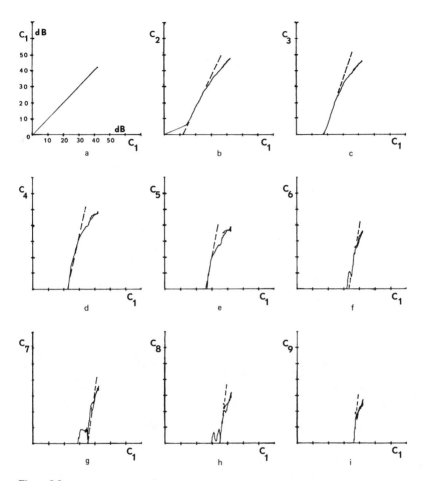

Figure 8.9
NIHR curves for original cornet tone. Dashed straight lines have slopes of 1, 2, ... , 9, corresponding to harmonic number.

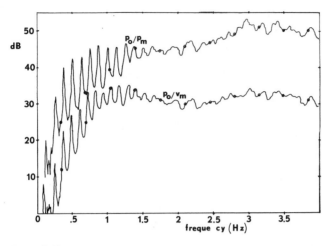

Figure 8.10
Transmission response graphs for cornet (Conn 80A, no valves depressed). Upper curve: output pressure over mouthpiece pressure. Lower curve: output pressure over mouthpiece velocity. Responses sampled at harmonics of 350 Hz.

depressed are shown in figure 8.10. The transmission curves of figure 8.10 were sampled at multiples of 350 Hz to produce values of $H_{dB}(kf_1)$. This allowed deduction of the d_k harmonic amplitudes from a specific C_k vector for a particular value of C_1. Equation 9 was then used to compute the nonlinear-processor coefficients a_k, which it was hoped would allow a reasonable replication of the original tone by means of equations 3 and 4 with appropriate variation of the amplitude α.

One can choose $\alpha(t)$ so as to force a perfect match with the original $c_1(t)$ envelope, or with the original envelope for any harmonic. (It could also be chosen to match the rms amplitude of the tone.) This is a matter of constructing a tabular function for c_1 versus α and inverting the function to get α from c_1. The original $c_1(t)$ function becomes the "driver" of the synthesis model, and it is guaranteed that the amplitude of the output signal's first harmonic will exactly match the original.

There were some problems in combining the data obtained in Benade's laboratory with the data reported in my 1975 paper. The most difficult problem was that the transmission curves contain several resonances, and harmonic samples that occur on the steep slopes of these resonances are subject to significant changes as the frequency of the tone and other factors such as temperature and humidity change. Another problem was that the microphone position used in Benade's lab was about 6 inches from the bell, as opposed to the 66 inches used for the other data (which were actually collected around 1967); however, this was expected to affect only frequencies below the radiation cutoff (about 1,500 Hz). Nevertheless, I decided to combine the two sets of data to see if a useful result could be obtained. The results were positive.

The analysis-and-synthesis procedure based on the NIHR and transmission data for the cornet can be summarized as follows: From the NIHR curves of figure 8.9 (for the *mf* case), select a value of C_1 and corresponding values of $C_2, C_3, \ldots$ (the C_k vector). Using one of the transmission curves of figure 8.10 (the p_o/p_m curve seemed to work best) and the C_k vector, derive the D_k vector and from that the corresponding d_k vector using the equations

$$D_k = C_k - H_{dB}(350k) \qquad (12a)$$

and

$$d_k = 10^{D_k/20}. \qquad (12b)$$

Use equation 9 to compute the polynomial coefficients a_k with α_o set to unity. Using equations 3 and 4b (setting $k = 1$), derive c_1 as a function of α; this makes it possible to obtain the inverse function to get α from c_1. From the original first harmonic envelope for each of three tones (played *pp*, *mf*, and *ff* at the same pitch), use the inverse function obtained in the preceding step to generate three different $\alpha(t)$ envelopes. Use these $\alpha(t)$ envelopes with equation 3 to generate $d_k(t)$ functions for each of the three tones. Use equation 4b to compute the $c_k(t)$ envelopes and equation 4a to compute the output waveform $z(t)$ (with $\beta = 1.0$) for each of the three tones. The NIHR curves for the synthetic case are also generated by variation of α and use of equations 3, 4b, and 5a.

The synthesis procedure just described is an additive-synthesis equivalent of the direct nonlinear-synthesis technique illustrated in figure 8.1. Of course, the direct nonlinear technique using equation 1 is the preferred one of the two for reasons of computational efficiency. It involves a table lookup to get $\alpha(t)$, an increment and a table lookup to get $\cos(2\pi f_1 t)$, a multiplication to get $\alpha(t)\cos(2\pi f_1 t)$, a table lookup to get $F[\alpha(t) \times \cos(2\pi f_1 t)]$, and a final digital filter operation. The filter can be approximated by a second-order high-pass type requiring five additions and three multiplications.

The harmonic amplitude envelopes resulting from the procedure described are shown in figure 8.11. These should be compared with the original envelopes of figure 8.8. The match was selected to be perfect for all harmonics for the times at which $c_1 = 64.0$. Note that the $c_1(t)$ envelopes match perfectly, whereas the other envelopes match only at one amplitude value. The NIHR curves for the synthetic tone are shown in figure 8.12. These should be compared with the original NIHR curves of figure 8.9.

Despite some visible differences between the original and the synthesized envelopes, the perceptual difference between the synthetic and the original tones is very small. This is true for the *pp* and *mf* cases and to a lesser extent for the *ff* case. The entire experiment was repeated using a second-order Butterworth high-pass filter with -3 dB cutoff at 1,800 Hz. The resulting synthetic tones were not as close (visually or perceptually) to the originals as those obtained with the data of figure 8.10, but they were still close.

The data derived for the nonlinear processor (the a_k coefficients), the matched harmonic amplitudes (c_{k_0}), and the corresponding filter samples $[H(350k)]$ are given in table 8.1 for the two filter responses used. Also given are the maximum values of A required for the three dynamic levels.

A plot of one of the derived nonlinear-processor functions (f) is shown in figure 8.13. It is generated by the a_k coefficients given in the rightmost column of table 8.1. Note the resemblance of this function (derived from cornet data) to that of figure 8.6 (derived from trombone data).

Summary and Conclusions

The acoustics of the lip-mouthpiece interaction leads one to conclude that a nonlinear process is responsible for tone formation in the mouthpiece. Any smooth nonlinear process can be represented by a polynomial, and its effect in distorting a sine wave can be predicted in terms of the harmonic spectrum it produces for changing values of the sine wave's amplitude.

Given a harmonic spectrum, one can compute the coefficients of the polynomial needed to produce it. The spectrum of a brass tone evolves in a particular way as the intensity changes. One can match the spectrum at one point and attempt to imitate the spectral evolution by using the

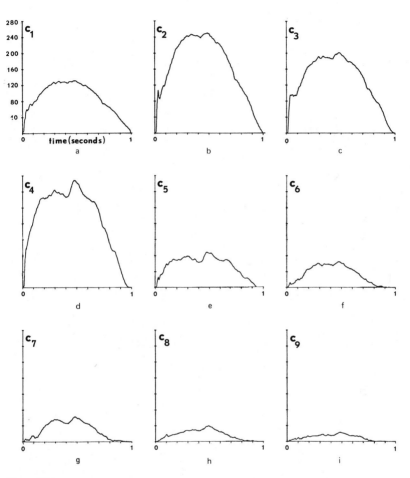

Figure 8.11
Harmonic amplitudes of synthesized cornet tone. Compare with figure 8.8.

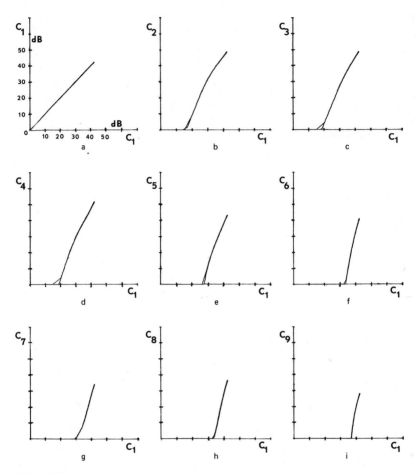

Figure 8.12
NIHR for synthesized cornet tone. Compare with figure 8.9. Match points are for
$c_1 = 36\,dB$.

Table 8.1
Data for nonlinear synthesis of analyzed cornet tone.

k	c_{k_0}	Filter data[a] $H(350k)$	a_k	Second-order Butterworth filter approximation $H(350k)$	a_k
1	64.0	0.0562	489.1	0.0378	1,023.1
2	109.8	0.1380	193.5	0.1488	−170.4
3	85.4	0.2985	646.4	0.2810	690.7
4	104.8	0.5888	1,873.1	0.5159	2,114.7
5	28.5	0.5370	−959.6	0.6853	−996.3
6	5.69	0.6095	−2,151.9	0.8046	−2,194.6
7	4.67	0.6839	2,878.4	0.8800	2,820.7
8	3.68	0.8913	3,786.4	0.9242	3,802.3
9	0.15	1.12	−2,483.9	0.9506	−2,533.5
10	0.65	1.00	−3,300.7	0.9668	−3,346.7
11	0.89	1.00	915.5	·0.9769	935.7
12	0.59	1.00	1,210.5	0.9835	1,229.4
		α_{max}		α_{max}	
pp		1.10		1.10	
mf		1.21		1.25	
ff		1.46		1.40	

a. Source: figure 8.10.

derived nonlinear polynomial to distort an amplitude-varying sine wave. However, the spectrum is guaranteed to match only at the matched point. A closer overall imitation can be obtained by using a filter at the output of the nonlinear processor which simulates the transmission response of the brass pipe. The "goodness" of the imitation can be estimated by visual comparison of the nonlinear interharmonic relationship (NIHR) curves for the original and synthetic cases.

Once the parameters of the nonlinear-synthesis model are established, tones can be synthesized with different articulations by supplying different $\alpha(t)$ functions describing the envelope of the input sine wave. The $\alpha(t)$ functions can be derived from some amplitude parameter of the original tone, such as the amplitude of the first harmonic. It is guaranteed that this parameter will be matched exactly, and one hopes that the other

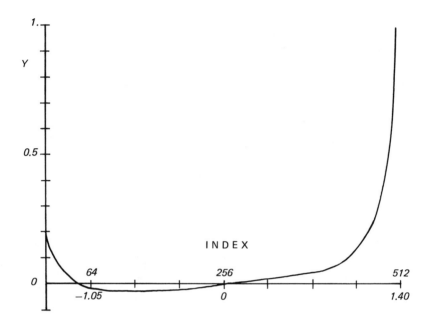

Figure 8.13
Nonlinear-processor function used to distort sine wave for synthesis of cornet tones with model of figure 8.1. This assumes that a second-order Butterworth high-pass filter with −3 dB cutoff of 1,800 Hz is also used. Compare with the derived trombone nonlinear function shown in figure 8.6.

parameters will "follow along" close enough for a reasonable imitation of the original sound.

When this procedure was tried for actual cornet tones, using a filter response derived from actual measurement, the synthetic tones sounded very close to the originals.

The nonlinear-synthesis model is a practical one for synthesis using a computer music program such as Music V or Music 4BF (Beauchamp 1979). In computational efficiency it compares favorably with FM, and it has the advantage of a strong theoretical basis for matching spectra.

References

Backus, J., and J. C. Hundley. 1971. "Harmonic generation in the trumpet." *Journal of the Acoustical Society of America* 49: 509–519.

Beauchamp, J. 1975. "Analysis and synthesis of cornet tones using nonlinear inter-harmonic relationships." *Journal of the Audio Engineering Society* 23: 778–795.

Beauchamp, J. W. 1979. "Practical sound synthesis using a nonlinear processor (waveshaper) and a high-pass filter." *Computer Music Journal* 3(3): 42–49.

Benade, A. H. 1976. *Fundamentals of Musical Acoustics*. New York: Oxford University Press.

Suen, C. Y. 1970. "Derivation of harmonic equations in nonlinear circuits." *Journal of the Audio Engineering Society* 18: 675–676.

Worman, E. W. 1971. Self-Sustained Nonlinear Oscillations of Medium Amplitude in Clarinet-Like Systems. Ph.D. diss., Case Western Reserve University.

9 An Analysis/Synthesis Tutorial

RICHARD CANN

This is a tutorial on an analysis/synthesis system I have been using to facilitate the performance of digital musique concrète using Music 4BF (Fortran). Section 1 describes several pieces that have been realized using this system and introduces signal modeling in the context of human speech. Section 2 describes (in nonmathematical terms) the analysis of speech on the basis of this model. Section 3 presents the mathematics, including an introduction to the concept of linear prediction. A list of Fortran programs, a user's manual, and copies of the pieces discussed are available from me at Box 329, Route 13, Skillman, New Jersey 08558.

1

Analysis/synthesis is a technique that involves taking an acoustic signal, analyzing it in order to extract information about certain aspects, and then using this information to synthesize the signal and/or its derivatives. The technique has been developed and widely used in communications and digital signal processing, where analysis/synthesis of signals such as speech has become attractive for many reasons, such as the reduction of data in telephone transmission lines and the automatic recognition of speech. In music, analysis/synthesis has been used as a form of musique concrète in which the same information a telephone company might use to synthesize an operator's voice can be used to synthesize "singing" or *Sprechstimme*.

Analysis/synthesis departs from the classical analog tape-studio musique concrète in that it relies heavily on the use of digital computers and it necessitates a preanalysis modeling of the signal involved (the analog studio is quite passive in the latter respect). It has a great advantage over the analog technique in that once the relevant information has been analyzed in the source signal there is almost no limit to the derivatives of that signal that can be synthesized. Before we delve into the specifics of analysis/synthesis, let us look briefly at several pieces that have been realized using this technique.

Originally printed in *Computer Music Journal* 3(3): 6–11, 1979; 3(4): 9–13, 1979; and 4(1): 36–42, 1980.

Figure 9.1
"Normal" piano envelope played in reverse.

Figure 9.2
The reversed envelope of figure 9.1 modified for use in *Piano Music*.

An Experiment with Four Piano Notes

Several years ago, I recorded four piano notes—the lowest four D's, *mf*, no pedal. They were digitized and then analyzed (a week's work). The analysis looked at the piano notes in small segments (1/100 sec) and reported information about the amplitude (envelope) and resonant properties (formants) of that segment. This information was then stored and used as input to a Music 4 synthesis orchestra.

The system was designed so that the original four notes could be reconstructed exactly, although such reconstruction was never the intent. Rather, the desire was to have the ability to resynthesize the original resonant properties with arbitrary pitch and rhythmic characteristics.

Piano Music *Piano Music* was supposed to sound like a piano over large registral spans. It didn't. There were many interesting effects, however. Synthesizing the notes backwards (like reversing a tape) produced "cellolike" sounds, especially when the envelope was modified from the "normal" backward piano (figure 9.1) to look as shown in figure 9.2.

Banjo Music Here the idea was to synthesize notes using the piano's resonant properties but totally unpianolike pitch curves. Notes were constructed using pitch curves such as that shown in figure 9.3. The instrument sounded "plucked," like a banjo.

Figure 9.3
Pitch curve used in *Banjo Music*.

Alillia   When the funny "banjo" pitch curves were spread out in time and combined with the backward "cello" reconstruction and microtonal tuning, "hornlike" sounds emerged.

Maentwrog, Music for Soleil   This piece used different inputs. First, a poem was read and then analyzed. Next, a guitar piece was recorded and digitized but not analyzed. During synthesis, the resonant properties of the voice that had been analyzed were placed on the guitar piece. The result was a "talking" guitar.

Requirements for Analysis/Synthesis

Three things are required for analysis/synthesis: a model must be derived that represents those features of the signal that we wish to extract, an analysis algorithm based on this model must be devised, and a synthesis program must be developed. (In this case, the program must be adaptable to music synthesis.)

The remainder of section 1 will deal with signal modeling. Since almost all available analysis/synthesis literature uses human sbeech as the signal to be modeled, I will also develop this model. Please bear in mind that analysis/synthesis is not speech-dependent, as the piano pieces discussed above demonstrate.

A Model of the Human Vocal Mechanism

In modern signal-processing techniques, the procedures for analyzing a signal make use of all the information that can be obtained in advance about the structure of the signal. The first step in signal analysis is thus to make a model of the signal. (Atal and Hanauer 1971)

The human vocal mechanism is part of the respiratory system, and as we breathe, air is passed through it (figure 9.4). As this air passes through, we can produce noise—snoring, for instance. Speech, whistling, and singing are refined versions of the snore in which we consciously mani-

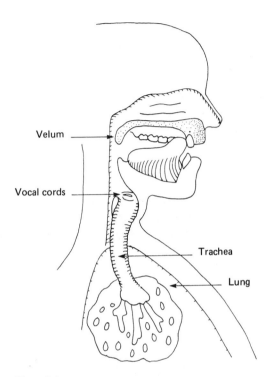

Figure 9.4
The human vocal mechanism.

pulate various parts of the mechanism in order to produce a larger variety of timbres.

We can make sounds both as we take air in and as we let it out. The basic snore involves both intake and exhaust, while most speech we are familiar with is produced only during exhalation. When we exhale, air is pushed out of the lungs, up through the trachea (windpipe), and into the resonant vocal-tract cavity.

The vocal tract consists of the acoustical tubing beginning at the top of the trachea (the vocal folds reside here) and ending at the mouth and/or nose (the sound radiates here). Within the vocal tract, the air pressure wave excites *resonant* and *attenuant* nodes, which cause changes in the spectral characteristics of the wave. This helps to determine the timbre of the radiated sound wave.

As we vocalize, we change the spectral characteristics of the sound wave generated by the air coming from the lungs, first by the use of the vocal folds and next by the configuration of the vocal tract. The former is accomplished by applying different tensions to the folds. The latter is done by moving various cranial parts—the lips, the jaw, the tongue, and the velum (which opens and closes the passageway to the nose); these parts are known as the *articulators*. The vocal folds and the articulators, working in concert, produce almost all the differentiations in the timbre that constitute human vocal sounds.

Whispering

Whispering is a subtle refinement. As in whistling, the only vocal-tract input used is an unabated air flow; however, in contrast with whistling, the articulators take on a variety of settings and are usually in constant motion.

Whistling

When we whistle, the vocal folds are idle (no tension is applied) and air is pushed directly into the vocal tract. Depending upon the shape of the tract, different frequencies of pressure waves set up by the air flow are resonated and attenuated. The amateur whistler has a hard time arranging the articulators so that only one of these frequencies is resonated, but when that is accomplished only slight rearrangement of the oral cavity shape is needed to produce a variety of pitches. In whistling, the vocal-tract input is always an unabated air flow, while the vocal-tract output (the actual sound) can vary widely in frequency and timbre.

Speech

In speech, as in whispering, we use a large variety of vocal-tract configurations. However, in contrast with whispering or whistling, we use our vocal folds to create different vocal-tract inputs. In normal speech, we can use the folds as follows.

Option 1: As in whistling and whispering, the folds can simply be relaxed, letting the air flow enter the tract undisturbed.

Option 2: The folds can be tensed, in which case they will cover the trachea and block the air flow. When this happens, pressure is built up behind the folds until it forces them open. Now the air passes through in a burst, after which the folds close again. The cycle is repeated as long as the folds are tensed, and as it is repeated the vocal tract is continually excited by these pulses of air. This repetition can occur several hundred times per second, causing us to hear a pitch.

Option 3: The folds can be made to operate in both of these states simultaneously; that is, they can be held slightly open at all times, letting air through unabated, but still be tense enough so that the vibratory pulsing takes place. (Some people seem to have this as the only option to relaxed vocal folds; that is, they never quite close their folds completely. This causes their speech to be "breathy" or "gravelly.")

Once the vocal folds are operating in one of these states, the remainder of the vocal tract acts as in whispering, and various frequencies of the input are resonated and attenuated according to the shape of the oral cavity.

Voicing: Options 1–3 Renamed   Unvoiced: When we produce speech sounds with the vocal folds held open, it is called unvoiced speech. The |sh| of sugar is an example of this.

Voiced: When we produce speech sounds with the vocal folds vibrating, it is called voiced speech. Vowel sounds fall into this catagory.

Mixed voice: When we produce speech sounds in the combination mode, it is called mixed voice. The |z| of azure is an example of this.

Articulators   Within a particular voicing, differentiations of speech are made by the positions of the articulators. Let us look at the American vowel sounds, because they can rather easily be described and pictured.

The vowels a, e, i, o and u are all normally voiced. Their production is not pitch-dependent; that is, we can produce any of the vowels for any given vocal-fold vibration rate. (They are not even input-dependent, viz. whispering.) The velum is (usually) closed so that no sound goes into the nasal cavity, and the mouth remains open at all times. Thus, the jaw and tongue positions uniquely determine these vowels. The jaw can move from a closed position to an open one, and the tongue can travel from the front of the mouth to the back of the mouth. Within these placements, all the vowels occur (as do the vowels of all other languages). Figure 9.5 shows the placements of several vowels.

We are now in a position to make a useful model of the human vocal mechanism: The vocal folds are considered to be the determinant of the type of excitation signal that the vocal tract is to receive. The articulators are filters that resonate and attenuate the amplitude of frequencies contained in this excitation signal and are the determinant of many of the differentiations of speech—the vowels in particular.

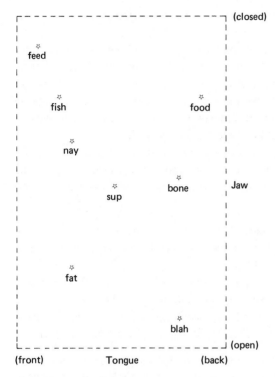

Figure 9.5
American vowel chart.

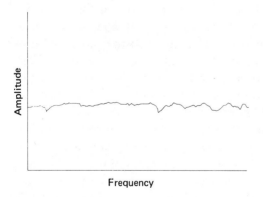

Figure 9.6
The fairly flat spectrum of the white-noise-like signal produced when the folds in the vocal tract are relaxed.

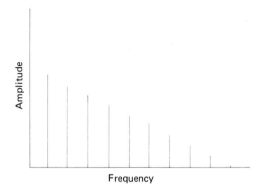

Figure 9.7
Simplified spectral plot of the triangular pulses produced by the folds in the vocal tract.

The Vocal Folds   Now let us look at some of this information in acoustic terms. During the production of unvoiced speech, or whenever the folds are relaxed to let air pass through undisturbed, the vocal tract is receiving a type of white noise that has a rather broad and flat spectrum (figure 9.6).

During the production of voiced speech, or whenever the folds are tensed and forced to vibrate, the vocal tract is receiving a series of pulses whose spectrum is very complicated and not well understood. These pulses are somewhat triangular in shape, and assuming this we get a spectrum as approximated in figure 9.7. This spectrum is harmonic and falls off rather rapidly, at a rate of around 12 dB per octave.

An even cruder approximation of the vocal-fold pulse is a pulse of very narrow width, that is, a pulse that would be created if the vocal folds opened and closed extremely rapidly within the total cycle. This is displayed by the spectrum shown in figure 9.8. The spectrum here is also harmonic, with all partials having equal amplitude. One could speculate that this pulse train, if passed through a low-pass filter, might be an acceptable substitute for the real vocal pulse, and it turns out that it is. To make all the further discussions a bit easier, let us assume that the voiced vocal-tract input is indeed one of these very narrow pulse trains.

The Articulators (Vowel Examples)   As mentioned above, the articulators serve to change the shape of the vocal tract, thus changing its resonant characteristics. As the articulators can be considered independent

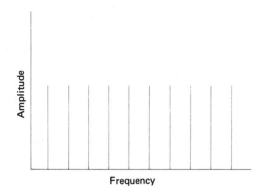

Figure 9.8
Spectrum produced if the folds in the vocal tract open and close extremely rapidly in
comparison with the total duration of one cycle.

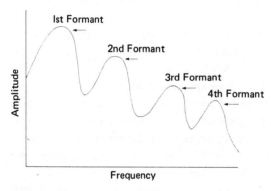

Figure 9.9
Typical plot of the frequency response of the vocal tract.

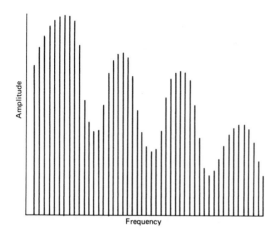

Figure 9.10
Spectral plot for a vowel, shown from 0 to 7,000 Hz.

of the particular use of the vocal folds, their frequency response curves do not change with respect to the input pitch. Vocal tract responses can be plotted, and a typical curve might look like figure 9.9.

The peaks of these response curves are thus fixed only with respect to the vowel to be uttered, and are called *formants*. If we were to look at this type of response for many vowels, we would notice that the first two formant frequencies tend to move around the most and that the upper formants tend to remain in place. (The two lowest formants are affected the most by the positions of the jaw and the tongue, each of which can make a large change in the shape of the oral cavity.) We would also notice that, for vowels, the largest amount of spectral energy is to be found in one of the lower formants, if not the lowest.

Vocal Folds and Articulators in Combination In our model, speech is considered a vocal-tract input that is resonated and then radiated. We look now at the different components of this system in terms of frequencies. Figure 9.10 is the spectrum of the middle of a vowel sound—an "instantaneous" example of voiced speech. Now, if we connect the tops of the output spectral lines of figure 9.10, we get figure 9.11. This curve is called the *spectral envelope*. If we consider the vocal-tract input to be a narrow pulse train (all harmonics of equal amplitude), the spectral envelope of the final signal also represents the response curve of the

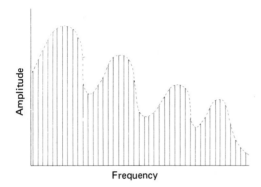

Figure 9.11
The spectral envelope is the curve connecting the peaks of the spectrum shown in figure 9.10.

articulator formants. Thus, we might expect a pulse train of arbitrary pitch, filtered so as to produce the spectral envelope, to talk. It does.

Summary

The spectral envelope is a way of capturing the resonant characteristics of speech without capturing the original input pitch. This separation is the crux of analysis/synthesis, and it is not speech-dependent: All acoustic instruments display the characteristic of having an input signal resonated at the instrument's particular formant frequencies.

In the synthesis of the aforementioned piano-derived pieces, the spectral envelope of the original piano notes was used in conjunction with pulse generators at arbitrary (that is, unrestricted) pitches. On the other hand, *Maentwrog* used spectral envelopes from an analysis of my poem reading, with the guitar piece used as the input signal.

Just for Fun

• The oral cavity can be excited from two directions, as we let air in or out. For instance, if the articulators are set for whistling (fingerless) and then held in place, you should be able to whistle continuously, on both intake and exhaust. You should also be able to talk on intake, but it will sound funny.

• Ventriloquists shape a cavity in the back of the throat that is equivalent in volume to the oral cavity, and thus are able to effect speech with little or no movement of the articulators. This, in essence, became the principle for early voice-talking machines. Air was pushed through a series of tubes that could take on shapes equivalent in volume to the vocal tract, then the shape of the tubes was changed by the depression of keys.

• Set your articulators up for the production of the |i| in "keep." Now, while keeping this position, produce a pulsed (voiced) input and glissando up and down as far as you can. The first two formant frequencies can be heard to remain constant, the second especially if you can glissando above the frequency of the first resonance.

• When we inhale gases lighter than everyday air, we sound like Donald Duck. Here, not only do the vocal folds vibrate faster than usual but the formant frequencies are also raised (the speed of sound in the cavity has changed). The same effect is noticed when a tape-recorded voice is reproduced at a different speed than that at which it was recorded. Not only does the pitch change, but so does the whole timbral quality, as the formant frequencies have also been shifted.

• "[Alexander Graham] Bell's youthful interest in speech production also led him to experiment with his pet Skye terrier. He taught the dog to sit up on his hind legs and growl continuously. At the same time, Bell manipulated the dog's vocal tract by hand. The dog's repertoire of sounds finally consisted of the vowels |a| and |u|, the dipthong |ou| and the syllables |ma| and |ga|. His greatest linguistic accomplishment consisted of the sentence, 'How are you Grandmama?' . . . This, according to Bell, is the only foundation to the rumor that he once taught a dog to speak." (Flanagan 1972)

2

Presumably, one of the characteristics to which we might initially pay serious attention in the electronic synthesis of speech is intelligibility—or, more generally, the "human" sense. On the basis of the model presented in section 1 and such empirical experiences as the sped-up-tape effect, it appears that the precise definition of the formant frequencies is crucial to achieving this end. In any case, if one of our musical goals is to be able to arbitrarily reconstruct speech at any pitch level, or with any rhythmic configuration, then a separation of the formant information from that of the vocal-tract input is in order. Such a process is called *formant extraction*, and the analysis/synthesis system about to be described is based on this process.

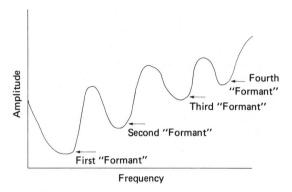

Figure 9.12
The inverse of the filter shown in figures 9.8–9.10.

Initialization

For the purpose of aiding the following discussion, assume that we are considering a very small speech segment, 1/50 sec in duration. Consider that this segment came from the middle of the production of an isolated vowel, as the |e| in "hey." Figures 9.10 and 9.11 represent some idealized characteristics of such a segment. Figure 9.10 shows the spectrum of this segment, and figure 9.11 outlines the spectral envelope. Recall from section 1 that we can, for simplicity, consider the envelope of voiced speech to be the response curve of the formant filters we wish to capture. Henceforth, the spectral envelope will be referred to as the *formant filter* response.

Inverse Filtering

Inverse filtering has been one of the most successful approaches to formant extraction. The basic idea is to create a filter whose response represents the inverse of the desired formant filter response. Thus, if we wish to extract the formant filter represented by figure 9.9, an inverse filter would be constructed that looked like figure 9.12. When this inverse filter is applied to the original speech segment, the resultant signal should represent the original vocal-tract input with no formant effects.

As it is only possible to construct an inverse filter that approximates the inverse of the original formants, this filter, when applied to speech, gives as output not the vocal-tract input but a signal that is close to it and has many useful characteristics. For instance, we can use this signal

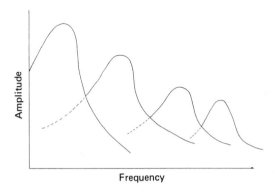

Figure 9.13
The filter of figures 9.8–9.10 can be approximated by a series of different filters, one for each formant peak.

to help determine whether the input speech was voiced or unvoiced; if it was voiced, the fundamental frequency can be extracted. This output signal is referred to as the *residual*.

After we have constructed and applied the inverse filter, obtaining the residual, if we reverse the process—putting the residual through the inverted inverse filter (i.e., the estimated formants)—we obtain an exact duplicate of the original speech (K. Steiglitz, personal communication of an experimental result).

More Approximations Are In Order

Historically, the formant filters of speech have been represented as a series of band-pass resonators. That is, a formant-filter response curve such as the one in figure 9.9 would be represented as a cascade of filters, as shown in figure 9.13. This approximation turns out to be fairly good for most speech sounds, and also tends to make both the mathematics and the implementation of the system much easier. (The error in this approximation will be discussed in section 3).

When this band-pass approximation is used, the estimated formant filter is referred to as the *all-pole-model*, since a band-pass filter of the type just described is, in its digital implementation, a two-coefficient, two-pole filter. The inverse filter that we are looking for is called an *all-zero filter*. Poles are equivalent to resonance; zeros are equivalent to antiresonance or attenuation.

The estimated formant filter is an all-resonance filter, and the estimated inverse formant filter is an all-attenuation filter.

The first step in finding the proper inverse filter is to determine how many band-pass filters it should be represented by; that is, how many filters will adequately represent, yet not overspecify, the original formants. The problem has both theoretical and empirical solutions, which will be discussed below; for now we could imagine simply scanning existing formant data (Fant 1960) and determining that in the first 4,000 Hz of the vowel spectra four formant peaks would be the right number. Hence, if our speech were band-limited (that is, run through a filter such that only frequencies from 0 to 4,000 Hz were present), our inverse filter should have four attenuation points.

Telephones are band-limited such that there is a range of only 3,000 Hz between the lowest and the highest frequencies transmitted. This is why, in general, the statement "It doesn't sound like you" actually makes sense. All of your upper formants are missing! The effect is worse during transmission of unvoiced sounds, where these upper formants play a critical role in our identification of the speech. Thus, as Paul Lansky once pointed out, "sink or swim" often comes across as "fink or fwim."

Demand Minimization of the Residual

Once we have determined the optimum number of band-reject filters to put in our inverse filter, the problem becomes one of placing these filters in the frequency domain. To do a good job we would want to put one band-reject at the exact location of each formant peak. We would not want, for instance, to have two band-reject filters on top of one peak. We would like to leave the placement of these filters up to the analysis program, and therefore we need to find a mathematical criterion for this placement.

Since most of the energy in the speech signal falls under the formant regions, it follows that if we correctly cancel these formants with our inverse filter, there will be substantially less energy in the residual signal than if we miss the formants completely or double up on one formant while missing another.

Further, if we require that the inverse filter be configured such that the energy in the residual is at an absolute minimum, we are equivalently demanding the inverse filter to be optimally placed, which is our goal. This requirement can be easily met mathematically; see section 3.

Inverting the Inverse Filter

Now we invert our inverse filter. This gives a filter approximating the original spectral envelope, and it can be used to reconstruct speech in two ways: Either the leftover signal (residual) or some approximation of the residual can be run through it. If (as assumed in our model) we use a pulse to approximate the vocal-tract input, the output is extremely humanoid, albeit a bit "buzzy." Thus, we're not that far off the mark.

Figures 9.14–9.16 show some examples of the effects of inverse filter placement. Each of these figures contains three parts: the actual formants, the formants as derived from inverse filtering, and the residual displacement-time signal. In figure 9.14 the inverse filter has smeared over the last two formants, causing the high-frequency component to remain in the residual. In figure 9.15 the inverse filter has missed the first formant, causing the residual to have a very large amplitude. In figure 9.16 the inverse filter has done a good job of fitting the spectral envelope.

Some Musical Applications

One of the musical applications of analysis/synthesis (figure 9.17) is in the choice of the input signal during resynthesis. There is virtually no restriction as to the type of signal to be fed through the derived formant filters. It can have arbitrary pitch and harmonic characteristics, and is limited only by the desired output.

In my piece *Maentwrog, Music for Soleil,* I took an analog guitar piece (multitracked guitar with tape reverb for sustain) and fed it through a formant analysis of my reading of a Hopkins poem. The result was intelligible speech, but with a very unusual timbre. At one point, I had scraped the lower guitar strings with a pick. The resultant "speech" was a harmonically rich whisper.

Further, we can decide at the outset of the analysis how often we wish to extract a new formant filter. (Once every 1/50 second produces very smooth speech.) We can then store these filters and use them for reconstruction in arbitrary order with arbitrary duration. In my piano-derived pieces, the "cellolike" sounds resulted from using the derived piano formants in reverse order, from the end of the note to the beginning. In *Alillia* the reconstructed formants were changed very slowly, so that the original one-second piano note was stretched over a period of up to 30 seconds. Again, I was able to specify arbitrary pitch and harmonic input, resulting in "hornlike" sounds.

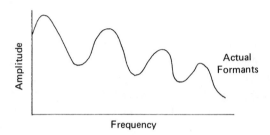

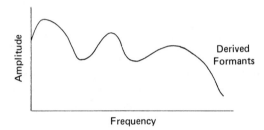

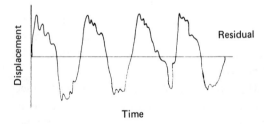

Figure 9.14
The formant filter (middle) misses the top two formants, so that the high-frequency components of the signal (top) show up in the residual (squiggly lines at the top and bottom of each cycle in the waveform at the bottom).

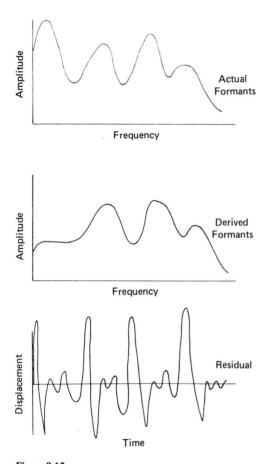

Figure 9.15
The formant filter misses the first formant, so that the amplitude of the residual is quite large.

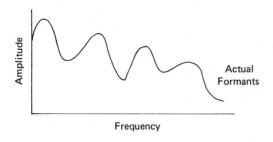

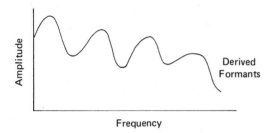

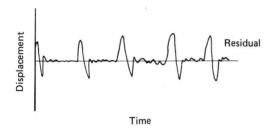

Figure 9.16
The formant filter (middle) provides a close approximation to the original formants.

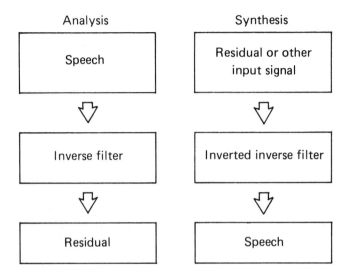

Figure 9.17
Summary of the analysis/synthesis system.

Summary

Inverse filtering is an analysis method that allows for the separation of the formant effects (spectral envelope) of speech from the vocal-tract input. It can be viewed in the following steps: A short speech segment is digitized and passed through a filter constructed to represent the inverse of the formant effects for that segment. We (mathematically) place this filter so that it removes as much energy from the source as possible, leaving a signal that (ideally) represents the vocal-tract input. This filter can then be inverted, thus representing the effects of the articulator formants. If either the residual signal or an approximation (pulse) is fed through this filter, we obtain high-quality speech.

This procedure is not speech-dependent, and will "work" for many varied types of systems that can be modeled as input signal → formants → output signal.

3

This section presents the mathematics of the inverse filtering technique described in section 2, including an introduction to the concept of linear prediction. Those who are already familiar with the theory of digital filters can skip to the subsection "General Inverse Filtering."

AllPole, an All-Pole Digital Filter

This subsection is devoted to a description of a simple band-pass filter:

```
PROCEDURE allPole (input, output, coef, pastOut);
BEGIN
    output ← input + coef[1] * pastOut[1] + coef[2] * pastOut[2];
    pastOut[2] ← pastOut[1];
    pastOut[1] ← output;
END;
```

This filter has been chosen for discussion because an understanding of a simple band-pass filter will make the general formulation in the next subsection a bit easier to understand. In Music 4BF this filter is called RESON. The corresponding unit generator in Music V is FLT.

As can be seen in the following prototype music-synthesis program for using allPole, the filter is initialized once before the filtering begins and is called every time a sample is generated.

```
BEGIN "use AllPole"
    REAL bandWidth, centerFreq, e, pi, unfilteredSignal, filteredSignal;
    INTEGER samplingRate;
    REAL ARRAY coef[1:2], past[1:2];
        :
    e ← 2.71828;                           COMMENT base of natural
    pi ← 3.14159;                          logarithms;
        :
    samplingRate ← ···                     COMMENT in Hz;
        :
    COMMENT initialize filter parameters here;
    bandWidth ← ···                        COMMENT in Hz;
    centerFreq ← ···                       COMMENT in Hz;
    past[1] ← 0;
    past[2] ← 0;
    coef[2] ← −e ↑ (−2*pi*bandWidth/samplingRate);
        COMMENT " ↑ " means "raised to the power of";
    coef[1] ← (4*coef[2])/(coef[2] + 1)*cos(2*pi*centerFreq/
    samplingRate);
        :
    COMMENT generate samples of sound signal here;
    unfilteredSignal ← ···
```

COMMENT for each sample, a new value of unfilteredSignal is calculated, and then allPole is invoked;
allPole (unfilteredSignal, filteredSignal, coef, past);
    COMMENT filteredSignal has now been filtered by allPole;
   ⋮
END "useAllPole";

The array "pastOut" contains past outputs of the filter allPole, and is initialized to 0 at the beginning of the program since the filter does not yet have any past outputs. The array "coef" contains the filter coefficients derived from the given center frequency and bandwidth of the desired filter.

The guts of allPole lie in the line just after "BEGIN," which means "the present output is equal to the present input, plus the most recent past output times the first coefficient, plus the penultimate past output times the second coefficient." The past outputs are then updated every sample.

AllPole is, of course, a very specific digital filter. With it, we are able to specify a center frequency and bandwidth and have the filter coefficients produced for us. In inverse filtering procedures, we must search for coefficients and, late in the game, decide what these coefficients might mean in terms of center frequencies and bandwidths.

Terminology   First, some substitution terms will be stated. All present and past inputs to filters will be represented by x_k, where x represents the value of the input for sample number k. Hence, x_{k-1} would be the input value of the previous sample. All present outputs to filters will be represented by y_k, where y represents the value of the output and k the sample number. Thus, y_{k-1} would be the previous output value. Coef $[1]$ and coef $[2]$ will be represented by a_1 and a_2, respectively. (The computer program for this prototype filter should also include a "gain" factor, which is omitted here and assumed to take on the value of 1.)

In this new terminology, the algorithm implemented in allPole would be represented as

$$y_k = x_k + a_1 y_{k-1} + a_2 y_{k-2}.$$

Now let us assume that this last "equation" is really an equality, that is, that the equals sign doesn't mean "takes on the value" as it does in some programming languages. Thus, we can rewrite it as

$$y_k - a_1 y_{k-1} - a_2 y_{k-2} = x_k.$$

The z Transform   To go one step further, it would be useful to stop looking at individual samples of a signal (say, x_k in the preceding equation) and consider what the spectrum of the signal looks like—the frequencies and amplitudes of the individual spectral components. To do this, we will invoke what is known as the z *transform*. Taking the z transform of our signal (all the x_k s that occur across time) yields information about the spectrum, which is then called $X(z)$; the upper-case X implies what is known as the *frequency domain* (used in talking about spectra), and the lower-case x implies the *time domain* (for the individual samples of the signal as they pass by in time).

The z transform is also useful because it simplifies the mathematics of working with time-shifted signals, such as the "past" outputs of the filter allPole (notated as y_{k-1} and y_{k-2} in the preceding equation). Taking the z transform of some unshifted signal y_k would yield a spectrum denoted as $Y(z)$. But if the samples of y_k have been shifted in time by n samples (resulting in the signal y_{k-n}), then the z transform changes this into the spectrum of the unshifted signal $Y(z)$, multiplied by z raised to the negative nth power. So the spectrum of y_{k-n} is said to be $z^{-n} Y(z)$. Now we can rewrite our equation as

$$Y(z) - a_1 z^{-1} Y(z) - a_2 z^{-2} Y(z) = X(z).$$

(This is meant to be an intuitive explanation of a complicated mathematical concept.) This allows us to regroup, bringing $Y(z)$ out:

$$Y(z)(1 - a_1 z^{-1} - a_2 z^{-2}) = X(z).$$

Traversing the equals sign again, we get

$$Y(z) = \frac{X(z)}{1 - a_1 z^{-1} - a_2 z^{-2}}.$$

The Transfer Function   If we let everything except $X(z)$ on the right-hand side of the preceding equation be represented by $H(z)$, then we get

$$Y(z) = H(z)X(z).$$

This may be interpreted as "The output spectrum of the filter is equal to a function of z times the input spectrum." Clearly, the characteristics of the filter (its bandwidth and center frequency) are going to be determined by the characteristics of $H(z)$.

$H(z)$ is called the *transfer function* of the filter. It contains the coefficients a_1 and a_2 and the gain, if any is present (not in our case). We are interested in how this transfer function effects the frequency response of the filter, so let us look at $H(z)$:

$$H(z) = \frac{1}{1 - a_1 z^{-1} - a_2 z^{-2}}.$$

Viewing this as a polynomial in z, we can multiply $H(z)$ by $z^2/z^2 \ (= 1)$ and then factor it:

$$H(z) = \frac{z^2}{z^2(1 - a_1 z^{-1} - a_2 z^{-2})}$$

$$= \frac{z^2}{z^2 - a_1 z^1 - a_2}.$$

Factoring the denominator as

$$(z^1 - p_1)(z^1 - p_2),$$

we can find the roots of this polynomial by solving

$$z^2 - a_1 z^1 - a_2 = (z^1 - p_1)(z^1 - p_2) = 0$$

for an appropriate value of z.

Poles We can interpret p_1 and p_2 as follows:

● p_1 and p_2 are associated with the coefficients a_1 and a_2.
● p_1 and p_2 represent points at which H can become very large or even infinite; that is, they are points of resonance, called *poles*.
● Each pole represents the center frequency of a band-pass filter.
● In those cases relevant to our discussion, the poles p_1 and p_2 come in mirror-image pairs, each pair representing a single resonance.
● If we know the coefficients a_1 and a_2, we can find the poles p_1 and p_2. Conversely, we can find the coefficients a_1 and a_2 if we know the pole positions p_1 and p_2.

Poles are the roots of the polynomial when $H(z)$ is of the form

$$H(z) = \frac{1}{\text{polynomial}}.$$

Poles represent points of resonance.

AllZero, an All-Zero Digital Filter

We looked at an all-pole, two-coefficient filter as

$$Y(z) = H(z)X(z).$$

When the gain was equal to unity, the transfer function $H(z)$ took on the form

$$\frac{1}{1 - a_1 z^{-1} - a_2 z^{-2}}.$$

If we were to invert this transfer function, we would have a filter of the form

$$Y(z) = (1 - a_1 z^{-1} - a_2 z^{-2})X(z).$$

This is an all-zero band-reject filter whose frequency response is just the inverse of the frequency response in the band-pass case. That is, if we solve for

$$(z^{-1} - s_1)(z^{-1} - s_2) = 0$$

we find roots that represent zeros of the transfer function rather than poles. (Clearly s_1 and s_2 will be identical in value to p_1 and p_2, but because of their location in the transfer function they will have a different interpretation.)

Working back "upward" to the time domain, we can take

$$Y(z) = X(z) - a_1 z^{-1} X(z) - a_2 z^{-2} X(z).$$

Removing z by using the "inverse z transform," we obtain

$$y_k = x_k - a_1 x_{k-1} - a_2 x_{k-2},$$

which can be implemented in a computer program as follows:

```
PROCEDURE allZero (input, output, coef, pastIn);
BEGIN
    output ← input − coef[1] * pastIn[1] − coef[2] * pastIn[2];
    pastIn[2] ← pastIn[1];
    pastIn[1] ← input;
END;
```

This is allZero, a prototype all-zero digital band-reject filter that could be used in place of allPole in the prototype music-synthesis program given above. Notice the minus signs in the first line after BEGIN, rather than the plus signs that occured in allPole. Also, input is saved in pastIn[1] here, whereas output was used in allPole.

Poles and Zeros: Summary

Note the difference between all-pole and all-zero filters: AllPole adds terms and uses past outputs, whereas allZero subtracts terms and uses past inputs. If the same coefficients are used, the frequency responses of these filters are exactly inverse to one another. We can see this by taking the filter

$$y_k = x_k - a_1 x_{k-1} - a_2 x_{k-2} + a_3 y_{k-1} + a_4 y_{k-2}$$

and letting $a_1 = a_3$ and $a_2 = a_4$. Then $y_k = x_k$ satisfies this equality, which was to be demonstrated.

General Inverse Filtering

Let us take a segment of n speech samples,

$$x_1, x_2, x_3, \ldots, x_n,$$

which we will represent as

$$x_k, \qquad k = 1, 2, 3, \ldots, n.$$

Now, apply an all-zero filter to this sequence. Assume the filter to have i coefficients.

$$y_k = x_k - a_1 x_{k-1} - a_2 x_{k-2} - \cdots - a_i x_{k-i},$$
$$k = i + 1, i + 2, \ldots, n.$$

(In allZero, i was equal to 2.) We must start with $k = i + 1$, since we need i past inputs for the filter, and inputs before $k = 1$ are undefined. In the cases of allPole and allZero, these nonexistent past inputs were initialized to 0. (This means that a digital filter may give "wrong" answers when it first starts to operate.) Another representation of the last equation is

$$y_k = x_k - \sum_{j=1}^{i} a_j x_{k-j}, \qquad k = i + 1, i + 2, \ldots, n.$$

Now let's spend some time playing with this.

Interpretation 1   The output of the filter y_k is equal to the input x_k minus some signal p_k, where

$$p_k = \sum_{j=1}^{i} a_j x_{k-j}.$$

Now, if p_k were to come out exactly equal to x_k, the output of the system would be exactly 0. That is to say, if x_k were a speech segment and p_k were its exact representation, the filter output would be 0.

Interpretation 2 p_k is a linear combination of coefficients and past inputs (i.e., no square terms, roots, etc.) and can be considered to be a prediction of the speech signal x_k. This is where the name *linear prediction* comes from.

Now let us give the filter output y_k a new name. This output represents the remainder after the predicted signal is subtracted from the original signal p_k. It is therefore a "leftover," or error signal. As was previously mentioned, this signal is known as the residual. Figure 9.18 shows two typical residuals.

If we square each sample value of the residual and then add up the answers for all samples $i + 1, \ldots, n$, we have a useful error measurement. (We square the error so that error values like -1 and $+1$ don't cancel each other out. That is, if $y_1 = -1$ and $y_2 = +1$, the sum will be 0, but $y_1^2 + y_2^2$ is 2, which tells us more about the response of the system than does the value 0.) Figure 9.16 also shows measurements of the sum of the error samples and the sum of the squares of the error samples for each residual. We call this latter sum the *squared error*, and denote it by E:

$$E = \sum_{k=i+1}^{n} y_k^2$$

$$= \sum_{k=i+1}^{n} \left(x_k - \sum_{j=1}^{i} a_j x_{k-j} \right)^2.$$

In operating a speech-analysis system, we want to have as small an error as possible with respect to each of our filter coefficients $a_1, a_2, \ldots, a_i$. This is to ensure that our formant peaks will be optimally placed. Mathematically, this is accomplished by taking the derivative of the squared error E with respect to each individual coefficient (here denoted as a_q) and setting the result equal to 0:

$$\frac{dE}{da_q} = 0, \qquad q = 1, 2, \ldots, i.$$

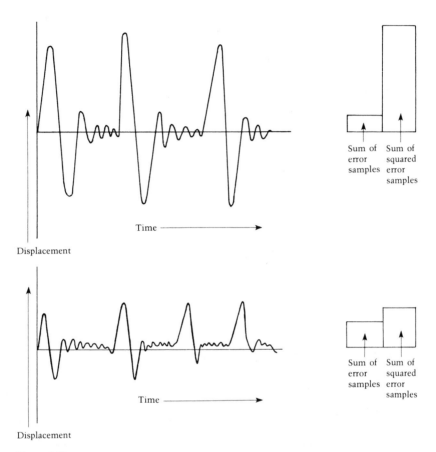

Figure 9.18
Residuals from two typical analyses of a speech signal. For each residual, two possible measures of error are shown. In the upper plot the speech formants have not been captured well; thus, the residual is large, making the sum of the squared residual samples large. In the lower plot the formants have been captured well, making both the residual and the sum of the squared residual samples small.

This gives

$$\frac{d}{da_q} \sum_k \left(x_k - \sum_j a_j x_{k-j} \right)^2 = 0,$$

$$q = 1, 2, \ldots, i$$

$$2 \sum_k \left(x_k - \sum_j a_j x_{k-j} \right) x_{k-q} = 0,$$

$$q = 1, 2, \ldots, i$$

$$2 \sum_k \left(x_k x_{k-q} - \sum_j a_j x_{k-j} x_{k-q} \right) = 0,$$

$$q = 1, 2, \ldots, i.$$

The constant 2 disappears by division, and we take through the sum over k, leaving

$$\sum_k x_k x_{k-q} - \sum_k \sum_j a_j x_{k-j} x_{k-q} = 0,$$

$$q = 1, 2, \ldots, i.$$

With some more rearranging, this becomes

$$\sum_j a_j \sum_k x_{k-j} x_{k-q} = \sum_k x_k x_{k-q},$$

$$q = 1, 2, \ldots, i.$$

Hence, we have i equations in i unknowns, these unknowns being the filter coefficients a_j. We know all of the input x_ks, since these are our original speech samples, and we can solve this last set of equations with standard equation solvers.

These are precisely the equations that the analysis program sets up and solves.

Summary

The inverse filtering analysis system discussed in section 2 is implemented as an all-zero filter p_k such that

$$y_k = x_k - p_k$$

where

$$p_k = \sum_j a_j x_{k-j}.$$

The all-zero filter p_k can be thought of as the predicted signal, giving rise to the term *linear prediction*. The output y_k can be thought of as the error signal, and is given the name *residual*.

The desired formant filter is obtained by setting the derivative of the sum of the squared residual values (E) equal to 0 with respect to each of the inverse filter coefficients a_j. In all cases we are talking about a small number of coefficients a_j as compared with the number of actual speech samples x_k (a ratio on the order of 1:20). Finally, once we have obtained the coefficients of the all-zero filter, we can construct an all-pole filter by changing the sign of the coefficients and applying them to (past) outputs (instead of past inputs).

As previously mentioned, this all-pole filter, if applied to the residual y_k of the system, will produce speech of perfect quality. If applied to an approximate vocal-tract input signal, it will produce good-quality speech.

Postscript

Once the formant filter coefficients have been derived, they can be modified before they are used for music. For instance, the filter polynomial can be solved to determine the frequencies of the formants. These frequencies can then be transposed and new coefficients derived. It is thus possible to alter drastically the characteristics of the original analog input. For instance, a male speaker can be made to sound female, a soprano saxophone can be made to sound like a double bass, and so forth. Interpolation is also possible: By interpolating between the formant filters of a piano and a human voice, one can get the effect of hitting a piano note, having it sound like a piano, and ending up at the tail end of the note with speech.

Clearly, the possibilities are enormous. Have fun!

Acknowledgments

The code listings were supplied by John Strawn.

References

Atal, B. S., and S. L. Hanauer. 1971. "Speech analysis and synthesis by linear prediction of the speech wave." *Journal of the Acoustical Society of America* 50: 637–655.

Fant, G. 1960. *Acoustic Theory of Speech Production*. The Hague: Mouton.

Flanagan, J. L. 1972. *Speech Analysis, Synthesis, and Perception*. New York: Springer.

Other Recommended Reading

Howe, H. S., Jr. 1975. *Electronic Music Synthesis*. New York: Norton.

Makhoul, J. 1975. "Linear prediction: A tutorial review." *Proceedings of the IEEE* 63: 561–580.

Markel, J. D. 1976. *Formant Trajectory Estimation from a Linear Least-Squares Inverse Filter Formulation*. Document AD734679. Springfield, Virginia: National Technical Information Service.

Markel, J. D., and A. H. Gray Jr. 1976. *Linear Prediction of Speech*. New York: Springer.

Mathews, M. V., with J. E. Miller, F. R. Moore, J. R. Pierce, and J.-C. Risset. 1969. *The Technology of Computer Music*. Cambridge, Mass.: MIT Press.

Moore, F. R. 1978. "An introduction to the mathematics of digital signal processing, Part II." *Computer Music Journal* 2(2): 38–60.

Randall, J. K. 1972. "Compose yourself—A manual for the young, Part II." *Perspectives of New Music* 11(1): 77–91.

Steiglitz, K. 1974. *An Introduction to Discrete Systems*. New York: Wiley.

10 Granular Synthesis of Sound

CURTIS ROADS

Granular synthesis of sound involves generating thousands of very short sonic grains to form larger acoustic events. Granular synthesis is a fruitful technique for the exploration of a different class of computer-generated sound spectra than those produced by additive, subtractive, or modulation techniques.

According to an acoustical theory put forth by Gabor (1947), a granular or quantum representation could describe any sound. This conjecture was verified mathematically by Bastiaans (1980). To generate even a fairly simple sound, however, requires a massive amount of control data, in the form of parameters for each of the grains. If n is the number of parameters of each grain and d is the mean grain density (per minute), it takes $d \times n$ parameter values to specify one minute of sound. Since d is often in the range 1,000–5,000, it is clear that for the purpose of compositional control a higher-level unit of organization for the grains is necessary.

A front-end processor that allows the user to specify granular sound events with just a few parameters greatly eases the burden of work. Such a front-end processor can automatically calculate the thousands of grain specifications required for complex sound events. The grain generator may be defined in software (as an instrument in standard music-synthesis programs in the Music V family) or with digital synthesizers.

Theoretical Background

Gabor (1947) took exception to the notion, derived from Helmholtz, that subjective hearing was best represented by Fourier analysis. As Gabor noted: "Fourier analysis is a timeless description in terms of exactly periodic waves of infinite duration. On the other hand it is our most elementary experience that sound has a time pattern as well as a frequency pattern. ... A mathematical description is wanted which *ab ovo* takes account of this duality." (p. 591)

Gabor's solution involved the correlation of two new representations: acoustical quanta and the discrete limits of hearing. First, Gabor formed a mathematical representation for acoustical quanta by relating a time-domain signal $s(t)$ (such as one might view on an oscilloscope screen) to a frequency-domain spectrum $S(f)$ (Fourier spectrum, real part). Gabor

This is a revised and updated version of an article that originally appeared in *Computer Music Journal* 2(2): 61–62, 1978.

then mapped an energy function from $s(t)$ over an effective duration Δt into an energy function from $S(f)$ over an effective frequency width Δf, to obtain a characteristic cell or acoustical quantum. As in Fourier analysis, the uncertainty relation between time and frequency obtains. That is, in Fourier analysis it is well known that to obtain a high degree of frequency resolution requires a large number of samples (a large time window). On the other hand, analyzing windows of fine temporal resolution can result in coarse frequency measurements (Rabiner and Gold 1975, pp. 384–385).

The acoustical quanta produced by relating the time-signal energy to the frequency-spectrum energy are units of acoustical information. They can be represented as elementary signals with harmonic oscillations at any audible frequency f, modulated by a finite duration envelope (Gaussian curve). An arbitrary signal can be expanded in terms of such signals by dividing up the information area (time versus frequency) into unit cells and associating with each cell a complex amplitude factor.

Gabor noticed further that the quantum of sound was a concept of significance to the theory of hearing, since human hearing is not continuous but is strictly bounded by audible difference thresholds. Gabor suggested that within a certain very short time window (10–21 msec) the ear is capable of registering only one distinct "sensation," that is, one event at a specific frequency. Since similar just-noticeable differences obtain in the frequency and amplitude domains, Gabor reasoned that hearing does not involve infinite degrees of resolution but is governed by quanta of difference thresholds in frequency, time, and amplitude discrimination (see also Whitfield 1978).

Wiener presented an argument similar to that advanced by Gabor. He contrasted the view (expounded by Leibniz in the eighteenth century) that time, space, and matter are infinitely subdivisible (continuous) with Planck's quantum-theory notions: "In light as in matter, there is a granular rather than a continuous texture" (Wiener 1964, p. 539). At the same time, Wiener noted that Newton's notion of deterministic physics was gradually supplanted by Gibbsian statistical mechanics—a "qualified indeterminism." These shifts in paradigm occurred because "the laws of ordinary magnitudes do not continue down into the range of the very small" (p. 544). Wiener, as Gabor, was skeptical of the timeless Fourier analysis as the best representation for music: "To start and stop a note involves an alteration of its frequency composition which may be small but is very real. A note lasting only a finite time is to be analyzed as a band of simple harmonic motions, no one of which can be taken as the only

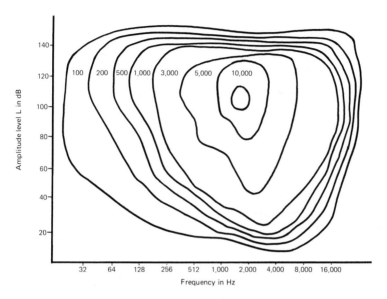

Figure 10.1
Map of the audible domain in the plane: sound pressure level versus frequency of sine waves. The closed curves indicate the level of acoustical information: number of quantified squares $\Delta L \Delta f$ per unit of surface. After Moles 1968; reproduced with permission of University of Illinois Press.

simple harmonic motion present. ... " (pp. 544–545) Going further, Wiener stressed the importance of recognizing the scope of a model of measurement: "The laws of physics are like musical notation—things that are real and important provided that we do not take them too seriously and push the time scale down beyond a certain level" (p. 545).

Moles was interested in segmenting the audible space (figure 10.1) into small units for the purpose of measuring the information content of a sonic message. Moles described this segmentation as follows: "We know that the receptor, the ear, divides these two dimensions [pitch and loudness] into quanta. Thus each sonic element may be represented by an elementary square. A pure sinusoidal sound without harmonics, unlimited in length, would be represented by just one of these squares" (1968, pp. 108–109). He estimated the power of the ear to resolve small differences in frequency and amplitude: "Because thresholds quantize the continua of pitch and loudness, the repertoire is limited to some 340,000 elements (figure 10.2). Physically, these elements are smaller and denser

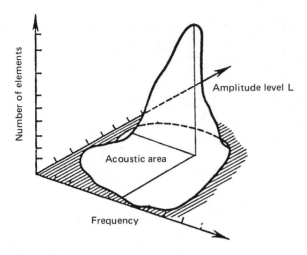

Figure 10.2
Extent of the repertoire of pure elementary sounds of limitless duration. Since the "resolution" of the ear is greater toward the center of the audible area, this repertoire assumes the form of a mountain, the base of which is circumscribed by the audible area. Hence, the vertical axis shows the ear's ability to resolve small differences in frequency and amplitude. After Moles 1968; reproduced with permission of University of Illinois Press.

toward the center of the sonic domain, where the ear is more acute; " . . . in most cases, each symbol [in a sonic message] is a combination of elements, that is, of a certain number of these squares. . . . " (Moles 1968, p. 110). Moles estimated the "temporal perceptual quantum" to be about 60 msec.

Xenakis (1971) was the first to explicate a compositional theory for grains of sound. He began by adopting the following lemma: "All sound is an integration of grains, of elementary sonic particles, of sonic quanta. . . . All sound, even continuous musical variation, is conceived as an assemblage of a large number of elementary sounds adequately disposed in time. In the attack, body, and decline of a complex sound, thousands of pure sounds appear in a more or less short interval of time Δt. . . . If we consider the duration Δt of the grain as quite small but invariable, we can ignore it in what follows and consider frequency and intensity only." (pp. 44–45) In attempting to characterize the necessary properties of grains for synthesis purposes, Xenakis took a pragmatic approach. He describes a possible approximation to Gabor's model for sonic quanta in

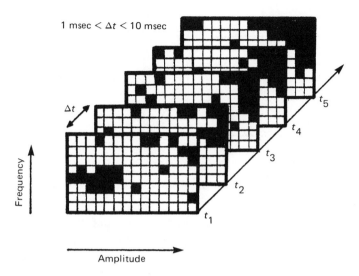

Figure 10.3
A book of screens containing simultaneous grains. Each screen represents a time slice in the evolution of a complex sound. In practice, the mesh on each screen would be much finer.

the context of an analog synthesis implementation. This model uses sine waves of 40 msec duration with a rectangular envelope. As a higher-level compositional unit, Xenakis suggests organizing the grains into entities called *screens*. The screens are time and frequency planes upon which are scattered hundreds of grains (the number of grains is determined by the mean density d). Each screen is like a time slice. A *book* of screens constitutes the evolution of a complex sound object (figure 10.3).

Implementing Grains of Sound

In order to test the various proposals for granular synthesis, I implemented an automated system in 1975 at the University of California at San Diego, using a Burroughs B6700 computer running Music V (Mathews 1969; Leibig 1974). The main goals of this project were to design and code a working granular-synthesis system, to fine-tune the synthesis parameters for optimum sound quality and flexibility, to develop high-level controls over the synthesis, and to experiment with compositional applications of the technique. There was no attempt to experimentally verify the com-

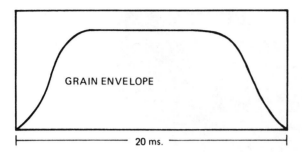

Figure 10.4
Grain envelope, with Gaussian attack and decay and sustained steady-state portion.

pleteness of the acoustical theories proposed by Gabor and Wiener. Each grain of sound had a fixed duration and amplitude function, but the waveforms, amplitudes, and frequencies varied. The proponents of granular synthesis have suggested grain durations between 10 and 60 msec. After several listening tests, an upper bound on grain durations of 20 msec was set. Grains of 10 msec are quite effective. Green (1971) has suggested that temporal auditory acuity (the ability of the ear to detect discrete events and discern their order) extends down to durations as short as 1 or 2 msec. According to Green, this is true for transients and noise bursts as well as for continuous periodic stimuli. This suggests that, in some cases, very short grains (duration < 10 msec) might also be useful. (Shorter grains can be computationally costly, since the shorter the grains are, the more grains are needed to fill in a given event's time span.)

Another critical synthesis parameter is the shape of the grain envelope. Experiments indicated that the pure Gaussian curve did not have enough effective amplitude, and the rectangular envelope proposed by Xenakis produced objectionable transients in the audio output. The envelope I finally settled on combines the Gaussian curve suggested by Gabor with the rectangle suggested by Xenakis, thus achieving a smooth rise and decay and a sustained peak (figure 10.4).

A Granular-Synthesis Instrument

Since the complexity of granular-synthesis sounds is produced by combining hundreds or thousands of grains into various constellations, the instrument used to produce an individual grain may be quite simple. The following is a Music V definition:

```
INS 0 1;
OSC P5 P6 B3 F4 P30;
OSC B3 P7 B4 F3 P29;
OSC B3 P7 B5 F1 P28;
ITP B4 B5 F1 P8;
OUT B2 B1;
END;
```

In this implementation the first oscillator is used in degenerate mode to produce one cycle—a fixed-duration envelope for the grain. F4 is the envelope function. The second oscillator produces a sine wave; F3 is the waveform function. The third oscillator produces a band-limited pulse; F1 is its waveform function. The ITP unit generator interpolates between the two oscillators. From the user standpoint, the waveform, frequency, and amplitude of each grain can be varied: P5 determines a grain's overall amplitude, P7 determines the frequency, and P8 determines the waveform content.

In the 1975 implementation, the waveform varied (from grain to grain) between a sine and a band-limited pulse (Winham and Steiglitz 1970), the frequencies took on values between 40.4 and 9,999 Hz at a 20 kHz sampling rate, and the amplitudes varied between 30 and 72 dB. The 20-msec grains were computed to a resolution of 16 bits, and up to 32 grains could be playing simultaneously. This means that up to 1,600 grains (50 × 32) could be packed into one second.

Events: Higher-Level Organization of Grains

Because of the massive amount of data required for moderately dense granular synthesis, it is impractical to require the grain specifications to be typed by a composer. It is necessary to organize collections of higher-level units with fewer parameters. In my implementations, the composer works with units called *events* (figure 10.5), which are characterized by the beginning time and duration (>20 msec), the initial waveform and waveform rate-of-change (slope) between a sine at one extreme and a band-limited pulse at the other, the initial center frequency and frequency slope, the initial bandwidth and bandwidth slope, the initial grain density and density slope, and the initial amplitude and amplitude slope. (As I discuss later, sound files containing any sound can also be granulated.) Within the boundaries of an event, grains are automatically scattered according to the tendencies specified by the event parameters. For example, if the initial

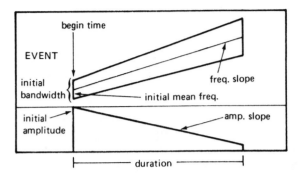

Figure 10.5
Parameters of an event.

density of an event is sparse, few grains will be scattered towards the beginning; if the grain density slope is positive, more and more grains will be generated toward the end of the event.

Details of the 1975 Implementation

The granular-synthesis (GS) program was implemented as a front-end processor interfaced to a Music V installation. The dual-processor Burroughs B6700 computer (an Algol stack machine) generated the grains and computed the sound samples. The GS program was written in Extended Algol, which is more or less directly executed by the B6700 computer without translation into assembly code.

The program interpreted composer-written event specifications and generated a Music V NOT (the Music V term for note) record for each grain of sound. Because of the number of notes generated, it was necessary to tune Music V (in particular the IP array) to allow adequate note storage. Function table lengths for the GS instrument were set at 1,024 16-bit quantities. The GS program was called in Pass 1 of Music V. After Pass 1, computation of sound was just as in any other Music V task. A simple Music V instrument for granular synthesis with waveform interpolation and delay is shown in figure 10.6.

Extensions of Granular Synthesis: The 1981 Implementation

In 1981 I undertook another implementation of granular synthesis at the MIT Experimental Music Studio. This implementation was coded in the

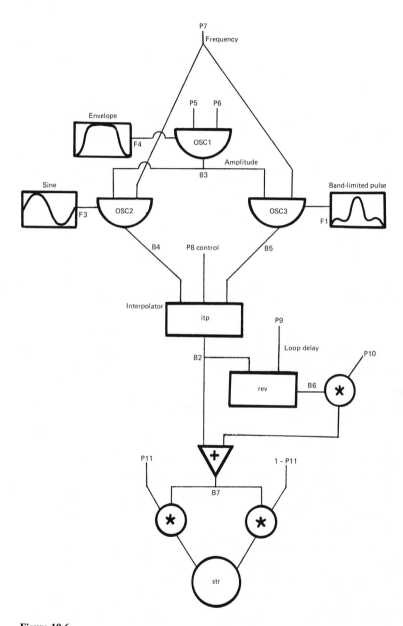

Figure 10.6
A Music V instrument for automated granular synthesis with reverberation and spatial positioning. P1 = NOT, P2 = start time, P3 = instrument number, P4 = duration, P5 = amplitude, P6 = envelope frequency, P7 = audio frequency, P8 = waveform interpolation factor, P9 = reverberation delay, P10 = amount of reverberation, and P11 = spatial position.

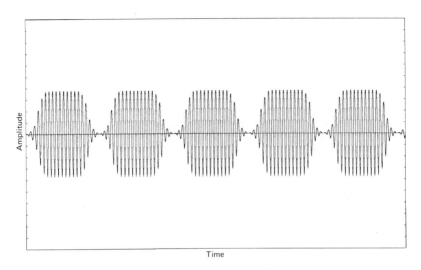

Figure 10.7
A chain of five 20-msec grains with a frequency of 1,000 Hz, sampled at 20 kHz.

Music 11 sound-synthesis language for a DEC PDP-11/50 computer with a floating-point processor. Tests were run at a 40-kHz sampling rate using 1,024-word function tables.

Signal-Processing Aspects of Granular Synthesis

The envelope shown in figure 10.4 has a predictable effect on the spectrum of the waveform fed into it. In this section, I briefly discuss what happens to the spectrum of a chain of grains at a fixed frequency as a guide to the effects on more complex signals. The signal is a chain of 20-msec grains with a sinusoidal carrier wave multiplied by the envelope of figure 10.4. This time-domain signal is plotted in figure 10.7.

In general, for each sinusoidal component in the carrier the time envelope will contribute a series of sidebands to the final spectrum. The sidebands are separated from the original sinusoidal component in the frequency domain by a distance corresponding to the inverse of the period of the envelope function. For the 20-msec envelope used in these tests, the sidebands in the output spectrum are spaced at 50-Hz intervals (figure 10.8). The acoustical effect is that of a "formant" surrounding the carrier frequency. That is, instead of a single line in the spectrum (denoting one

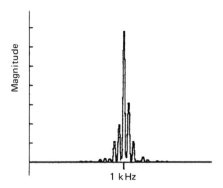

Figure 10.8
A fast Fourier transform (FFT) plot of the signal shown in figure 10.7 (with a Hamming window). The peak component is at 1,000 Hz, with sidebands spaced regularly every 50 Hz. The strongest sidebands are about 12 dB down from the 1,000-Hz components; the other components slope off rapidly.

spectral component), the spectrum looks like a hump (denoting a group of frequencies around the carrier). In practice, strictly sequential chains of grains are a boundary case, since the appearance of a grain at a particular timepoint in the event is determined by a call to a random function. Using a random onset time for the grains has the advantage of reducing the effect of the 50-Hz envelope components. A plot of the fast Fourier transform of a chain with just a 2-msec (maximum) random deviation in onset is shown in figure 10.9. A close examination demonstrates how the spectrum is smeared: The regular 50-Hz-spaced sidebands are attenuated.

Implementation of Granular Synthesis with Digital Hardware

An economical method for granular synthesis would involve committing the actual computation of grain samples to a digital synthesizer; the host computer would only need to compute grain specifications from a high-level musical specification and update the list to the hardware. The designs for programmable digital synthesizers that have been appearing could easily be adapted for multiple-voiced granular synthesis in conjunction with other methods.

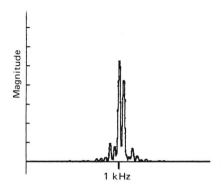

1 kHz

Figure 10.9
An FFT plot of a chain of grains in which the onset of the grains has been randomized by a factor of 2 msec maximum.

Musical Applications

Automated granular synthesis provides the user with a means of precise specification of complex timbral events. Sound spectra can vary from a single, isolated pitch (formed by a chain of grains at a given frequency) to groupings of simultaneous frequencies, glissandi, and clouds of granular particles over the entire audio spectrum. These variations may be controlled by manipulating just one or two event parameters.

Thus, granular synthesis provides a means for realizing Varèse's dream of "the movement of sound masses, of shifting planes," so that "in the moving masses you would be conscious of their transmutation when they pass over certain layers, when they penetrate certain opacities, or are dilated into certain rarefactions" (Varèse 1966, pp. 25–26).

The sounds produced by granular synthesis can be represented by a graphic notation similar to that used for Stockhausen's *Studie II* (1964). However, the notation (and the sound) is freer, since Stockhausen's composition uses rectangles to describe sonic events whereas this granular synthesis can model in sound any polygon inscribed on the frequency-versus-time plane (figure 10.10).

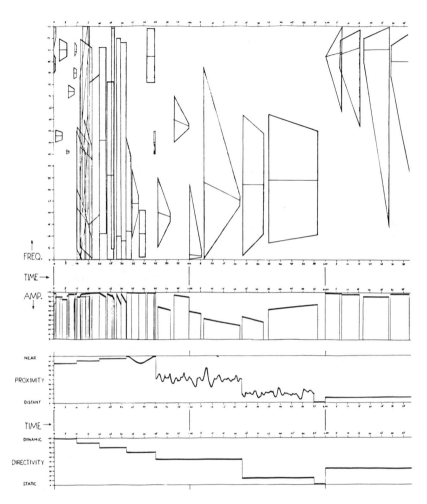

Figure 10.10
Excerpt from the graphic score for the composition *prototype* (C. Roads, 1975), realized
with granular synthesis. Each polygon inscribed on the frequency-versus-time plane
represents an event. The graphs at the bottom of the score specify variations in proximity
(amount of reverberation) and directivity (spatial changing, or panning).

Table 10.1
Compositions by the author in which granular synthesis is employed.

Composition	Date	When used (min:sec)
prototype	1975	Throughout
Objet	1977	8:29–8:43
nscor	1980	4:30–4:41, 5:00–5:40
Field	1981	3:10–3:16

Compositional Experience with Granular Synthesis

Granular synthesis has been employed in several of my compositions (table 10.1). In addition, musical experiments using digitized natural sounds have been carried out. I have "time-granulated" many soundfiles, including the sounds of snare drums, cymbals, and tom-toms. Various types of four-channel rolls and sound clouds have been developed with these basic ingredients. My most recent work has centered on the time granulation of digitized saxophone sounds, using multiple soundfiles as input. Varying the duration of the individual grains, the density of grains within an event, and the number and type of soundfiles used as input to the granulating instruments makes a wide range of textures achievable.

Extensions of Granular Synthesis

Granular synthesis could be coupled with an analysis subsystem that would allow the user to granulate an existing sound in both the frequency and the time dimension. (See Risset and Wessel 1982 for a general discussion of analysis/synthesis techniques, including granular synthesis.) A number of interesting effects could be achieved. First, by the cumulative deletion of grains over time, a sound could be made to "evaporate." The opposite tack, a "coelescence effect," could be implemented by starting from a sparse matrix of grains and gradually filling in the matrix to constitute the sound. Other effects, such as shifting the original time, frequency, and amplitude values of the grains in an analyzed segment, could be used to produce variations of or enrichments to the original sound.

Summary

Granular synthesis adds to the palette of new sound colors made available by digital synthesis. The main strengths of granular synthesis are its accessible composer interface, by which high-level events can be specified with just a few simple parameters, and its ability to accurately realize the kinds of gestures that can be captured in graphical scores.

Acknowledgments

I am indebted to John Stautner of the MIT Experimental Music Studio for his kind assistance in generating some of the plots shown in this chapter and for his consultation on the fine points of the Music 11 system. I also thank John Strawn for his helpful comments on the manuscript.

References

Bastiaans, M. 1980. "Gabor's expansion of a signal into Gaussian elementary signals." *Proceedings of the IEEE* 68: 538–539.

Gabor, D. 1947. "Acoustical quanta and the theory of hearing." *Nature* 159 (4044): 591–594.

Green, D. 1971. "Temporal auditory acuity." *Psychological Review* 78(6): 540–551.

Leibig, B. 1974. A User's Guide to Music V on the B6700. Internal report, University of California, San Diego, Center for Music Experiment, La Jolla.

Mathews, M. V., with J. E. Miller, F. R. Moore, J. R. Pierce, and J.-C. Risset. 1969. *The Technology of Computer Music*. Cambridge, Mass.: MIT Press.

Moles, A. 1968. *Information Theory and Esthetic Perception*. Urbana: University of Illinois Press.

Rabiner, L., and B. Gold. 1975. *Theory and Applications of Digital Signal Processing*. Englewood Cliffs, N.J.: Prentice-Hall.

Risset, J.-C., and D. Wessel. 1982. "Exploration of timbre by analysis and synthesis." In D. Deutsch, ed. 1982. *The Psychology of Music*. New York: Academic.

Stockhausen, K. 1964. "Elektronische Studien I und II." In *Texte*, Vol. 2. Cologne: Du-Mont.

Varèse, E. 1966. "The liberation of sound." In B. Boretz and E. Cone, eds. 1971. *Perspectives on American Composers*. New York: Norton.

Whitfield, J. 1978. "The neural code." In E. Carterette and M. Friedman, eds. 1978. *Handbook of Perception*, vol. IV, Hearing. New York: Academic.

Wiener, N. 1964. "Spatial-temporal continuity, quantum theory and music." In M. Capek, ed. 1975. *The Concepts of Space and Time*. Boston: Reidel.

Winham, G., and K. Steiglitz. 1970. "Input generators for digital sound synthesis." *Journal of the Acoustical Society of America* 27(2): 665–666.

Xenakis, I. 1971. *Formalized Music*. Bloomington: Indiana University Press.

11 PILE—A Language for Sound Synthesis

PAUL BERG

PILE is a computer language for direct sound synthesis. A program written in PILE operates in real time once it has been compiled. There is no external data storage. Up to four channels of sound may be produced. Groups of machine operations form the basis for PILE instructions. It is possible to program distinct sounds and a structure for them. It is also possible to program a structure that produces sound. The PILE compiler is available on the PDP-15 computer at the Institute of Sonology in Utrecht.

The above statements indicate certain aspects of PILE that are uncommon among the work being done in computer sound synthesis. It is a language and not a program. It actually operates in real time; calculations, decisions, and bookkeeping all occur as the sound is produced. This means that this language is also suitable for use with a limited hardware configuration. A large computer system is unnecessary. In contrast with other more or less real-time systems, PILE can simultaneously produce several sounds or layers of sounds. It is not limited to monolinear strings of sounds.

PILE instructions are based on groups of machine operations, not on a particular acoustical model. Parameters such as frequency, timbre, envelope, and duration are not specifically referenced. Rather, the available instructions fall into the following categories: manipulation of the accumulator, manipulation of external devices, manipulation of variables, manipulation of lists, and manipulation of program flow.

Given this basis, one can use PILE to produce music, musical structures, and musical sounds. Because PILE works in real time, the structures can be tested immediately. In one program, separate sounds can be described and ordered in a structure. A different possibility is to describe a structure in a program without referring to what could be distinct sound events, and then listening to the result of that structure. Probably the most uncommon aspect of PILE is that one can work with it in both of these ways.

Originally published in *Computer Music Journal* 3(1): 30–41, 1979.

Background

A myriad of sound-synthesis programs are based on models related to instrumental music or to the design of a traditional analog electronic studio. Some work in real time. Some work with extreme accuracy. Some provide for convenient interaction between the operator and the machine. They all require the use of a computer because of the magnitude of the task. For many, this is perhaps the only reason why a computer is needed. It is a valid reason, but it is certainly not the most interesting one. More interesting ones are to hear that which could not be heard without the computer, to think that which would not be thought without the computer, and to learn that which would not be learned without the computer. To ask what a computer can do for a composer or what you can learn from a computer is obviously within the realm of music. After all, a composer may certainly ask what a clarinet can do, or what the sound properties are of any other instrument or object used as an instrument. A performer often tries to learn something about a type of music by playing on various types of instruments. Playing "old" music on "old" instruments is a common example of this practice.

Computers produce and manipulate numbers and other symbolic data very quickly. This could be considered the idiom of the computer and used as a basis for musical work with the computer. In 1974–75 I performed a series of experiments with the production and output of numbers to a digital-to-analog converter within the framework of sound synthesis. These experiments led to the ASP (Automated Sound Programs), a collection of 22 programs written in Macro-15 (the assembler language for the PDP-15). These programs are fairly simple models of number manipulation and temporal distribution systems. Counting, calculating, comparing, choosing, and repeating are common procedures in the programs. Structures were described using strings of LACs (load accumulator), ANDs (logical and), XORs (exclusive or), TADs (two's complement addition), SRRANs (shift random-number generator and read into the accumulator), etc. The programs are self-contained and automatic—given a start number for the random-number generator, the programs will continue until externally halted. The output is variable—if one begins with a different start number, a different output results, and yet the output can be repeated by beginning the program with the same start number.

The most accurate statement of the relationships that occur in a program is found in the program text. This is because the structural relation-ships are defined in terms of the programming language. Since Macro-15 is not a widely used language, an example (ASP 11) will be described using a flowchart (figure 11.1) and the following description:

A number series with repetitions is output. This series is calculated using randomly selected logical operations. The clock is varied using values derived from variable A. Six logical functions are defined as macros—conjunction, antivalence, disjunction, equivalence, implication, and ex-clusion. A 12-bit random value is chosen as A. Its two's-complement is stored to use later in determining when a new A should be calculated. A 12-bit random value is chosen for B. The five right-hand bits are two's-complemented and used later to determine when to calculate a new value for B. Depending on the number read from the HRG (hardware random number generator), the program performs one of the six logical operations between A and B. The result, C, is trimmed to 12 bits and sent to the con-verter when a clock flag is detected. A check is made if a new value for the number of clock pulses should be calculated. If yes, the two's-complement of the right-hand six bits of A become the new value. The count for a new repetition mask is incremented. If zero, the count is reset to the two's-complement of C. The repetition mask is this complement masked by the octal value of 4137. The value of the repetition mask has great influence on the sonic output. Next, the repetition factor is checked. If the value of C just sent to the converter is to be repeated, the program jumps to SOUND, where the clock is loaded, enabled, and C is output. Otherwise a new value for the number of repetitions of the next C is calculated. The new repetition value is the antivalence of A and B, which is masked by the repetition mask, and two's-complemented. The previously-derived value for NEWB is incremented. If it equals zero, the program jumps to cal-culate a new B and from there continues the program. Otherwise, the check for a new A is performed. The program continues then either from the calculation of a new A value, or from the switch point where the logical operation was chosen. (Berg 1975)

As can be seen in this example, each sample produced necessarily results from all the program parts and all the program calculations. The program is an explicit description of what must happen and what has happened.

The 22 ASP programs demonstrated that it was possible to construct a number of programs with a variety of ideas and output. It also became clear that several groups of Macro-15 instructions were frequently used in various programs. These groups of instructions could be considered valu-able concepts in writing this type of synthesis program. One could gen-eralize these groups of instructions and use them as a basis for a language.

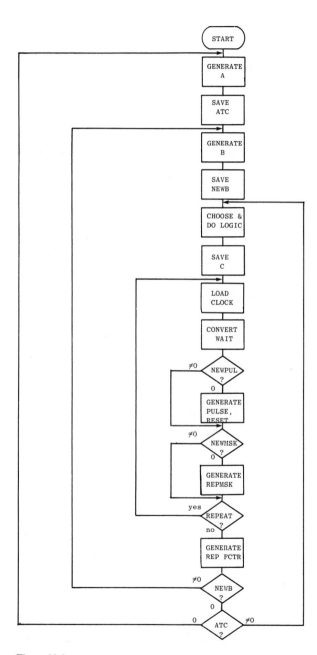

Figure 11.1
Example of a sound-synthesis procedure in one of the ASP programs (Berg 1975).

This was the basis for PILE. A frequently recurring group of instructions was generalized to one PILE instruction. The usefulness of the instructions had already been demonstrated in the ASP programs. The generalization to one instruction made the groups easier to use and to oversee and gave more insight into the processes of this type of sound synthesis. PILE instructions are not limited to groups used in ASP. The need for additional instructions became apparent with use, but the ASP groups did provide the starting point for the PILE instructions. The PILE language and the compiler for it were designed and written in 1976–77.

A Short Description of the Language

The available instructions are described in the appendix. An instruction in PILE contains the name of an operation on the first line and further information on the following lines. This may involve several applications of the operation stated on the first line. The last line of an instruction is terminated with a semicolon, e.g.,

```
CONVERT
    SEND:VAR
    CHANNEL:0;
```

An instruction may be given a label (address). If a label is used, it must be the first symbol(s) of the first line of an instruction. The first symbol of an instruction must be a tab or space. After that, any number of tabs and/or spaces may be used to align the instruction as desired.

Some Programming Examples

The available instructions are combined in programs, which are compiled and then executed. Sample values are sent directly to a digital-analog converter with the CONVERT instruction. Important considerations when programming are the succession of operations and amount of time they take. A given combination of instructions could work too slowly to result in an audible output.

One difficulty in describing programming examples is that the sound is not heard by the person reading this description. This limitation is less serious when one is working from a known model. Therefore, the first example will be of a known sound: noise.

```
TOP    RANDOM;
       CONVERT
              SEND:–
              CHANNEL:1;
       BRANCH
       TO:TOP;
```

The idea is to produce noise by sending random values to the converter. TOP is the label for the instruction RANDOM. That instruction reads a random number into the accumulator. The following instruction sends the contents of the accumulator to converter channel 0. The hyphen after SEND indicates a default condition, in this case the contents of the accumulator instead of a particular variable or constant. Program control branches to the instruction labeled TOP; that is, it returns to the first instruction. The speed at which this program operates is the speed of the assembed machine instructions.

The following is a sample program written in PILE. Figure 11.2 is a flowchart for this program.

```
             SEED
                  7;
             STORE
                  SAVE;
START        INIT
                  REF:1
                  NEW3:–1
                  NEW2:–1
                  NEW1:–1;
CHANGE  CHECK
                  NEW2
                  NCNT,–
                  NEW3
                  MSEL,–;
             SEL N
                  B:12–15
                  ST:NEW3;
             CAL
                  REF:REF*2
                  MASK3:REF–1
                  COMP:4096–REF;
             ZERO?
                  Y:END;
MSEL         SEL
                  M:MASK3
                  ST:MASK2;
             SEL N
                  B:12–17
                  ST:NEW2;
```

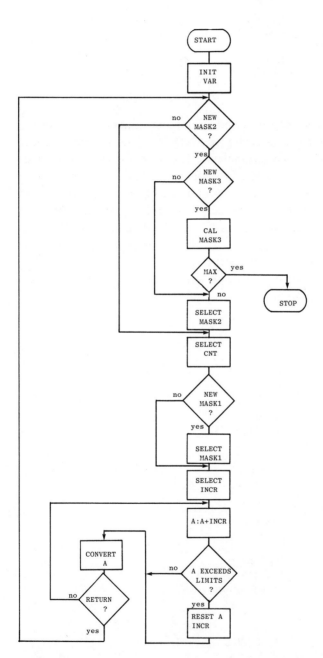

Figure 11.2
Flow chart for a sample PILE program.

```
NCNT      SEL N
                    B:MASK2
                    ST:CNT;
          CHECK
                    NEW1
                    NINC,-;
          SEL
                    B:8-17
                    ST:MASK1;
          SEL N
                    B:15-17
                    ST:NEW1;
NINC      SEL
                    M:MASK1
                    ST:INCR;
TURN      CAL
                    A:A + INCR      ←—————
                    MAX:4095-A;
                         NEGATIVE?
                         MAX
                         -,GOON;
                              INIT
                              A:4095
                              INCR:-INCR;
                              BRANCH
                                 TO:GOON2;
GOON                          NEG?
                              A
                              -,GOON2;
                         INIT
                         A:0    -
                         INCR:-INCR;
GOON2     CONVERT
                    SEND:A
                    CHANNEL:0;
          CHECK
                    CNT
                    TURN,CHANGE;
END
          FINISH?
             EXT:SAVE;
          DECLARE
                    NEW1,NEW2,MASK2,CNT,MASK1,INCR,A,
                    MAX,REF,COMP,SAVE,NEW3,MASK3;
```

The value A is incremented with INCR (see arrow). The result is
sent to the converter. This happens CNT times. If A becomes greater
than 4,095, the sign of INCR is changed and A is set to 4,095. If A be-

comes less than 0, the sign of INCR is changed and A is set to 0. If CNT and INCR are large, more or less regular triangle patterns are formed. If that is not the case, various other forms occur. After A has been incremented CNT times, several conditions are CHECKed to determine which variable should receive a new value.

In most cases the values for variables are produced with SELECT (SEL), which assigns a nonzero random value to a variable. This random value is limited in size by bits which can be specified; for example, if bits 15–17 are used the random value will be between 1 and 7. A variable can be used as a mask instead of specifying the bits. In that case a logical AND is performed between the variable and the tentative random number. The result, if nonzero, is stored in the variable. The boundaries for a random number therefore change every time the variable used as a mask changes its value. Thus, describing how mask values change in a program can be an important structural aspect. The values for INCR are determined with a variable, MASK1. A new value for this variable is occasionally chosen with a bit specification. CNT also has a variable mask, MASK2. Values for MASK2 are occasionally chosen, masked by MASK3. In the course of the program, MASK3 gets larger and larger. MASK3 has an initial value of 1. When it reaches 4,095, the program halts.

The result of selecting values for MASK2 from MASK3 is that CNT tends to become larger. But this is not a linear change. This results in a more interesting structure and a more interesting development in the sound. Since a large CNT usually implies a larger regularity and since CNT tends to get larger as the program progresses, the relatively complex sounds in the beginning gradually tend to become more regular and less complex.

An obvious way to expand this program would be to describe a more directed change of MASK1 which relates to INCR. This was realized in Tape 1 from my composition *Locks and Dams* for two two-track tapes and trombone. The program for Tape 1 produced two channels of sounds simultaneously. One channel is similar to the example given here. In the second channel, the mask for INCR tends to increase while the mask for CNT is selected with an unchanging bit specification.

In the following procedure, the results of a series of arithmetic calculations are sent to the converter. This is followed by a waiting loop. The length of the waiting loop varies in the course of the program. Three groups of these calculations are found in the sample. One of the groups is chosen. Control stays with the chosen group until it returns to the top of the program. Another choice of group is then made. The way in which the waiting time changes is important to the changes heard in the sound. The fourth group produces silence by sending zeros to the converter. Figure 11.3 is the corresponding flowchart.

```
                        SEED
                        41;

             INIT
                        A:1
                        B:37;
             SEL N
                        B:6-16
                        ST:NUTIME
                        B:14-17
                        ST:TIME;
CHO          FINISH?
                        EXT:0;
             SEL N
                        B:8-17
                        ST:RETURN;
             CHOOSE
                        GROUP1,GROUP2,GROUP3,GROUP4;
GROUP1       CAL
                        A:A+1
                        B:B+7
                        C:A*B/3
                        D:C/67;
             CONVERT
                        S:C
                        CH:0
                        S:D
                        CH:1;
             INIT
                        WAIT:TIME;
DELAY                           CHECK
                                WAIT
                                DELAY,-
                                        NUTIME
                                        TEST,-;
             SEL N
                        B:13-17
                        ST:TIME
                                B:5-16
                                ST:NUTIME;
```

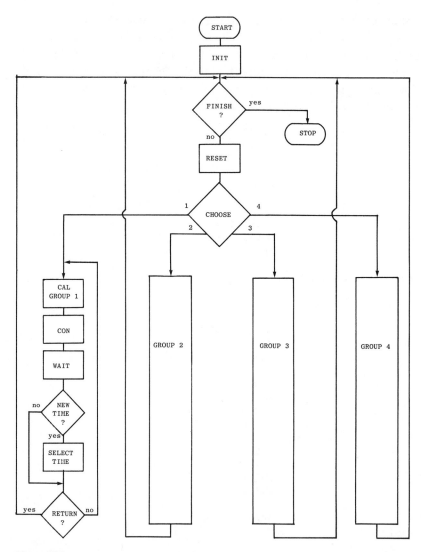

Figure 11.3
Flow chart for the third code example (pp. 169, 171–172). Details of the structure of each group are shown for the first group only.

```
TEST              CHECK
                  RETURN
                  GROUP1,CHO;
GROUP2   CAL      A:A−5
                  B:B+16
                  C:A∗B;
         CONVERT
                  SEND:C
                  CHANNEL:1;
         INIT
                  WAIT:TIME;
DELAY2            CHECK
                  WAIT
                  DELAY2,−
                  NUTIME
                  TEST2,−;
                  SEL N
                       B:13−17
                       ST:TIME
                       B:6−12
                       ST:NUTIME;
TEST2             CHECK
                  RETURN
                  GROUP2,CHO;  ·
GROUP3   CAL
                  A:A+A−267.
                  B:B+7
                  C:A∗B/4;
         CONVERT
                  S:C
                  CH:0;
                  INITIALIZE

                  WAIT:TIME;
DELAY3            CHECK
                  WAIT
                  DELAY3,−
                       NUTIME
                       TEST3,−;
                  SEL N
                       B:14−17
                       ST:TIME
                       B:6−16
                       ST:NUTIME;
TEST3    CHECK
                  RETURN
                  GROUP3,CHO;
```

```
GROUP4   CONVERT
                   S:0
                   CH:0
                   S:0
                   CH:1;
         INIT
                   WAIT:TIME;
DELAY4             CHECK
                   WAIT
                   DELAY4,–
                       NUTIME
                       TEST4,–;
                       SEL N
                           B:11–17
                           ST:TIME
                           B:6–12
                           ST:NUTIME;
TEST4
         CHECK
                   RETURN
                   GROUP4,CHO;
         DECLARE
                   A,B,C,D,NUTIME,TIME,RETURN,WAIT;
```

This example has a rather simple hierarchical structure. However, from the basic concept it is clear that more extended and varied hierarchical decision making could be programmed. An example of an extended version of the basic idea of this example can be found in Tape 2 of *Locks and Dams*.

The two preceding examples contain simple illustrations of the following techniques, which are often used in describing structures in PILE programs: shifting of masks, timing of the variation of variables using CHECKs, hierarchical changing of masks, control of program flow with CHOOSE and SWITCH, and representation of sound as calculations and delays. They illustrate the use of PILE to program a structure and then listen to how it sounds. As already mentioned, one could instead program distinct sounds and a structure using them. This should be clear from the instruction set and the examples already given. The instructions CREATE LIST and INSERT LIST are very useful for this. Less obvious is the possibility of simulating fixed-waveform synthesis with amplitude modulation and FM synthesis. It has even been possible to program the *Internationale* in PILE. I do not claim that PILE is the ideal tool for FM synthesis or for producing melodies; I mention this only to demonstrate the versatility of PILE.

Hardware Implementation

The PILE compiler is implemented on a PDP-15 at the Institute of Sonology in Utrecht. The compiler produces code in Macro-15. PILE instructions with random aspects use the hardware pseudo-random-number generator built by Scherpenisse (1974). This generator, linked to the computer's I/O bus, generates a random number in 3–4 microseconds. The clock instructions assume a variable programmable clock as designed by Scherpenisse. This clock allows the frequency as well as the number of steps before a flag to be programmed. The clock instructions in PILE are, however, seldom used. It is very conceivable that a version of PILE would be made without any clock instructions.

Compositional Example

I Never Knew You Cared is a 13-minute stereo piece for computer-synthesized sounds. It has been recorded on tape. The entire composition is described in the program for it. No external mixing, reverberation, or editing occurred. One performance possibility for the piece is via tape playback. It also can be performed "live" with any computer equipped with a PILE compiler and two channels of digital-to-analog conversion.

PILE is a language for sound synthesis. The score for *I Never Knew You Cared* is expressed in this language. The score consists of the instructions a computer received to produce this piece. This score was realized on the PDP-15 computer at the Institute of Sonology in 1978 and recorded on tape. Because of the length of the score, it was divided into two sections for realization: section 1 included parts 1–4; section 2, parts 5–8. Part 7 of the score is reproduced here:

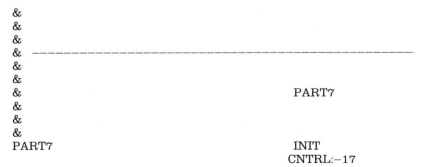

```
&
&
&
&     _____
&
&
&                              PART7
&
&
&
PART7                        INIT
                             CNTRL:-17
```

```
                              PEAK:40
                              CNT:−1
                                ENVNO:0
                                M:1
                           C:2
                          A:0;
                          BRA
                          T:G12;
G1
                          SEL
                          B:9−11
                          ST:SWEEP
                          B:13−17
                     ST:CFREQ
                        B:11−16
                        S:PEAKA;
                     CALCULATE
                        PEAKA:PEAKA+PEAK;
                        SEL N
                           B:12−15
                             ST:DUR;
                           CAL
                           MFREQ:CFREQ*M/2/C;
G2                           INITIALIZE
                          CNT:DUR;
                     SAMPLE LIST
                          N:MODAMP
                        S:80
                        I:1;
                     STORE
                        SWEAMP;
                     CALCULATE
                        SWEVAL:SWEEP*SWEAMP/PEAK;
                     SAMPLE LIST
                          N:CAMP
                        S:80
                          I:1;
                     STORE
                        AMP;
                        ZERO?
                        Y:G12;
G3                   SAMPLE
                     N:MOD
                   S:360
                        I:MFREQ;
                     STORE
                     MODSAM;
```

```
                    CALCULATE
                    INC:MODSAM*SWEVAL/100+CFREQ;
                    SAMPLE LIST
                    NAME:CAR
                    SIZE:720
                    INCREMENT:INC;
                    STORE
                    CARSAM;
                    CAL
                    OUT:CARSAM*AMP/PEAKA;
                 SWITCH
                 POSIT
                 G4,G5,G6,G7,G8,G9,G10;
G4               CALCULATE
              OUT2:OUT/8
              OUT3:OUT-OUT2;
           CONVERT
           S:OUT2
        CH:0
           S:OUT3
        CH:1;
        BRA
        T:G11;
G5         CAL
           OUT2:OUT/4
           OUT3/OUT-OUT2;
              CONVERT
              S:OUT2
              CH:0
              S:OUT3
              CH:1;
              BRA
              T:G11;
G6            CAL
                 OUT2:OUT/8*3
                 OUT3:OUT-OUT2;
                 CONVERT
                 S:OUT2
                 CH:0
                 S:OUT3
                 CH:1;
                 BRA
                 T:G11;
G7                  CAL
                    OUT2:OUT/2;
                    CON
                    S:OUT2
                    CH:0
                    S:OUT3
```

```
                        CH:1;
                        BRA
                        T:G11;
G8                      CAL
                        OUT2:OUT/8*5
                        OUT3:OUT-OUT2;
                        CON
                        S:OUT2
                       CH:0
                        S:OUT3
                       CH:1;
                      BRA
                     T:G11;
G9                      CAL
                        OUT3:OUT/4
                        OUT2:OUT-OUT3;
                        CONVERT
                        S:OUT2
                          CH:0
                          S:OUT3
                          CH:1;
                          BRA
                          T:G11;
G10                         CAL
                            OUT3:OUT/8
                            OUT2:OUT-OUT3;
                            CON
                            S:OUT2
                            CH:0
                            S:OUT3
                            CH:1;
G11                         CHE
                            CNT
                            ·G3,G2;
G12                         CON
                            S:0
                            CH:0
                            S:0
                            CH:1;
                            CHECK
                            CNTRL
                            -,DIV;
                            INIT
                            WHICH:1;
                            SEL
                            B:15-17
                            ST:POSIT;
```

G13   CALCULATE
                                             ENVNO:ENVNO+1
                                             MAX:5−ENVNO;
                                             NEGATIVE
                                             MAX
                                             −,G14;
                                             INIT
                                             ENVNO:1;
G14   CREATE LIST
         N:ENVDAT
         S:8;
         SWITCH
         ENVNO
         G15,G16,G17,G18,G19;
G15   SAMPLE
                     N:ENV1
                     S:8
                     I:1;
                     STORE
                                 E;
                                 BRANCH
                                             T:G20;
G16   SAMPLE
                     N:ENV2
                     S:8
                     I:1;
                     STORE
                                 E;
                                 BRANCH
                                             T:G20;
G17   SAMPLE
                     N:ENV3
                     S:8
                     I:1;
                     STORE
                                 E;
                                 BRANCH
                                             T:G20;
G18   SAMPLE
                     N:ENV4
                     S:8
                     I:1;
                     STORE
                                 E;
                                 BRANCH
                                             T:G20;
G19   SAMPLE
                     N:ENV5
                     S:8
                     I:1;
                     STORE
                                 E;

```
G20      END LIST
            SAVE:E;
                      INIT
                        A:O
                          CNT:-1;
                   SWITCH
                     WHICH
                     G21, G25;
G21                                    CREATE LIST
                                       N:CAMP
                                       S:80;
                                       CHECK
                                       CNT
                                       G24,-;
                                       INIT
                                       SKIP:-2;
G22                                    SAMPLE
                                       N:ENVDAT
                                       S:8
                                       I:1;
                                       CHECK
                                       SKIP
                                       -,G23;
                                       STORE N
                                       CNT;
                                       BRANCH
                                       T:G22;
G23                                    STORE
                                       AINC;
G24                                    CAL
                                       A:A+AINC;
                                       END LIST
                                       S:A;
                   INIT
                     WHICH:2;
                   BRANCH
                     T:G13;
G25                                    CREATE LIST
                                       N:MODAMP
                                       S:80;
                                       CHECK
                                       CNT
                                       G28,-;
                                       INIT
                                       SKIP:-2;
G26                                    SAMPLE
                                       N:ENVDAT
                                       S:8
                                       I:1;
                                       CHECK
                                       SKIP
```

```
                              -,G27;
                              STORE N
                              CNT;
                              BRANCH
                              T:G26;
     G27                      STORE
                              AINC;
     G28                      CAL
                              A:A+AINC;
                              END LIST
                              SAVE:A;
                                SEL N
                                B:3-11
                                  ST:CNT;
                                  SEL N
                                  B:14-16
                                    ST:CNT2;
     G29                              CONVERT
                                      S:0
                                        CH:0
                                        S:0
                                          CH:1;
                                          CHE
                                          CNT
                                          G29,-
                                          CNT2
                                          -,G1;
                                            SEL N
                                            B:3-11
                                              S:CNT;
                                              BRA
                                              T:G29;
     &
     &
     &
     &
     &
     &
     &   -------------------------------------------------------
     &
     &
     &
     &
```

Appendix: PILE Instruction Set

This list is excerpted from Berg 1978. The following conventions are
used in the description: CON indicates that a constant is to be inserted

by the programmer. VAR indicates that a variable is to be inserted by the programmer. LAB indicates that a label is to be inserted by the programmer. VAL indicates that either a constant or a variable may by inserted. arith indicates an arithmetic expression (+ or − or * or /). log indicates either antivalence, conjunction, disjunction, equivalence, implication, or exclusion.

Manipulation of Program Flow

1. BRANCH
      TO:LAB;

LAB is a label found in the program. The next instruction executed in the program will be the instruction marked with LAB. Execution will continue from that instruction.

2. CHOOSE
      LAB1, LAB2,... LAB8;

Randomly choose to branch to the instruction marked with one of the given labels (LAB1, LAB2,...).

3. ZERO?
      YES:LAB;

If the contents of the accumulator are 0, the program continues execution from the instruction marked with LAB.

4. CHECK
      VAR
      LAB1, LAB2;

or

      CHECK
      VAR
      LAB1,−;

or

      CHECK
      VAR
      −, LAB2;

Increase the value of VAR by 1. If it is not 0, the program branches to the instruction marked with LAB1. If it is 0, the program branches to

the instruction marked with LAB2. A dash may be used instead of
LAB1 or LAB2. In that case the program continues to the next instruction if that branch is chosen.

5. FINISH?
    EXTERNAL:VAL;

or

FINISH?
    INTERNAL:VAL;

The program terminates if the number set on the console accumulator
switches (external) or if a number supplied by the hardware random
number generator (internal) is the same as VAL.

6. NEGATIVE?
    VAR
    LAB1, LAB2;

or

NEGATIVE?
    VAR
    −, LAB2;

or

NEGATIVE?
    VAR
    LAB1,−;

Variable VAR is tested. If it contains a negative value, the program
goes to LAB1. Otherwise it goes to LAB2. Either LAB1 or LAB2 can
be replaced with a dash which indicates that the program continues to
the next instruction. The instruction may be applied several times in
succession.

7. SWITCH
    VAR
    LAB1, LAB2,..., LAB9;

The program switches to LAB1, LAB2, etc., depending on the value of
VAR. (If VAR is 1, the program switches to LAB1, etc.). A maximum
of nine labels may be used.

Manipulation of Variables

8. INITIALIZE
   VAR:VAL;

VAL can be positive or negative. VAL is assigned to VAR.

9. GET
   VAL;

The value is placed in the accumulator.

10. STORE
    VAR;

or

    STORE NEGATIVE
    VAR;

The number currently in the accumulator is stored in VAR. If STORE
NEGATIVE is indicated, the sign of the number is changed before it is
stored.

11. READ SWITCHES
    STORE:VAR;

The number set on the console switches is read and stored in VAR.

12. CALCULATE
    VAR1:VAL1arithVAL2 ...;

or

    CALCULATE
    VAR1:log,VAL1,VAL2;

No more than eight arithmetic operations may occur in one line. Operations are performed left to right. The result of the performed operations
is stored in VAR1. Multiplication and division of negative numbers is
not possible. Only one logical operation may occur in a line. The result
of the performed operation is stored in VAR1. Logical and arithmetic
operations may not occur in the same line, but they may occur in consecutive lines.

13. SELECT
    BITS:CON1,CON2,CON3–CON4 ...
    STORE:VAR;

or

    SELECT
        MASK:VAR
        STORE:VAR1;

or

    SELECT NEGATIVE
        BITS:CON1,CON2,CON3 ...
        STORE:VAR;

or

    SELECT NEGATIVE
        MASK:VAR
        STORE:VAR1;

A random number is selected, limited (masked), and, if then not equal to 0, stored in VAR. The process is repeated until a nonzero value can be stored in VAR. In the case of SELECT NEGATIVE the sign of the number is changed before it is stored. The number may be limited in two ways; the bits may be specified either separately or between two limits, e.g., BITS:3–10 (both ways may be combined), or a mask may be specified. A logical AND (conjunction) is performed with the random number and the mask. The use of the mask limits the range of the random number.

14. DECLARE
        VAR1,VAR2,VAR3 ...;

All variables used in the instructions may be declared so that storage can be saved for them. The names of lists should not be declared.

Manipulation of Lists

15. CREATE LIST
        NAME:VAR
        SIZE:CON;

VAR is the name to be given to the list. CON is the size of the list. In general, the total size of all lists should not exceed 2,500. After this instruction other instructions should be given to formulate values which would be used in creating the list. Instructions may be chosen from most of the other available instructions, e.g., CALCULATE, RANDOM,

SELECT, etc. This group of instructions should end with the instruction
END LIST.

16. END LIST
        SAVE:VAR;

This instruction indicates the end of the group of instructions used to
create a list. The value of VAR is stored in the created list. The instructions after CREATE LIST are again executed, the next value for VAR
is found, etc. until the list has been filled.

17. SAMPLE LIST
        NAME:VAR
        SIZE:VAL1
        INCREMENT:VAL2;

VAR is the name of a list previously made using CREATE LIST or
INSERT LIST. VAL1 is the size of the list. VAL1 must be less than or
equal to the size declared in CREATE LIST or INSERT LIST. VAL2 is
the increment. SAMPLE LIST places one value from the list into the
accumulator. The first time SAMPLE LIST is executed, the first value
will be placed in the accumulator. With each succeeding execution of
SAMPLE LIST the number VAL2 positions further in the list will be
placed in the accumulator, *e.g.*, if VAL2 is 5, every fifth number in the
list will be sampled. The current value for size will be maintained for the
rest of the program after the first execution of SAMPLE LIST.

18. INSERT LIST
        NAME:VAR
        SIZE:CON
        CON1,CON2,..., CON3;

VAR is the name of the list. CON is the size of the list. CON1, CON2,
etc., are constants which are the list. The list containing CON1 through
CON3 is inserted in the program. The maximum size of a list depends
on how many lists are used and how long the program is. INSERT LIST
may occur at any point in a program.

Manipulation of the Accumulator

19. RANDOM;

This is the only instruction which is complete on one line. A random
number (18 bits) from the hardware random number generator is placed
into the accumulator.

20. KEEP
    BITS:CON1,CON2–CON3,CON4 ...;

Certain bits of the number in the accumulator may be kept. The accumulator contains 18 bits, numbered 0–17 from left to right. CON1, CON2, etc., represent the numbers of the bits which have been selected. The bits may be expressed separately, e.g., BITS:1,5; or between limits, e.g., BITS:3–10; both ways may be combined.

Manipulation of External Devices

21. CONVERT
    SEND:VAL
    CHANNEL:CON;

or

    CONVERT
    SEND:–
    CHANNEL:CON;

VAL is sent to converter channel CON. VAL should be between 0 and 4,095. CON may be 0, 1, 2, or 3. If the accumulator contents are to be sent, a dash is used instead of VAL.

22. SEED
    VAL;

or

    SEED
    –;

A seed (start number) is specified for the hardware random-number generator. Each time the same number is specified, the same number (series) is produced by the hardware random-number generator. If VAL is a variable, it must be assigned a value before this instruction is used. VAL may not be 0. If one wishes to insert the start value from the console switches, one should use a minus sign instead of VAL.

23. CLOCK CON
    FREQ:VAL;

Two clocks are available. CON should be either 1 or 2. VAL should be positive and is expressed in microseconds. The minimum value is 10. This instruction sets the speed at which the clock will count, *i.e.*, not how long it will count, but how fast.

24. CLOCK CON
      COUNT:VAL;

CON should be either 1 or 2 for Clock 1 or Clock 2. VAL should be positive. It indicates how high the clock should count (at the speed specified in instruction 23).

25. CLOCK CON
      START;

CON should be either 1 or 2. The corresponding clock is started. This means it will begin counting.

26. CLOCK CON
      WAIT;

CON should be either 1 or 2. The program waits for the clock to finish counting (if it is not already finished) before continuing.

27. CLOCK CON
      STOP;

CON should be either 1 or 2. The clock is stopped. The clock should be turned off after WAIT.

Note: Some instructions fall into more than one of the above categories.

Additional Comments Concerning the Instruction Set

Example of the Use of CALCULATE

```
CALCULATE
   A:A+10
   B:A/C-1
   D:B*A
   STX1:ANTIV,B,3
   VAR2:IMPLIC,B,D
   E:A*B+C/D-STX1*VAR2/5+79;
```

Example of the Use of CREATE LIST

```
CREATE LIST
   NAME:HERMAN
   SIZE:500;
      CALCULATE
         C:EQUIV,25,D
         D:D+D;
```

```
END LIST
   SAVE:C;
```

Use of Abbreviations   Operations in the first line of an instruction can be abbreviated to the first three letters of the operation. In an instruction that could change sign (SELECT, STORE) NEGATIVE may be shortened to N. In all instructions except the clock instructions abbreviations of only one letter are tolerated before the colon; e.g.,

```
CONVERT
   SEND:ALL
   CHANNEL:0;
```

could be

```
CON
   S:ALL
   TO:0;
```

Except for the clock instructions, different words could be inserted before the colon. This can not be done in instructions where variables occur left of the colon (INITIALIZE, CALCULATE).

References

Berg, P. 1975. *ASP Report*. Utrecht: Institute of Sonology.

Berg, P. 1978. *PILE2—A Description of the Language*. Utrecht: Institute of Sonology.

Scherpenisse, J. 1974. "A pseudo-random number generator." *Interface* 3: 187–190.

II SYNTHESIZER HARDWARE AND ENGINEERING

Overview

JOHN STRAWN AND CURTIS ROADS

When the first successful facility for digital audio synthesis was established at Bell Laboratories in the 1950s (Roads 1980), the computer used for synthesis was a vacuum-tube device. Since then, digital audio synthesis has been implemented on various generations of transistorized and integrated-circuit computers. More recently, special-purpose digital synthesizers have appeared; these are usually connected to general-purpose computers of various sizes. The articles in this section focus on the design and construction of these special-purpose digital synthesizers and processors.

The assumption in many of the articles here is that the designer is interested in creating an audio signal with the highest quality possible. A great deal of interesting music can be created using systems that are less extensive or less expensive than those discussed here, but the same theoretical and practical questions must be answered. Recent commercial developments suggest that, as digital hardware continues to improve and costs decline, digital audio of even the highest quality will not be ruled out merely on the basis of financial considerations.

Design Requirements For Digital Audio Synthesis

Speed

In order to produce signals that cover the entire bandwidth of human hearing, sample rates approaching 50 kHz are often used. This means that the synthesizer must produce a digital number (sample) every 20 microseconds per channel.

Such speeds can now be achieved for musical sound of reasonable complexity only in special-purpose digital synthesizers. Moorer (1977) reviews the steps necessary to compute one sample with a single sinusoidal oscillator: three additions, one multiplication, and one memory access for wavetable lookup (assuming one section of a piecewise-linear amplitude envelope and one section of a piecewise-linear frequency envelope). Typically, 32-bit register-to-register integer addition on a large mainframe computer such as the Digital Equipment Corporation VAX-11/780 requires 0.4 microseconds; this means that such a computer could barely support 50 such oscillators in real time at a sample rate of 50 kHz, even if memory lookups and multiplications could be ignored. Memory access time is another limiting factor in wavetable-lookup synthesis schemes. Memory access requires 1–5 times as long as addition on computers like the VAX 11/780. The lone multiplication in the prototypical oscillator turns out to be the major bottleneck, in terms of both time and hardware. On the VAX 11/780, multiplication is typically 3–16 times slower than addition, and it is more costly in hardware. As a result, a considerable amount of effort has been devoted to finding ways to circumvent the necessity for multiplication. Some commercial digital synthesizers (Alonso et al. 1976; Strawn 1980), as well as the SSSP synthesizer, have used multiplying digital-to-analog converters. In article 12 Buxton et al. discuss the advantages and disadvantages of this approach. LeBrun (1977) and others have proposed numerical solutions to this problem, involving multiplication using additions and table lookups which are much simpler to implement. Saunders (article 3) has discussed Purcell's suggestion of exploiting trigonometric identities to achieve amplitude control of sinusoids, which is incorporated in Alles's work (1979, 1980).

As digital hardware continues to develop, it is reasonable to expect that the limits on speed required for real-time audio synthesis will become less of a stumbling block to the design of high-fidelity systems.

Precision

The process of digital audio recording and reproduction is not inherently distortion-free. Fortunately, the sources of noise can be isolated and kept within suitable tolerances; thus, digital audio can be said to be noise-free and distortion-free given a suitable investment in time and hardware. (This does not hold as well for analog means, which face intrinsic limitations such as the physical properties of the magnetic tape used in recording.)

Digital processing of signals can introduce noise. The effects of finite word lengths in digital filters are fairly well understood (see Rabiner and Gold 1975, chapter 5). Similar effects occur, even in the case of the simple oscillator mentioned above, when a signal is scaled in amplitude. An analogous problem exists with the process of wavetable lookup. When a sinusoid is stored in a wavetable of finite length with finite word size, inaccuracies in the waveform synthesized from that wavetable can manifest themselves as additive noise. Snell and Moore discuss some theoretical and practical constraints governing this problem in articles 19 and 20, respectively.

The frequency resolution of a given hardware synthesis scheme (that is, how accurately any specific frequency may be produced) can usually be specified within some more or less arbitrary bounds, depending on the number of bits used to select the frequency. It remains an acid test to cause a digital synthesizer to generate a slowly varying glissando in the lower frequency ranges and listen for the "steps" characteristic of frequency quantization. Vibrato can be equally troublesome. Sometimes these problems can be alleviated under appropriate software control (Alles 1979, p. 31; Kaplan 1981; Loy 1981, p. 48).

It is not sufficient on a generalized synthesizer to provide only equal-tempered tuning (with equal-tempered semitones given by the twelfth root of 2). Nontempered tunings have been explored compositionally by a wide variety of composers in computer music (Chowning's *Stria* comes immediately to mind) as well as by well-known keyboardists such as Terry Riley. Fortunately, most of the commercial devices on the market can be retuned (Strawn 1980, 1981). Digital control of tuning and spectra promises to open up new compositional paths which have hardly been explored to date—possibilities that are sometimes not appreciated fully in the engineering community.

Reliability

Analog synthesis circuitry, and analog audio circuitry in general, have long been plagued with variations in performance of the system due to such more or less uncontrollable variables as temperature, humidity, and unpredictable manufacturing variations among components. Such problems certainly exist for digital synthesis systems as well. Fortunately, their effects do not manifest themselves in the same way. For example, in a digital oscillator a minor change in temperature or humidity is not likely to produce a change in pitch, as it might in an analog system. Digital synthesizers thus provide a significant improvement in performance over their analog counterparts.

Digital equipment is not error-free. One of the few advantages of the patch cords on analog synthesizers is the ability to "trace" a patch from the initial sound source to the output amplifier. For debugging purposes, traceback facilities are a proven technique in digital systems, and they are included in some synthesizer designs as well. According to Moorer (1981), the ability to tap a signal at virtually any point in its path has proved advantageous and should be incorporated in future designs where possible.

Digital-synthesis design benefits further from the experience gathered by engineers in designing large-scale digital systems, no matter what the intended application. It is sobering to learn that some 10 percent of the 2,500 integrated circuits in one well-known synthesizer are dedicated strictly to hardware diagnostics. Experience in debugging and using the device indicates that this investment in hardware was indeed worthwhile.

The Question Of Architecture

Off-Line or Non-Real-Time Synthesis

In view of the high sample rates required for high-quality audio synthesis and the speeds of early general-purpose computers, it is not surprising that the first efforts at digital synthesis were strictly non-real-time. Off-line synthesis remains the practice at many installations around the world using Music V, Cmusic, and similar systems. Even studios intending to operate fully in real time often start by first implementing a slower music compiler (this was the case at IRCAM). In light of the development of 32-bit microprocessors, the cost of non-real-time software synthesis systems continues to drop.

The Hybrid Experience

An early method of obtaining real-time synthesis was to retain the advantages of digital control, storage (for scores), and perhaps even patching, but to remain in the analog domain for synthesis itself. The Groove system (Mathews and Moore 1970) remains an outstanding example of the possibilities for real-time editing, control, and performance of musical scores. Pioneering work in hybrid performance systems was carried out by S. Martirano (see Pellegrino 1983, pp. 95–98), by E. Kobrin, by M. Bartlett (1979), and by the E-mu synthesizer corporation (Rossum 1981) (see also Chamberlin 1980).

Digital Synthesizers

A wide variety of special-purpose digital hardware synthesizers have been attached to just as wide a spectrum of general-purpose computers, both large and small. Commercial keyboard-oriented synthesizers developed along these lines are already available (Strawn 1980, 1981).

No single answer to the question of which architecture(s) might be ideal for digital audio synthesis has been formulated. Not even a method for measuring synthesizer performance has been established. These questions are especially important for the stand-alone digital synthesizers appearing on the market (Kaplan 1981).

Four principal design strategies influencing architecture have appeared:

• Modularized systems, such as the FRMBox (Moore 1977), the SSSP synthesizer (Buxton et al., article 12), and the system discussed by Alles (article 14). Independent oscillator card designs such as those by Snell (article 19) and by Alles (1979, 1980), if considered as individual modules, fall into this category as well. In such a system, individual modules might well be constructed following the lead of the other design traditions being discussed here. There are many advantages to modular design. One potential drawback is the question of communication between individual modules. It might be tempting to design one oscillator module and one envelope module, for example, but then the data-flow requirements between the two modules become a design issue.

• A collection of suitable primitive elements, such as memory, arithmetic-logic units, shift registers, and multipliers, connected by one or more busses and controlled through microprogramming. These microprogrammed systems are conceptually simple (once the hardware has been debugged) and thus easier to program. The DMX-1000 discussed by Wallraff in article 13 is one commercially available example. A different design, based on bit-slice processor units, is presented by Allouis in article 18. The oscillator module in the SSSP synthesizer is likewise modified by what is effectively microprogramming, in order to select among the available synthesis techniques. Considerable experience was gained with the two-bus 4C (designed by G. diGiugno) constructed at IRCAM and discussed in article 17 by Moorer et al. (see also Abbott 1981a). The 4U, a more generalized microprogrammable unit, has found its way into the 4X machine at IRCAM (diGiugno et al. 1980, 1981). Moorer (1981) discusses some of the lessons learned from these architectures and presents another design based on this scheme, which has the added advantage of parallel processing. Lessons learned from this design have been incorporated into the much larger device at Lucasfilm Ltd. (Abbott 1981b; Moorer 1982; Snell 1982).

• The "pipelining" approach used by Snell (article 19) and by Samson (1980). There is another example in the oscillator module of the SSSP synthesizer (article 12). One advantage of this approach is the great synthesis power that can be achieved with a relatively small amount of hardware. A major disadvantage lies in the difficulty of knowing precisely where a datum might lie in the pipeline. It can also be difficult to repatch a highly pipelined instrument "on the fly," although some synthesizers take care of this by flushing the pipeline every sample.

• General-purpose (micro or mini) computer architectures. Of course, direct digital synthesis can be performed with 16-bit or even 8-bit microprocessors (see, for example, article 33 and Chamberlin 1980). More promising is the appearance of fast 32-bit microprocessors with built-in floating-point instructions or an auxiliary arithmetic processor.

Multiprocessor Systems and Microcomputer Networks

Special-purpose digital synthesis peripherals continue to grow in complexity and capability. Many of the designs discussed here qualify as general-purpose computers in their own right; they execute instructions, access memory, evaluate conditional expressions, and perform elaborate control sequences. Connecting such devices to a commercially available computer system creates a multiprocessor configuration, with all the concomitant advantages and disadvantages. A similar situation ensues when the modules of a modular system are designed to be dependent on data or control emanating from other modules.

No study has yet been completed on the interconnection of several digital sound synthesizers. This might seem surprising, since music synthesis inherently involves parallel processing at several levels (Moorer 1981). However, it has been more reasonable to design a single hardware system to fulfill several of these parallel obligations.

At another musical level, some compositional experience has already been gained with closely coupled networked microcomputers, as discussed by Bischoff et al. in article 33. With the availability of more powerful microprocessors with multiprocessor support features, it can be expected that others will follow this lead.

Design Considerations

Power

Computer performance measurement, toward which a great deal of effort has been expended, has not evolved any absolute criteria. The main tools used are benchmarks.

Because of the historical importance of additive synthesis based on sinusoids, it is not surprising that various synthesizers are often described in terms of the number of sinusoidal oscillators they can produce. Whatever the number might be for a given system, it is misleading to assess a system's musical capabilities solely on this measure. This becomes immediately apparent when one compares (to cite a reductionistic example) the large number of oscillators required to generate a given steady-state spectrum using additive synthesis, with a small number using frequency modulation.

This raises the question of which synthesis technique(s) to implement. But measuring the power of a synthesizer in terms of synthesis techniques is more difficult than it might seem at first glance. A hardware-design decision can exert considerable influence over the power and flexibility of a given technique. In the SSSP synthesizer, for example, it was apparently easy to allow for single-modulator FM, but adding further modulator inputs would have apparently caused a substantial increase in hardware.

From another point of view, the number of "notes per second" a synthesizer can generate might be taken as a measure of power. (We prefer the more generalized "musical events" or "sound objects" to "notes.") In such terms as these, the 4A synthesizer used to generate D. Wessel's *Antony* (1977) must be seen as a powerful instrument, as enough individual events are generated that the overall impression is that of a scintillating but continuous sheet of sound. However, as an objective measure of synthesizer performance, this leaves open the question of the complexity of each event. The question of how quickly such musical events can be changed (that is, how quickly the synthesizer parameters can be updated) is also relevant here.

In short, a set of criteria for measuring the capabilities might prove useful in evaluating design considerations in digital synthesizers, but a clear-cut definition of a synthesizer's power has not yet been formulated.

Synthesizer versus Signal Processor

From a performer's standpoint, it seems insufficient to suggest that only twelve "reasonably complex" voices (one each for ten fingers and two feet) will be adequate. Even with real-time control, it is reasonable to expect a synthesizer to generate additional musical material from prepared scores and to process digitized sound material.

Many of the devices discussed here incorporate the possibility of manipulating digitally recorded signals, whether or not in real time. [See also Moorer's (1981) discussion of "studio" and "performance" devices.] Typically, such operations include filtering and the addition of reverberation. Even more exotic operations such as "flanging" or pitch change are sometimes required by composers (McNabb 1981).

Input/Output Bandwidth

It is not sufficient, however, to discuss the power of a synthesizer/processor by itself. Instead, in order to evaluate a system's musical capability, the synthesizer together with the controlling computer must be analyzed as a whole. If the computer cannot keep up with the data rate required by the synthesizer, then the power of the synthesizer is wasted. Historically, it has happened more than once that a promising synthesizer has been brought to its knees by a slow host computer or input/output (I/O) bus. Composers have then been faced with the unappetizing task of spending large amounts of time optimizing command assemblers in order to obtain the musical effects desired; see Rolnick's description in article 25.

The problem is compounded by the nature of the information shared between the host computer and the synthesizer. Obviously, at the start of a given synthesis process there must be initialization information, such as the sample rate and the interconnections among synthesis and processing elements. If the synthesis involves a precompiled score, the commands controlling the musical events must be fed to the synthesizer. The problem of creating those commands is complex, to say the least (Rolnick, article 25; Abbott 1981a; Loy 1981). The synthesizer, in turn, may send back information to the control computer, such as "envelope n completed," which increases the I/O bandwidth requirements. Hardware devices accessible to the user (keyboards, knobs, switches) may provide control information; merging the commands from a precompiled file with those from hardware I/O devices is a tricky problem, as discussed by Rolnick (article 25) and by Moorer (1981). Finally, provision must be made for reading in one or more streams of digital samples.

To accommodate this flow of information, the designer may choose to provide more than one data path between the synthesizer and the host. Alternatively, part or all of the synthesizer's control inputs and outputs may live in the address space of the computer's main memory. In either case, it is misleading to calculate the average flow rate the system can support. Experience has shown that the burst rate is a critical factor. Moorer (1981), Kahrs (1981), and Kaplan (1981) discuss this question in detail for different machines.

User Input Devices

Almost every device available for computer input has been explored in one musical setting or another. Two examples: The Fairlight CMI keyboard synthesizer includes a lightpen for drawing envelopes, and the Toronto SSSP studio has pioneered the use of a graphics tablet and a hand-held cursor (Buxton et al. 1980). This idea of using readily available computer input devices does not seem doomed to failure; experience with analog synthesizers has shown that a control so mundane as a knob or a switch can be musically effective when used properly. On E. Kobrin's Hybrid IV system, developed in the 1970s at the University of California at San Diego, even an alphanumeric keyboard was adequate (if not inspiring) for controlling four separate channels of sound.

There have also been attempts to copy traditional musical transducers, such as piano and organ keyboards. The question whether a traditional musical interface encourages a musician to approach synthesis in traditional terms is beyond the scope of this overview. See Mathews and Abbott 1980.

Digital technology promises to allow even more innovative methods of human control over musical performance than have been achieved in past electronic music. S. Martirano's hybrid SalMar Construction, with its palette of touch-actuated switches, is a notable example. The menu-driven approach has been used effectively in the system at Toronto (article 22), in W. Kornfeld's Lisp Machine music editor at the MIT Artificial Intelligence Laboratory [see the covers of *Computer Music Journal* 4(2) and 4(3), 1980], and elsewhere. Many new computer systems incorporate the graphics screens necessary to support this mode of interaction. Especially promising results have been achieved with touch-sensitive keyboards. With digital control, even the mapping between keys on a keyboard and musical events can be established under user control, as discussed by Manthey (1977).

Long before the advent of electronic music, mechanical hardware had been constructed to record the actions of performing pianists. Analog and hybrid synthesis quickly developed recording sequencers, which usually were based on digital technology and allowed some post-performance editing (the Groove system at Bell Laboratories has already been mentioned in this regard). In a completely digital system, it becomes possible to record the player's motion with a high degree of accuracy and then edit parts of the recorded "score" before playback. The 63-track Pseudo-Tape on the EGG synthesizer is one example of such capabilities (Manthey 1977). Most of the commercial keyboard synthesizers currently on the market contain some form of sequencer, with or without an editing capability (Strawn 1980, 1981).

Dividing the Pie between Hardware and Software

Computer music has existed long enough for a pattern to have emerged: More and more of what was once accomplished in software is being turned over to hardware. It seems reasonable to expect that this trend will continue. Moorer (1981) foresees a reduction in complexity of what he calls the "merge problem" (blending separate processes into one command stream) through a hardware solution.

A constant theme running throughout the articles in this part is maximizing "bang per buck," to quote Mark Kahrs (Strawn et al. 1981, p. 42). Some significant decisions must be made on such a basis. The decision to use multiplying DACs in the SSSP synthesizer comes to mind.

The design tradeoffs that are finally reached have a nasty habit of popping up where least expected. Consider the question of scaling an arbitrary envelope function in time and amplitude. In article 25 Rolnick discusses the problems encountered in attempting to perform this scaling with the 4B hardware, which lacks a multiplier independent of the oscillators (that is, an oscillator must be sacrificed to perform the multiplication). The alternative of having the PDP-11/03 control computer perform the calculation for the 4B is also less than ideal, because it is too slow to perform the necessary calculations in real time.

Sample Rate

There are two major issues surrounding the sample rate: whether it should be variable or fixed and what the sample rate(s) should be.

For fixed-rate synthesizers, a variety of sample rates are in use. The 4C machine, although equipped with options of 16, 32, 64, and 128 kHz (see Moorer's article), runs for much of the time at 16 kHz (Abbott 1981a). The system built by H. Alles for Bell Laboratories (the system is now at Oberlin) runs at 30 kHz. The SSSP synthesizer at Toronto runs at 50 kHz.

In light of the "ideal" sample rate mentioned earlier in this overview, it is instructive that practical and useful music-making systems have been constructed using slower sample rates.

In the 4B synthesizer the envelopes were generated at 4 kHz, with an audio sample rate of 32 kHz. Hardware that would otherwise be required for the generation of the envelopes could thus be dedicated to the generation of signals (before amplitude scaling). In a similar vein, but in referring to the DMX-1000, Wallraff writes in article 13 that "envelopes may often be implemented in the master computer at sub-audio rates with acceptable results." However, in their article on the 4C machine, Moorer et al. warn that an annoying "chirp" can be caused in some—unfortunately unpredictable—situations. Thus, the shortcut of allowing a slow sample rate for control functions must be used with caution.

There are several reasons for choosing a variable sample rate. Consider the case of synthesis by instruction, discussed by Berg in article 11. At a given sample rate, the description of a given sound implies a certain period. To change that period (and thus presumably the pitch of the generated sound), one must change either the length of the description (and thus quite possibly the spectrum of the sound generated) or the sample rate. Seen in another light, variable sample rates are especially sensible for the time-multiplexed style of synthesizer already reviewed. If only a few of the available time slots are needed for some musical applications, then the sample rate can be raised—often to well beyond the 50 kHz given as an ideal minimum. On the other hand, when the sounds to be generated require more computational complexity the requisite hardware becomes available through time multiplexing by lowering the sample rate. The synthesizers discussed by Allouis and Wallraff, among others, are designed around a variable sample rate for this reason.

Consider further the well-known formula

$$\text{frequency} = \frac{\text{increment} \times \text{sample rate}}{\text{table length}}.$$

In implementing synthesis by wavetable lookup (which has the advantage of allowing the user to load the table with any arbitrary waveform), the designer may decide to require all of the wavetables to be of the same length. For a given increment (in some cases, equal to 1), variation in frequency can be achieved only by varying the sample rate. This is the method used in the Synclavier and Fairlight keyboard synthesizers currently on the market (Strawn 1980).

The variable sample rate is not without difficulties, however. Ideally, the smoothing filter following the digital-to-analog converter should be designed specifically for a given sample rate. With a variable sample rate, this is of course impossible. One solution is to require the user to select one of several filter settings. Another is to disable any hardwired smoothing filter entirely, so that the user can supply a filter. Experience at Stanford University suggests that these are reasonable solutions. For interchange of digital audio media, the use of the Audio Engineering Society standard sampling frequencies (48 kHz and 44.1 kHz) seems wise.

Perhaps the biggest stumbling block in the implementation of variable sample rates is the problem of digitally mixing samples generated at different sample frequencies. The general solution to this problem is to change the sample rate with interpolation and decimation (Schafer and Rabiner 1973). Similar problems will of course occur in implementing FM with the carrier and the modulator at different sample rates.

Which Technology?

Because of the tight computational constraints on digital audio synthesizers and sound processors, it might seem surprising that many of the devices built to date and discussed in this part of the volume have incorporated off-the-shelf transistor-transistor logic (TTL). Of the other high-performance technologies that are available, perhaps emitter-coupled logic (ECL) has the worst "image problem." In article 21 Hastings discusses some widely held misconceptions about ECL and offers some practical insights into his working with it. ECL is considerably faster than TTL, so it is not surprising that the large synthesizers built for Lucasfilm Ltd. incorporate ECL (Abbott 1981b; Moorer 1982; Snell 1982). It seems reasonable to expect other high-performance designs to be based on ECL in the future.

Commercial Applications

The first commercially available digital synthesizer cards designed for widespread use by the general public were note generators limited to generating square-wave signals. These devices, designed specifically to interface with the S-100 microcomputer bus, were incorporated into inexpensive commercial microcomputer music systems. Fortunately, more sophisticated synthesis cards for the general public have appeared on the market. With the current trend toward home computing, it is reasonable to expect that the market for such devices as these will continue to grow and that their quality will improve. On the other end of the commercial scale, several fully digital keyboard synthesizers have reached the market-place (Strawn 1980, 1981). As the music industry becomes accustomed to digital technology, it is to be expected that more home organs, film-studio-type sound-effects generators, and nonkeyboard digital instruments (such as a digital wind instrument) will appear on the market.

Conclusion

In this overview we have attempted to account for some of the major considerations in the design of digital audio synthesizers and processors. Of course there are many other arbitrary design goals, such as attempting to make a unit fit on one circuit card, or building a portable unit, or reaching some preordained number of sinusoidal oscillators.

As for the future, there is no doubt that very-large-scale integration (VLSI), which compresses tens of thousands of digital gates onto one chip, is revolutionizing the design of digital hardware and will bring special-purpose music processors within easy reach of those interested. Signal processing computers implemented in VLSI are now available. Other designs are in the works, and synthesizer companies such as Yamaha are already exploiting the possibilities. VLSI may revolutionize our manner of thinking about digital audio synthesis if it suddenly becomes economical to implement previously unwieldy synthesis techniques in hardware.

References

Abbott, C. 1981a. "The 4CED program." *Computer Music Journal* 5(1): 13–33.

Abbott, C. 1981b. Microprogramming a Generalized Signal Processor Architecture. Presented at the 1981 International Computer Music Conference, North Texas State University, Denton.

Alles, H. G. 1979. "An inexpensive digital sound synthesizer." *Computer Music Journal* 3(3): 28–37.

Alles, H. G. 1980. "Music synthesis using real-time digital techniques." *Proceedings of the IEEE* 68(4): 436–449.

Alonso, S., J. Appleton, and C. Jones. 1976. "A special-purpose digital system for musical instruction, composition, and performance." *Computers and the Humanities* 10: 209–215.

Andersen, K. H. 1976. "A digital sound generation unit." *Electronic Music and Musical Acoustics* 2: 25–42.

Buxton, W., W. Reeves, G. Fedorkow, K. C. Smith, and R. Baecker. 1980. "A microcomputer-based conducting system." *Computer Music Journal* 4(1): 8–21.

Chamberlin, H. 1980. *Musical Applications of Microprocessors.* Rochelle Park, N.J.: Hayden.

diGiugno, G., and J. Kott. 1980. The IRCAM Real-Time Digital Sound Processor. Presented at the 1980 International Computer Music Conference, Queens College, New York.

diGiugno, G., J. Kott, and A. Gerzo. 1981. Progress Report on the 4X Machine and its Use. Presented at the 1981 International Computer Music Conference, North Texas State University, Denton.

Hastings, C. 1978. "A recipe for homebrew ECL." *Computer Music Journal* 2(1): 48–58. Revised and updated version in this volume (article 21).

Kahrs, M. 1981. "Notes on very-large-scale integration and the design of real-time digital sound processors." *Computer Music Journal* 5(2): 20–28.

Kaplan, S. J. 1981. "Developing a commercial digital sound synthesizer." *Computer Music Journal* 5(3): 62–73.

LeBrun, M. 1977. "Notes on microcomputer music." *Computer Music Journal* 1(2): 30–35.

Loy, D. G. 1981. "Notes on the implementation of MUSBOX: A compiler for the Systems Concepts digital synthesizer." *Computer Music Journal* 5(1): 34–50.

McNabb, M. 1981. "*Dreamsong:* The composition." *Computer Music Journal* 5(4): 36–53.

Manthey, M. 1978. "The Egg: A purely digital real time polyphonic sound synthesizer." *Computer Music Journal* 2(2): 32–36.

Mathews, M. V., with C. Abbott. 1980. "The sequential drum." *Computer Music Journal* 4(4): 45–59.

Mathews, M., and F. R. Moore. 1970. "GROOVE—A program to compose, store, and edit functions of time." *Communications of the Association for Computing Machinery* 13(12): 715–721.

Moore, F. R. 1977. Real-Time Interactive Computer Music Synthesis. Ph.D. diss., Department of Electrical Engineering, Stanford University.

Moorer, J. A. 1977. "Signal processing aspects of computer music—A survey." *Proceedings of the IEEE* 65(8): 1108–1137.

Moorer, J. A. 1981. "Synthesizers I have known and loved." *Computer Music Journal* 5(1): 4–12.

Moorer, J. A. 1982. "The Lucasfilm Audio Signal Processor." *Computer Music Journal* 6(3): 22–32.

Pellegrino, R. 1983. *The Electronic Arts of Sound and Light.* New York: Van Nostrand.

Rabiner, L. R., and B. Gold. 1975. *Theory and Application of Digital Signal Processing.* Englewood Cliffs, N.J.: Prentice-Hall.

Roads, C. 1980. "Interview with Max Mathews." *Computer Music Journal* 4(4): 15–22.

Rossum, D. 1981. "A computer-controlled polyphonic synthesizer." *Journal of the Audio Engineering Society* 29(12): 895–901.

Samson, P. R. 1980. "A general-purpose digital synthesizer." *Journal of the Audio Engineering Society* 28: 106–113.

Schafer, R. W., and L. R. Rabiner. 1973. "A digital signal processing approach to interpolation." *Proceedings of the IEEE* 61: 692–702.

Snell, J. 1982. "The Lucasfilm real-time console for recording studios and for the performance of computer music. *Computer Music Journal* 6(3): 33–45.

Strawn, J. 1980. "Report from the 1980 Audio Engineering Society convention in Los Angeles." *Computer Music Journal* 4(3): 66–73.

Strawn, J. 1981. "Prism synthesizer." *Computer Music Journal* 5(4): 85–86.

Strawn, J., with C. Abbott, T. Blum, N. Earle, D. Gross, L. Hollander, and L. Smith. 1981. "Report on the International Computer Music Conference, Queens College, November 1980." *Computer Music Journal* 5(2): 36–44.

12 An Introduction to the SSSP Digital Synthesizer

WILLIAM BUXTON, E. A. FOGELS, GUY FEDORKOW, LAWRENCE SASAKI, AND
K. C. SMITH

One of the main interests of the Structured Sound Synthesis Project
(SSSP) is to develop a highly interactive environment to serve as an aid in
the composition of music. We would like to do this within the context of a
small, inexpensive, accessible system. In order to resolve the conflict between the high computational demands of sound synthesis and these
design objectives, we have developed a special-purpose digital sound
synthesizer. Work on this project began in January 1977, and the device
was functioning in a limited state by December of that year.

The design owes much to the Dartmouth synthesizer (Alonso et al.
1976) and the VOSIM oscillator (Kaegi and Tempelaars 1978). Generally
described, the synthesizer consists of one "real" oscillator, which is time-
division-multiplexed so as to function as sixteen oscillators. There are two
aspects of the device that we see as particularly significant. First, it was
designed to incorporate in hardware five important techniques of sound
synthesis; the fixed-waveform, frequency-modulation, additive-synthesis,
waveshaping, and VOSIM techniques. Second, the device can be easily
interfaced with most digital computers.

The generators are essentially fixed-sampling-rate, accumulator-type
digital oscillators. The sampling rate of each oscillator is 50 kHz, with a
system bandwidth of 20 kHz. The dynamic range is well over 60 dB, and
the frequency resolution is approximately 0.7 Hz (linear scale) over the
entire bandwidth. The output signal of each oscillator can be fed to one of
four analog output busses, which may then be fed either directly to an
amplifier or to a channel distributor (Fedorkow 1978; Fedorkow, Buxton,
and Smith 1978). Not only may the waveform output by each be defined
by the user—up to eight waveforms are available at one time—but one
may switch waveforms in mid-cycle. This is possible since the sixteen
oscillators share a 16K buffer of 12-bit words to store waveforms. This
16K of random-access memory is partitioned into eight 2K blocks, one for
each of the eight possible waveforms defined by the user or system.

An important point to note is that the uses of various sound-synthesis
modes are not mutually exclusive. That is, it is perfectly possible to synthesize an eight-partial tone using additive synthesis while utilizing

This is a revised and updated version of an article that originally appeared in *Computer
Music Journal* 2(4): 28–38, 1978.

VOSIM, FM, and fixed-waveform modes at the same time. The flexibility of the arrangement is obvious, as is its benefit. This goes a long way toward a "universal module"—that is, all modules of a uniform type (with the resulting ease of conceptualization and communication). Although this is in direct contrast with analog synthesizers, a very wide repertoire of sounds is possible (including all phonemes in Indo-European languages, for example).

Technical Details

In this section we shall give the design details of the digital synthesizer. Details will not, however, be taken to the logic level. Rather, the purpose is to illustrate and discuss the design approach to a level that enables the reader to evaluate the appropriateness of this design as compared to the alternatives.

General Architecture

The general layout of the device is shown in figure 12.1. The synthesizer itself is made up of four main modules: the controller, memory, oscillator, and digital-to-analog converter modules. Communication among the modules is via a single high-speed data bus, which is under the supervision of the controller module. Communication with the host computer is achieved via a parallel bus connecting the controller with an address decoder residing on the host computer's input/output bus.

By isolating the synthesizer from the host, we are able to power down, test, repair, and/or modify the synthesizer without having to also power down the host. Furthermore, the host is protected from damage due to faults or damage in the synthesizer. These were important considerations, because the synthesizer was initially hosted by an expensive time-sharing system. Other users could not be allowed to suffer because of work being undertaken on the synthesizer. All of this was even more important because we take the same iterative approach to implementing hardware as we do for software: The device was up and running in the simple fixed-waveform mode well before—one by one—the other modes were added.

Frequency Control

The basis of the digital oscillator is the sampling of a stored function. In this case, the function stored is one cycle of a selected waveform. The

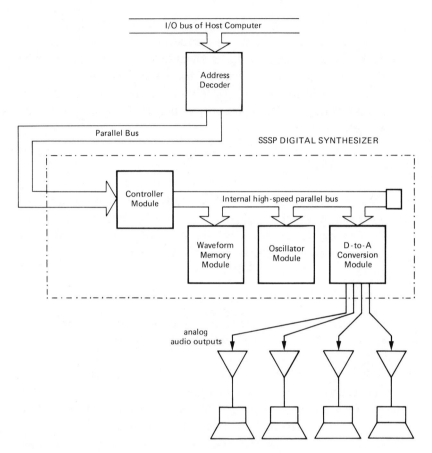

Figure 12.1
Block diagram of the architecture of the digital synthesizer.

waveform is stored as 2K 12-bit samples in a random-access memory internal to the synthesizer. Sound is generated by outputting (scaled) samples from this table through a digital-to-analog converter (DAC), which is connected to some transducer such as a loudspeaker.

Since the waveform buffer (WFB) contains only one cycle of the wave-form, frequency (cycles per second) is controlled by the number of times per second we cycle through the samples of the buffer. This can be con-trolled two ways. One is to sequentially output each sample of the buffer every cycle. Since the number of samples output per cycle is constant—as is the WFB size—the rate at which samples are output must vary for each frequency. The second alternative is to keep the sampling rate constant and vary the number of samples output each cycle; for example, if at frequency f every sample is output, then to output the frequency $2f$ we would output every second sample in the buffer. (Outputting half as many samples—equally spaced throughout the buffer—at the same rate doubles the frequency.) In the first case frequency is specified in terms of the sampling rate, in the second in terms of the offset between subsequent samples in the buffer.

Both approaches have been used with success. The variable-sampling-rate oscillator is used in the Dartmouth synthesizer (Alonso et al. 1976) and the VOSIM oscillator (Kaegi and Tempelaars 1978). However, two major problems must be overcome in taking this approach. First, when a bank of such oscillators is used—each at a different frequency—their samples are output asynchronously. This makes it difficult to mix or process them digitally. Hence, each oscillator in the Dartmouth synthe-sizer has its own DAC. The second problem is that at low frequencies the sampling rate may enter into the audio band (below about 16 kHz). This requires special consideration in terms of the output filters following the DACs. Consequently, the cutoff frequency of the low-pass filters may be required to vary with the sampling rate.

In our system, we have chosen to take the more straightforward fixed-sampling-rate approach. The technique is well understood (it is the basis of the Music V software oscillators), the sampling of different oscillators is synchronous (making the time-division multiplexing of several oscil-lators rather straightforward), and the final-stage filters have a fixed cut-off frequency. As stated above, frequency in this type of oscillator is controlled by specifying the offset in the WFB between subsequent

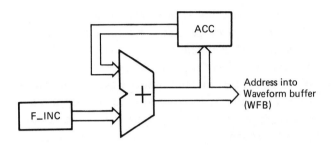

Figure 12.2
Simple ramp generator.

samples. This offset—or increment—we call F_INC ("frequency increment"). Given the address A_n of any sample n, then,

$A_{n+1} = (A_n + \text{F\_INC})$ modulo WFB size.

A generalized view of this mechanism is shown in figure 12.2. Here it is seen that the sum of the addition (and hence the address of the current sample) is accumulated in the register ACC, to be used in calculating the address of the next sample. The modulo arithmetic is accomplished by simply ignoring the carry bits. Converting frequency from hertz to F_INCs is straightforward, given the sampling rate and WFB size. This is effected using the formula

F_INC = FREQ*WFBS/SR

where FREQ is the frequency in hertz, WFBS is the waveform-buffer size, and SR is the sampling rate.

Fixed Waveform

We obtain the fixed-waveform mode of operation through a slight extension of figure 12.2. A simplified presentation of this mode is made in figure 12.3. Here, the principal components added concern the WFB table lookup and the DAC mechanism. In addition to F_INC, four new addressable registers appear: WF_SEL, OP_SEL, ENV, and VOL.

As was stated above, there are eight buffers in which waveforms can be stored. Therefore, besides calculating the address within any particular WFB (the process illustrated in figure 12.2), one must also specify from which of the eight WFBs the samples are to be taken. This is the purpose

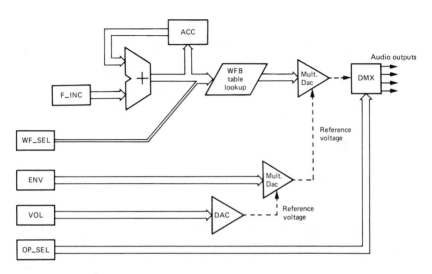

Figure 12.3
General view of simple fixed-waveform digital oscillator.

of the register WF_SEL ("waveform select"), which is simply a 3-bit value concatenated onto the address calculated by the ramp generator. One benefit of being able to easily change waveforms is the potential for minimizing distortion due to aliasing, or foldover. This can be accomplished simply by substituting simple sine tones for complex signals whose fundamental frequency is above a certain threshold. Since the harmonics of such signals would fall outside of the bandwidth of human pitch perception, the substitution would not be perceived and the generation of partials above the Nyquist frequency is avoided.

There are four audio output channels in the synthesizer. The output of each of the sixteen oscillators may be routed to any one (and only one) of these four channels. The purpose of the register OP_SEL is simply to specify to which of these output channels the oscillator's output is to be routed.

Once a sample is obtained from the WFB, it is generally scaled in amplitude so as to be able to produce sounds of different loudness. One technique of doing so is to digitally multiply the sample by a scaling factor and then output the product through a normal DAC. This is the technique used by Alles and diGiugno (1977), for example. At the time of design, however, it appeared more economical to take an approach similar to that of the Dartmouth synthesizer. Here we carry out the scaling through the use of multiplying DACs, which were less expensive and complex than digital scaling. The waveform sample is placed in a 12-bit multiplying DAC and the output is scaled according to a reference voltage input. Thus, even at low amplitudes there are 12-bits of resolution of the waveform, resulting in a better dynamic range than would be possible with an ordinary "fixed-point" 12-bit converter.

One interesting idea of Alonso's which is incorporated into our design deals with the derivation of this reference, or "scaling" voltage (Alonso et al. 1976). Rather than coming from a single amplitude value, separate notions of "envelope" and "volume" are carried over into hardware. That is, the envelope of a sound is scaled in hardware rather than software, thereby saving valuable central processing unit time. Amplitude scaling is, therefore, accomplished by three DACs in series. The first is the volume DAC. The second and third—both multiplying DACs—are the envelope and waveform DACs, respectively. The output of the volume DAC (as determined by the contents of register VOL) is used to scale the output of the envelope DAC (whose unscaled output is determined by the contents of register ENV). The scaled output of the envelope DAC is then used as the scaling voltage for the waveform DAC. One point worth noting in the current implementation concerns the volume DAC. Since loudness varies more logarithmically than linearly, a logarithmic DAC is used. Thus we have an example where psychoacoustic research has affected hardware design.

Additive Synthesis: Bank Mode

In the preceding subsection we saw how we can generate a sound having a particular fixed waveform and a varying amplitude contour. Given the principles of additive synthesis (Risset and Mathews 1969; Grey 1975), we see how a group of fixed-waveform oscillators can be used to generate complex sounds having time-varying spectra. In this case, we have one oscillator corresponding to each partial to be synthesized. Since the technique simply involves the use of a group of fixed-waveform oscillators, we refer to it as *bank mode*. For the same reason, we see that the technique requires no special-purpose hardware beyond that already described.

VOSIM

The basis of VOSIM (Kaegi and Tempelaars 1978) is the ability to output one cycle of a particular function (such as a cosine pulse) followed by a

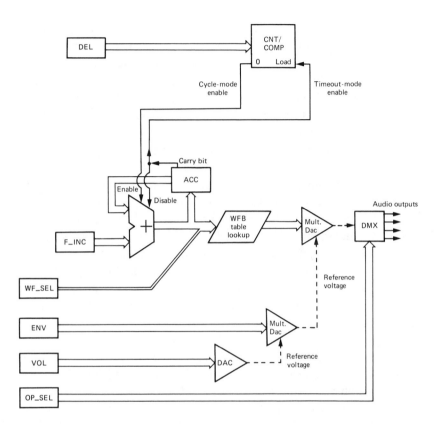

Figure 12.4
Simplified version of VOSIM oscillator.

controlled delay before the next cycle is output. [The actual form of the pulse is arbitrary. However, since one is trying to control the partial content, one typically wants to generate a pulse with few spurious components (Kaegi and Tempelaars 1978; Roads 1985)]. Let us assume that the function is stored in one of the WFBs. Our method of implementation, then, incorporates a mechanism that outputs one cycle of the function stored in the WFB (the period controlled by F_INC) and then steps into a time-out mode for a specific delay period. A simplified illustration of our implementation of this mechanism is shown in figure 12.4. Here it is seen that the period of delay is controlled by the contents of the register DEL. The oscillator functions in two modes: cycle and timeout. Cycle mode ends and timeout is triggered when there is a carry bit out of register ACC (i.e., at the peak of the ramp, or when the WFB addressing "wraps around"). At this time—timeout—the contents of DEL are loaded into the count/compare (CNT/COMP) register, which is decremented every 1/50,000 second. When the content of this register equals zero, the cycle mode is retriggered and the CNT/COMP register disabled. Thus, when DEL equals zero we are continually in the cycle mode and therefore effectively in the fixed-waveform mode of operation.

The VOSIM mechanism as described thus far is oversimplified to facilitate the presentation of material. What the description omits is the method for controlling random deviation, or noise in the sound. The mechanism employed is illustrated in figure 12.5. Again, the register CNT/COMP is loaded at the start of each timeout cycle. Similarly, CNT/COMP containing the value zero still triggers the cycle mode, while an overflow from ACC still triggers timeout. The difference, however, is in the value loaded into CNT/COMP. Instead of simply loading the value contained in register DEL, as diagrammed in figure 12.4, one loads the value contained in DEL plus a random value. The range of this random value is plus or minus some specified percentage of the contents of DEL. This percentage value is determined by the contents of the register DEV (% deviation). The actual origin of the random value is the random-number generator labeled RNG. It is clear from figure 12.5 how the actual delay—the value loaded into the register CNT/COMP—is arrived at. A few points are worth noting, however. First, when the content of DEV equals zero, we have effectively the situation diagrammed in figure 12.4. Second, when the content of DEL equal zero, we still effectively have the fixed-waveform mode. Finally, the effective (average) fundamental frequency in the VOSIM mode is determined by a combination of the contents of both the F_INC and DEL registers.

Frequency Modulation

The synthesizer has sixteen digital oscillators. Frequency modulation (Chowning 1973) is implemented such as to allow any oscillator n to frequency-modulate oscillator $n + 1$ (modulo 16). Though this format does not allow the use of multiple modulators of a single carrier wave (such as described in Schottstaedt 1977), this deficiency is largely made up for by our ability to use modes other than FM (including combinations of modes, such as passing the output of an FM instrument through a wave-shaper). At the time the device was designed, the tradeoff was weighted toward economy and accessibility rather than generality.

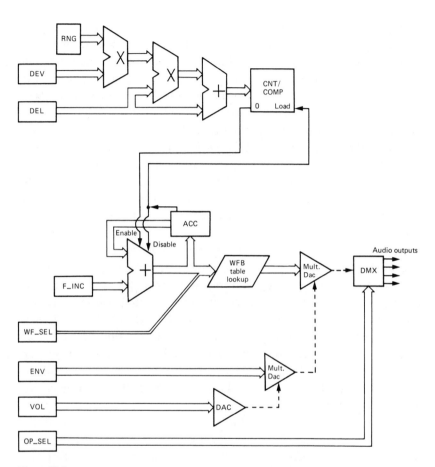

Figure 12.5
VOSIM mechanism.

Implementing FM required certain extensions of the basic oscillator described thus far. These fall into two categories: those that enable the oscillator to be modulated and those that enable it to modulate. The method of implementation is shown in figure 12.6. Here a pair of oscillators are shown. For simplicity's sake the VOSIM components have been omitted. (As in the fixed-waveform mode, register DEL would be set to zero.) Similarly, since the DACs of the modulating oscillator are not used (i.e., are set to zero), they are not shown. Finally, the diagram is made such that the first oscillator shows only the modulating mechanism, while the second shows only the additions to allow it to be modulated. It should be remembered, however, that the oscillators are in fact identical. This is seen in figure 12.7, which shows a single oscillator that includes the mechanisms for all oscillator modes.

Returning to figure 12.6, we see several points of interest. First, the maximum deviation of the frequency of the carrier oscillator is determined by the product obtained by multiplying the contents of the registers F_INC and MOD_INDEX of the modulating oscillator. Second, the actual instantaneous amount of deviation (MODULATION) is derived by multiplying the maximum deviation by the current sample taken from the WFB (again, of the modulating oscillator). Finally, the actual modulation is effected by adding the MODULATION to the contents of the register F_INC of the carrier oscillator. The sum of this addition is then input into the ramp generator.

There are a few additional points to note in the above. First, both the modulator and the carrier may address any one of the eight WFBs through the use of their WF_SEL registers. Thus, we are not restricted to FM with sine waves. Second (and not so obvious), every oscillator is always modulating its neighbor. However, in the fixed-waveform mode, for example, these MOD_INDEX registers are set to zero—effectively switching off the modulation. Finally, the richness of sound obtainable through FM is gained at the expense of two oscillators per sound. In complex structures this makes the low number of oscillators (sixteen) felt rather strongly. (This is equally true in the waveshaping mode, and even more true in additive synthesis.) The user must, therefore, be resigned to resources comparable to a quartet or an octet rather than a symphony. Given the other benefits of the system, however, these limitations seem not so serious. There has, after all, been a great deal of "acceptable" chamber music written over the years.

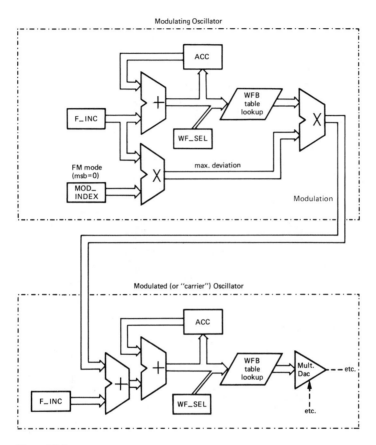

Figure 12.6
Simplified diagram of frequency modulation.

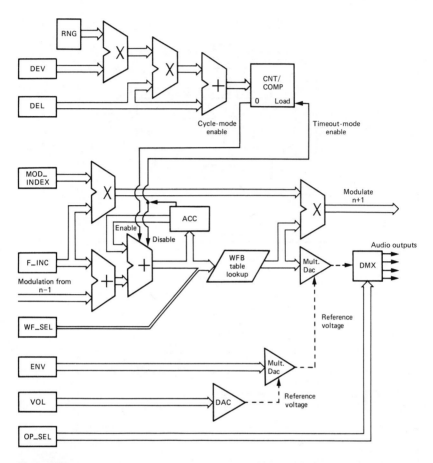

Figure 12.7
Composite view of digital oscillator. The multiplexed portion includes all the adders and
multipliers and the two lowest digital-to-analog converters (connected to the ENV and
VOL registers).

Waveshaping

Inspired by LeBrun (1979) and Arfib (1979), we decided to determine whether we could incorporate waveshaping into the hardware structure. (See Roads 1979 for a tutorial on this technique.) This turned out to be easier than expected, and the result is a slight variation on the FM mode already described. A functional representation of the waveshaping implementation is shown in figure 12.8. As in figure 12.6, we see only the critical components of two oscillators. However, instead of referring to the oscillators as "modulator" and "carrier" as in FM, we will refer to them as "excitation" and "distortion" respectively.

Starting with the excitation oscillator, note that the configuration is just as in FM except that the multiplication of the contents of the F_INC and MOD_INDEX registers is missing. The contents of MOD_INDEX, therefore, function as a simple scaling factor for the samples taken from the WFB. Second—concerning the distortion oscillator—notice that the entire ramp-generating mechanism for WFB address calculation (including ACC) is missing. In this mode, the content of F_INC is set to a value such that (by itself) it addresses the sample midway into the WFB. The output of the excitation is then simply added onto this constant, and the sum is used as the address into the distortion WFB. The sample thus addressed is then output to a DAC, thereby completing the basic waveshaping process.

It still remains to present how the mechanism shown in figure 12.8 is obtained using that shown in figure 12.6. The key to doing so lies in having the MOD_INDEX register function in two different modes. The current mode is determined by the most significant bit of the MOD_INDEX register. When this bit is zero, we have regular FM as described in the preceding section. However, when this bit is equal to 1 for a particular oscillator, the following happens:

• In the multiplication of the contents of the F_INC and MOD_INDEX registers, the F_INC factor is replaced by the constant 1. This effectively nulls the effect of the multiplication. F_INC still controls the frequency of the excitation oscillator.

• The ACC register of the next oscillator (i.e., that of the distortion oscillator in the pair) is cleared after every sample. This effectively disables the ramp generator in the way diagrammed in figure 12.8.

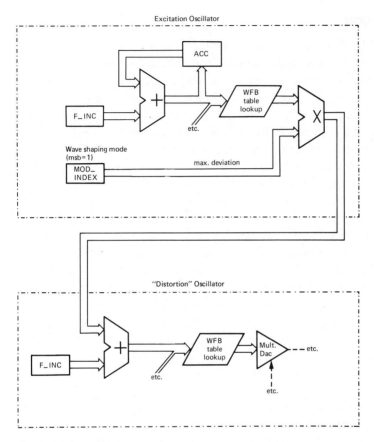

Figure 12.8
Functional diagram of waveshaping mechanism.

Figure 12.9
The SSSP digital synthesizer: detail of the oscillator card.

Thus, the requirements of waveshaping are straightforward, and the implementation not difficult.

Musical Experience with the Synthesizer

At present, the synthesizer is connected to a Digital Equipment Corporation (DEC) LSI-11/23 microcomputer. This system can function in a standalone mode in performance situations or function as a slave to our DEC PDP-11/45 in the studio context. In the studio the system has been used by numerous composers, resulting in works that have been heard around the world. In the portable performance configuration (Buxton et al. 1980) the system has stood up well to the rigors of being on the road. That this synthesizer, which was never intended to leave the security of the lab, works after being jostled on the road from Toronto to New York City is still one of the greatest sources of wonder for the designer.

Summary

An outline of the implementation of the various modes used in the digital synthesizer has been presented. Perhaps the most significant point about the implementation is that all of the oscillators are, in effect, functioning in all modes at all times. The effects are simply made invisible by "nulling" appropriate registers. The effect of this is that the synthesizer's resources can be easily distributed so as to permit sounds utilizing different acoustic models to be synthesized simultaneously with very little overhead on the CPU. In addition, though the FM mode does not allow the use of multiple modulators for a single carrier, the hardware does allow for obtaining similar effects by using the output of waveshaping mode as the modulator in FM, or waveshaping the output of FM. The device is designed so as to produce good audio quality and is able to be easily interfaced with a large number of different computers.

One aspect of the design that is now somewhat questionable is the method of implementing the digital-to-analog conversion process. While we would retain the control mechanism (that is, the method of scaling the waveform using the ENV and VOL registers), the actual scaling would be done digitally rather than using multiplying DACs. Digital scaling would then enable us to use only four DACs in total. The current design was made in the interest of economy and has served well in terms of fidelity and reliability. The modular nature of the architecture enables us to change one module with only minimal trauma to the others.

Other drawbacks of the device are the limited number of oscillators and the lack of generality in comparison with, for example, Music V. These are limitations we are willing to accept for the time being, given that our prime interest is in the relationships among sounds rather than in the intrinsic value of the sounds themselves. That is, we see our main priority in developing the software to manipulate the sounds currently in our repertoire (see, e.g., Reeves et al. 1979) rather than in expanding that repertoire. Finally, the lack of hardware ramp generators to control time-varying phenomena has proved unfortunate because of the additional computational overhead on the host computer and the limited time resolution of envelopes defined in software.

Acknowledgments

The work described in this article was undertaken as part of the research of the Structured Sound Synthesis Project (SSSP) of the University of Toronto. The SSSP is an interdisciplinary project whose aim is to conduct research into problems and benefits arising from the use of computers in music composition. This research can be considered in terms of two main areas: the investigation of new representations of musical data and processes, and the study of human-machine interaction as it relates to music.

The research of the SSSP is funded by the Humanities and Social Sciences Research Council of Canada under grant S76-0099. Logistic support comes from the Computer Systems Research Group (CSRG) of the University of Toronto. This support is gratefully acknowledged.

Appendix: Synthesizer Register Summary

DEL	Nonzero value implies VOSIM mode. DEL is the average delay, or timeout period, between instances of cycle-mode.
DEV	The percentage of random deviation in the value DEL. Used to control degree of nonperiodicity in VOSIM sounds.
ENV	The current value of the (as yet unscaled) amplitude envelope. ENV is scaled by VOL, and the product is used to scale the waveform sample to be output.
F_INC	Used for frequency control. F_INC is the increment added to the address of the last waveform sample output in order to derive that of the next sample.
MOD_INDEX	Controls the amount of modulation that the current oscillator n effects on oscillator $n + 1$. When the most significant bit is zero, the mode is FM. When the most significant bit is 1, the mode is waveshaping.
OP_SEL	Used to select to which of the four audio output busses the oscillator's output should be fed.
VOL	The maximum volume to which the envelope (ENV), and consequently the waveform, is to be scaled. VOL is logarithmic scale.

WF_SEL   A value to select from which of the eight waveform
                buffers the waveform sample is to be selected. Used
                to change waveforms.

References

Alles, H., and G. diGiugno. 1977. "The 4B: A one-card 64-channel digital synthesizer."
Computer Music Journal 1(4): 7–9. Article 15 in this volume.

Alonso, S., J. Appleton, and C. Jones. 1976. "A special-purpose digital system for musical
instruction, composition, and performance." *Computers and the Humanities* 10: 209–215.

Arfib, D. 1979. "Digital synthesis of complex spectra by means of multiplication of nonlinear distorted sine waves." *Journal of the Audio Engineering Society* 27(10): 757–779.

Buxton, W., W. Reeves, G. Fedorkow, K. C. Smith, and R. Baecker. 1980. "A microcomputer-based conducting system." *Computer Music Journal* 4(1): 8–21.

Chowning, J. 1973. "The synthesis of complex audio spectra by means of frequency modulation." *Journal of the Audio Engineering Society* 21(7): 526–534. Article 1 in this volume.

Fedorkow, G. 1978. Audio Network Control. M.S. thesis, Department of Electrical Engineering, University of Toronto.

Fedorkow, G., W. Buxton, and K. C. Smith. 1978. "A computer-controlled sound distribution system for the performance of electroacoustic music." *Computer Music Journal* 2(4):
33–42.

Grey, J. 1975. An Exploration of Musical Timbre. Ph.D. diss., Department of Music,
Stanford University.

Kaegi, W., and S. Tempelaars. 1978. "VOSIM—A new sound synthesis system." *Journal of
the Audio Engineering Society* 26(6): 418–425.

LeBrun, M. 1979. "Digital waveshaping synthesis." *Journal of the Audio Engineering Society*
27(4): 250–266.

Reeves, W., W. Buxton, R. Pike, and R. Baecker. 1979. "Ludwig: An example of interactive
graphics in a score editor." In C. Roads, ed., *Proceedings of the 1978 International Computer
Music Conference*, vol. 2. Evanston, Ill.: Northwestern University Press.

Risset, J.-C., and M. Mathews. 1969. "Analysis of musical instrument tones." *Physics Today*
22(2): 23–30.

Roads, C. 1979. "A tutorial on nonlinear distortion or waveshaping." *Computer Music
Journal* 3(2): 29–34. Article 7 in this volume.

Roads, C. 1985. "Digital sound synthesis techniques." In C. Roads and J. Strawn, eds.
Computer Music Tutorial. Cambridge, Mass.: MIT Press.

Schottstaedt, B. 1977. "The simulation of natural instrument tones using frequency modulation with a complex carrier." *Computer Music Journal* 1(4): 46–50. Article 4 in this volume.

13 The DMX-1000 Signal-Processing Computer

DEAN WALLRAFF

The DMX-1000 is an ultrafast 16-bit minicomputer designed especially for audio signal processing. The DMX-1000 is mostly digital. It synthesizes sound by calculating sampled waveform values and converting the stream of samples to analog form with one or more digital-to-analog converters.

The DMX-1000 is designed to be added as a peripheral unit to another computer, called the *master*. It gives this master computer, which is probably a slower, more general-purpose machine, the ability to digitally synthesize high-quality audio signals. The DMX-1000 does the high-speed repetitive "number-crunching" required for the synthesis, and the master controls it in real time. It is by microprogramming that the master computer controls the DMX-1000. The master provides a program and a set of parameters for it; the DMX-1000 executes the program over and over. Each execution of the program produces an output sample. Since the DMX-1000 has no branch instructions, any program will take the same amount of time to run each time it is executed; the samples will be evenly spaced.

There are two high-speed memories in the DMX-1000: the program memory and the data memory. The master computer may write into either of these at any time. The master provides the program for the DMX-1000 by writing it into the program memory. The data memory is used to hold constants, parameters, state variables, waveform lookup tables, and so forth.

It is partly through parallelism that the DMX-1000 achieves its high speed. Figure 13.2 shows in simplified form the architecture of the DMX-1000. All the units shown are controlled by the microcode in the control memory. The data paths shown are all 16 bits wide. The arithmetic-logical unit (ALU) is the heart of the machine. It adds, subtracts, ands, ors, *etc.* The multiplier multiplies two 16-bit numbers to give a 32-bit product. The data memory stores data for later lookup. Finally, the digital-to-analog converter (DAC) provides analog output. All these units operate in parallel. The multiplier may be multiplying two numbers

This is a revised and updated version of an article that originally appeared in *Computer Music Journal* 3(4): 44–49, 1979.

Figure 13.1
Dean Wallraff working with a DMX-1000 system. The left-hand equipment rack contains
the following equipment: at the top, a dual floppy disk unit, connected to the DEC
LSI-11 microcomputer just below it; next, a DMX-1000 signal processing computer;
below that, other DMX-1000 units in various states of construction.

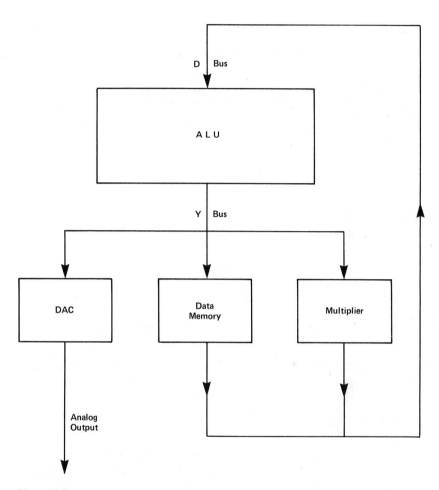

Figure 13.2
Overview of the DMX-1000 architecture.

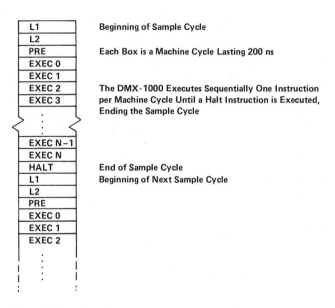

Figure 13.3
DMX-1000 timing, showing the list of instructions executed on each sample cycle.

while the ALU is adding two others and the data memory is fetching a datum.

Machine Timing

The timing of the DMX-1000 is illustrated in figure 13.3. When the machine is running, it begins a sample cycle by executing three special machine cycles: L1, L2, and PRE. During L1 and L2, the master computer interface has a chance to update one location in either the program memory or the data memory. During PRE, the first instruction to be executed is fetched from the program memory into the microinstruction pipeline register. Actual microprogram execution begins in the fourth machine cycle, when the first instruction is executed. After this, instructions are executed sequentially, one per machine cycle. There are no branch instructions for the DMX-1000, so the instruction executed in any given cycle is always the one immediately following, in the program memory, the one executed the cycle before. Sequential execution continues until a halt instruction is executed, at which time the sample cycle is over.

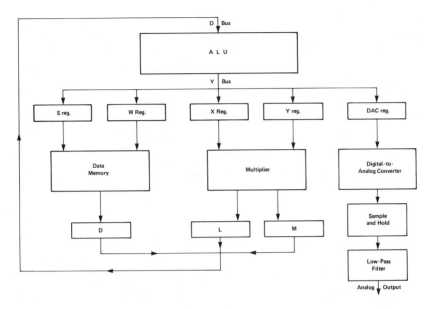

Figure 13.4
DMX-1000 minimum configuration.

The next machine cycle will be L1 again, followed by L2, PRE and the next execution of the microprogram.

The location of the first halt instruction in the program memory determines the sampling rate. The sampling rate may be computed by dividing 5 MHz (the machine cycle rate) by the address of the first halt instruction plus 4. For example, when the halt instruction is in location 100, the sampling rate is 5 MHz/104 = 48,077 Hz. The minimum sampling rate, when the halt is in location 255, is 5 MHz/(255 + 4) = 19,305 Hz.

Architecture

Figure 13.4 shows the architecture of the DMX-1000 in more detail. It depicts the minimum configuration, with only one DAC channel, no delay memory, and no ADC channels. The reader may want to refer to this diagram during the discussion of the DMX-1000's components that follows.

ALU

The 16-bit ALU is made of standard 2901 chip-slice components and performs arithmetic, logical, and switching operations. It contains 17 internal 16-bit registers and has two 16-bit busses: the D (or input) bus and the Y (or output) bus. Other components in the system may supply ALU operands via the D bus. The Y bus, in most cases, conveys the result of the last ALU operation to the other components in the system. The ALU performs one operation per 200-nanosecond machine cycle. During that cycle, the program memory (the microprogram currently running) provides signals that tell the ALU what to do.

Data Memory

The data memory holds 4K 16-bit words and is connected to the ALU output (Y) bus via the S and W registers and to the ALU input (D) bus via the D register. These are pipeline registers, used to hold the results of one unit's operation for subsequent use by another unit.

S and W are called *peripheral input pipeline registers*; there is a bit in the microcode word that corresponds to each of them. When one of these bits is set in an instruction, the DMX-1000 will load the result of that instruction's ALU operation (on the Y bus) into the corresponding register at the end of the machine cycle. The S register addresses the memory. When a number less than 4,096 is loaded into the S register, it will cause the contents of the memory location whose address is in the S register to be loaded into the D register. This operation will take one machine cycle, so the action time of the data memory is said to be one cycle. When a microcode instruction loads the S register, it will be loaded at the end of the machine cycle; the result of the memory lookup will not be available in the D register at the start of the next microinstruction, but rather at the start of the one following. After changing the S register, the microprogram must wait one machine cycle (probably doing something else) before the result will become available.

The D register is a *peripheral output pipeline register*. There is a field in the microinstruction word that allows selection of the contents of one (and only one) of the peripheral output pipeline registers onto the D bus for use as an ALU operand, at the beginning of a machine cycle.

The W register is used by the microprogram to update the contents of the data memory. Loading a value into W causes that value to be written in the data memory location addressed by S.

The use of the peripheral input and output pipeline registers makes it easy for the data memory to operate in parallel with the ALU. The ALU may initiate a data memory operation and do something else while that operation is being performed. The result will be held in the D register until it is convenient for the microprogram to use it. The other peripheral units in the system will be connected in much the same way, via pipeline registers, to the Y and D busses. The units will operate upon their inputs in some defined action time and will propagate the results to the output registers, where they may be used as ALU operands.

Multiplier

The multiplier (figure 13.5) performs signed multiplication of two 16-bit twos-complement quantities. The result is a 31-bit number, which is loaded into the two output registers. The multiplier inputs are the X and Y registers, and they are used to hold the two numbers being multiplied. The outputs are two registers, called L and M, which will hold the lower-order and higher-order halves of the product, respectively. The action times are one machine cycle for the higher-order half of the product and two cycles for the lower-order half.

Digital-to-Analog Converter

To the programmer, the DAC is just a peripheral input pipeline register. Loading a number into the DAC register causes a voltage proportional to the number to be presented at the analog output. Up to four 16-bit DACs may be present in a DMX-1000. Each will have its own pipeline register.

Analog-to-Digital Converter

The analog-to-digital converter (ADC) is an option not shown in figure 13.4. To the programmer, the ADC is just a peripheral output pipeline register whose contents may be selected onto the D bus by the microprogram. Doing this obtains the last converted sample from the ADC and causes that unit to sample again and to start conversion.

Delay Memory

The delay memory, an option not shown in figure 13.4, is a large, slow memory used mostly to implement delays and reverberation units. Its operation is similar to that of the data memory; it has registers, called DS, DW, and DD, that are identical in function to the data memory's S,

Figure 13.5
A look at the interior of the DMX-1000, showing the multiplier (chip marked "TRW"),
the bit-slice processors (four large chips next to the multiplier), the DAC systems (large
modules at the back of the box), and other components.

Figure 13.6
DMX-1000 microcode instruction format (32 bits).

W, and D registers. There are two main differences between the units. First, the delay memory is larger: it has 16K 16-bit words. Second, it is slower; its action time is six machine cycles.

Microinstruction Format

Figure 13.6 shows the format of a DMX-1000 microinstruction. Its bits are numbered from 0 to 31. Descriptions of the individual fields follow.

A, B select the two working registers that the ALU may use as operands. These are 4-bit fields, allowing the specification of any of the ALU's 16 internal working registers.

ALOAD tells the ALU what to do internally with the result of the operation. It may be shifted and loaded into one of the general registers or into a special register called the Q register.

AOP tells the ALU what operation to perform on what operands. Some of the AOPs are ADD, SUBTRACT, AND, OR, XOR, XNOR, MASK, INCREMENT, DECREMENT, CLEAR, MOVE, COMPLEMENT, and NEGATE.

X, Y, S, W are 1-bit fields corresponding to the X, Y, S, and W peripheral input pipeline registers. Putting a 1 in one of these fields causes the corresponding register to be loaded, at the end of the machine cycle, with the datum on the Y bus at the time. Any combination of these registers may be loaded in the same machine cycle.

OUTSEL serves a function similar to that of X, Y, S, and W. It selects one of up to seven other peripheral input pipeline registers to be loaded with the contents of the Y bus.

CN is the carry bit into the ALU, logically part of AOP.

CND is the conditional field, specifying conditions under which the microinstruction is to be executed. There are four condition codes set by the ALU to indicate the result of each microinstruction; they indicate zero result, negative result, arithmetic overflow, and carry. CND may specify that a microinstruction is to be unconditionally executed, or that

Table 13.1
Values of DMX-1000 command bytes and their corresponding functions. These values are sent by the master computer to the DMX-1000.

Command byte value	Number of data bytes	Function performed
0	0	Halt the DMX-1000
1	0	Single-step the DMX-1000
2	0	Start DMX-1000 microprogram execution
3	4	Load a data memory location
4	5	Load a program memory location

it will be executed if a particular condition code was set by the previous instruction, or that it will be executed if a particular condition code was cleared by the previous microinstruction.

INSEL is used to select one of the peripheral output pipeline registers onto the D bus, presumably to be used as an operand for the current instruction. The operand will be put on the D bus at the beginning of the machine cycle.

Master Computer Interface

The DMX-1000 is run by another computer, the master computer, which directs the activity of the DMX-1000 by giving it commands through an interface. Interfaces for various master computers are available, but they all convey information to the DMX-1000 in 8-bit bytes. All commands consist of an integral number of bytes and begin with a *command byte*, which is followed by a number of *data bytes*. The five DMX-1000 commands are summarized in table 13.1.

Sending a 0 command byte halts microcode execution in the DMX-1000. This allows very quick update of the data and control memories.

Sending a 1 command byte causes the DMX-1000 to execute its microprogram once; it will run for a single sample cycle. This feature is intended to provide the hardware support necessary for a software debugger.

Sending a 2 command byte starts the DMX-1000 executing microcode repetitively. While the DMX-1000 is running, the data and control memories may be updated only once per sample cycle. This is about as fast as most master computers will run.

Sending a 3 command byte indicates to the DMX-1000 that the next four bytes that are sent are to be interpreted as the address of a location in data memory and a value to be loaded into that location.

Sending a 4 command byte indicates to the DMX-1000 that the next five bytes that are sent are to be interpreted as a value to be loaded into a location in control memory and the address of that location.

Using an 8-bit parallel format for the master computer interface makes it easy to connect the DMX-1000 fairly easily to just about any general-purpose computer. Interfaces are available for several mini- and micro-computers.

Programming the DMX-1000

Direct Microprogramming

Directly programming the DMX-1000 involves giving it both a micro-program to run in the program memory and a set of parameters in the data memory. These memories are updated in real time during sound synthesis by the master computer.

Most of the time, in the system composed of the two computers, the DMX-1000 will be programmed to do only the processing that must be done at the audio rate. Its instruction set is well suited to audio signal processing. For example, a basic oscillator whose amplitude, frequency, and waveshape are controlled by the master computer may be implemented in ten DMX-1000 instructions. The master will do whatever processing may be done at a lower rate. This will include calculations that are done at the beginning of each note or event, as well as those that are done at regular intervals (typically between 1 and 20 msec) for the duration of each note or event. Envelopes may often be implemented in the master computer at subaudio rates with acceptable results. They may also be programmed in the DMX-1000 so that they run at the audio rate.

Microprogramming Example: Frequency-Modulation Instrument   Connecting two oscillators so that the scaled output of one (called the modulator) is continuously added to the phase of the other (called the carrier) results in a frequency-modulation instrument. The following program implements this sort of instrument.

```
(0)   CLR    ,XO,B,S       ;reset parameter pointer
(1)   CLR    ,XF,B         ;clear output accumulator
(2)   NXT
```

(3)	MOVD	,X1,B,D	;400 ramp scaler
(4)	NXT		
(5)	MOVD	,X2,B,D	;1000 table center address
(6)	NXT		
(7)	MOVD	,X4,B,D	;ramp increment from [2]
(8)	ADDDA	X4,X3,B,D	;add ramp value from [3]
(9)	MOVD	,X3,B,D,,IFMI	;use old value for ramp if
			;over 77777
(10)	MOVA	X3,,,,W	;write ramp value back to [3]
(11)	NXT		
(12)	NXT		
(13)	MOVD	,X5,B,D	;modulator SI from [4]
(14)	ADDDA	X5,X5,B,D,WY	;add to phase, write back [5]
(15)	MOVA	X1,,,,X	;scaler
(16)	NXT		
(17)	ADDDA	X2,,,M,S	;add table address for lookup
(18)	MOVD	,,,D,X	;modulation index from [6]
(19)	MOVA	X3,,,,Y	;times ramp
(20)	MOVD	,,,D,X	;times table lookup result ,
(21)	MOVD	,,,M,X	;(ramp times index)
(22)	NXT		
(23)	MOVD	,X5,B,M	;high order of modulator
(24)	NXT		
(25)	ADDDA	X5,X5,B,D	;add carrier SI from [7]
(26)	MOVD	,X4,DB,L	;low-order modulator
(27)	ADDDA	X4,X4,B,D,W	;add low-order carrier phase
			;from [8]
(28)	INCB	,X5,B,,,IFCS	;add carry from low-order
			;phase to high-order phase
(29)	NXT		
(30)	MOVA	X1,,,,X	;ramp scaler
(31)	ADDDA	X5,,,D,WY	;add high-order phase from [9]
(32)	NXT		
(33)	ADDDA	X2,,,M,S,	;add table address—lookup
(34)	MOVD	,,,D,X	;amplitude from [10]
(35)	MOVA	X3,,,Y	;times ramp
(36)	MOVD	,,,D,Y	;table lookup value
(37)	MOVD	,,,M,X	;times ramp * amplitude
(38)	NXT		
(39)	ADDDA	XF,XF,B,M	;add result into output
			;accumulator
(40)	MOVA	XF,,,DAC	

DATA MEMORY LAYOUT

[0] 400—Ramp scaler (octal)
[1] 1000—Table center address (octal)
[2] Ramp increment
[3] Current ramp value

[4]   Modulator SI
[5]   Modulator phase
[6]   Modulation index (* carrier SI)
[7]   Carrier SI
[8]   Low-order word of carrier phase
[9]   High-order word of carrier phase
[10]   Amplitude
[400]–[1400]   Sine table

Some conventions should be noted. A mandatory HALT instruction
has not been shown in this listing. The sampling rate is assumed to be
19.3 kHz. Register 0 (XO) is used to address parameters in data memory.
These parameters are placed in that memory starting at location 0, in
order of use. The abbreviation "NXT" stands for "INCB, XO, B,, S"
which increments XO and loads it into the S register, which addresses the
data memory. After another machine cycle, the next parameter will be
available in the D register. Register 15 (XF) is used by convention to
accumulate the output sample that is to be strobed into the DAC. In
discussing programs, particular instructions are referred to by their
control memory addresses in parentheses. Numbers in brackets refer
to corresponding data memory locations.

The instrument uses a setup fairly common for frequency modulation,
where the envelope function, in this case a linear ramp, also controls the
modulation index during the attack. The dynamic spectra that result give
a lifelike quality to the attack.

The ramp envelope function is implemented in (6) through (11). It is
similar to the sawtooth ramp generator used as input to the table lookup
in an oscillator, except that it does not wrap around. It increases to its
maximum value at a rate determined by the ramp increment in [2] and
then stops. The ramp value in [3] is presumably set to zero at the start of
a note. This construction and its variations are very useful for generating
envelopes. As it stands, it will generate most piecewise-linear envelopes if
the master computer updates the parameters at the start of each linear
segment. A similar double-precision ramp may be programmed when
slower or more precisely timed segments are needed. An exponential
version is easily implemented by multiplying the two parameters instead
of adding them. More complex envelope functions could be read from a
table in the data memory by using this ramp as a table index. Those
functions could be interpolated, if necessary. And so on.

The modulating oscillator is implemented in (12) through (22). The oscillator output is multiplied by the ramp function, to achieve the dynamic attack spectrum, and by a constant in [6]. This constant is not exactly the modulation index as described in the program's comments, but rather a constant proportional to it. In particular, the actual modulation index at the height of the attack (when the ramp reaches maximum value) will be the contents of [6] divided by the carrier SI. The rest of the program is the double-precision carrier oscillator. The double-precision output of the modulator (in M and L) is added to the single-precision carrier SI and the double-precision carrier phase accumulator. As usual, the phase is scaled and used as an index for a table lookup. The output is multiplied by the ramp function, which gives the signal an envelope, and by the amplitude. Seven of these instruments will fit in the DMX-1000.

Music Programming: The Music-1000 Language

Direct microprogramming is cumbersome both as a means of programming the DMX-1000 and as a means of musical expression. Music-1000 is a software package that runs on a DEC LSI-11 (or PDP-11) master computer and the DMX-1000. It is similar to such languages as Music V and Music 11 but runs in real time. The composer describes a piece of music to Music-1000 in a score file and an orchestra file. The Music-1000 score language is similar to that of most other music languages: there is one line of information, containing several numeric values, per note or event in the score. It is assumed that most composers will want to use some sort of automatic score preparation aid.

The orchestra is a program describing how to synthesize the piece; it reads the score as input and produces sound output in real time. The Music-1000 orchestra language is similar to that of other music systems. An instrument (which plays one voice in the orchestra) is composed primarily of units (equivalent to analog synthesizer modules) that are interconnected in the language. Instruments and units have program codes that run at different rates. The I-time code is executed once at the beginning of each note that the instrument plays. The K-time code runs on the PDP-11 at the control rate, either 100 Hz or 1,000 Hz. And the X-time code runs in the DMX-1000 at the audio rate. Named variables are used to pass values from one unit to another. These variables are, in a sense, signals, each being updated at a particular rate. The most important rule regarding the interconnection of units is that fast signals may not be connected to slow inputs; the hardware is not capable of conveying audio-rate information from the DMX-1000, where it is generated, to the PDP-11, where control-rate and I-time processing is done. The reverse is allowed—I-time signals may be connected to K-time and X-time inputs, and K-time signals may be connected to X-time inputs.

The orchestra language translator is currently implemented as a collection of macros for the PDP-11 assembler. These macros assemble the orchestra into real-time PDP-11 code and DMX-1000 microcode. The advantage of this implementation is the relatively small amount of programming effort required. The user interface is not ideal, however. The orchestra needs to be compiled and linked, which can take up to a few minutes. The compile-time error messages are often obscure, especially when they are generated by the assembler. And run-time checking is limited. The second version of Music-1000 will feature an interactive incremental compiler that will give much clearer error messages and that will reduce to a few seconds the waiting time from the end of orchestra definition to the beginning of sound generation. In the meantime, the current implementation provides the same basic features with much less programming effort. An example of a Music-1000 program follows.

Music-1000 Programming Example: Frequency Modulation Instrument
The Music-1000 frequency modulation instrument shown below is similar to the microcoded one described earlier. The line numbers shown in parentheses in the left-hand column are for reference and are not part of the instrument. The instrument is made up of units, one per line. The unit name (for example, oscillator) is the first thing on the line, followed by a number of parameters separated by commas. The first of these is generally the unit's output; the others are inputs. Comments (ignored by the computer) may follow semicolons at the right of each line.

```
(1)   INSTR    1
(2)   LOCAL    <MODAMP,ENVLOP,DECAY>
(3)   IMUL     MODAMP,P4,P5        ;MODAMP = P4 * P5
(4)   ISUB     DECAY,P1,P2         ;DECAY = P1 - P2
(5)   LINSEG   X8,0,P2,MAX,DECAY,0 ;X-TIME LINE SEGMENTS
(6)   XMUL     X9,X8,MODAMP        ;X9 = X8 * MODAMP
(7)   OSCIL    X9,SINE,P3,X9       ;MODULATOR
(8)   XADD     X9,X9,P5            ;X9 = X9 + P5
(9)   XMUL     X8,X8,P6            ;X8 = X8 * P6
(10)  OSCIL    X9,SINE,X9,X8       ;CARRIER OSCILLATOR
(11)  OUT      X9                  ;OUTPUT TO LEFT CHANNEL
(12)  ENDIN                        ;END OF INSTRUMENT
```

P1   Duration of note
P2   Attack time
P3   Modulator pitch
P4   Modulation index
P5   Carrier pitch
P6   Note amplitude

This instrument uses an envelope made of X-time line segments. This same envelope modulates both the carrier and the modulator; it is scaled differently for each one.

The INSTR statement (1) designates the code that follows, up to the ENDIN, as instrument number 1. (2) declares MODAMP, ENVLOP, and DECAY to be variables local to this instrument. (3) multiplies at I-time (once at the start of the note) P4 times P5 to give MODAMP—the amplitude of the modulating oscillator. (4) calculates the duration of the decay by subtracting the attack time from the note's duration. (5) is an X-time line segment generator. It specifies that the X-time variable X8 (which is actually the DMX-1000 register X8) will contain a line segment signal that begins at 0 at the start of the note, goes to maximum value over the attack time (P2) and then decays to 0 over the remaining duration of the note. The LINSEG unit contains DMX-1000 microcode to generate the line segments at the audio rate and PDP-11 code to update the slope and limit of the line segments at the breakpoints. (6) scales this signal so it can be used as the modulator amplitude; it is multiplied by MODAMP and put in X9. The XMUL unit generator as invoked in (6) contains code for both the DMX-1000 (the audio-rate multiplication) and the PDP-11 (updating MODAMP in the DMX-1000 at the control rate). (7) is the modulating oscillator. It outputs into X9 a sine signal (the SINE function should be defined elsewhere in the orchestra) of pitch P3 and amplitude X9. The old value of X9 (the scaled line-segment envelope) is overwritten with this new signal, which causes no problems as long as the old signal isn't needed later in the instrument. (8) adds this oscillator output to P5, putting that result in X9. (9) scales the line-segment envelope for use as the carrier envelope. (10) is the carrier oscillator, putting in X9 a SINE signal with frequency X9 and amplitude X8. (11) adds the signal to the accumulator for the first output channel (XF).

The Music-1000 version of the frequency modulation instrument is a great deal easier to understand and modify than the version implemented

Figure 13.7
The DMX-1000.

directly in microcode. It does a great deal more, besides: it specifies in
detail how the PDP-11 will update the DMX-1000 in real time to produce
music.

Flexibility

Most digital synthesizers designed to date are collections of digital implementations of analog synthesizer components—digital oscillators, envelope generators, filters, and the like. The components are connected
via some sort of intelligent bus that allows the routing of signals from unit
to unit to be controlled by the master. The advantage of this approach is
that these basic units are quite efficient, being implemented directly in
hardware. But a penalty is paid in flexibility. Using this sort of synthesizer,
one may run out of one type of unit while those of another type are unused.
One could, for example, use all the oscillators and wish for more, while
most of the filters were idle. Furthermore, this architecture limits the
choice of sound synthesis methods. Some synthesizers will not do *waveshaping*, for example, because their components were not designed for it
(LeBrun 1979; Roads 1979).

The DMX-1000, rather than being a digital synthesizer per se, is a
general-purpose computer whose architecture and instruction set have
been optimized for audio signal processing, while retaining as much as
possible of the flexibility of the general-purpose machine. It provides a

certain amount of computational capacity—256 microinstructions, executed each sample period. These 256 instructions may be used to implement exactly what the user needs and nothing else; they may be used, for example, to implement 25 oscillators, or one oscillator and 14 filters.

Since units are programmed in microcode rather than implemented directly in hardware, the details of their operation may be easily changed. Oscillators, for example, may have single- or double-precision phase accumulators for medium- or high-frequency resolution. They may truncate the phase for the table lookup, for speed, or may interpolate between table values, for less lookup noise. Envelope generators may produce linear or exponential segments at the audio rate, or may be implemented in the master computer at a slower rate.

The flexibility of the DMX-1000 means that virtually any type of unit or synthesis method may be implemented. Filters, noise generators, reverberation units, delay lines, waveshaping, and linear predictive synthesis may easily be implemented, in addition to more standard methods like additive synthesis and frequency modulation.

Precision

The DMX-1000 employs 16-bit data paths throughout, which is adequate for most purposes. When more precision is necessary, double-precision calculations may often be done. The multiplier gives a 32-bit product when multiplying two 16-bit numbers, and the ALU will add and subtract 32-bit quantities. For example, the basic frequency resolution of 0.29 Hz at the lowest (19 kHz) sampling rate may be improved by a factor of 2^{16} by using a 32-bit sampling increment and phase accumulator.

Speed

The DMX-1000, with its pipelined, somewhat parallel architecture, is several times as fast in audio signal-processing applications as the fastest general-purpose minicomputers. At a 19.3 kHz sampling rate it will implement, for example, 24 simple oscillators, or 16 oscillators with ramp envelope control, or 8 voices of frequency modulation, or 20 first-order filter sections, or 10 second-order filter sections, or 30 white noise generators, or various combinations of the above, such as 12 oscillators and 4 voices of frequency modulation.

Conclusion

The DMX-1000 is a 16-bit minicomputer whose architecture and instruction set have been optimized for audio signal processing. It is fast, because of its pipelined parallel architecture and its use of bipolar chip-slice technology. And it is flexible, because of its high degree of programmability.

References

LeBrun, M. 1979. "Digital waveshaping synthesis." *Journal of the Audio Engineering Society* 27(4): 250–266.

Roads, C. 1979. "A tutorial on nonlinear distortion or waveshaping." *Computer Music Journal* 3(2): 29–34. Article 7 in this volume.

14 A Portable Digital Sound-Synthesis System

H. G. ALLES

A complete, real-time, digital sound-synthesis system has been designed and constructed at Bell Laboratories (see figure 14.1). In one compact unit—42 inches wide, 25 inches high, and 18 inches deep, weighing approximately 300 pounds—a microcomputer system, a performer interface, a versatile digital sound synthesizer, and an array of timers have been integrated into a working system for the musician (figure 14.2). Approximately 1,400 integrated circuits are used in the system (Alles 1977a).

Microcomputer System

The microcomputer system is based on the Digital Equipment Corporation LSI-11 central processing unit (CPU). The CPU is augmented by 64 Kwords of 16-bit mappable memory for system tables and input/output buffering, two floppy disks with direct memory access (DMA) controllers, and an ASCII and graphics video terminal with a full ASCII keyboard.

Performer Interface

The performer interface samples and independently filters the positions of 256 input devices with approximately 7 bits of resolution. This yields about 100–200 different positions for each device. These devices are sampled at a 250-Hz sampling rate (Alles 1977b). Among the input devices are two 61-key organ-type manuals. The position of each key on the manual is measured 250 times per second with a 7-bit resolution. In addition, four three-axis joysticks and 72 slide potentiometers are provided.

Digital Synthesizer

The sound-generating core of the system is a 16-bit digital sound synthesizer that can produce a wide variety of polyphonic audio signals

This is a revised and updated version of an article that originally appeared in *Computer Music Journal* 1(4): 5–6, 1977.

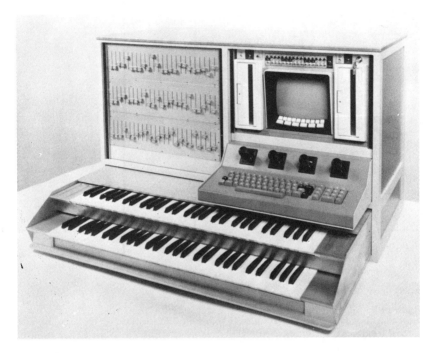

Figure 14.1
A portable digital sound-synthesis system designed by Harold Alles at Bell Laboratories.

(figure 14.3). For example, at a 30-kHz sampling rate, the device will produce 32 frequency-modulation (FM) oscillators (0.002-Hz frequency resolution and 14-bit accuracy); 32 FM oscillators that directly generate the first n harmonics of a specified frequency (for $1 \leqslant n \leqslant 127$) (figure 14.4); 32 completely programmable second-order digital filters (two pole and one zero) that may be signal controlled; 32 AM (four-quadrant) multipliers; and 256 envelope generators (linear or logarithmic). In addition, the synthesizer offers a two-second (64-Kword) digital reverberation and/or signal-driven lookup table. Sixty-four taps are allowed into this table space. There is also an array of 192 accumulating registers for interconnecting all the devices in any arbitrary way, under program control. The synthesizer can process natural sounds through two 14-bit analog-to-digital converters (ADCs). Sound is distributed to four 16-bit digital-to-analog converters (DACs).

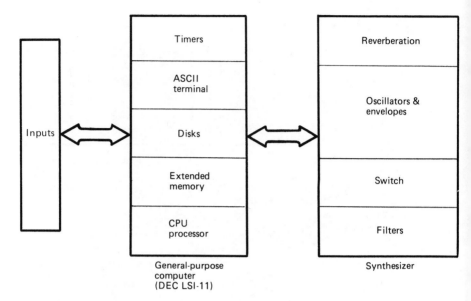

Figure 14.2
Block diagram of the system. Users interact with the synthesizer through the general-purpose computer.

Timers

For timing and synchronizing musical events, an array of 255 independent timers (with a 1-millisecond resolution) is provided with the system. Sixteen first-in-first-out (FIFO) stacks are available for storing and sorting timing events.

Discussion

All the devices in the system are interfaced to the LSI-11 microcomputer's Q-bus. Hence, all the control words for the system appear in the LSI-11's address space, which takes up approximately 6 Kwords of the microcomputer's memory space.

A major design goal was to ensure that all the system's components complement each other's capabilities. Toward this end, special-purpose hardware was constructed to perform those tasks that are repetitious and time consuming (such as filtering the performer input and timekeeping).

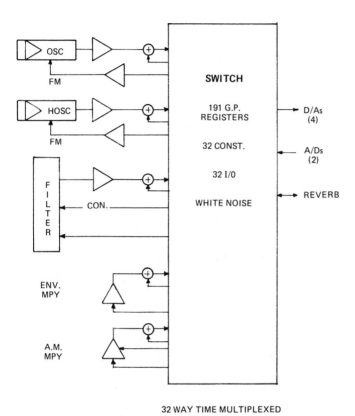

Figure 14.3
The architecture of the synthesizer. Thirty-two virtual copies of this configuration are available to the user in real time.

Since there are no hard-wired connections between the input devices and the synthesizer hardware, and since synthesizer interconnections are accomplished through program-loaded control registers, the whole system may be used in a variety of ways. For example, all the control parameters may be specified in real time and at performance time. This makes the machine into an instrument for improvisation. Alternatively, several files may be prepared in real-time interaction, but before the performance. Then at performance time the files may be played with some subset of the control parameters supplied during performance.

A third alternative is to prepare files incrementally in several sessions, editing and revising the original performance.

Harmonic synthesis equation:

$$\sum_{i=1}^{n} \cos{(i\omega t)} \propto \frac{\sin[(2n + 1)\omega t/2]}{\sin(\omega t/2)} - 1$$

Spectrum:

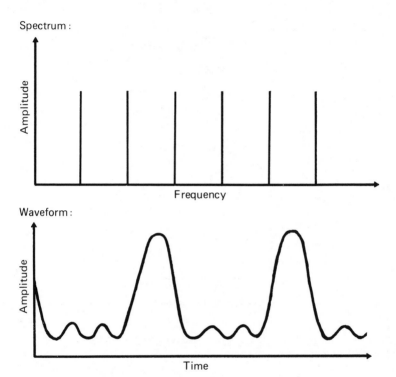

Waveform:

Figure 14.4
One of the modules in the sound-synthesis subsystem will compute the first n harmonics of a specified frequency. The resultant signal is shown in both the frequency and the time domains, that is, as a spectrum and as a waveform.

Capacity

The total real-time synthesis capacity depends, of course, on the type of sound synthesis techniques used by the performer. The LSI-11 microcomputer and the floppy disk subsystem can support approximately 1000 parameter changes per second throughout the system. These parameters can be used to specify frequencies, envelopes, configuration (interconnection) changes, graphic displays, and other values in the system. This data rate should be able to generate approximately 100 reasonably complex notes per second.

Summary

This complete system is perhaps the first representative of a new generation of musical instruments that combine in one relatively portable unit all the hardware and interfaces necessary for complicated real-time interactive work. The complexity of the sounds produced approaches that of a modest-sized orchestra. The system is now installed and being used at the Oberlin Conservatory in Oberlin, Ohio.

References

Alles, H. G. 1977a. "A modular approach to building large digital synthesis systems." *Computer Music Journal* 1(4): 10–13.

Alles, H. G. 1977b. "A 256-channel performer-input device." *Computer Music Journal* 1(4): 14–15. Article 16 in this volume.

15 The 4B: A One-Card 64-Channel Digital Synthesizer

H. G. ALLES AND G. DI GIUGNO

Real-time digital music synthesis is becoming more practical as digital integrated circuit technology improves. Figure 15.1 is a block diagram illustrating one oscillator function of the 4B synthesis card. Although only one circuit is used, it can calculate one complete oscillator function in approximately 0.5 microsecond. The circuit is used 64 times each 32 khz sample period, with different control parameters each time to provide in effect 64 independent oscillator functions. (The circuit may be modified to operate at other sampling rates, but higher sampling rates will reduce the number of independent oscillator functions available.)

The 4B synthesizer provides 64 frequency-modulation (FM) oscillators, 128 envelope (ramp) generators, and 15 accumulating registers for interconnecting the oscillators. Approximately 160 integrated circuits were used, mounted on one wire-wrap card, 8 inches by $10\frac{1}{2}$ inches. The synthesizer is interfaced to a Digital Equipment Corporation LSI-11 microcomputer via the LSI-11's Q-bus. All control parameters for the synthesizer appear in 1 Kword of LSI-11 address space and may be manipulated by any LSI-11 instruction (see Figure 15.2).

The Oscillator Function

The oscillator phase is calculated by a 24-bit accumulator that provides a frequency resolution of approximately 0.002 Hz. The phase is used as the address to a 16-Kword by 14-bit wavetable. The samples in the wavetable are loaded by the LSI-11 so that any waveshape may be used. This size table produces a signal-to-noise ratio of approximately 84 dB. Additionally, the 16-Kword table may be divided into two independent 8-Kword tables, four 4-Kword tables, or one 8-Kword and two 4-Kword tables. A control word for each oscillator is used to specify the size of the table and which table is used by that oscillator (see figure 15.3). Thus, up to four different waveshapes are available simultaneously. One of the wavetable sections may be loaded while other sections are being used.

The 14-bit wavetable output is multiplied by a 16-bit (signed) amplitude function, and 24 bits of the resulting product are retained. An array of

This is a revised version of an article that originally appeared in *Computer Music Journal* 1(4): 7–9, 1977.

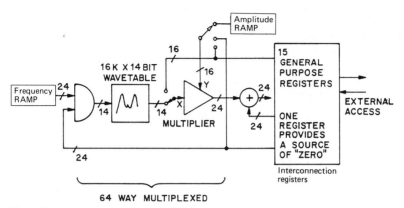

Figure 15.1
Digital oscillator internals. The waveform is read and values from it are multiplied by the ramp (envelope).

1k WORD MEMORY MAP

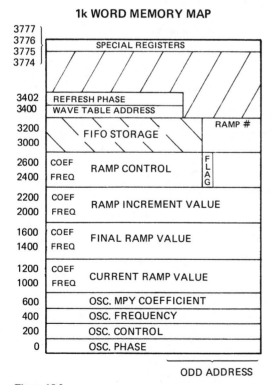

ODD ADDRESS

Figure 15.2
The control parameters of the digital synthesizer as they appear in the memory space of the LSI-11 microcomputer.

OSCILLATOR CONTROL WORD (odd address)

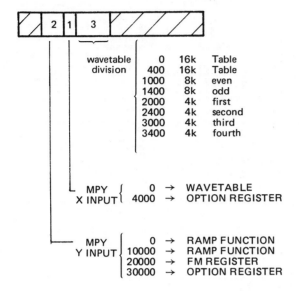

wavetable	0	16k	Table
division	400	16k	Table
	1000	8k	even
	1400	8k	odd
	2000	4k	first
	2400	4k	second
	3000	4k	third
	3400	4k	fourth

| MPY X INPUT | 0 | → | WAVETABLE |
| | 4000 | → | OPTION REGISTER |

MPY Y INPUT	0	→	RAMP FUNCTION
	10000	→	RAMP FUNCTION
	20000	→	FM REGISTER
	30000	→	OPTION REGISTER

OSCILLATOR CONTROL WORD (even address)

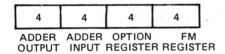

4	4	4	4
ADDER OUTPUT	ADDER INPUT	OPTION REGISTER	FM REGISTER

Figure 15.3
The oscillator control-word formats.

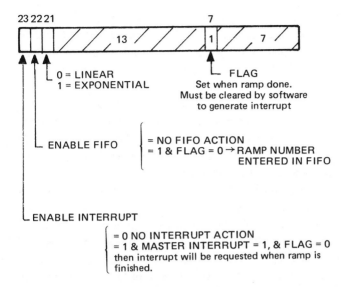

Figure 15.4
The control-word format for a ramp process.

15 general-purpose registers is provided to interconnect oscillators and combine their signals. A sixteenth register is available as a source of "zeros" and as a sink for unused output data. Each oscillator accesses the array four times. The actual registers used are specified by different 4-bit fields in the oscillator control word. The oscillator output may be added to the contents of any register and the sum loaded into any other register.

The oscillator frequency and amplitude values are generated by ramp processes that calculate new values at a 4-kHz rate. Each ramp is controlled by four words in LSI-11 address space: the start (current) value, the final value, the increment value, and a control word (see figure 15.4). The increment is added (4,000 times per second) to the start value until the final value is equalled or exceeded; then the final value is continually used until new values are loaded by the LSI-11. Since 24-bit registers are used, ramp times as long as 30 minutes are available. Any combination of positive and negative values may be specified. There is full protection against all types of overflow.

Any ramp process may be optionally enabled to generate an LSI-11 interrupt when the final value is reached. A first-in-first-out (FIFO) buffer structure is included to queue the interrupt events so that only one address need be accessed to find which ramps have reached their final value (see figure 15.5).

The current ramp value may be optionally exponentiated before it is used as the amplitude (or frequency). A read-only memory conversion table and shift technique yields 0.2% accuracy over a 90-dB (or 15-octave) dynamic range. Thus, exponential attacks and decays are simply produced and octave frequency scaling is easily done.

Each oscillator's phase is calculated using two inputs: the ramp process and the data from one of the 16 registers. Thus, the output of one oscillator may be used to linearly modulate the frequency of another oscillator.

As shown in figure 15.1, the multiplier may be used in some optional ways. Data in an array register (rather than the wavetable) may be used as the x input to the multiplier. This allows the amplitude of some complex signal (additive synthesis) to be controlled by a single ramp function (with the sacrifice of one oscillator). The multiplier y input may come from a register also. This allows one oscillator to modulate the amplitude of another oscillator. Finally the x and y inputs may both come from registers so that the outputs of two oscillators may be multiplied together. The multiplier options and the 15 general-purpose registers provide a good deal of flexibility. For example, a second-order filter section (two poles and two zeros) may be implemented using five oscillator sections.

Input and Output

The address, data in, and data out signals of the 15 registers are available to external devices for a 0.5 microsecond period every 2 microseconds. Data may be read from or written into any of these registers by an external device during this time. If no external address is supplied, the contents of the last register are put out during this time. In the simplest case, a signal from the synthesizer may clock the data to a digital-to-analog converter. However, more complex networks of these synthesizers and other units may be built by using some external circuitry for interconnection.

Control bits are provided so that the phase and ramp processes may be started and stopped synchronously. This allows the synthesizer to be used in a variety of non-real-time applications. For example, it could be used

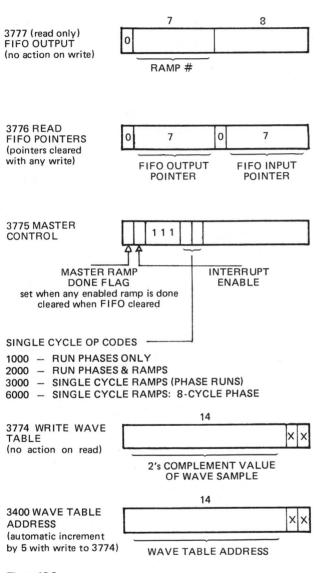

Figure 15.5
Special registers in the synthesizer for control of synthesis processes.

with a Music V system as a peripheral processor where the synthesizer output data is read into the general purpose computer for further processing.

Summary

This versatile synthesizer provides substantial real-time capabilities on one compact circuit card. Combined with a floppy-disk operating system for the LSI-11 computer, it provides a powerful synthesis system for a relatively small price.

The first oscillator circuit was designed and built with the assistance of G. diGiugno while the author was on a leave of absence at IRCAM in Paris. A second version was built by W. C. Fischer. See article 25 for a description of the software developed for the 4B.

16 A 256-Channel Performer-Input Device

H. G. ALLES

Performer Interface

A generalized interface between a performer and a Digital Equipment Corporation LSI-11 microcomputer for use with a digital music synthesizer has been designed and built at Bell Laboratories (Alles 1977a; 1977b). It is capable of encoding the positions of 256 independent devices with up to 8-bit resolution at 250 samples per second (64,000 eight-bit samples per second). In this system, 122 of the devices are the keys of two organ-type manuals, 72 devices are "slide pots" (potentiometers), 20 devices are pots on joysticks, and 4 devices are touch-sensitive sliders. The remaining channels are available for future use.

The Processor-Encoder

The processor-encoder and LSI-11 interface is built from approximately 80 integrated circuits (ICs) on a wire-wrap board the same size (8 inches by $10\frac{1}{2}$ inches) as the LSI-11 computer card. An additional small printed circuit card (approximately 6 inches by $14\frac{1}{2}$ inches) containing five ICs is required for each group of eight devices. Groups of eight such cards are connected to the processor via a "daisy-chained" 16-wire flat ribbon cable. Thus, only four ribbon cables are required to connect the processor-encoder to the 256 devices (figure 16.1).

Two Device Cards

There are two different types of device cards. One card type encodes the position of any variable resistor. Slide pots may be directly soldered onto this card, or the wires from a separate variable resistance device may be soldered to the board. The second card type is used to interface the organ manual keys. A novel capacitive coupled "antenna" is used to sense the key position. Eight antennae, their amplifiers, and an 8-to-1 multiplexer are mounted on one printed circuit card. The antennae are spaced to

This is a revised version of an article that originally appeared in *Computer Music Journal* 1(4): 14–15, 1977.

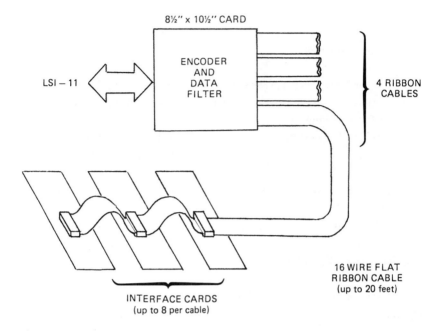

Figure 16.1
The connection between the encoder and data filter and the interface cards, via a 16-wire ribbon cable.

match the key spacing. The cards are simply mounted below a standard keyboard so that the normal switch pins make mechanical contact with the antennae. The mechanism can resolve approximately 100 different positions of a key (figure 16.2).

The keys have been weighted and extra-strong return springs are used to produce a more pleasing "feel." Rubber bumpers are mounted below the keys; they quickly increase the effective spring constant after the keys have been depressed approximately 70% of their allowed travel.

The position-versus-time information from a key may be processed by the LSI-11 in a variety of ways to derive interesting control parameters. The velocity may be accurately obtained by taking the first difference of successive samples. The static position during the last 30% of travel is a function of the key pressure. More complex types of motion may be

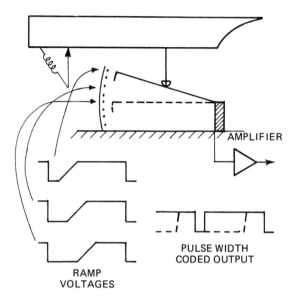

Figure 16.2
The position-sensitive key used in the organ manuals attached as input devices. A key-position detector generates a pulsewidth-modulated representation of the relative position of the key.

detected and used to specify any variety of control parameters (figure 16.3).

Reducing Redundant Information

A digital filter process is provided to reduce redundant position information. Each sample period, the current device position is compared to the last position sent to the computer. The computer is interrupted only if the difference exceeds a programmable threshold. A separate threshold for each device is provided. When processing key motion, the threshold is changed by the software, depending upon the key position (see figure 16.3).

Construction

This interface system is particularly clean in appearance and easy to maintain. Since the device cards are physically close to the devices they

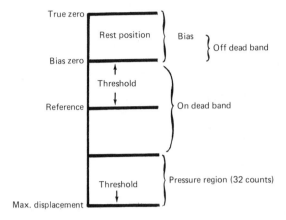

Figure 16.3
As a key is pressed on the organ manual, it first passes from a rest position to a dead band and then to a pressure region where 32 levels of pressure may be detected.

are encoding, and since the cards are daisy-chained together in groups, very few wires are required for the complete interface. This greatly simplifies construction, debugging, and maintenance. Individual device cards are interchangeable and simple to replace. Since the interface to the keys does not use any moving electrical contact or switch, it is relatively trouble-free.

Summary

This interface provides an extremely broad-band data path from the performer into a computer. It should be able to encode all the information a musician can produce in real time, including those subtleties often missed by conventional music keyboards. (The "Multidevice Position Digital Encoder" is described in detail in U.S. Patent 4,190,826.)

References

Alles, H. G. 1977a. "A portable digital sound-synthesis system." *Computer Music Journal* 1(4): 5–6. Article 14 in this volume.

Alles, H. G. 1977b. "A modular approach to building large digital synthesis systems." *Computer Music Journal* 1(4): 10–13.

17 The 4C Machine

JAMES A. MOORER, ALAIN CHAUVEAU, CURTIS ABBOTT, PETER EASTTY, AND
JAMES LAWSON

The 4C machine is one of a series of sound processors developed by or associated with the IRCAM staff, notably one G. diGiugno, and built by Alain Chauveau. It is but one of a series of machines, the design of which has been evolving continuously for quite a few years now. It follows most recently the 4B machine, which was developed at IRCAM jointly by Alles and diGiugno (1977). Among the goals of this design project was the desire to alleviate some of the difficulties of the previous machines, and especially the limitations imposed by the 4B machine, some of which are mentioned by Rolnick (1978), notably the following:

• The machine ran at a 32-kHz sampling rate, but the envelopes were generated at 4 kHz, thus causing an annoying "chirp" on some very fast envelopes.

• The "module definition" was hard-wired [into programmable read-only-memory (PROM) microcode memory] such that only a very limited number of interconnections could be realized.

• The memory used for interconnections and the memory for parameter storage (for frequencies, envelope data, and so forth) were not connected, so that it was not easy to mix these quantities.

The 4B machine did have a number of options in the programming of each module, so that most of the desired functions could be achieved, but only at the expense of "burning" oscillators to use them for other purposes, such as envelope scaling or generation. Thus one could achieve sophisticated applications only by the use of large numbers of oscillator modules (of which there were exactly 64) for various special purposes. The question was, Is it possible to build a machine of the same general size (one single wire-wrap card of about 160 integrated circuits) that is more flexible? The 4C machine represents one answer to this question.

We do not consider the 4C machine to be in any sense the best or most wonderful processor. We present it just as an example of such a machine with the purpose of drawing attention to the choices the designer and the programmer are forced to make when thinking about such systems

This is a revised and updated version of an article that originally appeared in *Computer Music Journal* 3(3): 16–24, 1979.

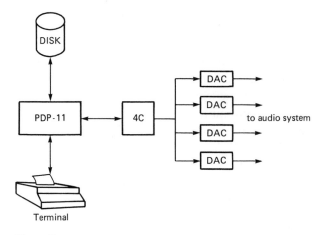

Figure 17.1
A basic 4C configuration, with the 4C connected to a PDP-11 minicomputer, and to four digital-to-analog conversion channels.

(Moorer 1981). It must also be emphasized that the 4C machine was designed principally for use as a single component in a larger, more comprehensive signal-processing system. The fact that it can be useful in an individual application is a fortuitous byproduct of the design. The other point we must emphasize is that the 4C and its relatives are developing machines and that development has continued (see Asta et al. 1980).

One of the problems with the 4C machine is that it was constrained, by a design decision, to be entirely on one wire-wrap board. This forced a consequent series of decisions about what functions could or could not be accommodated that represents a tradeoff of design goals. Some things were eliminated from consideration in this particular machine (like wave-table interpolation) that will be covered in future machines in larger, multi-board systems (Moorer 1981).

A word about notation: All the numbers in this article are decimal except for those preceded by an apostrophe ('), which are octal.

Overview

The 4C systems currently exist in at least three different forms at IRCAM. There is the "standard" 4C system, as shown in figure 17.1. This involves the use of a PDP-11 system, a single 4C processor, and up to four digital-

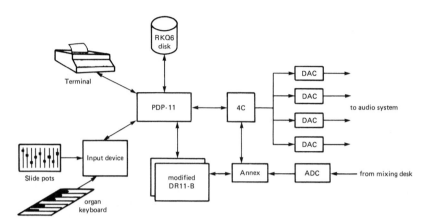

Figure 17.2
The IRCAM PDP-11/34 system, with the 4C machine, input devices, analog-to-digital converter (ADC), Eastty annex, and a direct memory access controller (DR-11B).

to-analog converters (DACs). This allows real-time synthesis of up to 64 oscillators, 32 envelopes with amplitude scaling, and various other functions at a sampling rate of 16 kHz, giving an effective audio bandwidth of 6.4 kHz. The sampling rate may be raised by two, four, or eight, with a corresponding sacrifice in the number of units available. With this configuration the PDP-11 can write directly into any of the 4C registers and may read data back from the registers.

Figure 17.2 shows an extended 4C system that was made possible by a switching annex, built by Peter Eastty. This annex allows the connection of an analog-to-digital converter (ADC) and a DR11-B direct memory access for exchange of sample-time data in a synchronous fashion, thus permitting digital recording and processing of live sound, as well as post-processing of recorded sound. The ADC used is the unit offered by Tim Orr and seems to be of quite high quality. We will refer to this in what follows as the "PDP-11/34 system" with the understanding that it is unique.

Hardware Description

Figure 17.3 is a functional or logical block diagram of the machine. There are seven programmable read-only memories (ROMs) that realize this

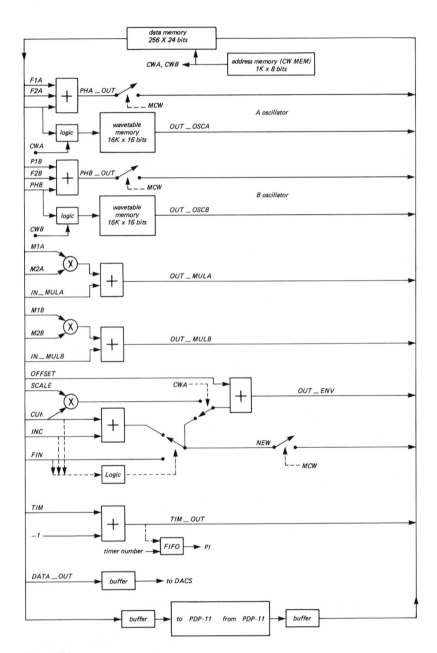

Figure 17.3
A functional block diagram of the 4C machine.

set of functions. These seven memories can be considered to be the "program" of the machine.

The 4C machine that is available to the user consists of a data memory (256 words of 24 bits), an address memory (1,024 words of 8 bits), a wavetable memory (16 Kwords of 16 bits), a certain number of functional units shown in Figure 17.3, and a lot of other stuff. Probably the best way to describe what it really does is to go through and describe the functional units and their timing.

The 4C machine makes one major cycle every 62.5 microseconds. It executes exactly the same "program" every cycle. This major cycle is broken up into 32 minicycles of 1.953 microseconds each. Each minicycle is divided into 32 microcycles of 61.035 nanoseconds each. On each microcycle, an 8-bit address comes out of the address memory and goes to the address of the data memory. What is done with this data is a fixed program that is executed every minicycle. There are 1,024 microcycles in a major cycle, corresponding to the 1,024 addresses that are stored in the address memory. A 62.5-microsecond cycle corresponds to a sample of sound, giving an effective sampling rate of 16,000 Hz.

Each minicycle, the machine can execute two 3-input adds and table lookups, two multiply-and-accumulates, one envelope generate with scaling, one interval timer, one access from the PDP-11, and one send of a sample to an output register (a DAC, for instance).

Multipliers

There are two multiplier-accumulators available in each minicycle, denoted A and B. The two inputs to the A multiplier are denoted M1A and M2A. The multipliers take the high-order 16 bits of the inputs and multiply them. The high-order 24 bits of the product are added to another input, called IN_MULA, and the accumulated sum, called OUT_MULA, is written back into the data memory. Likewise, the parameters for the B multiplier are M1B, M2B, and IN_MULB for input, and OUT_MULB for the accumulator output. All multipliers in the 4C are two's-complement fractional multipliers. In two's-complement fractional notation, the largest positive number ('37777777) is considered to be 1-ε, where ε is the smallest positive number expressible in the machine ('00000001). (There is nothing new here—this is standard two's-complement notation.)

There is no scaling in the multiplier. Since the arithmetic is fractional, the magnitude of the result is always smaller than or equal to the magnitude of either of the two inputs. The consequence of this is that there is virtually no way to make numbers bigger inside the machine except by adding them to themselves. In many cases this is not fatal, but for certain uses (like wavetable interpolation or scaling filter output) it can be limiting.

Adder-Wavetable

The adder-wavetable unit consists of a three-input adder, one input of which is delivered as an address to the wavetable. There are two adder-wavetable units available in each minicycle. The three inputs to the adder are denoted F1A, F2A, and PHA for the A adder, and F1B, F2B, and PHB for the B adder. One of the inputs (PHA and PHB) is used to address the wavetable. The addressing mode of the wavetable is controlled by the oscillator control word. There is one control word for the A oscillator and one for the B oscillator, called A_OSC_CW and B_OSC_CW, respectively. We could call these things oscillators instead of adder-wavetable units since they perform all the computations necessary for a simple oscillator (capable of frequency modulation): PHA is the current angle value that addresses the wavetable; F1A can be thought of as the frequency, or address increment; and F2A is the frequency (phase) modulation input. The output of the three-input adder is called PHA_OUT or PHB_OUT and the output of the wavetable is called OUT_OSCA or OUT_OSCB.

The two control words determine how the 16-Kword wavetable will be broken up. There is really only one 16 Kword table (even though figure 17.3 shows two tables, they are the same physical memory), so both the oscillators in a given minicycle really reference the same table. The wavetable can be broken up into units of 1 Kword, 2 Kwords, 4 Kwords, 8 Kwords, or 16 Kwords. The information on how it is to be broken up is stored in the address memory. This means that there are things in the address memory that are not really addresses, but are instead oscillator control words. Thus to our description of the oscillator above, we must add two inputs, A_OSC_CW and B_OSC_CW, which are the control words for each of the two oscillators. These control words are fundamentally different from the other data in the address memory: With the other data, the number from the address memory specifies the location of a 24-bit integer in the data memory that is used as the input to the oscillator; whereas with the control word, it is the actual 8-bit address byte from the address register that is used as a control word, and not the contents of the data memory at that address. It is a kind of "immediate" mode datum. This is a design choice, not an error, in that otherwise it would require another memory, or space in the data memory, to hold this control information. Using the address memory for "immediate" data is a reasonable economizing decision for this kind of machine.

The way the control word is decoded and the coding of the wavetable are a bit tricky. The right-hand 5 bits of the control word specify a number from 0 to 37 (octal) that determines the partitioning of the wavetable. This is summarized in table 17.1. A particular "part" is distributed as follows: For 16 Kword units, the partitioning is simple in that the single 16 Kword block is contiguous. The 14 high-order bits of the data become exactly the 14 high-order bits of the address. For any smaller division, a certain number of low-order bits are replaced by the part number from the low-order bits of the control word. For instance, with the 8 Kword table, the high-order 13 bits of data are sent directly to the high-order 13 bits of the table address and the low-order (the 14th) bit comes from the low-order bit of the control word. With 4 Kword tables, it takes the high-order 12 bits from the data and the low-order 2 bits from the control word, and so on. This gives the logical division as described above. The only time this detail makes itself evident for the user is when loading this table from the PDP-11. For example, if you decide to divide the table into four parts of 4 Kword samples each, then the samples of each part will be interleaved. This means that the first four samples in the 16 Kword table will be the first sample of each of the four parts in order. The next four samples will be the second four samples of the four parts, in order, and so on. This gets a bit more confusing when you use mixed table sizes—for example, one part of 8 Kword and two parts of 4 Kword—but the machine is perfectly capable of doing it.

Since the wavetable control word has only the low-order 5 bits occupied, one might ask what the high-order 3 bits do. We will get to this later: they control the enabling of the envelope generators and the timer interrupts.

The wavetable is 16 bits wide, and these 16 bits are read into the two high-order bytes of the 24-bit word. Since the wavetable just takes a word from the data memory to address it, you can use it for transformations, such as nonlinear distortion or waveshaping synthesis (LeBrun 1979), as well as for simple oscillators.

Table 17.1
Decoding of the control words (A_OSC_CW and B_OSC_CW) for wavetable
segment (part) selection. Note that the B_OSC_CW has only the low-order 4 bits
available, thus forcing all the B-oscillator tables to be 2Kword samples or longer.

Code	Length	Part	Comment
0	16K	1	Only one possible part so the second code here is redundant.
1	16K	1	
2	8K	1	Parts are actually interleaved on a 1Kword basis.
3	8K	2	
4	4K	1	For 4Kwords, this can be computed as follows:
5	4K	2	Code = 16/(length in Kwords) + part − 1.
6	4K	3	
7	4K	4	
10	2K	1	
11	2K	2	
12	2K	3	
13	2K	4	
14	2K	5	
15	2K	6	
16	2K	7	
17	2K	8	
20	1K	1	
21	1K	2	
22	1K	3	
23	1K	4	
24	1K	5	
25	1K	6	
26	1K	7	
27	1K	8	
30	1K	9	
31	1K	10	
32	1K	11	
33	1K	12	
34	1K	13	
35	1K	14	
36	1K	15	
37	1K	16	

Envelope Generators

There are 32 envelope generators. It is actually something of a misnomer to call them envelope generators, since they do many different things. DiGiugno suggests the term "logic unit," but we will stick with "envelope generator" here just for maximum confusion value. Each has two different parts. One part is a linear ramp generator with inputs CUR, INC, and FIN, and with an output NEW. The idea is that CUR is the current value of the ramp, INC is the increment that is added to the current value, and FIN is the final value. There is logic that tests the signs of these numbers both before and after updating the ramp value such that when the current value reaches the final value, the final value is gated directly into the new value so that it will never go beyond the final value. The logic is clever enough to know about positive and negative slopes and about positive and negative values. It is presented in table 17.2. A plus sign in this table means greater than or equal to zero, minus means strictly negative, and X means "don't care," that is, either + or −.

This logic can be used to do things like max and min functions, thresholding, clipping, and other nonlinear functions. For instance, one can point the INC input to zero (a "positive" number), and the output will then be the minimum value of the CUR and FIN inputs. Likewise, if you set INC to a very small negative number ($-\varepsilon$, for instance), the output will be the maximum of CUR and FIN. If you are doing regular breakpoint envelopes, you set INC, CUR and FIN to what their names imply. The envelope generator will add INC to CUR and if it goes past FIN, will just produce FIN. The decision table is set so that you can use the entire range of numbers on the machine with no difficulty. Please note that this implies that there is a correct order in which to set these things. If your envelope has come to a breakpoint and you are about to give it new INC and FIN values you should give it the INC first and then the FIN, because if you give it the FIN first it might just try to jump immediately to that final value, thinking that it was already done.

The other side of the envelope generator is another multiply-accumulate part. It takes the current value as one input to the multiplier, and an input called SCALE for the second input. The product is then added to the OFFSET input and the sum is put out as OUT_ENV. This makes one complete envelope generator. You can either use the envelope directly and stuff the output of an oscillator into SCALE and use OFFSET to add it into, say, the channel 1 output stream; or you can use the SCALE

Table 17.2.
Decision table for the envelope generator ramp. CUR is the current envelope amplitude. INC is the increment applied to the current value. FIN is the final value of the ramp. FIN-NEW is the difference between the final and the new value. NEW is the tentative value of the envelope. The value actually used for the amplitude of the envelope is either the new value or the final value, as determined by this table. This allows not only the common use of an upgoing or downgoing ramp such that it will "hang" at the final value, but also provides such logical functions as max or min. A plus sign in this table means greater than or equal to zero; minus means strictly negative. X means "don't care," that is, either + or −.

CUR	INC	FIN	FIN-NEW	NEW	Action
+	+	+	+	+	Output NEW value
+	+	+	+	−	Output FINAL value
+	+	+	−	×	Output FINAL value
+	+	−	×	×	Output FINAL value
+	−	+	+	×	Output FINAL value
+	−	+	−	+	Output NEW value
+	−	+	−	−	Output FINAL value
+	−	−	+	+	Output NEW value
+	−	−	+	−	Output FINAL value
+	−	−	−	×	Output NEW value
−	+	+	+	×	Output NEW value
−	+	+	−	+	Output FINAL value
−	+	+	−	−	Output NEW value
−	+	−	+	+	Output FINAL value
−	+	−	+	−	Output NEW value
−	+	−	−	×	Output FINAL value
−	−	+	×	×	Output FINAL value
−	−	−	+	×	Output FINAL value
−	−	−	−	+	Output FINAL value
−	−	−	−	−	Output NEW value

and OFFSET inputs to scale the envelope and then use a separate multiply-accumulate unit to multiply it by the oscillator signal.

This is where one of the high-order bits of the control word A comes in. Bit 5 ('40) controls whether the accumulator takes the output of the multiplier or the new value of the envelope generator. Thus you can bypass the multiplier and accumulate (or offset) the envelope value directly. A zero in this bit selects the new envelope value, and a one in this bit selects the multiplier output (note that this is in the A control word only).

Timers

There are 32 timers available on the 4C machine. A timer just counts down the high-order 16 bits of a data memory word and can produce an interrupt when the result goes negative. One timer works on each minicycle. Each timer has associated with it two data memory addresses that determine the read word and the write word. Every four milliseconds, all 32 timers are decremented by '400 (the timer is considered to be just the high-order 16 bits of the word) and the result is stored into the write word. If the subtraction causes the sign of the result to be negative, something will happen depending on the high-order 2 bits of the A-oscillator control word, A_OSC_CW. The high-order bit ('200 bit, PI_ENB) says to cause an interrupt at the first negative result. The next bit ('100 bit, FIFO_PUSH) causes the timer number (which is its mini-cycle number, 0 to 31) to be pushed onto the timer first-in-first-out (FIFO). The FIFO also maintains two bytes, accessible to the PDP-11 program, that represent the number of entries in the FIFO (FICOUNT) and an indirect cell that gets you successive FIFO entries (FIDATA). The FIFO itself is the last 32 words of the data memory, using the low-order 8 bits of each 24-bit word. Note that this means that if you intend to use the FIFO, you must not use those high-order 32 words for internal patching. The PDP-11 can read the contents of the FIFO by doing successive reads from the FIDATA word, which automatically increments, such that each read gets you the next timer number that underflowed. The number of such entries is in the FICOUNT word. After you service as many FIFO entries as you wish (presumably all of them), then you must reset the FIFO pointers. You do this by issuing any write operation on the count byte. This has the effect of clearing unconditionally both the count and the data byte.

Since the FIFO only uses the low-order 16 bits, the high-order 16 bits are available for general use, but one must be careful not to clobber the low-order 8 bits. For instance, the PDP-11 can write in the high-order 16 bits and the low-order 8 bits separately, so these last 32 words in the data memory could be loaded by the PDP-11 with constants that are used in multiplications, since the multiply just takes the high-order 16 bits. We must also mention that if, on a given major cycle, a large number of counts go negative, and interrupts are enabled on each of these timers, only one interrupt is immediately produced. We do not get one interrupt for each timer that fires, but rather one single interrupt that directs the attention of the PDP-11 to the fact that there is something in the FIFO it should look at.

At this point, let us describe the extra functions in the B-oscillator control word (B_OSC_CW). The low-order 4 bits are for wavetable selection just as in the A-oscillator control word. The high-order 4 bits, however, have other uses, which differ on the various 4C machines around. For instance, the "standard" configuration has the high-order 4 bits controlling the DAC output triggering. The bits are decoded as follows:

Bit 4	'20	DAC 1 out
Bit 5	'40	DAC 2 out
Bit 6	'100	DAC 3 out
Bit 7	'200	DAC 4 out

Eastty's modification to the PDP-11/34 4C machine, on the other hand, uses only the high-order 3 bits. These high-order 3 bits are decoded as a 3-bit number as follows:

0	no-op
1	ADC in (two-cycle overlap)
2	DMA input (two-cycle overlap)
3	DMA output
4	DAC 1 out
5	DAC 2 out
6	DAC 3 out
7	DAC 4 out

This two-cycle business goes as follows: normally, there is a micro-cycle for DAC output, called DATA_OUT (see the next section on microcycle timing). For input, however, the data is not really there yet, so an input operation (codes 1 and 2 above) does not take place on this minicycle, but on the next minicycle. It uses the data memory address in the DATA_ OUT timing position into which to write the appropriate data. Note that it takes three cycles to do an input followed by an output: two for the input (the first to trigger it, the second to do the data memory write) and one for the output. Note also that you can send more than one sample to a DAC in a major cycle. Unless you know what you are doing, this can result in certain forms of astonishment. For example, you can double the effective sampling rate to the DAC by issuing a DAC write on minicycle N and on minicycle $N + 16$, which splits are major cycle in two. Likewise, you can increase the effective sampling rate by any power of 2 up to 32. Depending on what DACs are connected to the machine, one may not be able to actually do the conversion to analog at the very high sampling rates, but nonetheless, the 4C can deliver the samples to the converters at these rates. On the IRCAM PDP-11/34 system, we have attached two DMA channels for transfer of sampled data between the PDP-11 and the 4C machine.

Minicycle Timing

The timing for a single minicycle is shown in table 17.3. The number on the left is the microcycle number within the minicycle; this is actually a key to what the addresses in the address memory are. For example, on the very first minicycle, the first 32 microcycles will use the first 32 addresses in the address memory, and these will be decoded in the manner described above: some used as read addresses, some used as write addresses, and some used as oscillator control words. On the next minicycle, the second 32 addresses in the address memory will be used, but their meanings will be the same as described above. Note that in all cases except the envelope scale input, the inputs are read and the output appears a few microcycles later. This means that if you wish to use a piece of data, you will want to reference it some time after it has been written. If you reference it before it has been written, you will get the value for the last sample (major cycle), which means that that word in the data memory has been occupied for an entire major cycle (and you better not have clobbered it by writing into it with another unit). Since data memory locations are at a premium, you will want to reuse every interconnection cell as soon as possible; you will want, for instance, to put the unit that

Table 17.3
Microcycle ordering within a minicyclè. The microcycle number corresponds
exactly to the low-order 5 bits of address for the address memory. The high-order
5 bits are just the minicycle number. Notice also the effect of the pipelining: the
phase update for oscillator bank A, for instance, occurs on cycle 15, after the reads
for the A-bank multiplier input. Note that the PDP-11 cycle (3) and the FIFO
write cycle (29) do not use the address memory. These registers can be used as
extra storage by the PDP-11, since their contents do not affect the functioning of
the machine.

Number	Function	Read/Write	Comment
0	CUR	READ	Envelope current value
1	INC	READ	Envelope increment
2	FIN	READ	Envelope final value
3	PDP-11	READ/WRITE	PDP-11 gets its chance here (address ignored)
4	A_OSC_CW	READ	Oscillator A control word
5	OFFSET	READ	Envelope offset (after scale)
6	NEW	WRITE	Envelope new value
7	B_OSC_CW	READ	Oscillator B control word
8	DATA_OUT	READ	DAC output word
9	OUT_ENV	WRITE	Envelope output, scaled and offset
10	PHA	READ	Oscillator A current angle
11	F1A	READ	Oscillator A frequency (increment)
12	F2A	READ	Oscillator A FM input
13	M1A	READ	Multiplier A first input
14	M2A	READ	Multiplier A second input
15	PHA_OUT	WRITE	Oscillator A new angle
16	PHB	READ	Oscillator B current angle
17	F1B	READ	Oscillator B frequency (increment)
18	F2B	READ	Oscillator B FM input
19	IN_MUL_A	READ	Multiplier A accumulator input
20	PHB_OUT	WRITE	Oscillator B new angle
21	OUT_OSC_A	WRITE	Oscillator A wavetable output
22	M1B	READ	Multiplier B first input
23	M2B	READ	Multiplier B second input
24	OUT_MUL_A	WRITE	Multiplier A output
25	TIM	READ	Timer count input

Table 17.3 (*continued*)

Number	Function	Read/Write	Comment
26	IN_MUL_B	READ	Multiplier B accumulator input
27	TIM_OUT	WRITE	Timer count output
28	OUT_OSC_B	WRITE	Oscillator B wavetable output
29	FIFO	WRITE	FIFO write cycle (address ignored)
30	OUT_MUL_B	WRITE	Multiplier B accumulated output
31	SCALE	READ	Envelope scale input (for next minicycle)

uses the data memory location on the following minicycle so that the data memory location is occupied for the minimum amount of time. Note that the FIFO uses built-in addresses, so the number you put in the address memory for the FIFO cycle will be ignored. This is also true of the PDP-11 time slot, since the PDP-11 delivers its own address data directly to the machine.

The importance of table 17.3 for the reader lies not so much in the details it provides of the function of each cycle, but rather in the way it shows that the location of the various address bytes in the address memory is determined uniquely by the minicycle number and the microcycle number. When programming the machine, you know, for instance, that address memory locations $32*N + 10$ where N is between 0 and 31 (inclusive) will be the address in the data memory for the phase data for an A-bank oscillator. (Note that even though this memory consists of 8-bit bytes, they are addressed from the PDP-11 as the low-order byte of the 16-bit word. Since the PDP-11 is byte-addressed, the above formula must be doubled.)

Memory Management

The 4C machine occupies exactly 1 Kword of the PDP-11 address space. Since the internal memory is somewhat larger than that, one might well ask how the PDP-11 gets at all the various registers. The answer is that it does so 1,024 words at a time. You write a code byte into the memory management register, which determines which 1 Kword block will be in the PDP-11's address space. The coding of this byte is shown in table 17.4.

Table 17.4
Decoding of the memory management register. The PDP-11 has a 1Kword "window" into the internal memory of the 4C machine. The 6 bits in the register determine which 1Kwords of the various internal memories will be "on-line" on the UNIBUS.

Code	Meaning	Comment
0	Data memory	A MOV gets the high-order 16 bits, a MOVB to addr + 1 gets the low-order 8 bits.
20	Address memory	Bytes in the memory correspond directly to PDP-11 words.
40	Wavetable, 1st 1K block	Remember the interleaving on 1 Kword,
41	Wavetable, 2nd 1K block	2 Kword, 4 Kword, and 8 Kword table
42	Wavetable, 3rd 1K block	sizes. These addresses are physical, not
43	Wavetable, 4th 1K block	logical, memory.
44	Wavetable, 5th 1K block	
45	Wavetable, 6th 1K block	
46	Wavetable, 7th 1K block	
47	Wavetable, 8th 1K block	
50	Wavetable, 9th 1K block	
51	Wavetable, 10th 1K block	
52	Wavetable, 11th 1K block	
53	Wavetable, 12th 1K block	
54	Wavetable, 13th 1K block	
55	Wavetable, 14th 1K block	
56	Wavetable, 15th 1K block	
57	Wavetable, 16th 1K block	

Programming

The process of programming this machine consists of giving the read and write addresses of the functional unit parameters in the data memory, setting the oscillator control words to the desired functions, and loading the wavetable with the functions needed. Run-time support must include taking timer interrupts to start and stop notes, as well as to feed the breakpoints of piecewise-linear functions into the envelope generators one point at a time. One makes an instrument definition, for example, by putting a frequency and initial phase angle into the data memory and setting the oscillator input addresses to read from those words in the data memory. The output of the oscillator can then be deposited anywhere in the data memory. This data can subsequently be read by any other functional unit, such as the DAC port, an envelope generator, or an adder (to add several oscillators together). For more details on a language to control the 4C, see Abbott 1981.

Here we might mention something else about sampling rate. To some, the limitation of 16 kHz may seem a bit restricting. The point is that the machine is actually capable of mixed sampling rates internally. To run the machine at, say, twice the basic rate, you just reproduce the first 512 bytes of the program (entries in the address memory) in the last 512 bytes of the address memory. This causes the same program to be run twice in one major cycle, thus achieving a doubling of the sampling rate. It is thus clear that one need not duplicate all the modules in this fashion. One can have, for instance, a filter running at 32 kHz, which means that there will be two instances of the calculation for the filter during the major cycle, but an envelope for this filter might be simultaneously running at 16 kHz by having only one instance of the envelope calculation in the major cycle. This way, key paths can be made to run at the 32-kHz rate necessary for high quality, and other paths (vibrato, envelopes, etc.) can run at the lower 16-kHz rate to conserve units.

Inside

Figure 17.4 shows the major elements that constitute the machine. There are three independent memories: the data memory, the address memory (marked CW memory in the figure), and the wavetable memory (marked Wavetable MEM). The arithmetic is performed by the TRW multiplier (marked X) and the arithmetic and logic unit (ALU) in the center of the drawing. The pipelining is done by the multitudes of registers scattered around the drawing. The main data path is from the data memory into either the ALU or the multiplier, then from their outputs back to the data memory. The wavetable memory (and the PDP-11, of course) may also write into the data memory. All sequencing is controlled by a series of microcode ROMs that are addressed largely by various bits of the microcycle counter (not shown explicitly in the figure). Extra paths exist throughout the machine to allow PDP-11 access to each of the memories. The wavetable address mapping is done by a memory (labeled MEM) that interprets the control word from the address memory and the high-order bits from the data memory to produce the wavetable address. The PDP-11 address bypasses this memory. The microcycle proceeds at 62.5 nanoseconds with no further subdivisions. A series of delay units of 5 nano-

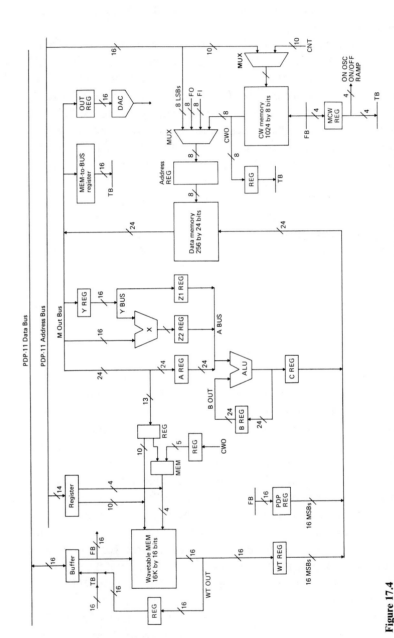

Figure 17.4
Physical block diagram of the 4C machine. TB and FB go to and from the PDP-11 UNIBUS, respectively. MCW is the master control word. FI and FO are the FIFO address counters. CWO is the 8-bit datum from the address memory (here labeled CW memory). All units are assumed to be connected to microcode ROMs, which are not shown. These ROMS are addressed by the microcycle count, CNT. Any place where the outputs of many registers are connected together implies that they have tri-state outputs.

seconds each produces various different phases of the clock that are used to adjust the timing.

Conclusions

The 4C machine is a one-board digital processing device capable of realizing certain of the operations useful for music synthesis. These include 64 oscillators with up to 16 different waveforms at any given time, 32 envelopes, and various other timing and control functions. All the internal address and data registers are in the address space of the PDP-11 and can be written and read asynchronously with the functioning of the machine. The machine is one of a series of sound-processing devices developed and realized at IRCAM. One implementation of this machine at IRCAM is endowed with analog input and the ability to read and write sample data in the memory of the PDP-11. It must be emphasized that the machine by itself can only be considered a component of a system—it requires at the least a computer to run it and a set of DACs for sound output. The utility can be further increased by the addition of some kind of user controls, such as knobs, slide pots, or an organ keyboard, but these things are not part of the 4C machine itself.

Acknowledgments

The *4n* series of sound processors was designed largely by G. diGiugno. The early machines, including the prototype 4C, were constructed entirely by Alain Chauveau at IRCAM. This work was made possible by the visionary guidance of Luciano Berio. Since the 4C machine came to life, Didier Roncin has been charged with the construction of several other replicas. Peter Eastty wrote programs to produce wire-wrap tapes for semi-automated construction of these machines and later modified the PDP-11/34 machine for real-time analog input and digital recording applications. Software for the machine was written by Curtis Abbott, Jim Lawson, and Jean Kott, and was extensively tested by Tod Machover. James A. Moorer did virtually nothing in this project except get into trouble and write this article.

All of this would not have been possible without the support of Pierre Boulez and IRCAM. This support is gratefully acknowledged.

References

Abbott, C. 1981. "The 4CED program." *Computer Music Journal* 5(1): 13–33.

Alles, H. G., and G. diGiugno. 1977. "The 4B: A one-card 64-channel digital synthesizer." *Computer Music Journal* 1(4): 7–9. Article 15 in this volume.

Asta, V., A. Chauveau, G. diGiugno, and J. Kott. 1980. "The real-time digital synthesis system 4X." *Automazione e Strumentazione* 27(2): 119–133.

LeBrun, M. 1979. "Digital waveshaping synthesis." *Journal of the Audio Engineering Society* 27(4): 250–266.

Moorer, J. A. 1981. "Synthesizers I have known and loved." *Computer Music Journal* 5(1): 4–12.

Rolnick, N. 1978. "A composer's notes on the development and implementation of software for a digital synthesizer." *Computer Music Journal* 2(2): 13–22. Article 25 in this volume.

18 Use of High-Speed Microprocessors for Digital Synthesis

JEAN-FRANÇOIS ALLOUIS

A processor specialized for the synthesis and processing of sound signals, realized with bipolar bit-slice microprocessors, has been studied in the music department of the Institut National de l'Audiovisuel (INA), within a project aiming at the development of digital systems for sound processing with real-time control (SYTER Project). A prototype has been built with the help of Denis Valette. The main characteristic of this processor is that it is completely programmable, which makes it possible to use many existing methods of synthesis or to adapt it to new methods without modifying the hardware. Three other points have also been crucial for the conception of the processor: the possibility of directly treating sounds sampled by an analog-to-digital converter; the possibility of connecting several units in a multiprocessor structure to multiply the capacity for treatment; and a simple interface with the control system. All the data controlling the functioning of the processor are stored in a dual-port memory that can be used as a main memory block by a host microprocessor or minicomputer.

General Structure

Fundamentally, the SYTER digital processor is a microprogrammable 16-bit machine. There are two data paths, A and B (figure 18.1). The arithmetic and logic unit (ALU) is composed of 16 general-purpose registers accessible to the user, while multiplications in the system are carried out by a 16-bit multiplier (TRW MPY-16). Special shift circuits for the multiplier and the random-access memory (RAM) have been constructed for the manipulation of the fixed-size function tables (of 64 words at present). Intermediate (pipeline) registers (not on the figure) allow the simultaneous execution of several elementary operations.

Instruction Set

There are three general modes of memory addressing—immediate, direct, and indexed by a general-purpose register—plus a special mode allowing the use of a 64-word array beginning at an address multiple of 64. Every

This is a revised and updated version of an article that originally appeared in *Computer Music Journal* 3(1): 14–16, 1979.

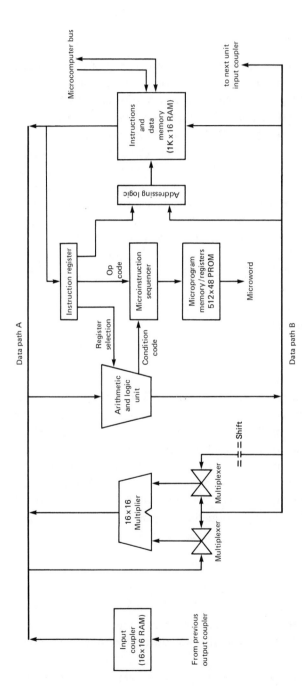

Figure 18.1
General structure of the SYTER processor, showing the bus arrangement and functional devices.

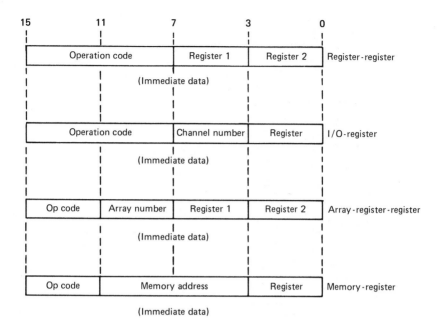

Figure 18.2
Instruction formats for SYTER.

instruction is coded on a 16-bit word divided into four fields of four bits each with four possible formats (figure 18.2).

The instruction set (figure 18.3), which was realized by microprogramming, includes a minimal set of "classical" instructions similar to those of a microcomputer—arithmetical and logical instructions, transfers, and so on—and special instructions designed for signal processing. This instruction set also allows for experimentation with various synthesis methods before later translating the corresponding instructions into microcode for faster execution.

Control of the Processing

Access to the main memory is realized by an external bus. This access is transparent and does not affect the functioning of the processor. The basic sampling rate is programmable and corresponds to an execution range going from 32 to 256 microcycles, that is to say, at present: 20 kHz $\leqslant$ $S \leqslant$ 160 kHz.

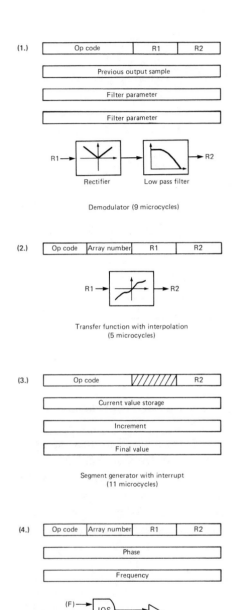

(1.)

Op code	R1	R2

Previous output sample

Filter parameter

Filter parameter

R1 → Rectifier → Low pass filter → R2

Demodulator (9 microcycles)

(2.)

Op code	Array number	R1	R2

R1 → (transfer function) → R2

Transfer function with interpolation
(5 microcycles)

(3.)

Op code	/////////	R2

Current value storage

Increment

Final value

Segment generator with interrupt
(11 microcycles)

(4.)

Op code	Array number	R1	R2

Phase

Frequency

(F) → IOS
R1 → IOS → + → R2
R2 →

Interpolation oscillator (8 microcycles)

Figure 18.3
Some synthesis instructions.

At the beginning of each cycle, control is transferred to an address among 16 stored at the beginning of the memory (figure 18.4). Thus, certain control subsequences can be executed at frequencies that are a multiple of $S/16$ (envelope generation, for example). Moreover, the connecting instructions can—if required—transfer control to certain instruction sequences co-resident in the memory, which makes high-speed commutation of several synthesis programs possible. The execution of an instruction may set a flag, thus sending an interrupt request to the external bus. The address of the instruction is then stored in the first word of the memory and further requests are masked until this word is demanded by the external control system.

Present Realization

The prototype includes 120 integrated circuits distributed on three cards. The basic cycle is 200 nanoseconds, which allows, for example, the realization of 16 randomly connected linear interpolation oscillators and the corresponding envelope controls (sampling rate: 30 kHz) (figure 18.5). The experimental system (figure 18.6) includes a Motorola 6800 microprocessor, which controls a chain composed of an analog-to-digital converter multiplexed on four channels, one or several synthesis processors, and four 16-bit digital-to-analog converters (figure 18.7).

Possible Extensions

The accuracy of 16 bits in fixed-point arithmetic seems sufficient for most cases, except for complex filter realizations. Although it is possible to make calculations in double precision, the resulting drop in performance seems generally prohibitive. The calculation power of the processor is mainly limited by the speed of the bipolar microprocessors (AMD 2901). If we work with more recent versions of the 2901, it seems possible to multiply this power by a factor of almost 2.

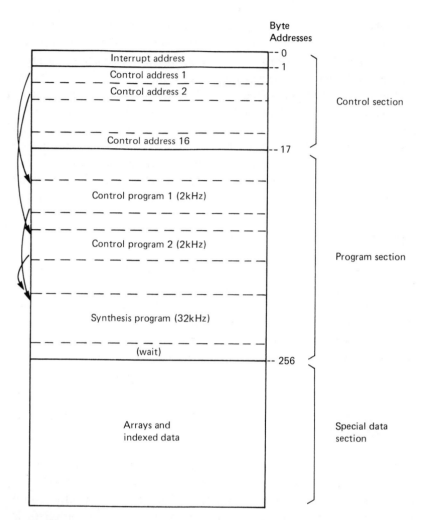

Figure 18.4
Memory map example, showing the flow of control from one section to another.

Figure 18.5
The interior of the SYTER processor, showing, from left to right: the analog-to-digital converter card; the three cards constituting the synthesis unit; the digital-to-analog converter card; two cards for the control microprocessor; and a card for generating clock signals.

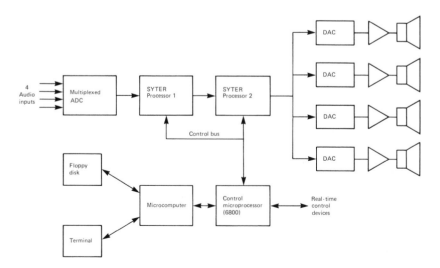

Figure 18.6
Schematic of the experimental SYTER system.

Figure 18.7
The complete SYTER system at the Group de récherches musicales/Institut national de
l'audiovisuel (GRM/INA) studio.

19 Design of a Digital Oscillator That Will Generate up to 256 Low-Distortion Sine Waves in Real Time

JOHN SNELL

In experimenting with nontraditional tone colors or timbres it is instructive to determine which parameters of sound need to be controlled in order to generate sounds which could come from acoustic musical instruments. Once these parameters are determined, they may be played with or varied to produce nontraditional sounds that are just as interesting in timbre as the sounds from acoustic musical instruments.

The sine wave illustrated in figure 19.1 is the most pure or simple sound. Theoretically, any sound may be generated by adding together a number of sinusoidal components (cosine or sine waves) for which the amplitude and frequency may be independently varied. Using additive synthesis, tones have been synthesized from the analysis data of the partials of acoustic instruments that are "indistinguishable numerically, theoretically, and perceptually from the original" (Moorer 1976).

A partial is a harmonic if it has a frequency that is equal to the fundamental frequency (usually related to the pitch) multiplied by an integer (1, 2, 3, 4, 5, ...). Partials may be inharmonic if their frequency equals the fundamental frequency multiplied by a noninteger, such as 2.31. Backus (1969, p. 96) adds some useful information here: "The term 'overtone' has frequently been used in reference to complex tones, such a tone being described as consisting of a fundamental and its overtones. This introduces a certain amount of confusion; in the sound produced by the vibrating string, the first overtone is the second harmonic. Similarly, in the sound produced by the closed tube, where the second harmonic is missing, the first overtone is the third harmonic. Because of this unnecessary confusion, it is best not to use the term 'overtone' at all—especially since we do not need it." A translator's footnote in Helmholtz 1863 (p. 25) states: "The term 'second harmonic' will always refer to a partial whose frequency is precisely twice that of the fundamental; this partial may or may not be present in a tone, but there is no ambiguity."

The partials are often found to be slightly inharmonic. Even the frequency of each partial varies within one single tone or note from most acoustic instruments. 256 sinusoidal components might be utilized in generating 16 voices or instruments, each having 16 partials. A large

This is a revised and updated version of an article that originally appeared in *Computer Music Journal* 1(2): 4–25, 1977.

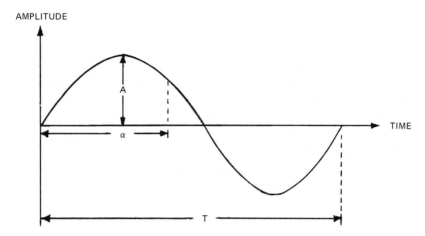

Figure 19.1
Representation of one cycle of a sine wave, where T is the period (the time for one 360°
cycle to occur); $F (= 1/T)$ is the frequency in hertz, and is related to the pitch of the sine
wave; A is the amplitude, which is related to the loudness of the sine wave; and α is the
phase angle. The sine wave may be generated by continuously evaluating $\sin(\alpha)$ for a
phase angle α increasing continuously and linearly in time.

number of sinusoidal components is also useful in generating choral
cloudlike tone clusters or tone fields somewhat like the music that György
Ligeti has often produced with a traditional orchestra (in, for example,
his *Atmospheres*).

Let's look at a method for generating one low-distortion sine wave
(or any waveshape). Then it will be found that one digital oscillator may
be used to generate a large number of sinusoidal components with
independently variable frequencies and independently variable amplitudes. This oscillator will also perform frequency-modulation (FM)
synthesis (Chowning 1973) with multiple modulators and/or carriers. A
sine/cosine generator is basic to many of the equations for timbre synthesis, such as those briefly discussed in Moorer 1977.

A sine wave may be represented digitally as a series of pulses or steps,
as shown in figure 19.2. If the steps or changes in pulse amplitudes are
made infinitely small, a smooth analog waveshape will result. The steps
should be made small enough so that the ear is incapable of hearing the
difference between a smooth analog waveshape and the digital waveshape.
Thus there will be no audible distortion or noise. Each of these steps is a
pulse whose amplitude may be represented by a number in a computer.

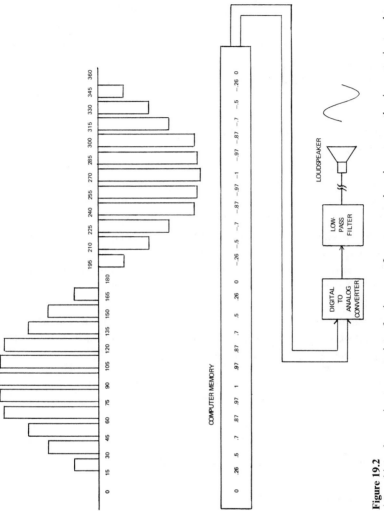

Figure 19.2
A graphic and numeric representation of a sine wave. In a computer's main memory, the sine wave is stored as a series of numbers that are read sequentially and sent through a DAC and a low-pass filter to produce electrical voltages that drive loudspeakers.

If one cycle of a digitized waveform is stored in computer memory (called the waveform memory), the numerical values of the pulse amplitudes may be read out by repeatedly incrementing the memory address (which corresponds to the phase angle). When the end of the waveform cycle is reached, the memory address will jump back to the beginning of the waveform memory. In other words, every time the phase angle (memory address) is incremented to a value greater than or equal to 360°, 360° will be subtracted from the phase angle. Then the phase angle will continue to be incremented as before. If this waveform memory output is fed to a digital-to-analog converter (DAC) followed by a smoothing filter, amplifier, and loudspeaker, a continuous sine wave will be heard. (To avoid a noisy output, the DAC is first followed by a sample and hold device or a track or ground switch. This will eliminate the spikes ("glitches") that may occur when the input of the DAC is changed.) The DAC changes the numbers into pulses whose amplitudes are controlled by the numbers read out of the waveform memory. The smoothing filter (low-pass filter) rounds off the pulses so that a continuous waveform results as shown in figure 19.2.

The frequency of the output waveform will be equal to the rate at which these pulses are generated (called the sample rate) divided by the number of pulses in one waveform cycle or period (Mathews 1969):

$$\text{frequency (Hz)} = \frac{\text{sample rate}}{\text{samples/waveform cycle}}.$$

One can see that the units check:

$$\text{frequency} = \frac{\text{samples/second}}{\text{samples/cycle}} = \text{cycles/second}.$$

As mentioned earlier, each of the numbers in the waveform memory has an address that corresponds to a phase angle α. Thus, if a particular address α is given, the memory will output the number $\sin(\alpha)$ contained at that address.

The sample rate is crystal-controlled for ultrastable tuning and is constant. If every number in the waveform memory is generated one after another at this constant sample rate, the frequency of the sine wave will be constant. This would result from incrementing the address of the waveshape memory by 1. If a higher frequency is desired, the address (phase angle) may be incremented by a larger number. If a lower frequency

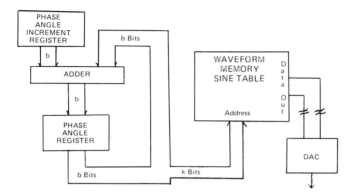

Figure 19.3
Schematic for reading a sine wave from a waveform memory with special hardware for
incrementing the phase.

is desired, the address may be incremented by a smaller number. The
phase angle is truncated to form the address for the waveform memory
as illustrated in figure 19.3. The phase angle increment register holds the
value of the increment to the phase angle. This phase angle increment
will be added to the phase angle once for each sample of the sine wave.
When the address is near the end of the waveform memory (360°), an
increment may be added that will overflow the phase angle register, thus
placing the address back at the beginning of the waveform cycle. This is
equivalent to subtracting 360° from the phase angle every time it is
incremented to a value greater than or equal to 360°.

Sampling Theory

At first glance, one might think that this technique would result in a large
amount of distortion if the phase angle increment were as large as 180°.
This would result in a frequency of half of the sample rate. With this
phase angle increment value, only two pulses would be generated per
waveform cycle. It can be shown mathematically (Carlson 1968) that if a
signal contains only frequency components whose absolute values are
less than some maximum frequency F_{max}, the signal may be completely
described by the instantaneous sample values uniformly spaced in time
with period $T_S \leqslant 1/2F_{max}$. If S is the sample rate, the sample period is
$T_S = 1/S$. Alternatively, the Nyquist sampling theorem states that if a

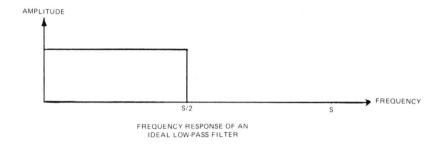

FREQUENCY RESPONSE OF AN
IDEAL LOW-PASS FILTER

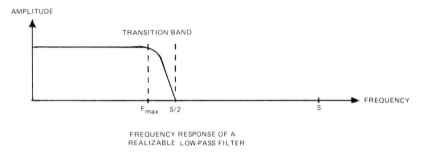

FREQUENCY RESPONSE OF A
REALIZABLE LOW-PASS FILTER

Figure 19.4
Frequency responses of low-pass filters: (a) ideal low-pass filter, (b) realizable low-pass
filter.

signal has been sampled at the Nyquist rate of $2F_{max}$ or greater $(S \geqslant 2F_{max})$, and the sample values are periodic weighted impulses, the signal can be exactly reconstructed from its samples by an ideal low-pass filter of bandwidth B where $F_{max} \leqslant B \leqslant (S - F_{max})$.

Let's look at the problems that arise when we apply this theorem to generating sound. Any practical (nonideal) low-pass filter will require a transition band to go from unity gain to 0 gain as shown in figure 19.4. To avoid distortion, the maximum output frequency should be below this transition band. The maximum sinusoidal component frequency is usually limited to 36%–40% of the sampling rate $(F_{max} \leqslant 0.4S)$.

It might be noticed that realizable samples from the DAC will not be impulses; they will have finite pulse widths. If the pulse widths are as wide as the sampling period, the frequency response will be attenuated very little if at all for very low frequencies and attenuated up to 4 dB down, at frequencies which approach half of the sample rate. The reconstruction filter (low-pass filter) may be designed to compensate for this. A different reconstruction filter should be used for each sample rate anticipated.

The theorem states that the samples from the DAC should be uniformly spaced, so the sample period jitter should be minimized. If the sample period jitter error is to be 82.6 dB below the root-mean-squared (RMS) level of a sine wave, the sample period jitter should be less than $(1.18 * 10^{-5})/F$ where F is the output sine wave frequency. So if F is 10 kHz (10,000 cycles/sec), the sample period jitter should be less than 1.18 nanoseconds (a nanosecond is one billionth of a second). But listening with a good ear is the ultimate test of a sound synthesis technique. Some of the 16-bit linear pulse-code modulation (PCM) digital audio tape recorders have provided a convincing demonstration of the Nyquist theorem to audio applications.

Frequency Resolution

As mentioned earlier, the frequency of the output waveform is the sample rate divided by the number of samples in one period of the waveform:

$$\text{frequency} = \frac{\text{sample rate}}{\text{no. of samples/cycle}}.$$

The number of samples in one cycle of the sine wave is determined by the sine table length (number of words in waveform memory) divided by the phase angle increment:

$$\text{no. of samples/cycle} = \frac{\text{sine table length}}{\text{phase angle increment}}.$$

Substituting this expression for the number of samples per cycle into the above equation for frequency:

$$\text{frequency} = \text{sample rate} * \frac{\text{phase angle increment}}{\text{sine table length}}.$$

or

$$F = S(I/L). \tag{1}$$

The sample rate S and the sine table length L will be held constant, so the frequency F may be changed by changing the phase angle increment I.

The smallest increment in frequency (frequency resolution) will be determined by the number of bits b used in the phase angle increment register (see figure 19.3). The phase angle register should also contain this many b bits. Rakowski 1971 indicates that under ideal listening conditions a very discriminating ear is capable, at best, of noticing a pitch change of between approximately 0.03 Hz and 0.08 Hz around 160 Hz. To specify frequencies to an accuracy of 0.03 Hz would require 19.3 bits, plus a sign bit for FM synthesis (Chowning 1973) in the phase angle increment register if the maximum output frequency is 20,000 Hz, as determined from the following equations:

$$\frac{N_{max}}{N_{min}} = \frac{I_{max}}{I_{min}} \tag{2}$$

where

I_{max} = the maximum phase angle increment that will produce the maximum desirable frequency of any sinusoidal component (F_{max})

I_{min} = the minimum phase angle increment that will produce the minimum step or change in frequency (F_{min})

N_{max} = the maximum number expressible with b bits. For FM synthesis, positive as well as negative increments (or decrements) to the phase angle will be needed. An extra sign bit will be needed in any registers that handle frequency or phase angle information. So $N_{max} = 2^{(b-1)} - 1$.

N_{min} = the minimum number expressible with b bits = 1.

Equation 1 may be used to determine the phase angle increment I, in terms of the frequency F, sample rate S, and sine table length L:

$$I = (F/S)L.$$

This equation may be substituted into equation 2 for I_{max} and I_{min}:

$$\frac{N_{max}}{N_{min}} = \frac{(F_{max}/S)L}{(F_{min}/S)L} = \frac{F_{max}}{F_{min}}.$$

Then replacing N_{max} and N_{min} results in

$$\frac{2^{(b-1)} - 1}{1} = \frac{F_{max}}{F_{min}}. \tag{3}$$

Hence

$$b = 1 + \log_2 \left(\frac{F_{max}}{F_{min}} + 1 \right)$$

$$= 1 + 3.32 \log_{10} \left(\frac{F_{max}}{F_{min}} + 1 \right)$$

F_{max} may be set to 20 kHz. A minimum step in frequency of $F_{min} = 0.03$ Hz should be inaudible to most musicians. Substituting these values into the above equation, we get

$$b = 1 + 3.32 \log_{10} \left(\frac{20{,}000 \text{ Hz}}{0.03 \text{ Hz}} + 1 \right) = 20.3.$$

Thus a 21-bit phase angle increment register should be capable of generating a glissando or vibrato that will be perceived as smooth. Minimum changes in frequency should be inaudible as steps to a listener with very discriminating ears, even in an ideal listening environment. A computer may update the frequency (incrementing by 1 the phase angle register) at the right time intervals to generate as slow a change in frequency as is desired. Alternatively in hardware a 28-bit frequency envelope may be added to the phase angle increment. For musical purposes a 20-bit phase angle increment register should be fine, with the following possible exception: If the sound were played in a soundproof room to a listener who had an extremely discriminating ear, who had previously sat in silence for 15 minutes, and who listened specifically for steps in frequency in a slow glissando in the lower part of the audible frequency range, then the steps might just barely be noticed sometimes. Rakowski's tests were done under similar ideal conditions. He was looking for information would serve as a basis for speculations concerning the action of the hearing mechanism. Table 19.1 shows the resulting values of the minimum step in frequency for different values of the number of bits b in the phase angle increment register and for different maximum frequencies.

A musical interval is often measured in cents instead of as a step in hertz. A cent is $1/1{,}200$ of an octave, or $1/100$ of an equally tempered semitone in the chromatic scale. An interval or ratio of one semitone is equal to the twelfth root of 2.

1 semitone $= 2^{(1/12)}$

1 cent $= 2^{(1/1{,}200)}$

Table 19.1
Frequency resolution. This shows the resulting values of the minimum representable step in frequency F_{min} and the corresponding minimum representable interval (or tuning accuracy) C_{min} measured in cents around 65.4 Hz and 160 Hz, for different values of the number of bits b in the phase angle increment register and different maximum frequencies. 20 kHz was chosen as a F_{max} since it is the highest audible frequency for many people. 16,384 Hz was chosen since it is a power of 2; so the true frequency could be read directly from the phase angle increment for human comprehension. Any maximum frequency that is not a power of 2 will need a translation program to convert encoded values of phase angle increment to the true frequency value. For this reason 8,192 Hz and 4,096 Hz were also included. 15 kHz, 12.8 kHz, and 10 kHz were included as maximum frequencies since they correspond to 40% of the useful sample rates of 37,500 samples/sec, 32,000 samples/sec, and 25,000 samples/sec respectively.

			C_{min}	
			Around	Around
b	F_{max}	F_{min}	65.4 Hz	160 Hz
(bits)	(Hz)	(Hz)	(cents)	(cents)
21	20,000	0.019	0.5	0.2
20	20,000	0.038	1.0	0.4
19	20,000	0.076	2.0	0.8
18	20,000	0.15	4.0	1.65
17	20,000	0.31	8.1	3.3
16	20,000	0.61	16.1	6.6
20	16,384	0.031	0.83	0.34
18	16,384	0.125	3.3	1.35
16	16,384	0.50	13.2	5.4
20	15,000	0.029	0.76	0.31
18	15,000	0.114	3.03	1.24
16	15,000	0.46	12.1	4.94
20	12,800	0.024	0.65	0.26
18	12,800	0.098	2.58	1.06
16	12,800	0.39	10.3	4.2
20	10,000	0.019	0.51	0.21
18	10,000	0.076	2.02	0.83
16	10,000	0.305	8.1	3.3
20	8,192	0.016	0.4	0.17
18	8,192	0.063	1.65	0.68
16	8,192	0.25	6.6	2.7
20	4,096	0.008	0.2	0.09
18	4,096	0.031	0.8	0.34
16	4,096	0.125	3.3	1.4

A minimum interval (which is an indication of how accurately an instrument can be tuned) measured in cents C_{min} may be related to the minimum step F_{min} as follows:

$$F_{min} = F(2^{(C_{min}/1,200)}) - F$$

$$= F(2^{(C_{min}/1,200)} - 1)$$

where F = the frequency around which the minimum frequency step is made. Solving for C_{min}, we get

$$C_{min} = 1,200 \log_2 \left(\frac{F_{min}}{F} + 1 \right)$$

$$= 3,986.31 \log_{10} \left(\frac{F_{min}}{F} + 1 \right). \tag{5}$$

F_{min} may be determined from equation 3:

$$\frac{2^{(b-1)} - 1}{1} = \frac{F_{max}}{F_{min}}.$$

Hence

$$F_{min} = \frac{F_{max}}{2^{(b-1)} - 1}. \tag{6}$$

Substituting equation 6 into equation 5 results in

$$C_{min} = 3,986.31 \log_{10} \left(\frac{F_{max}}{F(2^{(b-1)} - 1)} + 1 \right). \tag{7}$$

A minimum frequency step (F_{min} of 0.038 Hz) around a frequency of 65.4 Hz is an interval or ratio of 1 cent. 65.4 Hz is the frequency of C_2 or the note C one octave above the lowest note C on a piano tuned to $A_4 = 440$ Hz in equal tempered tuning. This same step of 0.038 Hz around 160 Hz is an interval or ratio of 0.4 cents. 160 Hz is a little below the note E_3, which is in the octave below middle C on the same piano. Table 19.1 shows the resulting value of the minimum intervals or tuning accuracy measured in cents, C_{min}, around 65.4 Hz and 160 Hz for each different value of the number of bits b in the phase angle increment register and for different maximum frequencies.

Moore (1977a) points out that a *portamento* from 50 Hz to 100 Hz will not sound smooth if a 16-bit phase angle increment (frequency control) and phase angle are used with a Nyquist frequency (half of the sample rate) of 16,384 Hz. As an alternative to making both the phase angle increment and the phase angle be wider words, it is suggested to only make the phase angle register wider. Then the 16-bit phase angle increment may be shifted left or right for variable frequency resolution and range. This phase angle increment shifting technique is useful for controlling the oscillator with a small computer which can do 16-bit data word arithmetic and movement. Even the 8-bit microprocessors have the capability of performing 16-bit arithmetic. However, they are very slow when working with 16-bit data. A useful integrated circuit (IC) for implementing this shifting technique is the 8-bit position scaler made by Signetics, the 8243. It is expandable to handle wider word widths and is capable of shifting up to 7 bit positions at once instead of requiring 7 clock periods like a shift register. If this shifting technique is used, an arithmetic operation such as addition of a low frequency to a high frequency would first require shifting inside the computer to line up equally weighted bits. Once added, the frequencies might have to be shifted left or right before being sent to an output port. This would slow down the shipping of frequency control data to the oscillator.

However, in the oscillator I describe in this article, the control words are 20 bits wide. Thus, a 16- or 32-bit microcomputer is preferable as the host system.

Sine Table

The size of the waveform memory or sine table will affect the signal-to-noise ratio. If all 20 bits of the phase angle register were used to address the sine table, the sine table would be 1 million words long. Fortunately this is not needed. Fewer bits may be used to address the sine table without affecting the frequency resolution if the number of bits in the phase angle register and phase angle increment register is not reduced. If the 12 most significant bits of the phase angle register are used to address a 360° sine table (truncating the 8 least significant bits), $2^{12} = 4,096$ words of sine table memory would be needed. (For more details, see Moore 1977a.) If the address of the sine table memory is rounded off to 11 bits instead of truncating it to 12 bits, the table length may be reduced to $2^{11} = 2,048$ words while maintaining the same signal-to-noise ratio obtained by truncating the address to 12 bits. It is not worth the computation time to make an interpolating table for real-time operation. Some of the sine tables in university computer music software use 512 words with the interpolation technique. This corresponds to a signal-to-error noise ratio of 95.1 dB. For non-real-time operation, interpolation is very useful.

A listening test to determine the necessary size of the sine table was conducted at the Center for Computer Research in Music and Acoustics (CCRMA) at Stanford University. Different memory sizes were tried for the table in generating a low-frequency FM tone that was believed to be the worst case. A 4,096-word-by-12-bit/word table for 360° of a sine function was perceived to be just as distortion-free as a 65,536-word-by-16-bit/word table. However, a 1,024-word-by-10-bit/word table generated an objectionable amount of noise. The truncation method of addressing the sine table was used. The test indicates that if the round-off method of addressing is used, 2,048 words will be needed for a 360° sine wave with negligible distortion.

In examining one cycle of a sine wave, it may be noticed that the first half (0° up to 180°) of the cycle is identical to the second half except that the sign is changed. One may store only 180° of the sine function in the sine table and then change the sign of the output sine wave every time the waveform memory address is incremented to or past 180° (or decremented below 0°, as in FM synthesis). The sine function may be generated from only 90°; in my design, however, the control functions for incrementing (and decrementing) the phase angle with a 90° sine table required more ICs than are needed with a 180° sine table.

As shown in figure 19.5, the output of the sine table is fed into one data input of a multiplexer. The other multiplexer input is fed by the inverted output of the sine table. The most significant bit from the round-off adder is used to select the inverted or noninverted half of the sine wave, resulting in a sine wave with a positive half cycle and a negative half cycle. The addition of 1 to finish forming a twos-complement negative number was assumed to be insigificant and thus was not included.

The sine table size experiments at Stanford indicate that a 1,024-word-by-11-bit/word, 180° sine table memory will generate a negligible amount of distortion if round-off addressing is used. The phase angle may be rounded off by adding bit 8 of the phase angle to the 11-bit word formed by bits 9 through 19. As mentioned earlier, the most significant bit from this round-off addition is used to determine the sign of the sine wave. Bits

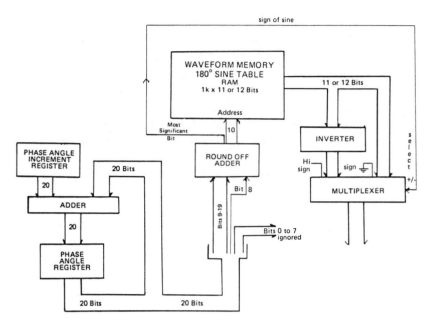

Figure 19.5
Hardware schematic for a digital oscillator circuit that automatically inverts the sine wave beyond 180°.

0 to 7 of the phase angle are ignored in addressing the sine table. However, the full 20-bit angle is used in calculating the phase angle so that accurate frequencies are generated.

Since fast random-access memory chips (RAMs) are less expensive than fast programmable read-only memory chips (PROMs), RAMs were chosen for the sine table. This also enables the sine table memory to be loaded with another waveshape if desired; however, I doubt this feature would be used because of the time multiplexing of the sine table. The generation of a few hundred sine waves is probably more useful than the generation of a few hundred of any other waveshape. The 180° sine table may be stored in three 1K-by-4-bit RAM ICs, such as the AMD (Advanced Micro Devices) 9135, or Intel's 2114, or the fast VMOS RAM from AMI (American Microsystems, Inc.). Alternatively, the sine table could be made with eleven of the less expensive 1K-by-1-bit-RAM ICs, such as the Intel 2102A or the 9102. For high speeds the AMD 9135J RAM or the VMOS RAM from AMI will be useful.

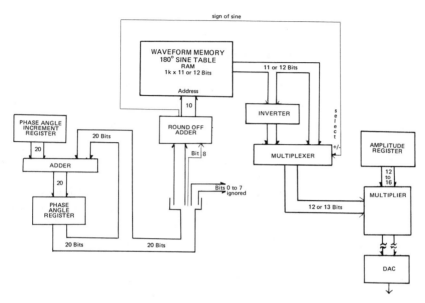

Figure 19.6
Hardware schematic for a digital oscillator circuit using a multiplier to control the amplitude.

The output from the sine table will have a constant amplitude. The amplitude of the sine wave is fed into a multiplier, which multiplies the sine wave by an amplitude that may vary in time as illustrated in figure 19.6. In an analog synthesizer this is similar to connecting the output of a voltage-controlled (control-of-frequency) oscillator to a voltage-controlled amplifier signal input. The control input of the voltage-controlled amplifier would be used to vary the amplitude in time (often controlled by an envelope generator). The frequency of the digital oscillator is binary-number controlled as is the amplitude input of the multiplier.

How wide a multiplier is needed? If a 12-bit sine wave is multiplied by the contents of an amplitude register of infinite width, the resulting signal-to-noise ratio is only 6 dB above that which results from using a 12-bit wide amplitude register. If 16 bits are used in the amplitude register, the signal-to-noise ratio of the product is about 0.5 dB less than that resulting from an amplitude register of infinite width.

Generation of Many Sinusoidal Components

If one desired over a hundred sinusoidal components, building a separate oscillator for each would be expensive. However, one low-distortion digital oscillator may be time-multiplexed to generate a large quantity of low-distortion sinusoidal components (with independent control of each frequency and independent control of each amplitude). The number of sinusoidal components that the oscillator will generate is determined by the speed of the ICs and the sample rate.

If the sample rate is set to 40,000 samples/sec, a new sample must be generated every 25 microseconds (a microsecond is one millionth of a second). Each output sample from the DAC is the sum of the samples from each of the sinusoidal components. If 100 sinusoidal components are desired, each will be allotted 25 microseconds/100 = 250 nanoseconds to compute its sample. With a sample rate of 25,000 samples/sec, 40 partials can be generated if each sinusoidal component sample is calculated in 40 microseconds/40 = 1 microsecond.

The number of sinusoidal components that may be generated is inversely proportional to the sample rate (and thus to the maximum output frequency). It is possible with very fast ICs to generate 512 partials at a sample rate of 50,000 samples/sec, thus enabling a maximum frequency of 20 kHz. To achieve this would require a very large quantity of expensive, heat-generating emitter-coupled logic (ECL) ICs, including a very high-speed multiplier. A couple of less expensive implementations that require fewer ICs and generate a maximum of 256 sinusoidal components (depending on desired audio bandwidth) will be described.

What kind of modifications must be made to the digital oscillator in order to generate many sinusoidal components? In figure 19.6, the phase angle increment register must be replaced by a RAM that contains the phase angle increment (frequency) of each sinusoidal component. As shown in figure 19.7, a phase angle RAM is used to hold the phase angle of each sinusoidal component. The amplitude register is replaced by a RAM that contains the amplitude of each sinusoidal component. Following the multiplier is an accumulator to sum the sinusoidal components. A counter is used to address the RAM's to determine which sinusoidal component parameter is to be accessed. The number of desired sinusoidal components will be placed in a register. This number will be compared with the output of the counter. When the two are equal, the counter will be cleared and start counting over again.

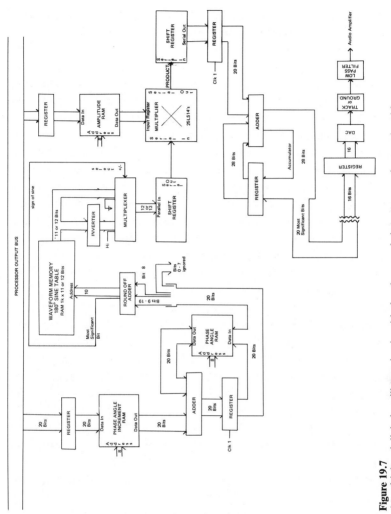

Figure 19.7
A multiplexed digital oscillator circuit, with the phase angle increment register replaced by a RAM that contains the phase angle increment of each sinusoidal component.

If one had to perform all of the operations on one sinusoidal component before starting the operations on another, one would not be able to calculate many sinusoidal components during the sample period. The registers allow one sinusoidal component to have its phase angle increment added to its phase angle while another sinusoidal component is being looked up in the sine table, while still another sinusoidal component is being multiplied by its amplitude, while another sinusoidal component is being summed in the final accumulator. The individual component samples cannot move from one stage to the next until all the other stages have finished their operation. Then all the stages will simultaneously move their contents to the following stage, and each will accept a new content from its input. Thus the slowest stage of the pipeline will determine the throughput rate. Since the throughput rate is increased, more sinusoidal components may be generated in real time.

A relatively inexpensive digital oscillator may be constructed if the multiplier is made with two of the Am 25LS14 integrated circuits from Advanced Micro Devices and a few inexpensive shift registers. These multiplier ICs are slow. A 16-bit-by-12-bit multiplication will require a maximum of 1.2 microseconds; a 12-bit-by-12-bit multiplication will require a maximum of 1.04 microseconds. With this speed, the multiplication stage is definitely the pipeline bottleneck; so inexpensive slow RAMs such as the Intel 2101A-4 may be used in the phase angle increment, phase angle, and amplitude RAMs. A read followed by a write to the same address will require 700 nanoseconds maximum, well under the time required for the Am 25LS14 multipliers. Eleven or twelve of the inexpensive 2102A-6 RAMs from Intel may be used in the waveform memory.

When this Am 25LS14 multiplier is used, a wide bandwidth (high maximum frequency) is not obtainable simultaneously with a large number (such as 100) of sinusoidal components. A wide bandwidth (such as a maximum frequency of 20,000 Hz) is obtainable if fewer sinusoidal components (approximately 20) are desired. If double the number of sinusoidal components is desired simultaneously with a wide bandwidth and small additional cost, a couple of multipliers made from the Am 25LS14 chips may be used. Two numbers to be multiplied are latched into the input registers of the first multiplier; then the second two numbers to be multiplied are latched into the second multiplier. Following this, the third two numbers are latched into the first multiplier at the same time that the first product is being read from the first multiplier. Then the second product is read from the second multiplier at the same time that the fourth two numbers to be multiplied are being latched into the input registers of the second multiplier. This cycle continues, thus halving multiplication time. With this faster multiplication stage, the faster 2101A-2 ICs can be used in the phase angle, phase angle increment, and amplitude RAMs. The waveform memory can now be constructed with 2102A RAMs, which are faster than the 2102A-6 RAMs.

Thus far, no provision has been made in this oscillator for FM synthesis. The output of the multiplier should be available as an input (through the FM register) to the adder that follows the phase angle increment RAM, as illustrated in figure 19.8. This will allow one sinusoidal component to modulate the frequency of another. First the FM register is cleared so that the modulation frequency will not be modulated. Then the modulation frequency is read from the phase angle increment RAM into the adders. After the fifth clock tick, the corresponding sample (the instantaneous modulation amplitude) of the modulating sine wave will be clocked into the FM register. The modulation index will be controlled by the amplitude RAM and the multiplier. The resulting instantaneous modulation amplitude will be added to the carrier frequency read from the phase angle increment RAM, thus modulating it. If the carrier frequency is not ready to be read from the phase angle increment RAM, the FM register will not be clocked. However, the register that feeds the FM register will hold this instantaneous modulation amplitude until it is needed. Meanwhile, the accumulator that follows the multiplier may be used to sum other sinusoidal components.

A few composers have been generating interesting timbres by using several different modulation frequencies, each with a small index of modulation, thus avoiding typical FM clichés (LeBrun 1977; Schottstaedt 1977). Many modulating sinusoidal components, each with an independently variable modulation index, may be summed together in the accumulator that follows the multiplier, as shown in figure 19.8. This sum may be used to modulate a carrier frequency by clocking it into the FM register. Obviously, multiple carriers are easily generated. Timing must be carefully arranged so that the correct instantaneous modulation amplitude is added to the appropriate carrier frequency.

The address of the phase angle increment RAM, the phase angle RAM, and the amplitude RAM may be controlled by one 8-bit up-counter.

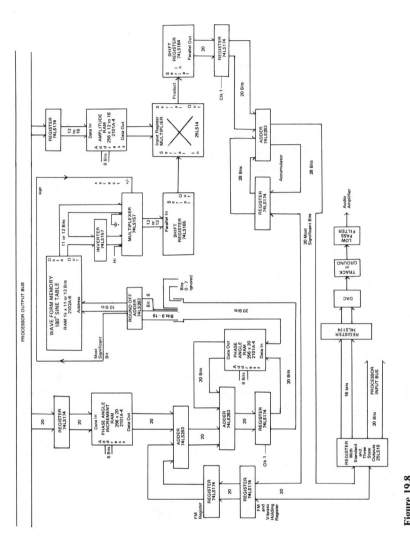

Figure 19.8
An inexpensive, slow, multiplexed digital oscillator with FM synthesis capability.

As shown in figure 19.9, the output of the counter is compared with the number (N) of desired sinusoidal components. If they are equal, the counter will be reset. When clocked, the output of the counter will be changing; the comparator might erroneously try to reset the counter. A one-shot is utilized to prevent the counter from being reset just after the counter is clocked. A second one-shot guarantees that a minimum clear pulsewidth will be provided.

The 8-bit register that holds N is loaded from the computer output bus. To avoid the possibility of loading the N register at a time when the counter might need to be reset, the 4 most significant bits of the counter are used to prevent the N register from being loaded unless the counter is in the early part (counter output of 0 to 15) of its counting sequence. The controlling computer places the value N on its output bus and then sends a ready signal to strobe N into the N register.

When the frequency of the second sinusoidal component is read from the phase angle increment RAM, the amplitude of the first sinusoidal component is read from the amplitude RAM. With this timing, a sample of the first sinusoidal component from the sine table arrives at one input to the multiplier at the same time that the amplitude of the first sinusoidal component arrives at the other input of the multiplier. The computer that updates the RAMs must realize that the counter addresses the frequency of the nth sinusoidal component at the same time that it addresses the amplitude of the $(n - 1)$th sinusoidal component. The method of updating the frequency is shown for the phase angle increment in figure 19.9. The digital oscillator frequency control is allotted (hardwired to) a group of 256 of the available computer addresses. The 8 least significant bits of the computer address bus are compared with the counter output, while the most significant bits of the computer address bus are compared with the allotted (hardwired) address of the digital oscillator frequency control. If both are equal, and the update frequency is ready, and clock 1 is at a high level, then the new frequency value will be written into the phase angle increment RAM. The amplitude RAM is updated similarly. Amplitude envelopes as well as frequency envelopes may be generated in the controlling computer's software and used to update the corresponding amplitudes and frequencies. Simple hardware envelope generators are used in the oscillator shown in figure 19.10.

The track or ground is a bipolar switch, so it may be constructed from a few transistors, which cost next to nothing. The DAC, however, will be

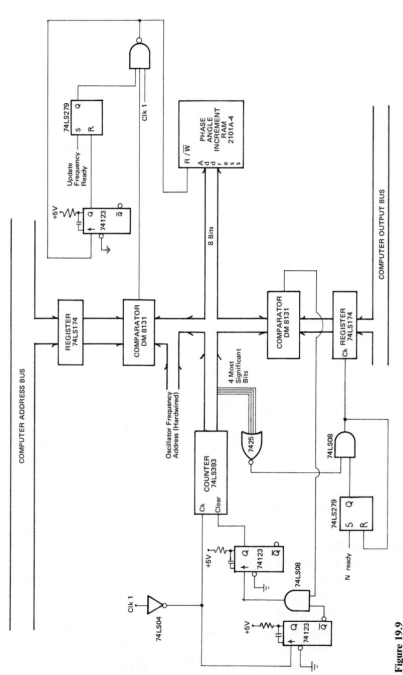

Figure 19.9
Logic circuit for addressing and updating the RAMs in the slow oscillator.

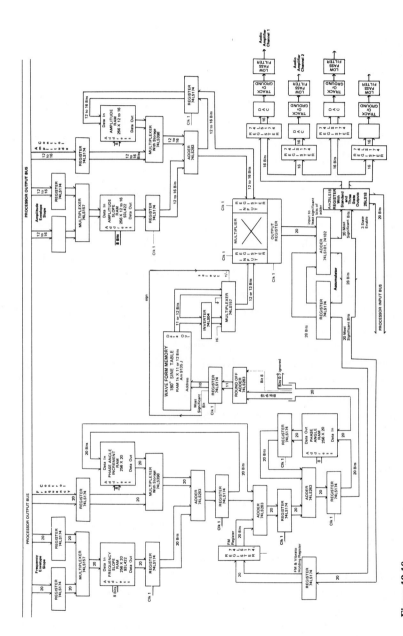

Figure 19.10
A high-speed multiplexed digital oscillator circuit.

a major expense. Datel manufactures a 16-bit DAC called the DAC-HR 16 B, and Analogic makes a high-quality DAC called the MP1926.

The low-pass filter needs to be maximally flat in its pass band and to have a very sharp frequency roll-off above the cut-off frequency (seven-pole filters are recommended). A voltage-controlled low-pass filter would enable the cut-off frequency to be dynamically changed as the sample rate was dynamically varied among several fixed values. With a dynamically variable sample rate, high frequencies could be generated with a few sinusoidal components during one section of the music, while in another section a large number of sinusoidal components could be generated with a lower maximum frequency. However, voltage-controlled seven-pole low-pass filters are difficult to design. CCRMA at Stanford University has used several of the J77C low-pass filters made by T. T. Electronics of Los Angeles, California. These are low-noise and low-distortion filters (since they are passive) and have approximately 0.5 dB of ripple. The transition bandwidth from the cut-off frequency of zero output is narrow enough to allow output frequencies of 40% of the sample rate. T. T. Electronics also makes a newer filter series, the J87C, that has an even narrower transition bandwidth. Every time the sample rate is changed, a different low-pass filter is needed. This can be expensive if several different possible sample rates are desired.

Table 19.2 lists the number of sinusoidal components that may be generated with a given sample rate using the inexpensive slow oscillator shown in figures 19.8 and 19.9.

High-Speed Oscillator

If more sinusoidal components are desired with a wide bandwidth, then faster, more expensive RAMs and a faster, more expensive multiplier will be needed, as mentioned earlier. As illustrated in figure 19.10, a pipeline register will be placed after each basic operation to speed up throughout rate. A timing diagram for the phase angle RAM stage of this higher-speed pipeline is provided in figure 19.11. Identical timing is used for the phase angle increment and amplitude RAMs. Clk 1 clocks all of the pipeline registers in figure 19.10. A 20-bit addition stage will occur during the period of Clk 1. The address is supplied by an 8-bit counter (such as the 74LS393 manufactured by Texas Instruments)

Table 19.2
Trade-off between the number of sinusoidal components that may be generated and the sample rate for the slow, inexpensive oscillator shown in figures 19.8 and 19.9. The 25LS14s in the multiplier are the main speed bottleneck in this oscillator. For more sinusoidal components at a wide bandwidth, see the faster oscillator shown in figures 19.10 and 19.11, and table 19.3.

Sample rate (samples/sec)	Maximum output frequency of any sinusoidal component (40% sample rate) (Hz)	Number of generatable sinusoidal components	
		For a 12-bit-by-12-bit multiplication	For a 12-bit-by-16-bit multiplication
50,000	20,000	19	16
40,000	16,000	24	20
37,500	15,000	25	22
32,768	13,107	29	25
25,000	10,000	38	33
20,000	8,000	48	41
16,384	6,554	58	50
13,000	5,200	73	64
10,000	4,000	96	83

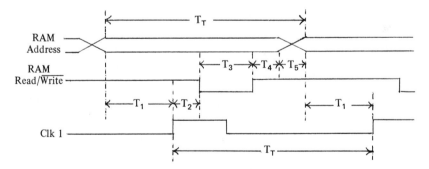

Figure 19.11
Timing diagram for the oscillator shown in figure 19.10. T_1 is the read address access time of the RAM plus the data setup time of a register, T_2 is the clock-to-output delay of a register plus the data setup time (before the beginning of the write pulse) of the RAM, T_3 is the RAM write pulsewidth, T_4 is the RAM address hold time, T_5 is the time needed to change the address, and T_T is the total delay time of one pipeline stage. The counter that generates the address already has the next address, so the pipeline register (between the counter and the RAM) clocks in the next address; thus, T_5 will simply be the clock-to-output delay time of a register.

through a pipeline register to the RAM. So the time required to change the address is simply the clock-to-output delay of a register.

The stage in which the phase angle increment is added to the phase angle is one of the slowest stages in the pipeline. Either this stage or the multiplication stage is the bottleneck. The speed of the phase angle computation stage will be very dependent on the speed of the RAM. A two-port RAM would be very useful for the phase angle RAM. One port could be read from at the same time that the previous address was being written.

Fairchild manufactures a fast 256 by 4-bit RAM (not multiport), the 93L422, which draws typically 60 milliamperes—75 milliamperes maximum—of power supply current, so it should not become hot. Only five of these ICs are needed in the phase angle RAM. The read address access time is typically 45 nanoseconds, with a maximum of 60 nsec and the write time plus address hold time is typically 30 nsec with a 50-nsec maximum. Data setup time is 5 nsec, maximum.

Signetics makes a 256 by 1-bit RAM, the 82S116. Address access time for the 82S116 is typically 30 nsec with a maximum of 40 nsec. The data setup time is specified from the end of the write pulse-width and is the same width as the write pulse-width. The write pulse-width is typically 15 nsec, 25 nsec maximum. The address may typically be changed 5 nsec before the end of the write pulse, and at worst changed exactly at the end of the write pulse. Thus the time required to read, then write to the same address is 40 nsec according to typically specifications, with a maximum of 65 nsec.

When one is attempting to minimize the number of ICs required but still to obtain high speed, the 93L422 is a good choice for the phase angle RAM. To minimize costs at the beginning of the project, 2101A-2 RAMs made by Intel can be used. Later, when a wider bandwidth with a large number of sinusoidal components is desired, these RAMs can be unplugged from their IC sockets and replaced with the pin-compatible higher-speed 93L422 RAMs. The 2101A-2s are 256 by 4-bit static RAMs. The read address access time is 250 nsec maximum, and the write time is a maximum of 150 nsec if writing to the same address as the read address.

In looking for fast RAMs, it was assumed that the phase angle calculation stage of the pipeline would require more or about the same amount of time as the multiplication stage. This assumes that the multiplier can multiply two words in less than 200 nsec and preferably in approximately 100 nsec. The TRW MPY-16AJ will latch and multiply two 16-bit words in a maximum of 190 nsec. The MPY-12AJ will latch and multiply two 12-bit words in a maximum of 175 nsec. Monolithic Memories' 67558 expandable 8-bit multiplier should also be considered for high speed. Unfortunately these high-speed multipliers are still expensive.

Using the design shown in figure 19.10, table 19.3 shows the time delay of one pipeline stage as summed from the individual IC time delays within the pipeline stage. The left half of the table assumes that the phase angle computation stage will be the slowest pipeline stage. The right half assumes that any 20-bit addition stage will be the pipeline bottleneck (which is unlikely). Most of these times assume that TRW will be able to manufacture a faster high-resolution multiplier so that the multiplier does not become the bottleneck. If TRW's 190-nsec multiplier, MPY-16AJ, is used for a multiplier, I would recommend using the Fairchild 93L422 RAM and low-power Schottky ICs for adders and registers. The parts picked in figure 19.10 assume that a multiplier with a typical multiply time of 125 nsec and a maximum of 157 nsec is used. A parallel pipeline multiplier constructed from Monolithic Memories' 67558 ICs should also meet this specification. The bottom of table 19.3 shows the number of sinusoidal components that may be generated depending on the sample rate and the ICs that are used (assuming that no other pipeline stage is a bottleneck).

ICs were chosen for the oscillator in figure 19.10 with speed and relatively low power consumption in mind (so that little heat is generated). If the heat generated by the ICs is minimized, the number of fans (which are acoustically noisy) needed to cool the circuit will also be minimized. Rotron manufactures a very quiet fan that would be useful for cooling the multiplier circuit. If still higher speed is desired, the low-power Schottky ICs could be replaced with their pin-compatible Schottky parts. The Signetics 82S116 could be used in the 256-word RAMs and 1K-by-1-bit bipolar RAMs such as the Fairchild 93415 could be used in the waveform memory. Price and power consumption, however, would take a quantum leap.

Envelopes are generated by straight line segment approximations to the envelope curve. If infinitesimally short line segments were used, any curve could be generated. The slope of the envelope at the beginning of a line segment is loaded into the appropriate RAM (through its temporary

Table 19.3
Number of sinusoidal components that may be generated depending on the time delay of the slowest pipeline stage. The time delay of a pipeline stage is summed from the time delays of the ICs within that pipeline stage. The delays of several different possible combinations of ICs within a pipeline stage are shown. The left half of the table assumes that the phase angle computation stage will be the slowest pipeline stage. The right half assumes that any 20-bit addition stage will be the pipeline bottleneck (which is unlikely). The bottom of table 19.3 shows the number of sinusoidal components that may be generated depending on the sample rate and the ICs that are used (assuming that one is willing to buy or build a fast enough multiplier—the multiplier will likely be the bottleneck).

Cause of time delay	Manufacturer part number	Delay time in RAM stages as a function of which ICs are used (nanoseconds)						Delay time in adder stages as a function of which ICs are used (nanoseconds)
RAM data setup time before leading edge of write pulsewidth	82S116			40	40	60	60	250
	93L422							
	2101A-2							
Register data setup time	74LS174	20		20	20	20		20
	74S174		5	5		5		
Register clock-to-output delay	74LS174	30		30	30	30		30
	74S174		17	17	17	17		
RAM data setup before leading edge of write pulsewidth	82S116			0	0	5	5	0
	93L422							
	2101A-2							
RAM write pulsewidth	82S116			25	25	45	45	150
	93L422							
	2101A-2							
	82S116			0	0			

Component timing contributions (microseconds / ns as listed):

Parameter	Device	Value
RAM address hold time	93L422	30
	2101A-2	30
Address change time	74LS174	30
	74S174	17
Register clock-to-output delay	74LS174	30
	74S174	17
Addition time	74LS283	107
	74S181, 74S182	69
		44
Register data setup time	74LS174	20
	74S174	5

Total time delay of one stage (per configuration):

125	150	109	145	104	195	154	480	157	129	119	91	66

Number of sinusoidal components that may be generated:

Sampling rate (samples/sec)	Sample period (microseconds)	Maximum frequency (Hz)													
50,000	20	20,000	158	131	181	135	190	100	127	39	125	153	166	217	256
40,000	25	16,000	198	164	227	170	238	126	160	50	157	191	208	256	256
37,500	26.7	15,000	211	175	242	181	254	134	171	53	167	204	222	256	256
32,768	30.3	13,107	242	201	256	208	256	154	196	61	192	234	254	256	256
25,000	40	10,000	256	256	256	256	256	203	256	81	252	256	256	256	256
20,000	50	8,000	256	256	256	256	256	254	256	102	256	256	256	256	256
16,384	61	6,554	256	256	256	256	256	256	256	125	256	256	256	256	256
12,000	83.3	4,800	256	256	256	256	256	256	256	171	256	256	256	256	256
10,000	100	4,000	256	256	256	256	256	256	256	206	256	256	256	256	256

holding register) by the processor. This slope is repeatedly added to the current amplitude (or frequency for frequency envelopes) until the slope of the envelope changes. Then a new envelope slope is loaded into the RAM. This is a simple-minded method of envelope generation; however, minimal extra hardware is required as compared to other methods of envelope generation of which I am aware. One of the problems with this envelope generation technique is that the software that updates the slopes must load the new slopes at the right times.

I would be interested in other techniques for envelope generation that allow a different envelope to be used for every individual note. A function table generates the same envelope shape for every note. A group of function tables may be multiplexed for more generality. Perhaps the simplest method of enveloping would be to use an input controller with pressure sensitivity so that envelopes could be generated by the musician in real time. Then the slope RAMs and corresponding logic would not be needed in figure 19.10, thus reducing the cost by over a hundred dollars.

Other Synthesis Techniques and Professional Quality Audio

Waveshaping (LeBrun 1979) and discrete summation formulae (Moorer 1976) may be performed with minor modifications to the architecture shown in figure 19.10. A larger version of the waveform RAM is used to store waveshaping transfer functions as well as other general functions such as $\log(x)$, $\ln(x)$, $\exp(x)$, $1/x$ (for use in performing division), as well as $\cos(x)$, $\sin(x)$, and other waveforms. The clear function of several of the registers will now be utilized. For example, in waveshaping synthesis, the register that holds the output of the phase angle accumulator must now be cleared when the FM feedback path is utilized in running a waveform through the transfer function. A fast RAM of 256 to 1 Kwords by 16 to 24 bits with a direct path back to the multiplier should replace the accumulator register (which holds the output of the arithmetic-logic unit (ALU) that follows the multiplier). For professional quality audio, a 16-by-16 multiplier and preferably a 24-by-24 multiplier should be used to avoid round-off noise. VOSIM (Kaegi and Tempelaars 1978) may be implemented with this architecture with minor modifications. (See the implementation described in Buxton et al. 1978.)

For added flexibility in generating other synthesis techniques and for professional quality audio, a larger waveform memory RAM (such as

64 to 128 Kwords by 16 to 24 bits) should be used. By interpolating between the values in the memory, many small tables may be stored in this large RAM. An additional multiplier immediately following this RAM should be added for performing the interpolation. In this case the memory should be composed of two 64 Kword parts (with each part being at least 16 bits wide) that are accessed simultaneously. One part will hold the sampled points in the function and the other part will hold the differences between the sampled points. The difference (between the sampled points in the function) will be multiplied by the least significant bits of the memory address (which were previously rounded off). The product will be added to the sample point in the other part of the memory. A full cycle of each function should be stored for simplicity in working with nonsymmetrical functions; hence the round-off logic will be removed. Logic for shifting and masking the memory address will now be needed for addressing many functions of various sizes.

For additional speed the transistor-transistor logic (TTL) could be replaced by Fairchild's "FAST" logic. Fairchild claims to be working on a 256-by-4 RAM, the 93F422, with much faster access times; two multipliers may also be used in parallel to increase their throughout.

Overview and an Alternative Architecture

This digital oscillator should be thought of as one module that plugs into a modular synthesizer with other modules, such as digital filters, pitch detectors, envelope followers, phase vocoders, reverberators, and so on. F. R. Moore's digital synthesizer is built around this modular concept (Moore 1977b). The oscillator architecture may be broken up into simpler, more general components hanging on two busses for software-controlled patching between the components, as in figure 19.12. These are useful basic components in synthesis, analysis, and modification of sound. This horizontal architecture may be microprogrammed to perform digital filtering, reverberation, phase vocoding, pitch detection, envelope detection, phase shifting, and many other algorithms. Microprogramming this sort of horizontal architecture is less difficult than microprogramming a long pipeline of components with programmable interconnections, such as a version of the digital oscillator extended to do digital filtering (Abbott 1979, 1985). Two busses are used, since many of the components use two operands. The architecture was originally

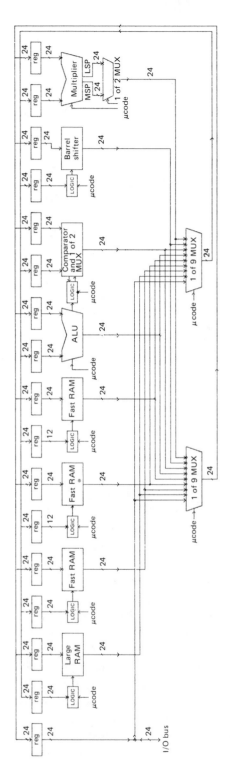

Figure 19.12
The long pipeline oscillator architecture may be broken up into simpler, more general components hanging on two busses for software-controlled patching between the components, such as the architecture shown here. This real-time, digital audio signal processor module has the advantage of being able to run many different algorithms for synthesis, modification, and analysis of sound by changing the microprogram stored in the RAM shown in figure 19.13. Extra address bits are provided for future expansion of the RAMs.

conceived in 1977, with whole oscillators and filters hanging on the busses in addition to simple components (but without the barrel shifter and comparator/multiplexer components). A year and a half later, J. A. Moorer (1978) described a version of his horizontal architecture that had all simple components (including the barrel shifter and multiplexer/comparator), but only one bus; and it passed the output data from all of the components through one fast RAM back to the inputs of the components. In order to avoid the bottleneck of the RAM, I moved the fast RAM to a position hanging on the busses (treating it just like the other general components) and added a second fast RAM for simultaneous access of two operands.

The microprogram is stored in a fast RAM of 1 to 16 Kwords by 64 to 80 bits as shown in figure 19.13. Each microinstruction is held by a pipeline register. Following this are many microinstruction decoders that control the basic elements of this horizontal architecture. For simplicity in figure 19.12, these control bits are shown as μcode.

The basic components of the architecture are as follows. A 24-by-24 multiplier generates a 48-bit product. Microcode is used to select (by controlling the multiplexer) the 24 most significant bits or the 24 least significant bits of the product to go to the busses. The microcode also determines whether signed, unsigned, or mixed arithmetic will be performed, as well as whether or not to round off the product. The number of places to shift data in the 24-bit barrel shifter is controlled by data or by microcode. The barrel shifter may be used in performing floating-point arithmetic. The comparator/multiplexer component is used for decision making and branching. Selections are based on the data or on results from arithmetic and logic operations. This was one of J. A. Moorer's ideas for avoiding jumps or branches in the microprogram so that the audio sample rate is held constant. The audio sample rate is the microinstruction rate divided by the number of instructions. If the number of executed microinstructions changes, then the audio sample rate will change. Another alternative is to use first-in-first-outs (FIFOs) between the audio converters and the signal processor. These FIFOs allow a variable length of microprogram (and thus branches) as long as the average microprogram length is constant. The microcode also tells the ALU what operation to perform. The RAMs may be addressed by microcode or by the data. The large RAMs have additional logic for shifting and masking their addresses. This logic may be used to access multiple

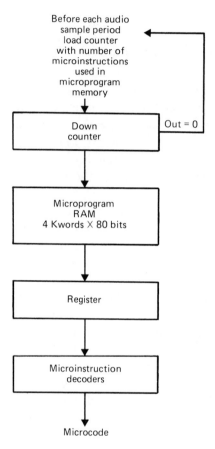

Figure 19.13
Microprogram controller. A counter counts through the sequence of microinstructions each audio sample period. Each microinstruction is decoded to control (μcode) the architecture shown in figure 19.12.

tables of various sizes within the large RAMs, as well as to employ the large RAMs as delay lines for reverberation, autocorrelation, and other signal processing algorithms. Extra address bits are sent to all of the RAMs for easy future expansion of the memory. The leftmost "component" is an input-output connection to other modules, audio converters, and to the controlling computers.

This sort of horizontal architecture has the advantages of flexibility (the ability to run many different algorithms for synthesis, analysis, and modification of sound) and relative ease of programming. However, it cannot generate the large number (such as 256) of virtual oscillators or filters that long pipelines can. A useful system would have a combination of special-purpose pipelines (such as a 256-oscillator bank or a 256-filter bank) for frequently used algorithms, plus many general-purpose, horizontal modules, with an architecture such as that shown in figure 19.12, for algorithms that are used less often. This could also be used for easy development of and experimentation with new algorithms. Since the horizontal architecture cannot generate a large number of oscillators and performs less filtering, etc., it would be appropriate to implement this sort of architecture in emitter-coupled logic (ECL). This would speed up the design considerably. A slow multiplier would be a real bottleneck in signal-processing algorithms. A 50-nsec multiply cycle is possible with the 100K ECL available today. This would match the microinstruction cycle time, if the microprogram memory and microinstruction decoders are implemented in ECL. The input registers should also be implemented in ECL to lower their clock-to-output delay time. With this much of the design implemented in ECL, it doesn't make sense to implement the rest of the design in TTL because of the large number of ECL-TTL translator ICs that would be required. However, the large RAMS should be implemented in *n*-channel metal oxide semiconductor (NMOS) in order to lower the cost of this expensive beast. The rest of the signal processor would be ECL. Registers should be added on the outputs of all the components to avoid race conditions.

In order to optimize the architectures described here, one should use faster components as they are developed. However, it is a good idea to keep the components balanced in speed. A 1-nsec multiplier would not be worth its cost if the rest of the components in the architecture were 50-nsec components. In a few years, designs such as these will become less expensive as today's state-of-the-art components become more commonplace.

Acknowledgments

I would especially like to thank J. A. Moorer for his unending guidance and inspiration in digital audio design concepts. I would also like to thank Jeff Goldstein, Dick Moore, Efrem Lipkin, and G. diGiugno for their willingness to discuss openly their digital synthesizer designs. It is hoped that more flexible high-fidelity music instruments will evolve with this open communication of ideas. A foundation for these designs was provided by *The Technology of Computer Music* by Max Mathews et al. Thanks must go to Peter Samson, who pioneered real-time digital synthesizer design; to Renny Wiggins, Maria Kent, John Strawn, and Judy Wasserman; and last, but certainly not least, to Curtis Roads for his careful editorial work in helping to bring this article up to date.

References

Abbott, C. 1979. "Machine tongues V." *Computer Music Journal* 3(2): 6–11, 28.

Abbott, C. 1985. "Automated microprogramming for digital synthesizers: A tutorial." Article 26 in this volume.

Advanced Micro Devices. 1975. *Schottky and Low-power Schottky Bipolar Memory, Logic, and Interface.* Sunnyvale, Calif. Advanced Micro Devices.

Backus, J. 1969. *The Acoustical Foundations of Music.* New York: Norton.

Buxton, W., E. A. Fogels, G. Fedorkow, L. Sasaki, and K. C. Smith. 1978. "An introduction to the SSSP digital synthesizer." *Computer Music Journal* 2(4): 28–38. Article 12 in this volume.

Carlson, B. 1968. *Communications Systems: An Introduction to Symbols, Signals, and Noise.* New York: McGraw-Hill. See especially pages 272–288.

Chowning, J. 1973. "The synthesis of complex audio spectra by means of frequency modulation." *Journal of the Audio Engineering Society* 21(7): 526–534. Article 1 in this volume.

Fairchild. 1976. *Bipolar Memory Data Book.* Mountain View, Calif.: Fairchild Corporation.

Von Helmholtz, H. 1863. *Die Lehre von den Tonempfindungen als physiologische Grundlage für die Theorie der Musik.* Translated as *On the Sensations of Tone as a Physiological Basis for the Theory of Music.* A. Ellis, tr. 1954. New York: Dover.

Intel. 1977. *Data Catalog 1977.* Santa Clara, Calif.: Intel Corporation.

Kaegi, W., and S. Tempelaars. 1978. "VOSIM—A new sound synthesis system." *Journal of the Audio Engineering Society* 26(6): 418–425.

LeBrun, M. 1977. "A derivation of the spectrum of FM with a complex modulating wave." *Computer Music Journal* 1(4): 51–52. Article 5 in this volume.

LeBrun, M. 1979. "Digital waveshaping synthesis." *Journal of the Audio Engineering Society* 27(4): 250–266.

Mathews, M. V., with J. E. Miller, F. R. Moore, J. R. Pierce, and J.-C. Risset. 1969. *The Technology of Computer Music.* Cambridge, Mass.: MIT Press.

Moore, F. R. 1977a. "Table lookup noise for sinusoidal digital oscillators." *Computer Music Journal* 1(2): 26–29, 1977. Article 20 in this volume.

Moore, F. R. 1977b. Real-Time Interactive Computer Music Synthesis. Ph.D. Diss., Department of Electrical Engineering, Stanford University.

Moorer, J. A. 1976. "The synthesis of complex audio spectra by means of discrete summation formulae." *Journal of the Audio Engineering Society* 24: 717–727.

Moorer, J. A. 1977. "Signal processing aspects of computer music—A survey." *Proceedings of the IEEE* 65(8): 1108–1137.

Moorer, J. A. 1978. "The use of the phase vocoder in computer music applications." *Journal of the Audio Engineering Society* 26: 42–45.

National Semiconductor. 1976. *TTL Data Book*. Santa Clara, Calif.: National Semiconductor Corporation.

Rakowski, A. 1971. "Pitch discrimination at the threshold of hearing." In *Proceedings of the Seventh International Congress on Acoustics*, vol. 3. Budapest.

Schottstaedt, B. 1977. "The simulation of natural instrument tones using frequency modulation with a complex modulating wave." *Computer Music Journal* 1(4): 46–50. Article 4 in this volume.

Signetics. 1976. *Data Manual*. Sunnyvale, Calif.: Signetics Corporation.

Texas Instruments. 1976. *The TTL Data Book for Design Engineers*. Second edition. Dallas: Texas Instruments Corporation.

Texas Instruments. 1977. *Bipolar Microcomputer Components Data Book for Design Engineers*. Dallas: Texas Instruments Corporation.

20 Table Lookup Noise for Sinusoidal Digital Oscillators

F. RICHARD MOORE

Several means of frequency generation have been reported in the signal-processing literature (Rabiner and Gold 1975), including generation of sinusoids from difference equations and complex arithmetic involving the number e to an imaginary exponent; but the most economical method by far seems to be the table lookup method. The basic hardware elements required to implement this method are shown in figure 20.1. A number determining the frequency, called the increment, is repeatedly added to a register (called the sum-of-increments, or phase, register) at each clock pulse; the clock frequency is taken here to be equal to the sampling rate. By a suitable choice of register width and table length, the modulus arithmetic is automatically performed by ignoring the register overflow, and the contents of this register are used to address a waveform memory containing 2^k samples of one period of the (periodic) waveform to be generated. The exact method of forming the table address is important in determining the quality of the digital output signal. The increment value is related to the frequency of the output waveform by the following formula (Mathews 1969):

$$\text{Increment} = \frac{\text{Frequency} * \text{Table length}}{\text{Sampling rate}},$$

which implies that

$$\text{Frequency} = \frac{\text{Increment} * \text{Sampling rate}}{\text{Table length}}.$$

We see that the increment represents the size of the step taken through the table for successive values of the output waveform. If the increment is equal to 1.0, each period of the output waveform will contain exactly as many samples as there are in the table, yielding a frequency equal to the sampling rate divided by the table length. Doubling the increment doubles the frequency, and vice versa. However, most frequencies do not yield integer values for the increment, so normally one of three methods is used to handle such cases: the truncation method, in which the integer part of the sum of increments is used directly to address the table; the

This is a revised and updated version of an article that originally appeared in *Computer Music Journal* 1(2): 26–29, 1977.

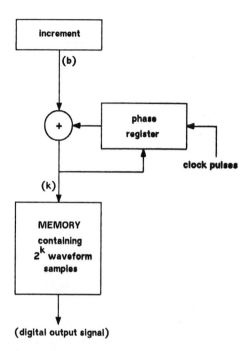

(digital output signal)

Figure 20.1
Block diagram of the hardware required for the table lookup oscillator. At each clock
pulse (where the clock frequency is equal to the sampling rate), the signed, b-bit increment
is added to the sum-of-increments, or phase, register. The uppermost k bits of this phase
value are used to address a random-access (possibly read-only) table memory containing
samples of one period of the waveform to be produced. Extensions of the basic method
shown above include rounding the k-bit address by the $(k + 1)$th bit of the phase value, or
interpolating between adjacent table entries. The quality of the digital output signal is
affected by slight errors due to the finite length of the table (called phase jitter) and
amplitude quantization errors due to the finite wordlength of the table entries.
Measurements of the effects of these errors are given in tables 20.1, 20.2, and 20.3 for
three different table-addressing schemes: truncation, rounding, and interpolation.

rounding method, in which the sum of increments is rounded to the nearest integer, which is then used to address the table; or the interpolation method, in which some form of interpolation between successive table values is used.

How Large Should the Sine Table Be?

In order to determine how large to make the sinusoid table (that is, how many entries and how much precision it need have), we can compare the signal quality for each of the three methods given above (truncation, rounding, and interpolation) to the quality of an "ideal" digital waveform. This signal is ideal in the sense that it is computed to the full accuracy of a 36-bit general-purpose computer at each sample, so that both phase jitter due to the finite length of the table and quantization noise are at minimum value. Further, it is assumed that these minimum values are well within the tolerance levels of acoustic perception; that is, the ideal digital waveform sounds as pure as the other audio equipment will allow.

The method for making the comparison is as follows: The addressing mode is chosen, and the table length and width are set to selected values. Only table lengths that are powers of 2 are considered, because of their convenience in hardware implementation. A computer program then simulates the operation of the hardware built to these specifications, and the computed waveform is compared against the ideal waveform. The percentage root-mean-square amplitude of the error signal is determined according to the following formula:

$$\text{Percentage r.m.s. error} = \psi \sqrt{\frac{\sum_{n=0}^{k-1} [f_{\text{ideal}}(n) - f_{\text{test}}(n)]^2}{k}}$$

where $f_{\text{ideal}}(n)$ represents the nth of k samples of the ideal waveform at times nT, $n = 0, 1, \ldots, (k-1)$ and T is the sampling period; $f_{\text{test}}(n)$ is the analogous waveform generated by the hardware simulator; and ψ is a normalizing factor equal to $100/0.707$ to yield r.m.s. in percent.

It is found that the r.m.s. error depends on the relationship of the table length to the frequency of the generated sinusoid. By trying several frequencies the worst-case error can be empirically approximated. In most instances the worst case appears when the increment values are close to but not equal to 1.0. If the error signal itself is considered to be a noise

Table 20.1
Approximate worst-case signal-to-error noise ratios (SN_eR, in dB) for the truncating oscillator, listed according to waveform memory size. If the truncating addressing scheme is used with a waveform table containing 512 samples of one period of a sinusoid, and each sample has 8 bits of magnitude, the noise due to phase jitter and quantization errors will be 42.1 dB below the signal level, according to this table (see text for an explanation of how these values are calculated). No improvement is gained by adding more bits of precision to the table beyond the last value in each row of the above table, since at this point virtually all the noise in the digital signal is due to the finite table length. Using this data, one can design digital hardware or software with "optimum" waveform memory sizes.

Memory length (one period, in words)	Memory wordlength (in bits, not including the sign bit)								
	4	5	6	7	8	9	10	11	12
32	18.4	18.6							
64	24.1	24.1	24.3						
128	27.9	29.8	30.0	30.4					
256	30.5	34.2	35.6	36.3	36.3				
512	31.7	36.6	40.0	41.6	42.1	42.4			
1,024	32.0	37.7	42.7	46.1	47.7	48.2	48.4		
2,048	32.1	38.0	43.6	48.6	52.1	53.6	54.2	54.4	
4,096	32.1	38.0	43.9	49.6	54.6	58.1	59.7	60.2	60.4

Rule for truncating oscillator: if the table has 2^k entries, then each entry should optimally be specified to k bits of precision (not including the sign bit), and the SN_eR achievable will then be $6(k - 2)$ dB.

added to the ideal waveform, and if the amplitude of this noise is compared with the overall amplitude of the signal, we can infer a signal-to-error noise ratio (SN_eR); the results of such calculations are shown in tables 20.1, 20.2, and 20.3.

In table 20.1 the SN_eR values are given in decibels for the truncation method, and the last value in each row indicates the largest ratio achievable for a given table length. Apparently, adding more bits of precision does not increase this value because the error is then principally due to the finite length of the table, resulting in instantaneous phase errors in the test signal. Inspection of the table yields the rule that when the truncation method of table lookup is used, if the table is 2^k words long, then the signal can benefit from no more than k bits per table entry (not including

Table 20.2
Approximate worst-case signal-to-error noise ratios (SN_eR) for the rounding oscillator. If the rounding addressing scheme is used with a waveform table containing 512 samples of one period of a sinusoid, and each sample has 8 bits of magnitude, the noise due to phase jitter and quantization errors will be 47.6 dB below the signal level, according to this table (see text for an explanation of how these values are calculated).

Memory length (one period, in words)	Memory wordlength (in bits, not including the sign bit)								
	4	5	6	7	8	9	10	11	12
32	22.7	23.4	23.5						
64	27.4	28.9	29.7	30.2					
128	30.5	33.8	35.2	36.2	36.3				
256	31.6	36.7	39.9	41.7	42.1	42.3			
512	32.1	37.7	40.5	45.9	47.6	48.2	48.3		
1,024	32.1	38.0	43.6	48.7	52.0	53.6	54.2	54.4	
2,048	32.1	38.0	43.9	49.6	54.7	58.0	59.7	60.2	60.4

Rule for rounding oscillator: if the table has 2^k entries, then each entry should optimally be specified to $k + 1$ bits of precision (not including the sign bit), and the SN_eR achievable will then be $6(k - 1)$ dB.

a sign bit), and the limiting SN_eR is approximately $6(k - 2)$ dB. This makes intuitive sense from an information theoretic viewpoint, since we would expect that k bits of information input cannot yield more than k bits of information output. Similar results are shown for the rounding and interpolation methods in tables 20.2 and 20.3. It can be seen that rounding increases the SN_eR by about 6 dB compared to truncation for a given table size, since rounding allows the output signal to benefit by one more bit of table precision. (Again, from the standpoint of information theory, we "take account" of $k + 1$ bits of inputs, so we get $k + 1$ valid bits of output.) This 6 dB improvement is due to a better phase match between f_{ideal} and f_{test}. Since the ear is generally insensitive to such constant phase errors, however, the rounding method is not likely to yield an improvement in sound quality in most cases.

Interpolation greatly increases the output signal accuracy and is clearly of interest when memory must be conserved. Interpolation requires additional arithmetic and memory access, however, so it is intrinsically

Table 20.3
Approximate worst-case signal-to-error noise ratios (SN_eR) for the interpolating oscillator. If the interpolating addressing scheme is used with a waveform table containing 512 samples of one period of a sinusoid, and each sample has 8 bits of magnitude, the noise due to phase jitter and quantization errors will be 56.5 dB below the signal level, according to this table (see text for an explanation of how these values are calculated).

Memory length (one period, in words)	Memory wordlength (in bits, not including the sign bit)										
	8	9	10	11	12	13	14	15	16	17	18
32	48.0										
64	57.1	60.1	58.9								
128	62.5	67.5	70.1	71.1	71.3						
256	56.3	61.5	68.9	73.7	79.5	82.3	83.4				
512	56.5	61.6	68.8	73.5	79.8	85.6	92.6	94.8	95.1		
1,024	56.1	61.7	68.4	73.9	80.2	85.8	92.3	98.7	103.9	106.0	107.0
2,048	56.0	61.9	68.0	74.1	80.2	86.0	92.4	98.4	104.0	110.2	115.4

Rule for interpolating oscillator: if the table has 2^k entries, then each entry optimally should be specified to $2(k-1)$ bits of precision (not including the sign bit), and the SN_eR achievable will then be $6k$ dB.

more time-consuming than either of the other methods. The method of interpolation is as follows: if we take i and f to be the integer and fractional parts of the sum-of-increments register, then interpolation involves evaluation of either

$$\sin(i + f) \approx \text{sintable}(i) + f[\text{sintable}(i + 1) - \text{sintable}(i)] \qquad (1)$$

or

$$\sin(i + f) \approx \text{sintable}(i) + f\,\text{costable}(i). \qquad (2)$$

The second method is based on the fact that $\sin(x) \approx x$ for small x expressed in radians. Unfortunately f is not expressed in radians, so this otherwise attractive method does not compare favorably with the method of equation 1 which was used to compute table 20.3. Next, the precision of the increments has to be considered. In order to represent both positive and negative frequencies (the latter occur in frequency-modulation synthesis of complex audio waveforms), the increment must be a signed quantity of, say, m bits. If the increment and sum registers each contain m bits, then the frequency range of the oscillator from 0 Hz to the Nyquist frequency is simply divided into 2^{m-1} equal steps. For example, a sampling rate of $2^{15} = 32,768$ Hz and an increment size of 16 bits (including sign) divides the frequency range of $0-2^{14}$ Hz into 2^{15} equal steps, each 0.5 Hz in width. This is sufficient accuracy to be psychoacoustically acceptable above about 200 Hz, but this resolution becomes increasingly intolerable at lower frequencies (Roederer 1973). For example, a smooth-sounding, slow glissando between about 50 and 100 Hz would be impossible, since the abrupt changes of 0.5 Hz are sufficiently large to be audible, producing a kind of graininess in the sound of the changing frequency.

This problem may be solved either by making both the increment and the sum register longer or by simply making the sum register more precise and allowing the increment to be arithmetically shifted to the left or right, thus making the range and frequency resolution of the oscillator variable. For each bit the increment is shifted to the right, the maximum frequency achievable is halved and the frequency resolution is doubled in accuracy— exactly the kind of relationship desired, since frequency resolution is more of a problem at low frequencies than at high. The increment-shifting scheme also minimizes the bit width of the required signal paths for controlling the oscillator with a time-varying increment control signal. Also, it is possible to apply not only scaling to the frequency specification, but ranging as well. Suppose we are shifting the 16-bit frequency value to the right by one bit. Then we have an upper frequency limit of about 8 kHz instead of 16 kHz, and a frequency resolution (minimum step size) of 0.25 Hz instead of 0.5 Hz. If we provide a mechanism for inverting bit 1 (the bit just to the right of the sign bit), then we can select whether the frequencies will be those between 0 and 8 kHz or those between 8 and 16 kHz. This is a typical application of the control bits that come in with the frequency specification; if some are used to set the scale, then others can be used to set the range. (Note that the range bits must be *exclusive* *or*ed into the scaled frequency bits in order to give proper results for twos-complement numbers.)

Economizing Memory

Finally, it is possible to take advantage of the quarter-wave symmetry of the sinusoid to reduce the amount of table memory by a factor of 4, with only a slight increase in the amount of hardware needed to form the table address and to interpret the data read from the table. By storing only the first quadrant of the waveform it is also possible to reduce the width of the table by one bit, since all of the values of the sine function in this quadrant are positive. The details of this method are as follows.

Assume that we have available a W-word memory, where $W = 2^n$, typically 512 or 2,048. Assume also that each word in this memory contains B bits of data (the optimum number of bits may be determined from table 20.1, 20.2, or 20.3, according to the addressing mode). We fill this memory with positive binary fractions representing the values of the first quadrant of the sine function according to the formula

$$\text{Memory}[I] \leftarrow 2^B \sin\left(\frac{I\pi}{2W}\right), \qquad I = 0, 1, 2, \ldots, W - 1$$

where each fractional value is truncated to B bits of precision. For simplicity, let us assume that the truncation method is used to address the table. Referring to figure 20.1, we take the uppermost k bits of the phase register to address the table. Since our quarter-wave table is only one-fourth as long as a full-wave table, we use the uppermost $k = n + 2$ bits of the phase register. The most significant of these k bits (let us call it $k0$) provides the sign of the output value (normally, 0 for positive and 1 for negative), and the second of these k bits ($k1$) determines whether we should negate the remaining n bits in the address for the table (note that $k0$ and $k1$ together form a quadrant number for our sine function: 00, 01, 10, or 11). The low-order n bits are used directly to address the table if bit $k1$ is a 0; the twos complement of these bits is used if bit $k1$ is equal to 1, with one exception: when the low-order n bits are all 0 and bit $k1$ is a 1 (that is, the phase corresponds to either 90° or 270° exactly), then twos-complementing the low-order bits will result in an incorrect address of 0. This particular case must be treated specially by substituting the maximum address (all ones) for this value. This is accomplished in hardware by simply *or*ing the carry-out bit of the twos complementer with the remaining n bits. It might seem that using a ones complement rather than a twos complement here would solve the problem, but unfortunately the more economical ones complement can lead to a distortion of the output waveform around the zero crossing. The rounding operation may be included in this twos complementation, if it is used.

The value read from the memory at the calculated address is a positive fractional value upon which we "superimpose" the sign bit by twos-complementing the B bits whenever bit $k0$ is equal to 1 and retaining $B + 1$ bits of the result (that is, we retain the overflow bit), resulting in a $B + 1$ result. Again twos-complementing is necessary to avoid generating the "illegal" fractional value -1.0. Thus a rounding oscillator with a 512-word-by-12-bit quarter-wave table can achieve a worst-case SN_eR of about 60 dB, which compares favorably to the noise level of high-quality analog equipment. Tables 20.1, 20.2, and 20.3 can be used to determine the SN_eR for smaller widths than the optimum as well, for it can be seen that using a 512-word-by-11-bit table (instead of 12 bits) has a very small effect on the quality of the generated signal.

A quarter- or half-wave table may be used whenever the waveform to be generated possesses the appropriate symmetry. The table lookup procedure provides the basic method for sinusoid generation needed for music synthesis, and its implementation in hardware is relatively straightforward.

References

Mathews, M. V., with J. E. Miller, F. R. Moore, J. R. Pierce, and J.-C. Risset. 1969. *The Technology of Computer Music*. Cambridge, Mass.: MIT Press.

Rabiner, L. R., and B. Gold. 1975. *Theory and Application of Digital Signal Processing*. Englewood Cliffs, N.J.: Prentice-Hall.

Roederer, J. G. 1973. *Introduction to the Physics and Psychophysics of Music*. New York: Springer.

21 A Recipe for Homebrew ECL

CHUCK HASTINGS

Emitter-coupled logic (ECL) is understood by most computer designers to be the fastest stuff available—which it is—and as too difficult for anyone but the largest companies to design with—which it isn't. If an appropriate recipe is followed, ECL systems can be developed with very limited resources with as good, or better, chances of technical success as with equivalent transistor-transistor logic (TTL) systems. Thus, homebrew ECL is a viable alternative for applications that require very high-speed processing. Such applications may occur in some technical approaches to music synthesis, speech analysis (Cann 1979, 1980), or simply fireside number crunching involving matrices, partial differential equations, or Fast Fourier Transforms.

Such a recipe isn't written down anywhere—existing ECL tutorials make ECL design sound formidable. However, a careful amateur can achieve a reliable 100-MHz small system today. This paper will present a practical recipe, used once successfully, for designing, building, and troubleshooting a small ECL system with the level of resources available in a well-equipped homebrew lab.

This recipe was developed during the course of one task in a project at Racal-Milgo, a medium-sized Florida company with no previous ECL systems experience. The circumstances were in many ways quite similar to those of a homebrew project. The outcome of the task was a 24-bit general-purpose stored-microprogram computer, capable of 6 million three-address fixed-point add/subtract/Boolean instructions or 900,000 fixed-point multiply instructions per second, which was completed and has since been operated 10 hours a day for several months in a signal-processing system.

Why ECL?

Why ECL? For openers, the industry-standard 10,000 series ECL (hereafter referred to as 10K) offers at least twice the net speed of Schottky TTL when actually designed into typical systems. 10K provides a more

This article first appeared in *Proceedings of the Second West Coast Computer Faire*, available from P. O. Box 1579, Palo Alto, California. A revised version appeared in *Computer Music Journal* 2(1):48–59, 1978. That version has been further revised and updated here.

natural and less brute-force approach to high-speed signal transmission than Schottky, and is in a number of respects actually easier to use.

ECL has probably not been considered for many applications where it would have been appropriate, both in industry and more recently in hobby work, because people tend to be scared to death of it. Frankly, ECL has an image problem. Like many image problems, this one has some basis in truth; but there has been a considerable overlay of exaggeration, distortion, and mythology, which I will do my best to dispel based on the results obtained in one medium-sized computer hardware development project.

Much of what I have to say concerns a subject euphemistically called "interconnection practice," which means all the things you have to do to keep your logic from being thoroughly confused by its own noise after you turn it on. Except as occasionally noted, all of my remarks concern 10K in a wire-wrap environment. Later on, I'll have a little to say about other ECL families, such as MECL III, PECL III, and Fairchild 100K.

A good wire-wrap board, believe it or not, is an excellent signal environment for high-speed logic. I have met people who solemnly claimed that one can't wire-wrap ECL, but it just isn't so. Communications Satellite Corporation, and National Advanced Systems, have both done it for years. I have also met people who claimed that wire-wrap fabrication was something one does only for prototypes and that it is too expensive to be a manufacturing technique; but Modular Computer Systems in Florida has been cranking out wire-wrapped minicomputers since about the beginning of the 1970s. Much of the wire-wrap equipment used in industry is made by Gardner-Denver, and many hobbyists use Gardner-Denver rechargeable battery-operated wire-wrap guns. There is also a company called OK Machine and Tool Corporation which makes a line of low-cost wire-wrap equipment specifically marketed for use by hobbyists. (See the appendix for a list of addresses.)

Since most hobbyists probably prefer to have their systems work without a major initial checkout hassle, my interconnection-practice recipe probably errs on the side of overkill. If for some underground entrepreneurial reason you are intensely concerned with the cost of replicating a homebrew ECL system once it is working, you can do a cost-reduction job by deleting some of the practices I am advocating one by one until the system goes bananas. But don't start out doing an el cheapo job—if the system doesn't work at all, you may not have the equipment, resources, or patience to find out why. Big companies do have the luxury of trading off more product-development engineering hours against lower manufacturing costs, but you probably don't. The first time you do it, do it right.

The fear of ECL in the industry is so great that it requires some chutzpah on my part to state straight out that you too can successfully build, debug, and operate ECL systems in your spare bedroom, garage, or rumpus room—just like TTL and metal oxide semiconductor (MOS). You don't have to have the vast resources of a company like Control Data, Univac, IBM, or Burroughs behind you to succeed—or even those of a rather unusual small company such as Cray Research or Biomation, to name two with some obvious ECL expertise.

I make this statement on the basis of successfully developing a medium-sized, high-performance ECL midicomputer under what might be called primitive industrial conditions at a company (Racal-Milgo) having no prior experience building either ECL systems or digital computers. The company management did not particularly understand digital computers, although they did have some expertise in analog computers. The backup resources which one expects to find in place in even a small computer mainframe house simply weren't there.

To top it all off, I myself am a computer systems type—ones and zeroes, architecture, logic design, machine-level software, microprogram-ming—with very little expertise in, say, linear circuit design or electro-magnetic field theory. All the same, with one sharp technician working with me full-time plus part-time help from a few other people, I was able to get a high-performance digital system of about 900 ECL 10K chips developed and operating in about 15 months. Thereafter, for several months, it was operated many hours a day, five or six days a week, as part of a larger signal-processing system, with very few maintenance problems. If I can do something like that, probably you can too.

The Miami Number Cruncher

The architecture of this midicomputer is not the main point of my presentation, so I'll say just enough about it to put it in perspective. It is three-address format, with a 48-bit instruction word and a 12-bit data word. Instructions and data come from separate memories with separate addressing spaces ("Harvard architecture"). Arithmetic is generally 24-bit two's-complement, with some 12-bit operations also available. The minor cycle (*clock interval*) is about 10.17 nanoseconds, which is the reciprocal of the 98.304-MHz basic frequency. One microprogram step requires a major cycle consisting of 5 to 12 minor cycles according to a 3-bit microprogrammed field.

Normal execution time for a 24-bit add or subtract instruction is 163 nanoseconds, and a Boolean instruction requires one minor cycle less; instructions of both these types require two major cycles. The time of 163 nanoseconds is for a *memory-to-memory* operation, not merely register-to-register, since the main data memory (4K 12-bit words) is comprised of 20-nanosecond-access 1K-by-1-bit ECL memory chips (type 10415A/10146). Two copies of all main memory words are implemented, in order to avoid the penalty of an extra major cycle on each execution of one of these instructions.

The approximate times for some other 24-bit three-address operations are: 1.1 microseconds for multiplication, 3.5 microseconds for division, and 13 microseconds for the square root of a sum. There are both single-word and blocks oriented input and output instructions, and an external command instruction, with a fully asynchronous handshake control philosophy. All instruction sequences are controlled entirely by stored-microprogram techniques.

The computer itself, including both data and instruction memories, occupies three large [418 dual in-line package (DIP) locations] wire-wrap boards mounted in aluminum frames and draws a little more than 300 watts. It is part of a larger experimental signal-processing system for a proprietary real-time application and was never intended to be a product in its own right.

Test Equipment

Probably the scale of this machine is larger than should be attempted under home lab conditions. Nevertheless, the only important resources I had that would be difficult to match in a well-equipped homebrew lab were a much larger test equipment budget and other people to do some of the work.

By far the two most important pieces of test equipment were a Tektronix type 485 portable 350-MHz oscilloscope and a Data I/O model VI programmable read-only memory (PROM) programmer. The 485 is a marvelous scope, but is much higher in performance than needed for routine measurements, even in ECL work, and is priced out of the reach of most hobbyists. I had previously used a Tektronix 150-MHz type 454 scope for TTL work, and this model should be quite adequate for ECL. A 50-MHz or 60-MHz scope such as a Tektronix type 547 or type 453 could be used effectively as long as its limitations were understood and conservative design practices were followed (more on this later).

As for the PROM programmer, this was needed because Miami is, for digital systems work, an isolated area far from the bright lights of technology. In Silicon Valley, Los Angeles, or Boston, an enterprising hobbyist should be able to buy preprogrammed ECL PROMs from a distributor or even a manufacturer, although it may still be a while before they are sold over the counter in every shopping center.

ECL Transmission Lines—Image and Reality

Perhaps the single statement that scared me most, as I embarked on the development of Racal-Milgo's ECL number cruncher, was this one: "In high-speed systems, the inductance, capacitance, and signal delay along interconnections cannot be ignored. The only practical way of dealing with these factors is to treat interconnections as transmission lines" (Fairchild 1977). This statement is, of course, literally true in a technical sense, and yet it is enormously misleading. It raises vivid mental images of huge steel towers marching across the wasteland, with long wires dangling from brown insulators in catenary curves. It tends to scare hell out of people who are used to treating logic signals simply as wires from one point to another, as in garden-variety or low-power Schottky TTL.

The truth is that any type of logic operating at relatively high speeds has to be treated with extreme care—not just ECL. I have found that there is essentially no difference between the care that must be taken in designing a good Schottky TTL system, with respect to interconnection practice, and that needed in designing a good ECL system; but the ECL system will run somewhat more than twice as fast, is actually easier to debug and get running, springs fewer nasty surprises on you during the checkout process, and tends on the whole to come closer to treating you right if you have treated it right.

Actually, all the transmission-line property means in practice is that the last thing attached to each and every signal wire in an ECL computer is a resistor.

If your system is entirely wire-wrapped, as mine was, on a board with good voltage planes (more on that later), the characteristic impedance of each wire is that of a "wire over ground" and is somewhere between 100 and 120 ohms. And if you wade through all the formidable equations in Z's and i's in Motorola's various handbooks, one of the things you discover is that nothing really bad happens—just a few percent reflection —if there is a fair amount of mismatch between the line and the terminating resistor. Because the wire over ground on a wire-wrap board full of other wires is at a varying height anyway, and the characteristic impedance depends on that height, the characteristic impedance of that wire is bound to be "smeared out" and not very precise.

Appropriate Resistors

I used two types of resistors: thick-film, which come in 16-pin DIPs costing $1.25 to $2.50 each, depending on quantity, from Beckman, Bourns, and other vendors, with 11 individual resistors per DIP; and 1/8-watt carbon resistors, which are so tiny that the leads can be wire-wrapped around backplane pins. Most of the resistors overall were of the thick-film DIP variety, and the ratio of ECL integrated circuit (IC) DIPs to resistor DIPs was roughly 3:1.

There are also single-in-line (SIP) resistor packages, and "active terminators" (Fairchild type 10014) with a nonlinear current-versus-voltage characteristic. In any case, the other end of the resistor is terminated to a supply voltage (V_{TT}) intermediate between the two usual supply voltages (V_{CC} and V_{EE}).

The *Thevenin equivalent* scheme is a second way of terminating a signal line in its characteristic impedance. This approach avoids having a V_{TT} plane at all and presumably also inflicts less noise from the logic on the main power supplies in some cases; however, it dissipates about 11 times as much extra power per line termination as does the previous method. In the Thevenin equivalent scheme, the termination point for each signal line is connected to both V_{CC} and V_{EE} by resistors whose values are chosen to form a voltage divider (Thevenin network) such that the voltage drop produces V_{TT} at the termination point. Beckman also makes Thevenin network thick-film termination resistor packs, with four such networks per DIP.

To be sure, there are other ways of approaching signal interconnection besides my recipe for terminating each and every signal line in its characteristic impedance, especially if you are (a) skilled in linear circuit design, and/or (b) a masochist. You can simply not terminate the line, and compute out the maximum number of inches or tenths of an inch allowable for line length under each given set of conditions for each signal line. Or you can use *series termination*, in which there is a resistor between the output stage of your gate, or whatever, and the input that is being driven. (There is just one input per line, but with many lines fanning out from one original output.) Possibly in a big company environment where one is using 17-layer etched circuit boards like those used in the Texas Instruments Advanced Scientific Computer, there are real advantages to these schemes. In the wire-wrap world there aren't any, and it is better to terminate each and every signal line in a resistor and then relax, since you have thereby at one stroke slain most of the big, scary goblins of high-speed logic systems—crosstalk, ringing and reflections, limits on line length, and so forth.

Some Good News

And now for some pleasant surprises. First, 10K outputs are *open-emitter* and may be tied together in almost the same way as TTL open-collector outputs, but with wire-ORing of outputs viewed as assertive-high and wire-ANDing of outputs viewed as assertive-low. However, since the termination resistor has a value determined by the characteristic impedance of the signal line, one no longer has to recompute this value every time the number of driving outputs or the number of driven inputs changes, as one is supposed to do when stringing together open-collector TTL. ECL isn't slowed down much by stringing together open-emitter outputs: Motorola estimates 50 picoseconds per additional output. When five or more outputs are strung together, one may start to see minor glitches in the waveform; I never tried that. Stringing together open-emitter outputs turns out to be a valuable technique in ECL, for two reasons: It does an extra level of logic with essentially no extra logic delay and no additional gates, which together with the usual two-rail outputs makes ECL small-scale integration (SSI) much more powerful per gate package than TTL SSI. Also, it allows in-circuit stimulation of ECL devices while your system is running, or trying unsuccessfully to run, at full speed; any logic point can be tied to a logic "1" source with impunity in order to change what is happening so that you can study it. This is a very powerful troubleshooting technique. (It is normally forbidden in

TTL troubleshooting because of an unfortunate tendency to melt IC output transistors in totem-pole devices.)

Second, since virtually any ECL IC output stage will drive a 50-ohm line, it will also drive two properly terminated 100-ohm lines going to different places, which is very useful, for instance, when driving a lot of memory address lines. By way of comparison, there are only a few TTL devices—the 74S140 dual NAND buffer and the 74128 quad NOR buffer, for instance—that will drive such low-impedance lines.

Third, once you have bitten the bullet and terminated a signal line in its characteristic impedance, you can stop worrying about how long that line is, at least as long as it doesn't go off the board away from the ground plane. The boards I used were roughly a foot wide and almost two feet long, and some signal lines were longer than two feet, which would be rather unacceptable using TTL gates since the usually quoted line length limit is ten inches. (For TTL tri-state buffers it is much longer.) ECL signals that go off the board should be differential, but even that turns out to be less frightening than it sounds, as will be discussed later on.

Fourth, in ECL the only limitation on fanout that matters is that each additional input connected to a line adds a few picofarads of capacitance, just as additional TTL or MOS inputs do in other systems; and as the number of inputs increases, the rise and fall times lengthen a bit. But instead of a fanout of 10 as for garden-variety or Schottky TTL, or of 21 as for low-power Schottky TTL, the fanout limit imposed by driving capability is something like 92, which is as good as infinity for most purposes. I never really had to test this proposition out: it usually was not necessary to go beyond driving 10 to 12 loads with one output, except in special situations like driving memory IC address inputs with buffer gates; and even there I stayed conservative.

Voltage Planes and "Positive Earth"

ECL, even the easier-to-use 10K, should still be built on a good board for best results. "Good" here means that the voltage plane or planes occupy at least 50% of the available area of the board as it is viewed from above, say by Superman with X-ray vision if the board is multilayer with internal voltage planes. I knew where to get really deluxe boards, from a successor company (Kleffman Electronics, Minnetonka, Minnesota) to one I once worked for, with four complete voltage planes, but up until now these boards have not been offered for public sale. However, the designer of

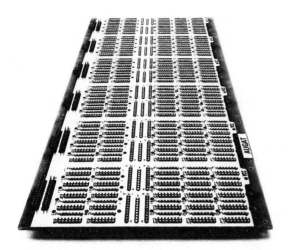

Figure 21.1
Top view of Augat wire-wrap board.

these boards, Gary McPherson, is now in business for himself, so you can try contacting him (see the appendix at the end of this chapter). A number of circuit-board companies do now offer wire-wrap breadboards that look satisfactory for ECL and in some cases state such a design objective (see the list in the appendix). Augat pioneered in this area, with a three-layer board, and boards with a similar design philosophy are now also available from Excel, Garry, Mupac, and SAE. Interdyne has a rather different type of board, which also looks plausible. These boards do, of course, cost more than vector board—probably $200–$300 for one to accommodate 150 or so DIPs. In most cases the DIPs plug directly into the holes in the round pins on the board, and no additional IC sockets are needed.

Figures 21.1 and 21.2 show an Augat board in top view and in local cross section, and figure 21.3 shows Mupac's Sponge board. Doucet (1974) is a useful technical note available from Augat on wire-wrapping ECL logic using their boards.

One of the disconcerting facts about ECL that seems to baffle every person newly introduced to the stuff is that V_{CC}—yes, I did say V_{CC}—is normally specified as $+0.0$ volts, or "positive earth," as British car aficionados say. After all, everyone who has designed TTL or MOS systems knows that V_{CC} has to be $+5.0$ volts and that it is the other

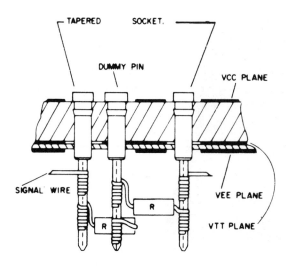

RESISTOR TERMINATION

Figure 21.2
Cross section of Augat wire-wrap board.

voltage supply that is at $+0.0$ volts—why, it is even called ground. What, then, is this V_{EE} that is specified as -5.2 volts? Why isn't V_{CC} specified as $+5.2$ volts and V_{EE} as ground? Certainly the logic doesn't care what the dc potential of various circuit points is relative to Mother Earth, does it? For that matter, why can't ECL run on a 5.0-volt spread between the two main supply voltages as TTL does?

It turns out that when Motorola originally instituted this now-universal $+0.0/-5.2$ specification, the goal that they were in a subtle way trying to achieve was to get their customers to use the best plane on the board for V_{CC} rather than for V_{EE} in case there was any difference in the extent of the planes. The circuit properties of ECL are such that system performance is affected much more by inadequacy of the V_{CC} plane than by, say, a V_{EE} plane that only covers part of the board and shares the same surface with the V_{TT} plane. To keep the internal workings of ECL ICs from being confused by electrical transients due to their own output stages, most of them (except the ones with particularly serendipitous internal layout)

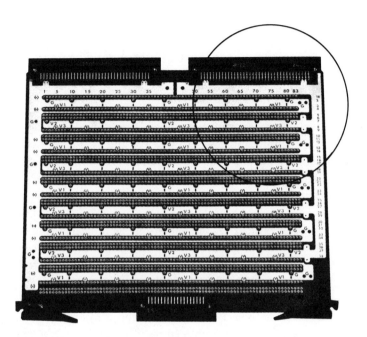

Figure 21.3
Top view of Mupac wire-wrap board.

have two or even three separate V_{CC} pins. Do not, however, draw the conclusion that you must actually connect these different pins to different V_{CC} planes—they don't want you to do that, but rather to connect them separately to the same V_{CC} plane. It makes sense if you think about it: you don't want the potentials at different V_{CC} pins to diverge—you only want to convey the output switching noise to ground without it going through the tender internal gates.

The Kleffman boards I used had two complete ground planes and two other voltage planes, having been designed to accommodate a mixture of Schottky MSI devices with linears that often required a -5.0-volt supply in addition to the normal TTL supply voltages. I adapted these boards for ECL by using the ground planes for V_{CC} (after all, it is at ground), the TTL V_{CC} planes for V_{EE}, and the -5.0 plane for V_{TT}.

Now that the upside-down supply voltage polarity issue has been disposed of, you will know what I mean when I state that V_{TT} (or the equivalent individual termination points if the Thevenin-equivalent voltage divider scheme is used) is normally specified as -2.0 volts.

Decoupling Capacitors

In any high-speed logic system, not just ECL, there should be an easy path for high-frequency noise to get between the two main supply-voltage planes without passing through the logic and confusing the hell out of it on the way. Lower-frequency noise is usually dealt with by connecting a fairly large tantalum electrolytic capacitor, say 22 microfarads or larger, between the two main supply voltages (for ECL, V_{CC} and V_{EE}) at the point where they are brought onto the board, and perhaps at other points on the board also. High-frequency noise is similarly shorted out using little ceramic disk capacitors scattered all over the board, mingled with the semiconductors.

Although I have seen printed recommendations as mild as using an 0.01-microfarad disk capacitor for every few ICs, again—as in the case of signal-line termination—my recipe calls for doing it right everywhere to start with and finishing off the goblins for good. Here, doing it right means using one 0.1-microfarad disk capacitor (ten times as large) for each and every DIP on the board, which thoroughly slays many noise problems otherwise likely to be encountered in either ECL or Schottky systems. AVX (née Aerovox) is the brand I have used, and there are some other vendors also whom I haven't personally calibrated. These capacitors are physically quite small and cost in the range of 20¢ each in modest quantities.

The reason why I—and the people who write ECL applications notes for semiconductor manufacturers—insist on using disk capacitors for this application is that they provide the best practical way to get just a capacitor, without at the same time getting an inductor and a resistor willy-nilly into the bargain. The last thing you need is to have all your little decoupling capacitors turn into little tank circuits scattered all over your printed circuit board.

The Kleffman boards I used and some of the commercially available boards, such as Augat's (see figure 20.2) and Interdyne's, provide yet one more weapon in the battle against supply-voltage noise. A pair of supply-voltage planes are physically separated by only a very small thickness—an 0.004-inch mylar layer in the case of the Kleffman boards—so that there is in effect a distributed capacitor, sufficiently large to severely restrict the magnitude of the very-highest-frequency noise (say 150 Mhz and up), between all points on these planes.

Keeping Supply Voltage Smooth

The ever-present possibility of ac noise on the power-supply voltages is probably the real reason for the general industry concern with power-supply-voltage margins in digital logic. It isn't hard today to build a fairly economical power supply with very tight regulation—0.1% to 0.2%—according to what one seasoned power-supply designer once told me. The non-trivial part is getting that precise voltage conveyed to each and every DIP. ECL, by the way, is normally specified as having a $\pm 10\%$ supply-voltage tolerance, and one major vendor (Fairchild) offers 10K logic with internal voltage compensation. In contrast, normal commercial-grade TTL is specified to tolerate just $\pm 5\%$ supply-voltage misbehavior.

Why, then, is 10K specified for a 5.2-volt main-supply-voltage spread rather than a 5.0-volt spread if it is so tolerant of funny power-supply levels? Simply for optimization of other circuit parameters. Under normal circumstances, 10K will run perfectly well on a 5.0-volt spread.

Although I did not find it necessary to do this in my system, and I doubt that you will either, it is worth noting that an ECL system can be designed to present an invariant load to the power supply—in contrast to a TTL system, since some TTL gate packages may draw as much as seven times as much supply current with all outputs low as with all outputs high, and thus full-word-complementing operations may result in high-frequency supply-voltage hiccups.

One of the world's fastest computers, the CRAY-1, capable of 138,000,000 floating-point arithmetic operations per second on a sustained basis, is designed according to this invariant-power-supply-load philosophy (Russell 1978, p. 72; IEEE Computer Society 1976). A number of rather extreme measures have been taken in the CRAY-1 to control various types of noise, for obvious reasons. The non-memory portions are designed largely with simple gates (Fairchild type 11C01) having "two-rail" outputs (the output and its complement, on separate leads), with both outputs terminated even if both are not used. In this configuration, each 11C01 presents an invariant load to the power supply. Single-rail output devices such as memory ICs use Thevenin termination. The 72-bit (64 information plus 8 checking), 1,048,576-word CRAY-1 main memory is comprised entirely of 1K-by-1 ECL memory ICs essentially similar (and actually bought to a longer access-time specification) to the ones I used. Of course, I only needed about 200 of them rather than 74,000 or so.

Off-Board Interconnection

Probably one could, at least in some cases, get away with running a properly terminated signal line right off one board onto another, if all the precautions already discussed were taken. I never tried it. In the first place, one can't assume that the voltage-plane potentials on one board exactly match those on some other board the way they're supposed to, even if one has used 0.1 microfarad capacitors like popcorn as I have recommended. In the second place, there has to be some way to keep the signal lines at the same characteristic impedance, without discontinuities, as they leap through space between boards—and, worse yet, to keep them shielded from various forms of electromagnetic interference (such as each other) now that they are no longer safely close to a ground or other voltage plane.

Again, there is a simple, seemingly drastic, very effective way of solving the problem which pretty well decimates the goblins. As I stated in the previous section, many ECL gates have two-rail outputs. (This may be an unfamiliar idea to TTL chauvinists; except for flipflops, one multiplexer configuration, and a rather little-known two-rail buffer called the 74265, TTL devices don't usually offer this feature.) ECL gate circuit parameters are such that any two-rail gate can be used to drive a differential line, with all of the implied advantages of common-mode-noise rejection and insensitivity to temperature and dc-voltage discrepancies between different boards. Since such a line may in principle be as long as a few hundred feet before purely circuit-design-parameter alligators start snapping at you, there is no abrupt length limit of concern to a hobbyist. Of course, remember that a nanosecond is approximately a "light foot" and that electrons in a wire only travel about 2/3 as fast as light travels. Thus you may observe, at least if you can borrow a 485 scope for a while, that each 6-inches to 8-inches of signal line requires another nanosecond for the signal to traverse it, for differential as well as for single-ended signals. I was at one point rather startled to realize that some 15-inch signal lines were actually a bigger delay factor in one data path than a whole row of 2-nanosecond buffers with short signal lines coming and going.

At the other end of the differential line, on the other board, one uses a differential receiver element with a resistor between the two differential line ends. These elements come in four flavors: three types of triple elements with two-rail outputs (type 10116 for plain vanilla, 10114 for hysteresis, and 10216 for extra blazing speed) and one (type 10115) with quadruple elements with single-rail outputs.

For more details see Blood 1974, which also describes how to turn one of the triple two-rail devices into a Schmitt trigger circuit. Two cautions: First, any unused elements in a differential receiver DIP should be "strapped" to force their outputs into one logic state or the other, as otherwise they will hover right at the logic threshold point and the on-chip bias networks will get screwed up and confuse the elements that are being used. Also, we found that the resistor values suggested for use with the receiver elements by Blood (1974) were not the right ones for our interconnection system, and we wound up using resistors with values close to 300 ohms for all three resistors shown in figure 3 of that reference.

Cabling

There are probably other acceptable physical means for getting these differential signals from one board to another, but the one I recommend is flat ribbon cable, available in various forms from 3M, Augat, Elco, Spectra-Strip, and probably other companies. Specifically, what I have used is 40-wire 3M cable, which is physically surprisingly small. Many such cables stack neatly in a small thickness, and fairly abrupt turns and at least some limited hinge action are possible. 3M supplies little press-on connectors and a tool to crunch them into place, one at each end of the cable.

The electrical shielding properties of this cable are excellent if one does not get greedy about how many logic signals pass through a single cable. There should be one or more ground wires at each edge of the cable, and alternating signal and ground wires within the cable. This means that one can only transmit nine differential logic signals in one 40-wire cable, since doing just that according to the recipe demands a minimum of 37 wires. The cable format is, of course,

$$G \ G \ S_1 \ G \ \bar{S}_1 \ G \ S_2 \ G \ \bar{S}_2 \ G \ \ldots \ G \ S_9 \ G \ \bar{S}_9 \ G \ G \ G$$

When one stacks several such cables, the signal-ground-signalbar-ground philosophy should also prevail along the "z axis," that is, in the direction perpendicular to the plane of each cable as one goes through successive cables. Thus, in the cables immediately above and below the one whose format has just been given, there would be three edge G's on the left and two on the right, and so forth, so that the signal wires are staggered.

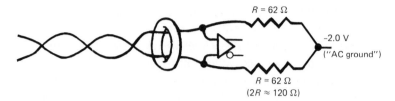

Figure 21.4
Receiving board termination scheme.

For shipping differential signals around on a board, say from ribbon cable connectors to differential receiver ICs, use *twisted-pair* wire. To make your own, begin with two 15-foot lengths of different colors of wire-wrap wire, secure one end of each wire to something across the room from yourself, clamp the other end of each wire into the chuck of a small electric drill, back up holding the drill until both wires are taut and close together, and gun the drill for a few seconds until the two wires are twisted together for their entire lengths with a satisfactory number of twists per inch. Inevitably there will be a slightly greater density of twists at the end of the wires close to the drill, but don't let that worry you.

Another Off-Board Interconnection Scheme

The following scheme is the work of Norm Winningstad of Floating Point Systems, who is expert in such matters. I haven't tried it myself, but there are plausible physical reasons why it should work even better than the previous scheme. It is different in three respects.

First, within each ribbon cable, use a different signal format, namely,

$$G \ G \ G \ S_1 \ \overline{S}_1 \ G \ G \ S_2 \ \overline{S}_2 \ G \ G \ \ldots \ G \ G \ S_9 \ \overline{S}_9 \ G \ G \ G$$

This makes good sense: the closer S_j and $\overline{S}_j$ are physically, the more nearly their externally produced electromagnetic fields cancel. The z-axis signal-ground-signalbar-ground approach remains in effect as in my method, since from one cable to another the signals aren't necessarily related in phase and thus won't cancel. Don't try to economize by using just one ground wire between each pair of signal wires; having two wires there provides much better isolation, since stray fields from each signal-wire pair basically have a whole ground wire to themselves on each side.

Second, use the termination scheme illustrated in figure 21.4 on the receiving board, rather than the one described by Blood (1974). Any of the four aforementioned types of 10K differential receiver elements will work. The *bifilar ferrite toroid* is optional. ("Bifilar" means that both wires go through it; a "ferrite toroid" is, of course, a small doughnut-shaped magnetic core.) If it is used, however, it will nicely throttle un-wanted common-mode noise transients while letting the desired signal pass almost unscathed, since the latter produces almost no net external electromagnetic field to sweep across the toroid—at least, if the toroid is physically close enough to the −2 volt termination point. This is the case, so that the signals on both sides of the differential line are still essentially in phase at that point, and hence are equal and opposite.

Third, use flexible plastic sheets between successive stacked ribbon cables to increase the physical distance between their wires. Note that this plastic is not a conductor—it isn't intended to be. Shielded ribbon cable is a different game, outside the scope of this discussion; for one thing, the stuff with built-in shielding is physically much stiffer and doesn't bend as readily.

Keeping It All Cool

If one firmly grasps a 1K-by-1 ECL memory IC (type 10415A/10146) after the computer has been running for a few minutes, one can get second-degree burns. This IC type dissipates as much as 3/4 watt, and we measured ceramic DIP case temperatures as high as 60° C. Up-down counters (type 10136) and hex D-flipflops (type 10186) also run pretty hot, although not quite that hot. Oddly enough, 256-by-4 PROMs (type 10149) run much cooler—about 45° C. The average power dissipation for all ICs in the entire midicomputer, including SSI and medium-scale integration (MSI) types as well as large-scale integration (LSI) types such as the 10149 and 10415A, is about 1/3 watt. Of course, probably about 1/10 of that is dissipated as heat, not within the ICs themselves but within the termination resistor DIPs.

Despite all that, we encountered no problems attributable to heat. The ICs simply sat out in the open, on large boards that were mounted vertically like pages of a book on a central vertical post, free to flop back and forth through a small arc since they were interconnected by ribbon cable as described. Although we had a forced-air cooling scheme figured out, we never had to use it and relied purely on convection and radiant cooling. I also found that ECL ICs, once installed and running properly, very rarely died of natural causes, at least as compared with TTL ICs in similar applications. Probably the very high percentage (about 78) of voltage plane on our boards helped a lot to conduct the heat efficiently away from the ICs. Also, Augat has done studies which show that wire-wrapped boards run cooler than etched boards with equivalent circuitry on them.

An ECL system installed within a closed metal cabinet, particularly if the boards are mounted horizontally, should doubtless be cooled by some more active technique, such as forced air. As for what the big-machine people do, Control Data's big computers are Freon-cooled, with lots of little pipes running along chassis structural members. The CRAY-1 uses not only Freon cooling but heavy gauge heat-conductive copper sheets. (And, even though the CRAY-1 main frame itself is physically small enough to fit into your spare bedroom, the auxiliary cooling apparatus might drive you out of the rest of the house.) Some large IBM computers use chilled-water cooling. Some day, an ingenious hobbyist trying to cool a really massive homebrew ECL system may wind up using the refrigeration unit from a used Sears Coldspot, but open-rack convection cooling or forced air should do the trick for most systems.

There were a few Saturdays when we worked on the Racal-Milgo system and Plant Engineering forgot to turn on the air-conditioning until the middle of the morning; and in Miami during the summer an unventilated room is bad news for people as well as for computers. The system didn't run too well on those days until the air-conditioning had been on long eough to pull the temperature in the lab down below, say, 90° F. However, we really had no reason to believe it was the ECL that was giving problems. We were using a semi-homebrew IM6100-based, PDP-8-compatible microcomputer to control the larger ECL machine, which is also a likely technique for a hobbyist who already has one or two other microcomputers. Most of the system reliability problems that we were actually able to pin down turned out to be trouble with the 2102-type MOS memory ICs used with the IM6100, and the specific symptom of trouble we had on those hot Saturday mornings was usually inability to load the ECL midicomputer instruction memory from the IM6100. Nevertheless, if you do choose to rely on open-rack convection cooling, your ECL homebrew number cruncher may run a bit better if you keep your spare bedroom at a temperature that you also find agreeable.

If Your Scope Isn't Fast Enough

ECL 10K output stages have a nominal logic swing from about -0.900 volts (considered to be a "logic 1" or "high") down to about -1.750 volts ("logic 0" or "low"), with the logic threshold being around -1.290 volts. (Now you know what these negative numbers really mean.) If you have followed the interconnection recipe of the preceding paragraphs faithfully, you should see picture-book square waveforms everywhere, although they do look just a bit cleaner at the end of a signal line close to the termination resistor than at points along the way. Even with a 485 scope, which shows every little wiggle, the ECL waveforms I observed looked very clean compared to the grassy ones sometimes seen in high-speed TTL systems.

If you must use a slower scope for economic reasons, you will, of course, observe even cleaner waveforms (which aren't exactly real) with slightly rounded corners, which may not deceive you very much about anything essential as long as you remember why it is that they look so clean. The principal danger is that, now and then, there will be a glitch on some signal line that is insufficiently wide to show up on the scope, or at least to look to you as if it is of sufficient magnitude to reach the logic threshold—when, all the while, here is an up-down counter (type 10136) or hex D-flipflop (type 10186) or other edge-sensitive device whose clock input is connected to that signal line, which sure is acting as if it is getting an edge at just about that time. Probably it is, and you just can't see it because your scope has smoothed it out for you. Realizing that such must be the case, you have your choice of (a) getting hold of a more expensive scope, or (b) "reading between the lines" of what your humbler scope is telling you, terminating that clock line better, and seeing if the problem doesn't then go away. Or perhaps the clock-line glitch is really due to a switching hazard in the logic you designed to control that clock line.

Product Families

To oversimplify things a bit in a manner meaningful to a ones-and-zeroes type like me, ECL is one type of current-mode logic. The state of an ECL gate is determined by which of the two output legs the main current is being steered through, and the resulting voltages at the output points are interesting side effects but are not the basic switching phenomenon.

In TTL and MOS, on the other hand, the output voltage states are where the action is, and the currents tag along after the voltage as interesting (and often inconvenient) side effects. In Schottky TTL logic, for instance, the voltage states you actually see on a scope are about $+0.2$ volts for a logic 0 and $+4.1$ volts for a logic 1. Incidentally, since Schottky TTL rise times are probably a bit faster than the 3.5-nanosecond to 4-nanosecond times characteristic of ECL 10K, you may notice that the "voltage slew rate," or whatever that parameter should be called, is many times greater for Schottky TTL, and is in fact roughly equal to the corresponding rate for the very fastest ECL families.

There are lots of custom families made by IC manufactures for direct sale to large computer companies that fall into the general category of current-mode logic. However, most of these are not available for sale to the general public. There are six product families, more specifically considered to be ECL, that are sold to all comers:

● ECL I, contemporary with diode-transistor logic (DTL) and now obsolete and not used in new designs.

● ECL II, contemporary with and somewhat akin to H-series TTL, and recently also declared obsolete by its manufacturer (Motorola).

● ECL III, extremely fast, but with only a modest selection of SSI and MSI types.

● ECL 10K, the only one that I consider well adapted to homebrew use.

● ECL 95K, much like 10K, but a marketplace also-ran.

● ECL 100K, the fastest one of all.

The first four of these families were introduced by Motorola, and the last two by Fairchild. Fairchild, Motorola, and Plessey also have various other ECL products that are not really organized into families—for instance, Fairchild's 11C01 OR/NOR gate (used in the CRAY-1), which is 100K-technology devide offered in a non-100K package. The last four families are, or can be made to be, electrically compatible so that with some care devices may be mixed in a system.

The Even Faster Stuff

A hobbyist willing to hand-solder, rather than wire-wrap, all interconnections to that part of his system might with due care succeed in making some limited use of ECL III and/or ECL 100K (Blood 1980). (A few turns of wrapped wire, it turns out, can function all too well as an inductor when hit with the 900 or 700 picosecond edges respectively characteristic of those families, and the resulting impedance discontinuities make reflections.) The technology required to build a system of any size using one of these families, however, remains more difficult at the present time than the technology for ECL 10K. Nevertheless, the three papers by Barry Gilbert of the Mayo Clinic (Gilbert and Harris 1980; Gilbert, Krueger, and Beistad 1980; and Gilbert 1982) describe a very practical approach to wire-wrapped use of ECL 100K.

There are two ECL III devices of some interest to a hobbyist: type 1648, which is called a voltage-controlled oscillator, and type 1658, which is called a voltage-controlled multivibrator. There is no announced ECL 10K product matching either of these descriptions, and they are useful. I used a 1648 once in an otherwise all-TTL system to provide a hand-adjustable system clock source for testing clock margin—that is, how fast the system could be made to go before it failed. It worked fine after being well shielded.

Those ECL 10K parts having type numbers of form 102XX (106XX in military temperature) form a subfamily with appreciably different properties. Hand-soldered connections are also advisable when using any of these. They are quite a lot faster than their normal ECL 10K equivalents and consume essentially no more power, so they sound like a supergood deal. Alas, this greater speed has been obtained by cutting very short the leisurely rise and fall times deliberately designed into normal ECL 10K. To oversimplify a bit, normal ECL 10K rise and fall times are perhaps 3.5 to 4 nanoseconds—much longer than the nominal logic delay of 2 nanoseconds or so; whereas 102XX rise and fall times are probably not much different from the logic delay, which I have observed to be about 1.25 nanoseconds. Reluctantly, I concluded that system noise problems would be minimized by restricting the use of 102XX parts to those situations where that last ounce of speed is really required, for instance in the clock generation circuits. The only example of proven crosstalk trouble in the Racal-Milgo midicomputer was due to an unnecessarily long wire being driven by a type 10212 buffer; it was eliminated by relocating a few ICs so that that buffer was closer to its load. (Note: The more recent Motorola "10KM" parts, with numbers like 10K101, claim to offer better trade-offs, and you should investigate these; they weren't available in time for my Racal-Milgo project.)

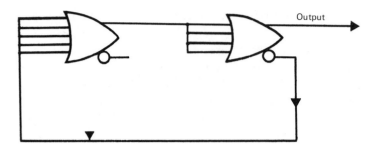

Figure 21.5
Fixed-frequency oscillator.

One other simple and plausible use of ECL III or ECL 100K is for building high-speed, fixed-frequency oscillators. Two type 1688 OR/NOR gates on the same IC in series make a dandy oscillator (see figure 21.5), which we observed to generate various frequencies from 100 MHz to 170 MHz depending on which particular Motorola or Plessey sample we were using. Probably an 11C01 would produce a somewhat higher frequency. Don't try to build this type of oscillator with a single gate—it won't even oscillate, but just hang in there with its output at about the threshold voltage. If swapping ICs around doesn't get you the frequency you are shooting for, try hanging very small capacitors on gate outputs to slow them down. (Caution: With ECL III at least, the speed of oscillation may depend on the ambient temperature.)

Logic-Drawing Conventions

If one wishes to think "assertive-high"—that is, the more positive of the two output voltage states represents a 1 and the more negative state represents a 0—then it follows that in TTL logic the simplest and most natural gate structure is the NAND gate, whereas in ECL logic it turns out to be an OR/NOR gate. It is fairly clearcut in both cases what is really the simplest circuit for the silicon people to build.

Since the ORing together of "min-terms" seems to be more natural to human psychology than the ANDing together of "max-terms," part of learning to use ECL consists of learning to use "mixed-logic" conventions in some form. These conventions allow you to think of—and draw—a given physical gate circuit as performing either an OR function or an AND function, and then to consider as a separate issue the assertiveness of that gate's input and output signals.

Soaking up the mixed-logic viewpoint should also be part of learning to design with TTL, but unfortunately it isn't always (Grossman 1973; 1978). In fact, many erudite polemics have been written defending older and less general viewpoints that I feel are now best understood as evolutionary stages on the way to the full-blown mixed-logic viewpoint. One of these older viewpoints is the one that results in the dozens of busy little black and white triangular flag symbols on the inputs and outputs of ECL 10K parts as drawn on Motorola's data sheets.

I can only say that once I forced myself to give up my Bronze-Age viewpoint and learned to use mixed-logic conventions, within a week I was wondering why I had ever used anything else. If one uses an additional logic symbol to denote "psychological inversion"—implying that although the electrical polarity of some signal (say, for example, BANANAS) hasn't changed, one's perception of its meaning or "psychological polarity" has changed (in the example, to YES WE HAVE NO BANANAS), then logic drawings can be made almost as semantically precise and self-checking as logic equations. This is not an academic exercise; it helps you spot real mistakes before you wire the machine up wrong and waste a lot of time trying to figure out why it isn't working.

Kintner 1971 is an eminently sane paper on this whole dogma-ridden subject; I have relied on it for several years for guidance as to logic drawing conventions. Recently there have been more papers in the same vein. I have just one minor quibble with Kintner: the symbol suggested there for psychological inversion, a small line drawn across the signal line at right angles, tends not to show up too well on blueline copies. A little solid triangle or arrowhead drawn next to the signal line shows up much better, and there is a hole of the right shape on most templates. (See figure 21.5 again.)

Figure 21.6 shows the same physical gate element, one of the two-input elements from a type 10105 triple OR/NOR gate part, drawn first with assertive-high inputs as an OR/NOR gate and second with assertive-low inputs as an AND/NAND gate. You get the idea. The pins are all still in the same relative positions. If one uses the standard inversion bubbles correctly, one doesn't really need the additional symbols such as triangular flags—they in fact introduce one too many degrees of freedom and just confuse the issue. I suggest the proper use of mixed-logic con-

Figure 21.6
Two representations of the same gate.

ventions as a sort of software adjunct to the rest of my homebrew ECL recipe.

Finale

I have used references sparingly, because many of them tend to give ECL system design an air of awesome complexity and desperate peril, and this is exactly what I am trying to tell you isn't necessarily so. However, if you get seriously into ECL you probably will want to get hold of Motorola's set of application notes pertaining to ECL 10K, as well as some worthwhile material published by Fairchild and Signetics (figure 21.7). Good luck, and may the Force be with you.

Acknowledgments

There are several people who were at Racal-Milgo when I was, without whose efforts the number cruncher would never have happened and I wouldn't have been able to tell you about it. Two deserve particular mention. Dick Joerger is the sharp technician referred to in this paper; he built most of the machine with his own two hands. Rick Johnston did the preliminary design of the control section and improved it greatly from what I had originally planned; he made it a pipelined, overlapped, stored-microprogram machine with a self-restarting main timing circuit.

There are also three electronics industry veterans without whose wise opinions I would not have had the temerity to try to build the machine out of ECL. They are Stan Bruederle of Signetics, Rob Walker of LSI Logic (at that time still at Fairchild), and Norm Winningstad of Floating Point Systems. Everything each of them told me about ECL turned out

Figure 21.7
A modern ECL chip: the Motorola MC10901, which multiplies two 8-bit quantities in
25 nanoseconds.

to be absolutely correct, and much of it appears in this paper. If I am
wildly off-base on any topic, it's because I didn't get their complete
message.

References

Blood, W. 1974. Interfacing with MECL 10,000 Integrated Circuits. Application note
AN-720. Phoenix, Ariz.: Motorola Semiconductor Corp.

Blood, W. 1980. *The MECL System Design Handbook*. Phoenix, Ariz.: Motorola Semiconductor Corp.

Cann. R. 1979, 1980. "An analysis/synthesis tutorial." *Computer Music Journal* 3(3): 6–11,
3(4): 9–13, 4(1): 36–42. Article 9 in this volume.

Doucet, L. 1974. Packaging High-Speed ECL Integrated Circuits. Attleboro, Mass.: Augat,
Inc.

Fairchild Semiconductor. 1977. The ECL Databook. Mountain View, Calif.: Fairchild
Semiconductor.

Gilbert, B., and L. Harris. 1980. "Advances in processor architecture, display, and device technology for biomedical image processing." *IEEE Transactions on Nuclear Science* NS-27(3):1197–1206.

Gilbert, B., L. Krueger, and R. Beistad. 1980. "Design of prototype digital processors employing subnanosecond emitter-coupled logic and rapid fabrication techniques." *IEEE Transactions on Components, Hybrids, and Manufacturing Technology* CHMT-3(1): 125–134.

Gilbert, B.1982. "Architectures, tools, and technologies for the development of special-purpose processors." In S. I. Kartashev and S. V. Kartashev, eds. *Supersystems of the Eighties*, vol. 2 of *Modular Computers and Systems*. Englewood Cliffs, N. J.: Prentice-Hall.

Grossman, M. 1978. "Fast logic no problem for wire-wrapped boards." *Electronic Design*. 6 December 1978.

Grossman, S. 1973. "ECL, TTL get together on same board." *Electronics*. 6 December 1973.

IEEE Computer Society. 1976. "CRAY-1: The smaller supercomputer." *IEEE Computer* 3:53.

Kintner, P. 1971. "Mixed logic: A tool for design simplification." *Computer Design* 8:55–60.

Russell, R. 1978. "The CRAY-1 computer system." *Communications of the Association for Computing Machinery* 21(1): 63–72.

Appendix

Here is a list of vendors of various items that you will need, arranged in alphabetical order by topic. My listing them here does not imply any warranty that you will find them utterly perfect, but I have had positive dealings with many of them.

ECL Logic and Memories

Fairchild Semiconductor
464 Ellis Street
Mountain View, CA 94042

Motorola Semiconductor Products, Inc.
Box 20912
Phoenix, AZ 85036

NEC America, Inc.
Electron Devices Division
3070 Lawrence Expressway
Santa Clara, CA 95051
(Head office: Japan)

Plessey Semiconductors
1674 McGaw Avenue
Santa Ana, CA 92715
(Head office: Swindon, U.K.; specialty products only)

Signetics Corporation
811 East Arques Avenue
Sunnyvale, CA 94086

ECL Memories Only

Advanced Micro Devices
901 Thompson Place
Sunnyvale, CA 94086

Fujitsu America, Inc.
2945 Oakmead Village Court
Santa Clara, CA 95051
(Head office: Japan)

National Semiconductor Corporation
2900 Semiconductor Drive
Santa Clara, CA 95051

Siemens Corporation
Salzufer 6-8
Postfach 110560
1000 Berlin 11
West Germany

ECL-Grade Logic Breadboards

Augat, Inc.
33 Perry Avenue
Attleboro, MA 02703

Excel Products Company, Inc.
401 Joyce Kilmer Avenue
New Brunswick, NJ 08903

Garry Manufacturing Company
1010 Jersey Avenue
New Brunswick, NJ 08902

Interdyne, Inc.
14761 Califa Street
Van Nuys, CA 91411

Gary C. McPherson
P. O. Box 1044
Minnetonka, MN 55343

Mupac Corporation
646 Summer Street
Brockton, MA 02402

Stanford Applied Engineering, Inc. (SAE)
340 Martin Avenue
Santa Clara, CA 95050

Flat Ribbon Cable

Augat (see above)

Elco Corporation
2250 Park Place
El Segundo, CA 90245

Eltra Spectra-Strip
7100 Lampson Avenue
Garden Grove, CA 92642

3M Company
Industrial Electrical Products
3M Center
St. Paul, MN 55101

Ceramic Disk Capacitors

AVX Ceramics
P. O. Box 867
Myrtle Beach, SC 29577

Centre Engineering
2820 East College Avenue
State College, PA 16801

Resistor Packages

Beckman Instruments, Inc.
2500 Harbor Boulevard
Fullerton, CA 92634

Bourns, Inc.
1200 Columbia Avenue
Riverside, CA 92507

ILC Data Device Corporation
Airport International Plaza
Bohemia, Long Island, NY 11716

Wirewrap Equipment

Gardner Denver Company
1333 Fulton Street
Grand Haven, MI 49417

OK Machine and Tool Corporation
3455 Conner Street
Bronx, NY 10475

III SOFTWARE SYSTEMS FOR MUSIC

Overview

CURTIS ROADS

These articles are devoted to the programming of digital music systems. The dominant theme is the prudent use of available hardware and software—getting the most out of limited resources. Within the limits of resources, each project in music programming must balance at least three software goals: ease of use, coherence of program design, and efficiency of code. Achieving all these goals is not easy, as they sometimes conflict. A key to reaching these goals is the use of powerful software tools (programs that aid the software developer).

In the 1950s, little was known about the writing of such essential tools as rudimentary compilers (Baur 1976) and operating systems (Strachey 1959). We can scarcely appreciate what it must have been like in 1956 to be the first to conceive and implement a machine-language program to produce a score according to the rules of common-practice harmony, as Hiller and Isaacson (1959) did.

In today's highly interactive personal computing environments, it is difficult to imagine how Mathews could have coded and debugged the synthesis language Music III in 1960 without the luxury of even a macro assembler or an interactive terminal (Roads 1980b). These early achievements remind us of how far we should be able to take today's programming tools if we use them carefully.

Underlying any effort at computer-music programming is someone's conception of a musical task and, ultimately, a musical idea. As these articles point out, the technical and musical goals must be coordinated. The price of a lack of coordination is a system that is musically weak or technically dysfunctional. Another common problem with poorly designed and poorly executed musical software is a lack of "robustness." Such systems are prone to frequent breakdowns or unreliable behavior, requiring extraordinary efforts to get any useful work done with them.

The Language Hierarchy of a Computer System

Computer software is organized in layers. High-level languages, such as Pascal, Lisp, and C, are used throughout music systems. They incorporate data and control structures in a syntax that enables programmers to express algorithms in a relatively "natural" manner. High-level languages give programmers expressive power while hiding much of the underlying detail of the computer system from them. This is especially valuable in the coding of large and complex problems whose logical structure is already very complicated. High-level languages are typically easier to read than their assembly-language counterparts. This makes them much easier to modify and extend. Some major software systems (such as Music V, Cmusic, and the Unix operating system) have been coded almost entirely in high-level languages for just these reasons. One major advantage of high-level languages is that code written in them is more portable (i.e., machine-independent).

Assembly languages were developed before high-level languages. They are closer to the function of computer hardware. In simple assembly language, every line of a program contains a mnemonic code word for a machine instruction, along with appropriate arguments. This provides a rudimentary syntax, such as

operation   operand-1   operand-2

in which the operation takes the two operands as arguments. More powerful assemblers have facilities for macros in which long sequences of instructions may be given names and then be called by the macro name. A knowledge of assembly-language programming can be useful in implementing real-time applications, where every instruction counts. (Knuth 1972 is a good introduction to this art.) It is still possible to find input/output device drivers—the routines that handle many real-time tasks—written in assembly language.

Below the assembly language in level is the machine language, a series of binary digits (zeros and ones, e.g. 110101011011101111011000) directly understood by the machine. Machine language is simply assembly language without mnemonic code words and without macros. Machine language is a binary representation of the macroinstructions (the basic instruction set of the computer).

Microcode controls the hardware data paths through which information flows inside a computer. In a general-purpose computer the microcode is largely fixed, remaining resident within the machine. In contrast, many digital synthesizers, such as the DMX-1000 discussed by Wallraff in article 13, use microcode much more dynamically. For each "orchestra" (an internal configuration of signal-processing functions such as filters and oscillators) there is a separate microprogram. Because the other software layers are built on top of microcode, efficiency at this level is a higher priority than it is with high-level languages. This is one of the reasons microcoding has earned its reputation as a difficult and time-consuming task. The difficulty of microcoding is exacerbated by the usual absence of high-level programming tools. In article 26, Abbott discusses a possible solution to this dilemma.

Operating Systems and Device Drivers

All tasks in a computer run under the supervision of an operating system, a set of supervisory procedures that manage the machine's resources. For example, the operating system schedules processes, handles low-level interaction with the file system, and attends to network transactions.

Device drivers—the programs that communicate directly with hardware peripherals attached to the computer, such as disk storage units or printers—are essential components of an operating system. In music systems, various device drivers transfer sound samples to and from audio converters, update the memory registers of a digital synthesizer, display graphics on a screen, and read the potentiometer settings of a mixing console. Computer sound-processing systems, such as Abbott's INV design (article 27), require substantial programming effort at the device-driver level. These high-speed event-driven processes are often embedded in the operating system.

On some systems (e.g., Lisp Machines) the distinction between the operating system and the language environment is blurred. Programmers can readily access predefined system functions and embed them in their own programs.

Along with the operating system are the utilities, which perform common tasks for the user. The utilities include font and text editors, text formatters, file-management subsystems, mail systems, debugging tools, and other software.

Representations for Music

Music systems can include synthesis compilers, music theory models, real-time systems, sound-analysis algorithms, computer-assisted composition systems, and other subsystems. A major implementation question is: How shall we represent music within the computer and to the user? Three views are presented in this part. Chadabe and Meyers have based their PLAY system (article 28) on a process model of music, with functions and timers not unlike those in models derived from analog synthesis. Buxton and his associates at Toronto have posited a music representation based on hierarchical data structures (articles 22 and 24). Instances of these data structures are created in order to represent specific compositions.

Article 23 surveys various music representations based on grammars and lays out the strengths and weaknesses of linguistic models. Evidently, different musical tasks require different representations within the computer. For example, a composer may want to specify a composition in terms of a combination of sound-object specifications and musical processes, while the digital synthesizer requires long lists of musical events and the display hardware needs graphics commands. How can these representations be designed so as to be coordinated with one another, allowing updates in one to ramify into the others? Many of the best ideas for solving these problems are coming from the field of artificial intelligence (Minsky 1981; Roads 1980a; Winston 1984). Certain knowledge-representation techniques may be used to specify active objects that can model information from several perspectives simultaneously.

The User Interface

An area that is receiving increasing attention is the design of the user interface—the protocols that allow a person to perform tasks (musical or not) at the computer (Kay and Goldberg 1977). Many modern user interfaces are based around graphic windows and menus (which prompt the user with a set of choices) selected by a hand-held pointing device such as a "mouse" (Newman and Sproull 1979). The user interface can also include traditional alphanumeric command languages and software to control musical input devices such as organ keyboards, potentiometers, and special display devices (Snell 1982). (So far, voice communication has been little used in computer music for control of musical processes.)

Laske (article 30) calls this level of interaction the musical task environment. He takes a procedural view of music, seeing it as a schedule of tasks.

After an analysis of different kinds of human memory used in working with music, he stresses the need for user interfaces that will lighten the burden on the user's memory.

Real-Time Versus Non-Real-Time Systems

"Real-time" systems are those with more or less instantaneous response and functionality. "Non-real-time" systems, such as the Music V software synthesis programs, involve computational delays before results are obtained. Probably the first real-time computer music system was that used by P. Samson in his 1959 demonstration of four-voice square-wave synthesis on a PDP-1 computer. Since then, the unaided general-purpose computer has rarely been used for real-time music synthesis. [Exceptions include work in instruction synthesis by Berg (article 11) and Holtzman (1979).] This is because digital music synthesis requires very fast arithmetical processing. Generating a single channel of digital audio at a 50-kHz sampling rate requires a new sample every 20 microseconds. In many computers, this leaves only enough time for a few instructions, such as very simple synthesis or processing algorithms.

One of the first real-time applications of the smaller computers that appeared in the mid-1960s was the control of analog synthesis hardware. This idea has continued as a low-cost entry to computer music work (Oppenheim 1978). For a small system, the best strategy may be to define a personalized musical system, as Bartlett describes in article 29. The resulting design conforms to an individual musician's aesthetic at the time, which may be all that is required. Because the cost is so low, it may be possible to update or replace the microcomputer system without a great investment in software, hardware, and development time.

Programming Digital Synthesizers

The tremendous musical potential opened up by real-time digital sound synthesis and processing brings with it stringent programming demands. Many of the articles in this part discuss approaches to the complicated problems of programming and controlling real-time digital synthesizers.

The Institut de Recherche et Coordination Acoustique/Musique (IRCAM) invested in digital signal processors from its inception. The programming lessons learned in IRCAM's 4B synthesizer project are reported by Rolnick in article 25. These lessons may steer future implementers of microcomputer-controlled synthesizers away from the pitfalls the IRCAM team encountered. Among the lessons the IRCAM team learned are that creating an image of the control registers in the host computer's memory makes possible simultaneous updating of all control words, that software access to the low-level hardware is important, and that the hardware for generating interrupts should not interfere with the host computer, which is already busy servicing interrupts. Another point proved in the 4B experience is that the ability to evaluate arbitrary expressions is a desirable feature of both the score and the orchestra part of the sound-synthesis language.

More recent approaches to programming digital synthesizers, such as 4CED (Abbott 1981) and Music 1000 (discussed in article 13) provide a high-level language, similar to an enhanced Music V (Mathews 1969). One of the main extensions of these languages is the inclusion of "hooks" for real-time input device. With these hooks, the user can specify that the value of a synthesis parameter (e.g., frequency) will not be stated in the score but will come in real time from a switch or a knob on the synthesizer. Interpreting musical control information emanating from many switches and knobs in a finite amount of time requires substantial ingenuity (Moorer 1981). Special considerations enter into projects that must satisfy commercial constraints of cost and portability and still meet a musical need (Kaplan 1981).

Software Synthesis

The earliest generally available software synthesis systems were Music IV and Music V, both developed at Bell Laboratories in the late 1960s. A major feature of these languages is the use of *unit generators*—software modules for signal processing. Musicians learned to connect unit generators to create an unlimited number of software instruments. Languages based on the concept of the unit generator have been the foundation of most research in digital sound-synthesis algorithms to date. (Indeed, both Music IV and Music V are still running at some sites.)

Despite the advantages of real-time synthesizer work, there remains a place for non-real-time systems run on general-purpose computers or special hardware. Such systems are valuable for testing new sound-analysis and sound-synthesis algorithms and for experiments with "virtual" instruments too large or complicated to synthesize in real time on any device.

Specialized Systems

The high degree of generality provided by such a language as Music V must be supported by substantial computing resources. In efforts to build a sound-synthesis system on a more modest computer, some have taken a route in the digital domain that is similar to Bartlett's in the analog domain. These researchers have implemented one-of-a-kind, special-purpose systems that allow one kind of sound synthesis with a limited but well-defined musical aesthetic (Truax 1977; Holtzman 1979).

Trends in Music Software

The future of music software is contingent on musical developments and technological changes. Although we can scarcely predict the long-term future, certain trends appear promising.

High-Level Languages

In programming practice, there is a strong trend away from assembly languages toward high-level languages. The present push is toward languages that explicitly support object-oriented programming (Hewitt 1976; Kornfeld 1980; Krasner 1980; Lieberman 1982). The main elements of this approach are active objects and messages. The active objects bind together data and procedures, while the messages are the means of intercommunication between active objects. Sending messages to active objects causes the objects to perform a computation. A main benefit of the object-oriented style of programming is that it lends itself to a particularly lucid kind of modularity.

Even with better programming tools, rigorous programming methodologies such as program specifications or "structured walk-throughs" proposed by industry (Bergland 1981) are not often possible in musical research. Trends toward standardization of music software might alleviate this condition.

The User Interface

As operating systems and compilers have become well understood and standardized, much attention has turned to the design of the user interface. In the past, the user interfaces to many time-shared computer music systems tended to be rigid and one-dimensional. The design of a comfortable and flexible user interface is now recognized as a difficult and important endeavor.

Many systems are being designed around real-time synthesis and processing, using interactive graphics (see article 22). One of the major software problems in this area is supporting the musician's creative context switching in a rapid and consistent manner. Much creative work is characterized by rapid shifts of attention from high-level musical architecture to low-level details of gesture and back. It is difficult to anticipate the strategy of creative thought and action. Hence, it is necessary to avoid arbitrary software restrictions that would hamper the musician's movement from one activity to another.

Microcoding Tools

More productive programming of digital synthesizers will require better microcoding tools and techniques. Simulation is a time-tested means of developing reliable software quickly. Abbott's work on the Lucasfilm digital audio processor is a classic example of the efficacy of this approach (Abbott 1982). Long before microcode could be loaded on the hardware (which did not exist at the time), Abbott wrote a software simulator of the processor and tested his microcode on it. The software simulator made systematic debugging possible; at each step of the execution of the code the machine state could be examined in detail.

Parallel Processes

Many aspects of music lend themselves to computer implementations based on parallel processes. Although parallelism has been exploited in a few computer music projects (Loy 1981; Roads 1976; Smoliar 1971), its use has been slow in proliferating. This is due mainly to a lack of appropriate parallel hardware and standard parallel languages. The situation is beginning to change as the notion of parallel microprocessors takes hold.

Coherent Design

Two hardware trends are affecting the development of software for computer music. First, the networked personal computer is replacing time sharing at many computer music centers. Second, sound-synthesis software is being offloaded to special real-time hardware. A major unsolved problem is putting all of the software components together to form a unified music system with a consistent design philosophy.

In many cases, obtaining a coherent design from a team of programmers requires better communication among them. This is aided by the adoption of a software environment that supports a team of programmers, such as the package construct in which different modules may be distinguished from one another according to their origins even if they have the same name (Weinreb and Moon 1981).

Efficiency and Complexity

For some years it has not been possible to conceive of music software as a monolithic program written by one person running on a batch computer. Rather, computer music software exemplifies the trend, already noted in artificial intelligence and other fields, toward large systems written by many people (Winograd 1979). The early preoccupation with efficiency has been supplemented by a concern over software complexity.

Complexity has two facets: Complexity that is visible to the user makes a system seem ridden with layers of arbitrary detail and can stifle creativity; complexity that is visible to the programmer stymies program development and makes program modification difficult or impossible. As more musicians approach the computer, the proper management of complexity becomes a decisive factor in evaluating the musical success of a software system. The illusion of simplicity can require enormous effort.

References

Abbott, C. 1981. "The 4CED program." *Computer Music Journal* 5(1): 13–33.

Abbott, C., 1983. "A symbolic simulator for microprogram development." *IEEE Transactions on Computers* C-32(8): 770–774.

Baur, F. 1976. "Historical remarks on compiler construction." In F. Baur and J. Eickel, *Compiler Construction: An Advanced Course*. New York: Springer, 1976.

Berg, P. 1979. "PILE—A language for sound synthesis." *Computer Music Journal* 3(1): 30–41. Article 11 in this volume.

Bergland, G. 1981. "A guided tour of programming design methodologies." *Computer* 14(10): 13–37.

Hewitt, C. 1976. Viewing Control Structures as Patterns of Passing Messages. A. I. Memo 410, M.I.T. Artificial Intelligence Laboratory.

Hiller, L., and L. Isaacson. 1959. *Experimental Music.* New York: McGraw-Hill.

Holtzman, S. 1979. "An automated digital sound synthesis instrument." *Computer Music Journal* 3(2): 53–61.

Kaplan, S. J. 1981. "Developing a commercial digital sound synthesizer." *Computer Music Journal* 5(3): 62–73.

Kay, A., and A. Goldberg. 1977. "Personal dynamic media." *Computer* 10(3): 31–41.

Knuth, D. 1972. *The Art of Computer Programming,* vols. 1–3. Reading, Mass.: Addison-Wesley.

Kornfeld, W. 1980. "Machine tongues VII: Lisp." *Computer Music Journal* 4(2): 6–12.

Krasner, G. 1980. "Machine tongues VIII: The Design of a Smalltalk music system." *Computer Music Journal* 4(4): 4–14.

Lieberman, H. 1982. "Machine tongues IX: Object-oriented programming." *Computer Music Journal* 6(3): 8–21.

Loy, D. 1981. "Notes on the implementation of MUSBOX: A compiler for the Systems Concepts digital synthesizer." *Computer Music Journal* 5(1): 34–50.

Mathews, M. V., with J. E. Miller, F. R. Moore, J. R. Pierce, and J. C. Risset. 1969. *The Technology of Computer Music.* Cambridge, Mass.: MIT Press.

Minsky, M. 1981. "Music, mind, and meaning." *Computer Music Journal* 5(3): 28–44.

Moorer, J. A. 1981. "Synthesizers I have known and loved." *Computer Music Journal* 5(1): 4–12.

Newman, W., and R. Sproull. 1979. *Principles of Interactive Computer Graphics,* second edition. New York: McGraw-Hill.

Oppenheim, D. 1978. "Microcomputer to synthesizer interface for a low-cost system." *Computer Music Journal* 2(1): 6–11.

Roads, C. 1976. A Systems Approach to Composition. Honors thesis, University of California, San Diego.

Roads, C. 1980a. "Interview with Marvin Minsky." *Computer Music Journal* 4(3): 25–39.

Roads, C. 1980b. "Interview with Max Mathews." *Computer Music Journal* 4(4): 15–22.

Smoliar, S. 1971. A Parallel Processing Model of Musical Structures. A. I. Technical Report 242. MIT Artificial Intelligence Laboratory.

Snell, J., 1982. "The Lucasfilm Real-time Console for recording studios and performance of computer music." *Computer Music Journal* 6(3): 33–45.

Strachey, C. 1959. "Time-sharing in large fast computers." In *Proceedings of the International Conference on Information Processing.* Paris: UNESCO.

Truax, B. 1977. "The POD system of interactive composition programs." *Computer Music Journal* 1(3): 30–39.

Wallraff, D. 1979. "The DMX-1000 signal processing computer." *Computer Music Journal* 3(4): 44–49. Article 13 in this volume.

Weinreb, D., and D. Moon. 1981. Lisp Machine Manual. Fourth edition. MIT Artificial Intelligence Laboratory.

Winograd, T. 1979. "Beyond programming languages." *Communications of the Association for Computing Machinery* 22(7): 391–401.

Winston, P. 1984. *Artificial Intelligence*. Second edition. Reading, Mass.: Addison-Wesley.

22 The Evolution of the SSSP Score-Editing Tools

WILLIAM BUXTON, RICHARD SNIDERMAN, WILLIAM REEVES, SANAND PATEL, AND
RONALD BAECKER

This article traces the evolution of score-editing tools developed by the Structured Sound Synthesis Project (SSSP) at the University of Toronto. The focus is on the use of interactive computer graphics to assist a composer in the editing of a file of information detailing a musical score. In this context we examine some of the issues involved in designing user interfaces involving interactive graphics systems. We outline an overall design strategy that has been used successfully in the designing of SSSP hardware and software.

Background

The SSSP is an interdisciplinary project whose aim is to conduct research into problems and benefits arising from the use of computers in musical composition (Buxton 1978; Buxton and Fedorkow 1978; Buxton et al. 1978a). This research can be considered in terms of two main areas: the investigation of musical data and processes, and the study of musician-machine communication.

In designing the system, we decided early on to adopt a highly interactive approach to the design of the human interface. Batch processing as in Music V (Mathews 1969) is an alternative, but it widely separates the composer and the program, causing serious delays in the feedback loop. A score editor must be interactive, because there are facets of the task that demand control and aesthetic judgment by the composer in an interactive and exploratory manner. Several modes of interaction have previously been investigated in music systems, such as alphanumeric text as in MUS10 (Tovar and Smith 1978), voice recognition (Tucker et al. 1977), and piano-type keyboards. In our work we have adopted a bias toward graphics-based interaction (Baecker 1979; Newman and Sproull 1979) in the belief that this approach can make a significant contribution to an effective human interface. First, music lends itself well to representations in the visual domain. Second, the task of editing music is complex in the sense that there are many parameters and commands to be manipulated and controlled; this complexity can be reduced by the

Originally published in *Computer Music Journal* 3(4):14–25, 1979.

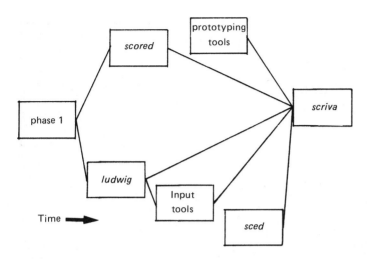

Figure 22.1
Evolution of the SSSP score-editing tools.

graphic representation of information. Third, previous work (Pulfer 1972; Tanner 1972; Vercoe 1975) indicates that more congenial interfaces can be constructed using dynamic graphics techniques.

The hardware environment centers on a PDP-11/45 running under the UNIX time-sharing operating system (Ritchie and Thompson 1974) and a digital sound synthesizer (Buxton et al. 1978b) with its own LSI-11. The graphics hardware includes a vector-drawing graphics display, a digitizing tablet with accompanying cursor box, and a slider box. Several terminals with alphanumeric keyboards are also available for non-graphical processing.

Overview

The main area of SSSP activity has been the development of high-level "front-end" programs that would give the musically sophisticated (but technologically naive) user a high degree of access to the potential offered by the computer-synthesizer combination. Thus, the development of score-editing tools was initiated even before such tools could be "hooked up" to the synthesizer, and has proceeded continuously since. Figure 22.1 charts this development, and the following sections detail the salient features of each stage.

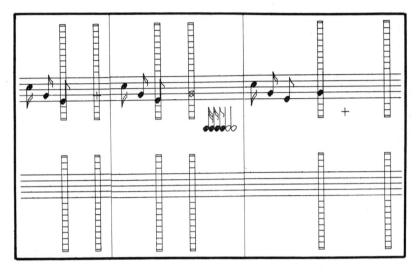

Figure 22.2
Input of a note in three stages.

In the Beginning

We first needed to quickly address some of the fundamental issues concerning graphical interaction as applied to score editing. This led to the design and implementation of an editing environment that was never used in conjunction with the synthesizer. However, it was at this early stage that techniques of graphically realizing entities of musical notation were developed—techniques that were used and built upon in subsequent work.

It was also at this stage that an interactive method of note input was devised which has remained the major note-input tool to date. The first panel of figure 22.2 shows the note-input tracking cross being positioned over the desired pitch. When the button on the cursor is depressed, a "marker note" symbol appears at the indicated pitch. Concurrently, the tracker is replaced by a sequence of notes. This is shown in the second panel of the figure. This sequence of notes "tracks" or follows the motion of the cursor on the tablet. The roles of the tracking cross and the menu are now reversed. Instead of the conventional stationary menu and moving pointing tool, we have a moving menu and a stationary pointer. By placing the note of the desired duration over the marker note symbol (i.e., moving the menu) and releasing the cursor button, a note is input. This is shown in the third panel of figure 22.2. The ledger lines, tail direction, bar lines, and note spacing are handled automatically.

This note-input tool is very flexible. By positioning the marker note in the first set of ledger lines, the new note is "chorded" with all notes above or below it. This allows polyphonic scores to be edited. By manipulating other input transducers, the composer can also enter ties, delete the last note, and make pitch corrections on the last note. A rest-input tool was also included, the protocol for which is identical to the note tool except that the sequence of notes becomes a sequence of rests.

This prototype score editor was discarded soon after completion. Valuable lessons had been learned, and the cost of development was not so great as to discourage quick replacement. This latter point serves as the cornerstone of SSSP design strategy: No prototype should be so costly as to make it unfeasible to discard it upon completion. If that is not the case, then the time should be spent in the development of tools to assist prototype design rather than in the development of the prototypes themselves.

ludwig

ludwig (Reeves et al. 1978) was the first score-editing program to be used by composers in conjunction with the synthesizer. Although both it and its precursor use common music notation (CMN) to represent musical events, this does not imply an affinity for or a bias toward CMN. Rather, CMN was used to present the new computer-related concepts to composers in a familiar environment. It was recognized that CMN is just a special case of notation in a Cartesian space, using notes and other special symbols placed in some relation to staves. In fact, an editor using "piano-roll" notation was developed at the same time.

Various issues were addressed for the first time during the course of *ludwig*'s development. One of the more important issues was motivated by the rather facile observation that music is not usually monolinear. Take for example any Bach *two-part invention*. Such a work could be entered into the computer as a sequential stream of notes, from start to finish. In this case, however, one does not think of the composition as a linear sequence of notes, but rather as a layering of parallel voices (figure 22.3). In notating the invention a more reasonable approach would be to notate each voice separately. Thus, two distinct modes of note input are apparent: the insertion of notes into a score and the merging of notes with a score. The former mode is referred to as *splice* and is analogous to the cutting and joining of recording tape; the latter is referred to as *mix* and is analogous to the *voice-over-voice* function available on many tape recorders.

Once this distinction was made, the problem had to be solved of how to keep a line of music being generated in *mix* mode in its proper relation with the parallel layers of music. The nature of the problem becomes apparent when one realizes that the underlying data structure used to represent musical events in our environment is a single linear linked list. The problem is compounded by the fact that notes can be entered anywhere in the Cartesian space being used. The solution, transparent to the user, involves a sophisticated manipulation of the pointers that constitute the linkages of the list.

Another issue considered in the *ludwig* design was that of score navigation—how to enable the composer to "get around" the score, the notes of which may or may not be currently displayed on the screen. Two major techniques were developed. The first involves scrolling the score across the screen in "real time" at the touch of one of the hardware sliders. The second involves pointing at the light button "Search" and pressing a cursor button. As shown in figure 22.4, a time line representing the entire duration of the score appears on the screen. Two angle brackets indicate the portion of the score currently visible. Thus the user can readily answer the question "Where in the score am I?" Furthermore, by placing the tracking cross anywhere on the time line and depressing the cursor button, the corresponding portion of the score will become visible.

The problem of simplifying the composer's task in inputting and outputting score files was tackled in *ludwig*'s design. Computer-science-related nomenclature (read/write) was initially used for these operations but was not understood readily by the composers. More user-oriented nomenclature (retrieve/save) met with far greater success. It was also apparent that the burden should not be placed on the composer to remember the file names and to type these file names in, correctly spelled, each time they were to be retrieved. This led to the development of a *window* onto the dictionary of a composer's score names. As shown in figure 22.5, if a change of score name is desired, the "Score" light button

Figure 22.3
A Bach invention notated with *ludwig*.

Figure 22.4
The *ludwig* Search command.

Figure 22.5
A directory window.

is "hit" and a listing of the currently available scores appears. The name of the "current" score is highlighted. By then "hitting" the name of the desired score, the change is effected. Alternatively, the hardware slider can be used to scroll through the list of scores until the desired name is highlighted.

The final feature of *ludwig* to be examined is the tool used to orchestrate the notes of a score. This technique is often called the "paint pot" technique, for .reasons which will become obvious. After selecting the "orchestrate" light button, the tracking cross becomes a paintbrush, and the palette of timbral "colors" (instruments) appears as a menu below the displayed portion of the score. The color currently on the brush is highlighted. Simply pointing at notes with the brush and depressing the button will orchestrate them with the current instrument. At any time, the composer is able to change the color of the brush, either by dipping into the palette (i.e., pointing at the desired instrument in the instrument menu) or by scrolling through the list of instruments (using the hardware slider) until the desired instrument is the one that is highlighted.

This is a successful interactive tool for various reasons. No typing is done in accessing the various instrument files, nor must the composer recall the instruments in the directories or their spelling. This is because *directory windows* are used in orchestration in the same manner as described for file input. Also, since the sliders are used to change the instrument in the palette, the cursor can remain on the score itself. Orchestration is thus carried out with the cursor in one hand and the sliders in the other. The resulting economy of motion results in a smooth, efficient, and congenial interface whose use can be extended to other contexts.

Scored

The various problems tackled in *ludwig* were approached in the context of CMN primarily because it offered a familiar environment to the designers and the users. Although the program was used successfully by musicians, it had obvious shortcomings. We have already alluded to CMN being a specific case of a more general concept, namely the representation of musical events in a Cartesian coordinate space. *Scored* was intended as a parallel experience to *ludwig* in which the same problems were approached in alternative ways. The major feature was the use of piano-roll notation (figure 22.6).

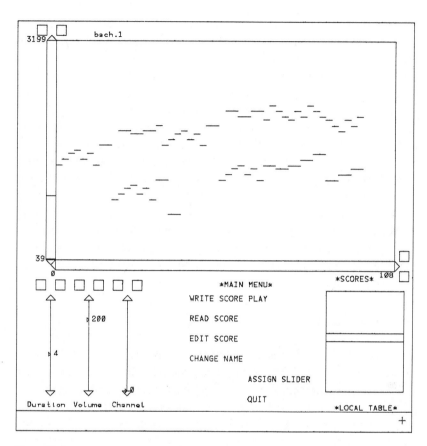

Figure 22.6
The Bach invention of figure 22.3 notated with *scored*.

The primary issue here is the distinction being made between the external representation of a score and the internal representation, meaning the underlying data structures (Buxton et al. 1978c). Since there is no graphical information about notation stored when a score is saved, the underlying musical representation is notation-independent. Thus, scores in different notations are completely compatible, and any single score can be viewed using any notational scheme. The disadvantage of this is that it is not possible to realize a "perfect" CMN representation of a score. The lack of stored graphical information means that, when a score is retrieved for display purposes, certain representational decisions have to be made by the program. As a result, the newly-displayed score may not be the same as the composer's original notation. This drawback is outweighted by the advantages gained by being able to view a score in various ways. A musical justification is the fact that the expression of different musical ideas has been facilitated by the availability of alternative forms of notation.

Note-Input Tools

It was clear during the development of *ludwig* that the mix/splice issue affected not only the input of notes but the reading of entire scores as well—i.e., should a score file being input be appended to or merged with the current score? It was realized that, conceptually, our note-input tool and score reading were two variations on the same operation. The literature shows various other techniques that have been used to perform this operation. Examples include techniques involving specially built hardware input transducers (Pulfer 1972), alphanumeric command languages entered on typewriterlike keyboards (Smith 1972), and graphical interaction via sets of displayed menus (Murray, Beauchamp, and Loitz 1978). A major unanswered question was how to compare different note-input techniques in order to evaluate their effectiveness.

In order to study this problem and to investigate techniques for benchmarking and comparison, several note-input tools have been implemented (Hogg and Sniderman 1979).

One input technique implemented was based on the GUIDO music education system (Hofstetter 1975). As the term implies, the *graphical keyboard technique* employs a graphical representation of a piano keyboard, primarily to aid the user in choosing pitch information. The motivation for the idea comes from the fact that many musicians use a piano as an aid when composing. Thus, a graphical keyboard should be a visual aid with which the composer is comfortable. As figure 22.7 shows, the keyboard consists of two octaves, the range of which is indicated by the vertical position of the "ladder" on the score. This range can be raised or lowered by depressing the cursor button when the tracking cross is positioned over the head of the upward- or downward-pointing arrow. A note itself is chosen by depressing the cursor button when the tracking cross is positioned over the desired key. At this point a note appears on the score at the appropriate position within the "ladder." To choose a duration, the user moves the cursor along the length of the piano key with the button pressed. Each piano key is divided into invisible segments corresponding to different durations. When the note of desired pitch and duration is displayed, the user releases the button and the note is set in the score.

A second technique, the *total menu technique*, employs menus to aid the user in making the decisions needed to specify the time and pitch information of notes. The motivation for the idea comes from the fact that a menu listing all options is a clear and unambiguous way of presenting choices open to the user. Examine the menus as pictured in figure 22.8. The user indicates the name, octave, accidental, and duration of a note by hitting the appropriate light buttons, which are then intensified to indicate visually the choices made. When the desired choices have been made, the user hits the "ENTER" button. Contrast this system of menus with those of the PLACOMP language (Murray, Beauchamp, and Loitz 1978), from which it is derived. (See figure 22.9.)

Char-rec is a "shorthand" technique that employs a character recognizer to decode a set of symbols (figure 22.10) designed to represent notes of varying durations. To enter a note, the tracking cross is placed over the desired pitch on the appropriate ladder and the cursor button is depressed. An "ink trail" is laid down until the button is released, during which interval the user draws the desired duration symbol. On the basis of the starting point and the shape of the symbol, the pitch and duration of the desired note are decoded. The lengths of the line segments constituting a symbol are immaterial if they are greater than a fairly small size. However, the directional changes in a symbol must be drawn distinctly to ensure correct recognition. Figure 22.11 shows a sixteenth note being entered.

Research with the techniques described follows two lines. The first

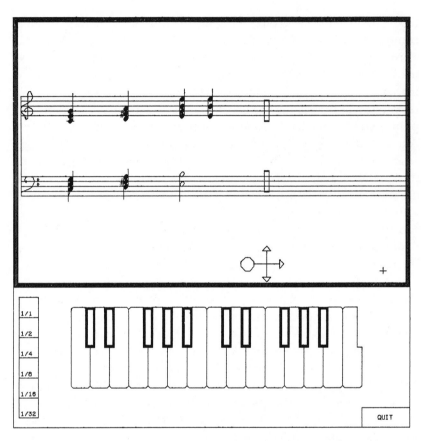

Figure 22.7
A typical screen layout of the graphical keyboard technique.

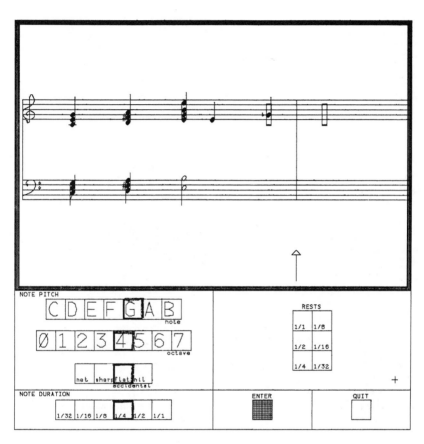

Figure 22.8
A typical screen layout for the total menu technique.

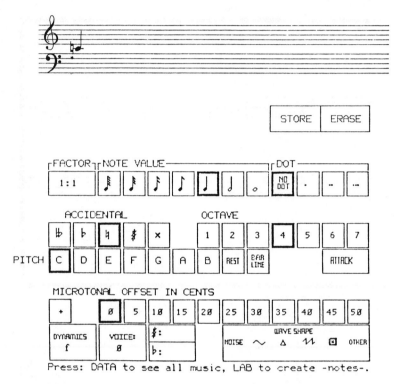

Figure 22.9
A typical screen layout from *PLACOMP*. Source: Murray, Beauchamp, and Loitz 1978.

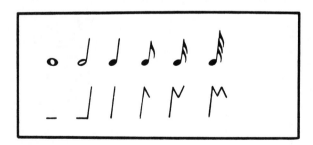

Figure 22.10
Char-rec duration symbols.

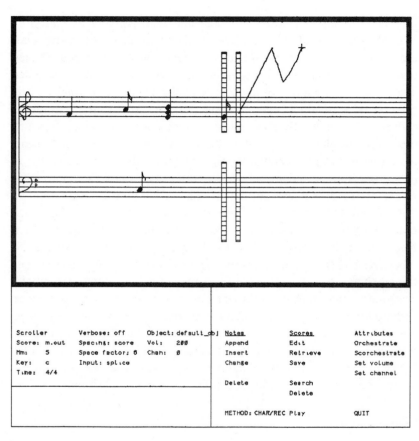

Figure 22.11
Appending a sixteenth note with *Char-rec*.

involves looking at features with the aim of classifying designs. For example, the original technique uses vertical movements of the tracking cross to make pitch choices and horizontal movements of a menu of notes to make duration choices. The graphical keyboard technique, on the other hand, uses horizontal movements along the keyboard to make pitch choices and vertical movements along individual keys to make duration choices. Both alternatives are natural in the context in which they are used. The graphical keyboard technique is similar to the total menu technique in that, conceptually, the keyboard is being used exactly as menu—each key is a light button, and each key is subdivided into individual (invisible) segments forming a menu of durations.

As stated, the second line of research involves evaluation of the ease of use of these tools. Preliminary observations indicate that the character recognizer makes possible a fluency of transcription that far exceeds the others, despite the fact that it is the more difficult to learn because to get the maximum use out of it one must memorize the duration symbols. The total menu system, on the other hand, requires no memorization, since each option for every choice that must be made is clearly listed. Although it is therefore easy to learn, it is of minimal use in a composition environment because many hand motions must be made to enter each note. It has, however, proved useful in other contexts, such as computer-aided instruction, which have different constraints than composition.

Consolidation

At this stage, the focus shifted to an evaluation of the effort being expended by the programmers implementing the score-editor designs. It was becoming increasingly clear as more software was developed that various transactions were being programmed repeatedly. There was an obvious need to eliminate this duplication of effort. Some software was also being written by groups, so protocols had to be repeatedly established for interfacing their work. Thus, it was evident that before more ambitious score editors could be developed it was necessary to work on a library of sophisticated prototyping tools.

First, we developed a library of basic transactions to be performed on the musical database and on the digital synthesizer. Second, we implemented standard routines for displaying and modifying directory windows. Finally, we noticed that all of our interactive graphics programs involved at least a one-level command menu, so we implemented a standard command menu for use in all programs. Software tools were thus developed to free the programmer from the low-level effort involved in programming database transactions, directory windows, and command menus. At the same time, the method of use of these tools was documented in *The SSSP Programmer's Manual* (Buxton et al. 1979).

The result of such a stage of consolidation is the pushing back of a "barrier of complexity." This makes the programmer's work more productive. Additionally, software employing these tools becomes more maintainable—an important fact when programs are being updated almost daily. Finally, the design process as a whole not only is sped up but also becomes more cost-effective. Less effort is expended, so the resulting programs are more expendable. When a prototype is being developed as part of an evolutionary process and not as an intended "final product," this reduction in cost is attractive.

sced

The next score editor written, *sced* (Buxton 1981a), was a marked departure from its predecessors in that is was driven alphanumerically rather than graphically (figure 22.12). The reason for this was twofold. First, we had a number of conventional terminals with alphanumeric keyboards but very few graphical hardware resources. The availability of an alphanumeric score editor was thus necessary to increase access to the system. It also provided an environment in which to develop and test the various primitives discussed in the preceding section (and those about to be discussed) in a concise manner, avoiding the complexity and cost of using the graphics.

One new type of transaction developed in *sced* involved the definition and use of scope (Buxton et al. 1981). A scope is a subset of the musical events of a score, selected according to some criteria. This scope may then be operated on in some way, thus conceptually becoming the operand of an operation. Refer to figure 22.3, which illustrates *ludwig*. There are two "Delete" commands available, one for individual notes and one for the entire score. The "Play" command is available only for auditioning entire scores. These two facts point out that *ludwig* suffered from one of the main inadequacies of many other score editors: that the user can deal only with notes or scores. In the case where one operation is applicable

```
% sed
Type 'h' for help.
?
* r bach.1
input mode: s
93
* 1,40L
1          freq: 494      dur: 1/16     obj: default_obj     vol: 200     del: 0/16
2          freq: 147      dur: 1/2      obj: default_obj     vol: 200     del: 1/16
3          freq: 262      dur: 1/16     obj: default_obj     vol: 200     del: 1/16
4          freq: 294      dur: 1/16     obj: default_obj     vol: 200     del: 1/16
5          freq: 330      dur: 1/16     obj: default_obj     vol: 200     del: 1/16
6          freq: 349      dur: 1/16     obj: default_obj     vol: 200     del: 1/16
7          freq: 294      dur: 1/16     obj: default_obj     vol: 200     del: 1/16
8          freq: 330      dur: 1/16     obj: default_obj     vol: 200     del: 1/16
9          freq: 262      dur: 1/16     obj: default_obj     vol: 200     del: 1/16
10         freq: 392      dur: 1/8      obj: default_obj     vol: 200     del: 0/8
11         freq: 147      dur: 1/16     obj: default_obj     vol: 200     del: 1/16
12         freq: 131      dur: 1/16     obj: default_obj     vol: 200     del: 1/16
13         freq: 523      dur: 1/8      obj: default_obj     vol: 200     del: 0/8
14         freq: 147      dur: 1/16     obj: default_obj     vol: 200     del: 1/16
15         freq: 165      dur: 1/16     obj: default_obj     vol: 200     del: 1/16
16         freq: 494      dur: 1/8      obj: default_obj     vol: 200     del: 0/8
17         freq: 175      dur: 1/16     obj: default_obj     vol: 200     del: 1/16
18         freq: 147      dur: 1/16     obj: default_obj     vol: 200     del: 1/16
19         freq: 523      dur: 1/8      obj: default_obj     vol: 200     del: 0/8
20         freq: 165      dur: 1/16     obj: default_obj     vol: 200     del: 1/16
21         freq: 131      dur: 1/16     obj: default_obj     vol: 200     del: 1/16
22         freq: 587      dur: 1/16     obj: default_obj     vol: 200     del: 0/16
23         freq: 196      dur: 1/8      obj: default_obj     vol: 200     del: 1/16
24         freq: 392      dur: 1/16     obj: default_obj     vol: 200     del: 1/16
25         freq: 440      dur: 1/16     obj: default_obj     vol: 200     del: 0/16
26         freq: 98       dur: 1/8      obj: default_obj     vol: 200     del: 1/16
27         freq: 494      dur: 1/16     obj: default_obj     vol: 200     del: 1/16
28         freq: 523      dur: 1/16     obj: default_obj     vol: 200     del: 0/16
29         freq: 147      dur: 1/4      obj: default_obj     vol: 200     del: 1/16
30         freq: 440      dur: 1/16     obj: default_obj     vol: 200     del: 1/16
31         freq: 494      dur: 1/16     obj: default_obj     vol: 200     del: 1/16
32         freq: 392      dur: 1/16     obj: default_obj     vol: 200     del: 1/16
33         freq: 587      dur: 1/8      obj: default_obj     vol: 200     del: 0/8
34         freq: 147      dur: 1/16     obj: default_obj     vol: 200     del: 1/16
35         freq: 196      dur: 1/16     obj: default_obj     vol: 200     del: 1/16
36         freq: 784      dur: 1/8      obj: default_obj     vol: 200     del: 0/8
37         freq: 220      dur: 1/16     obj: default_obj     vol: 200     del: 1/16
38         freq: 247      dur: 1/16     obj: default_obj     vol: 200     del: 1/16
39         freq: 698      dur: 1/8      obj: default_obj     vol: 200     del: 0/8
40         freq: 262      dur: 1/16     obj: default_obj     vol: 200     del: 1/16
* ▷
```

Figure 22.12
The score of figures 22.3 and 22.6 in *sced* notation.

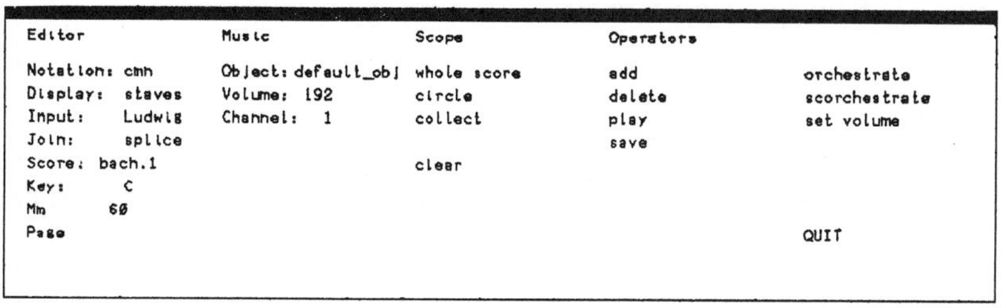

Editor		Music	Scope	Operators	
Notation:	cmh	Object: default_obj	whole score	add	orchestrate
Display:	staves	Volume: 192	circle	delete	scorchestrate
Input:	Ludwig	Channel: 1	collect	play	set volume
Join:	splice			save	
Score:	bach.1		clear		
Key:	c				
Mm	60				
Pase					QUIT

Figure 22.13
The *scriva* command window layout.

to either, two versions must be included. This motivated the feeling that composers should be able to define a group of notes on the basis of their own constraints (a scope as defined above) and operate on such a group. *sced* was therefore used to debug and test procedures for handling scope, with the aim that this powerful tool would be used in subsequent editors.

As mentioned, from the user's point of view *sced* allowed work to progress even when the graphics resources were employed. However, a somewhat unexpected benefit developed. The SSSP software provides a wide repertoire of commands to the software user that are alphanumerically driven (Buxton 1979). Thus, the issue arises of how to make this repertoire extendable by allowing the user to define special commands. It is feasible with the UNIX shell and text editor (Kernighan 1974) for the user to build higher-level commands using predefined utilities; such an option has proved useful. The point is that *sced* is based on the UNIX text editor. Although this probably has not resulted in the most efficient score editor, the consistency of approach has made it relatively easy for the user to learn enough of the UNIX text editor to create tailor-made commands.

scriva

scriva (Buxton 1981b) was designed to integrate and expand upon the ideas examined so far (figure 22.13). It is a graphical score editor, and is intended as a critical mass of many ideas realized in a simple environment for purposes of experimentation.

The concept of independence of notation and data structures is built upon by allowing scores in *scriva* to be viewed in different ways, each of which highlights a different aspect of the score. Figure 22.14 shows a

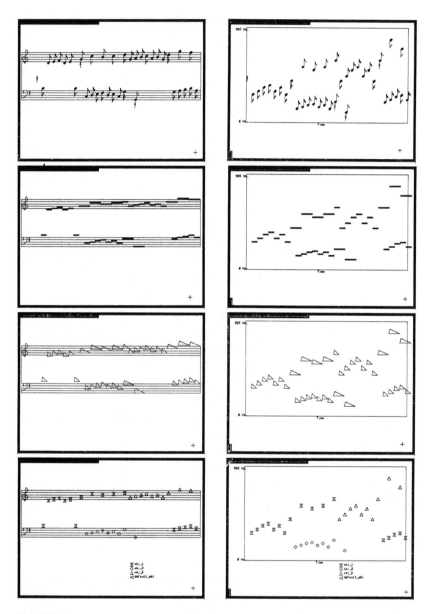

Figure 22.14
Notational flexibility in *scriva:* the score-display portion of eight screens.

portion of a score displayed in four different notational schemes, each of which is displayed on staves and in Cartesian coordinate space. The four notational schemes are CMN, piano roll, object highlighting, and envelope highlighting. For the purposes of the discussion, an object is equivalent to a timbre and an envelope is equivalent to an amplitude/loudness contour.

The concept of scope is built upon by providing various techniques to facilitate definition of groups of notes of interest, and by providing operators such as "Delete" and "Play" that act on these defined groups. One method of scope definition involves positioning the tracking cross over each note to be included and then depressing the cursor button. This is another application of the "paint-pot" technique mentioned with respect to orchestration in *ludwig*. Another method involves simply "inking" a circle around notes of current interest, as shown in figure 22.15. To exclude notes from within a larger circle, the user may draw yet another circle around those not to be included.

The concept of file reading as just another input tool is built upon by including this operation as one of the alternative methods of input rather than as a separate operation. As shown in figure 22.16, the user has just hit the "Input" light button and a list of available input methods has appeared. Note the inclusion of score input along with the various methods outlined above.

A final point to note is the logical organization of the command layout as shown in figure 22.13. Commands pertaining to the score-editor environment, to the musical environment, and to scope definition, and operators that act on scopes, have been grouped in separate columns. The purpose is to provide a basic organization to aid the composer in remembering each command's function.

Evaluation

The evolution detailed represents a large amount of work accomplished on a minimal budget and with minimal manpower. This fact alone tends to validate the design approach. The other major indication is the success with which the system has been utilized by musicians, for whom it was designed.

By taking an iterative approach to the design process, we are able to catch flaws before they are irrevocably embedded. By always ensuring the availability of usable software, we have been able to provide the user

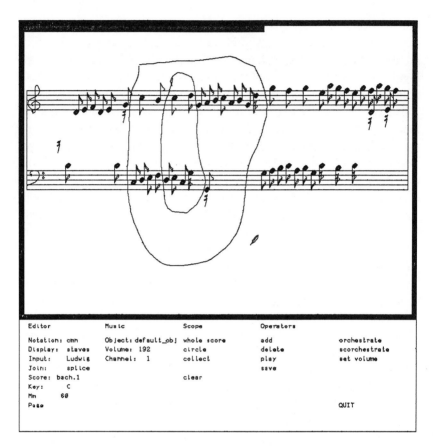

Figure 22.15
Scope definition by circling in *scriva*.

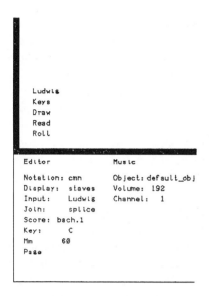

Figure 22.16
Input options in *scriva:* the lower left portion of the display screen.

community with resources from the project's inception. This has been a critical factor in obtaining the involvement of musicians from the beginning, and has allowed us to glean results from their work on a continuing basis. By periodically shifting emphasis to the development of tools to aid the design process, we are able to make subsequent work more cost-effective.

Future Directions

One area of future work is the extension of the system's capabilities to tree-structured scores. Although it was mentioned previously that the underlying data structure is a single linked list of notes, this is actually a special case of the data structure. Any single element in the list can in fact be a pointer to yet another score—a subscore. In this case we are dealing not with a linear list of notes but with a tree of notes and subscores. The linear restriction has been imposed until now to simplify the issues of graphical display, score navigation, and scope definition. Our next step is thus to use the alphanumeric score editor *sced* to isolate and test those transactions that are essential to the handling of subscores.

The problems associated with large scores will also be investigated. In many cases these are quite different from, and often more complex than, those associated with smaller score fragments. For example, in dealing with a short passage it is often the case that the entire passage can be displayed at once. Thus, navigation is rather simple since the user can point at the notes of interest. However, how does one provide the user with the mechanism to navigate to any portion of the score? How is the time length of the score to be represented visually to aid this navigation? This problem has been touched on already in *ludwig*, as shown in figure 22.4. Approaches to be considered include the use of rehearsal markings and grids in conjunction with time lines. A related issue is the desirability of having a score scroll as it is being played. A program to assist in "real-time" scrolling, *sview*, has thus been written.

The third area is the continuation of the work on note-input tools described above. Methods of evaluating and benchmarking their performance will be investigated. Also, an analysis of the protocols required to accomplish the task of note input may shed light on the design of a more general tool to accomplish this task.

Acknowledgments

The research of the SSSP has been made possible by a grant from the Social Sciences and Humanities Research Council of Canada. This support is gratefully acknowledged. In addition, the authors wish to acknowledge the contributions to the research made by the musicians associated with the project and by colleagues from the Computer Systems Research Group of the University of Toronto. In particular we would like to thank Mark Green, John Hogg, Steve Hume, James Montgomery, and Rob Pike.

References

Baecker, R. 1979. "Towards an effective characterization of graphical interaction." Presented at the International Federation of Information Processing, Workshop on Methodology of Interaction, Selliac, France.

Buxton, W. 1978. Design Issues in the Foundation of a Computer-Based Tool for Music Composition. Technical report CSRG-97, Computer Systems Research Group, University of Toronto.

Buxton, W. 1979. Music Software User's Manual. Internal report, Structured Sound Synthesis Project, University of Toronto.

Buxton, W. 1981a. "A tutorial introduction to SCED." In W. Buxton, Music Software User's Manual, second edition. Computer Systems Research Group, University of Toronto.

Buxton, W. 1981b. "A tutorial introduction to SCRIVA." In W. Buxton, Music Software User's Manual, second edition. Computer Systems Research Group, University of Toronto.

Buxton, W., and G. Fedorkow. 1978. The Structured Sound Synthesis Project (SSSP): An Introduction. Technical report CSRG-92, Computer Systems Research Group, University of Toronto.

Buxton, W., G. Fedorkow, R. Baecker, W. Reeves, K. Smith, G. Ciamaga, and L. Mezei. 1978a. "An overview of the Structured Sound Synthesis Project." In C. Roads, ed., *Proceedings of the 1978 International Computer Music Conference*, vol. 2. Evanston, Ill.: Northwestern University Press.

Buxton, W., E. A. Fogels, G. Fedorkow, L. Sasaki, and K. C. Smith. 1978b. "An introduction to the SSSP digital synthesizer." *Computer Music Journal* 2(4): 28–38. Article 12 in this volume.

Buxton, W., W. Reeves, R. Baecker, and L. Mezei. 1978c. "The use of hierarchy and instance in a data structure for computer music." *Computer Music Journal* 2(4): 10–20. Article 24 in this volume.

Buxton, W., W. Reeves, S. Patel, and T. O'Dell. 1979. SSSP Programmer's Manual. Internal document, Structured Sound Synthesis Project, Computer Systems Research Group, University of Toronto.

Buxton, W., S. Patel, W. Reeves, and R. Baecker. 1981. "Scope in interactive score editors." *Computer Music Journal* 5(3): 50–56.

Hofstetter, F. 1975. "Guido: An interactive computer-based system for improvement of instruction and research in ear-training." *Journal of Computer-Based Instruction* 1(4): 100–106.

Hogg, J., and R. Sniderman. 1979. Score Input Tools Project Report. Internal document, Structured Sound Synthesis Project, Computer Systems Research Group, University of Toronto.

Kernighan, B. 1974. A Tutorial Introduction to the UNIX Text Editor. Technical memorandum 74-1273-17, Bell Laboratories, Murray Hill, N.J.

Mathews, M. V., with Joan E. Miller, F. R. Moore, J. R. Pierce, and J.-C. Risset. 1969. *The Technology of Computer Music*. Cambridge, Mass.: MIT Press.

Murray, D., J. Beauchamp, and G. Loitz. 1978. "Using the PLATO/TI980 music synthesis system." In C. Roads, ed., *Proceedings of the 1978 International Computer Music Conference*, vol. 1. Evanston, Ill.: Northwestern University Press.

Newman, W., and R. Sproull. 1979. *Principles of Interactive Computer Graphics*, second edition. New York: McGraw-Hill.

Pulfer, J. 1972. *MUSICOMP Manual*. Ottawa: National Research Council.

Reeves, W., W. Buxton, R. Pike, and R. Baecker. 1978. "Ludwig: An example of interactive computer graphics in a score editor." In C. Roads, ed., *Proceedings of the 1978 International Computer Music Conference*, vol. 2. Evanston, Ill.: Northwestern University Press.

Ritchie, D., and K. Thompson. 1974. "The UNIX time-sharing system." *Communications of the Association for Computing Machinery* 17(7): 365–375.

Smith, L. 1972. "SCORE—A musician's approach to computer music." *Journal of the Audio Engineering Society* 20: 7–14.

Tanner, P. 1972. *MUSICOMP, An Experimental Aid for the Composition and Production of Music.* Ottawa: National Research Council.

Tovar and L. Smith. 1978. *MUS10 User Manual.* Department of Music, Stanford University, Stanford, Calif.

Tucker, W., R. Bates, S. Frykberg. R. Howrath, W. Kennedy, M. Lamb, and R. Vaughan. 1977. "An interactive aid for musicians." *International Journal of Man-Machine Studies* 9:635–651.

Vercoe, B. 1975. *Man-Computer Interaction in Creative Applications.* Cambridge, Mass.: MIT Experimental Music Studio.

23 Grammars as Representations for Music

CURTIS ROADS

In a lecture at Stanford University, the linguist and philosopher Noam Chomsky posed this question: "Is music a language?" (Chomsky 1979) He spoke to the question immediately after posing it. It all depends on one's definitions, he said; the question is ultimately unnecessary, and one should not be diverted by it.

I take this as the starting point of this essay. Being not too concerned whether "music is a language," I would like to pose several concrete questions about the application of linguistic concepts and tools to music: Can techniques from linguistics be applied usefully to music? Can the use of grammar representations be effective in describing and specifying musical structures? Are grammars intrinsically normative, i.e., are they fit only to describe traditional music? What are the limitations of various grammar representations? Is the notion of syntactic context used in formal language theory adequate for representing musical context? What are some alternatives to grammar representations? This article explores the literature surrounding these questions and offers answers based on the current state of research.

The Grammar Revival

The idea of viewing music in terms of a musical grammar is not new. Powers (1980, p. 49) cites a ninth-century Latin passage that portrays song forms through a linguistic analogy. A number of sixteenth-century composition manuals treated composition as a form of rhetorical expression. A later example of a linguistic analogy is the book by Busby (1818).

Recent years have seen a resurgence of this perspective (Baroni 1981). In part, this has been prompted by the success of linguistics, particularly since Chomsky's *Syntactic Structures* (1957). The trend in computational linguistics toward the development of natural language understanding systems has also pushed musical research forward. Studies in the semiotic analysis of poetry (Greimas 1970; Jacobson 1973) had a strong influence on the linguistically-inclined music research of Molino (1975), Nattiez

This is an expanded and revised version of an article that originally appeared in *Computer Music Journal* 3(1):48–55, 1979. Another version appeared in Italian as "Le grammatiche come rappresentazioni della musica" in *Musica e elaboratore*, ed. A. Vidolin (Venice: Biennale di Venezia, 1980).

(1975), and Ruwet (1972, 1975). Another influence has been the need in computer music for more advanced score representations. The goal of these representations is to capture more parts and dimensions of musical structure than the note lists provided in sound-synthesis languages such as Music V (Mathews 1969).

Language as a Metaphor for Music

It is natural that musicians, and in particular the music theory profession, would gravitate toward an approach perceived as more powerful and consistent than the *ad hoc* methods of the past. However, this gravitation has generated its own counterforce in the form of a running controversy over the appropriateness of applying certain linguistic concepts to music. (See, for example, Boretz 1969, 1970; Nattiez 1975; Narmour 1977; Powers 1980.)

One major issue is how far the analogies between linguistics and music studies should be taken. Applications of linguistic theory to music range over the following tasks:

sound analysis, where the tools of phonology can be applied to the study of musical sound (Bright 1963),

composition, where musical structure can be characterized in terms of the abstract expressions of formal language theory (see, for example, Jones 1981), and

cognitive theories of music, which include at least three applications: viewing music as a kind of utterance that is more or less directly akin to spoken language (Bernstein 1976), using formal languages to construct a cognitive theory of musical listening (Laske 1975), and using linguistic methodology (e.g., theory construction and verification techniques such as segmentation) (Lerdahl and Jackendoff 1983).

It should be clear from this list that there is a wide range of opinion as to what aspects of music should be modeled via linguistic representations. For example, some studies try to account for only the notes on the printed score, others concentrate on the sound, and still others try to model the perceived music in the listener's mind. Critics of linguistic methodology have tended to focus on one application of linguistics to music. For example, the critiques of the linguistic analogy found in the writings of

Narmour, Nattiez, and Powers are aimed primarily at the "music as natural language" idea, espoused by Bernstein among others. Whatever one's position, it is a mistake to look upon linguistics as a conceptual monolith. As Winograd (1983) points out, linguistics has several competing branches, each of which is based on a metaphor derived from yet another field of study. Among the branches are comparative linguistics (linguistics as biology), structural linguistics (linguistics as chemistry), generative linguistics (linguistics as mathematics), and computational linguistics (linguistics as the study of knowledge-based communication). For each strain of linguistic theory, a corresponding interpretation in the musical field has been preferred.

Chomsky's linguistic theories (concerning transformational generative grammars) have inspired a large number of musical projects, for example Bernstein's book. In his writings, Chomsky attaches a great deal of importance to metatheoretical issues such as goals and methodology. His monographs are peppered with discussions of discovery rules, descriptive adequacy, the existence of universals, and the innateness of language. Much of the debate concerning the applicability of grammar theory to music has focused on these metatheoretical issues (Narmour 1977; Nattiez 1975; Powers 1980) rather than on the content of the generative rules themselves or on the tradeoffs involved in using various representations.

Another metatheoretical issue that has surfaced both in linguistics and in music is the degree of mentalism associated with a representation. Mentalism debates focus on whether a representation corresponds to psychological reality (see Jackendoff and Lerdahl 1980; Keiler 1980).

Iconic, Symbolic, and Score Representations

What is a representation? For the purpose of this discussion, it is useful to establish certain working definitions and to clarify certain concepts. First, it is necessary to distinguish between iconic and symbolic representations. As Sebeok states, "A sign is said to be iconic when there is a topological similarity between the signifier [the sign] and its denotata [what it represents]." (Sebeok 1975, p. 242) An example of such an iconic representation is a sequence of numbers stored in a computer memory that correspond in value to the shape of an acoustic signal. In computer music, a common form of iconic information is raw, uninterpreted data, usually obtained by applying a transducer to the physical manifestation of sound. In this case, the patterns of the number values mirror the patterns of the waveforms.

In contrast, a symbol can be defined as "a sign without either similarity or contiguity but with only a conventional link between its signifier and denotata" (Sebeok 1975, p. 247). Symbols are most often combined into formal languages. The symbols and their syntactic arrangement have functional meaning within the language, so they can be interpreted. Such symbols do not usually mirror the surface structure of a composition; rather, they represent the *background* interrelations (or *deep structure*). An example of a symbolic notation for traditional music can be found in the language of chords and chord sequences (e.g., "V–I–VI–II$_7$–VII^6– III–I^6") or in the labeling of structural relationships (e.g., "AbbaA").

Standing between the iconic and the symbolic are most scores, which are intermediate representations. Graphic scores and tablature tend to be more iconic, while traditional staff notation contains more formal elements such as note heads and stems, dynamic terms (*ppp*, *pp*, *mp*, etc.), accidentals, and the like. In both cases, there is typically room for performance and analysis interpretation, wherein the background or macrostructure, only implied by the score, is articulated or explicated.

Basic Concepts of Grammar

A grammar of music is a symbolic representation. In musical applications, a grammar is usually used to represent a generic class of compositions. Specific compositions can be represented within a grammar as a selection of *production rules* or *rewrite rules*. (The latter term is usually preferred to avoid confusion with rules used in production systems in artificial-intelligence research.) A grammar can be represented graphically by means of a *parse tree*, as shown in figure 23.1. At the highest level of the tree, a composition or class of compositions is represented by a single symbol, called the *root token*. Other tokens, standing for subunits of the grammar, are derived from the root token by tracing downward. The general term *token* is used to denote any symbol in a grammar or parse tree.

One of the major distinctions drawn in much linguistic study is the difference between syntax and semantics. A working definition of musical syntax follows. If a given piece of music can be segmented into elementary

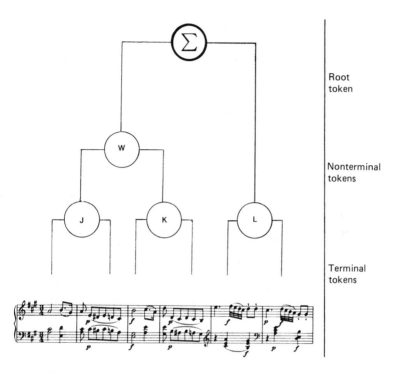

Figure 23.1
A simple parsing of a fragment of music, showing a hierarchical structure.

lexical units (such as notes), its syntactic structure consists of groupings of contiguous lexical units into categories. Typical musical syntactic categories include "the first four measures," "section 1," "the counter-subject," "the third movement," and "the entire piece." The notion of musical semantics is defined differently by various scholars. It can refer to things as disparate as the intentions of the composer, associations prompted in the listener, instructions in the score (e.g., "with feeling"), common properties between syntactically separate events (e.g., "all loud notes"), and acoustical factors such as timbre and articulation. For the purposes of this article, the scope of the term *semantics* need not be defined precisely. I will use the term simply to refer to all "extrasyntactic" aspects of the music. Some studies that focus on musical semantics are Bernstein 1976; Imberty 1976, 1981; Laske 1973; Lidov 1975, 1980; Meyer 1956; Minsky 1981; Nattiez 1975; and Powers 1976, 1980.

Limits and Powers of a Grammar Approach

One of the limits of a grammar approach is implied in the distinction made earlier between iconic and symbolic representation systems. Before a sound signal can be represented symbolically, it must be transformed into the discrete, symbolic domain. As Saussure noted, this discreteness is not given in nature. In a computer-aided sound-analysis system, considerable signal processing is necessary to obtain the pertinent data necessary to transform musical sound from the low-level acoustic domain through the intermediate level of score representation and finally into a high-level, symbolic notation (Moorer 1975; Chafe et al. 1982; Foster et al. 1982). For compositional uses, this situation is slightly less restrictive, in that composers can coordinate symbolic and sonic representations by working in each domain separately and mapping the symbolic to the sonic. In this case it makes sense to treat the sonic domain as composed of discrete *sonic objects* similar to the *objets sonores* of Schaeffer (1977). Naturally, objects can be linked and blended for a continuous musical flow.

As is the case in any representation system, the use of grammars relies on certain biases. The notation system for formal grammars is very useful for representing multilevel macrostructures where broad macrosections encapsule substrata consisting of sound objects on the lowest level. Clearly the musical scope of such a representation system is very large. However, while it may be "theoretically possible" to generate "any" structure with any one system, there is always a sharp pragmatic distinction between what can be done easily and what is difficult to do—between what can be done with some elegance and what requires *ad hoc* patchwork. Of course, to be of any use, the grammar model itself must embody a certain explanatory strength (for purposes of analysis) or expressive power (for purposes of composition). A weak or trivial grammar model of a composition is probably less effective than a strong, nongrammar model.

Nevertheless, some words about the power and scope of a grammar representation are in order. A very broad range of music can be described naturally using grammars. Theorists have applied grammar concepts to chorales (Baroni and Jacoboni 1978) and to Venda music (Blacking 1971). Any music that can be segmented can be described by a grammar. Furthermore, a great deal of study has already been invested into the properties of abstract grammars; their features are well understood. A collection of powerful software tools has developed around these grammars through computer science, including lexical analyzers, parsers, compilers, reverse-compilers, and compiler-compilers or parser-generators. In some cases, these tools have been adapted for musical purposes.

Last, grammars provide a unified, multilevel generative model. Parse trees have proven useful in describing known compositions, and grammars can be used to test both compositional and analytical hypotheses.

More specific criticisms of the grammar formalism will be discussed later. Now the properties of formal grammars will be explained and some musical applications of grammars will be synopsized.

Introductory Notes on Formal Grammars

In this section the basic properties of various classes of formal languages are summarized. More detailed information on formal grammars is readily available; Salomaa 1973 and Aho and Ullman 1972 are excellent sources.

Formal languages stand in contrast with *natural* languages such as English and Chinese. A formal language consists of an alphabet of abstract symbols, which are combined in various ways to form sentences. One way to specify a language is to list all the sentences in it. When the number of sentences is infinite, a more compact system of rules is used. The rules for combining symbols into valid sentences constitute a *formal grammar*. For musical purposes, statements within music grammars are representations of music structures—collections of sounds conforming to some compositional syntax.

The notation system for abstract grammars is a collection of *graphemes* or characters, e.g., a, b, ... or 0, 1, ..., n. Out of one or more graphemes are composed individual *tokens* or symbols, e.g., aa, bb, ab, ... This collection of tokens along with the null token φ make up the *vocabulary of tokens, V*. Within the vocabulary of tokens is defined the *alphabet of terminals, T*. The terminals are the lowest-level tokens; they correspond to the lowest level of microstructure that the grammar describes (the "surface structure"). A *language, L,* is defined as the subset of finite concatenations of tokens in T. The terms *sentence, word*, and *string* are often used synonymously in different articles on formal language theory to denote sequences of terminal tokens in L. An *alphabet of nonterminals, N*, is defined in V; these represent categories of macrostructures (or "deep structure"). A *sentential form* is simply a sequence of nonterminals.

The expression

$$\alpha \rightarrow \beta$$

is a *production rule* or *rewrite rule*. The right side of the expression is a replacement for the left side; this constitutes an algorithm for generating sentences. A *derivation* is a complete sequence of rewrite rules leading from the highest nonterminal token to a terminal; for example,

$$\Sigma \rightarrow A1,$$

$$A1 \rightarrow A2,$$

$$A2 \rightarrow z$$

is a derivation from the root Σ to the terminal z. Finally, a *generative grammar*, G, can be characterized as a quadruple:

$$G = (N, T, \Sigma, P)$$

where N is the alphabet of nonterminals, T is the alphabet of terminals, Σ is the root token, and P is the collection of rewrite rules of the form $\alpha \rightarrow \beta$ where $\alpha, \beta \in (N \cup T)^*$ and $(N \cap T) = \varnothing$. (The asterisk denotes the set containing all strings over the specified domain.)

A Brief Consideration of Grammar Types

Distinguishing some of the relevant properties of the major grammar types is useful as a prelude to studying how various grammars have been or might be applied to music. The grammar types to be discussed include the following:

type 0 (free)

type 1 (context-sensitive)

type 2 (context-free)

type 3 (finite-state)

transformational

systemic

regulated

array

augmented transition network (ATN)

The first grammars to be discussed are the four types (0, 1, 2, 3) identified by Chomsky (1957).

Type 0 (Free)

A type 0 grammar is a theoretical construct that imposes no restrictions on the form of the rewrite rules. Null rewrite rules $(A \rightarrow \varphi)$, infinite rewrite rules, and erasing rewrite rules (which destroy or modify the effects of earlier rules) are all legal in a type 0 grammar.

Type 1 (Context-Sensitive)

A type 1 or context-sensitive grammar derives its name from the rewrite rule $A\alpha B \rightarrow A\beta B$, where α produces β in the context of the tokens A and B. The length of α must be less than the length of β. A type 1 grammar is less open than a type 0 grammar. In particular, the null rewrite rule $\alpha \rightarrow \varphi$ is not legal.

Type 2 (Context-Free)

Whereas a type 1 grammar allows strings on both sides of a rewrite rule, a type 2 grammar expands only one nonterminal token, on the left-hand side of a rule. An example of a type 2 rewrite rule is $A \rightarrow BcD$, where B and D are nonterminals and c is a terminal token.

Type 3 (Finite-State)

A type 3 or finite-state grammar is characterized by the restriction that no more than one nonterminal token can appear on each side of any rewrite rule. $A \rightarrow b$ or $A \rightarrow bC$ is an example of a *right-linear* finite-state grammar, where A and C are nonterminals and b is a terminal. The name right-linear is derived from the position of the nonterminal C.

Consideration of the Chomsky Grammar Types for Music

Some questions to ask in considering the application of a grammar type as a recognizer or generator for a musical style are the following:

Is this grammar adequate to represent this musical style?

Is a more powerful grammar needed?

Is this grammar reasonably efficient? Can I keep track of this grammar by hand? Or can this grammar be implemented practically on a computer?

This section attempts to resolve these questions.

Type 0 A type 0 grammar, because it allows infinite rewriting, is not practical. In particular, it is not possible to build a recognizer for a type 0 grammar. As for generative operations, since a type 0 grammar allows null rewrite rules and erasing rules, keeping track of its output could be very confusing.

The erasing rules mean that a type 0 grammar can generate intermediate strings that expand and then contract, producing the curious case of a "phantom macrostructure" for which there is no corresponding microstructure. While this may at first glance seem useless, the idea of erasing rules becomes attractive when one is trying to simulate processes such as variations on a theme. Often notes from the original theme are deleted as variations are made, and an erasing rule is a possible means of modeling this process. As we shall see later, it is possible to incorporate erasure without embedding it in the production rules, through devices such as transformations.

Type 1 A strong case can be made for the utility of including context sensitivity in musical grammars. Type 1 (context-sensitive) grammars are one means of achieving this. However, certain complications appear when context-sensitive rewrite rules are used.

These complication are of two kinds. First, since the well-formedness of strings generated by a type 1 grammar is undecidable (Chomsky 1963a), ambiguous rules are quite legal. This means that there is no way of recovering a unique parsing (derivation) from sentences generated by a type 1 grammar. The situation is made complex by the fact that either side of a type 1 rewrite rule may be a string of tokens. The second complication involves implementation. The use of a type 1 grammar (in a musical analysis or generation system) would entail multiplying the number of rewrite rules by the number of contextual possibilities. This has two ramifications. First, it makes the specification of the grammar a rather onerous task. Second, the number of recognition steps in a parser of such a grammar becomes combinatorially explosive, since continual cross-references must be made to the rewrite tables.

Fortunately, as with erasing rules in type 0 grammars, it is possible to incorporate context-sensitive features into a grammar with simpler (type 2) rewrite rules. This feature can be implemented via transformational devices or through the use of control procedures in a regulated grammar.

Type 2 Type 2 grammars have been proved useful for many applications in programming-language parsers and in computational linguistics, primarily because of their relative ease of implementation. Parsing complexity is a simple linear function of the number of rewrite rules in a derivation. The power of type 2 grammars for music lies in their ability to represe..t multilevel syntactic formations. Any nonterminal (which could represent a structural category such as section, phrase, or motive) may generate a string of tokens (including other nonterminals) at a lower level.

As in type 1 grammars, ambiguous rewrite rules are also allowed. However, the tracing of their derivation is simplified, since any terminal need only be reduced to a single nonterminal rather than an entire string.

Type 3 Type 3 rules are quite restricted. The ability of a type 3 rule to represent any kind of multilevel tree structure (such as a musical composition that exhibits a simple, hierarchical form) is extremely limited. This is because the definition of a type 3 grammar limits it to producing only one nonterminal on the right side of a rewrite rule.

By contrast, type 2 grammars can generate a string of nonterminal tokens in a single rewrite rule. This makes type 2 grammars more powerful for representing musical structure. The strongest advantage of a type 2 grammar over a type 3 grammar results from rewrite rules of the form $A \rightarrow \alpha A \beta$, where A is a nonterminal and α and β are members of V. Rules of this form are called *self-embedding*. In music, they result in nested motivic formations. This issue convinced Chomsky (1957) that type 3 grammars were too weak to handle phrase-structured languages. A representation for music should have the power to generate at least nested phrases and motives, constructions technically excluded from type 3 grammars.

Chomsky characterized Markov-chain process as type 3 grammars (1957, 1963b). Markov chains have been used in algorithmic music-composition systems (Hiller and Isaacson 1959; Moorer 1972; Xenakis 1971). Chomsky pointed out the inability of Markov chains to handle phrase structure. This inability has nothing to do with the issue of a stochastic process versus a deterministic process. Indeed, a type 2 musical grammar can be made stochastic (see Jones 1981). The issue is rather in the form of the rewrite rules. A Markov system is limited to a linear, step-by-step rewriting process, whereas a type 2 rule can generate a complete phrase (string of nonterminal tokens) at once. Since type 2 grammars are not difficult to specify or program, there seems to be no reason for limiting a musical grammar to type 3 rules.

Transformational Grammar

Transformational generative grammar was proposed by Chomsky (1965) to describe the structure of natural language. The grammar for English is made up of three parts: a *phrase-structure grammar*, which generates abstract kernel sentences; a set of *transformation rules*, which map kernel sentences into English sentences; and a set of *morphophonetic rules*, which map English sentences into streams of phonemes (spoken sequences). Chomsky's reasons for adopting a mediating level between phrase structure and morphophonetics stem from certain complexities associated with natural-language constructs. These constructs include active-passive verb relations, auxiliary verbs, and negation. Bernstein (1976) argued that direct analogies exist between these syntactic structures (and all natural-language structures) and syntactic structures in music. Such a literal analogy between this natural-language theory and music theory is debatable.

Whatever the justification, a transformational process at the output of the abstract rules does increase the power and flexibility of a musical grammar. If the abstract rules are kept the same, transformational rules can adapt generated material to a specific context. For example, given a phrase generated by an abstract rule, a transformational rule may change a quarter note into two eighth notes, or delete a note, or add a rest as an offset to a rhythmic figure.

The addition of a transformational layer to a parser adds ambiguity and complexity. For example, if a parser is able to "almost match" an input string with a syntactic category in a stored grammar, how much transformation is valid in order to get the string to match exactly? There comes a point at which any string can be viewed as a transformation of any other string, and specifying the limits of valid transformations is difficult.

If we iimit the scope of the rewrite rules to the production or analysis of the printed score, then the process of morphophonetics—associating abstract tokens output by a grammar to a lexicon of sounds—has a pertinant musical analogy in the process of orchestration.

Systemic Grammar

Systemic grammar is a linguistic model developed in the 1960s by M. A. K. Halliday and his associates at University College, London (Halliday 1961, 1967, 1973). The basic technical notion is that of a formal *system*—with

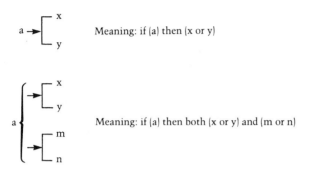

Figure 23.2
Halliday's systemic grammar notation.

the term used in a specialized sense to mean a set of options with an entry condition. This can also be expressed as a number of possibilities from which a choice has to be made if the specified conditions of entry are to be satisfied. Halliday's notation is shown in figure 23.2. Figure 23.3 illustrates Winograd's (1968) musical application of this notation. [Winograd (1969) also used the systemic grammar model in constructing a program to parse natural language.]

An advantage of systemic grammar is the ease with which syntax and semantics can be intermingled in the grammar rules. Meaning in a systemic grammar can be encoded as a system of semantic options alongside the syntactic ones.

The theoretical basis of systemic grammars rests on the observation that there is a high correlation between the context-dependent features of natural language and the semantic interpretation of the constituents that exhibit them. In practice, this means that symbols in the grammar can have additional features that may control their expansions. These features may include semantic tests for plausibility and meaningfulness. For example, we may recognize that an E-G-C chord is (syntactically, anyway) the tonic of the key of C major in first inversion. However, if this is the last event in a piece that has been up to this point in E minor, it is not very meaningful to characterize the chord as related to C major. Winograd used the features of systemic grammar in precisely this way to differentiate meaningful chord names from merely syntactically legal ones.

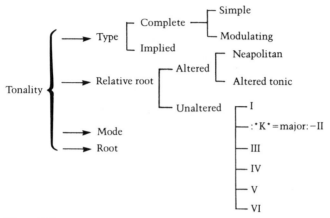

Figure 23.3
Winograd's musical application of Halliday's notation to tonal harmony.

Regulated Grammar

A regulated grammar typically involves a context-free (type 2) grammar controlled by procedures that determine not the form of the production rules but rather at which point they are to be applied (Cleaveland and Uzgalis 1977). Through the use of control procedures or a control language the generative capacity of a context-free grammar can be greatly increased. A variety of regulated grammar systems were devised by Salomaa (1973), and in Roads 1978 I discussed the design of a composing language incorporating control procedures as well as a lexical mapping system regulated by a control language.

Control systems over a grammar can be straightforward and useful ways of handling such special cases as productions with several alternatives (a control procedure can resolve the ambiguity) and recursive productions (a control procedure can control when the recursion will stop). Another device besides control procedures is available. A *control language* works by assigning a label to each production rule. The control language is said to function *over* the grammar. It contains expressions that are simply sequences of labels that determine what production rules are valid at any stage in the parsing process.

Multidimensional Grammars

One of the more obvious distinctions between natural languages and music is the presence of syntactic parallelism in music. It is difficult to say two different sentences simultaneously! The inherent parallelism in much music, for example in chords and polyphony, requires appropriate representation mechanisms.

Other aspects of musical structure, such as the shape of acoustic waveforms, are suited to two or more dimensions of representations. Since most formal language representations were spawned from sequential linguistic theories, generative devices with more than one dimension and with parallelism were developed only later. The need to develop grammars that define and recognize two-dimensional pictures provided the initial impetus for research in multidimensional grammars (Rosenfeld 1971). Much of this work is classified under the rubric of *syntactic pattern recognition* (Fu 1974).

Another use for multidimensional grammars is for the coordination of several musical parameters simultaneously. For this purpose, more than two dimensions are needed. *Array grammars* (Rosenfeld 1973) are a generalized multidimensional grammar mechanism. An array grammar defines a language of *n*-dimensional arrays of symbols. Rewrite rules in an array grammar specify subarray substitutions. If, during the generation process, the array contains a subarray identical to the left side of a rule, the right side of the rule may be substituted for that subarray. This was the approach taken by Strawn (1980) in his analysis of waveforms. Jones (1981) used a generative device similar to an array grammar called a *space grammar*, and applied it to algorithmic composition. Other types of multidimensional generators, such as graph, plex, tree, pattern, and shape grammars, define languages of graphs, plex structures, trees, patterns, and shapes, respectively (Gips 1975).

Augmented-Transition-Network Grammars

The augmented-transition-network (ATN) grammar is a paradigm and a computer program developed by Woods (1970, 1975a, 1980) for parsing natural language. It incorporates many of the operations of Chomsky's transformational grammar while overcoming the need for a separate (and, as Woods shows, highly inefficient) transformational component.

An ATN is built out of a basic transition network (BTN), a standard finite-state automation to which recursion has been added. The result is no longer a finite-state device but is formally equivalent to a context-free grammar. This is due to the inclusion of so-called PUSH arcs labeled with the names of phrase structures. Another special feature is a JUMP arc,

Section — Introduction

Section — Introduction Phrase-1

Section — Introduction Phrase-1 Phrase-1

Section — Introduction Phrase-2

Section — Introduction Phrase-1 Phrase-2

Section — Introduction Phrase-1 Phrase-1 Phrase 2

.

.

.

Section — Introduction (Phrase-1 (Phrase-1)) (Phrase-2)*

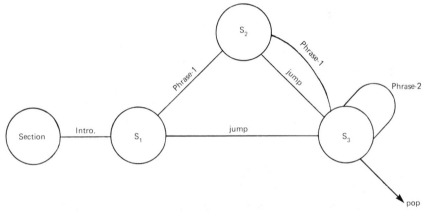

Figure 23.4
Merging the right side of context-free rules in a basic-transition-network grammar
representation. (top) Separate context-free rules. (middle) Merged representation.
(bottom) Graphical form of merged representation.

which allows the parser to progress to a new rule without consuming
more input. The BTN formalism allows one to merge the common parts
of what would be different context-free rules (figure 23.4).

ATNs are augmented to carry a set of register contents in addition to
state and stack information. Also, arbitrary computational tests and
actions (coded in Lisp) may be associated with the state transitions. If
the test associated with traversing an arc is satisfied, then the action builds
tree structure. The actions may extend to any Lisp function, providing
Turing Machine equivalency. As in transformational grammars, the
typical functions of the actions include reordering, restructuring, deleting,
and copying constituents.

ATN grammars can be used for both generating and parsing phrase-structured information. Although ATN grammars have been used extensively in studies of natural language, they have never been adapted for musical use, though it appears they could be useful. For example, Woods (1980) proposed that a series of ATN grammars be used for parsing speech sounds, including an ATN for phonology and one for lexical analysis as well as higher-level ATNs.

A Survey of Grammars Applied to Music

Having discussed the properties of the various types of grammars, it is now feasible to survey the use of grammars in music studies by a number of researchers.

Ruwet

The studies of Nicholas Ruwet fall into two periods, with somewhat contrasting visions as to the place of grammars in music studies. In his 1966 article "Méthodes d'analyse en musicologie" (in Ruwet 1972), Ruwet the musicologist proposed a method of analysis which applied techniques of segmentation (or *partitioning*) based on criteria of repetition (equivalences), opposition, and transformation. He used linguistic techniques to analyze fourteenth-century *Geisslerlieder* and extracts from works by Rameau and Debussy. He emphasized the use of formal grammars as a tool for *verification of the analysis* (through a test of synthesis based on the grammar constructed from the analysis) and as a *unified formal model* of necessarily disunited analysis techniques.

By 1975, however, Ruwet, by then an established generative grammarian linguist, had altered his views on music theory construction (Ruwet 1975). Following a line of reasoning argued earlier by Chomsky, Ruwet preferred a more *top-down* approach to music analysis, in which the construction of a theoretical model precedes the testing of its validity. He contrasted this top-down approach to the *bottom-up* method used in his earlier articles and in the work of Nattiez, which is strictly empirically based. To Ruwet, the top-down approach is more scientific, in that like a theoretical physicist, one validates a theory by attempting to falsify it. Like Chomsky, he argued that there are no procedures for discovering theories; there only exist methods of falsifying them. Thus, strong, general, interesting music theories need to be intuitively proposed, and only then scientifically validated or invalidated. Ruwet went on to suggest that a form of generative grammar [in detail not equivalent to Chomsky's *Aspects* schema (1965) for natural language] could be an excellent model for such a purpose. The function of a grammar is thus shifted from that of a validating device of an inductive (bottom-up) theory to that of a starting point in the construction of a hypothetico-deductive (top-down) theory. Lastly, Ruwet asserted that music analysis cannot simply be scorebound, but rather must treat the sonic domain more comprehensively.

Nattiez

The position of J.-J. Nattiez was different from that of Ruwet. In particular, Nattiez took an empiricist's approach; he did not believe that it is possible to propose a significant set of synthetic (generative) rules without first passing through a process of detailed taxonomic description (Nattiez 1974, 1975). Based on taxonomical procedures of the early Ruwet [who, in turn borrowed from early poetic analyses by Jacobson (1973)], Nattiez gave examples of analyses on scores by Stravinsky, Brahms, and Varèse. He went beyond the early Ruwet in asserting the need for inter-textual analyses of whole families of scores in order to recover pertinent stylistic traits. As regards grammars, he suggested that "syntagmatic grammars" may be constructed to represent an analysis of a single work in the form of a system of generative rules for the specific signs in a piece. However, a large part of Nattiez's book is devoted to arguing the semiological specificity of music as distinct from natural language. Thus, he criticized the bald translation of Chomsky's *Aspects* schema for natural language to music. While noting that one or another part of the theory may be useful, he specifically attacked the notion of importing a "transformational" stage into a music grammar.

   Nattiez noted the analogy between Schenker's hierarchical graph notation and the parse trees which he himself used. But he criticized the identification of Schenker's *Ursatz* (or *fundamental structure*; see Forte 1977) with Chomsky's semantically tied *deep structure*. He felt this led to a normative conception of music.

Laske

A common thread running through all of Laske's early writings is the grammar form. He based his explorations into a "generative theory of music" on a grammatical conception which, in form, corresponds to

Chomsky's schema (1965). This grammar conception was, in Laske's mind, to be founded on "an explicit and formal model of empirical musical activity" (Laske 1975). The construction of the theory rested on what he called a "sonological/psychological base." Finding an integrated model for such a base to be nonexistent, Laske, in his later work, turned to the "investigation of the strategical task environment of such grammars." He characterized this work as "studies in musical cognition." Its purpose was to study the formal properties of cognitive tasks undertaken in processing musical input. Instead of producing a taxonomic analysis of music structures, Laske turned to what is essentially a project in cognitive psychology.

One of the most useful concepts of Laske's earlier essays is the notion of *sonology*, a generalization of the linguist's *phonology*, which is said to "express the relationship between the syntactic structure of a music and its physical representation in so far as this relationship is determined by grammatical rules" (Laske 1975, section 1, p. 31). The issues involved in sonology are vital to composition, as well as musical analysis and theory, since they touch upon systems of orchestration and psychoacoustics.

In later essays, Laske used the notion of a grammar particularly as a model for musical task strategies. In particular, Laske adopted the use of "programmed grammars" (a form of regulated grammar) which specify the order in which task-production rules are to be applied. In his book (Laske 1977) he retained a grammar conception of musical structure (as multiple layers of musical phrases linked by production rules).

Smoliar

For the purposes of this discussion, it makes sense to partition Smoliar's writings on grammars and music into two phases. In the first phase, Smoliar suggested the use of grammatical constructs for an analysis procedure which would proceed to parse a music signal from the bottom up. Specifically, Smoliar's proposed music analysis system would "decompile" the electroacoustic signal of some music by generating what he calls "antiproductions." Such a decompilation process would ultimately produce a model of music perception, to be characterized in terms of a "high-level language" (Smoliar 1976).

In the second phase, Smoliar implemented an interactive language for music theorists in which structural descriptions of music compositions may be encoded. The program generated music strings based on the structural descriptions. The primitives of the language were a clever adaptation of Schenker's functional model of the tonal language. Starting from a musical *proto-structure* (Smoliar's term for Schenker's *Ursatz*) the theorist may specify various commands which invoke rewriting rules that derive a surface structure from the proto-structure. In graphic terms, the program generated a tree from the root; commands generated branches, deleted branches, rearranged the levels of the tree, and so on (Smoliar 1977, 1980).

Lidov and Gabura

Lidov and Gabura (1973) concentrated on a generator for melody—specifically, 32-note melodies in an 8-measure, 2/4 frame, using the C major diatonic scale. The goal of their study was the development of a computer program to emulate the "common-practice" melodies found in Haydn and in folk and popular music.

Their system incorporated two grammars. One generated a rhythmic base (a string of durations with indexes for tonal stress). The rhythmic grammar used context-sensitive rules. Each node in the grammar generated two subordinate nodes. The right part allowed a random choice for the tonal weight.

The pitch grammar interpreted the stress indexes, assigning pitches to the rhythmic base. It relied on a context-free set of rules, with the most-stressed notes (tonics) chosen first. The context-free rules were augmented by a set of "melodic contour" rules that ensured a reasonable melodic shape. Each pitch interval was marked according to the melodic contour index in which it was produced. In particular, a notion of *waves*—high-level melodic shapes—was defined. The melodic contour rules formed a "filter" through which the grammar-generated melodies were passed. Lidov and Gabura summarized this work by stating that a convincing syntax was easier to achieve than a convincing contour.

Baroni and Jacoboni

Baroni and Jacoboni (1975, 1978) undertook the definition of a grammar of melodies for a selected corpus of Lutheran chorales. Rejecting statistical procedures, they developed a set of 56 rules (a grammar) which generated "correct" (as distinct from aesthetic) melodies. The rules were derived from an analysis of 60 chorales harmonized by J. S. Bach. Baroni and Jacoboni did not propose a grammar in the sense of Chomsky's description (which is supposed to indicate how an utterance is heard by a listener). Indeed, they doubted the existence of musical deep structure, since they insisted that performance is so tied to the "sense" of music. Hence, they asserted that syntactic structures are not strictly correlated to semantic context.

Baroni and Jacoboni have not insisted on the primacy of the rules they derived. According to them, there could be many functionally equivalent sets of rules. They used a computer program to verify their generative hypotheses. They revised their original plan between 1978 and 1982 to a more complete form (Baroni 1982). Their later work used analysis of the final notes in phrases (seen as pivotal to melodic structure) and an "analogies tree" (essentially a transformational grammar that derives musical surface structures from a kernel through a series of transformations) to generate melodic forms. Ongoing work is devoted to automatically harmonizing the melodies.

Bernstein

Bernstein 1976 is a transcription of a series of television broadcasts aimed at applying Chomsky's model of transformational grammar more or less directly to tonal music. Starting from a speculative assumption of musical monogenesis (without reference to Rousseau's 1754 speculations on linguistic monogenesis along the same lines), Bernstein built an argument for "universals" in music. He identified the overtone series, the tonic-dominant opposition, and innate musical-grammatical competence as universals.

Bernstein claimed that music's phonological level is based on the overtone series. On this foundation, he went on to make concept-for-concept correspondences between categories in generative grammar theory and music. He related the letters of the alphabet to musical notes, and different alphabets to different scales. He found a correlation between the nouns, verbs, adjectives, and adverbs of languages and the tonal syntax of keys, motives, and rhythmic figuration in music.

In order to model the transformations of generative grammar, Bernstein equated interrogative sentence forms with unresolved musical chords, and negation of a sentence with a shift from a major to a minor tonality. The analogies were stretched further as he related large-scale rhetorical forms such as anaphora, asyndeton, and alliteration to forms in music.

Jackendoff (1977) and Keiler (1978) have both criticized Bernstein's unadulterated transfer of a specific linguistic theory to music theory. Keiler disputed the whole notion of using the overtone series as a basis for musical phonology. He found Bernstein's noun = melody, verb = rhythm, and adjective = harmony equations to be forced. He was likewise unconvinced by Bernstein's general conclusions concerning serialism versus tonality.

Lerdahl and Jackendoff

Lerdahl and Jackendoff (1977) introduced a music-analysis methodology that derives much metatheoretical inspiration from Chomsky while not importing specifically linguistic models to music. Their generative model is specifically a theory of tonal music, with implications for other musics and for musical cognition in general. The model uses four types of analysis to derive layers of musical organization in pitch and metrical structure (the only domains of organization they discuss). Though they did not assert that all music is at all times organized on multiple levels, they concentrated on hierarchical aspects. The rules that assign structural descriptions are of three types: *well-formedness rules*, which assign possible (tree) structures, *preference rules*, which select more coherent and compelling structural descriptions from possible ones, and *transformational rules*, which are needed to describe certain special cases such as elisions.

The "transformational rules" were not meant to be exactly equivalent to their linguistic counterparts. Though Lerdahl and Jackendoff introduced the notion of transformations into their description system, they admitted that then "the problem is to constrain admissible transformations," since any phrase may be characterized as a transformation of any other. They also suggested that in Chomskian linguistics the role of transformations has been weakened somewhat in favor of an enriched phrase-structure grammar. They presented examples of their analysis technique and showed how it differs from Schenker's (see Forte 1977 for a synopsis), which they found too inexplicit. The use of the term *deep structure* was debated in connection with the notion of archetypal music forms. While dismissing the normative connotations of *archetypes*, Lerdahl and Jackendoff suggested that they may be a way of classifying perceived regularities or congruencies in phrase structures (particularly for tonal music), which may in turn suggest how music is processed by listeners.

Lerdahl and Jackendoff's later studies focus on generative theories of the hierarchical aspects of homophonic tonal music (Lerdahl and Jackendoff 1981, 1983; Jackendoff and Lerdahl 1981). They applied four types of analysis to a composition: *grouping analysis*, which breaks up a piece into a hierarchy of sections, phrases, and motives; *metrical analysis*, which finds metrical hierarchies such as two consecutive groups of three notes that are a part of a larger six-note group; and *time-span reduction* and *prolongational reduction*, which isolate pitch hierarchies (see Jackendoff and Lerdahl 1982).

In time-span reduction, pitch importance is measured with respect to other pitches in the same time-span, where a time-span is defined as a rhythmic unit constructed out of an interaction of grouping and metrical structures. Prolongational analysis emphasizes the connections among pitch events, establishing their continuity and progression and their movement toward tension or relaxation. Lerdahl and Potard (1982) have proposed the use of these four forms as an aid to composition.

Balaban

Balaban (1981) wrote a doctoral dissertation on a "generalized concept model" representation for tonal music. Although she did not use specific grammar formalisms, she related all her work to earlier linguistic and formal linguistic theories. The generalized concept model is a synthesis of ideas from the theories of relational databases (Chen 1976), attribute grammars (Knuth 1968), and semantic networks (Quillian 1968; Woods 1975b).

Balaban's overall goal was to formalize basic tonal-music theory and develop appropriate computer representations for the formalization, thereby laying a cornerstone for systematic musical research. Pitch and duration are the only musical parameters studied. She begins with a formalization of notes and intervals, leading to formal representations of *tonal-music-strings*, which she says are analogous to the *deep structures* of Chomsky's transformational generative grammar theories. For any piece, a tonal-music-string is a linear representation containing "the union of all sets describing occurrences of notes and rests, or of intervals, in that piece" (p. 67). It is clear from this definition that the tonal-music-string concept "actually describes any piece [consisting] of the twelve tones, and has nothing to do with the not-so-easily-defined concept of tonality" (p. 144).

The computerized representation system is built on the following notions: *concepts* (distinguishable musical "things" such as notes and chords), *attributes* attached to concepts, (e.g., the chord concept has the attribute number-of-notes), and *relationships* among the concepts (e.g., a chord *is-a* tonal-music-string).

A formalization for the Skeletal System—a "common denominator" of music theories dealing with melodic and harmonic aspects of tonal music—was coded in Lisp. Balaban notes: "From the musical point of view, the Skeletal System is clearly not 'interesting,' as it simply formalizes conventional tonal music terminology, suggesting no specific claims about it. The importance of the system lies in its being the basic step in the complete formalization of 'interesting' musical theories." (p. 132)

Strawn

Strawn (1980) used the grammar formalism as a means of classifying the characteristic shapes of envelopes for amplitude and frequency functions in a digital sound analysis/synthesis system. Strawn's goal was to construct a grammar of perceptually important *features* to be retained in simplified representations of the waveforms. His research was based on techniques of syntactic pattern recognition in the analysis of waveforms (Fu 1974).

Strawn called the terminal tokens *primitives*. These primitives of the waveform grammar were line segments of length x or $2x$ which were classified as horizontal, sloped upward, or sloped downward. His parsing algorithm grouped the line segments into three syntactic levels. The automatic syntactic approximations have the potential of being equal to or superior to approximations made laboriously by hand.

Roads

The subject of Roads 1978 is the notion of using *composing grammars*, in conjunction with a grammar interpreter run on a computer, as a means of organizing music structures. The paper briefly surveys some applications of grammars to music, and introduces some conceptual and notational ideas from formal language theory. These ideas are used to describe the structural properties of various grammars. The second part of the paper is about the design of a graphic and symbolic notation for specifying grammars as shorthand notations for compositional structure. The designs of two languages, TREE (a grammar-specification language for music) and COTREE (a composing language), are given. Compositional expressions coded in COTREE are compiled into a score using the grammar specified with TREE. Both languages use a context-free grammar augmented by control procedures. As an extension of the sequential languages used in formal language theory, the notion of parallel rewrite rules is introduced in order to specify musically concurrent events. The final part of the paper discusses the mapping from an abstract syntactic form generated by COTREE into a lexicon of sound objects. An example of the process of composing with grammars is given.

Other Studies

A number of other studies involving grammars have been undertaken. Lindblom and Sundberg (1970) applied the generative-grammar approach to the study of simple melodies; the methodological approach of this paper is probably of more general interest than the specific results. Rader (1974) followed a similar tack. Ulrich (1977) described a system for analyzing chords and their functions in harmonic jazz compositions, with the goal of modeling a form of jazz improvization (harmonic rhapsodizing). Though Ulrich's system uses a chord grammar for identifying chords, different kinds of comparison procedures are used to identify key centers, and a functional analysis of the chords involves a table-lookup process.

In a separate musical context, there have been several other instances of grammatical models embedded in composing languages for computer music. One of the earler grammatical constructions was implicitly embedded in Smith's SCORE language, in that a *motive*-specification facility effectively defined a context-free production. Transformations such as rhythmic offsets and retrogression could be applied to the motives (Smith 1972, 1973). Buxton's hierarchical data structures (Buxton et al. 1978) allowed a composer to work with what was essentially a parse tree of a composition. The composer could work at any level of the tree (represented as a linked list) to define an abstract syntactic structure, which was mapped to a lexicon of sound objects in a separate phase of composition.

S. Haflich and J. Snell have both proposed generative theories for tonal music. Haflich proposed a model of the competence manifest in classic-era compositions, in particular, the piano sonatas of Mozart (personal communication, 1981). Haflich's goal was to write a program that would produce a myriad of fragments of music that would exemplify aspects of Mozart's style. Snell's planned research (based on rules derived from Bach's *Well-Tempered Clavier*) has not been published.

In several studies, formal logic has been used to construct devices very similar to grammars. Kassler (1967) devised a logical procedure for determining the "admissibility" of a piece of music to the "twelve-note-class-system." Kassler has also used formal logic to implement the *middleground* portion of Schenker's theory of tonality. Kassler's system was designed to recognize instances of the tonal language (this is a major function of a grammar) and produce derivations of the composition from a root token (akin to Schenker's *Ursatz*). Rothenberg (1975) used formal logic to describe a composing system that operated much like the rewrite rules of a grammar.

Problems of Grammar Representations

Grammar representations have been criticized on various technical and musical grounds. This section poses the following questions and attempts to assess their significance: Must grammars be strictly hierarchical structures? Is the notion of musical context adequately represented by syntactic categories? What cognitive processes use and construct grammars? What are some alternatives to the grammar approach?

Hierarchy versus Ambiguity

Grammar representations have been criticized for being strictly hierarchical. Indeed, in much if not most music a segmentation of events into purely hierarchical syntactic structures is not convincing (Levy 1973; Lidov 1975). An inspection of such music reveals overlapping contexts, suggesting several possible parsings. Not all grammars are strictly hierarchical, however. An *ambiguous grammar* allows more than than one way to parse or generate a syntactic structure.

Here is an example of ambiguity in a set of simple rewrite rules:

$E \rightarrow ab$,

$F \rightarrow a$,

$G \rightarrow ba$,

$H \rightarrow b$.

If we attempt to trace the derivation of the string "abba," we find it could have been produced by EG, by FHHF, by EHF, or by FHG. Ambiguous grammars resemble network graphs rather than pure tree structures (figure 23.5). Ambiguity can add to the representational power of a grammar, at a cost of introducing increased complexity. Even so, some fundamental problems in representing musical context are not solved by adopting an ambiguous grammar representation. As Lidov and Gabura (1973) note, "It is not clear whether our present [grammar-based] approach can ever be adequate to mirror the total ambiguity which is so important in music, of the boundary between new figures and variations of an old one" (p. 139). Lidov made a similar statement: "The linguistic strata of word, sentence, and discourse are (for nearly all purposes) unambiguously distinct, and 'sentence' can be defined by reference to the grammar of sentences (a subject plus a predicate makes a sentence). . . . The case in music is quite different because so many of the same constructive relations, for example tonic and dominant, can appear at any level—motive, half-phrase, phrase, period, or section." (Lidov 1980, p. 68; see also Boretz 1969, p. 55) The meaning of these "constructive relations" depends, obviously, on their context. It is precisely in their concept of context that formal grammars are lacking. More powerful models for context are needed.

Musical Context

In nearly every study surveyed here, the rewrite rule by itself has been shown to be insufficient as a representation for music. This is particularly the case for context-free grammar models. Why are "context-sensitive" rewrite rules not an adequate solution?

It is not easy to characterize a moderately complex system with context-sensitive rules. This is due primarily to their intrinsic cross-referencing structure. When rules are nested, the complexity increases, making it harder to follow the logical chain. This human factor, together with their known computational inefficiency, makes context-sensitive grammars unattractive as working tools. Several of the extended grammar types discussed in this essay (transformational, regulated, systemic, and ATN) were designed to add more context sensitivity without adding to the complexity of the rewrite rules.

A more fundamental criticism of context-sensitive rules can be made, however. The whole notion of context sensitivity as embodied in formal language theory is inadequate for music. In formal language theory, "context" is typically a sequential concept. The exception is arraylike

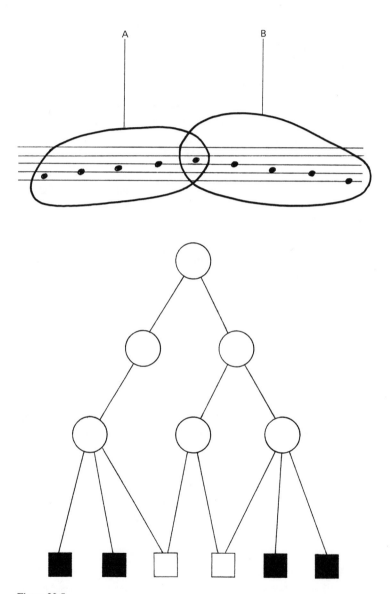

Figure 23.5
An example of ambiguity in parsing. (top) In a simple case—a pitch sequence without
other traits to distinguish it—there are many ways to segment the structure. Two obvious
ones are shown here. (bottom) Graphical representation of ambiguity in a parse tree; the
ambiguous tokens are shown in white.

grammars, in which a parallel context can be specified. In music, however, neither sequential strings nor multidimensional arrays are adequate models for musical context, because musical context extends beyond syntactic categories. Improvisation provides many examples of extra-syntactic context in music. In improvised music, one instrumentalist might play a fragment similar to a well-known tune, provoking a flood of associations in the minds of the other players who may respond with a variation of it or with another similar fragment.

Other contextual cues occur when players alter their style of playing. When a saxophonist shifts the tone from smooth to rough, this timbral marker can signal numerous changes in the performance. It can trigger a change in the overall loudness of the ensemble; it can signal a transformation in the rhythm. Typically, it shifts the emotional direction of the piece toward more intense gestures. A timbral marker can occur in any pitch or rhythmic context, but its meaning is clear: Change now.

However, couldn't "similar" melodic fragments, styles of playing, timbral cues, and other phenomena be classified as syntactic categories and represented within a sparsely filled array grammar? At what point do we limit our definition of syntax, and what will this limit buy us? This is a major conundrum in the application of grammars to music.

Reexamining Syntax and Semantics

Minsky (1965) objected to the way new and specious syntactic categories have been introduced in natural-language understanding systems in order to resolve essentially semantic ambiguities. One of the studies Minsky cites introduced a syntactic category for a physical phenomenon in sentences discussing elementary physics: "While this [strategy] is moderately successful in 'explaining' some syntactic behavior, surely it is a step along a most treacherous path. For it is a sort of pun to represent a *physical* category ... as a *syntactic* type." (p. 22)

The same problems arise in formulating syntactic categories for parsing music. Winograd (1968) uses the labels of traditional harmony to categorize chords, Lerdahl and Jackendoff (1983) use criteria of contiguity and metric stress to isolate different groups, Ruwet (1972) uses criteria of repetition and duration in isolating units, Narmour (1982) labels notes as either a reversal of a previous event or a continuation, Forte (1973) applies the concept of pitch-class-sets to atonal music analysis, and

Deutsch (1982) cites eight perceptual grouping mechanisms. Innumerable other criteria are possible.

The multiplicity of categories for parsing music suggests that the special status accorded to syntax in linguistic theory may be misleading in music studies. We can define *syntax* in whatever way we like, but ultimately any syntactic analysis is merely one viewpoint on a complex phenomenon.

Alternatives to Grammars

Representations that allow multiple viewpoints stand a better chance of accounting for context (musical or otherwise). A number of alternatives to the transformational-grammar paradigm have been developed in the fields of computational linguistics and artificial intelligence (Wilks 1977; Winograd 1977). In order to convey a sense of the features needed to represent musical context, I will sketch the outlines of three multiple-viewpoint representation schemes that have been applied to music. (For a broader survey of representations for music, see Roads 1982a, 1982b.) In the first scheme, called *conceptual dependency*, the importance of syntax in analyzing an utterance is greatly diminished. In the second, a *procedural model* uses multiple processes to construct the different perspectives embodied in intelligent systems. In the third, called *constraints*, interdependencies between the viewpoints allow consistency to be maintained within several partial descriptions of objects.

Conceptual Dependency Frames

Conceptual dependency theory (CD) stands in explicit opposition to a syntactic approach to language processing (Schank 1973). CD was developed by Schank and his associates for applications in natural language understanding. In the CD approach, syntactic structure is used merely as a clue to solving the problem of capturing the underlying conceptual structure of utterances. One of the reasons for their faith in the effectiveness of extrasyntactic processing can be traced to the human ability to understand incomplete and ungrammatical utterances, such as those that make up most conversations.

According to Schank, the internal representations of text used in his systems are "language-free." A tenet of the CD approach to text understanding is that any two sentences that are identical in meaning shall have only one representation of that meaning in conceptual dependency (Schank and Abelson 1977, p. 11). Because CD attempts to represent meaning (as opposed to syntactic structure), new words and concepts enter CD representations that were not in the original sentence. For example, in the sentence "Adam ate the apple" the word *ate* might be replaced by the primitive *ingest*, which captures the essential meaning, without keeping the exact form of the utterance. This is a fundamental distinction between CD diagrams and parse trees of sentences.

Conceptual dependencies are often implemented using frames (Minsky 1974). CD frames are a special kind of semantic network in which events and things are described in terms of several "atomic" entities with a limited number of interrelationships. Schank proposed 14 basic relations for natural-language processing, including *move, propel, look-at,* and *listen-to*. High-level CD frames model large-scale structures as *scripts* of stereotypical behavior and *plans* for future action.

CD frames are designed to account for expectations in parsing. If one object that fits a frame's slot is found, a CD system tries to find objects that fill the other slots. In a musical application, the frame can thus activate "default" structures, which are not heard immediately. For example, if we hear several notes in sequence, we can often infer a scale even in the absence of the tonic.

Meehan (1980) proposed CD as a model for the implication/realization tonal music theory of Narmour (1977). CD frames are used in Laske (1982) to represent musical concepts.

Procedural Models

Minsky has criticized grammar-based approaches to representation of music for being static representations of the temporary state of an active cognitive process (Roads 1980; Minsky 1981). He does not question the grouping of musical events into units, but he laments the lack of emphasis on the parsing process that leads to a grammar. He feels that the study of the properties of grammars in the abstract leads away from the fundamental scientific question of how music is processed in the mind (Roads 1980).

As Narmour has pointed out, the subject of rule formation (the generation of rules by lower-level phenomena) never arises in transformational grammar theory. By contrast, rule formation is a natural consequence of

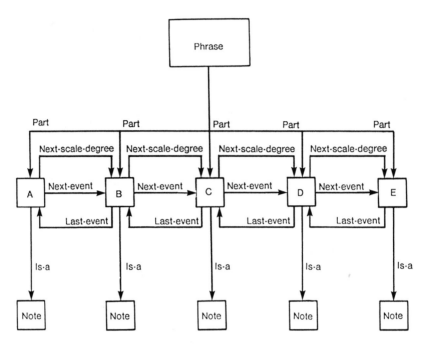

Figure 23.6
Semantic network representation of a musical phrase from the pitch A to the pitch E.
Musical relations such as NEXT-EVENT, LAST-EVENT, NEXT-SCALE-DEGREE,
and IS-A bind the notes into a unit.

a procedural approach. In a procedural model, a "listening process" is always scanning the input stream. Its first goal is akin to lexical analysis: to scan the basic units in the input stream and convert them into tokens for further processing. If the score is encoded, this is a trivial task. If the score is in the form of an acoustic waveform, this can be a major undertaking. Once the listening process has labeled all the tokens, it begins the second stage of parsing. Using stored knowledge, it tries to identify groups of events and groups of groups. This has traditionally been associated with syntactic analysis, except that in the procedural model multiple parsings according to different criteria are legal. Simultaneously, all the "extrasyntactic" features and associations are recorded. A "web of meaning" is constructed and integrated with existing knowledge (figure 23.6). Once the listening process has noted all the associative interconnections it can, it is compelled to start a new task: inventing processes to quickly recognize large-scale parts of the structures it has just built. This is the rule-formation phase. The listening process both uses and builds on a "grammar" of knowledge. However, this quasi-grammar is merely a temporary state of an active learning process that is constantly modifying the contents of memory. (See also Michalski, Carbonell, and Mitchell 1983.)

Constraints

Constraints are an intrinsically multiple-viewpoint representation. A simple constraint can be visualized as a network of devices connected by wires (Sussman and Steele 1981). Data values may flow along the wires, and computation is performed by the devices. A device computes only locally available information, and places newly derived values on other locally attached wires. Computed values are propagated in this way.

In a constraint network, some of the values of the variables in the devices are dependent on the values of other variables in other devices. This notion of dependent variables is familiar; it is just the same as that in an algebraic equation such as $(x*y) + z = 3$. This constraint is no more about how to compute x given y and z than it is about how to compute z given x and y. The point is that we can compute the value of any of the dependent variables from this constraint.

Constraints are not limited to modeling quantitative relationships. They can be used to represent qualitative semantic dependencies as well. Just as "story problems" may be decomposed into elementary algebra, the essentials of other kinds of relationships can be expressed with constraints. A simple example of a constraint in a musical application is shown in figure 23.7.

A key to the progress of the constraint paradigm is the development of languages that support the specification and manipulation of constraints. Languages for expressing constraint relationships have been developed by Borning (1979), Steele (1980), and Steels (1982).

Two musical applications of constraints are recorded in the literature. Steels (1979) used constraints to reason about tonal structures in music. His system could solve the "passing-chord" problem, which inserts a chord that is harmonically "near" to both its predecessor and successor. Levitt (1981) used the concept of constraints in organizing a description system for melodies and a set of procedures that performed melodic improvisation. Levitt's system worked within jazz idioms.

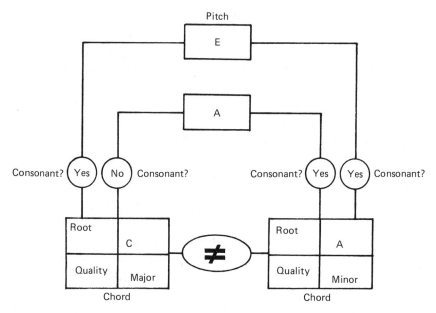

Figure 23.7
Musical knowledge about two chords (the triads C major and A minor) and two pitches
(E and A) represented as a constraint network. The circles and ellipses represent
constraints, The Consonant? constraints describe the relations of the pitches to the two
chords, while the Not-equal (≠) constraint describes the relation between the two chords.

Conclusion

It appears that the linguistic techniques of segmentation and parsing may
be useful in music analysis. The construction of rewrite rules and multilevel grammar representations facilitates verification of musical theories.
The notational convenience of rewrite rules and associated interpreters
allows composers to work with musical macrostructure as easily as with
individual notes.

The range of grammars is extensive, and their expressive scope is broad.
Thus, there is no intrinsic reason why grammars should be useful only in
representing traditional music. Composing languages (Roads 1978;
Buxton et al. 1978; Green 1980; Holtzman 1981; Jones 1981) demonstrate
that the specification of parse trees for compositions or composing
grammars has become available as a composition technique.

In sum: The grammar form, though not a perfect model for music, has clarified many issues involved in the representation of music structure. As shown, the major limitation of grammar formalisms for music is their treatment of context. Grammar forms have been superseded by multiple-perspective knowledge representations in many artificial-intelligence applications.

Musical knowledge representations may lead to intelligent musical devices. These devices will be able to convert the acoustical signal into symbolic form and to recognize not only frequency, amplitude, and duration, but also larger forms such as phrases and other macrostructures as well as "semantic" aspects of music. Acting from a base of programmed or acquired musical knowledge, such devices will be able to listen and respond intelligently not just to sound, but to music.

Before all the recent emphasis on grammars, music had long been the subject of a variety of formalizations. Ultimately, the question is not whether music conforms to the structure of formal grammars but whether particular grammars can be designed that are useful representations of certain compositions. Grammars with embedded procedures can be effective tools of expression and description. However, we can be sure that formal languages will evolve, and that representations of musical knowledge, whatever they are called in the future, will grow more powerful and elegant.

Acknowledgments

I extend gratitude to Curtis Abbott for his consultation on a draft of this article and to John Strawn for his insightful comments.

References

Aho, A., and J. Ullman. 1972. *The Theory of Parsing, Translating, and Compiling.* Englewood Cliffs, N.J.: Prentice-Hall.

Balaban, M. 1981. Toward a Computerized Analytical Research of Tonal Music. Ph.D. thesis, Weizmann Institute of Science, Rehovat, Israel.

Baroni, M. 1981. "Sulla nozione di grammatica musicale." *Rivista Italiana di Musicologia* 16(2): 240–279.

Baroni, M. 1982. "A project of a grammer of melody." Presented at the First International Conference on Musical Grammars and Computer Analysis, Modena.

Baroni, M., and C. Jacoboni. 1975. "Analysis and generation of Bach's chorale melodies." In G. Stefani, ed., *Proceedings of the First International Congress on the Semiotics of Music.* Pesaro, Italy: Centro di Iniziativa Culturale.

Baroni, M., and C. Jacoboni. 1978. *Proposal for a Grammar of Melody.* Presses de l'Université de Montréal.

Bernstein, L. 1976. *The Unanswered Question.* Cambridge, Mass.: Harvard University Press.

Blacking, J. 1971. "Deep and surface structures in Venda music." *Yearbook of the International Folk Music Council* 3: 69–98.

Boretz, B. 1969. "Meta-variations: Studies in the foundations of musical thought." *Perspectives of New Music* 8(1): 1–74.

Boretz, B. 1970. "Sketch of a musical system (Meta-variations, part II)." *Perspectives of New Music* 8(2): 49–111.

Borning, A. 1979. Thinglab—A Constraint-Oriented Simulation Laboratory. Report SSL-79-3, Xerox Palo Alto Research Center.

Bright, W. 1963. "Language and music: Areas for cooperation." *Ethnomusicology* 7: 26–32.

Busby, T. 1818. *A Grammar of Music: To Which are Prefixed Observations Explanatory of the Properties and Powers of Music as a Science and of the General Scope and Object of the Work.* New York: Da Capo, 1976.

Buxton, W., W. Reeves, R. Baecker, and L. Mezei. 1978. "The use of hierarchy and instance in a data structure for computer music." *Computer Music Journal* 2(4): 10–20. Article 24 in this volume.

Chafe, C., B. Mont-Reynaud, and L. Rush. 1982. "Toward an intelligent editor of digital audio: Recognition of musical constructs." *Computer Music Journal* 6(1): 30–41.

Chen, P. 1976. "The entity-relationship model—Toward a unified theory of data." *ACM Transactions on Database Systems* 1(1): 9–36.

Chomsky, N. 1957. *Syntactic Structures.* The Hague: Mouton.

Chomsky, N. 1963a. "Formal properties of grammars." In R. Luce, E. Bush, and E. Galanter, eds., *Handbook of Mathematical Psychology,* vol. 2. New York: Wiley.

Chomsky, N. 1963b. "Formal analysis of natural language." In R. Luce, E. Bush, and E. Galanter, eds., *Handbook of Mathematical Psychology,* vol. 2. New York: Wiley.

Chomsky, N. 1965. *Aspects of the Theory of Syntax.* Cambridge, Mass.: MIT Press.

Chomsky, N. 1979. Immanual Kant Lectures in Philosophy. Stanford University, Stanford, Calif.

Cleaveland, J., and R. Uzgalis. 1977. *Grammars for Programming Languages.* New York: Elsevier.

Deutsch, D. 1982. "Grouping mechanisms in music." In D. Deutsch, ed., *The Psychology of Music.* New York: Academic.

Forte, A. 1973. *The Structure of Atonal Music.* New Haven, Conn.: Yale University Press.

Forte, A. 1977. "Schenker's conception of music structure." In M. Yeston, ed., *Readings in Schenkerian Analysis and Other Approaches.* New Haven, Conn.: Yale University Press.

Foster, S., W. A. Schloss, and A. J. Rockmore. 1982. "Toward an intelligent editor of digital audio: Signal processing methods." *Computer Music Journal* 6(1): 42–51.

Fu, K. 1974. *Syntactic Methods in Pattern Recognition.* New York: Academic.

Gips, J. 1975. *Shape Grammars and Their Uses.* Basel: Birkhäuser.

Green, M. 1980. "PROD: A grammar-based computer composition program." In H. S. Howe, Jr., ed., *Proceedings of the 1980 International Computer Music Conference.* San Francisco: Computer Music Association.

Greimas, A. 1970. *Du Sens*. Paris: Editions du Seuil.

Halliday, M. 1961. "Categories of the theory of grammar." *Word* 17: 241–292.

Halliday, M. 1967. "Notes on transivity and theme in English." *Journal of Linguistics* 3:199–244, 4:179–215.

Halliday, M. 1973. *Explorations in the Function of Language*. London: Edward Arnold.

Hiller, L., and L. Isaacson. 1959. *Experimental Music*. New York: McGraw-Hill.

Holtzman, S. 1981. "Using generative grammars for music composition." *Computer Music Journal* 5(1):51–64.

Imberty, M. 1976. Signification and Meaning in Music: On Debussy's *Préludes pour le piano*. Monographies de sémiologies et d'analyse musicales III. Montréal: Groupe de recherches en sémiologie musicale.

Imberty, M. 1981. *Entendre la musique*. Paris: Dunod.

Jackendoff, R. 1977. "Review of *The Unanswered Question* by Leonard Bernstein." *Language* 53:883–894.

Jackendoff, R., and F. Lerdahl. 1980. "Discovery procedures versus rules of a musical grammar in a generative music theory." *Perspectives of New Music* 18(1–2):503–510.

Jackendoff, R., and F. Lerdahl. 1981. "Generative music theory and its relation to psychology." *Journal of Music Theory* 25(1):45–90.

Jackendoff, R., and F. Lerdahl. 1982. "A grammatical parallel between music and language." In M. Clynes, ed., *Music, Mind, and Brain*. New York: Plenum.

Jacobson, R. 1973. *Questions de poétique*. Paris: Editions du Seuil.

Jones, K. 1981. "Compositional applications of stochastic processes." *Computer Music Journal* 5(2):45–61.

Kassler, M. 1967. "Toward a theory that is the twelve-note-class-system." *Perspectives of New Music* 5(2):1–80.

Kassler, M. 1975. Proving Musical Theorems I: The Middleground of Heinrich Schenker's Theory of Tonality. Technical report 103, Basser Department of Computer Science, University of Sydney.

Keiler, A. 1977. "The syntax of prolongation I." *In Theory Only* 3(5):3–27.

Keiler, A. 1978. "Bernstein's *Unanswered Question* and the problem of musical competence." *Musical Quarterly* 64(2):195–222.

Keiler, A. 1980. "Reply to Lerdahl and Jackendoff." *Perspectives of New Music* 18(1–2): 511–516.

Knuth, D. 1968. "Semantics of context-free languages." *Mathematical Systems Theory* 2:127–145.

Knuth, D. 1971. "Top-down syntax analysis." *Acta Informatica* 1(1):79–110.

Laske, O. 1972. "On musical strategies with a view to a generative theory of music." *Interface* 1:111–125.

Laske, O. 1973. *Musical Semantics: A Procedural Point of View*. San Francisco: Computer Music Association.

Laske, O. 1975. Introduction to a Generative Theory of Music. Sonological report 1b, Institute of Sonology, Utrecht.

Laske, O. 1977. *Music, Memory, and Thought*. Ann Arbor, Mich.: University Microfilms.

Laske, O. 1982. "Keith: A rule system for making music-analytical discoveries." Presented at International Conference on Musical Grammars and Computer Analysis, Modena.

Lerdahl, F., and R. Jackendoff. 1977. "Toward a formal theory of tonal music." *Journal of Music Theory* 21(1): 111–172.

Lerdahl, F., and R. Jackendoff. 1981. "On the theory of grouping and meter." *Musical Quarterly* 67(4):479–506.

Lerdahl, F., and R. Jackendoff. 1983. *A Generative Theory of Tonal Music*. Cambridge, Mass.: MIT Press.

Lerdahl, F., and Y. Potard. 1982. A Computer Aid to Composition. Unpublished manuscript.

Levitt, D. 1981. A Melody Description System for Jazz Improvisation. M.S. thesis, Department of Electrical Engineering and Computer Science, MIT.

Levy, M. 1973. "On the problem of defining musical units." In G. Stefani, ed., *Proceedings of the First International Congress on the Semiotics of Music*. Pesaro, Italy: Centro di Iniziativa.

Lindblom, B., and J. Sundberg. 1970. "Towards a generative theory of melody." *Swedish Journal of Musicology* 52:77–88.

Lidov, D. 1975. On Musical Phrase. Monographies de sémiologie et d'analyse musicales. Groupe de recherches en sémiologie musicale, Université de Montréal.

Lidov, D. 1980. Musical Structure and Musical Significance, Part 1. Toronto Semiotic Circle, Victoria University.

Lidov, D., and J. Gabura. 1973. "A melody writing algorithm using a formal language model." *Computer Studies in the Humanities* 4(3–4):138–148.

Mathews, M. V., with J. E. Miller, F. R. Moore, J. R. Pierce, and J.-C. Risset. 1969. *The Technology of Computer Music*. Cambridge, Mass.: MIT Press.

Meehan, J. 1980. "An artificial intelligence approach to tonal music theory." *Computer Music Journal* 4(2): 60–65.

Meyer, L. 1956. *Emotion and Meaning in Music*. University of Chicago Press.

Michalski, R., J. Carbonell, and T. Mitchell. 1983. *Machine Learning*. Palo Alto, Calif.: Tioga.

Minsky, M. 1965. *Semantic Information Processing*. Cambridge, Mass.: MIT Press.

Minsky, M. 1974. A Framework for Representing Knowledge. A. I. memo 306, MIT Artificial Intelligence Laboratory.

Minsky, M. 1981. "Music, mind, and meaning." *Computer Music Journal* 5(3): 28–44.

Molino, J. 1975. "Fait musicale et sémiologie de la musique." *Musique en Jeu* 17: 37–62.

Moorer, J. 1972. "Music and computer composition." *Communications of the Association for Computing Machinery* 15(2):104–113.

Moorer, J. 1975. On the Segmentation and Analysis of Continuous Musical Sound by Digital Computer. Ph.D. diss., Computer Science Department, Stanford University. Department of Music report STAN-M-2.

Narmour, E. 1977. *Beyond Schenkerism*. University of Chicago Press.

Narmour E. 1982. "The melodic, harmonic, and rhythmic functions of implication and realization in tonal music: Toward an analytical symbology." Presented at International Conference on Musical Grammars and Computer Analysis, Modena.

Nattiez, J.-J. 1974. "Sémiologie musicale: l'etat de la question." *Acta Musicologia* 61(2): 153–171.

Nattiez, J.-J. 1975. *Fondements d'une sémiologie de la musique.* Paris: Union Generale d'Editions.

Powers, H. 1976. "The structure of musical meaning: A view from the Banaras." *Perspectives of New Music* 14(2)/15(1): 308–334.

Powers, H. 1980. "Language models and musical analysis." *Ethnomusicology* 24(1): 1–60.

Quillian, M. 1968. "Semantic memory." In M. Minsky, ed., *Semantic Information Processing.* Cambridge, Mass.: MIT Press.

Rader, G. 1974. "A method for composing simple traditional music by computer." *Communications of the Association for Computing Machinery* 17(11): 631–642.

Roads, C. 1978. "Composing grammars." In C. Roads, ed., *Proceedings of the 1977 International Computer Music Conference.* San Francisco: Computer Music Association.

Roads, C. 1980. "Interview with Marvin Minsky." *Computer Music Journal* 4(3): 25–39.

Roads, C. 1982a. "An Overview of representations for music." Presented at the International Conference on Musical Grammars and Computer Analysis, Modena.

Roads, C. 1982b. "Music and artificial intelligence: A research overview." In *Annual Conference Proceedings, AICA 1982.* Padua: Associazione Italiana per il Calcolo Automatico. Reprinted as "Musik und künstliche Intelligenz: Ein Forschungsüberblick" (tr. O. Laske), *Feedback Papers* 31: 3–36.

Rosenfeld, A. 1971. "Isotonic grammars, parallel grammars, and picture grammars." In B. Meltzer and D. Michie, eds., *Machine Intelligence 6.* New York: American Elsevier.

Rosenfeld, A. 1973. "Array grammar normal forms." *Information and Control* 23(2): 173–182.

Rothenberg, D. 1975. "A nonprocedural language for musical composition." In J. Beauchamp and J. Melby, eds., *Proceedings of the Second Annual Music Computation Conference,* part 2. Urbana: Office of Continuing Education and Public Service in Music, University of Illinois.

Rousseau, J.-J. 1754. "Discours sur l'origine et les fondements de l'inégalité parmi des hommes." In B. Gagnebin and M. Raymond, eds., *Jean-Jacques Rousseau: Oeuvres completes,* vol. 3. Paris: Gallimard, 1964.

Ruwet, N. 1972. *Langage, musique, poésie.* Paris: Editions du Seuil.

Ruwet, N. 1975. "Théorie et méthodes dans les études musicales." *Musique en Jeu* 17: 11–36.

Salomaa, A. 1973. *Formal Languages.* New York: Academic.

Schaeffer, P. 1977. *Traité des objets musicaux,* second edition. Paris: Editions du Seuil.

Schank, R. 1973. "Identification of conceptualizations underlying natural language." In R. Schank and K. Colby, eds., *Computer Models of Thought and Language.* San Francisco: Freeman.

Schank, R., and R. Abelson. 1977. *Scripts, Plans, Goals, and Understanding.* Hillsdale, N.J.: Erlbaum.

Sebeok, T. 1975. "Six species of signs: Some propositions and strictures." *Semiotica* 13(3): 233–260.

Smith, L. 1972. "Score: A musician's approach to computer music." *Journal of the Audio Engineering Society* 20: 7–14.

Smith, L. 1973. "SCORE: A musician's approach to computer music." *Numus-West* 4–73: 21–29.

Smoliar, S. 1971. A Parallel Processing Model of Musical Structure. Technical report 242, MIT Artificial Intelligence Laboratory.

Smoliar, S. 1976. "Music programs: An approach to music theory through computational linguistics." *Journal of Music Theory* 20: 105–131.

Smoliar, S. 1980. "A computer aid for Schenkerian analysis." *Computer Music Journal* 4(2): 41–59.

Steele, G. 1980. The Definition and Implementation of a Programming Language Based on Constraints. Report AI-TR-595, MIT Artificial Intelligence Laboratory.

Steels, L. 1979. Reasoning Modeled as a Society of Communicating Experts. Report AI-TR-542, MIT Artificial Intelligence Laboratory.

Steels, L. 1982. "Constraints as consultants." In *Proceedings of the 1982 European Conference on Artificial Intelligence*. University of Kaiserslautern.

Strawn, J. 1980. "Approximation and syntactic analysis of amplitude and frequency functions for digital sound synthesis." *Computer Music Journal* 4(3): 3–24.

Sussman, G., and G. Steele. 1981. Constraints: A Language for Expressing Almost-Hierarchical Descriptions. Memo 502A, MIT Artificial Intelligence Laboratory. Reprinted in *Artificial Intelligence* 14: 1–39.

Ulrich, W. 1977. "The analysis and synthesis of jazz by computer." In *Proceedings of the Fifth International Joint Conference on Artificial Intelligence*, vol. 2. Los Altos, Calif.: William Kaufmann.

Wilks, Y. 1977. "Natural language understanding systems." In A. Zampoli, ed., *Linguistic Structures Processing*. Amsterdam: North-Holland.

Winograd, T. 1968. "Linguistics and computer analysis of tonal harmony." *Journal of Music Theory* 12: 2–49.

Winograd, T. 1977. "Five lectures on artificial intelligence." In A. Zampoli, ed., *Linguistic Structures Processing*. Amsterdam: North-Holland.

Winograd, T. 1983. *Language as a Cognitive Process*, vol. 1. Reading, Mass.: Addison-Wesley.

Woods, W. 1970. "Transition network grammars for natural language analysis." *Communications of the Association for Computer Machinery* 13(10): 591–606.

Woods, W. 1975a. Syntax, Semantics, and Speech. Report 3067, Bolt, Beranek, and Newman, Inc., Cambridge, Mass.

Woods, W. 1975b. "What's in a link: Foundations for semantic networks." In D. Bobrow and A. Collins, eds., *Representation and Understanding: Studies in Cognitive Science*. New York: Academic.

Woods, W. 1980. "Cascaded ATN grammars." *American Journal of Computational Linguistics* 6(1): 1–12.

Xenakis, I. 1971. *Formalized Music*. Bloomington: Indiana University Press.

24 The Use of Hierarchy and Instance in a Data Structure for Computer Music

WILLIAM BUXTON, WILLIAM REEVES, RONALD BAECKER, AND LESLIE MEZEI

One of the most important aspects in the design of any computer system is determining the basic data types and structures to be used. The main consideration is the manner in which the data must function in their intended application. In defining the data structures for the music system of the Structured Sound Synthesis Project, we have been guided by our projection of the interaction between the tool we are developing and the composer. In this regard, we view the composer's action as consisting of four basic tasks:

• Definition of the palette of timbres to be available. This we call *object definition*. It is analogous to choosing the instruments for the composer's orchestra. The main expansion on the analogy is that the composer also has the option to "invent" new instruments.

• Definition of the pitch-time structure of a compostion, a process which we can call *score definition*. In conventional music, this task would be roughly analogous to composing a piano version of a score.

• The *orchestration* of the score. Generally stated, this consists of attaching attributes (such as the objects defined in the first step) to the scores defined in the second step.

• The *performance* of the material developed thus far, whether it is an entire (orchestrated or unorchestrated) score, or simply a single note (to audition to particular object, for example).

(We include performance as part of the compositional process on the basis of the opinion that a piece of music is not completed until it is heard. Although some theorists would dispute the need for performance, we would argue that composers of conventional music have always had such aural feedback in the mind's ear, enabled by a familiarity with the long tradition of Western music—a tradition that does not exist for the composer of contemporary music.)

From this taxonomy of tasks derives one of our first major decisions: to have two major data types, *objects* and *scores*, which relate to the sonic level and the deeper structural level, respectively. Because composers work in different ways, a second important consideration was to structure

This is a revised and updated version of an article that originally appeared in *Computer Music Journal* 2(4): 10–20, 1978.

the system so that there would be no order imposed on the sequence in which the user undertakes the above four tasks. A composer is allowed to perform a score before it has been orchestrated, for example. The implication is that the system should be capable of coping with incompletely specified data. The obvious solution is to ensure that the low-level structures can support an elegant system of defaults. Finally, it was seen as important to design the data structures so as to facilitate the definition of the scope of operators which the composer would be invoking to affect the data base. The composer must be provided with a "handle" on the data beyond the note-by-note approach prevalent in most systems today.

In this article we present the design of a data structure developed in light of these considerations. We begin by giving a general background and motivation for scores and objects; we then present the details of the actual implementation.

Scores

The Hierarchical Representation of Scores

In the literature it can be seen that most systems to date have gravitated toward one of two extremes: dealing with the score note by note (e.g., Vercoe 1975) and dealing with the score as a single entity (e.g., Xenakis 1971). It is obvious, however, that structures falling somewhere between the note level and the score level play an important musical role. Therefore, systems that lean toward the note and/or the score level are seen as largely inadequate in dealing with these middle-level structures. Truax (1977) recognized this, and his POD system was an attempt to deal with the problem. His approach, however, was based on the use of stochastic processes, and therefore assumed other problems of compositional programs. The problem of dealing with the different structural levels of a composition—from note to score—remains largely unresolved.

Two observations concerning the above provide the basis of our approach to the problem. First, what have hitherto been considered two extremes are seen as two instances of the same thing. Both deal with the composition *chunk-by-chunk*. The only real difference is the size of the chunk: a note or an entire score. If we could provide a structure through which the composer could cause an operator (e.g., *play, transpose*, etc.)

to affect any chunk of the composition, from note to score, we will have gone a long way in overcoming the problems of previous systems.

The key to allowing this chunk-by-chunk addressing lies in our second observation: that the discussion of structural *levels* immediately suggests a hierarchical internal representation for scores. Such a structuring of the data goes a long way toward making it possible to specify the scope (define the chunks) of operators. A *play* command, for example, can affect a terminal node (single note) or some nonterminal node (thus causing the subtree or *subscore* below that node to be played). The important point to note is that such a structuring of the data allows any chunk of a score to be treated in exactly the same manner as a single note, with the same ease and clarity, regardless of chunk size.

The Musical Event

In light of the temporal nature of music, it is "natural" that we define a *score* as "an ordered sequence of musical events." What we mean by a *musical event*, however, is central to an understanding of our hierarchic representation of scores. By a musical event we mean simply an event that occurs during the course of a composition that has a start time and an end. Thus, the entire composition constitutes a musical event (the highest level), as does a single note (the lowest level). Similarly, chords, motives, and movements are all musical events. In fact, any of the chunks described in the previous section can constitute a musical event. This notion of an event being either a simple sound or a more complex struc- ture is somewhat similar to the use of *sound pattern* (simple) and *gemisches* (complex) in the system of the Institute of Musicology at Aarhus, Den- mark (Hansen 1977; Manthey 1978). Thus, any musical event (e.g., a motif) can be made up of composite musical events (e.g., chords and notes); hence the basis for our hierarchy.

In considering the concept of a musical event, it is important to realize that the starting time of the next event is completely independent of the duration of the current one. Therefore, as in figure 24.1, the same two events (G4 and C5) can occur in sequence (bar 1) or parallel (bar 2), or in some combination of the two (bar 3). Similarly, as in figure 24.2, each of the four parts in a string quartet can be considered as a separate musical event (each made up of events of a lower level).

With the musical events, there are two autonomous notions of time: *duration* and *entry delay*. The first is self-explanatory; the second is the

Figure 24.1
Temporal relationships between simple musical events. Measure 1: sequence (melodic).
Measure 2: parallel (chord). Measure 3: mixed.

Figure 24.2
Example of high-level musical events. Each line in the quartet can be considered as a
single musical event. The events overlap in a relationship similar to measures 2 and 3 in
figure 24.1. (Score example from B. Bartok's *String Quartet No. 4*, first movement.)

delay before the onset of the next event in the sequence. In melodic
figures the two are equal. In a chord the entry delay is equal to zero. The
important thing to note is that in performance they can be modified
independently or together. Changing both will vary tempo while adjusting
the articulation proportionally. Adjusting duration independent of entry
delay will result in a change in the articulation of notes, for example.
Thus, there is a great deal of potential for the "conducting" of a score
built into the underlying structure.

We can express the notion of musical event as a simple grammar (where
Mevent is an abbreviation for musical event):

Composition ::= Mevent;
Mevent   ::= Mevent*|Score|note;
Score   ::= Mevent;
note   ::= terminal (i.e., some musical note);

(The grammar is expressed in BNF, where " ::= " means "is defined as,"
"|" means "or," and "*" means "may be repeated." Nonterminals begin
with upper-case characters.)

Besides the ability to isolate different components of the composition, this structure has the benefit that the tree structure actually represents a "recipe" of how the composition was put together. Thus, the additional features of being able to backtrack or reassemble scores are provided. Throughout, it should be kept in mind that the common simple list structure used to represent scores is covered by the model: a tree of level 1. Therefore, the user has a choice as to the score representation. Complexity is not forced upon the composer.

Instantiation

Our choice of a hierarchic score representation makes possible additional features not yet discussed. Consider, for example, the common case where a composition is made up of certain base material which is then repeated, developed, transposed, and so on. In this case, the score could contain several instances of a particular musical event, but each instance might be transformed in some way. One need only consider one of the examples in the literature of the "theme and variations" form to find a good illustration of this point. In terms of a tree structure, we see that this case could be described as one in which there is more than one instance of a particular subtree. We can derive power from this observation in stating that, consequently, there should only be one master copy of that subtree, and at each instance we store only the subtree identifier and the transformations to be effected for the particular instance. This notion of instance was developed and used extensively by Sutherland (1963) in his SKETCHPAD system.

There are a number of benefits to this approach. First, it is easy to isolate all instances of "motif A," for example. Second, the size of the score is reduced considerably, since only one copy of the motif is saved. (This is admittedly at the expense of speed. However, if we do have to do an expansion before the score can be performed, we are still no worse off than with the linked list representation of Music V, for example. Furthermore, we still have the hierarchical representation intact, as a master recipe that makes possible backup, transformation, etc.) Third, it is clear that our file system and data structures must be able to treat any musical event as a free-standing self-contained structure, a subscore. Therefore, any subscore can be played, edited, etc., on its own. Most important, any change to the master copy of any subscore in a composition will be reflected in every instance of that structure. Thus, if a recurring figure in our composition is an octave jump up, followed by a semitone fall, if the master copy of this figure were simply changed to a major triad, all instances would be similarly affected by this one action.

Summary

In the preceding discussion, an argument has been made for the adoption of a hierarchically based internal representation of scores. Through this approach we can provide the basis for composers to address themselves (and their commands) to the "chunks" of the score with which they are concerned. Furthermore, through the use of instantiation we are able to exploit the redundancies inherent in musical structures and gain savings in space and ease of operation.

Objects and Timbre Definition

If we are going to synthesize sounds, we have an obvious interest in being able to control "timbre." However, the nature of "timbre" for musical purposes is rather elusive. Traditional explanations (e.g. Helmholtz 1863) have restricted their description to the physical (acoustical) properties of sounds. Two things are clear, however: that ideally, timbre should be described in the perceptual rather than the acoustical domain, and that timbre is a multidimensional attribute of sound, such that the number of dimensions inhibits the understanding and control of the perceived phenomenon. Thus, our prime objective is to establish the underlying structures that will facilitate the implementation of different high-level external representations of our repertoire of timbres and support an effective editor for exploring the multidimensional attributes of this repertoire. Throughout, the intention is that initial work at the lower acoustical level will enable us to develop a control mechanism that will function at the higher perceptual level. As our insights into the nature of timbre improve through experience and experimentation, we are able to refine our external representations accordingly.

In our approach the analogy to the timbre of a musical instrument is an *object* (after Schaeffer 1977). By our definition, an object is "a named set of attributes that will result in sounds having different pitches, durations, and amplitudes to be perceived as having the same timbre." In our definition, it is significant that we have stated nothing about the nature of those attributes constituting an object. The notion of an object simply provides a conceptual framework in which composers can view their activities. Each object has a name, and all instances of a particularly named object sound "the same." (Note that we use the notion of instance here in exactly the same manner as during our discussion of scores. That is, there is only one master copy for any particular object. Any change to that master copy is therefore reflected in every instance of the object. This provides an efficient mechanism for refining the definition of a trumpet timbre, for example, or changing all "trumpets" to "flutes.") Conceptually, this is all that a composer need understand, plus the fact that there is an editor that will aid in controlling the palette of timbres (by defining and modifying a set of objects) and in "orchestrating" the notes in a score from this set of objects.

In contrast to the SYN4B system at IRCAM (Rolnick 1978), our approach to the problem is to take a few well-proven configurations of unit generators and "package" them so as to optimize on the ability of the composer to explore their full potential. Clearly this decision relates to the issue of strength versus generality. Our choice is to take the more limited but stronger approach. We are confident that research such as that of Moorer (1977) and LeBrun (1979) will help bring an ever-expanding repertoire of computer-based sounds to composers. Our prime concern is with the development of tools to aid the composer in controlling these sounds in a musical context.

Once we adopt this approach, the problem is to select the instruments or acoustic models we will support. The prime considerations are range of timbral palette, suitability to efficient implementation, ease of control protocol, and (perhaps most important) how well the model lends itself to the implementation of a user-congenial interface. Moorer (1977) gives a good survey of the alternatives. The models we have chosen to support, each of which is implemented in hardware in the SSSP digital synthesizer (Buxton et al. 1978), are the fixed-waveform, frequency-modulation, additive-synthesis, waveshaping, and VOSIM models.

Implementation

This section presents the implementation details of a data structure that conforms to the general description outlined in the previous section. A version of the structure has been implemented and utilized with success at the University of Toronto. An overview of this structure is presented in figure 24.3. Here we see that there are four main types of structures,

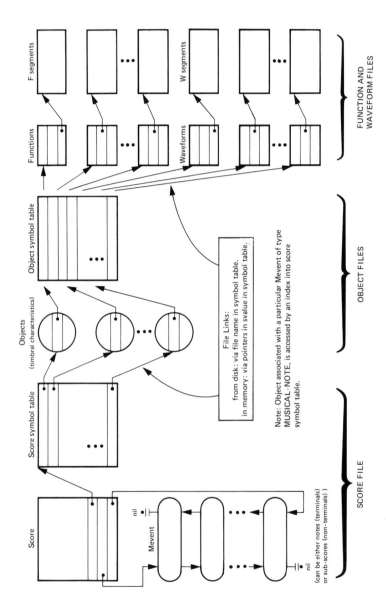

Figure 24.3
Overview of data structures, showing how score files, sound-object files, and function and waveform files are linked via a system of intermediate symbol tables and pointers.

each of which constitutes a particular type of *file*. These are scores, objects, functions, and waveforms. Each of these file types is made up of various composite structures. The purpose of this section, therefore, is to present the internal representation of each of these four types of files and to define the methods of communication, or links, among these files.

Since it is a structure common to various file types, and since it is the prime medium of interfile communication, we shall begin by presenting the form of the *symbol table* data structure. (In the discussion that follows, any name or value specified entirely in upper-case characters, as OBJECT or UNDEFINED, is a defined constant for the music system.)

Interfile Communication

The Symbol Table

The symbol table is the method of linking auxiliary files to both object files and score files. Therefore, both score and object files contain symbol tables.

A symbol table is an array of symbol structures, where the size of the array, or table, corresponds to the number of symbols, or entries, in that table. Examples of the structures used are presented in subsequent paragraphs. All examples are given in the programming language C (Kernighan and Ritchie 1978). In the examples, a structure is an aggregate of data. The name following the label "struct" is the name of the aggregate. The names within the curly brackets define a template for the data in the aggregate. The first value in each row indicates data type (char: 1 byte; int: 2 bytes; float: 4 bytes); the second value is the variable name. A value preceded by an asterisk is a pointer to data of the indicated type (such as a structure). A pointer occupies one word of memory. Memory for such structures may be dynamically allocated or freed, and several structures of the same type may be allocated space in contiguous memory to form a table, or vector, of structures (as with a symbol table). Variables terminating with a value in square brackets are arrays whose dimensions are contained within the brackets.

The symbol structures for a particular symbol table are stored in contiguous memory. In the programming language C, each entry in a symbol table has the following structure format:

struct symbol
{
    char name [FNAME__SIZE];   File name
    int stype;   Contains fields for type of symbol.
    int svalue;   Value of symbol (may be pointer)
    int nsrefs;   Reference count
};

The *name* field simply contains the name of the file associated with the symbol in question. The *stype* field then indicates the type of file this entry in the symbol table is. Valid symbol types include OBJECT, SCORE, FUNCTION, and WAVEFORM. Each of these symbol types corresponds to one of the file types mentioned above, and will, therefore, be dealt with in more detail below. If the file in question is in primary memory, the third field of the symbol entry—the *svalue*—contains a pointer to the file's core image. Finally, the *nrefs* field is a counter used in garbage collection.

We see, therefore, that access to subordinate files is accomplished through a symbol table, via the *name* fields for files not in primary memory (i.e., those requiring system input/output) and via the *svalue* field for others (thereby avoiding the time-consuming input/output). (WAVE-FORM files are a special case, where we interpret primary memory as the eight 2-Kword waveform buffers in the synthesizer. Thus, a non-NULL *svalue* for a WAVEFORM entry indicates which of the buffers contains the waveform.)

A particular symbol entry is accessed by providing an index into the table. An important convention to note in this regard is that the first entry in the table is accessed by an index of 1, not 0. An index of 0 into the symbol table has the special meaning that the symbol to be referenced is not yet defined; a default symbol of the appropriate type (context-dependent) is substituted. Thus, the mechanism for handling default situations is provided; the user never has to provide details beyond the current concern.

File Types

SCORE Files

For our purposes, a *score* is essentially a list, or sequence of musical events, called *Mevents*. Thus, it can be seen as a performance script for a composition. A great deal of effort has been spent in providing the flexibility in the data structures of a score to enable the structuring of a score in a hierarchic manner.

A SCORE file consists of three main data structures: a *score* structure, a linked list of *Mevent* structures, and a *symbol table*. We will now proceed to present the details of each of these structures.

score Structures   The *score* structure functions as the header to the SCORE file. Besides storing the file name and a "magic" number identifying the file as type SCORE, it contains pointers to the head and tail of its associated list of Mevents. Also, it contains a field indicating the total duration of the score, and links to functions affecting the score's performance.

When the score is saved on disk, all of the score structure is written first, followed by the symbol table, and then the Mevents in sequential order. Thus, the link fields are not needed on disk.

The detailed composition of the score structure is as follows:

```
struct score
    {
    int magic;                      Magic number
    char fname [FNAME__SIZE];       File name
    int nsyms;                      Number of entries in table
    struct symbol  * sym__table;    Pointer to symbol table
    float tot__dur;                 Total duration of score
    int nMevents;                   Total number of Mevents
    struct Mevent  * head;          Pointer to start of Mevent list
    struct Mevent  * tail;          Pointer to end of Mevent list
    };
```

The Mevent   As stated above, an essential component of a score is a sorted list of musical events which we call Mevents. Though there are various recognized types of Mevents allowable in this list, they all conform to a single structure template. It is important to note that the Mevent structure is simply a template. It functions as a generalization for the different types of events that may occur in a score, and is included for purposes of convenience. The structure template is as follows:

```
struct Mevent
    {
    struct Mevent  * flink;    Next event pointer
    struct Mevent  * blink;    Last event pointer
    int tag;                   Free field for application pro-
                               grammer
```

```
char del__num;        Entry delay: numerator (beats)
char del__den;        Entry delay: denominator (beats)
char type;            Type of event
char Mdum1;           Dummy fields
char Mdum2;
char Mdum3;
char Mdum4;
char Mdum5;
char Mdum6;
char Mdum7;
char Mdum8;
char Mdum9;
};
```

As can be seen from the above, Mevents are represented as a doubly linked list (i.e., pointers to both the previous and next Mevents). This is to facilitate insertions, searching, and other transformations on the list (playing the score in retrograde, for example).

Many music systems, such as that of Tucker et al. (1977), avoid linked lists in the score. Instead, "notes" are stored in contiguous memory; the pointers then are implicit. Though such a representation provides a more compact representation and a more efficient performance program, editing—the prime function of our system—is considerably less efficient. Furthermore, if in using the linked-list approach the performance is too complex for the system to keep up with in real time, we have found that enabling a score to be "compiled" into a more efficient representation is adequate.

In the list, the order of the linking specifies the order in which the Mevents are to be played. The del_num and del_den fields in each structure specify the time between the start of the current Mevent and the start time of the next. They are the numerator and denominator of a fraction of a beat. Thus, 1/4 would indicate that the next event starts a quarter note after the start of the first one. If the numerator is 0, the Mevents are played simultaneously (as in the case of a chord). If the fraction exceeds the duration of the Mevent, the result is a rest whose duration is equal to the difference.

The currently available types of Mevents (as specified in the *type* field) are MUSICAL_NOTE and SCORE. An Mevent of the MUSICAL_ NOTE type is simply a single sound event. A SCORE-type Mevent is just that: a (sub-) score that commences at a particular point in a composition. This implementation of the notion of *subscore* enables us to create hierarchically structured scores. More formally, we can view a score as a tree structure in which a SCORE Mevent (called Mscore) constitutes a non-terminal node and each MUSICAL_NOTE Mevent (called Mnote) constitutes a terminal, or *leaf*, in the tree.

In the above structure, one feature is of particular import: the choice of delta (i.e., entry delay) rather than absolute values for time. This choice is based on the ease with which several instances of the same subscore can be merged into another master score.

Since the interpretation of the Mevent structure fields Mdum 1–9 depends on the Mevent type, we shall now consider the individual types in detail.

THE MUSICAL_NOTE: MNOTE   An Mevent of the MUSICAL_NOTE type is a single sound event that has certain characteristics (or parameters) as defined by the following Mnote structure. (Note that this structure exactly follows the template of the Mevent structure.)

struct Mnote
```
{
    struct Mevent  *flink;      Next event pointer
    struct Mevent  *blink;      Last event pointer
    int tag;                    Free field for application pro-
                                grammer
    char del__num;              Entry delay: numerator (beats)
    char del__den;              Entry delay: denominator (beats)
    char type;                  Type of event
    char volume;                Volume of note
                                0 ≤ volume ≤ 255
    int frequency;              Note frequency
    char dur__num;              Duration: numerator (beats)
    char dur__den;              Duration: denominator (beats)
    int object__ind;            Object index
                                1 ≤ object__ind ≤ score.nsyms
    char chan__no;              Output channel of note
    char Mdum9;                 Dummy
};
```

THE SCORE: MSCORE   An Mevent of the SCORE type is called an Mscore. The fields of the Mscore structure are given below. Again, note that the structure format follows that of the Mevent.

struct Mscore
```
{
    struct Mevent  *flink;      Next event pointer
    struct Mevent  *blink;      Last event pointer
```

int tag;	Free field for application programmer
char del__num;	Entry delay: numerator (beats)
char del__den;	Entry delay: denominator (beats)
char type;	Type of event
char vol__factor;	Volume scaling factor
int score__ind;	Index into symbol table for subscore
char freq__nfactor;	Freq factor: numerator
char freq__dfactor;	Freq factor: denominator
char dur__nfactor;	Dur factor: numerator
char dur__dfactor;	Dur factor: denominator
char del__nfactor;	Entry delay factor: numerator
char del__dfactor;	Entry delay factor: denominator
};	

There are a few very important points to note regarding the use of subscores. First, each appearance of a particular subscore constitutes an *instance* rather than master copy of that subscore. The difference is that there is only one master copy of the subscore (accessed through the symbol table), and any changes to the original are reflected in each instance during a composition. Therefore, if we view a score as a tree structure, the scaling factor fields of the Mscore structure will effect transformations on the subscore (or subtree) below them. Musically, therefore, these fields allow for the occurrence of the subscore starting at any pitch (i.e., transposition), for the dynamics to be scaled, and for the augmentation and diminution of the time structure. The result is that we can obtain several versions of a single *score* while maintaining only one copy of the original.

SCORE Symbol Table   The types of symbols that are legal in a score's symbol table are FUNCTION, (sub) SCORE, and OBJECT. If the *stype* field of a symbol's entry is UNDEFINED, a default symbol is substituted. If the entry's *svalue* is nonzero (not UNDEFINED), there is an image of the symbol in primary memory and the *svalue* is a pointer to it; otherwise, the *svalue* must be UNDEFINED.

If the *nsyms* field of the associated score structure equals zero, there is no symbol table, the field **sym_table* should equal NULL, and default values of the appropriate type will be inserted during performance. The implications of this are (musically) important in that no ordering of operations is imposed on the composer, who may, for example, perform the pitch/time structure of a composition before any thought is given to orchestration. Furthermore, the user may orchestrate the score with yet undefined objects and still audition the work with default objects substituted. Finally, in either case the default object(s) substituted may be user-defined (i.e., the user may personalize the system by overriding the system-defined defaults).

OBJECT Files

One of the aims of the music system is to provide a facility whereby a composer can specify a palette of timbres to be used in a composition. Each set of timbral characteristics defined by the composer, called an *object*, is then stored in a file named by the composer. Notes in a score may then be "orchestrated" by establishing an association with a particular object file. This is accomplished via the object_ind field of the Mnote structure, in combination with the score symbol table (as outlined previously).

We saw above that there may be several instances of the same (sub-) score in a composition. Similarly, there may be numerous Mnotes of various durations, pitches, and amplitudes, all deriving their timbral characteristics from the same object. Furthermore, any change of the object file will cause that change to be reflected in all instances of that object in a score. We see, therefore, that the object functions as a type of timbral *template*. Finally, owing to this template nature of the object, the only restriction on how many instances of that object may occur simultaneously is the number of oscillators in the synthesizer. This is in contrast with the notion of *instrument* as developed in Music V (Mathews 1969), for example.

Though all objects serve the same musical purpose of timbral control, there exist different internal representations for object data. These differences primarily reflect the different modes—or acoustic models— whereby sound can be generated by the SSSP digital synthesizer. We will see, therefore, that there are three main data structures in an object file: the *object* structure and *symbol* (table) structure (both common to all objects, regardless of mode), and the *type_object* structure, which contains the data peculiar to the mode of that particular object.

Object Structures   The object structure contains information common to all objects, regardless of mode. Such information includes the object's name and mode, and a *magic number* to distinguish OBJECT files (from, for example, SCORE files) during various operations such as reading and writing. The structure also specifies the number of critical resources (i.e., synthesizer oscillators) required by that object. This information is represented as follows:

```
struct object
    {
    int magic;                          Magic number
    char fname [FNAME__SIZE];           File name
    int nsyms;                          Number of symbols in table
    struct symbol  * sym__table;        Pointer to symbol table nsyms
                                        long.
    int mode;                           Designates type of object
    int noscils;                        Number of oscillators needed
    union type__object {
        struct fixedwf__object fwfobj;
        struct fm__object fmobj;
        struct bank__object bankobj;
        struct ws__object wsobj;
        struct vosim__object
        vosimobj;
        } * data;                       Defines " * data" as a pointer to an
                                        object.
    char rigidfunc__ind;                Index into symbol table to access
                                        basis of function time-scaling.

    } ;
```

One field of the object structure warrants special attention. This is *rigid-func_ind*. As will be seen, each mode of object specification includes the specification of functions which determine how parameters vary over time. The time base of such functions, however, must be able to be scaled over Mevents (e.g., Mnotes) of various durations. This is in keeping with the notion that an object is a general template for timbre. One problem is, however, that in compressing and expanding functions we do not always want the scaling to be linear. That is to say, if we consider the x (or time) axis of a stored function as a spring, we do not always want the spring to be of uniform stiffness. In imitating sounds that occur in nature, for example, we would want the attack and decay portions of the amplitude function to be more "stiff" than the steady state. In other objects we might want just the opposite. In view of this problem, each object has associated with it a user-definable "rigidity" function, which determines how the functions of that object are to be scaled—in time—in their various instances throughout a composition. The *rigidfunc_ind* field provides, therefore, an index into the symbol table that identifies the "rigidity" function for that object.

Object Types   As stated above, there are different methods of representing objects that reflect the method of sound synthesis used. These modes are fixed waveform (FIXEDWF), frequency modulation (FM), pulse modulation (VOSIM), additive synthesis (BANK), and waveshaping (WAVESHP). The amount and type of data required differ for each of these modes. Therefore, a different type of structure is used for each. The definition of the structure peculiar to each object type is given below. The appropriate structure for a particular object's type-specific data is accessed via the *data field in the *object* structure, whose *mode* field indicates the structure's type.

FIXEDWF OBJECTS   The fixed-waveform synthesis mode utilizes a single oscillator as a function generator. The only parameters at the object level in this mode are the waveform, the amplitude contour (or *envelope*), and the frequency contour (or deviation over time). The amplitude and frequency contours are stored functions (see FUNCTION files, below) and are accessed through the object symbol table. The format for FIXEDWF data is as follows:

```
struct fixedwf__object
    {
    char fwf__ind;        Index into object symbol table to define
                          waveform
    char envel__ind;      Index into object symbol table for amp.
                          function
    char freq__ind;       Index into object symbol table for freq.
                          function
    };
```

FM OBJECTS   The FM mode of object specification makes it possible to synthesize sound by having one oscillator (*m*) modulate the frequency of another (the *c*, or carrier oscillator). The resulting relevant parameters include the ratio between the frequencies of the two oscillators (the $c:m$ ratio), the maximum degree of modulation and how modulation varies in time, and the amplitude and frequency contours (as seen with FIXEDWF objects). The format of FM mode data is as follows:

```
struct fm__object
    {
    struct fixedwf__object car;    Carrier waveform (as in FIXED__
                                   WAVEFORM)
    char mfwf__ind;                Index into object symbol table
                                   defining mod. waveform
```

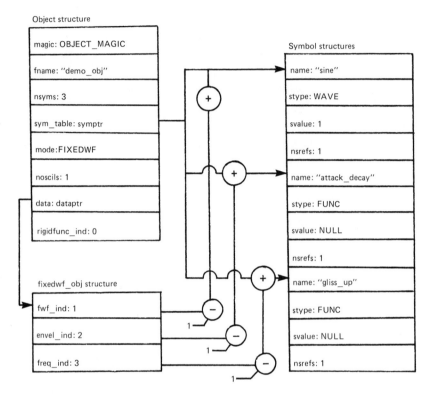

Figure 24.4
Fixed-waveform object representation, showing a fixed-waveform object with its three composite structures. In this case, the object refers to the three "sub" files, all of which are of type FUNCTION. These references are made via the symbol table. (See figure 24.5 for the internal structure of a FUNCTION file.)

char mdev—ind;	Index into object symbol table for mod. function
int maxindex;	Max. modulation index
int cval;	c term in $c{:}m$ freq. ratio
int mval;	m term in $c{:}m$ freq. ratio
} ;	

VOSIM OBJECTS   The VOSIM mode permits voice-type synthesis via a form of pulsewidth modulation. Different degrees of complexity are possible; generally, the more complex, the more oscillators or *VOSIM functions* must be used. Besides the pulse-shape (waveform) select and the amplitude and frequency functions, each VOSIM function also has the following parameters: the pulsewidth, how the pulsewidth varies in time, and the degree of randomization (to produce consonants, or noisy spectra). The format for the VOSIM data is as follows:

```
struct vosim—object
    {
    struct fixedwf—object vosfn;   As in FIXEDWF
    char maxdev;                    Maximum deviation (i.e., noise)
                                    factor
    char dev—ind;                   Index into object symbol table for
                                    dev./time function
    char pw—ind;                    Index into object symbol table for
                                    pulsewidth (i.e., formant) change
                                    function
    int pwf;                        Pulsewidth expressed as
                                    frequency
    };
```

Complex VOSIM objects utilize more than one VOSIM function or oscillator. When this is the case, a table of *vosim_object* structures is kept in a contiguous portion of memory. The number of entries in this table is given by the *noscils* field in the parent *object* structure.

BANK OBJECTS   This mode permits the use of several generators together, such that each oscillator functions as one component, or partial, in a complex tone. The frequency and amplitude of each component may vary over time. The actual frequency of any component is its partial number times the fundamental frequency (where the fundamental frequency is considered partial number 1). The data for the various partials in a particular object are stored in a table of *bank_object* structures. The format of these table entries is as follows:

```
struct bank—object
    {
    struct fixedwf—obj bnkmd;    As in FIXEDWF
    float partial;               Partial number (fund. = 1)
    };
```

The partial number is specified as a "float" value so as to allow arbitrary partial structures, and the number of entries (which are stored in contiguous memory) is given by the *noscils* field of the parent object structure.

WAVESHP OBJECTS   Waveshaping is a technique that makes possible the synthesis of complex sounds having time-varying spectra (Arfib 1979; LeBrun 1979; Roads 1979). The technique makes use of a form of controlled nonlinear distortion. Essentially, the output of one oscillator is scaled by an index (which may be a time-varying function) and then used as an address into a lookup table. The sample taken from the table (which contains the *distortion function*) is then used as a waveform sample, and is therefore scaled in amplitude and sent to a digital-to-analog converter. The technique utilizes two oscillator modules and has its parameters stored in the following structure format:

struct ws—object
{
char fwf—ind;	Index into object symbol table to define waveform previous to distortion
char envel—ind;	Index into object symbol table defining envelope of waveform after distortion
char freq—ind;	Index into object symbol table for frequency function
int dindex;	Index of distortion to which dist—ind function is scaled
char dindfn—ind;	Index into object symbol table specifying time-varying function for dindex
char distfn—ind;	Index into object symbol table indicating wave-form buffer containing distortion function
};

OBJECT Symbol Table   The only valid symbol types for object symbol tables are FUNCTION and WAVEFORM. Functions at the object level provide the means of specifying how parameters of the microstructure vary in time. This is essential for sounds to be of musical interest.

Just as with the score symbol table, if object.nsyms equals 0, or if any function named in the table is UNDEFINED, default functions will be substituted. Again, the user is able to override the system-defined defaults.

FUNCTION Files

Stored functions are used throughout the various hierarchies of the music system to control the variation of parameters over time. Just as there may be many instances of the same score or object in a composition, there may be several instances of the same function. In addition, each instance of the same function could quite conceivably be affecting a different parameter. Functions are stored as a set of straight line segments which approximate a continuous curve. Each file has a unique, user-defined name. In performance, each function is scaled in both the x and

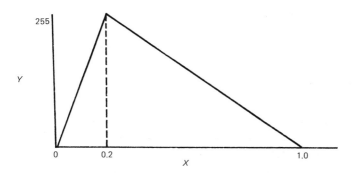

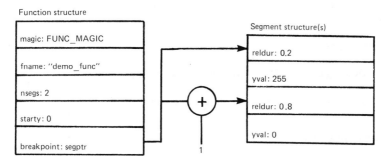

Figure 24.5
Example of a FUNCTION file. In this case, the two-segment function shown at the top of the figure is represented in the internal format of the two constituent structures of the FUNCTION file.

y domains according to application. Since there is no set number of segments in a function, we resort to using two different types of structures for their representation. These are outlined below.

function Structure   This is the *header structure* of a function. It contains the function's name, a *magic number* to identify the file as type FUNC-TION, the total number of segments, and a link to the segment data. The actual format of the structure is as follows:

struct function
 {
  int magic;   Magic number defining
                                        function
  char fname [FNAME_SIZE];   File name
  int nsegs;   Number of segments
  char starty;   Initial y value

    struct segment *breakpoint;   Pointer to breakpoint
                                       functions as:
                                       breakpoint [nsegs]
    };

segment Structure   The data for the actual segments are stored in a table of *segment* structures. There is one structure for each segment, and all structures are in contiguous memory. Rather than represent segments by integer breakpoints, we have chosen a slightly different approach that is computationally more efficient (when scaling functions during real-time performance). The y value is stored as would be expected, but the x value is stored as a fractional value representing that segment's relative duration with respect to the complete function. The format of the structure is as follows:

    struct segment
        {
        float reldur   Relative duration of segment
                         ($0 \leqslant$ reldur $\leqslant 1$)
        char yval;   End y value of segment
        };

WAVEFORM Files

Waveforms are a particular form of function which we choose to treat differently than FUNCTION files. In the case of a waveform, we store the function as a series of point samples, where the number of points equals the size of a synthesizer waveform buffer (i.e., 2048). Consequently, only the y value of the function need be stored; the x value is the index into the table. Besides storing the actual function data, the *waveform* structure also contains a magic number to distinguish it as type WAVE-FORM, and the actual waveform name. The data format for waveforms is

    struct waveform
        {
        int magic;   Magic number
        char fname [FNAME_SIZE];   File name
        int wfsamp [WFB_SIZE];   Waveform samples
        };

Acknowledgments

The work described in this article has been undertaken as part of the research of the Structured Sound Synthesis Project (SSSP) of the University of Toronto. The SSSP is an interdisciplinary project whose aim is to conduct research into problems and benefits arising from the use of computers in music composition. This research can be considered in terms of the investigation of new representations of musical data and processes and the study of human-machine interaction as it relates to music. The research of the SSSP is funded by the Humanities and Social Sciences Research Council of Canada. Logistic support comes from the Computer Systems Research Group (CSRG) of the University of Toronto. This support is gratefully acknowledged.

References

Arfib, D. 1979. "Digital synthesis of complex spectra by means of multiplication of non-linear distorted sine waves." *Journal of the Audio Engineering Society* 27(10): 757–768.

Buxton, W., E. A. Fogels, G. Fedorkow, L. Sasaki, and K. C. Smith. 1978. "An introduction to the SSSP digital synthesizer." *Computer Music Journal* 2(4): 28–38. Article 12 in this volume.

Hansen, F. E. 1977. "Sonic demonstration of the EGG Synthesizer." *Electronic Music and Musical Acoustics* 3.

von Helmholtz, H. 1863. *Die Lehre von den Tonempfindungen als physiologische Grundlage für die Theorie der Musik*. Reprinted as *On the Sensations of Tone as a Physiological Basis for the Theory of Music*. A. Ellis, tr. New York: Dover, 1954.

Kernighan, B., and D. Ritchie. 1978. *The C Programming Language*. Englewood Cliffs, N.J.: Prentice-Hall.

LeBrun, M. 1979. "Digital waveshaping synthesis." *Journal of the Audio Engineering Society* 27(4): 250–266.

Manthey, M. 1978. "The EGG: A purely digital real time polyphonic sound synthesizer." *Computer Music Journal* 2(2): 32–36.

Mathews, M. V., with J. E. Miller, F. R. Moore, J. R. Pierce, and J.-C. Risset. 1969. *The Technology of Computer Music*. Cambridge, Mass.: MIT Press.

Moorer, J. 1977. "Signal processing aspects of computer music." *Proceedings of the IEEE* 65(8): 1108–1137.

Roads, C. 1979. "A tutorial on nonlinear distortion or waveshaping synthesis." *Computer Music Journal* 3(2): 29–34. Article 7 in this volume.

Rolnick, N. 1978. "A composer's notes on the development and implementation of software for a digital synthesizer." *Computer Music Journal* 2(2): 13–22. Article 25 in this volume.

Schaeffer, P. 1977. *Traité des objets musicaux*, second edition. Paris: Editions du Seuil.

Sutherland, I. 1963. SKETCHPAD: A Man-Machine Graphical Communication System. Report TR-296, MIT Lincoln Laborators.

Truax, B. 1977. "The POD system of interactive composition programs." *Computer Music Journal* 1(3): 30–39.

Tucker, W., R. Bates, S. Frykberg, R. Howarth, W. Kennedy, M. Lamb, and R. Vaughan. 1977. "An interactive aid for musicians." *International Journal of Man-Machine Studies* 9: 635–651.

Vercoe, B. 1975. Man-Computer Interaction in Creative Applications. Cambridge, Mass.: MIT Experimental Music Studio.

Xenakis, I. 1971. *Formalized Music*. Bloomington: Indiana University Press.

25 A Composer's Notes on the Development and Implementation of Software for a Digital Synthesizer

NEIL B. ROLNICK

Composers generally have to approach computer music systems as a given fact of life, to be used toward the realization of musical sounds with very little thought as to why a system is the way it is. As a user of various computer music systems, I have often been frustrated at the awkwardness of achieving a particular result and wondered "Why has this system been designed in such a way as to make things difficult and time consuming?" I will try here to give other composers some insight into the answer to this question by outlining the process of development of SYN4B, a control language for a real-time digital sound synthesizer.

Although I will outline many of the features of SYN4B, I do not intend for this to be used as a manual for the language or as its main documentation. Instead, I will focus on the problems presented in designing a system that provides a maximum of flexibility and convenience for the composer while at the same time allowing access to the synthesizer itself at the lowest level possible. The problems faced in the development of SYN4B grew out of the conflict between the desire for an ideal system and the necessity of implementing that system on a particular hardware configuration. The specific points of conflict in any such project depend on the designer's concept of an ideal system and the specific hardware available. The problems involved in the design of a non-real-time system or a hybrid digital-analog system would, of course, be different from those described here. However, users of any system may benefit from seeing the kinds of problems encountered in the design and implementation of a language such as SYN4B. Other composers who find themselves in a similar position of responsibility for system development may be able to benefit from some of our solutions to specific problems we encountered. At the same time, I hope that users of any system might gain some understanding of the causes of the frustrations and annoyances they encounter by following the design and implementation of a computer music system and the many compromises necessary in order to reach workable solutions.

The Machine

SYN4B was written and designed by Phillipe Prevot and me to control the 4B Synthesizer, using a Digital Equipment Corporation LSI-11/03

This is a revised version of an article that was originally published in *Computer Music Journal* 2(2): 13–22, 1978.

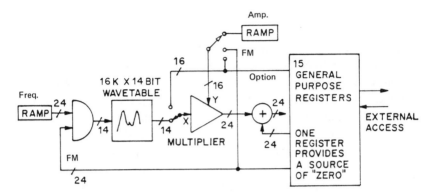

Figure 25.1
Functional diagram of an oscillator in the 4B synthesizer. The ramp and FM inputs are
added together, then added to the current phase. This new phase is saved for the next
current phase, and the result addresses the wavetable. The multiplier has several options
to allow for filtering and generalized arithmetic operators. The result can be stored
directly in a register (by adding the "zero" register) or summed with another register.

microcomputer. The 4B was designed and built by G. diGiugno and H. G.
Alles at IRCAM. (See Alles and diGiugno 1977.) To illustrate the problems involved in the software design, it will be necessary to restate briefly
a few features of the machine's design.

Figure 25.1 shows the design of one of the 64 oscillators available in
the machine. The ramps at the left side and the top of the diagram supply
data for the frequency and the amplitude of the oscillator, respectively.
These ramps are enabled or disabled by control words; they remain
at the current value if disabled and they move to a specified final value
if enabled. There is also a control word to enable the generation of an
interrupt to the system when a ramp arrives at its final value. The current
value in the frequency ramp is processed through the wavetable and then
given to the x input of the multiplier. The value contained in the amplitude
ramp is read at the y input of the multiplier. The output of the multiplier
is read by an adder, then passed into one of the 15 general-purpose
registers. The adder may also accept data from any register to be added
to the output of the multiplier. There are also switches at both the x
and y inputs of the multiplier. With these the user may access data stored
in any of the general-purpose registers via the OPTION and FM inputs,
one of which may also be used for the FM input to the wavetable, thus
permitting frequency modulation.

Any software for the 4B must set the proper control words in the 4B

memory to give values to the two ramps, and must set the switches for the
x and *y* inputs of the multiplier, the input register for the adder, and the
output register for each oscillator. We may begin by considering that
instruments are to be defined through the interconnections of oscillators
(setting the switches for the multiplier as well as for the input and output
of the adder), and the values of the frequency and amplitude ramps.

The switches controlling the input to the multiplier, the FM input,
and the input and output of the adder are all specified by bits in the control
words. The values of the ramps, however, present a slight problem. The
ramps are all linear, and they take as input a final value and an increment
(24 bits each). The current values of the ramps are contained in the memory
in such a way that the ramp may be forced to a given value by putting
that value into the "current ramp value" word. The potential difficulty
caused by this is twofold. First, the user will in many cases want to put
a series of ramp segments into the ramps rather than a single increment
and final value (such as data for an amplitude envelope). Second, most
musicians may be expected to think in terms of duration of the various
parameters controlled by the ramps. As far as the machine is concerned,
however, the duration of a ramp segment's ascent or descent to its final
value is a function of the increment and the difference between the initial
value and the final value. Any system software, then, must solve these
two problems by providing the user with a means of specifying a series
of consecutive ramps (again, an amplitude envelope is a good example)
and a means of scaling the consecutive ramps in time.

This machine in its present form contains no reverberation unit, no
filter unit, only one digital-to-analog converter (DAC) channel and no
analog-to-digital converter (ADC), so these problems are not addressed
by the software described in this paper. However, the software is designed
to be open ended, so that it can be adapted to new hardware modules
as they are developed, and also to new generations of the synthesizer
itself. However, the version of the SYN4B language described in this
paper will deal only with the control of the 4B synthesizer itself and with
a box of real-time controls (potentiometers, knobs, buttons, keyboards,
a pedal, and a joystick).

The First Problem

When we began working with the 4B, the only means of producing a
sound was to write a program in LSI-11 assembly language setting the

appropriate control bits and specifying the appropriate data for the ramp values. Having written such a program and loaded it into the machine, we had only two ways to change oscillator connections or ramp value data not taken from real-time inputs: modifying and recompiling the original program or using an on-line debugging program to change bits one by one in order to hear the effects in real time. With the latter technique, one quickly becomes aware that, once a ramp is enabled, it proceeds immediately on its course to the given final value. Two ramps cannot be enabled at the same time by this method.

After we got to know the machine in this way, some of the basic requirements for a control language became apparent. The first requirement was that there be two modes of use: a mode in which each line of code is scanned and interpreted, allowing the user to type in changes and hear the results immediately while communicating from the teletype keyboard, and a mode in which the prescanned code is interpreted and loaded into the synthesizer, giving control directly to the real-time input devices while disabling the teletype keyboard. This division of the language allows the user to build instruments first and test real-time devices on an interactive basis. Then, by getting rid of the scanner in the second mode, the LSI-11 is left free to process interrupts from the real-time control devices and from completed ramps.

The second fundamental feature of the language emerged from the impossibility of starting two ramps simultaneously when running the machine with the on-line debugging program. If the user is to interact with the synthesizer from the teletype, as in the first of the two modes described above, then it will be necessary to allow the user to amass all the data destined for the 4B's memory and send it to the synthesizer all at once. Another problem is that once the synthesizer has been given data enabling it to play, that part of the data that refers to current ramp values will be lost immediately as the ramps progress to their final values. Therefore, to replay the same note it is necessary on the lowest level to give all the current ramp-value data again. The solution we used for these problems was to build an image of the 4B's memory into the interactive mode of the SYN4B language. With this feature it is possible to enter all data into the image from the teletype, then copy the entire image into the synthesizer itself. This method of operation yields many benefits. First, since the image is independent of the changes in the 4B, a note may be replayed simply by recopying the image, thus resetting all the ramps automatically. This allows the user to make changes in any part of the input data and hear it at any time without having to retype anything other than the changes. And, of course, since all the data are transferred simultaneously from the image to the 4B, all the ramps will start simultaneously.

The last feature of the language decided on at this point was the necessity of permitting input and output through files. In this way, files may be created with a standard text editor to specify any input to the SYN4B program. Then a file may be read into the SYN4B program and tested and changed in real time. Once we had thus conceived of the possibility of using files as input to SYN4B, several other uses for files suggested themselves:

• It would be useful to save data entered by the user from the teletype in files to be used as input at some other time.

• The user may wish to enter one source file from another, read through the second file, and then return to the original file. This concept of *nested* files open up the possibility of creating complex modular musical events without the necessity of using files of unwieldy length.

• The user may also wish to save data that have been input and already scanned by SYN4B.

• Likewise, the user should have the option of saving any specific state of the 4B image in a file.

Syntax for Oscillator Connections

The next problem was to design a syntax for specifying oscillator connections to the 4B in a form that would be relatively easy for musicians without extensive computer experience to comprehend and use. At this point we made one of the most important decisions in the language design: to have the SYN4B language address the 4B at the lowest level possible. To do this, it was necessary to assume that anyone using the machine understands the structure of the oscillators as represented above. Then it is just a matter of finding a simple format to accomodate data for the switches and input for the FM and OPTION registers and input and output for the adder. Our solution to this problem was as follows:

*OSC# Rn = [Rm +] (FMx, FreqRamp. Opy or WavTabl, AmpRamp or FMx or OPy)

where Rn is the output register for OSC#, Rm is the optional adder input register, FMx is the register number from which the FM input is taken, OPy is the register number from which the OPTION input is taken, and FreqRamp and AmpRamp are variable names identifying the frequency and amplitude ramps associated with OSC#.

In view of the above explanation of how each oscillator is structured, this format for oscillator definitions should appear straightforward and not overly complex. The only feature that might not be obvious is the use of variables to identify the ramps for frequency and amplitude. This was done with the expectation that at some point it might be desirable to associate various functions with any particular ramp, perhaps in a score format for playing the 4B from a note list.

Each position is given a default value, so the use of the oscillator connection statement is made quite simple. For example, to specify that oscillator 1 is to have R0 as the FM register (i.e., no frequency modulation), that the ramps are to be connected to the two poles of the multiplier, that R0 is to be input to the adder, and that the oscillator output is to go to R15, the user simply types

OSC1 R15 = (,,,)

This format is really nothing more than a simple mnemonic form for the commands for the 4B's oscillator control words. This is important, however, because it means that the user of the SYN4B language is actually communicating with the synthesizer on the same level as if LSI-11 assembly language were being used. This means that the language will not limit the user's access to the machine at all.

To complete this kind of low-level access, we also defined simple mnemonics for the ramp control words:

< code > < osc# > < new value >
    where: < code > ≡ IF or IA (initial value freq/amp)
            ≡ FF or FA (final value freq/amp)
            ≡ DF or DA (increment freq/amp)
    < new value > ≡ < new value >
            ≡ real time input specifications (see the section on
            "Real-time Inputs.")

In the process of actually playing the synthesizer, these commands are awkward, to say the least, Generally, when these particular commands are used extensively to control the ramps, it becomes apparent that another, higher-level command is necessary. For example, a constant value of 2,000,000 in the amplitude ramp for oscillator 1 would be specified in this notation as

```
IA1   2000000
FA1   2000000
DA1   MAX        (full 23 bits as increment)
```

Instead it is possible to type

```
FA1   2000000
```

which sets the same bits as the three preceding lines of code. However, this ability to actually set the ramp control words directly from the high-level control language means that future users will not be limited by our present vision of how the machine can be used, or by simplified statements in which the user cannot really see what is going into the machine.

The best way to learn what each of the possible controls for the machine can do is to use the lowest level of the language when first using the machine. This helps take the mystery out of the higher-level command formats, which are used more frequently in actual practice, particularly in the case of ramp controls.

What the Machine Lacks

As was mentioned, there are several features that are desirable for a highly flexible software environment for computer music but are either awkward or downright difficult to implement from the lowest level of the language because of the hardware configuration of the synthesizer. These include the specification of a series of consecutive ramps in the form of breakpoint functions, the scaling of the breakpoint functions along both the x and y axes, the specification of durations rather than increments for single ramps or series of ramps, the specification of ramp values in terms of arithmetic equations, and the specification of constant ramp values.

Some of these features have already been implemented in the SYN4B language, some are in the process of being implemented, and some are still in the planning stage. The simplest feature to implement was the command for setting a constant ramp value, which has the following format:

PIn < value > (for frequency ramp #n)
PAn < value > (for amplitude ramp #n)

As mentioned, these commands simply allow the user to substitute one line of code for the three lines necessary at the language's lowest level. This may seem like a very minor improvement, but we have found that this feature has cut down the time necessary for entering an instrument definition and made our input files more easily comprehensible.

For the design and use of breakpoint functions we have used the following basic format:

```
FUN  BP  < value >
         y₀
x₁       y₁
x₂       y₂
.        .
.        .
.        .
100      yₙ
```

This format specifies the breakpoints on a grid of 100 by 100. The first value on the x axis is automatically set at 0, and the function is considered complete when the x value reaches 100. SYN4B then automatically sets the proper increment and final values for each ramp segment, as well as setting the interrupt enable control bits and sending the new values to the proper ramp each time an interrupt is generated by the arrival at the final value of the current ramp segment.

In order for such a function to have any real meaning for the synthesizer, it must be scaled on both the x and y axes. The need for this scaling is important to understand. Since we may safely assume that a breakpoint function will be used to control either an amplitude or a frequency ramp, we may consider that the y axis will represent either frequency or amplitude and the x axis will represent time. Now, our first question must be "What amount of time is to be represented by the 100 points along the x axis?" The second question is "How do we know that that amount of time has passed?" It is important to realize, in this regard, that the computer has no way of knowing what time it is unless you tell it. Therefore, some sort of timing mechanism must be built into the program that will allow us to measure time. This measurement must be made in terms of some basic unit of time, and only then may we consider that the 100 points along the x axis of our function have any meaning at all. Furthermore, unless all notes or events to be controlled by the function are to be of the same duration, its length (i.e., the x axis) must be adjustable in terms of time units. In other words, it must be scaled.

On the y axis the situation is different but equally significant. Let us assume that the values on this scale will be used as data for ramp final values. What is the range of these values inside the 4B? Not 0 to 100, but 0 to $2^{23} - 1$, or 8,388,607. This is so because the value is actually represented by a 24 bit binary word, with the leftmost bit saved to indicate the sign (positive or negative). Obviously, a value of 100 on a scale of 0 to 8,000,000 is not very significant. And things would not be improved by automatically scaling the function such that the maximum value of the function is 8,388,607, because this number is used to represent the maximum amplitude of the entire synthesizer. This means that the maximum amplitude for each oscillator must depend upon the number of oscillators being used for audio output. Therefore, again, it must be scaled by the user.

Scaling in time, as noted above, is dependent upon some sort of time unit. We have implemented a method by which users define their own time units, employing an oscillator for this purpose. This will be explained in more detail in the following section. One feature of scaling in time, however, should be discussed here. Assuming that the total duration of a breakpoint function is to be variable and user-specified for different notes or events, we may wish to have a portion of the function that will not vary regardless of the overall duration of the function. For example, if we use a breakpoint function to define an amplitude envelope, it may be desirable to set specific times for the attack and the decay, leaving only the central portion of the envelope to be scaled according to the duration of the note. We have built this feature into the breakpoint-function definitions by expanding the format as follows:

FUN BP   < name>
< att >, < dec >
           y_0
x_1 y_1
x_2 y_2 *
.   .   *
.   .   *
.   .
100   y_n

where ⟨att⟩ and ⟨dec⟩ are the attack and decay times in milliseconds and where the asterisks following any number of x and y coordinates indicate that those ramp segments are to be considered as part of the *steady-state* portion of the function. This means that the ramp segments appearing before the steady-state segments are calculated to have the exact duration specified in ⟨att⟩, and the ramp segments following the steady-state segments are calculated to have the duration specified in ⟨dec⟩, leaving only the steady-state portion of the function to be scaled in time.

Scaling the functions on the y axis presents a somewhat different problem. If breakpoint functions will again be used in part to describe amplitude envelopes, it will be necessary to multiply these functions by one or more scaling values. This can be done to a limited extent in the 4B itself if the oscillators are used as multipliers by connecting the OPTION register to bypass the wavetable. However, if we wish to scale by several factors at once, it becomes necessary to use many oscillators as multipliers, which considerably diminishes the power of the synthesizer. A further problem with this method of using the synthesizer to do arithmetic is that there are not direct inputs to the general-purpose registers. In order to put a given value in the general-purpose register so that it can be used for a hardware multiplication, it is necessary to set the frequency of an oscillator to 0, set the phase of that oscillator to 90° (assuming that there is a sine wave in the wavetable that has a value of 1 at 90°), and then put the value into the amplitude ramp. This method works, but is quite awkward and tends to consume too many oscillators to do simple arithmetic.

The other obvious solution to scaling is to do it all in the software, using a series of subroutines that allow us to do various kinds of arithmetic operations on single values as well as on breakpoint functions. Here we found a fatal flaw: The LSI-11/03 we are using to control the 4B is simply not fast enough to do very many multiplications in real time while servicing interrupts generated by ramps and real-time input devices.

To illustrate this problem, let us define a simple, single-modulator FM instrument using the 4B hardware for all the multiplications. We will assume that the ratio of carrier to modulating frequency is to be constant, and therefore the carrier will be expressed as

< basic frequency >*< carrier scaler >

and the modulating frequency as

$<$ basic frequency $>*<$ FM scaler $>$,

with the convention that scalers will be constant. If it were possible to use the software for arithmetic, our instrument could be represented as in figure 25.2. The use of the various scaling factors is quite important if we wish to have precise control over timbre. With software arithmetic, as shown in the figure, we need only two oscillators to define this instrument, which means that we could have up to 32 such instruments playing at once. If, however, we are forced to use the synthesizer hardware for our multiplications (assuming we can do the subtraction $I_2 - I_1$ by hand), and including the need to set the frequency to 0 and the phase to 90° in order to put an initial constant value into the general-purpose registers, we end up with the instrument shown in figure 25.3. In this diagram I have included only those parts of each oscillator that are actually used, in order to simplify the schematic representation. It should be clear, however, that instead of two oscillators we now must use eight. This means that we may only have a maximum of eight such instruments at once. In effect, we have had to diminish the capacity of the machine by a factor of 4 in order to do our scaling operations.

The need for scaling breakpoint functions and the problems involved in doing that scaling through the 4B hardware should now be clear. With the 4B synthesizer and the LSI-11/03, there seems to be no ideal solution for this problem or for the more general problem of doing arithmetic operations in real time via software for the LSI, short of having a high-speed arithmetic unit designed, built, and mounted on the LSI. Therefore, we have made a series of compromises concerning the scaling of the breakpoint functions along their y axis and the use of arithmetic equations.

For the breakpoint functions we have implemented a set of fixed scaling possibilities, thus expanding our format for the functions to the following:

```
FUN  BP   <name>  a, b, c
<att>, <dec>
          y0
x1        y1
x2        y2
.         .
.         .
.         .
100       yn
```

478   Rolnick

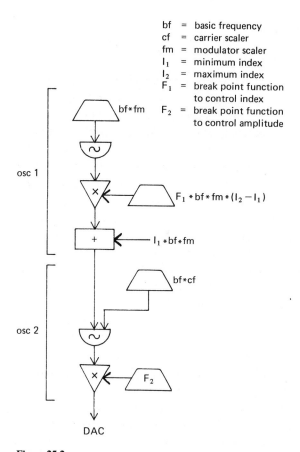

Figure 25.2
A single-modulator FM instrument in which scaling of the frequency terms is performed
by software in the LSI-11. In this diagram the trapezoid represents an input, which is
generally equivalent to the frequency or amplitude ramp in figure 25.1. The half-circle
represents phase accumulation and lookup, and the triangle stands for the multiplication.
The rectangle represents the addition before storage in a general-purpose register.

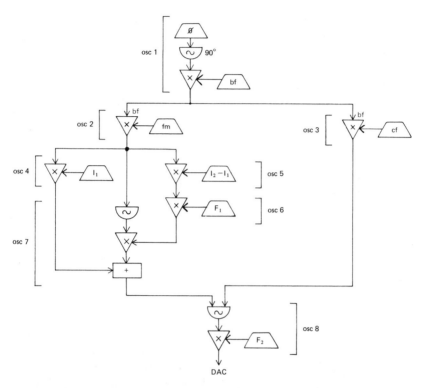

Figure 25.3
An expansion of the instrument illustrated in figure 25.2 that performs coefficient calculation in the hardware.

where a and b are additive and multiplicative factors, respectively, and c is a shift factor. This means that the value of each breakpoint is evaluated by the equation

$$\text{value}(n) := (a + b * y(n)) * 2^c.$$

That is, each y value of the function is multiplied by b, offset by a, and then the binary representation of that number is shifted c bits to the left (with a shift to the right if c is negative).

For the evaluation of more general arithmetic equations, we have made use of the previously described "hardware multiply" within the 4B, and also, to a more limited extent, devised a method for evaluating expressions in which all components of the expression are read from the real-time inputs.

Let me now return to the five features mentioned at the beginning of this section (multiple ramps, scaling of functions, use of durations rather than increments, evaluation of arithmetic expressions, and constant ramp values). It will be clear that all five have been implemented to some extent, but often with a certain amount of compromise. This makes for a language that at this time is in some ways more awkward to use than I would like. However, the awkwardness is primarily a function of the limitations of the machines, and we often had to decide between being able to do something awkwardly or not at all. In order to give users of the system the greatest possible flexibility, we have always opted to include features that might be a little cumbersome to use but allow for more complete control over the synthesizer.

Scores

Though we have specified the interconnections of oscillators and found a format for giving ramps the data they require, we still haven't dealt with the problem of how to play the 4B. In designing SYN4B, we began with the idea of two different modes of playing the synthesizer: with a note (or event) list and with the real-time input devices. The note-list mode, which can be thought of as a kind of musical score for the synthesizer to play, is not yet fully implemented, but it may be interesting to examine some of the planning that has gone into the development of this feature.

The basic questions which we had to answer in our planning were these: If we are to have a score, then we must have some way of specifying durations. How is this to be done, since there are no timers built into the synthesizer? What is the most easily comprehensible and at the same time most flexible format to use for notating a score? Should a score be monophonic or polyphonic? That is, do we want to specify events one voice at a time? Should the score be completely separate from the instrument definitions, as it is in non-real-time languages such as Music V or Music 10, or should it be possible to mix note list and instrument definition? Should input from the score be separated entirely from control by real time inputs? If not, how can the two methods of playing be used together?

First is the problem of specifying durations. This is done by using one or more oscillators as timers. To do this, the software needs to set a ramp with specific initial, increment, and final values to yield a user-specified duration for a basic unit of time. The user then expresses durations in the score in relation to this basic unit. The format for defining a timer is

TIM*n*   < duration >

where *n* is the oscillator number used for the timer and the duration is either expressed in milliseconds or as a real-time input specification. In expressing durations in the score, the symbol D is used to express the basic unit given to the timer. Other durations are then expressed as arithmetic expressions relative to this basic unit. For example, if we have set the basic unit for the timer to be 100 msec (0.1 sec), then D ∗ 2 would indicate a duration of 0.2 sec and D/2 would indicate a duration of 0.05 sec. Evaluating arithmetic expressions in the score need not present any problem for the LSI-11, with its relatively long multiply time, as long as the score is not to be interpreted in real time.

The problem of finding the appropriate format for the score has not yet been satisfactorily solved, but it may be interesting to examine the two possibilities we have considered. The first possibility is to use a fixed-parameter-field format, similar to that used for Music 10 note lists. In this case, the system would demand that a certain number of fields in the list for each note or event be used to express required data, such as duration, instrument name or number, and begin time. The remaining fields would then be associated with ramps, which would be specified in the oscillator definitions as P*n*. That is, if we define oscillator 1 as

OSC1   R15 = (,P3,,P4)

then we will know that the values or functions to be put into the frequency and amplitude ramps for oscillator 1 will be found in the third and fourth fields of data for each note. If OSC1 is defined as instrument 1 and if fields 1 and 2 are reserved for instrument number and duration, respectively, a line of score in this format might look like this:

1   D/7   200   40000000

One disadvantage of this system is that it is possible to imagine values which one would wish to specify in the score, but which may not be used directly in an oscillator connection statement. For this reason, it may be more desirable to ask the user to specify at the beginning of each score the definition of each field. For example, we may wish to have the same oscillator connection as above, but use breakpoint functions for both ramps, scaling the functions differently for each note. We might then begin by setting breakpoint functions called FRQ1 and AMP1, then define two new breakpoint functions:

FUN BP P3 = FRQ1∗FSCAL
FUN BP P4 = AMP1∗ASCAL

A line of our score input would then look like this, with instrument number indicated in the first line:

```
SCORE     INS1
(DUR      FSCAL ASCAL)
D/7       10     4000
```

To extend this possibility even further, we might assume that we can use different breakpoint functions for different notes. In this case we might assign FRQ1 and AMP1 as variable names and call on predefined break-point functions, which we will call F1 through F4. Two lines of score input would then look like this:

```
SCORE     INS1
(DUR      FRQ1      FSCAL      AMP1      ASCAL)
D/7       F1        10         F3        4000
D/2       F2        20         F4        5000
```

The advantage to this method is that it allows for considerably more flexibility than a fixed-field method. The disadvantage is that it may prove slightly more cumbersome to use, since the format for each score must be set up individually.

The next question in designing the score format for the 4B is whether we want to use polyphonic or monophonic scores. In a monophonic score, such as the examples above, we must indicate that a block of score data is to be applied to a specific instrument. Each event for that voice is then listed in chronological order. One can of course play several instruments at the same time using this method, but the score for each instrument must be entered separately. In a polyphonic score, on the other hand, each note for each instrument played must be listed in chronological order. This method, which is used in Music V and Music 10, requires an instrument name and a begin time for each note. The monophonic method appears preferable, again because it allows the user considerably more flexibility; several instruments may be played independently at the same time. In real-time performance (one of the capabilities of the 4B synthesizer), this flexibility might be employed by starting scores for various instruments at different times, to be decided at performance time. Similarly, it would be possible to use different timers for different instruments, and to control these timers from real-time inputs. In this way the tempi of different musical lines could be varied independently and in real time. The only advantage of a polyphonic score format is that the specifications for chords and for tightly controlled counterpoint may be somewhat simpler for the user, but this is counterbalanced by the loss of flexibility and the general awkwardness of this approach for nonchordal musical textures. The ideal solution for this particular problem may be to have both systems of score notation available to the user, although this has not yet been implemented in SYN4B.

The last two questions to be considered in the design of a score format have to do with how the score portion of the control language relates to other portions of the language. The solutions to these problems depend to a large extent on the real-time performance nature of the 4B machine. The questions are these: Should the note list coexist with or be separate from the instrument definitions? Should control from a score coexist with or be separate from control by real-time inputs? The answer is that the score should coexist with both instrument definitions and real-time inputs.

To consider the first of these problems, it helps to have some familiarity with the structure of music programs for large, non-real-time computer music systems, such as Music V or Music 10. In these programs the user begins by defining instruments and functions. As soon as a note list is begun, the program will accept no more instrument or function definitions, because it begins calculating a sound file for storage on disk. This is all quite reasonable, since these programs calculate music files rather than send information to a synthesizer. The 4B, however, has entirely different needs. Since the synthesizer is, in effect, always capable of producing sound with whatever oscillator connections and ramp data it has, there is no particular reason to separate the score from the instrument definitions. On the contrary, the potential of intermixing the two presents very interesting possibilities. For example, there is no reason why one could not have one set of instrument definitions, followed by scores for those instruments, followed by some modifications of the instruments, followed by more scores. In this way, very different sounds could be generated from the synthesizer at different times within the same performance without the need to enter any new input files for the SYN4B program.

This mode of operation might be even more interesting if, for example, we included the possibility of triggering the beginning of a score from a real-time input. This brings us to the final question in the design of the score portion of the program: whether one should be able to combine the score with real-time inputs. The use of a real-time input as a switch to trigger the beginning of a score is only one of the possibilities to consider in this combined mode of operation. Another possibility might be to trigger each event in a note list by pressing a key on the keyboard. This would mean that the note itself would be dependent upon the keyboard for nothing but its initialization, with all other aspects controlled in the score. Another possibility would be to have the timer for a particular instrument controlled by a real-time input device, so that, while the notes and relative durations would be fixed in the score, the tempo could be varied over a wide range in performance. Also of great interest might be the ability to notate certain parameters of an instrument in a score while controlling other parameters from the real-time control devices.

As should be obvious, the combination of real-time input with preset note-list data would appear to be one way in which the nature of the 4B as a digital synthesizer might be most fully exploited to yield great exactitude and tightly controlled complexity, which is almost impossible to achieve with an analog synthesizer, while having the potential for real-time user interaction with the machine in performance, which is generally not possible with computer-generated sound.

Because of this wish to take advantage of the potential for interacting with the score in real time, the actual code for creating the score portion of the program has become very much intertwined with the processing of the real-time input devices, particularly on the level of program interrupts generated by the real-time devices as well as by the ramps. A technical description of the inner workings of this part of the program is beyond the scope of this paper, but it may be of interest to mention the general approach we have taken to processing the several levels of program interrupts generated by actually playing the synthesizer in this way, which could easily overtax the LSI-11/03 (a slow computer). This has been done by implementing a *waiting loop*, which is in operation whenever data are not being taken in from the teletype. It is within this waiting loop that the SYN4B program processes data from the real-time input devices, keeps track of program interrupts, and determines when the next note or event is to be initialized.

One last idea that came out of the planning for the note-list format is the inclusion of a limited amount of decision-making capability for the program itself, in the form of **if-then**, **goto**, and **wait** commands, with the decisions determined by the state of one of the real time inputs. When used in the note list, this could allow the user the option of looping through one section of a score until a certain button is pressed, at which point the program could proceed through the rest of the note list, or be directed to an entirely different part of the score, or even be directed to a block of code that changed the oscillator connections and then sent the program back to another block of score input. This would provide a truly idiomatic use of the synthesizer by allowing the performer to make formal decisions about the music in performance without sacrificing the kind of tight control of detail that is available through the use of a score.

Real-Time Inputs

I have been referring to real-time input devices without being very explicit about what those devices are. We have been working with a box of real-time controls built by David Cockerell at IRCAM for use with the 4B synthesizer. This box includes a total of 48 slide potentiometers in two banks of 16 and 32 each, a two-direction joystick, and one foot pedal, each of which yields 8 bits of binary data. In addition there are two rows of buttons, which may be read in a number of ways, such as depressed or not and on or off (indicated by lights within the buttons). In addition, one row of buttons may be read as a 16-bit word, while the other may be used to access 16 virtual values of 16 bits each of which are set by means of a spin-wheel. Finally, there are two keyboards: a 61-key organ keyboard and an 8 by 9 button matrix. Any note or button on either keyboard is used to refer to a specific location in a user-definable table in the LSI-11 memory. We have used the following general format to identify real-time input devices:

< device type > (< number >)

where the ⟨device type⟩ may be either a single input or several inputs grouped together, and the number indicates the specific member of the group. The mnemonics for real time devices implemented at this time include the following:

PBA(n)   Pot #n of the first bank of slide pots
PBB(n)   Pot #n of the second bank of slide pots
PED   Pedal
KBD(n)   Keyboard 1 or 2
STV   Joystick, vertical scale
STH   Joystick, horizontal scale
SPW(n)   Virtual spinwheel #n, selected from lower buttons

This list should not be seen as definitive. It will be possible for users to define their own device names, in which they may include any of the specific real-time inputs desired, so that any number of inputs used to put together parameters for a particular sound may be grouped as a single real-time input device.

The first basic decision we made concerning the use of the real-time inputs was that ideally we would like to be able to use them anywhere in the program: to specify values for ramps, to define breakpoint functions, and as inputs for arithmetic expressions, as well as for logic in the **if-then** statements described in the previous section. It also is essential, particularly in the case of the keyboards, that the real-time inputs be able to trigger events, which means indicating to the waiting loop that the various ramps for a particular instrument are to be initialized.

The process for reading data directly from the real-time inputs into a ramp value is fairly straightforward. The only problem to be dealt with is the fact that, except for the keyboards, the data are all in either 8-bit or 16-bit format, whereas the 4B uses 23 bits for all ramp data. This means that if the value of a slide potentiometer, for example, is put directly into the final value of an amplitude ramp, it will be 2^{15} (32,678) times smaller than the maximum amplitude, which means that it will be virtually inaudible. The problem, then, is to find a simple means to scale the values read from the pots. We have implemented several different methods of doing this.

The first method is to concatenate three 8-bit pots into one 24-bit word. This is done with the format

$< code > < osc\# > < origin > (x, y)$

where $\langle$code$\rangle$ represents the symbolic name of the destination within the 4B (such as P11 for constant frequency of oscillator 1), $\langle$origin$\rangle$ is either PBA or PBB, and x and y indicate the first and last of no more than three pots to be concatenated. Using this format, we may indicate a constant value for the frequency of oscillator 1, to be determined by the concatenation of the first three pots in pot bank A, with the following statement:

PI1   PBA(1, 3)

While this was useful in the first stages of testing the machine and the SYN4B program, it became obvious that it would be quite inconvenient to operate the controls in this manner at all times. The obvious solution to the problem was to use some form of scaling so that a full 23 bits of information could be taken from an 8-bit pot. To do this we incorporated the scaling feature used in our breakpoint functions into the symbolic names for the real-time inputs, as follows:

< code > < osc# > < origin > a, b, c

where a, b, and c represent additive, multiplicative, and shift factors (as explained above). Thus, to take a full range of values on 23 bits from an 8-bit pot, we need to multiply the value in the pot by about 30,000, with the statement

PA1   PBA(1) ,30000,

which indicates that the pot is to have an additive factor of 0, a multiplicative factor of 30,000, and a shift factor of 0. Once one becomes accustomed to this method of scaling the output of the real-time inputs, it becomes quite simple to scale the values to have virtually any range desired. Furthermore, by using a combination of the scalers and the concatenation feature, it is possible to use the pots for a combination of wide range selection and fine tuning of values. For example, the following statement would assign the first pot of pot bank A to control the frequency of the first oscillator while allowing fine tuning with the second pot of the same pot bank:

PI1   PBA(1, 2) ,,7

Having in this way adopted the symbolic representation of the real-time inputs to the format of the breakpoint functions, we have also expanded the concept of these functions to include the possibility of a type of function defined simply by points. This *point function* simply returns the value of a given input, scaled with the same format as above. However, if a series of pots is listed, the function will return the value of the first pot the first time it is called, the second pot the second time it is called, the third pot the third time, and so on. When the last pot has been read, the function returns to the beginning of the cycle. The format for this type of function is

FUN PT < name > < origin > $(x, y) a, b, c$

where $a, b,$ and c are scale factors, as above, ⟨origin⟩ is either PBA or PBB, and x and y are the first and last pots to be read by the function. Using this type of function, it is possible, for example, to simulate an analog sequencer with up to 32 positions, controlled in real time, with the following format defining a function named SEQ:

FUN PT SEQ PBB(1, 32) ,4000,

This function might then be used as the frequency control for an oscillator with the statement

PI1 SEQ

We have also implemented the ability to define breakpoint functions with the real-time inputs, with a statement such as

FUN BP f1 PBA(1, 8)

in which breakpoints are set at eight equally spaced points on the x axis and the y value of each breakpoint is read from pots 1–8 in pot bank A.

Although, as mentioned before, we have not yet implemented the use of arithmetic expressions to be evaluated in real time with the SYN4B language, because of the speed limitations of the LSI-11, the ease of access to the values contained in the real-time inputs has allowed us to implement this feature on a limited scale, with the stipulation that all components of an arithmetic expression be read from the real-time inputs. This is another feature of the language that is more cumbersome than I would like it to be, but is certainly an improvement over the limitation of being able to do arithmetic only in the 4B itself or in the scalers used with real-time input assignment statements and function definition statements. With this feature, for example, it is possible to construct an FM instrument in which the ratio of carrier to modulating frequency and the range of modulation indices are set by values in four of the virtual spin wheels, while the basic frequency of each note is determined by the keyboard or by a score.

Final Thoughts

We have followed the development of the major features of the SYN4B language. In general, each feature was approached with a certain ideal form of implementation in mind, and very often that ideal had to be compromised to some extent by the limitations of the machines we were working with. To a greater or lesser extent this must be true of all computer music systems.

Many of the problems we encountered in the design of SYN4B can be instructive in the realm of hardware design for digital synthesizers. For example, the problems of scaling and the waste of oscillators for use in evaluating arithmetic expressions may be avoided altogether by separating the components of the oscillators so that adders and multipliers may be accessed independently. Similarly, the synthesizer may be constructed to include a number of timers so that oscillators would not have to be sacrificed for this purpose as well. These improvements, as well as many others that stem from the experience of using the 4B, have been incorporated into the design of diGiugno's 4C synthesizer (Moorer et al. 1979).

Though our solutions to the particular problems we encountered may help others solve similar problems, those who are simply users of computer music systems, and who will never be faced with the specific problems discussed in this paper, can benefit from having followed our progress. If one is to write "idiomatic" music for or with a computer, it is essential to have some understanding of why and how one's instrument (the computer) works. This may be seen as analogous to the way in which most instrumentalists who utilize new performing techniques find it essential to understand the physical and mechanical means by which their instrument produces sound. If computer music composers make a similar effort to understand why the software works the way it does, at the very least they may be led to write in a way that fits the machine idiomatically. Furthermore, if composers can understand a particularly troublesome feature as the result of a decision concerning a specific problem in the design of the system, they may be able to find another solution that is more suited to compositional needs.

Acknowledgments

The work documented here was made possible by the cooperation of a large number of people who gave freely of their time and ideas. Much of the formal structure of the language took shape under the influence of Max V. Mathews, James R. Lawson, and Bruce E. Leibig. Virtually all of the coding of the language was done by Philippe Prevot. I would also like to thank James A. Moorer for his careful reading of this paper and his many helpful suggestions, and G. diGiugno for his patience in guiding Philippe and me through the inner workings of his synthesizer.

References

Alles, H. G., and G. diGiugno. 1977. "The 4B: A one-card 64-channel digital synthesizer." *Computer Music Journal* 1(4): 7–9. Article 15 in this volume.

Moorer, J. A., A. Chauveau, C. Abbott, P. Eastty, and J. Lawson. 1979. "The 4C machine." *Computer Music Journal* 3(3): 16–24. Article 17 in this volume.

26 Automated Microprogramming for Signal Processing: A Tutorial

CURTIS ABBOTT

Automated microprogramming of processors having parallel elements is of interest to computer musicians because of its relevance to the use of generalized signal processors in analyzing and synthesizing sound. In particular, automated microprogramming tools for digital synthesizers would remove much of the tedium and would require less technical expertise to use the machines with the maximum of flexibility and efficiency. However, creating such tools will be difficult. Indeed, designers of digital synthesizers are only now recognizing the importance of microprogrammability.

This is not a report of new research. Rather, it is an attempt to present a coherent view of the problem and of the issues that surround it and grow out of it. Design considerations that affect programming will be discussed, as will heuristic approaches to the scheduling of computations, theoretical and practical aspects of the scheduling problem, and the choice of block or stream computation.

Microprogramming

Traditionally, microprogramming means programming a computer not in terms of the usual instruction set, but on a lower level: that of registers, functional units, and data paths, the basic hardware elements out of which computers are built. The traditional use of microprogramming is to define an instruction set, but the point of view taken here is broader: We consider the possibility of applying microprogramming to whole programming problems in a semiautomatic way.

Consider the usual schema wherein programming takes place: We write programs in a high-level language and invoke a compiler to translate this program text to a "more executable language" (perhaps a symbolic assembler, in which case another program is invoked to translate the program text to a machine-language program whose numbers are interpretable as machine instructions, addresses, constants, etc.). In many modern computers, there is a normally unseen level below this: a *microprogram*, which interprets these *machine instructions*, effectively translating them to the level of machine registers and functional units. Explicit translation to this lower level by a compiler-type program gives us a new potential for optimization and adaptation of the machine's resources to different situations. In a machine with different functional units that can operate in parallel, and in an application (such as digital synthesis) where enormous amounts of repetitive computation are called for, this possibility becomes attractive.

Definitions

As has already been stated, the basic elements of a computer are registers, functional units, and data paths. A *register* is memory organized into a word of some number of bits (the number depends on the use of the register). A *register file* is a collection of registers, each with an address. A *functional unit* is a hardware device that operates on data. A good example of a functional unit is an arithmetic logic unit (ALU) chip that takes two words of data input and some control input and produces one data word of output and some control output. Whether the output is an arithmetic or a logical function of the inputs depends on the control information. The control output typically tells something about the resulting data or the operation—for example, that there was an arithmetic overflow, or that the result is zero. Other functional units include multipliers, shifters, large memories used as lookup tables or delay lines, and possibly many more complicated and specialized functions. A *data path* is just a collection of wires allowing data to move from one register or functional unit to another. The architecture of a digital machine is the configuration of these elements.

Architectural Considerations

Architecture and programming are closely linked domains that interact strongly. Even the best microprogram cannot make a machine do something well that it was not designed to do at all. On the other hand, a machine can all too easily become so complex that microprogramming is next to impossible and automated microprogramming is unthinkable.

Processor architecture is an art of making choices. One of the kinds of choices that can be made is to select certain machine configurations as "important" and to make these the only configurations available to programs. Essentially, this is done by inserting a level of indirection in the hardware: The program chooses one of the possible configurations (represented as a number that indexes a list of the chosen "important" configurations), and the hardware translates this into the "underlying" configuration. This technique is called *verticalizing* and the resulting machine is called a *vertical microcode machine*. A machine in which microprograms have access to all the underlying configurations is called a *horizontal microcode machine*.

Vertical machines tend to be slower and/or more complicated, but they are typically less costly to build because microprograms select from a smaller set of possible configurations and can therefore be represented with fewer bits. This same fact may make microprogramming simpler, but the extra level of indirection introduces added complexity (at least when a program branch is taken). This needs a little explanation. Most processors of any interest make some use of the technique called *pipelining*. Pipelining is another way of making choices, but the choices are of a different kind than those that lead to verticalization of a processor architecture. Pipelining can take place as the result of limiting the possible data flow between different processor elements. An example of pipelining occurs when, during a given time slice, one instruction is being executed while the next instruction is being fetched from memory. In this situation, as long as we know where to fetch the next instruction without having executed the current one, we can make our machine run as fast as the maximum of the fetch time or the execution time. If we don't know this, as when an instruction causes a branch, then we cannot overlap and processing slows down. In a vertical architecture, there is often more pipelining associated with instruction fetch and execution because of the extra work involved in translating the microcode fields into their corresponding "underlying configurations." This tends to increase the penalty for branching in such machines.

A more application-dependent aspect of processor architecture is that of balancing resources. We can visualize a processor as having a set of resources, which are the capabilities of the processor's elements. Each element is associated with a cost, typically the time it takes an element to carry out an operation. Generally, the machines in which we are interested operate in terms of a repetitive cycle of fixed length; thus, we can express resources in terms of this cycle. For the machines in which we will be interested here, the period of this cycle will be between 50 and 500 nanoseconds.

The problem of resource balancing is to adjust the resources built into a machine to the kinds of algorithms to be programmed on it. A machine that can do four adds and one multiply per cycle is not well balanced if our algorithms typically call for two multiplies for every add. We must not forget to include data movement as a resource; the ability to get data from point A to point B in a machine may be the limiting factor in our use of it.

It was stated at the beginning of this section that machine architectures could render automated microprogramming infeasible by their complexity. One way to ensure complexity is to make the interconnection structure of processor elements complicated. In this situation, the constraints on data flow (the potential movement of data from one unit to another) combine with the already thorny constraints on the ordering of operations to make the problem of automated microprogramming much harder than it already is. Another potential source of problems is related to highly pipelined functional units. These become problematic if the program is to attempt to use them in different ways according to the needs of an algorithm. For example, with a functional unit that performs two multiplies, two lookups, and four additions, with one or several possible patterns of interconnection between these operations, attempting to match a part of an algorithm that needs one multiply, two lookups, and three additions to the given functional unit is hard for the same reason that complex interconnections are usually hard. In fact, deep pipelines typically exhibit complex interconnection structure, so the problems caused by excessive pipelining can be viewed as specializations of those caused by complex interconnection structures in general. If deep pipelines are to be used only as "originally intended," they are not a great problem.

The above discussion is intended only to give the broadest outline of the issues in processor architecture, a subject about which whole books (such as Bell, Mudge, and McNamara 1978) have been written. Though a given architecture helps define the environment in which microprogramming takes place, the latter can be discussed without consideration of the former.

Programming

Automated microprogramming is an extension of ordinary compiling. To make this clear, this section is divided into a short discussion of the usual problems associated with compiling and a longer discussion of the problems that are peculiar to a partially parallel, microprogrammed target machine.

Usual Problems with Compiling

Compiling involves handling a textual stream as input. Output may also be textual, but it is not always. The problems involved in dealing with textual input, recognizing meaningful units (tokens), and so on are often underestimated. On the other hand, this type of problem is quite well understood, and a variety of good software is available to help with it.

Another well-understood aspect of compiling is *parsing* (translating the input text into a set of symbol definitions and of data structures that represent the meanings of the expressions in terms of their constituent operators). The data structure used for this is usually called a *parse tree*, whereas symbol definitions occur in a *symbol table*. A parse tree is a representation of the computational structure of an expression.

In order to have something definite to speak about, let us consider a contrived example. The (modified) Music V notation for the example is in figure 26.1. The same algorithm in an expression form, such as might be used in a programming language, looks as follows:

```
T1  ←  OSC(SIN, MF2)*MI2;
T2  ←  OSC(SIN, MF1 + RS*SD)*MI1;
SD  ←  SD*M + C;
OUT  ←  OSC(SIN, T1 + T2 + CF);
```

This, then, is essentially a textual equivalent to the graphic form of figure 26.1. One slightly subtle but crucial point is knowing the ordering constraints that are present in a given expression. Essentially, this comes down to representing the expression in the program that is attempting to compile it.

Figure 26.2 is an example of a *directed acyclic graph* (DAG) (Aho and Ullman 1978). It has a simple interpretation: Each arc entering a node from the bottom represents something that must be done before the action represented by the node in question can be carried out. Figure 26.3, another DAG, is really not much more complicated than figure 26.1. It is turned upside-down, the oscillators are expanded into more primitive operations, and some of the lines are stretched so that all the memory reads are at the bottom. It is clear from figure 26.3 that some memory read must be the first action. After M and SD have been read, one multiply is permissible. After RS has been read, another is permissible (if the value of SD is still available), and so on.

A considerable number of other subtleties in the parsing and compiling processes are already well understood on sequential machines and only get

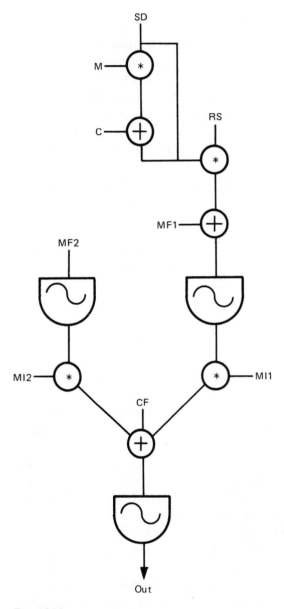

Figure 26.1
Music V–like notation for a frequency modulation (FM) instrument. Text symbols
represent memory locations, circles represent multiplication (∗) or addition (+), and
hemicircles represent oscillators. SD: random seed; M: multiplier; C: constant; RS:
random scaling; MF1: modulating frequency 1; MI1: modulating index 1; CF: center
frequency.

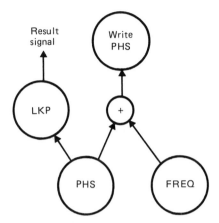

Figure 26.2
Expansion of a simple OSC to more fundamental operations. Here, LKP means look up in a wavetable and PHS is the instantaneous phase.

worse on parallel ones. One of the more important of these subtleties is that, in generating code for an expression on a particular machine, it is ordinarily necessary to create "secret" temporary variables to hold intermediate results (results of subexpressions). Ordinary machines typically have some processor registers in which these can be stored, and if we run out of registers (or are too lazy) temporary variables can be held in regular memory. In microprogramming, the situation is noticeably more complicated because of the proliferation of kinds of memory (fast small memory, slow large memory, registers) and the likelihood of complicated restrictions on each of them (typically brought about by their placement in the interconnection structure of the machine, or their interaction with clocks, use of bus cycles, and so on). The existence of these temporary variables and the different costs associated with different temporary variables are two factors that make optimizing difficult even on ordinary computers.

Extra Problems with Compiling

Operator Matching

The first kind of problem we will talk about here is one that applies to normal compilers as well, but in a somewhat different way. This is the

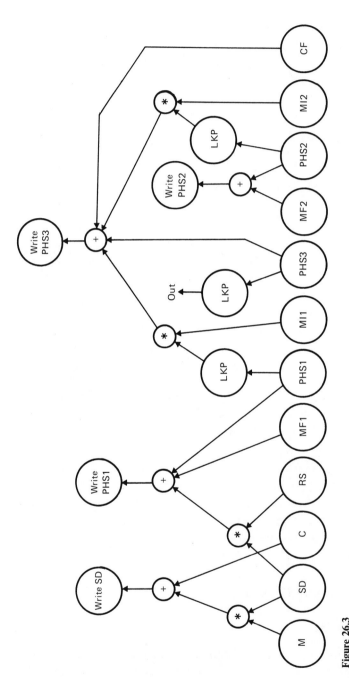

Figure 26.3
Version of figure 26.1 with oscillators expanded as shown in figure 26.2, and drawn as a DAG. This gives a level of detail appropriate to a relatively unspecialized (i.e., general-purpose) machine.

problem of matching the operators in a DAG (or a parse tree) to the operators that occur in the machine. This problem can be posed in a very general way, and can thus be made arbitrarily hard; however, for illustration let us consider a reasonably simple problem arising from the example presented above.

As explained in the legend of figure 26.1, the hemicircle indicates an oscillator (a unit that includes a lookup and an accumulating phase register). We will assume that our target machine does not have an oscillator unit wired into the hardware. This means that there is a mismatch between the DAG and the target machine.

The right thing to do in this situation is to expand each oscillator unit in the DAG into a set of operations that the machine can do and that together perform the desired oscillation. Figure 26.2 shows the DAG for an oscillator, and figure 26.3 shows a DAG corresponding to figure 26.1 with the oscillators expanded. This is about as good as we can do with such an expression without knowing much about the target machine.

Of course, there are other kinds of operator matching and adjustment. Here is another example from our contrived algorithm: It is likely that we want the multiply of SD by M to be an integer multiply (that is, to return the low-order bits of the result), because we are using this multiply to generate a pseudo-random sequence; the algorithm that generates it calls for an integer multiply. The multiply operations that perform scaling of signals are likely to be much easier to manipulate if they have the radix point elsewhere; this corresponds to taking a different set of bits from the answer as the result. It is necessary, in a real (as opposed to a contrived) situation, to deal with problems such as this. This necessity of operator matching impinges on the design of a programming language as well as on its compilation.

Scheduling Parallelism   Here we consider some heuristic techniques germane to the scheduling problem, then some theory. The results of the theory tell us that we are in the realm of inherently difficult problems.

Before discussing ways of solving the scheduling problem, it might be well to define it a little better. Consider, therefore, figure 26.3. If we draw imaginary horizontal lines from bottom to top, the first passes through twelve memory reads; the second through one addition, two multiplies, and three lookups; the third through two additions, two multiplies, and one memory write; and so on. (In this example, memory read and memory write are two classes of memory reference in a fast scratchpad memory. Lookup is a memory reference in a larger, slower memory, used for wavetables in this case.) This represents, naively speaking, what can be done in parallel. The limitation of resources creates all the interest. We wish to choose an ordering of operations subject to the constraints in the figure and those of the target machine such that the use of the parallel resources of the machine is maximized.

HEURISTIC APPROACHES   Perhaps the best way to define *heuristic* is to say that a heuristic gives a strategy for solving a problem without guaranteeing that the solution so obtained will be the best possible (or even that a solution will be obtained, in some cases). A more irreverent definition is to say that *heuristic* is a fancy word for educated guess. We use heuristics when we don't know what else to do. However, this should in no way be taken as a negative comment.

We will consider two kinds of heuristics for solving the scheduling problem with which we are faced. The discussion is rather brief and we will not show directly how to use these strategies, but only suggest how they might be applied.

The first strategy we will call *critical resource counting*. The idea here is that each operator in our expression corresponds to a unit of a machine having fixed resources, and we may be able to structure the scheduling of a particular expression by finding out which machine resources are most critical to it. In order to do this, we count how many units of each type of resource the expression uses in terms of the cost incurred for each. Consider the example in figure 26.3 and a machine for which the costs for memory reference, multiplication, addition, and lookup are 1, 3, 2, and 4 respectively in terms of time slices (the indivisible unit of time in the machine). We count the number of times each operation is used in the expression and get 12, 4, 7, and 3 respectively. (In hardware, addition is done two operands at a time. Thus, each three-operand addition is actually counted as two additions.) Then we multiply costs by resource-use counts to get 12, 12, 14, and 12 for the four operations. One thing this tells us is that no microprogram for this expression can take fewer than 14 time slices, since each addition takes two of them and there are seven additions to do. We can also gain some information about the expression by asking how different the resource counts are from each other. In this case they are not very different, and this means that the expression is well balanced with respect to the machine (in the sense discussed previously).

The idea in critical-resource counting is that we might use the counts to give priority to scheduling the different kinds of operations. This means in the example discussed above that we would try to schedule the additions one after the other, then try to schedule the other kinds of operations around these, in order of decreasing priority. This is likely to work less well if the expression is well balanced (as this one is), since other aspects of the expression may be much more important.

The second heuristic we will present, *critical-path scheduling*, is an accredited and rather well-known technique. The idea here is to determine the *critical path* of the expression. To define this, let us say that a *path* of an expression is a set of operations in the expression which are sequentially dependent, that is, which must be done one after another. Then a critical path (and there may be more than one) is that path or paths with the maximum total cost in terms of the machine operators present on it.

Like critical-resource counting, the critical path provides a theoretical minimum on the time in which the expression can be executed on the target machine. For our usual example, there are two critical paths: from the memory reference for either PHS1 or PHS2, through a lookup, a multiply, a quadruple addition, and a write to PHS3 (classified as a memory reference also). The time for these paths is 15 time slices each, broken down as 1 for the memory reference, 4 for the lookup, 3 for the multiply, 4 for the quadruple addition (implemented as 3 binary additions, 2 of which can be done in parallel) and 1 for the final write.

We can define subcritical paths as the critical paths of the expression that results from removing the critical paths from the original one. In our example, if we take out the two critical paths we have just identified, we uncover one critical path of length 9 (from SD or RS to multiply, triple addition, and write), then one of length 7 (from SD or M to multiply, binary addition, and write), and so on.

In a sense, we have chosen a good expression for demonstrating the problems with the heuristics discussed, since there are two critical paths and since the subcritical paths (those that remain when we remove the ones we have already identified) are also reasonably long. This means that the critical-path heuristic does not give us precise idea of how to schedule —nor does critical-resource counting, as we have seen. Paradoxically, what this kind of result means is that we have an expression that is well suited to a highly parallel microprogram.

Consider briefly how to apply heuristics to an actual problem. One suggestion that seems reasonable is to combine the two heuristics some-how, or at least to use them both. This is reasonable because they provide different kinds of information about the expression being scheduled. If either identifies an aspect of the expression that "sticks out" in the sense of badly balanced resource use or a critical path much longer than all subpaths, then we can use this as a starting point from which to attack the problem. We can also compare the theoretical minimum times for the expression obtained by each method and use the maximum of these to decide which is the more appropriate heuristic for the expression. Given that we have gotten started somehow (in the case of our example, we might even decide to flip a coin), we have then reduced the problem and can proceed by starting over with the smaller problem. Things get more com-plicated as we go on, because as soon as part of the expression is already scheduled we must work within the constraints imposed by that partial program—probably leaving ourselves the option of going back and chang-ing what has been decided already.

The method just outlined, of *reduce and conquer*, occurs over and over in many guises. It can even be seen to be related to the method of *stepwise refinement* advocated as a principle of structured programming. We will see it again in this article when we discuss the branch and bound algorithm. If an election were held to decide which are the fundamental principles of programming (or problem solving), it would surely be a winner.

ENUMERATIVE TECHNIQUES   Let us now turn to more theoretical subjects, to answer the question why we have to use heuristics at all and to get some perspective on our problem. We have said that a heuristic is not guaran-teed to give the best possible answer. Is it possible to imagine a method that is guaranteed to do so? The answer is yes, and the method is decep-tively simple: Given an expression for which we want a microprogram, we are going to make a list of all possible microprograms and choose the one that takes the least time. This can be generalized to any notion of "best possible" that we like; all that is needed is a way of measuring the *goodness* of each possible microprogram. We can choose as optimal the program that minimizes this measure.

There are two problems with this method, one obvious and one less so. First, we need a way to list all the possible programs. This is called *enumeration*. It is not a trivial matter to write a program that will enumer-ate the microprograms that implement a given expression. There is even the tricky question of whether the set of such microprograms is finite; it is easy enough to make it infinite, for instance, by allowing delays (no-ops) to be inserted anywhere in the microprogram. This instance is a good one, because there are expressions and machines for which the optimal micro-program contains instructions that start no functional units but only wait for previously started results to finish—a case that is hard to distinguish from a no-op. To formalize the notion of an acceptable microprogram and to guarantee that the resulting set is finite, we need to formalize the notion that each microprogram instruction should make a "positive contribu-tion" to evaluating the expression. The less obvious problem with enu-meration is even worse. The number of possible microprograms for an expression will tend to increase exponentially as the length of the expres-sion increases. Mathematically, this means that $P = a^L$, where P is the number of possible microprograms, L is the length of the expression, and a is some constant greater than 1. More descriptive terms exist, most of them having to do with explosions or catastrophes. To get an idea of what this exponential formula represents, recall that it is the same as the scientific notation used for large numbers: 10^3 is 1,000 (a reasonable number), but 10^{80} is the estimated number of elementary particles in the universe (clearly an unreasonable one).

Mathematicians and computer scientists measure the computational efficiency of algorithms according to a formula that relates the average number of computations needed as a function of some pertinent feature of the input. For example, the exponential formula above relates the number of programs (each of which can be checked for optimality in a relatively short fixed amount of time) to the number of operators in the input expression. It shows that the enumerative algorithm for optimal scheduling is "of exponential order," as the saying goes. This word *order* can take on several very different meanings in mathematical discourse. In this case, it means essentially *magnitude*. We have asserted nothing definite about the relationship between the number of operators and the number of possible microprograms, only that one grows as an exponential function of the other. This is the usual way of characterizing the efficiency of algorithms in computer science, and there is a useful notation: If n is the independent variable and $f(n)$ is any function of n, then $O(f(n))$ is the "order of $f(n)$" in the sense just discussed. For example, $O(a^n)$ for $a > 1$, is *exponential order*, while $O(n^k)$ for some fixed k is called *polynomial order*.

In practice, however, the effect of algorithms that are exponential in nature is not easily summarized. There exist problems for which the algorithms are exponential in their use of time or of space, but the exponential behavior happens only for certain inputs. A good example of this is the simplex algorithm for linear programming, which is well behaved "in practice" in spite of being theoretically exponential in its behavior. Another situation in which the use of an exponential-order algorithm can be justified is when it is guaranteed to be used only for small inputs. In this case, the exponential behavior cannot become overwhelming. Thus, if we can break a problem into small pieces, it is possible to solve each piece independently with an exponential algorithm. This cannot be done when the pieces are interdependent, as is typical for scheduling and similar problems.

NP-COMPLETENESS   By pursuing some theoretical ideas about the efficiency of algorithms a little further, we can understand the assertion that problems such as optimal scheduling for a microprogrammed processor are inherently hard. This area is theoretically incomplete and thus all the more tantalizing.

A whole class of problems in scheduling, graph theory, operations research, and other areas can be vaguely described as searches for optimal arrangements of complicated systems. Many of these areas are of considerable practical interest. A large number of these problems have been shown to be *NP-complete*. What it means for a problem to be NP-complete is that it is equivalent to all other NP-complete problems in the sense that, if an algorithm can be found for any one NP-complete problem that is theoretically better than exponential order, then such an algorithm can be found for any NP-complete problem. This is elusive enough to be worth restating in a more intuitive fashion: If any NP-complete problem can be efficiently solved, then all such problems can be. What makes the theory of NP-completeness of especial practical interest is that many of the problems in this class have been worked on for a long time and no efficient algorithm has ever been found to solve them. This is evidence (not proof) that NP-complete problems cannot be solved efficiently and are thus inherently hard. It seems that humans are no good at these kinds of problems either. All the tasks that humans can do a great deal better than computers (such as language, recognition of faces, and recognition of instruments in an orchestra) are problems not of optimal arrangement but of pattern recognition, which is fundamentally different.

THE BRANCH AND BOUND ALGORITHM   The branch and bound algorithm provides a systematic way of enumerating the possible solutions of an optimization problem, taking advantage as much as possible of the structure inherent in it.

We have already discussed the possibility of enumerating all the possible solutions of a scheduling problem. In the present case, these solutions take the form of microprograms. Given this list of microprograms, we find an optimal one by finding out how much each one costs (and, eventually, which one costs the least)—in other words, by applying a cost function to each microprogram in the list.

The first idea we need in order to understand the branch and bound algorithm is that we can extend the idea of a cost function to a microprogram that only partly solves the problem. Suppose we have a *partial microprogram* (an initial segment of one of the microprograms in our imaginary list of all possible ones). We can apply a cost function to such an initial segment just as easily as to a complete microprogram. The key observation is this: If the cost of any known complete microprogram is less than that of any known initial segment, then none of the complete microprograms that start with that initial segment can be optimal. This observation depends, of course, on the cost of a partial microprogram not shrinking as the partial microprogram gets longer.

This observation gives us a way to eliminate some elements of the list of all possible microprograms without explicitly generating them. What remains is to find a way to systematically generate and eliminate candidates for optimality. In order to make this presentation easier, we will first generalize the above observation a little. Consider the role of the "cost of any known complete microprogram" in the observation: Its purpose is to provide an upper bound on the possible cost of the optimal program. Indeed, given any complete microprogram, we know that no optimal microprogram could cost more than it. In light of this, let us restate the observation explicitly: Given a known upper bound U on the cost of the optimal microprogram, we know that any partial microprogram whose cost is greater than U cannot lead to an optimal microprogram.

It is not really necessary to find such an upper bound in advance, although this can help. First, let us outline the way in which the branch and bound algorithm systematizes the enumeration of possibilities. In this outline, we will act as if branch and bound is useful only for finding optimal microprograms, although this is far from true. However, to present branch and bound in as general a context as possible requires more confusion than seems necessary here. Another shortcut we will take is to present branch and bound in terms of abstract data structures and operations that might be horribly inefficient to implement as such. The point is to understand the principles of the algorithm.

We will use *steps*, abstract operations that can be thought of as procedures in a programming language. The main control algorithm will be presented, then the definition of the steps. Before either of these, we define the kinds of objects these steps will manipulate. First, we have the notion of a partial program. A description of a partial program includes its instructions (in sequence, of course) and its cost. Next, we need the notion of a set of partial programs. These are used to remember the state of the enumeration. (Remember that branch and bound is an enumerative procedure, though a systematic one.) We will use several of these sets during the computation, but there will always be exactly one of them that is currently of interest. This one we call *ATTN*, since we are paying attention to it. Other sets of partial programs will be organized on a stack. At some points in the computation we need to identify a single partial program as being of particular interest. We will call this *PP*, and it will always be obtained by picking and removing some set from *ATTN*. We also need to remember the best complete program so far discovered. This is called *OPT*, and the cost of *OPT* is the currently best upper bound, (which we call *U*). The initial value of *U* can be understood as a parameter to the branch and bound algorithm. It can be an impossibly large value, greater than that of any real microprogram, or it can be some heuristically generated value. The only constraint is that it not be less than the cost of the (initially unknown) optimal microprogram; if it is, the algorithm will enumerate all possible microprograms and never choose one.

The main control algorithm for branch and bound is

```
initialize;
while true do begin
    reject;
    pick;
    If PP is a complete microprogram then
        begin
            update;
            backtrack;
        end
        else generate;
    end;
```

Next, we define the steps (or operations) used above.

initialize: Generate *ATTN* as the set of all possible partial programs of length 1.

reject: Remove all elements from *ATTN* whose cost is greater than *U*.

pick: If *ATTN* is empty then backtrack. Now let *PP* be the set in *ATTN* with the least cost. Remove it from *ATTN*.

update: Let *OPT* be *PP* and *U* be the cost of *PP*.

backtrack: If the stack of sets of partial programs is empty, we are done. Otherwise, remove the top element of the stack, assigning it to *ATTN*. If this set is empty, repeat this step.

generate: Push *ATTN* onto the stack. Now generate a new *ATTN* set consisting of all possible extensions of *PP*.

We can gain a little more insight into how this algorithm behaves by watching *PP*. Initially, *PP* gets longer and longer. At some point, it becomes complete. Then we obtain a better upper bound, and backtrack, examining shorter partial programs until we find one that is less costly than the complete program we found before backtracking. We then elaborate from this new starting point. This elaboration may go faster, since the reject procedure has a sharper upper bound. This process continues until we have either explicitly enumerated all possibilities or implicitly rejected them.

It should be easy to see that the efficiency of this algorithm depends on the order in which we enumerate complete solutions (and, thus, new upper bounds). If we can find structure in our particular application of the algorithm that allows us to get a good initial upper bound, we can expect things to go faster. In our application, for example, we might generate a heuristic solution and initialize *OPT* and *U* with this solution and its cost respectively.

Block or Stream Processing

Until now, the discussion has centered on some of the technical problems associated with compiling for parallel and microcoded machines and a few of the mathematical ramifications of these problems. In this section, we take up an issue that is not so much technical as strategic but is important all the same. This is the question of how to organize calculations at the operator level: whether to let operators act on blocks of data or have them act on a single datum at a time. Before we consider the implications of this question, it would be well to define it a little better. If we are given a set of primitive operators (e.g., multiply, add, lookup, oscillation, and two-pole filter) and an algorithm for producing sound samples using these operators, the stream-processing approach applies the operators to one sample at a time. A block-processing approach would use operators adapted to act on an array of samples rather than a single one, and would therefore produce an array of samples as the output of a single application of the algorithm.

The advantage to be gained by block processing depends on the situation. For example, the CRAY-1 computer has many components which can act in parallel on blocks of up to 64 data elements. In this situation, the advantage of block processing should be quite obvious. (Unfortunately, the CRAY-1 is too expensive for computer musicians.) However, even if block-processing operators are implemented sequentially (or with a small amount of parallelism), one can gain an advantage if a block operator can set up its variables in the fastest available memory and then calculate the samples of its block with the least possible overhead. This option is important enough in practice to deserve an example. Consider an oscillator as a primitive operator. In a simple oscillator, we must read the phase, look up the waveform value, perhaps interpolate on the basis of the fractional value of the phase, add the phase increment (which corresponds to frequency) to the phase, and store the phase. In stream processing, this must be done for each sample. In block processing, however, if a faster memory is available than the one in which the phase is usually stored, we need only read the phase from the slower memory at the beginning of the block and store it at the end.

Another advantage of block processing is that it facilitates using control signals sampled at a rate that is the regular sampling rate divided by the number of samples per block. Control signals at such a rate can have their values updated at the end of each pass through an algorithm. The idea of control signals at lower sampling rates is a useful one for situations in which parameters of a digital instrument change slowly (relative to the sampling rate) but not in a stepwise fashion. However, block processing makes implementation of multiple and/or arbitrary control rates more difficult than with stream processing.

Perhaps the most important advantage of block processing for applications that go beyond pure synthesis is that a large number of classical algorithms (digital signal analysis algorithms in particular) can be implemented only in a block format. An obvious and important example is the FFT algorithm for spectral analysis. Many others are in the same category.

Let us turn now to the problems that can arise in block processing. One of these is that it is much more natural to express many algorithms (synthesis algorithms in particular) in terms of stream processing. This makes an automatic translation desirable. This is not completely trivial. In translating from stream to block, it is necessary to account very carefully for signal delays that may be introduced by the use of memory and operators in the instrument. Consider, for example, a one-pole filter with input X and output Y: $Y \leftarrow aX + bZ$; $Z \leftarrow Y$. What we wish to do is translate the assignment of Y to Z into a storage operation that goes to a location in an array of delay values. The array is as long as a block and gets completely rewritten on each pass. Typically, we can implement two-pole filters using only one such array of delay values, but with the added complexity of pointer manipulation (to keep track of where each newly generated delay value goes). In order to translate arbitrary expressions in a general way, a deeper analysis is needed; this is nontrivial and beyond the scope of this tutorial.

Just as block processing may be made advantageous by a given machine architecture, it may also be made disadvantageous. Thus, in a machine with a limited memory hierarchy (so that overhead remains high throughout the computation by an operator of a block of samples), or in a machine in which the chosen primitive block operators do not allow balanced use of the parallelism in the machine, block processing may not be such a good idea. (Of course, block processing can never lose for block algorithms such as the FFT.)

A relatively cursory examination will convince anyone that there is no fundamental difference between block and stream processing, in the sense that with an adequate machine anything that can be expressed as a stream algorithm can be translated to block-processing form. Thus, in the jargon of computer science, this translation is a *meaning-preserving transform*. Another adjective that can be applied to such transforms is *optimization*, since we do not usually trouble with them without reason. Thus, we are led to regard block processing of essentially stream algorithms as a means of optimizing their execution. As has already been pointed out, the utility of this depends on the machine. It is, in general, more economical to build a machine that is adapted for block processing than to build one that is not.

Summary

This article has been more concerned with raising problems than with solving them. We considered some of the ways machine architecture can affect automated microprogramming and some of the relationships between automated microprogramming and ordinary compiling of high-level languages. The problems associated with scheduling of expression operators in a partly parallel environment were discussed from heuristic and enumerative points of view. We also examined some of the theoretical underpinnings of the scheduling problem and saw that the hopes of finding an efficient, general solution are slim, since scheduling problems of any complexity have an annoying tendency to be NP-complete. Continuing our examination of enumerative methods, we considered a way of systematizing enumeration (branch and bound). Finally, we examined a strategy for optimization (block processing) that can be useful with certain very practical digital signal-processing machine architectures.

We have consistently glossed over a number of important and difficult programming problems involved in keeping track of the state of partially compiled expressions and deciding what constitutes a "positive contribution" to a partially compiled expression. This is a problem in defining and managing data structures. It is related to, but typically more complicated than, the analogous problems in ordinary compilers. Also untreated is an interesting model for representing and manipulating expressions that allows all their potential concurrency to be easily found. This model, called *Petri nets*, has received some attention from researchers, and some references are given below.

Bibliography

Aho, A., S. Johnson, and J. Ullman. 1977. "Code generation for expressions with common sub-expressions." *Journal of the Association for Computing Machinery* 24(1): 146–160. This paper, though difficult, discusses many of the key issues of the present tutorial in a more rigorous way and presents several proofs of NP-completeness. It can profitably be read in conjunction with Aho and Ullman 1978.

Aho, A., and J. Ullman. 1978. *Principles of Compiler Design*. Reading, Mass.: Addison-Wesley. This is probably the best book available on compiling. Of particular relevance to the topics discussed above are the sections on DAG generation, data-flow analysis, and code generation.

Bell, G., J. C. Mudge, and J. McNamara. 1978. *Computer Engineering: A DEC View of Hardware Systems Design.* Bedford, Mass.: Digital Press. This is an interesting historical look at the tradeoffs involved in designing several families of computers, from microprocessors to powerful mainframe systems.

Holt, A., and F. Commoner. 1968. *Events and Conditions.* Three volumes. Wakefield, Mass.: Applied Data Research. This introduces and develops Petri nets and related structures, develops some mathematical framework for extracting information about classes of concurrent structures as well as particular ones, and provides some hope of reducing the intractable general case of parallel scheduling to a more manageable size. Holt has reported on practical application of Petri nets to compiling for the CDC 6600.

Lawler, E., and D. Wood. 1966. "Branch and bound methods: A survey." *Operations Research* 149. This is useful for gaining a perspective on the variety of forms branch and bound can take.

Misunas, D. 1973. "Petri nets and speed independent design." *Communications of the Association for Computing Machinery* 16(8):474–481. This article discusses a machine all of whose modules are asynchronously coupled so that data can flow from one to the next as soon as one is finished, rather than in synchrony with some fixed cycle time as envisaged above, and discusses the use of Petri nets in working with this idea.

27 A Software Approach to Interactive Processing of Musical Sound

CURTIS ABBOTT

This article concerns a program I wrote during the latter part of 1976 and the early part of 1977. I describe here the intentions that led to the program, the results, and what can be learned from the work. Although the program is available (in principle) for others to use, this article is not intended to advertise the program but to view it as a way of approaching an important class of software problems that are encountered by computer musicians.

The program came to be called INV (for "invoke"). The initial motivation for INV was to provide a means to perform mixing and editing operations in an entirely digital context in order to produce pieces of music I had conceived but for which I couldn't face the prospect of nearly infinite amounts of tape duplication, splicing, and so on. Also, I wanted to test some routines I intended to write that would implement various interesting analysis and synthesis techniques (see Moorer 1977).

The result of this work can be most reasonably described as a simple high-level computer language. The elements of the language will be described below.

The Lowest Level

The lowest level of the language is concerned not with musical matters but with processing input commands. What I am calling the lowest level, then, might just as well be called the language proper. It can be understood roughly in terms of its lexicon and its syntax. The *lexicon* is the set of "kinds of things" that are recognized as meaningful in the input; the *syntax* is essentially the rules or conventions governing the form of the input.

The lexicon consists of constants (which may only be integers), known variables of several types, strings, parameters, the usual symbols for arithmetic and relational expressions (including the usual conventions about parentheses), certain keywords (**if, goto**), a convention for defining labels, an operator that assigns results to variables, and certain words in the input which may be the names of activities—either predefined (in

Originally published in *Computer Music Journal* 2(1): 19–23, 1978.

which case they are called *primitives*) or defined by users (in which case they are called *macros*).

The conventions governing the form of the input make a single line of input the natural unit for program activity. In fact, only one activity (primitive, macro, **if**, or **goto**) may be named on a line. If none of these kinds of activities are named, the line is assumed to be simply an assignment of the value of an arithmetic and/or relational expression. In any case, the result of the activity or expression can be assigned to one or more variables in the same line. (The **if** activity is implemented by evaluating the expression following the keyword and ignoring the next input line if the expression was true.)

This restriction of activities to a "one-line-at-a-time" format, which makes conceptualization and implementation of the language much simpler, is a significant restriction. Language experts will note that a number of common high-level computer languages (for example, C, the base language for INV) are less restrictive in at least two different ways. The first, which I think is less important, is a difference in formatting rules. What must appear in INV as two statements on two lines may be spread out over four lines or compressed onto one in many languages. The second kind of difference is that in many languages *activities* may be substituted for variables. Such activities are often called *functions* (as in FORTRAN and BASIC). I recommend a capability like this in a language not because it allows us to write apparently shorter programs, but because it seems to mirror something about the way we think and therefore makes a language more "natural."

Implementation of the Lowest Level

The computer to which I had access for this project was essentially a PDP-11/40 (actually, it was a Cal Data 100 emulating the latter) running under the operating system UNIX (Ritchie and Thompson 1974). This means that the program was written in a high-level language called C and that I had a sophisticated set of program development tools at my disposal. Without such tools, the program would certainly have taken longer than approximately two man-months to write. I want to emphasize in particular the help of a program called YACC (Johnson 1974). YACC is a parser generator that takes as input a formal definition of the lexicon of a computer language and a set of rules for the syntax, and produces as output a computer program that recognizes input in the language and performs specified activities whenever it has recognized significant fragments of such input.

The lowest level of the language functions as an interpreter and comprises a scanner, and a parser (the latter supplied by YACC and a collection of routines for recognizing and processing various kinds of strings as well as for manipulating data structures (notably the symbol table and calling-level stack)).

The Basic Primitives

With the primitives, we begin to approach musical matters. But the first primitives must be mundane, since nothing has been provided in the basic language to carry out such useful operations as defining variables, typing information on the terminal, and defining values for fundamental constants such as the sampling rate. In particular, this first set of primitives can set and print the sampling rate; type out a message, including values of any desired variables, on the terminal; accept a digit string from the terminal and return its value; and define and "undefine" (thereby reclaiming the space used by) variables of two different sorts. One of these is a variable in the ordinary sense and can take on an integer value. I chose to call the other kind of variable a *structure*, since that is the name of an analogous kind of entity in certain high-level languages (including C). A structure is an object with multiple parts, each of which can take independent values. Thus, a collection of two integer variables can be a structure. The advantage of structures is that they can be used to collect together logically related sets of variables. An example (which is heavily used in INV and in the examples below) is the *event structure* denoted by the keywords **stru event** in the language. It consists of two integer variables which represent the starting time and the duration (respectively) of an event.

When one wishes to pass a whole structure (that is, a whole collection of logically related variables) to a primitive or macro, one needs to name only the structure itself. In order to reference a component of a structure (that is, a single variable), more information is necessary, in the form of either a component name (certain component names are predefined) or the position of the component in the structure (which is a constant integer).

Other basic primitives are also concerned with supporting data structures implemented in the language. These include buffers and two kinds of files. *Buffers* are arrays that cannot be indexed except by primitives. *Data files* are intended for the storage of waveforms. *Parameter files* are intended for the storage of control information. The reason for the distinction is that data files must be stored in a physically contiguous way, which is not supported by UNIX. Therefore, the program contains a simple file-system manager for a physical device which is not used by UNIX. (This implies that an installation using this program must have at least two disks.)

Primitives that read files place their data into a buffer; primitives that write into files get their data from buffers. At this basic level, then, the program user is required to be aware of such considerations as the use of buffers in the process of duplicating a waveform or any other significant operation involving waveform data. This is required because buffering is a general-purpose mechanism, not because musicians ought to know about it. There is a mechanism for user-defined activities (*macros*, mentioned above) with which buffers can be made completely transparent to users.

Musically Oriented Primitives

I will discuss all the primitives in this category that were thoroughly designed, even though only the first three have been written. The first of these sends data (in a file, not a buffer) to a DAC. As parameters, it expects the name of an open file, an event structure, and (optionally) another event structure. Times in these structures (and generally in the program) are represented as hundredths of a second. The first event in the call tells what portion of the file to play. (Of course, an error is reported if this portion doesn't exist.) The second (optional) structure is used to record the time in the file at which a certain key was struck. This information is returned in the start-time portion of the structure and is intended to facilitate interactive *marking* of portions of sound.

The second musical primitive complements the first. Sound is recorded through an ADC and placed into a file. A file name and one event structure are expected and serve functions analogous those in the DAC primitive.

The third primitive scales data in a buffer according to either a constant or a table representing a scaling function. If a table is used, a structure must also be passed to tell the primitive which portion of the table to use on this buffer. By this means, a single scaling function can be used to scale a waveform many buffers long. Scaling is done entirely with integer arithmetic in this system. The scaling value is a 16-bit quantity interpreted as having 7 bits of fraction. In other words, each sample is scaled by a 16-bit integer multiply followed by a 7-bit right shift. A useful extension might be to allow users to decide how many fraction bits they want.

The fourth primitive "makes waves." It produces a waveform (sine, square, or sawtooth) at a normalized amplitude. The frequency of this waveform can be constant or can come from a table that represents a changing frequency. In the latter case a structure must be passed to say where we are in the table, just as for the scaling primitive. Also, an FM input may optionally be given. This will be a buffer, either produced by the wave maker already or input from a file. It is assumed that these two buffers (the FM buffer and the output buffer) are synchronized.

The fifth primitive adds one buffer to another. A similar primitive for buffer arithmetic negates all the values in a buffer. Another primitive rotates the values in a buffer by a given amount. These primitives, together with the scaling primitive, allow quite general arithmetic to be done on buffers.

A number of other primitives would be very useful but were neither carefully designed nor written by the time my work on this program ceased. One of these would plot data in a buffer on a display screen or an XY plotting device. This primitive would be best designed with an event structure as a parameter to say what portion of data to plot and with another event structure to say what portion of the screen to use. There need not be a fixed relationship between buffer length and the size of a graph. Another primitive could supplement the plotting primitive by drawing axes and perhaps by setting up scaling constants.

A large number of primitives could be designed to implement various algorithms found in the signal-processing literature. Some of these could be specialized—for example, decimation and interpolation filters for changing the underlying sampling rate without distortion. This would be essentially equivalent to changing tape speed (Crochiere and Rabiner 1975), equalization filtering, low-pass filtering, and so on. Some would be useful for signal analysis: linear predictive analysis (Makhoul 1975), discrete Fourier transform, Hilbert transform, and so on. Some could perform general types of filtering: second-order recursive and nth-order transversal filtering, for example. Still other interesting algorithms suggested for sound synthesis and processing could be included in this program by implementing them as primitives.

Implementation of all these ideas would result (after a lot of work) in a program of very general utility. (Never mind that all these subroutines would be unlikely to fit in the address space of a PDP-11!)

More Implementation Notes

I have already said that the lowest level of the language is implemented interpretively. This choice has the advantage that interactive usage of the language can be supported most conveniently. User-defined activities (macros) are defined using a separate program (an editor) that stores them in a library. During program execution, only the names of macros and their disk locations are stored in core, and this only for macros in libraries named when the program is initiated. When one of these activities is called on (by virtue of being named on a line), the program interprets it by the simple expedient of taking its input from the disk, starting at the stored location, and continuing until the end-of-macro symbol. Thus, the language used to define macros is essentially the same as that used interactively, except that certain symbols that are illegal in keyboard input are legal in macros, namely the **goto** symbol, label definitions, parameter references, and the end-of-macro symbol.

The calling-level stack is organized to allow invocation of macros from other macros (including recursive invocations) and deletion of all symbols defined in a macro. This last capability, along with the convention that the most recently defined instance of a particular variable name is used in any reference, allows one to effectively declare *local* variables in a macro and cause them to go away at the end of it.

Since primitives are compiled into the program, it is clear that they will execute much faster than macros. It is for this reason that primitives are the method of choice for "number crunching." Macros can then be relegated to the less time-consuming but more subtle function of controlling the flow of activity. Adding new primitives is not at all difficult; it merely involves programming them in a high-level language (C in this case) and adding their names to two internal tables. Thus, the program is relatively adaptable to unforeseen uses.

Extensions

One can make sensible decisions about how to extend a program only after having thought carefully about what one wants to do with it and what the limitations are in the current environment. One of the constraints that I found most severe in designing this program was the set of limitations inherent in a 16-bit world. Either 32-bit arithmetic or (better still) a floating-point representation of numbers would be most useful. Such changes are not as simple as adding new primitives, however; one must keep additional type information in the symbol table and access it regularly to find out what sort of arithmetic instructions to do, how much space a variable needs on the stack, and so on.

Another sort of extension that would seem natural if a program like this were to be used heavily would be the implementation of better control constructs (such as **while** and **if-then-else**). Although the current implementation is sufficient to generate any desired control sequence (in macros), it can hardly be described as convenient.

Conclusions

In closing, I'd like to comment briefly on the way I envision this program/ language being used. The examples below should make it even clearer that INV will be most accessible and immediately useful to persons who have some sophistication in computer-programming concepts. I feel that this could only have been avoided by making a different sort of program— one that, in a sense, "knows what you want to do" and can therefore allow you to express what you want to do in a simple, convenient manner. That approach is great until you want to do something a little different, at which point it falls apart.

For example, I was initially motivated to design INV by a desire to produce a particular piece of music, and I had in mind a set of processing techniques by which I would manipulate taped sounds, emphasizing their internal structures and interrelationships and imposing new, higher-level structures. INV does not actually make it extremely convenient to produce my piece, but it does allow me to define a set of macros that will.

If INV is viewed as a tool for musicians, its power is not in what it can do directly but in the variety of specialized versions of it that can be created with libraries of macros. This power derives from the fact that INV can be thought of not only as a program but as a language. I suggest that this orientation will be important as we move on to create more and more sophisticated software for computer music.

Appendix

The first part of this appendix supplies such details as the names of primitives and their expected parameters, conventions for definitions of labels, and so on. The second part provides examples of typical interactive usage and definition of simple macros.

Labels are two characters long, and are preceded by a colon at the beginning of a line with no intervening spaces. Lines that start with colon followed by space are ignored and can therefore be used for comments. Label definitions during keyboard input are illegal.

Any sequence of input characters that is surrounded by quotes is interpreted as a single string, as is any sequence of alphanumeric characters (starting with an alphabetic one) that is not a known name. A parameter name is given by % followed by a digit which represents the position of the parameter in the parameter list. The end-of-macro symbol is a semicolon.

The convention for accessing elements of structures is "⟨name of structure⟩ ⟨element⟩," where the element part can be either a predefined symbol (such as *stime* or *dur* for the event structure) or a constant. Certain structure types also have predefined names which can be used in the parameter list for the structure-definition primitive.

In the definitions, words enclosed in angular brackets mean *types of things*. For example, ⟨value⟩ in a parameter list can be the result of an expression, a parameter passed from higher up, or the value of a structure element. An asterisk appended to one of these *types of things* means a list of zero or more of them. Parentheses around something indicate that it is optional. I define below just those primitives needed by my examples.

v ⟨string⟩*
   Variable: Each string is defined as a simple variable.

stru ⟨value⟩ ⟨string⟩*
   Structure: Each string is defined as a structure ⟨value⟩ bytes long.

k (⟨value⟩)

Set and print the sampling rate (or just print if ⟨value⟩ is omitted).

m ⟨string⟩ ⟨value⟩

Make: Make a file called ⟨string⟩ of length ⟨value⟩/100 seconds (at the current sampling rate). The file name is interpreted later as a structure.

i ⟨value⟩ ⟨event struc⟩

Input: Record data from ADC. The ⟨value⟩ must be a file name's "fptr." The event structure says where to put the waveform in the file.

l ⟨value⟩ ⟨event struct⟩ (⟨event struct⟩)

Listen: Play a waveform on the DAC. The ⟨value⟩ is like ⟨value⟩ for input. The second event structure is for marking.

da Deletes all data objects declared at this level. At keyboard level, this deletes everything except predefined symbols.

b ⟨strings⟩ ⟨value⟩

Buffer: Declare a buffer. The parameters are like those for file creation.

g ⟨filename⟩ ⟨buffername⟩ ⟨event struct⟩ (⟨value⟩)

Get: Move data from file to buffer. The event structure tells what portion of the file to move, and the ⟨value⟩ is for a nonzero starting time in the buffer.

p ⟨filename⟩ ⟨buffername⟩ ⟨event struct⟩ (⟨value⟩)

Puts: Move data from buffer to file. Parameters are like those for "get."

Examples

The first two examples deal with interactive usage. In the first, we record data into a file we have created and listen to it.

```
k  20000            // set sampling rate
stru event input    // declare event structure
input. stime = 0
input. dur = 1500   // 15 seconds long
m  file input.dur   // "file" is also 15 seconds long
i  file.fptr input  // record. Program waits until you
                    // hit return again.
l  file.fptr input  // listen to it
```

In the second example, we mark a portion of the file, using an event structure to remember it.

```
stru event seg                    // declare another event
l   file.fptr input seg           // hit rubout key as the end of the
                                  // segment sounds
seg. dur = seg.stime              // save result
l   file.fptr input seg           // hit rubout keys as the start of the
                                  // segment sounds
seg.dur = seg.dur − seg.stime     // adjust duration
l   file.fptr seg                 // listen just to the segment
```

The next example defines two macros, the first of which calls on the second. Parameters are numbered 1, 2, 3, 4 and referred to as % 1, % 2, and so on.

rpt ⟨value⟩ ⟨file name⟩ ⟨string⟩ ⟨event struct⟩

Make a file named ⟨string⟩ long enough to hold ⟨value⟩ repetitions of the portion of ⟨filename⟩ described by ⟨event struct⟩ and copy the repetitions into the file. The variable "ofile" defined internally will serve as descriptor of the new file but the name of the passed string will work in the calling environment.

```
v ofile ifile ptime ctr           // declare variables
ofile = m %3 %1 * %4.dur          // make data file and assign result
                                  // to ofile.
ifile = %2                        // input descriptor gets a nice name
ctr = %1                          // initialize counter
ptime = 0                         // and offset time time in output
                                  // file.
:g1                               // beginning of loop
if ctr = = 0                      // done?
goto g2                           // yes
copy ifile ofile %4 ptime         // call copy macro
ptime = ptime + %4 dur            // update offest in output file
ctr = ctr − 1                     // and counter
goto g1                           // loop
:g2
da                                // detete all variables declared here
```

copy < filename 1 > < filename 2 > < event struct > < value >
copy the segment described by < event struct > of
< filename 1 > into < filename 2 > starting at time
< value > in the output file.

```
v cbuf cpytm                      // declare variables
cbuf = b cpybuf 10                // make a buffer 10 csec long
stru event cpyev                  // make an event structure
```

```
cpyev.stime = %4              // to describe output file
cpytm = %3.dur                // total duration
%3. dur = cpyev. dur = 10     // copy a buffer's worth at a
                              //   time

:g1
if cpytm < 10                 // almost done?
goto g2                       // yes
g %1 cbuf %3                  // get data into buffer
p %2 cbuf cpyev               // put it into output file
%3.stime = %3.stime + 10      // update input start time
cpyev.stime = cpyev.stime + 10 // and output start time
cpytm = cpytm - 10            // decrement time remaining
                              // to copy

goto g1                       // loop
:g2
if cpytm = = 0                // all done?
goto g3                       // yes
%3.dur = cpyev.dur = cpytm    // copy only time remaining
g %1 cbuf %3                  // get data
p %2 cbuf cpyev               // and put it away
:g3
da                            // delete all variables
;
```

References

Crochiere, R., and L. Rabiner. 1975. "Optimum FIR digital filter implementations for decimation, interpolation, and narrow-band filtering." *IEEE Transactions on Signal Processing* ASSP-23(5):444–456.

Johnson, S. 1974. YACC—Yet Another Compiler-Compiler. Murray Hill, N.J.: Bell Laboratories.

Makhoul, J. 1975. "Linear prediction—A tutorial review." *Proceedings of the IEEE* 63:561–580.

Moorer, J. 1977. "Signal processing aspects of computer music—A survey." *Proceedings of the IEEE* 65(8):1108–1137

Ritchie, D., and K. Thompson. 1974. "The UNIX time-sharing system." *Communications of the ACM* 17(7):365–375.

28 An Introduction to the PLAY Program

JOEL CHADABE AND ROGER MEYERS

PLAY was first written during the spring and summer of 1977 at the Electronic Music Studio at the State University of New York at Albany. It grew out of our knowledge of several programs and systems, particularly GROOVE and the Conductor program from Bell Laboratories (Mathews and Moore 1970; Mathews 1976), Donald Buchla's Series 500 Electric Music Box (available from Buchla and Associates, Berkeley, California), and Salvatore Martirano's Sal-Mar Construction (personal communication, 1977). Our intention in PLAY was to maximize a composer's flexibility in conceptualizing temporal processes. Consequently, although traditional musical problems may be easily solved with PLAY, the input formats of the program are not rooted in traditional concepts or notation. Further, because we felt that small, interactive systems offer important advantages to composers, we designed the program to be used with a small, portable computer controlling an external synthesizer (analog or digital, video or audio) in real time and with extensive interaction capability. The principles on which the system is based are described in Chadabe 1977.

As a specific example to convey the general principles of organization and operating processes of the program, we will describe PLAY1, a version of the program optimized for the PDP-11 computer at the Albany studio.

PLAY1 can be described as functioning in two stages: a design stage, where the composer designs a specific compositional process, using any of the modules available in the program, and an operation stage, where the composer's process plays back and the composer interacts with the playback according to the design.

The Design Stage

The design stage has three steps. First, the composer specifies *data generators*. A data generator can be a precise list of numbers determined by the composer or a random number generator, or data can be performed in real time. The data can be used to determine attributes of sound, such

This is a revised and updated version of an article that originally appeared in *Computer Music Journal* 2(1): 12–18, 1978.

as pitch, rhythm, envelope shape, and loudness; it can be used to control variables determined by the technical characteristics of the synthesizer; or it can be used to control variables internal to the organization of PLAY. The outputs from the data generators are simply numbers, and those numbers can be used, in digital form or converted to analog voltages, to control any variable in any synthesizer in any medium that deals with changes in time.

In the second step, the data generators are organized as modules which are interconnected with each other. One module may trigger changes in another, or one module may turn another module on or off, or the output rate of one module may be controlled by another module, or data may be added together, or subtracted, multiplied, or divided.

Third, the composer sets the rate of the system clock and the timing for each individual module. Although there is no absolute high or low limit, and extremely slow or fast rates are easily possible, a typical operating frequency for the system clock might be in the range of 20 Hz to 2 kHz. Every module is timed by a division of the system-clock frequency. For example, if the system-clock frequency is 2 kHz and if a module is timed by a divide-by-2 of that frequency, then the module will proceed at a rate of 1 kHz. The divider for each module is called the *clock period*, and the clock period for each module may be different. One module might divide by 2, another by 50, another by 100, and so on. A typical timing scheme would be a hierarchy of clocks within which each module divides the system clock into different periods. Since one module may use another module as a clock instead of the system clock, making the synchronization of one event with another conceptually easier, the timing hierarchy can become quite complex.

The Operation Stage

In the operation stage, the program plays back as it was designed to and the composer controls in real time whatever variables were designed to be controlled. An important feature of the program is that any of the specifications of data or module interconnections may be changed while the program is playing back. This allows for real-time adjustment, or "tuning," as well as for significant changes in module interconnections, without discontinuity in the playback.

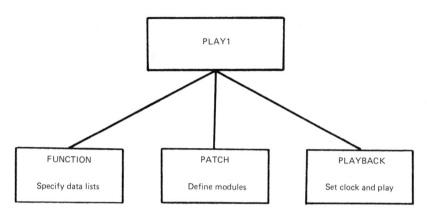

Figure 28.1
The subprograms of PLAY.

The Subprograms

PLAY1 is made up of three different subprograms: FUNCTION, PATCH, AND PLAYBACK (see figure 28.1). Each of these programs accomplishes certain specialized tasks in the design and operation stages. In FUNCTION, data lists are specified. In PATCH, modules are defined, their interactions with other modules are determined, rates are set, and transformation processes are specified. In PLAYBACK, the system-clock frequency is set and the program plays.

The three subprograms may be accessed in any order, and any of the subprograms may be called while the program is producing output. Changes may be made by recalling FUNCTION or PATCH. This is done without disturbing the playback, and the changes will be incorporated into the playback at the instant that PLAYBACK is recalled.

Operating Procedures

PLAY1 begins by asking which of its three subprograms will be used first. The composer answers by typing either PA, FU, or PL (PATCH, FUNCTION, or PLAYBACK), depending upon which program is chosen. The computer then accesses the chosen subprogram and prints an asterisk to show that it is ready to receive commands in the subprogram.

The FUNCTION Subprogram: Data Input and Editing

There are several commands in FUNCTION, by means of which data can be entered, changed, deleted, listed, and saved onto or read out from cassettes. In the following examples, what the computer types is set in boldface and what the composer types is set in ordinary type.

Example 1

* I
NAME MEL 1
X, Y 1, 1850

In this example, the command I, typed by the composer in response to the asterisk, instructs the computer that the composer would like to input data. The computer asks for a name for the number list, and the composer answers by typing the four-character name MEL1. The computer then prints **X, Y**, which asks the composer to designate a position in the list and a number in that position. In this example the composer has put the number 1850 in position 1. Any number from 0 to 32,767 ($2^{15} - 1$) may be specified, and the numbers will mean different things depending upon their use. In this case, if the number 1850 were converted to an analog voltage in a digital-to-analog converter, it would (in the Albany studio) be converted to approximately -1 volt.

There is a feature in the FUNCTION subprogram that aids in specifying line segments by automatically interpolating between different numbers. For example, if the number 3000 were in position 1 and the number 4,000 in position 6, the computer would calculate a difference of 1,000 in five steps and increment the numbers in each successive position 2 through 5 by 200. The input as starting values and endpoints and its interpretation by the program might be clearly shown as follows:

Input, typed by composer	Interpretation
1,3000	1,3000
6,4000	2,3200
	3,3400
	4,3600
	5,3800
	6,4000

However, if positions 1 through 5 were intended to contain the same numbers, and if there were to be a sudden change from 3000 in position

5 to 4000 in position 6, it would be necessary to specify only the number 3000 in position 5; the program would fill in the positions 2 through 4 as follows:

Input, typed by composer	Interpretation
1,3000	1,3000
5,3000	2,3000
6,4000	3,3000
	4,3000
	5,3000
	6,4000

There may be any number of positions in a list and as many lists as desired, subject only to limitations in the computer's memory size. Since PLAY1, as described here, is intended for use on computers with small memories, we have chosen to use memory for data storage rather than convenient and flexible input procedures. Consequently, in this version of the program, number typing is the only means for specifying data. Graphic and keyboard inputs, and other input procedures, exist in other versions of PLAY.

Example 2   This example illustrates editing procedures:

* L	list a function
NAME FUN1	list FUN1
FUN1	
1,1800	
4,3000	
5,2800	
9.5000	
12,1800	
* C	change (edit) the list
NAME FUN1	
I, D OR C D	insert, delete, or change?
X, Y 4,3000	delete
	position (x) and value (y)?
X, Y E	end
I, D OR C I	insert
X, Y 6,2700	
X, Y E	end
I, D OR C C	change
X, Y 9,4000	
X, Y 12,1832	
X, Y E	end
I, D OR C [CR]	done

```
* L                            list again
NAME FUN1
FUN1
     1,1800
     5,2800
     6,2700
     9,4000
    12,1832
* M                            exit from FUNCTION
PAT, FUN OR PLA                back to top level.
```

Module Formats in PATCH

It is probable that the composer would next call PATCH so that the data lists specified in FUNCTION could be integrated into modules. The PLAY program contains three types of modules, all of which are defined and interconnected in PATCH. There are *data-generating* modules, *timing* modules, and *output* modules.

Data lists specified in FUNCTION would be integrated into data-generating modules in accordance with the following constraints. A list can be on or off, i.e., it can be generating numbers or not. If a list is turned off and then on again, there are two possibilities: It can continue from where it was stopped, or it can reset to the first position in the list and start again at the beginning. A list can output from successive positions, or it can skip positions. Every time a number is output from a list, a trigger is also output, so that one module may be the clock for another. A module may also be timed by the system clock. We arrived at the following format for dealing with these variables:

MOD NUM1 NUM2 (NAME, CL_IN, ON/OFF, CYC/RST,
CL_PER, STEP_CT)

The module is labeled as MOD followed by two numbers. The NAME of the data list follows within parentheses, and this is followed by control assignments for the variables. CL_IN is the clock input (SYS or another module). ON/OFF is the state of the module (which can be changed by other modules). CYC/RST can be set to cycle automatically or reset. CL_PER is the clock period (this is the number of clock periods equalling a trigger). STEP_CT is the step count, which determines the number of positions the module will advance through the list at each trigger.

There are two other type of data-generating modules: *random-number generators* and *ADCs* (modules that convert analog voltages to numbers).

Their formats are, respectively,

MOD NUM1 NUM2 (RND, CL—IN, ON/OFF, CYC,
CL—PER, LO—LIM, HI—LIM)

and

MOD NUM1 NUM2 (AD NUM, CL—IN, ON/OFF, CYC,
CL—PER, STEP—CT)

Controls for the random-number generator are specified as in the other modules, except that the name of the list is always RND and the CYC/RST variable must always be CYC. The LO_LIM and HI_LIM (for low limit and high limit) set the range within which the random number will occur, and they can be fixed numbers or the names of other modules whose numerical outputs will determine the limits. In the analog-to-digital conversion modules, AD and a number are written to specify the channel of the analog-to-digital converter to which the analog voltage is applied. The controls are specified as in the other modules, except that CYC must always be specified and the step count must always be 1.

Timing modules are specified as are the timing sections of other modules, except that they begin with DIV and two numbers. The format is

DIV NUM1 NUM2(CL—IN, ON/OFF, CL—PER).

The output modules are written as DAC followed by a number and a module name or names as inputs written within parentheses. The format is

DAC NUM1(NAME).

Examples of Module Interconnections

The following examples introduce the notation used in PATCH and a variety of the elementary operations of the program. As a general rule, modules are written on the page so that lines of influence run upward. (This is a format that we have followed for easier comprehensibility; however, the program will allow for any arrangement of modules on the page.) Thus, a DAC module that is a destination for signals from other modules appears above the modules that are input to it. Insofar as is possible, any module is written above its inputs.

Outputs from PLAY1 come from DACs and are used to control analog equipment. The analog connections that will generate and modify the sounds are easy to visualize. In general, envelope outputs would be applied, through an analog interpolator, to the control inputs of voltage-controlled filters and amplifiers, and outputs would be applied to the control inputs of voltage-controlled oscillators.

Example 3

PAT, FUN OR PLA PA
* I
DAC0 (MOD01)
MOD01(MEL1, SYS, ON, CYC, 100, 1)

In this example, the composer calls PATCH and types I in response to the asterisk. The composer then proceeds to input module definitions and other specifications. The numerical output from MOD01 appears at DAC0. MOD01 is using a number list called MEL1. Since the clock period is 100, the clock input is SYS, and the step count is 1, MOD01 will output successive numbers from MEL1 at every 100 system-clock counts. If the system-clock rate were 1,000 Hz, MOD01 would output every tenth of a second.

Example 4

DAC0(MOD01)
MOD01(MEL 1, SYS, ON, CYC, 100, 1)
DAC1(MOD02)
MOD02(MEL6, MOD01, ON, CYC, 1, 1)

This example illustrates synchronous and parallel outputs from two modules. MOD01 is exactly as in example 3. MOD02 uses a list called MEL6. Since the clock input to MOD02 is MOD01 and the clock period of MOD02 is 1, MOD02 will output at every trigger from MOD01, so that the outputs from MOD02 and MOD01 are synchronized.

Example 5

MEL1
        1,1850
        20,3000
TIM1
        1,50
        3,50
        4,25
        4,25

```
DAC0(MOD01)
MOD01(MEL1, SYS, ON, CYC, MOD02, 1)
MOD02(TIM1, MOD01, ON, CYC, 1, 1)
```

This example illustrates one module controlling the timing of another. MOD01 is outputting MEL1, a list of 20 numbers of ascending value which, when converted in the Albany studio, would be voltages from approximately − 1 volt to approximately 5 volts. MOD02 is synchronized with MOD01 as in example 4. However, here the output from MOD02 is applied to the CL PER input of MOD01. As indicated by the numbers in TIM1, the rhythm of the output from MOD01 would be three longer durations followed by two shorter durations.

Example 6

```
DAC0(MOD01)
MOD01(RND, SYS, ON, CYC, MOD02, 1800, 3000)
MOD02(RND, MOD01, ON, CYC, 1, 10, 100)
```

This example illustrates the control of one random-number generator by another. MOD01 and MOD02 are related as in example 5, except that the clock period for MOD01 is a random number between 10 and 100 generated by MOD02. MOD01 will output random voltages at random time intervals.

Example 7

```
DAC0(MOD01)
MOD01(MEL1, SYS, ON, CYC, 5, 1)
DAC1(MOD02)
MOD02(MEL1, SYS, ON, CYC, 7, 1)
```

In this example, DAC0 and DAC1 are outputting MEL1, as listed in example 5, at different speeds in a relationship of 7 against 5.

Example 8

```
DAC0(MOD01)
MOD01(MEL1, SYS, DIV01&DIV02, CYC, MOD02, 1)
DIV01(SYS, ON&DIV01, 1000)
DIV02(MOD01, ON, 19)
MOD02(RND, MOD01, DIV01, CYC, 1, 2, 20)
```

This example illustrates a method for specifying a nonrepeating event. The timing principle for programming such an event is to keep track of time from the beginning of the playback by the use of DIV modules. DIV01 counts 1,000 clock beats before triggering the event. If another event were to occur later, another DIV module would count beats from DIV01, and then another DIV module would count beats from the second DIV, and so on for additional events. In this example, MOD01 is turned on by DIV01, at which time it outputs an ascending series of 19 values, whose timing derives from MOD02, after which it is turned off by DIV02. DIV01 turns itself off after triggering MOD01.

Example 9

```
DAC0(MOD01)
MOD01(MEL1, SYS, ON, CYC, 1, MOD02)
MOD02(RND, MOD01, ON, CYC, 1, 1, 20)
```

This example illustrates random selection from an array of fixed values. MEL1, as listed in example 5, is a series of 20 ascending values. However, since the step count of MOD01 is a random number between 1 and 20, the numbers of MEL1 will be output in random order.

Example 10

```
DAC0(MOD01&MOD02)
MOD01(MEL1, SYS, ON&DIV01&DIV02, CYC, 20, 1)
DIV01(MOD01, ON, 7)
MOD02(MEL6, SYS, DIV01&DIV02, CYC, 20, 1)
DIV02(MOD02, ON, 7)
```

This example shows an alternation between segments of two different lists. Notice that there are two inputs to DAC0 and to the ON/OFF control of MOD02, and three inputs to the ON/OFF control of MOD01. Any variable may have up to seven controls specified for it. The controls may be related by addition, subtraction, multiplication, division, or replacement (designated by &). MOD01 is turned off by DIV01 at the same instant that MOD02 is turned on. MOD02 is turned off by DIV02, and MOD01 is turned on. Any number of lists may be used in this fashion, and the length of each segment may be varied by changing the clock periods of the timing modules.

Example 11

```
ENV1
    1,1800
    4,3000
```

```
      7,2800
     12,2500
     19,1800
     20,1800
```

DIV01(SYS, ON, MOD01)
MOD01(RND, DIV01, ON, CYC, 20, 1, 7)
DAC0(MOD02)
MOD02(ENV1, DIV01, ON, CYC, 1, 1)
DAC1(MOD03)
MOD03(RND, DIV01, ON, CYC, 20, 1800, 3000)

This example illustrates an envelope synchronized with a melody. There are three groups of modules: a timebase, an envelope generator, and a random tune. The timebase, DIV01, divides the system-clock frequency into periods whose length is determined by MOD01. The system-clock frequency might be, in this example, 1 kHz. The duration of time between trigger outputs from DIV01 is changed only every 20 triggers, so that each complete envelope will be made up of segments of uniform duration. DAC0 outputs MOD02, which is the envelope shape described in the list ENV1. MOD03 is the melody. The timebase is common to the envelope and to the melody. The envelope outputs a new step at every trigger from the timebase, and the melody outputs a new step at every 20 triggers. Both melody and envelope change speed together as the rate of the triggers from the timebase changes. As the melody notes become longer, so do their envelopes.

Example 12

```
MEL5
      1,1
     20,40
     40,1
MEL6
      1,1800
     20,2200
     40,1800
```

DIV01(SYS, ON, MOD01)
MOD01(RND, MOD03, ON, CYC, 20, 1, 7)
DAC0(MOD02)
MOD02(ENV1, DIV01, ON, CYC, 1, 1)
DAC1(MOD03*MOD04 + MOD05)
MOD03(MEL5, DIV01, ON, CYC, 20, 1)
MOD04(RND, MOD03, ON, CYC, 40, 1, 10)
MOD05(MEL6, DIV01, ON, CYC, 20, 1)

This example illustrates the generation of slopes of different angles and amplitudes. Here the slopes are the basis of the melody, but the technique could as easily be applied to envelopes. The timebase and the envelope generator are as in example 11. The melody, output from DAC1, is a staircase up and down, but the timing and the height of each slope vary. The height varies because the basic triangular shape listed in MEL6 is added synchronously to MEL5, which is a triangular shape that changes amplitude. The changes in amplitude occur because every complete cycle of MOD03 is multiplied by a different random number between 1 and 10, generated by MOD04. Thus, every complete cycle of 40 steps up and down will have a different amplitude, and, since each half-cycle of 20 steps up or down will have a different timing, each slope (whether up or down) will have a different angle.

Example 13

```
DIV01(SYS, ON, MOD01)
MOD01(RND, DIV01, ON, CYC, 20, 1, 7)
DAC0(MOD02)
MOD02(ENV1, DIV01, ON, CYC, 1, 1)
DAC1(MOD05/50*MOD04 + MOD03)
MOD03(RND, DIV01, ON, CYC, 20, 2000, 2100)
MOD04(MEL5, DIV01, ON, CYC, 20, 1)
MOD05(AD0, DIV01, ON, CYC, 20, 1)
```

In this example the timebase and the envelope generator are as in example 11, but the pitch range over which the melody varies is controlled by an analog voltage such as might be generated by a joystick. The basic melody is output from MOD03, to which is added the numbers from MOD04 multiplied by the numbers derived from the analog-to-digital converter divided by 50. The ADC numbers must be divided by 50 to adjust their variance to a usable range; the ADC accepts a range of voltages between −2.5 and 2.5 volts and converts that to a range of numbers between 0 and 1,000, but since a range of numbers between 1 and 20 is needed the numbers between 100 and 1,000 must be divided by 50. (These numbers apply to the ADC in the Albany studio. Different specific numbers might apply in other studios.)

Setting the System Clock

After defining the system in PATCH, the composer would normally call the PLAYBACK subprogram. The system-clock rate is set by the composer when the PLAYBACK subprogram is called. It is expressed as a basic clock frequency of 100 Hz, 1 kHz, 10 kHz, or 1 MHz, divided by any number between 1 and 255. As an additional option, an external oscillator may be used as the system clock, in which case the composer may "perform" the system-clock rate by frequency-modulating that oscillator with, for example, a joystick.

Operation and Changes

After the system-clock frequency has been set, the program begins to operate. (We are using the word operate as a synonym for *playback* or *output*.) Example 13 can serve as an example of user interaction in two dimensions: the speed with which the system plays back (if the composer is using an external oscillator as the clock) and the range of pitches over which the melody varies. User interaction may be far more complex, or it may be more direct. The pitches themselves might be controlled from a keyboard, or specific music might be played back which a composer would "conduct" (as in Mathews's Conductor program) in terms of tempo, phrasing, or intonation (Mathews 1976).

As integral parts of PLAY, either FUNCTION or PATCH may be recalled while the program is operating. When the program begins to play back, after the system-clock rate has been set, the computer types **PAT, FUN OR PLA** as it does at the beginning, and the composer may recall PATCH or FUNCTION to introduce changes. If a detail in a particular list must be changed, for example, the composer types FUN, then C in response to the asterisk, and proceeds to make the necessary changes. When the changes are complete, the composer exits from FUNCTION by typing M and then types PLA in response to **PAT, FUN OR PLA**. At the instant PLAYBACK begins, the changes are incorporated into the playback. The playback is not interrupted while changes are made; this feature of PLAY is extremely valuable in performance.

Distinguishing Features

The two most important distinguishing features of PLAY are its great flexibility (i.e., its potential for use in a great variety of fundamentally different compositional situations) and its efficiency at different levels of complexity.

The description of PLAY as functioning in the two distinct stages of design and operation emphasizes the idea that PLAY gives composers the opportunity to perform in real time a compositional process of their own design. Because PLAY allows for the precise specification and storage of detailed data in the FUNCTION subprogram, and because there are random-number generators that generate data and analog-to-digital conversion modules that take in performed data, the PLAY program allows diversity in approaches to composition. A composer may work anywhere within a landscape bounded by the precise specification of every compositional parameter on the one hand and the automatic generation of compositional data on the other hand, with any degree of real-time interaction anywhere in the landscape. Further, the modularity of the structure of the program, the many possibilities for real-time transformation processes, and the flexibility with which the outputs from performance generators may be used make PLAY powerful with small computers. Of particular interest for real-time performance is the feature allowing for precisely specified data as well as the organization of the system itself to be changed while the system is operating.

Another aspect of the flexibility of PLAY is that there is no practical limit to the complexity with which the program can operate in real-time. Real-time operation may be defined as the ability of the computer to perform all the operations necessary to determine what its next output should be before the output occurs. Real-time control-signal generation, for which PLAY is intended, occurs typically in a range from 20 Hz to 2 kHz, a range within which PLAY normally operates.

The essential point is that it is the composer who sets the system-clock frequency. This allows the composer to find the fastest or the otherwise optimal rate for any level of complexity.

PLAY2

PLAY1, the first and simplest version of the PLAY program, is written in PDP-11 assembly language. PLAY2, written in XPL, exists in two versions: PLAY2A (intended for the control of analog equipment) and PLAY2D (intended for the control of the New England Digital Corporation digital synthesizer, the Synclavier I).

PLAY2 is in some ways easier to operate than PLAY1. There is a slightly different program structure, and the additional modules add considerable power. The FUNCTION subprogram from PLAY1 is replaced in PLAY2 with the DATA subprogram, which does not interpolate automatically between endpoints. That interpolation function is accomplished by a special interpolator subroutine module, which, since it can be used in interaction with the variables of any other module, has a wider, more general application than does interpolation in PLAY1. There is a comparator module, which generates a trigger if a "more than," "less than," or "equal to" condition is met. There is a clear format for the user to write subroutines in XPL, incorporate them into modules, and integrate them with the rest of the system. The subroutine feature is particularly important because it allows the user to devise modules.

In PLAY2A, a graphic input enables the user to specify data by using a joystick to draw an envelope or some other shape on the terminal screen. In PLAY2D, outputs to the digital synthesizer's waveform buffers allow the user to determine waveforms by specifying the individual amplitudes of their harmonics; thus, a data list intended to represent a waveform would be written such that the numbers would represent the relative amplitudes of each harmonic on a scale from 0 to 100. There are also outputs from PLAY2D to digital oscillators, allowing the user to specify frequency (in hertz), volume on a scale from 0 to 255, endpoints for amplitude envelopes, rise and fall rates for amplitudes envelopes (in milliseconds), endpoints for index of modulation envelopes, rise and fall rates for index of modulation envelopes, a range control for the index of modulation, and waveform. Keyboard-oriented input greatly enhances the program's potential for use in traditional performance situations.

Performance Experience

Working with the program during the past several years has led us to think that the main advantages of the PLAY program are that algorithms are clearly conceptualized in all but the most complex situations and that the program allows musicians to think in terms of musical processes happening simultaneously (rather than, as with traditional computer languages, one after the other). When used with analog equipment, PLAY is a powerful composing language. With digital equipment such as the Synclavier, which needs more control data than an analog system), PLAY is a useful sketchpad; it gives immediate access to the digital variables, but its internal modular communications are too time-consuming to achieve more than medium complexity. Several composers have used the PLAY program in its digital version. Warren Burt produced several compositions of considerable complexity very quickly and then exclaimed "I love to play with PLAY." We feel that the greatest problem with the PLAY program is that the input language is too complicated and slow, and we anticipate improvements in that area.

Closing Comment

We have intended this software for general use by composers, and it is our hope that PLAY will go far toward eliminating the software obstacles that many musicians encounter when working with computers (especially small computers for which software is not typically available).

The PLAY program is available by licensing agreement. The authors may be contacted at P.O. Box 8748, Albany, NY 12208 for further information.

References

Chadabe, J. 1977. "Some reflections on the nature of the landscape within which computer music systems are designed." *Computer Music Journal* 1(3): 5–11.

Mathews, M. 1976. "The conductor program." Presented at the 1976 International Conference on Computer Music, Massachusetts Institute of Technology.

Mathews, M. V., and F. R. Moore. 1970. "GROOVE—A program to compose, store, and edit functions of time." *Communications of the Association for Computing Machinery* 13(12):715–721.

29 Software for a Microcomputer-Controlled Synthesizer for Live Performance

MARTIN BARTLETT

In my experience with electronic music, the studio environment has always presented a major problem. Music is a social phenomenon; the musical act reaches fruition in performance. To work in the studio producing works that have their existence only as recordings seems artificial to me. Yet the cost and technical sophistication of electronic music facilities, particularly where computation is involved, seems to imply that "Mohammed comes to the mountain," and this approach has been further emphasized by the development of general-purpose computer music systems which are as far as possible without personality of their own and can supposedly serve the needs of a variety of composers. Furthermore, even in institutions that can afford such facilities it may be impossible to have a system dedicated totally to musical tasks.

Now I have nothing against the existence of sophisticated centralized facilities, and I have been delighted with the rare opportunities I have had to work with them. However, I believe that if the potential of computer music is to be realized, these facilities should be complemented by small personalized systems that can be used in live performance. My own approach to the implementation of such a system is the concern of this article.

The Black Box

In 1969 I began building a personal analog synthesis system. This was the Black Box. It has gone through many metamorphoses in its working life; it is still in use. Only recently, however, has it seemed feasible to extend the controlling means of this instrument with a microcomputer.

The Black Box is a collection of fairly conventional analog synthesizer modules. Many of the circuits were designed by William Hearn, with whom I collaborated from 1969 to 1972, though I am responsible for the overall configuration of modules, the construction, and various designed or undesigned "quirks." The basic premise was a low-cost live-performance voltage-controlled synthesizer capable of complex timbral textures and spatial location in four channels (see also Oppenheim 1978.) A large

This is a revised version of an article that originally appeared in *Computer Music Journal* 3(1): 25–29, 1979.

number of modules were built. The instrument has ten voltage-controlled oscillators, four voltage-controlled filters (two of them doubling as quadrature oscillators), eight envelope generators, twenty voltage-controlled amplifiers in a four-channel distribution matrix configuration, and two four-channel sequencers, in addition to noise generators, envelope followers, multipliers, and phase-locked loops. Absolute linearity and predictability of operation was in some cases sacrificed to module density, giving this instrument its own personality and sound and condemning me to eternal bondage to the soldering iron. There is no keyboard; the only tactile input is through potentiometers and switches. The performance philosophy is to realize by means of small adjustments the acoustic potential of a given patch in the way that an Indian musician might exploit the pitch and duration associations of a particular *raga* or *tala*. The instrument is in a continuous state of change, with modules retired and new ones constructed as my musical ideas and performance aims change.

Because of the absence of tactile input, the generation of complex event sequences has always been a problem. On occasion it has been attained through combinations of patching and parameter setting that have seemed almost beyond my control. The computer offered the possibility of transcending this problem, though the actual implementation of a practical system seemed even more daunting. In particular, many of the available low-cost microcomputer systems seemed to require the addition of memory boards, interfaces, terminals, and so on.

I decided at the time of the International Computer Music Conference at La Jolla in 1977 to start with a minimal system and allow expansion to be governed by experience. This approach led me to choose the MOS Technology KIM-1 computer. My choice was influenced by the work of several composers associated with the Contemporary Music Center at Mills College, particularly James Horton, Paul DeMarinis, David Behrman, and Rich Gold, all of whom have managed to make interesting and individual use of this microcomputer system (Bischoff, Gold, and Horton 1978).

Beginning in October 1977, and working largely unaided except by what I could glean from the literature, I set about implementing the KIM-1 as a control-voltage processor. Though I had no programming experience, after about two months I understood the essentials of writing and debugging 6502 machine code.

Interface

The next step was the construction of a digital-to-analog converter (DAC) and an analog-to-digital converter (ADC). I started with a very simple single-channel DAC designed by Chamberlin (1977). With this interface working, I began to write control programs based on stochastic algorithms, primarily for oscillator control and the generation of timing functions. Since it was obviously important to have as many output channels as possible, and also to have the capability of analog input to the computer, I looked for a suitable design for a multichannel interface. In January 1978 I built an eight-channel multiplexed DAC and ADC to the design of Kraul (1977). This interface uses a single inexpensive DAC for both ADC and DAC modes, with 8-bit resolution and a maximum bandwidth of approximately 100 Hz per channel, which, though modest in comparison with more elaborate installations, compares favorably with the sequencers available with most analog synthesizers.

The KIM-1 seems to me an elegant and versatile little machine. In addition to the 6502 CPU, the system includes two 6530 arrays providing 2 Kbytes of ROM for the system monitor, a hexadecimal keyboard, a TTY interface, an LED display, a cassette interface, and a programmable timer. In addition, the board accommodates 1 Kbytes of RAM, to which, until recently, all my programs have been restricted.

As well as the 1 Kbyte of onboard RAM, each 6530 contains an additional 64 bytes of RAM, and it is in this memory space that the program resides to refresh the DAC sample-and-holds and enable the ADC or DAC modes of the interface, which it does on an interrupt basis, deriving timings from the programmable timer. Some trial-and-error experimentation was needed to establish the optimal timing for this interrupt, especially since the programmable timer is used also as a system clock for timing output voltages. A system refresh and timing pulse of 200 Hz was ultimately decided upon, although part of the control program provides for altering this frequency as a function of an analog input.

Programming

The programs written for the system so far are for the generation of control voltages (mainly for oscillators) and trigger pulses to fire the synthesizer's envelope generators. Since the timing pulses are generally made to coincide with the generation of a new output voltage (the combination is called a *note* in musical terminology), I found it convenient to link these functions so that four of the DAC channels output voltages and the other four output the trigger pulses. This gives, therefore, four independent control channels.

The timing process must allow independent timings for each channel. The algorithm to accomplish this (NEWOUT) is diagrammed in figure 29.1. Decrementing the channel timing counters is done as part of the same interrupt routine that updates the DACs, so one's control over the output timing can be implemented in two ways: by programming the 6530 interval timer as part of the program or from an ADC input, or by choice of numbers loaded into the duration tables.

Frequency and Duration Tables

Analog output levels ("frequencies") and durations are chosen from tables. Parameters may be read from these tables sequentially, randomly, or by means of a number of "random walk" algorithms. Each output may choose data from its own separate table, or one table may be shared by two or more outputs. It is also provided that the choice of the table in use by a given output may be a function of an input voltage from one of the ADC channels.

Analog output levels are specified by numbers between 00 and FF(Hex). The DAC is adjusted so that 30(Hex) = 1 volt = 1 octave on the exponential-input oscillators. This gives frequency control of 48 bits per octave, or 1 bit = $\frac{1}{4}$ semitone, for a full range of a little over 5 octaves. This can hardly be called a high degree of resolution, but has proved adequate so far, especially since the oscillators are not models of precision themselves.

As already outlined, the duration tables contain hexadecimal values which effectively act as dividers of the programmable timer frequency. The most usual means of accessing the duration data so far has been by random choice of values from the table. Probability distributions are governed by the table length and weighted by duplication of data values in the table; a typical situation might be a table of 32 data elements containing only four different values, distributed, say 1, 3, 8, and 20.

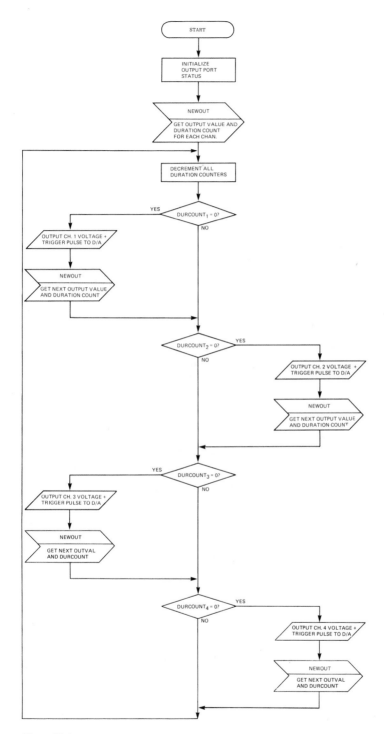

Figure 29.1
The timing algorithm NEWOUT.

Random Walks

One of the first "automatic melody" algorithms written for this system was the random walk diagrammed in figure 29.2. Each time the duration counter for a given channel reaches 0, a subroutine (NEWOUT2) is called which begins by choosing a random number between 0 and 3. If the result is 0, the new output value is the same as the previous one (a "repeated note"). If it is 1, the frequency table index pointer is incremented by 1 (the next "higher" note); if 2, it is decremented by 1 (the next "lower"); and if 3, a new pointer value is chosen randomly. Table values comprising different pitch sets, or tables arranged with irregular increments, naturally yield widely different musical results.

An article on stochastic music in *Scientific American* (Gardner 1978) interested me in the possibility of writing a random-walk program based on a $1/f$ distribution. The results are musically interesting, having that peculiar combination of volition and purposelessness that seems so characteristic of computers when they are feeling playful. This subroutine (NEWOUT3) is diagrammed in figure 29.3. A counter is incremented each time the subroutine is called. The lowest three bits of the counter value are tested, and, depending on which bits are set, one, two, or three new random numbers between 0 and 7 are stored in three memory locations. The contents of these locations are summed, and the result is the frequency table pointer value.

ADC Input

The system's eight ADC inputs are provided with voltage-divider potentiometers for manual control and jacks for control-voltage input from the synthesizer. The limited frequency response of the interface makes it impractical to use these inputs for audio-frequency signals. Nevertheless, there is potential for access to program parameters through these inputs.

As with the DACs, the inputs are adjusted so that 5 volts in gives the full-scale value of 255 (FF Hex). One of the ADC inputs is usually used to control the frequency of the programmable timer, giving overall system timing control. The range of control is adjusted so that even at the slowest setting there is no perceptible droop in the output from the sample-and-holds, while the fastest setting still allows sufficient time for interrupt

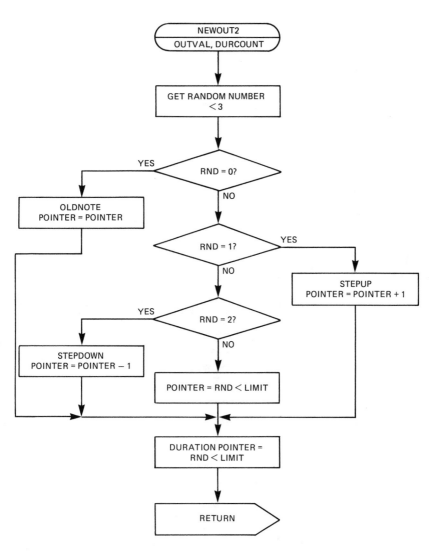

Figure 29.2
The subroutine NEWOUT2.

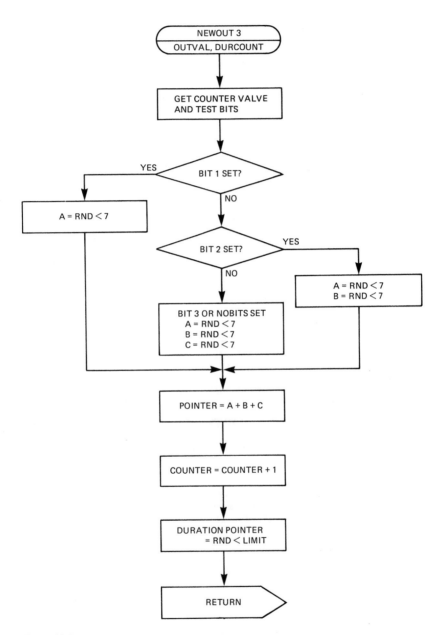

Figure 29.3
The subroutine NEWOUT3.

servicing and program execution. In this, as in other timing problems, I have used a trial-and-error approach.

At present, the ADC inputs are used in the following ways. First, they are used to determine which of a number of output-voltage selection algorithms are in use. (Should the table pointer step sequentially through the table? Should it move randomly? Should it employ one of the algorithms already described?) Second, ADC inputs are used to choose which of a number of data tables is being addressed by the pointer. These include tables containing different pitch sets ("modes"), including microtonal ones, and other tables loaded by random operations. Third, some of these ADC inputs determine choices among a number of timing possibilities: durations from a list, regular time intervals, and so on, including the option of whether or not trigger pulses will coincide with output voltage changes ("notes") or operate on a slower time scale ("phrases"). Fourth, one of the ADC inputs controls the frequency of the programmable timer that governs the data acquisition rate and also counts down the individual clocks for the output channels, giving overall system timing control. All these inputs may be addressed from either the potentiometers or the analog inputs, giving the possibility of structural variation by feedback from synthesizer control voltages. These ADC inputs make possible rapid and radical changes in control voltage structures and hence in musical output.

Musical Uses

Since February 1978 I have been using this system in live performance— solo, as part of an electronic-instrument improvisation ensemble (the Networks Orchestra), and more recently in a composed work for eight instruments and live electronics. It always functions very much as an addition to the capabilities of the analog synthesizer, at which timbral and dynamic control as well as structural decisions are exercised. As such I find it a very useful extension of the Black Box's capabilities, and considerably more versatile than an analog sequencer (see figure 29.4).

In *Air*, my composition for eight instruments and live electronics, the KIM-1 Black Box has a rather satirical role, as a "pseudo-instrument." Since the same algorithms determined many of the pitch-time decisions in the instrumental parts as are used by the computer, computer and instruments engage in a kind of mutual parody.

Figure 29.4
The microcomputer-controlled synthesis system for live performance. In the foreground
is the KIM-1; in the background is the Black Box analog synthesizer. (Photograph by
Joel Chadabe.)

Further Developments

The system has been expanded beyond its original minimal configuration by the addition of an 8K memory board with two extra output ports, sockets for four 2716 EPROMs, and an EPROM programmer. This permits assembly-language programming and an editor, which after a year of loading hexadecimal machine code on the KIM's calculator-type keypad, seems a great luxury. Other envisioned improvements are a faster data-acquisition system, and, of course, more extensive and ingenious programming.

As I get to know the capabilities of this system, I am impressed at the complexity and diversity of the music I can make with it. The countless hours of debugging hardware and software have been rewarded by the partial realization of a long-term goal: to perform a lively and intricate music full of timbral, tonal, temporal, and spatial variety, and to do so with my own resources wherever I may happen to be. The portability, personality, and minimum hardware cost of the system are persuasive advantages; its limitations are readily apparent and are accepted as part of that personality. As always, the musical results are the only real test of a system's validity.

Update (1981)

The KIM-1 has been replaced by a Rockwell AIM-65 with 32 Kbytes of RAM. This permits the use of much more ambitious software, including high-level languages. The antique Black Box has been replaced by a more compact (though still analog) synthesizer based on Curtis synthesizer modules. All control functions, including patching, are assigned by the computer.

Many composers working with microcomputers have discovered the usefulness of the Forth language. The speed and power of this language made it a natural choice for software development for the new system. The concept remains basically as described previously: An inner interrupt-driven loop controls system timings and sends data to the output devices when appropriate. It also monitors a multiplexed ADC for outside-world controls. Table loading, pointer manipulation, patching of analog modules, and assignment of different data tables to selected output parameters are all controlled by high-level Forth routines. The basic compositional bias is still toward an ever-growing library of stochastic algorithms, which may be constrained to the limits required for control of any parameter.

Since it makes its home in a surplus Hughes Aircraft equipment box boldly stenciled "Apogee Motor," the machine has been so named, and its controlling program is called APOGEE.

References

Bischoff, J., R. Gold, and J. Horton. 1978. "Music for an interactive network of microcomputers." *Computer Music Journal* 2(3): 24–29. Article 33 in this volume.

Chamberlin, H. 1977. "A sampling of techniques for the computer performance of music." *Byte* 2(9): 62–83.

Gardner, M. 1978. "Mathematical games: White and brown music, fractal curves, and one-over-*f* fluctuations." *Scientific American* 238(4): 16–31.

Kraul, D. 1977. "Designing multichannel analog interfaces." *Byte* 2(6): 18–23.

Oppenheim, D. 1978. "Microcomputer to synthesizer interface for a low-cost system." *Computer Music Journal* 2(1): 6–11.

30 Considering Human Memory in Designing User Interfaces for Computer Music

OTTO E. LASKE

In this article I discuss the parallels between computer music systems and a particular model of human memory. It would be of great methodological significance if general features that define human information processing could be used in formulating guidelines for the design of user interfaces for computer music tasks. As I try to show, interface design is ultimately concerned with establishing alternative possibilities to human memory transaction by sparing the need to remember everything at every level of composition.

Interactive composition involves a variety of tasks and a variety of kinds of knowledge. The article analyzes this environment for the purpose of establishing guidelines for memories and representations appropriate to these various kinds of compositional knowledge.

The Study of Musical Activity

Work in computer science, particularly in its subdiscipline of artificial intelligence, has over the years led to new ways of conceptualizing capabilities of the human mind. Musical activity is one of the least understood of the human capabilities. It seems to me that a link between computer science and studies in music can significantly advance our insight into the functioning of the human mind and of memory. Since the late 1950s it has become possible to explore human creative activity with empirical methods, and to describe aspects of it formally and explicitly. If this possibility is fully exploited, the time may come when it will be possible to establish a design science whose practitioners can help build optimized task environments for creative activity. The science of music could become absorbed into what Schafer (1977) has called *acoustic design*, a discipline for the design of humane sonic environments.

Data Structures, Programs, and Memory

In the philosophical tradition of Western culture, "mind" has often been defined with reference to consciousness and to conscious processing of sensory data. The nature of consciousness has remained a mystery, but

This is a revised version of an article that originally appeared in *Computer Music Journal* 2(4):39–45, 1978.

great advances have been made in understanding what is involved in the cognitive processing of sensory information. Realistic philosophies of the past were concerned mostly with the structural content of the mind, whereas idealistic approaches in philosophy dealt with the procedures that make a synthesis of data, or a perception, possible. From contemporary cognitive studies it emerges clearly that both aspects of mental activity are inextricably linked. Whatever of the human mind is observable is bound up with the functioning of memory, and memory contains both data structures and programs. It appears that the distinction between data and programs, or between structural content and operators acting on content, is a relative one. The distinction makes sense only outside of memory and is thus an expediency of representation rather than a difference in cognitive subject matter.

A Procedural View of Music

Since 1970, I have taken a *procedural* view of music, regarding it as a cognitive task domain. Music is a set of tasks people (like to) do, and theories of music that do not acknowledge the task dependency of musical knowledge are bound to exhibit a lack of common sense. There is very little in human information processing that can be generalized from one task to another. This task specificity of human cognition is in opposition to the view, taken in many artificial-intelligence studies, that there is an all-pervasive general intelligence interfaced to all the human task domains we know of. This Platonic view of human activity is a variant of rationalistic philosophies of the past, most of which were based on logic. However, the assumption of a general intelligence has a heuristic function; it is the easiest hypothesis to make when one starts to investigate human cognitive functioning.

Problem Definition and Problem Solution

Studies in artificial intelligence have most often dealt with so-called "well-defined problems." As Simon (1973) has shown, in this world there are no well-defined problems; there are only problems that have been given representations that make them appear well defined, or well structured. What it is that makes a problem well or ill structured has been specified in different ways. I consider most to the point the definition of ill-structuredness that links it to the size of the knowledge base (the set of knowledge sources) utilized in a task. However, it is not the size of the knowledge base per se that matters most. What matters are two entailments of the existence of a large knowledge base. The first is that a large knowledge base potentially gives rise to many different representations of knowledge, some of which may be available to a performance system (and, hence, to a user) simultaneously. The second is that a problem solver operating upon a large knowledge base is able to, or forced to, redefine the problem space during the performance of a task. Consequently, problem definition and problem solution may come along together. Musical composition is a case in point for both of these entailments. Original composition, by definition, implies the invention of representations for precompositional materials. It also implies that the composer works out compositional solutions in terms of these chosen representations. Most composers use visual, verbal, and auditory representations simultaneously. In working out these compositional materials, a composer often has to introduce new operators midway through a composition. This typically redefines the problem space and nullifies the original problem definition (Chadabe 1977).

Commonalities between Humans and Systems

Studies in the computer-aided composition of music are relevant both for providing tools for creative activity and for understanding such an activity. I consider it important that these two aspects of research be seen as related, and not only for pragmatic reasons. Since a user of an interactive system and the system itself are inextricably welded together, it is useful to seek commonalities that link the two subsystems. From a cognitive perspective, a commonality is provided by the concept of an information-processing system as a distributed memory system. I refer to the tradition in cognitive psychology in which the human mind is conceived as a set of distinct but procedurally interrelated buffers. The defining elements of these buffers are parameters such as the time constant of storage, the transfer rate, the access time of a buffer, or the capacity in number of symbols. Unfortunately, the notion of a memory system able to account for all of human task behavior is as problematic as the notion of a general intelligence.

Hypotheses for Musical Memory

As regards computer music systems, there is a justification for considering in parallel the different levels of functioning of an interactive music system and a human memory system. Intelligent interface design is based on understanding this parallelism. Notions concerning the structure of human musical memory are, of course, hypothetical, but they can be falsified. I refer to the possibility of falsifying a hypothesis concerning musical memory on the basis of so-called protocol data documenting the behavior of humans in some well-defined task. My own research in the past has been concerned with developing and testing hypotheses as to how musical memory functions (Laske 1977).

Real-Time Constraints

Human memory functions primarily by logging the temporal structure of occurring events and constructing successive internal representations of these events. In an interactive computer music system, the time structuring of sonic events and the alternatives available for transferring contents within human memory are significant design variables. The total set of real-time constraints in such a system might be partitioned into *audio-time*, *conscious-time*, and *interpretive-time* constraints.

Audio Time

Events in audio time change over periods of a few milliseconds. They are sonic phenomena whose rate of change is too fast to be detected by a human information processor except in terms of their total effect. The representation these phenomena are given in a computer music system and the way in which the "acoustic model" of these phenomena is made transparent to the user are crucial for design options at the superordinate levels of *conscious time* and *interpretive time*. Most of the work in computer music system design up to the present has been concerned with the level of audio time. Requirements of the subsequent temporal levels have typically been neglected until recently.

Conscious Time

On the next higher temporal level, that of conscious time, the system designer deals with sonic events lasting a fraction of a second to several seconds. Occurrence of events on this cognitive level is "conscious," in the sense that perceptual configurations exist of which a listener can be (made) aware. Perceptual configurations that inform musical experience are traditionally defined in several interdependent dimensions, such as tone height (pitch), tone loudness, tone chroma (a term sometimes used in psychoacoustics for describing intervallic content), tone duration, tone color (spectrum), and tone location (Deutsch 1975). To date, there is no convincing theory of how the different dimensions of conscious time interrelate. The notion of "timbre" is a metaphor for the enduring mystery of these interrelationships.

Interpretive Time

The third and highest cognitive level on which sonic events occur, and the most complex level of all, is that of interpretive time. A more neutral designation for this level would be *long-term time*, were it not a contradiction in itself. The illusion of lasting time is created by memory through interpretations of events on a high level of abstraction. It is therefore fair to say that the events stored over long periods are all past events. Thus, in musical cognition, long-term memory is a generator of remembrances that are musical pasts.

Two Musical Pasts

Musical memory is composed of musical pasts, be they personal experiences or parts of an enduring musical tradition. Two aspects of a music's past should be clearly distinguished, although they interact constantly in human cognitive processes: the *cultural past* to which a music and its associated conceptual and compositional software belong, and the *immediate past* into which sounds perceived as music are projected by memory during listening. The latter is often referred to as *musical context*. Musical context is a semantic model of the current auditory world of a listener. The burden of designing suitable music interfaces falls to whoever conceptualizes the level of interpretive time for the interface.

A Model for Human Memory

The human memory system depicted in figure 30.1 is constructed around a chain of submemories, along which more and more processing time becomes available. The system is a distributed memory system comprising *echoic memory* (EM), *perceptual memory* (PM), *short-term memory* (STM), *working memory* (WM), *contextual memory* (CM), and *long-term memory* (LTM).

Contextual Memory   Contextual memory is not actually separate from long-term memory; it is rather the currently active portion of long-term memory, which defines a musical context.

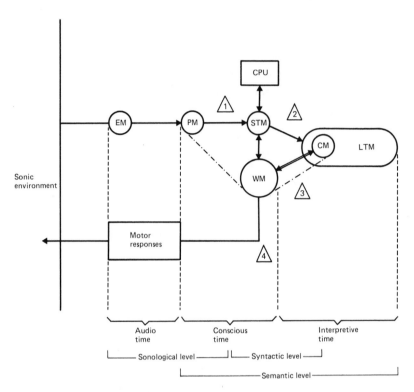

Figure 30.1
Hypothetical model of human memory for music. See note 1.

Working Memory Working memory is an extension of short-term memory. Depending on the problem to be solved, working memory may comprise elements stemming from perceptual as well as contextual memory. Contents in working memory define the musical present of which a musician can be conscious. The contents in long-term memory (as far as they become available in contextual memory and are retrieved into working memory) define the musical past existing for a musician. All information-processing decisions are made on the basis of the transitory contents residing in working memory. Working memory has an immediate-access connection with the central processor (CPU) via short-term memory.

The central processor is most conveniently thought of as a production system interpreter. Productions are of the general form "if C, then A"

$(C \rightarrow A)$, where C stands for a set of conditions true or false of the contents of working memory and where A is a set of actions that are carried out if and only if the conditions preceding it hold true. Actions in a production effect changes in the contents of the submemories that are under the control of the central processor. A set of productions is called a *production system*. It provides a metalanguage in which human performance programs can be made explicit (Newell 1973).

Echoic Memory Echoic memory is the cognitive buffer in which sonic events occurring in audio time are stored. This memory is pre-perceptual, in the sense that its contents are not perceived as such but become perceptible only once they have been stored in perceptual memory.

Perceptual Memory Perceptual memory stores acoustic data in configurations defined along several auditory dimensions and lasting up to several seconds. This buffer determines experiences in conscious time. In contrast to short-term memory, perceptual memory stores acoustic information in the form of perceptual traces (i.e., in analog form), not in the form of discrete chunks as imposed on information residing in short-term memory.

Short-Term Memory Musical short-time memory is probably significantly different from linguistic short-term memory, mainly in that music usually lacks units having assigned connotation. Short-term memory is defined not so much by some time constant of storage as by its limited capacity. Information pushed out of this memory, if not saved in contextual memory, is irretrievably lost; this fact explains the extraordinary importance of recoding information in more abstract terms (i.e., bigger chunks) in short-term memory.

Contextual Memory Of central importance for problems of interface design is contextual memory, the active portion of long-term memory. Contextual memory is intermediate between a memory storing information for an indefinite amount of time (LTM) and a memory storing information momentarily (WM, STM). The memory is called contextual because it stores the context in terms of which individual events are conceptualized and understood; it can thus be thought of as holding a model of the current musical world of a composer or listener. Contextual memory functions in two different but interrelated modes: a syntactic and a semantic mode. In whatever mode it may function, one best conceives of contextual memory as a network whose nodes represent verbal (syntactic) and nonverbal (semantic) concepts.

Syntactic and Semantic Concepts of Music

Syntactic concepts define events as part of some structural representation of music, thus making it possible to distinguish different levels. Their power to relate levels other than statically and hierarchically is quite limited. Semantic concepts are, rather, interpretive of structure and structural levels. They are time-bound and highly selective in that they concern musical remembrances (pasts) and, far from interpreting structures exhaustively, only highlight the structures selectively. Such concepts are presumably nonverbal and closer to images than to concepts proper. A music-syntactic network differs greatly from a music-semantic network, although both are stored in the same memory, or, more properly, are alternative representations given to contents of that memory. A network that stores syntactic concepts is a representation of a hierarchy of the structural levels of a music. A semantic network may be thought of as a linked list of interpretations. This linked list is composed of alternative "readings" of musical structure, which combine to form a cumulative reading.

Music-Syntactic Networks and Linguistic Phrase Markers

Music-syntactic networks are comparable to tree representations of linguistic phrase markers (figure 30.2). They are a set of nodes representing a hierarchy. This extends from musical events forming a sonic surface structure, through layers of intermediate structure such as phrases (microstructure), to the most abstract structural unit in terms of which a particular composition is designed (macrostructure). Musical surface structure is close in appearance to encodings in traditional notation, in which pitch events function as the smallest units. Top nodes in the network are associated with music-theoretical concepts that define temporal or other delineations of some music (movements, sections, and the like). The complexity of branching in a music-syntactic network represents the degree of differentiation between adjacent levels, i.e., the degree of syntactic articulation. Composers are obliged to deal neither with surface structure events nor with high-level structural concepts only; their major decisions concern intermediary levels. It is essential to be able to move from the bottom of a structural hierarchy upward (in order to generalize) and to move downward toward the terminal event string or surface structure (in order to instantiate higher-level concepts). Compositional

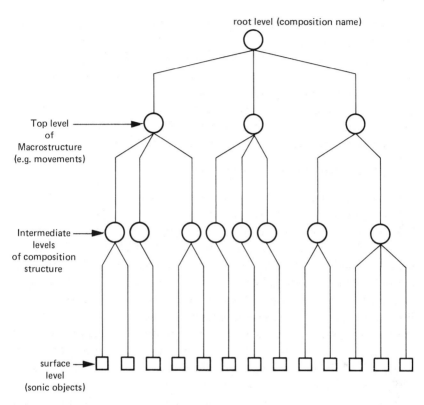

Figure 30.2
A music-syntactic network. See note 2.

activity is difficult to analyze because it is characterized by instantaneous changes in compositional strategy from top-down to bottom-up approaches to the material.

The Relationships between Syntactic and Semantic Concepts in Music

The cognitive relationship of syntactic to semantic concepts in music is little understood at present. Semantic concepts are bound to a music's past, i.e., to memory. The term "musical past" has two distinct but related meanings. It refers to personal experience, however recent, and to a musical tradition without which such an experience is inconceivable. Currently experienced sounds can function as carriers of musical meaning only when contacting categorizations of past acoustic events. Consequently, the nodes in a music-semantic network represent the alternative pasts of a music. They are of two kinds. First, semantic nodes are *perception-world* nodes at which important perceptual or syntactic features of some ongoing music are stored; second, they are *reflection-world* nodes at which musical interpretations are stored. These two classes of nodes are related by access lines, which represent inference relations between sets of features and semantic interpretations and between semantic interpretations having different degrees of strength.

How Music-Semantic Networks Function

Music-semantic networks function as follows: Some initial perceptual input gives rise to an initial interpretation, which in many cases is arbitrary. This interpretation is then used as a basis for further conceptualizing of perceptual input. Interpretations function as musical "laws" that define a current model of the auditory world. A musical law is "broken" if a currently effective musical interpretation is at odds with a set of currently perceived sonic or syntactic features. When this situation occurs, the listener is cognitively obliged to redefine the music's current law. That is, the listener must come up with a new, currently valid interpretation of the music that accounts for the currently perceived features. This reinterpretation of musical data is a complex task, since it necessitates a complete resynthesis of all of the structural material so far heard and memorized. Since the temporal flow of musical events does not cease until the music has ended, the listener operates under severely restrictive temporal conditions. Several listenings may be needed in order to generate a worthwhile semantic interpretation. A music-semantic network is the set of all interpretations a listener could have, or actually has, established during a task performance.

Interactive Computer Music Composition

The user of an interactive computer music system employs contextual memory in both the syntactic and the semantic mode. It becomes evident from observing users that they can switch from a conceptualization of syntactic levels to a conceptualization of musical interpretations of such levels (or laws) almost instantaneously. I consider the semantic model to be the basic mode of contextual memory functioning for two related reasons: First, as a composer, the user is essentially a designer of listening situations in which to function as the initial and authentic listener.

Second, human beings make syntactic decisions, in whatever cognitive domain, on the basis of goals, and the top goal of a task performance is never a syntactic notion but rather a semantic notion defining a purpose. The purpose may be interpretive or constructive; in either case, composers need a model of the current (auditory) world, and such a model is always a semantic model.

Switching from Semantic to Syntactic Modes

The possibility of switching from the semantic to the syntactic mode of functioning gives contextual memory its crucial relevance for creative pursuits. How and under what conditions contextual memory switches from one mode of functioning to the other is a problem with which cognitive researchers have barely begun to cope. The problem posed by this change in the mode of functioning relates to the problem of whether contextual memory is best conceived as an analog or a digital device. More specifically, the problem is how to relate the operational to the figurative aspect of human memory.

Operational and Figurative Aspects of Memory

From the operational viewpoint, contextual memory is inextricably linked to the intelligence that is essentially concerned with problem solving. From the figurative viewpoint, contextual memory is a generator of mental imagery, and such imagery serves the purpose of reconstructing the past of some cognitive experience. The unity of memory lies in that it functions both in an operational (*syntactic*) and a figurative (*semantic*) mode. To understand the interaction of concepts and images in memory and render their interaction formally and explicitly is probably the crucial problem of cognitive psychology. Music users employ both operational concepts and mental (auditory) imagery. In an interactive task environment, their actual behavior can be empirically documented. Interactive computer music systems are thus excellent experimental environments for studing the functional ability of memory.

The Question of Representation

Whether contextual memory functions as an image store (holding pictorial representations of musical information) or as a propositional network (encoding musical information symbolically) is at the center of the problems posed by the design of music interfaces. If in some task it is advantageous for a user to employ a pictorial representation of musical data and if no such representation is provided by the interface being used, human memory resources will be wasted. Problems will be less "well defined" than they would be if an adequate representation were available.

The User's Choice of Representations

The memory representation a user will choose at a given moment depends mainly on two things. The first is the user's internal encoding of the task environment, also called a *problem space*. The problem space is the set of all knowledge states the user can be in; the space can be formally described in terms of a Backus Normal Form (BNF) grammar listing all the cognitive items that enter into a particular task performance. The grammar explicates possible knowledge states as a list of valid expressions. The second determinant for choosing among memory representations is the set of problem determinants that characterizes a specific task, or, rather, the form in which these determinants are given to a user. One might conceive of problem determinants in the manner of input to a General Problem Solver. Of foremost relevance are seven problem determinants:

the top goal,

the difference between a goal state (syntactic or semantic) and a present state,

the operators changing current states,

an ordering of differences in terms of their difficulty of removal,

a table linking differences to the operators suited for removing them,

the stimulus repertory worked with, and

the current semantic interpretation assigned to some sonic or syntactic configuration.

In composition tasks, each of these problem determinants can assume one out of four cognitive appearances: The determinant may be *given* to the user (via instructions or comments), *inferred* by the user from what is given, initially *invented* by the user, or *evolved* over time (i.e., during the problem-solving session). Clearly, a task in which most of the problem determinants are given at the outset is of less cognitive complexity than a task whose problem determinants have to be evolved by the user alone. (In the latter case, no top goal exists that is significantly different from the current subgoal, and the problem to be solved is clearly defined only once it has been solved.) It is inconceivable to me how a system user can cope with a complex task without having recourse to problem representations that are pictorial, especially if the user changes the problem space along the way.

This leads me to think that interfaces incorporating graphic means are crucial for complex and ill-structured compositional tasks. Where the top goal appears as undefined, (i.e., still evolving), the music-semantic network held in contextual memory is itself incomplete and thus cannot control syntactic decisions absolutely. By contrast, where the top goal is semantically well defined, and the problem space thus fixed, music-syntactic levels can easily be specified and digital representations (either graphic or verbal) are appropriate.

Structures and Procedures

Human memory contains both data structures and procedures working on data structures. In a cognitive model, data structures might be represented in the form of networks, while procedures might be formulated as production systems. Structural networks represent the passive part of the memory, and procedures represent the active part. However, procedures may themselves function as data. According to my hypothesis, contextual memory comprises syntactic and semantic network structures and a set of procedures for working on these structures. Where these procedures appear in the form of productions, structures are embedded in procedures on the left-hand side of a production rule, since they define conditions under which memory transactions take place. Network structures thus function as constraints on the actions a performance system carries out. Among the productions that run a human performance system, self-modifying productions play a major role. These productions are capable of modifying other productions and of synthesizing new productions from old ones. Without self-modifying productions, the performance system is incapable of learning and developing. Feedback as it occurs in an interactive system would be useless if no self-modifying productions were available to the performance system.

Levels of User Interaction

Of major relevance for the kind of learning a user can accomplish in an interactive system is whether to use mainly data or procedure specifications. Data specifications in a computer music system can be made on three different levels: the sonic, the syntactic, and the semantic (figure

30.1). Such specifications are ultimately bound up with states of working memory whose transitory contents determine problem-solving decisions. Lowest in cognitive power are interfaces exclusively suitable for specifying data on the sonic level. Using such specifications, the user is in most cases restricted to working on a very low level of generality: that of single events or small groups of events. The user is forced to compose "from left to right" and without explicit guidance by higher-level concepts on the syntactic or semantic level. Compositional strategies demanding a top-down approach are not within the reach of the user of this type of system. Therefore, the designer of an interface that mainly uses data specifications should be aware of the severe restrictions such an interface imposes on potential users.

Top-Down Approaches to Composition

More suitable to top-down approaches in composition are procedural specifications. Procedure specifications are more abstract, since they may draw on data at any level of memory encoding. In the most general terms, procedures are concept-realization routines. Their generality is determined by the most general concept they incorporate and of which they are the specification. Syntactic concepts used in composition most often concern the layered nature of a piece of music, i.e., the way in which various structural levels interact with each other. Semantic concepts define the global structure of a piece of music, however it may be specified; they can be used only where routines for specifying syntactic subject matter already exist. There are as many ways of conceptualizing the global structure of a composition as there are ways of conceptualizing the compositional task itself. Semantic as well as syntactic concepts are thus dependent on the structure of the problem space in which a user chooses to work. That is, they are dependent on the cognitive items a user admits into the problem space, and on the modifications and tests that are chosen during performance. An interface that permits the user to employ procedure specifications is one in which procedures can be written by the user.

Conclusions

I have maintained in the foregoing that decisions guiding the design of music interfaces ultimately concern the alternative types of information transfer within a distributed human memory system. My memory model suggests the hypothesis that a music user can be simulated as an interpreter of production systems. Understanding user behavior presupposes that empirical observations concerning the timing of actions and concerning the operators used during a task performance have been carried out. Productions carry out the steps taken in a human performance program. This performance program specifies how and when to change the contents of a particular memory. Memory contents constitute the epistemic structure upon which the memory agents called productions operate.

Four main classes of productions might be distinguished. (For a specification of productions within a distributed memory system, see figure 30.1.) *Perceptual productions* effect the transfer between perceptual and working memory. *Semantic productions* effect the transfer between contextual memory and working memory, as well as long-term memory. If contextual memory functions in its syntactic mode, productions are needed that make segmental decisions as required by short-term memory; these productions might be called *syntactic productions*. Finally, one needs general agents that do the general bookkeeping for working memory; these agents might be called *general productions*. A music user is an assemblage of different interacting production systems.

Interfaces should be designed with a view to making the empirical observation of users feasible and obtaining documentations of a user's actions in the task environment. Behavioral data documenting musical activity can be analyzed in terms of the performance program that underlies the activity. Gaining insight into the performance program of users is important for improving interfaces as well as systems. In cognitive terms, the function of an interface is twofold: to optimize the transfer of information within human memory and to reduce task complexity. In the end these two functions are synonymous, because a complex task is a task that requires a great amount of memory transaction on the part of the problem solver.

Methodological Comment

The reader might feel that the memory model here proposed is too general, since it is not elaborated from within a particular musical context. This deficiency is due to two main reasons, one historical and the other personal.

The need for a transfer of ideas from cognitive psychology and computer science (artificial intelligence in particular) to music seems inescapable
in view of the state of musical science. As far as they exist at all, models
of musical processing and memory developed from inside the field of
music bear witness to a research tradition that predates information-
processing psychology and is therefore out of date. Only continued
research in artificial intelligence and music can bring about a change in
this situation.

Much of my own empirical research using the memory model here
proposed (or a variant thereof) is unpublished. However, an elaboration
of the model discussed here can be found in "An information processing
model of melody composition," in Laske 1981.

This paper was first presented at the University of Toronto during my
tenure as a Visiting Scholar in the Department of Computer Science and
the Structured Sound Synthesis Project. It was first published as Technical
Memo 4, in January 1978, by the Computer Systems Research Group
at the University of Toronto.

Notes

1. In the model of a musical information processor depicted in figure 30.1, submemories
are arranged according to their position along the time line leading from experiences lasting
a few microseconds (EM) to those lasting years and encompassing a musical tradition
(LTM). The time line is further subdivided into (hypothetical) parts called "audio time,"
"conscious time," and "interpretive time," according to criteria of musical perception.
(Stimuli occur in audio time, events in conscious time, and contexts of events in interpretive
time.) One event is thought to be processed on three different music-grammatical levels,
called the sonological, the syntactic, and the semantic. The overlapping of the semantic
level with the other two levels indicates that semantic decision making presupposes sonic
and syntactic results.

The distributed memory system depicted is a static "snapshot" of a dynamic system
executed by performance programs called productions. Each class of productions represents
a set of experts in a particular domain. [The central processing unit (CPU), which controls
the system, is thought to be "beyond time" in that it is responsible for all elements of the
time line.] Working memory (WM) is a collection of memories (PM, STM, CM) providing
problem spaces that comprise elements from more than a single memory; it thus provides
communication among memories. However, the CPU has direct access only to STM (the
holder of "attention"). LTM is the holder of musical traditions—as sedimented in personal
memories—as well as long-term memories of an individual. The focus of interactive work
with a computer music system is, of course, working memory.

2. The network description of music-syntactic memory, above, employs a tree structure to
depict relationships of adjacency (syntagmatic) and identical function (paradigmatic) among
sounding events. The model is not prescriptive but purely descriptive, viz. of the fact that

musical syntax is usually interpreted and understood in terms of different levels—the lowest level being formed by single events, the highest by entire movements.

Figure 30.2 depicts a musical structure of three parts showing that elements pertaining to one particular part have manifestations in other parts of the structure as well. One may think of a semantic interpretation of sounds (as music) as a set of readings of a syntactic network. In such a reading, elements shared between parts, although syntactically synonymous, have different meanings because of differing contexts.

References

Chadabe, J. 1977. "Some reflections on the nature of the landscape within which computer music systems are designed." *Computer Music Journal* 1(3):5–11.

Deutsch, D. 1975. "The organization of short-term memory for a single acoustic attribute." In D. Deutsch and J. A. Deutsch, eds., *Short-Term Memory*. New York: Academic.

Laske, O. 1977. *Music Memory and Thought*. Ann Arbor, Mich.: University Microfilms.

Laske, O. 1981. *Music and Mind: An Artificial Intelligence Perspective*. Boston: O. Laske.

Newell, A. 1973. "Production systems: Models of control structures." In W. Chase, ed., *Visual Information Processing*. New York: Academic.

Schafer, R. M. 1977. *The Tuning of the World*. New York: Knopf.

Simon, H. 1973. "The structure of ill-structured problems." *Artificial Intelligence* 3–4:181–201.

31 Interview with Gottfried Michael Koenig

CURTIS ROADS

Gottfried Michael Koenig (b. 1926, Magdeburg, Germany) is one of the directors of the Institute of Sonology at Utrecht State University in Utrecht, Holland.

Koenig's work as a composer includes instrumental as well as electro-acoustic compositions. From 1954 to 1964 he worked at radio station WDR in Cologne. Among other projects there, he assisted Karlheinz Stockhausen in the construction of his *Kontakte* (1960). Koenig's compositions available on record include *Terminus* (1966–67) and *Funktion Grün* (1967), which features computer-generated control voltages regulating analog equipment. Both compositions are found on DGG 137011 (Avant Garde Series). In addition, his *Funktion Gelb* (1967–68) is available on a 7-inch disk (Wergo WER 324). His concentrated *Übung für Klavier* (1969) was performed at the UNESCO Workshop on Computer Music in Aarhus, Denmark.

The Institute of Sonology is a center for contemporary electroacoustic and computer music. Distributed among its five studios are several computers, including small-scale (DEC LSI-11) and medium-scale (DEC PDP-15) systems as well as analog equipment. The Institute has its own technical department and staff.

This interview took place at the Institute of Sonology during the early afternoon of August 25, 1978.

Background

CBR Mr. Koenig, can you tell us about your early development as a composer?

GMK I started in a music conservatory and studied, besides music theory, acoustics, analysis and piano, also composition as a student of music; I started making or composing music as a child together with my piano education and developed that up to a certain level when it became necessary to study music professionally. After my studies in the conservatory I considered myself a composer until I met electronic music—which really meant to study anew.

Originally published in *Computer Music Journal* 2(3): 11–15, 29, 1978.

CBR When did you first become involved in electronic music?

GMK It was about in 1951, 1952 when the first night programs were broadcast by the Cologne radio station.

CBR When did you first start to work with electronic music?

GMK I went to Cologne in 1953 and started working in the Cologne electronic music studio one year later in 1954.

CBR Is it not true that you also studied computer programming at one time?

GMK Yes, that was about ten years later: 1963 and 1964. Until then there was no need. There was a large field of electronic music; computers were barely known; and when computers came into my field of view, it took some time before I met people who really made me aware of the possibilities. And that was at the beginning of the 1960s. I met somebody from the University at Bonn and started studying computer programming.

CBR When did you first write composing programs?

GMK Right from the beginning. In the computer programming class, exercises were given mostly in fields not related to music. When I said I would like to have some programming exercises in the music field, the teacher was very happy about it, of course. So I made little programs about making 12-tone series and some harmonic control and things like that. And after a couple of experiments like this, I started to write a larger composition program which later would be the PROJECT 1 program.

PROJECT 1 and PROJECT 2

CBR When was PROJECT 1 actually written?

GMK I suppose in the years 1964 to 1966.

CBR Can you tell us about PROJECT 1 itself?

GMK Yes. The basic idea was to make use of my experience in serial music and also the aleatoric consequences drawn from serial music. I tried to describe a model in which certain basic decisions were described, and where besides that the user—the composer—would have some influence over the musical variables. In that way you could ask for any number of variants which would evolve from the same basic principle; you could compare them and see to what extent the musical characteristics laid down in the program were really experienceable in music.

CBR And how did the PROJECT 1 program lead to PROJECT 2?

GMK Sometimes I call PROJECT 1 a closed program, because the composer can exert very little influence on the program itself. In contrast to that, I wanted a program which would, according to the experiences gathered with PROJECT 1, allow a composer to fill in his own variables, not only with respect to the musical material—what kind of pitches or loudnesses or durations—but also with respect to compositional rules— the way the elements are put together to form a musical context. To that purpose I designed PROJECT 2, which is actually a questionnaire of more than 60 questions. According to those questions, which refer to the musical material and the rules, the program would combine or compose a piece.

CBR So you not only specify elements, you specify operations in PRO-JECT 2—predicates, as it were, for composition.

GMK Yes.

PROJECT 1, PROJECT 2, and VOSIM

CBR Recently you've combined your PROJECT 1 program with the VOSIM oscillators. Are the VOSIM oscillators a kind of ideal synthesis output for PROJECT 1?

GMK I don't know yet. Maybe not, because the VOSIM system was designed for a very special task, namely for making speech sounds. They also offer the possibility of making a large variety of sounds not being part of any natural language. But still, it's not originally designed to replace an electronic music studio for instance. Now neither is PROJECT 1. PROJECT 1 actually is a program which designs instrumental music scores. But under certain conditions you could use this kind of structure also for electronic music; but there are restrictions in the program which are more on the side of instrumental music. I mean, I would personally design electronic music completely different from the design of instrumental music.

On the other hand, if we don't talk about electronic music, then it's a question of whether we could try to use the VOSIM system to add a sound part to PROJECT 1 which would replace the string quartet or the piano or the orchestra. I think that that is theoretically possible, not at the present stage, but in the future when all those instruments are properly described and can be just inserted in the program. But at that moment I think I would lose interest, because if I would want a piano I would take one, and not try to imitate it with any VOSIM generator in the world.

So what I am expecting from devices like VOSIM generators is a *new* field of sound, not speech sounds, not instrumental sounds, but something which I've tried to achieve in the electronic music studio and toward which I will keep striving. The VOSIM generator is just a convenient means of having a sound output for PROJECT 1 because the VOSIM system was developed at this Institute and it's just there.

CBR Can you tell us about the relationship between PROJECT 1 and the VOSIM system through the program VOSACS? What is the VOSACS program?

GMK The VOSACS program is a routine which enables you to test the VOSIM variables, nine of them at least, in a small number of steps. There's a certain variable which can have about 2,000 states or steps, of which the VOSACS routine only uses maybe four or eight spread over this range. Still, it gives a general view, and enables the composer to make up his mind what kind of VOSIM sounds he wants to use when playing a PROJECT 1 score.

CBR You said that PROJECT 1 was originally designed to make instrumental music. How about PROJECT 2?

GMK Yes, the same is valid for PROJECT 2. PROJECT 2, being kind of an extension to PROJECT 1, also was designed to make instrumental music. I have made scores with PROJECT 2, and the new version which is in preparation will also be given a VOSIM extension, so that the results of PROJECT 2 composition can be heard immediately.

Extensions to PROJECT 1 and PROJECT 2

CBR Are you planning a composing program to compose electronic music? And if so, what kinds of principles would it incorporate? How would it be different from PROJECT 1 and PROJECT 2 for instance?

GMK In instrumental music, my starting point is always the relationship to a well-defined musical material. You have the orchestral instruments, and all the division of labor that takes place in an orchestra, which results in harmony, in certain rhythmic patterns and even in the notation.

Electronic music is completely free from all those restrictions. So when I might in the future try to write a routine to make electronic music with a computer, I would not start with those traditional language-like features I just mentioned but from predescribed sound characteristics or ranges in which sounds could move. Then I would try to develop the grammar of the music according to the sounds and not the other way around.

Researcher and Composer

CBR In an interview with *NUMUS-WEST* (1973) you said that you were at that time a researcher, not a composer. Has this changed?

GMK Not really, I have been busy designing programs, correcting them, and testing them for many years besides other work I have had to do in these last years. I hope to become a composer again, maybe next year and the years after.

CBR Is this prompted by the new possibilities of PROJECT 1, PROJECT 2, and the sound synthesis systems here at the Institute?

GMK Actually I've waited for many years to put those programs to use. There were many interferences, not only because of my own work but also because of the computer development. Computers break down occasionally, and things like that.

SSP and "Nonstandard" Synthesis

CBR Can you tell us about your sound synthesis program SSP?

GMK Yes, this program uses what we call the "nonstandard approach" to sound synthesis. That means not referring to a given acoustic model but rather describing the waveform in terms of amplitude values and time values. My first intention was to go away from the classical instrumental definitions of sound in terms of loudness, pitch, and duration, and so on, because then you would refer to musical elements which are not necessarily the elements of the language of today. To explore a new field of sound possibilities I thought it would be best to *close* the classical descriptions of sound and open up an experimental field in which you would really have to start again. It would be the task of a later time or other people to map the new possibilities to the old experiences.

CBR What are the primary values of a nonstandard (or synthesis-by-instruction) approach vis-à-vis a standard (or synthesis-by-rule) approach?

GMK That's difficult to say. Even though I wrote the program, I don't have enough experience (with SSP) at this very minute to make a judgment about that.

(pause)

Primarily I'm very annoyed with composers using the most modern tools of music making, like electronic music, voltage control, even computers, and making twelve-tone series for instance, or trying to imitate existing instruments. That has, of course, its scientific value, but not necessarily a creative value in new music making. But if a system is designed to produce twelve-tone series and instrumental sounds, then it is very difficult to avoid that. So just to be able to avoid that, to open up new fields of sounds you would not be able to produce or would not think of describing in classical terms, I have chosen this nonstandard approach.

The Influence of Computers

CBR How have your compositional ideas been influenced by working with computers?

GMK Not so much. If I compare my own compositions of the pre-computer era to what I have tried to describe in my programming and what still fascinates me, then there is not so much difference. I mean I have gathered experience as a composer for many years, say 20 years, something like that. A program will not be able to describe 20 years of experience, but only a week of it or maybe a month. That means that I try to influence my programming by my experience instead of the other way round. I try to lay down what I know about music, and at this moment I think I know more about music than my computer program.

CBR Are your composing ideas influenced by the sounds that you're able to create with the systems at the Institute?

GMK Yes, especially in the field of electronic music. Then it's difficult to say. Have I chosen electronic music because of sound ideas, or have I composed in a certain style because of the sounds possible in the studio? I think there is a mutual influence. I think that the compositional technique should be in a very narrow and strong relation to the sound sources. That's my interest in programmed music—to put possible sound sources into a program which combines them instead of instrumenting a piano score.

CBR One kind of artificial intelligence task is that of a program itself knowing what kinds of sounds that it's dealing with, and altering the program logic according to these sounds. Do you see this as a possibility?

GMK Not only as a possibility, I think it is even a necessity. My own programming does not take that aspect into account as yet because the programs were meant to be instrumental music programs; but as soon as sound production is involved, you need some kind of feedback or relationship between the musical language structure and the structure of the sounds produced.

Composers and Computer Music

CBR What directions being pursued by other composers are of interest to you?

GMK When we talk about computer music we have to distinguish between the act of composing and the act of sound production. In many cases, the modern means of sound production of the computer are used to make, let's say, outmoded music to come into being, into sound. It's not always the most advanced structural design which is used in computer music. I think composers I admire most are not busy at this moment in the computer music field, while what I have heard in computer music attracts me more or less in terms of technical procedures and not so much as aesthetic results.

My general feeling is that computer music has seen a very fine development in programming, software, and hardware development, but composers have a strong tendency to instrumental music and sometimes it seems that they avoid computers. Maybe they feel that they wouldn't be able to express themselves the way they are able to with an orchestra using human beings and all the mechanical instruments of the musical past.

CBR Are composers afraid of the concept of programmed music?

GMK I think so.

CBR Why do you suppose that is?

GMK In the first place, in most musical institutions composers are not prepared to think of music in terms of a set of given rules. I mean, programmed music is not a concept taught in most music schools. That's one point. They're used to thinking in terms of what they can do with their own breath and hands, with musicians and conductors, and all the given conditions of musical life. They have to fit in. That's the place where they will earn the money.

Computer music is something hard to sell to a larger audience. Composers who are not paid by the government but working freelance have to consider this condition.

The Institute of Sonology

CBR I'd like to ask a few questions about the Institute. Can you tell us a little about some of the other work going on at the Institute right now?

GMK Yes. The Institute is busy in different ways. On the one hand we have the development of studio and computer facilities. Secondly there's an annual course, the subjects being signal processing, computer techniques, logic, and practical exercises in the studio. In the third place, we have composers who make use of our facilities to produce music compositions. In the fourth place, we have research in fields of musical structures and musical sounds—that means both analysis and synthesis of musical structures and musical sounds and of course the relationship between them. We organize a series of concerts every year both in Utrecht and Amsterdam including not only electronic music but also films in which modern music plays an important role. We gather documents—as many as possible, not only in the form of books and records, scores and periodicals, but also any kind of document which comes to our knowledge is filed and even stored on the computer for easier reference. We have our own electronic workshop to maintain the apparatus and also for new development of analog or digital hardware.

CBR There seems to be a great deal of collaboration among the people within the Institute. This seems difficult to achieve at some other institutions. What are the ingredients of this collaboration? Is it simply a matter of survival for all of you, i.e., you have to work well together, or are there organizational techniques that make this easier to achieve?

GMK Ja, in the first place the Institute has grown step by step. That means only people who were attracted to our way of working joined the staff. In the second stage of development we have tried to find an internal organization which optimizes the collaboration of the staff members and also everyone who comes from the outside.

CBR How is this actually implemented? Are there obligations and responsibilities that each staff member has? Must he or she fulfill a collaborative function within the group?

GMK Yes. We have three main committees which are re-elected every year or every two years, concerned with scientific research, artistic creation, and technology, that's one committee; the second committee sees to teaching, and the third committee about public relations, information, and publications. In that way, everything that is going on in those fields is talked over in the committee so that every subject can be examined from different aspects—it's a good coordination that way.

An Interactive Approach

CBR I notice one characteristic of the Utrecht studios seems to be that whenever you develop a synthesis technique you seem to have someone from the hardware section develop a device to carry out the synthesis. It seems that you optimize your computer resources towards interaction with composers, and leave the synthesis computation to the hardware generators. That seems to work well for you.

GMK Yes. We started with real-time synthesis without any hardware oscillators, but soon we reached the limits of that technique. It is still applied to certain approaches, but on the other hand the computer is just too slow to compute in real time complex sound structures, especially if they are also embedded in a complex language structure. Hardware generators make it much easier to compute these complex structures. I want to point out that if there is a new technical design, before it's carried out it's talked over with the artistic and scientific people at the Institute, and also the other way around. So nothing is done without an agreement from all sides.

CBR All of the systems here at the Institute are interactive. Is this by design? Was there an agreement among all the people at the Institute?

GMK A silent agreement I would say, and then at a certain moment one talks about it, and recognizes its usefulness.

CBR Almost all of the systems have immediate sound feedback!

GMK Yes. That's possible because we don't share the computer with other institutions. We own our own computers, and in that way we have the computer at our disposal—24 hours if necessary. That speeds it up; it's not necessary to make elaborate preparations in terms of programming and input data, then carry it to a computer center and wait for the output.

For extensive experimentation the immediate sound response is necessary; otherwise we wouldn't be able to carry out a large number of experiments which are necessary to develop programs which serve composers.

Future Projects

CBR What ideas are on the horizon for the Institute?

GMK One idea is to build hybrid studios, in which analog means and digital means are combined, up to a certain degree.

CBR This is already under way?

GMK This is already under way in one studio and I could imagine that we could follow that direction later on. The thing is, if you offer analog and digital means to composers, it's hard to know beforehand what they would turn to. I mean, there are composers who would prefer the analog audio studio even if you have the most modern computer facilities around, just because of their habit of music making.

Analog versus Digital

CBR As far as sound synthesizers go, it seems to me that some of the new digital synthesizers will have much the same composer interfaces as the analog equipment—only everything behind the knobs and dials will be digital. Some people, however, draw a great distinction between analog and digital. What are your thoughts?

GMK As long as only sound synthesis is involved I wouldn't bother so much—analog means are fine; digital means are sometimes better, sometimes not. All the precision you get from digital apparatus is not what every type of composer really wants. But still, then it wouldn't make much difference to the composer whether he handles analog apparatus *or* digital apparatus. But if you want to be involved at the same time in composing problems like programmed music or preconceived structural ideas, then I think the situation is slightly different because it affects the state of the mind of the composer and not only the state of the apparatus.

In that respect I think we need many years to develop computer programs for not only making sounds but composing structures, to develop things which are really attractive to composers and useful to composers so they can feel at home and express themselves.

Today, the composer who wants to work with preconceived structural ideas mostly uses his desk for that—not necessarily wanting sound immediately, but rather to put certain features, certain characteristics, certain items in certain configurations. But I could imagine a stage in which a computer would respond not only with sound but also with structures with such speed that the composer could have as many compositions to consider in real time as he's now able to consider sound characteristics.

Composer as Selector

CBR So are you interested then in the idea of composer as selector—the computer generates a number of examples of either a sound structure or a musical structure and the composer selects from the possibilities generated by the computer?

GMK Yes. It's hard to describe. I think he should not only select but also have some influence on the agents which prepare the selection options. But then I am asking myself whether the composer has not always selected, through the centuries, among given items like instruments and instrumentalists.

One should either offer the composer a wide variety of compositional means, in terms of programs and programming languages, or on the other hand, should educate him in such a way that he would be able not only to select among means but also create his own means.

But that's an educational problem. That depends not only on the psychology of the composer but also on society in general, on the role music plays in society. And that's changing.

CBR How is it changing?

GMK Faster sometimes than technology, I think. It takes years to develop electronic music studios according to the demands of a given time, and then it's always too late! The moment the studio is developed up to its original standards, the composers are miles away.

CBR What programs and technical devices need to be built? What systems do composers need today?

GMK The composers of the past (by that I mean the last 10 or 20 years) would not have been able to build their own hardware, or design their own studios, or to write their own software. So they had to accept anything that was prepared in their respective studios and institutions. But in the future, composers will be educated in a different way, or at least will have other possibilities of being educated, in terms of mathematics, sound synthesis techniques, linguistics, artificial intelligence, or what have you. Also the prices of digital hardware are decreasing. So I could imagine a future situation in which a composer would not wait for the Institute of Sonology to make things, but would rather buy his own computer, to design his own software in a much faster time period than the past. Even the technology of designing programs is progressing.

CBR Do you then see a situation of decentralization?

GMK I think so.

Collaboration among Computer Music Centers

CBR What about an intermingling among centers for computer music now? Do you foresee any of this? What are the difficulties or advantages of collaboration?

GMK But music is made by individuals. Composers compose alone. They don't form teams. Places like IRCAM or this institute or others are more or less centered around individuals who design the basic principles.

CBR And yet is not musical research—by the definition of what is scientific—socially communicable? Is it not something that should feed together to create a common body of knowledge that everybody can draw from?

GMK That's a very steady but slow-growing process; everybody talks about better communication between studios—one should come together

more often, have conferences, and the like. The computer music conference is now established, but it's in only one place in the world, and
for Europeans it's harder to get to the States. On the other hand, if it
were held in Europe it would be the same problem. You can't telephone
all day to everybody; it's too costly and you don't have the time. So it's
a theoretical wish that people have—to get together more frequently to
exchange ideas and knowledge. I would think that it's not really that
necessary to make an effort to bring people together more often, because
certain ideas lie in the air, so to speak. Some things are developed independently of each other at different places. You discover that it wasn't
really necessary to consult because you know actually what the present-
day problems are.

On the other hand, the exchange is difficult. Even the exchange of
computer programs seems to be difficult. Systems are different and
approaches are different. So collaboration is a little hypothetical.

The nice thing about different institutes is that you can have different
approaches to the same problem. Suppose we would try to imitate what
the French are doing in Paris, or they would try to imitate what we are
doing here. Then you would have the same institute twice. On the other
hand, if you are an individual walking in your own direction then you
want to know what's around you but you don't want to follow the others.
Exchange is sometimes necessary, but it doesn't always solve your own
problems.

CBR You see more of a collaboration on the level of ideas?

GMK Yes, and there are periodicals in which ideas and developments
are described. If you really are in need of certain knowledge, then you
can do as people have for centuries—just travel to the place and study
the problems there.

32 Controlled Indeterminacy: A First Step Toward a Semistochastic Music Language

JOHN MYHILL

I have been working on various ways of extending Xenakis's Stochastic Music Language (SML) for some years now. In particular, I have (with the assistance of my students Isaac and Solomon) implemented a form of SML that incorporates the improvements mentioned in Myhill 1979, and interfaced it with Music V. (The listing is available on request.) More recently, I have become interested in the region between stochastic and deterministic music, and have come to regard SML as one end of a continuum. I have been trying to develop a generalized SSML (semistochastic music language) that will permit the composition of continuity —for example, of film music—so that with a small number of computer instructions (which incorporate both the constraints of the film and the real compositional choices) one can generate long passages of appropriate accompanying sound. Naturally this involves giving up, or leaving only as options, some basic features of SML. For a trivial example, the lengths of the texturally contrasting sections of which an SML piece is composed would obviously not themselves need to be stochastically generated but could be coordinated with the action in appropriate ways. The quite practical problem of composing film music that, though stochastic in its general character, could have certain temporal structuring, climaxes, etc., because of its dramatic function, gradually led me to consider matters at once more philosophically basic and more technically manageable. These considerations centered on the definition of a music that would be at once deterministic and stochastic, or else stochastic in some parts and deterministic in some other parts, without any loss of stylistic coherence.

Different Forms of Determinism

I shall mention some of the thoughts that have occurred to me on this subject. There was first the problem of what one could possibly mean by deterministic music. Although there is probably a pretty general consensus (modulo some minor musical and mathematical details) as to what a *random* sequence of pitches or durations is, what we are seeking is a

Originally published in *Computer Music Journal* 3(3): 12–14, 1979.

continuum (called New Diapason in Xenakis 1979). In this continuum, randomness or "stochasticity" is one end, and there is no such uniformity, given the diversity of musical cultures and styles, as to what to put at the other end in the case of pitch. In other words, there seems no objective reason why we should contrast "random pitches" with eighteenth-century common practice as the other end of the spectrum, rather than with sixteenth-century polyphony, dodecaphony, or the ancient Korean style. There is, to risk repetition, a fairly well-defined notion of random pitch, but seemingly no culture-independent notion of nonrandom or deterministic pitch structure. (But see Rothenberg's series of articles in *Mathematical Systems Theory*.) So, though we have an idea of what it would be like to make music *more and more random* (for example, in a film where the progressive disintegration of a personality might be reflected in the increasing fragmentation of a theme or of a melodic style), what we mean by making music, at least in its pitch aspects, *less and less random* seems totally culture-bound and lacking anything approaching a precise mathematical definition. There is certainly one solution—namely, that nonrandom melody consists of a mere reiteration of one frequency—which makes impeccable musical and mathematical sense. This is the foundation of many of Hiller's compositions (e.g., some movements of *Computer Cantata*), yet I would feel happier with something more sophisticated and subtle. For example, one could accept as given a number of "common practices" and "modulate" between them. A typical exercise in this kind of modulation might be to write a lute piece that begins in the manner of Dowland and "modulates" to the style of eighteenth-century Japanese koto music. A starting point in this direction might be an analysis of Henri Pousseur's *Wild Horse Ride*, which takes us from Mozart and early Beethoven, via Schubert, Brahms, and Wagner, to Schoenberg and Webern. I know that the "modulations" are implemented by means of certain permutations of the integers 1 through 12 which take, e.g., major triads after a sufficient number of applications into "Webern triads" such as C − F − B or C − F$\sharp$ − B, but I have no idea whether this technique can be programmed. In any case, since I do not know how to do this, I pass to something less unapproachable, namely the contrast of regularity and randomness in regard to rhythm. Here the other end of the spectrum is simply and transculturally periodicity, and so I was led to the slogan *degree of periodicity*, which is the focus of this paper from here on in.

Periodic and Aperiodic Rhythm

A couple of my earlier attempts to work out a coexistence of periodic and aperiodic rhythm might be mentioned briefly here. One of them, the percussion piece *Dialectic* composed for Jan Williams at SUNY Buffalo, consisted of an underlying deterministic substructure (*background* in the Schenkerian sense, based on Joseph Schillinger's theory of rhythm) with a stochastic *foreground*. This seems to be a viable method of composition (somewhat like tachistic brushwork over a firmly limned geometrical drawing), but it is a bit off from our main task. Ultimately, we are aiming at a continuum or New Diapason incorporating both random and deterministic elements in controllably greater and lesser degree. Another venture of mine was an ill-fated collaboration with the composer and film-maker Victor Grauer aimed at formulating a mathematically precise and aesthetically viable notion of *degree of periodicity*, which he wished to employ in his one-second abstract movies. One second equals 24 frames, and I was driven to invent a measure of *degree of asymmetry* of 24 things in a row, which turned out, in my view at least, to be mathematically intractable and aesthetically unilluminating. "24 things in a row" meant both the 24 frames perceived temporally one after the other and the filmstrip of blacks and whites lying on my desk before me. This double meaning (spatial and temporal) of "24 things in a row" was in my view (though not in Grauer's) responsible for the failure of the project. A fundamental lesson I learned from this failure was the difference between space and time. (Another one was the slogan *degree of periodicity*, whose implementation I had long sought.)

Temporal and Spatial Distinctions

A rhythmic cancrizans (for example, in the manner of Messiaen) has an obvious symmetry to the eye—even more when laid out as a filmstrip than when written in conventional music notes—that is, more likely than not, completely imperceptible to the ear. Anthony Hill, the English constructivist artist, has made remarkable progress toward a definition of visual or spatial asymmetry (which makes the later works of Mondrian in a precise sense maximally asymmetric). I am convinced that this definition is not amenable to musical or temporal application. Speaking of rhythm in painting or of the symmetry of a musical phrase seems to me to lead necessarily to aesthetic disaster. I hold to this radical distinction between time and space because I am convinced of the primacy of change and because my philosophy stems more from Heraclitus than from Plato.

A Degree of Periodicity

That time is not space, and that motion is not the graphic and simultaneous representation of motion (as in the inert filmstrip or score lying on my desk) does not mean, however, that time and motion cannot be treated mathematically. My search for a concept of *degree of periodicity* in musical (and filmic) rhythm was facilitated by a serendipitous cross-fertilization between Xenakis and Eisler. Xenakis, following Poisson, teaches us that absolute aperiodicity corresponds to a logarithmic distribution of durations. That is, you take a random number between 0 and 1, take the negative of its logarithm (scaled by a constant), and get a unique distribution of durations. This distribution has the property that whether or not there is silence (no attack) during one time span has absolutely nothing to do with whether there was silence in the preceding time span—more precisely, the probability of no attack in time $t_1 + t_2$ is the product of the probability of no attack in time t_1 and the probability of no attack in time t_2. Eisler (1947) states this problem: How does one make music to describe the mobilization of an army? (Recall that, in Eisler's approach, music reflects the subjective aspect of the action on the screen.) At the beginning one sees, say, a mobilization notice, and observes people reading it, going home, preparing to depart for the war, bidding farewell to their families, and so on. The subjectivity is shocked and erratically numbed or painful. As they go out into the streets their subjectivity becomes more organized and anonymous; they think of themselves less and less as individuals, more and more as parts of One Thing (the *böse Kollektivität*). I asked myself, specializing Eisler's question, how this is reflected in the rhythmical character of the accompanying music. The answer was: Increase the degree of periodicity!

A Solution

Here is my solution (the fourth or fifth, which at last seems to make both musical and mathematical sense). Consider the extremes. In the Xenakis-

Poisson distribution, one picks random numbers from the whole interval (0, 1) with equal probabilities and takes their negative (natural) logarithms. At the opposite extreme, one takes one point (namely $1/e$) from this interval and takes repeatedly its negative logarithm, obtaining 1, 1, 1, 1, 1, or complete periodicity. A gradual narrowing of the interval from which the random numbers are selected before taking their logarithms corresponds to a gradual increase in periodicity. More specifically, if we define the degree of nonperiodicity of a continuity by

$$D = \frac{\text{Maximum duration} - \text{Minimum duration}}{\text{Average duration}} \tag{1}$$

(which may not be the best way, though I have found none better), the duration of a note (time between attacks) is determined as follows: Find x and y between 0 and 1 such that

$$x \ln(x) = y \ln(y), \tag{2}$$

$$x/y = e^D, \tag{3}$$

where D is the deviation defined by equation 1 above. Pick a random number k between x and y and set duration equal to $-\alpha \ln(k)$, where α is the average duration. Requirement 3 above amounts to

$$\ln(x) - \ln(y) = D, \tag{4}$$

i.e., to

Maximum duration − Minimum duration

$$= -\alpha \ln(y) + \alpha \ln(x)$$

$$= \alpha D$$

$= D \times$ Average duration required by equation 1.

Requirement 2 guarantees that $\alpha = -\alpha \ln(1/e)$ is indeed the average duration. Implementing these calculations by a computer program is straightforward and fast (using a table lookup of $x \ln(x)$ tabulated from 0 to 1 by increments of 0.01 to solve equations 2 and 3 for x and y).

But we can do more. We can obtain a type of polyrhythm in which, e.g., one voice may get more and more regular as another gets more and more irregular. The "score" of such a polyrhythm, to be fed in suitably

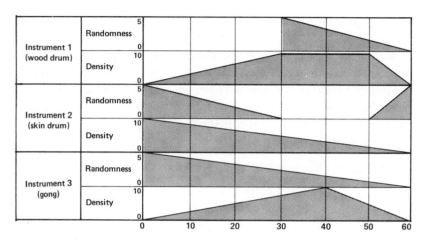

Figure 32.1
Percussion score showing degree of nonperiodicity (randomness) and event density (number of notes per second) versus time.

coded form to a computer, assigns to each instrument two graphs, one giving density ($1/\alpha$ number of notes per second) as a function of time, the other giving D of equation 1 as a function of time. Experiment shows that piecewise-linear graphs work well. After each note is terminated, D and $1/k$ are updated from the graphs, and the computation just described picks a new note length.

Proof

For the delight of the curious, I append a proof of the weird-looking formula 2. Consider a composition for one instrument consisting of N notes whose durations are determined by the formula

$$\text{Duration} = -\alpha \ln(k), \tag{5}$$

where k is flatly distributed between y and x ($0 < y < k < x < 1$). Let $(u, u + du)$ be a little subinterval of (y, x). Then the number of chosen numbers k that lie in that subinterval is $N\,du/(x - y)$, and the length of the note associated with such a k is $-\alpha \ln(u)$. So the contribution of $(u, u + du)$ to the length of the piece is $-\alpha \ln(u)N\,du/(x - y)$. Integrating with respect to u, we get

$$\frac{\int_y^x -\alpha \ln(u)\,N\,du}{x-y} = \frac{\alpha N[u\ln(u)-u]_y^x}{y-x}$$

$$= \alpha N \frac{x\ln(x)-x-y\ln(y)+y}{y-x} \tag{6}$$

as the length of the piece. The average note length is then

$$\alpha \frac{x\ln(x)-x-y\ln(y)+y}{y-x}, \tag{7}$$

and we need this to be equal to α. This will happen just in case the numerator and denominator of the fraction in brackets are equal, i.e., just in case 2 holds, Q.E.D. (If $D=0$, set $x=y=1/e$.)

References

Eisler, H. 1947. *Composing for the Film.* New York: Oxford University Press.

Myhill, J. 1979. "Some simplification and improvements in the stochastic music program." In *Proceedings of the 1978 International Computer Music Conference*, volume 1, ed. C. Roads. Evanston, Ill.: Northwestern University Press.

Xenakis, I. 1979. "Opening address." Ibid.

33 Music for an Interactive Network of Microcomputers

JOHN BISCHOFF, RICH GOLD, AND JIM HORTON

We describe here the music presented in concert on July 3, 1978, at the Blind Lemon, a music gallery in Berkeley, California.

An Overview of the Piece

Traditionally, music has involved more than one person, either in its composition, in its production, or in both. In fact, it seems to be one of the most social art forms. Although there has been individually produced music as well, computer music by its nature could until recently only be individual, solitary music. However, with the introduction of microprocessors at a reasonable cost, composers can now own microcomputers, and true computer bands, free from major institutions, are possible. Though such bands can take many forms, network music seems the most suitable and contemporary.

All three of us owned KIM-1 microcomputers, but aside from the fact that they simplified many of the input/output problems they were not significantly similar. Each composer had programmed his computer with a music program that was by itself able to produce music; however, the programs were also able to input data that would affect the musical content and to output data that would affect another computer's program. Each computer had its own musical output, either to a digital-to-analog converter (DAC) or to digitally controlled electronics.

It was decided that for the first concert a simple formation would be used. In this case, each computer sent data to one other computer and received data from one other computer, so that a circular data structure was effected. How the received data were used and what data would be sent were the individual composer's choice, though the bus structures were mutually agreed to by each pair of composers. The final musical output was mixed together and broadcast over a high-fidelity music system.

The exact configuration used during the concert was the following: Bischoff sent data to Horton, Horton sent data to Gold, and Gold sent data to Bischoff.

Originally published in *Computer Music Journal* 2(3):24–29, 1978.

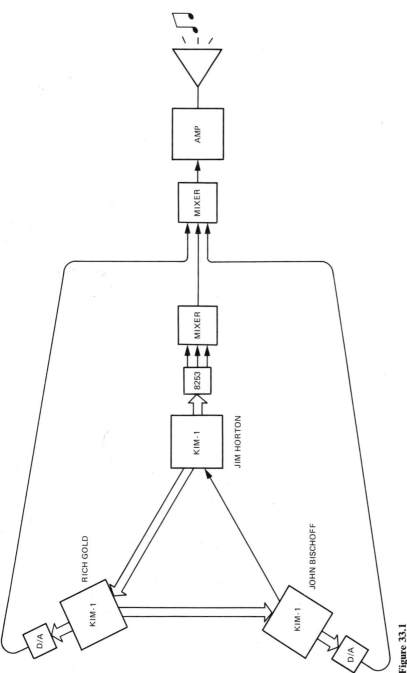

Figure 33.1

As can be seen here, the basic flow of information was circular. Bischoff's KIM sent one line of serial information (which served as both interrupt and data line) to Horton's KIM. Horton placed four bits of parallel information onto a latched data line for the use of Gold's KIM, while Gold gave information to Bischoff, also on a four-bit latched data line. Each of the three KIMs had its own musical output: Horton's machine featured digitally controlled circuits; Gold's and Bischoff's outputs were both direct digital-to-analog conversion. The three musical outputs were summed together and played to the audience at a goodly volume.

The Individual Programs

Bischoff's Program

John Bischoff's program was originally composed for a performance
with Phil Harmonic at the WORKS Gallery in San Jose, California,
in February 1978. The performance environment was casual, attentive,
and allowing of social interaction, and the music was designed around
the idea of long moments of rest interspersed with computer tones. The
occasional tones generated by the KIM served to punctuate the performance. The periods of rest between tones lasted up to one minute, and,
as Phil Harmonic pointed out, one could even forget that the KIM was
running. As heard in the network, the program played somewhat the
same complementary role but with more emphasis on the ensemble music
properties of the three parts moving in relation to one another.

All the choices in figure 33.2 are based on a continually renewed string
of random numbers. The output waveforms are routed through an 8-bit
DAC and are of a constant amplitude. There is no predetermined sequence
of pitches, as each run-through of the program involves one rest period
followed by one pitch event. There are four possible waveforms: sawtooth,
triangle, and two types of random waveshapes. The random waveshapes
generate particularly striking timbres and noticeable sidebands during
pitch slides. (Since 1978 this program has been modified and developed
extensively. It is currently run simultaneously on two microcomputers,
and is dynamically performed as a piece called *Audio Wave.*)

In April 1978, Horton modified his program so as to accept data
regarding the specific frequencies that Bischoff's computer was putting
out. Bischoff altered his program to enable it to send these data each
time it was ready to produce a tone.

A single line was connected between the two computers to act as both
an interrupt line and a serial data line. Before each tone and before each
rest, an interrupt was sent. This was followed by one bit of data, which
acted as a flag to indicate the upcoming event. In the case of a tone,
a floating-point representation of the frequency was then transmitted,
serially, following the flag bit. On receiving that, Horton's computer
calculated and played pitches that were in justly intoned harmonic intervals to the note it had received. His program jumped back into its independent mode when it received an interrupt followed by a *rest flag.*

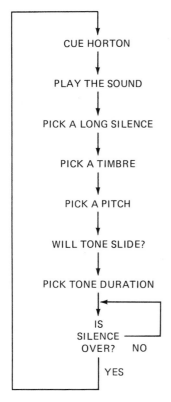

Figure 33.2
The musical flow of Bischoff's program.

Bischoff's computer was also connected, by four parallel lines, to Gold's computer, the information from which was used to influence frequency or rest duration, or both, or was ignored.

Gold's Program

From the equation

$$f(x, y) = z,$$

where x is the latitude and y the longitude of a traveler on a fairly smooth, basically continuous surface, where z is the altitude of that traveler, and where the traveler exhibits a continuous, closed motion about the surface, z can be shown to exhibit periodic-wave-like properties where the fre-

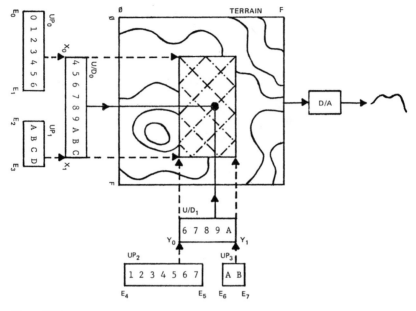

Figure 33.3
A block diagram of Gold's *Terrain Reader*. Each of the four upcounters controls one of
the four endpoints of the two up-down counters. The upcounters are updated at the
beginning of each new note. The up-down counters count at audio rates and specify a
point of the surface or terrain, which is held in one page of memory. The value of the
point specified is sent to the DAC. The tune, or the series of notes that results, is
determined by the eight endpoints of the upcounters, which are set, in this version of the
piece, by the information flowing from Horton's computer.

quency of the wave (z_w) is determined by the length of the traveler's closed
walk and the speed of the walking while the timbre of the wave, including
amplitude, is determined by the hills and valleys of the land. The problem
would become far more complicated if the traveler could move at more
than one speed; however, since in Gold's program the traveler can move
at only one constant speed, frequency is determined by the length of the
walk only. Further, if that traveler moves at a speed such that the periodicity of z_w usually falls between 20 and 20,000 Hz, and given the appropriate transducers, there is music.

The entire program, save a latched output port and a simple DAC,
was contained within the KIM's 1 Kbytes of memory. The surface f was
modeled in a 16 × 16 matrix, occupying page 3 of memory, and behaved

like a land on a torus. The continuous closed motion of the traveler was produced in a Lissajous-like fashion using two software up-down counters (triangular outputs). While the rate of update of the two counters remained constant, the four endpoints (a top and a bottom for each counter) were under program control. The fundamental frequency of z_w is determined not only by the length of the count, but also by the relationship between the lengths of the two up-down counters. Further, since the pattern could be relocated anywhere on the surface f, there was a way of altering the timbre of a given pitch.

The endpoints of the up-down counters were determined by four up-counters, one controlling each of the four endpoints. These were updated at the beginning of each new note or sound. The endpoints of these four upcounters were controlled by data input from Horton's machine. The "tune" was determined by the series of endpoints generated by the up-counters, given that at the beginning of each note they were all incremented by 1 and wrapped around (i.e., rotated) upon reaching maxima. The length of each note, the number of notes in each "song," and the length of silence between songs was determined from information coming from the surface. The durational information was sent to Bischoff's machine (as a four-bit word).

The program, called *Terrain Reader*, was part of a broad piece entitled *Fictional Travels in a Mythical Land*. What the *Terrain Reader* reads *is* the land, the shape of which was determined by the general "myth" from which the entire *Fictional Travels* piece was derived. That is, the program was not intended to be a general-purpose music program but rather to be an integral part of the piece itself.

Horton's Program

Horton's program did two separate but related things, one harmonic and the other melodic. The melodic program was written out of curiosity in order to listen to an aspect of Max Meyer's psychological theory of melody (Meyer 1901). Meyer's empirical investigations led him to conclude that no tone is in a specifically melodic relation with another unless the interval between them can be represented by one of the ratios 2-2, 2-3, 2-5, 3-5, 2-7, 3-7, 2-9, 2-15, 5-7, and 5-9, or else they are both related to a third tone by one (not necessarily the same) of these ratios. Meyer's notation represents classes of ratios (for instance, 2-3 indicates 3/2, 4/3,

3/1, 8/3, etc.), because according to his observations octave transposition does not make any difference in the kind of relationship perceived.

Meyer defines the "complete musical scale" as "the series of all tones which may occur in our melody, however complex this may be." He shows that according to his theory it "is represented by the infinite series of all products of the powers of 2, 3, 5, and 7." However, in his extensive analysis of existing melodies, including those of the highly chromatic music of his contemporaries, he found that 29 tones suffice for a complete description. None of these tones has a factor of $2 > 2^{10}$, of $3 > 3^6$, of $5 > 5^3$, or of $7 > 7^1$. This 29-tone-to-the-octave scale is arranged in figure 33.4 so that, with a little perusal, the melodic relationships are evident.

The program works by randomly selecting a note from the scale and calculating whether or not it and the note already sounding form an interval that falls within one of the ten melodic classes. Phil Harmonic has commented that this system "usually seems right on the edge of breaking into a recognizable tune."

Range, tempo, "rhythmic pattern," and density of rests are determined by simple algorithms whose parameters can be changed while the program is running. This is done by switching subroutines in or out or by changing values in memory. The program is designed so that any constant or parameter that might conceivably be changed is located in page 0 (00–FF hex). A section of the program allows the player to use a hex keyboard and an LED display to inspect any location in page 0 and to enter new data into a buffer. The player can then transfer the contents of the buffer to a memory location at the right musical moment.

Whenever a new note is played, data about the current "rhythmic pattern" is latched into an output port for the use of Gold's program. Audio is obtained by using an LSI device, the 8253 programmable interval timer. This chip contains three 16-bit down counters and a control-word register. Each counter is configured as a square-wave rate generator whose frequency is set by dividing a 1-MHz clock by a number supplied to it by the computer.

Any counter is always at the same pitch as the others but at a slightly different frequency. One is played at the scale frequency, another is offset from the first by a small fixed amount, and the third is offset by a randomly determined amount. The three components of the sound are mixed together to produce precisely controlled flanging.

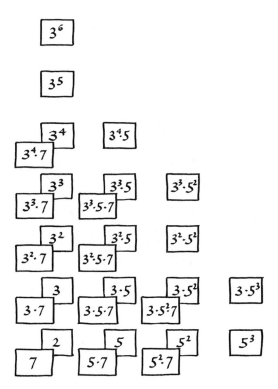

Figure 33.4
Meyer's empirically derived, 29-tone-per-octave scale arranged by fifths vertically, by major thirds horizontally, and by septimal minor sevenths perpendicular to the page (i.e., $3^1 \cdot 5^1$ should be read as $3^1 \cdot 5^1$ lying on the page and as $3^1 \cdot 5^1 \cdot 7^1$ floating just above the page). In order to project these tones into an octave they should be multiplied by some power of 2 so that they fall within the range 512–1,024. Each pair of tones can be seen to form two intervals with each other (i.e., $3^1 \cdot 5^2 \cdot 7^1 / 3^2 \cdot 5^1 \cdot 7^1 = 5/3$, a major sixth, and $3^2 \cdot 5^1 \cdot 7^1 / 3^1 \cdot 5^2 \cdot 7^1 = (2^1) \cdot 3^1/5^1 = 6/5$, a minor third). Only a subset of pairs falls within the class of the ten melodic intervals.

Figure 33.5
The League of Automatic Music Composers in Performance at 80 Langton Street, San
Francisco, California, 15 November 1980. From left: Jim Horton, Tim Perkis, John
Bischoff. (Rich Gold was not a participant in this event.) (Photograph by John Grau.)

Network Music

(The following section was written using a technique very similar to the
process used by the three computers in the *Network Piece* discussed in this
article.)

The event of three composers making music together using ideas and
structures developed independently without thought of future collaboration now seems a natural musical process. This is due in large part to the
work of John Cage.

Because nobody is only an ear, the *sound* of music, bracketed apart
from the projection of socially relevant images and meanings, is, while
often quite interesting, not necessarily the main focus of a composer's
work.

Very high technology is *about* working together in large-scale teams,
e.g. the space program. It should be no different for modern music.

Independent simultaneous activities viewed as one single activity always bring to mind the idea that groups can work wonderfully together without the anxiety of control structures that supposedly ensure success.

Yes! What a pleasure to play and be part of a dynamic musical cybernetic process! To explore catastrophe hypersurfaces in the relative safety and comfort of involvement with one's friends and neighbors!

At each stage in the development of the network the music changed unpredictably. It became clear that it was impossible to tell beforehand where the music was going to come from.

At this stage in the development of the experimental tradition it is thought well to develop a personal, even idiosyncratic, approach to music. To find such an approach is not always easy. The advent of not-very-expensive microsystems can help free the computer musician from the pressure to comform to the mores of highly structured business and academic institutions.

It seems obvious that three composers would write different music for subroutines in an IBM mainframe computer than for micros they personally own in a network. I suppose that if we hooked these routines together and the result was a Bach fugue with perfectly synthesized strings, we'd have to rewrite the programs.

Although the network seemed to have a sound more characteristic of one active musical intelligence, it could be viewed as three people making music and listening to each other continually along the way.

To bring into play the full bandwidth of communication there seems to be no substitute, for mammals at least, than the playing of music live.

For music exhibits the properties of both gyroscope and steering rocket for a society.

For instance, having one's own microcomputer reduces the need for contact with institutions just to do one's music, while at the same time it encourages collaborative work between artists. This latter situation is created by the possibility of everyone on the block owning roughly the same device.

It was John Cage who pioneered an important form of collaborative music: the simultaneous playing of compositions. An extension of that idea is to write "reactive" compositions that can interact with one another as well as with their players. This approach makes possible a collective style of music while allowing each composer the opportunity to invent and play complete designs not necessarily subordinated to other parts or wholes.

There are many ways of handling form other than putting the largest and fewest structures at the top and the smallest and most numerous at the bottom. In this case forms were distributed fairly evenly throughout.

Computers seem to start from such a low level of musical intelligence (in contrast with the impression that synthesizers give immediately) that the potential of modeling musical intelligence using computers appears promising.

However, at present, the philosophies guiding the development of general-purpose software systems and programs can be questioned. For instance, why the great effort to synthesize the sound of the violin and the piano? Why not the koto, the accordian, the Peyote ceremony's rattle? For that matter, how many composers are really committed to the idea that art should imitate nature anyway?

Music has that wonderful ability that when you have three pieces of music working together you still have music.

Though synthesizers always offered the potential of multisynthesizer group music, and there are some nice examples, microcomputers seem to fit the group-music situation even better. One can show up at a rehearsal or a performance with little more than computer in hand. Microcomputers are conceptually both a module and an entire system.

And ideally music should contain within itself all the information most important to a culture. An orchestra especially should have a structure that exhibits the best types of sociopolitical arrangements imaginable.

Though a single computer, micro or macro, is regal in nature, with its hierarchy of registers, a network of them isn't necessarily.

(Live concerts always seem to have a shared feeling between the performers and the audience that makes all the startings and stoppings enchanting.)

"The patterns of control in a system tend to reproduce the organizational chart of the institution that designed the system." Hierarchical design derives from the myth that militaristic kings are better at getting things done. The theory of heterarchical and anarchistic systems design has been underexplored, although experimental musicians have been engaged in the processes for years.

John Cage set up a new minimum, on the potential plane of music, away from the classical music valley but close enough to draw composers away from it. This allowed for the direct modeling of contemporary ideas (if we want to talk about networks, we build a network) and the use of the available technology for sound production.

The inexpensive microcomputer is a decentralizing influence on the way art involving technology is structured in society. This might help to balance the inherently centralist tendency of the arts and music in general.

Since computers are now as portable as other musical instruments, it is easier to think about grouping them into bands and orchestras.

In our band, each computer contained the program of one composer and produced a sound of its own. Furthermore, all three computers played those programs simultaneously and in the same real time. Beyond that, they were interactive in that each affected the next. That is to say, the piece unabashedly manifested all major trends in music composition of the last 5,000 years.

The sound of the piece as a whole is characterized by sudden overlapping sonorities and converging and diverging lines. There are moments of tuned correspondence where the three voices seemed to listen to each other; at other times they appear to be independent. There are also instances of odd grandeur.

When the elements of the network are not connected the music sounds like three completely independent processes, but when they are interconnected the music seems to present a "mindlike" aspect. Why this is so or why we can perceive some but not all activities as the product of an artificial intelligence is not understood.

The nonhierarchical structure of the network encourages multiplicity of viewpoints and allows the separate parts in the system to function in a variety of musical modes. This means that the moment-to-moment form the music takes is the result of the overlapping individual activities of all the parts, with the coordinating influence of the data exchanged between computers.

Since mistaken concepts and "bugs" seem inevitable, and since plans of any complexity usually break down, it is heartening to note the mystery that where several errors intersect they very often make an interesting pattern.

But how do you get three modern composers to work together? Micros, with their simple structures, provide an answer. On the other hand, large computer facilities and large electronic music studios seemed to be an extension of the older romantic idea of the individual composer writing notes in isolation from an audience and other musicians.

The structure of a circular system satisfies the desire for a symmetrical interactive network where the flow of influence emanates evenly from each point in the system.

Because musicians, since time immemorial, have been playing together, music has developed into a wide variety of "naturally occurring" parallel processing systems.

We created an interesting creature and spent an evening, in public, listening to it.

Editor's Note   A recording of the League of Automatic Music Composers is available from Lovely Music/Vital Records, 325 Spring Street, New York, N.Y. 10013: *John Bischoff, Paul DeMarinis, Phil Harmonic, Frankie Mann, Maggi Payne, and "Blue" Jean Tyranny* (record number VR-101-06).

Reference

Meyer, Max. 1901. *Contributions to a Psychological Theory of Music*. Volume 1. University of Missouri.

IV PERCEPTION AND DIGITAL SIGNAL PROCESSING

Overview

JOHN STRAWN

Part IV contains three major articles relating signal processing, psycho-acoustics, and digital synthesis. The design of reverberators for commercial and compositional applications is thorny, involving a high degree of sophistication in signal processing as well as attention to details of architectural acoustics and music perception. M. R. Schroeder's early work on an "all-pass" reverberator dominated the field for over a decade. In article 34 Moorer presents some significant improvements to Schroeder's original design and reviews experience gained in digital reverberation since Schroeder's original work appeared. Moorer's reverberator has been used to good effect in a large number of pieces at Stanford. One of these (*Nekyia*, by D. Gareth Loy) shows the robustness of Moorer's design. As Moorer discusses in some detail, a poorly designed reverberator can produce a metallic and/or ragged-sounding decay. At the end of *Nekyia*, Moorer's reverberator dies out over the space of almost a minute; near the end of this decay the reverberation itself turns into what might appear to be white noise scaled in amplitude.

Computer music has provided a fertile ground for the study of timbre. Timbre research, in turn, has inspired composers to explore this area of sound, which traditionally has been beyond rigorous compositional control. Timbre can even take on a functional significance in composition on the same level as pitch, following the lead of Schönberg's concept of *Klangfarbenmelodie*. This raises the question of transposition and other operations on a given timbral sequence. In article 35 Wessel explores the following question: Starting with a relationship between two timbres A and B, if the composer wishes to move to timbre C, how can a timbre D be specified so that A is to B as C is to D? Wessel discusses a parallelogram model, the validity of which has been confirmed through experiment.

Most of the studies of timbre performed to date have involved experiments based on one-note stimuli. Until recently, technological limitations precluded work with more complex material. However, the point has been reached at which is it reasonable to ask whether studies of timbre using isolated notes run the risk of reductionism. It can be shown that when a given instrumental timbre is placed into a musical context (either a mono-phonic phrase or polyphony) the ability of the ear to detect changes in the timbres of individual notes can be modified significantly. Such changes are not limited to the perceived timbres of individual notes. Higher-level perceptual and cognitive processes can cause the listener to hear a given musical event in one of several ways, depending on the context. The distinction between "timbre" and "note" can even be blurred. In article 36 McAdams and Bregman present a fascinating collection of phenomena that can and do occur in musical contexts. They place these phenomena into perspective by providing information about relevant psychoacoustical research. The fusion phenomenon discussed in this article has spilled over into the area of synthesis techniques, where the addition of a small amount of vibrato can cause sung voices to crystallize out of a set of spectral components that otherwise sound unrelated.

34 About This Reverberation Business

JAMES A. MOORER

When music is performed in a concert hall, a torrent of echoes from the various different surfaces in the room strikes the ear, producing the impression of space. This effect can vary in evoked subjective response from great annoyance or even incomprehensibility, in the case of speech presented in a highly reverberant auditorium, to sheer ecstasy, in the case of late romantic music in the Vienna Grosser Musikvereinsaal. Most music is heard these days in homes, in cars, or in university auditoriums, all of which generally have short reverberation times. For this reason, most recordings of music already have some amount of reverberation added before distribution, either by a natural process (as in the case of recordings made in concert halls) or by artificial processes (plate or spring reverberators). Computer music is an especially fertile ground for artificial reverberation in that it is rarely performed in highly reverberant concert halls. The use of the computer for the simulation of this reverberation also allows the composer to "tailor" the reverberation to the particular aural effect desired—for instance, by allowing each individual sound in the piece to carry an entirely different spatial aspect. In this article I review some of the work that has been done in the production of artificial reverberation by computer and present the fruits of my own labors along this line, both in the attempted simulation of the concert hall environment by computer and in the proliferation of different circuits for the realization of simulated room reverberation.

Historical Review

Although the study of acoustics may have started as early as the sixth century B.C., with Pythagoras's inquiries upon the discovery that halving the length of a string seemed to double its pitch, I will begin with the first published computer simulations of room reverberation (Schroeder 1961, 1962).[1] The two systems proposed by Schroeder are combinations of two unit reverberators, shown in canonical form in figures 34.1 and 34.2. The first one is the all-pass filter, shown in figure 34.1 in the one-multiply form. The second is the comb filter, shown in figure 34.2.[2]

Originally published in *Computer Music Journal* 3(2):13–28, 1979.

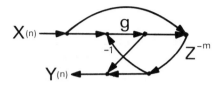

Figure 34.1
One-multiply all-pass. For stability, g must be less than 1.

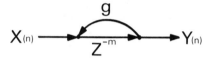

Figure 34.2
Comb filter. For stability, g must be less than 1.

The unit reverberators shown in figures 34.1 and 34.2 have, by themselves, the following transfer functions:

$$T(z) = \frac{g + z^{-m}}{1 + gz^{-m}}, \tag{1}$$

$$T(z) = \frac{z^{-m}}{1 - gz^{-m}}. \tag{2}$$

It is simple to show that the transfer function in equation 1 is indeed that of an all-pass filter, in that the coefficients in the numerator are in reverse order of those in the denominator and so force the zeros to be the reciprocals of the poles. This is sufficient for the filter to be an all-pass. We must remember, however, that the all-pass nature is more a theoretical nature than a perceptual one. We should not assume, simply because the frequency response is absolutely uniform, that the filter is perceptually transparent. In fact, the phase response of the all-pass filter can be quite complex. The all-pass nature only implies that in the long run, with steady-state sounds, the spectral balance will not be changed. This implies nothing of the sort in the short-term, transient regions. In fact, both the all-pass and the comb filter have very definite and distinct "sounds" that are immediately recognizable to the experienced ear.

To use these filters as a reverberation generator, we must combine them in some manner. Schroeder suggested two different combinations,

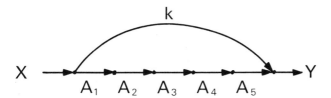

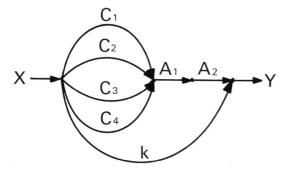

Figure 34.3
Series connection of all-pass networks. The direct signal is added in with a scaling of k.
The functional dependence on z has been dropped in the illustration.

Figure 34.4
Parallel combination of comb filters followed by series combination of all-pass filters. The
direct signal is added in with a scaling of k.

shown in figures 34.3 and 34.4. In these figures, A_i represents an all-pass filter and C_i represents a comb filter. Figure 34.3 thus shows a series connection of all-pass filters with a final addition of some proportion of the original signal. With the all-pass there is also a feedthrough of the original signal scaled by the gain g of the all-pass, so with the circuit of figure 34.3 we will find a total direct signal contribution of k plus the product of the gains of the individual all-passes. In figure 34.4, we see a parallel connection of four comb filters followed by two all-passes, again with a feedforward connection of a portion of the original signal. The idea with both of these is to use the unit reverberators to simulate the effect of wall reflections and the transit time of the wavefront as it passes from one wall to the other. The addition of the direct signal simulates the proximity of the source to the destination. As the destination listener moves away from the sound source, the perceived reverberation remains at about the same amplitude, but the direct sound intensity decreases by the usual reciprocal distance-squared term; thus, there is a distance at which the direct and reverberant sounds are equal in amplitude, such that at larger distances the reverberant sound field dominates. In these circuits, we attempt to simulate the wall reflections with the feedback paths and the transit time between reflections with the delay lengths. We shall see later that this is a somewhat crude way to simulate actual rooms. Both Schroeder and I have proposed refinements (which require corresponding increases in computer time).

In any case, the use of the reverberators in figures 34.3 and 34.4 implies that the various parameters (gains and delay lengths) of all the unit reverberators must be chosen somehow. It is generally thought important to make all the delay lengths mutually prime, in that this reduces the effect of many peaks piling up on the same sample, thus leading to a more dense and uniform decay.

Schroeder (1970) has reported on a way of simulating room reverberation while taking into account the exact geometry of the room. This study involves the simulation of the source as an omnidirectional pulsating circle (the study was done in two dimensions), following the paths of some 300 individual rays that are cast at equally spaced angles about the source. The presumptive linearity of the air and the walls makes it possible to transmit a single ideal impulse, thus obtaining the impulse response of the simulated room. The impulse response can then be convolved with musical sound to produce the sound of that music in that room. Schroeder suggested that a new reverberator could be made that would simulate exactly the first few echoes, then simulate the later echoes by means of a reverberator such as has been shown above. This design is shown in figure 34.5. The first delays and gains are chosen to follow the geometry of the room; then the reverberator $R(z)$ is chosen to simulate the decay of the room reverberation after the density has reached the level where the individual pulses cannot be separated.

Some New Unit Reverberators

In the course of studying the art of making artificial reverberation, I have explored several new unit generators. These include the oscillatory all-pass in figure 34.6 and the oscillatory comb in figure 34.7. In addition, we may also replace the gain terms with filters to produce decays, the lengths of

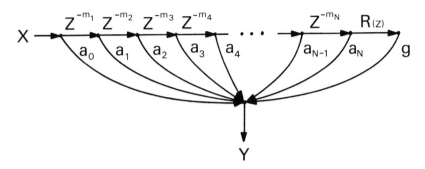

Figure 34.5
Form suggested by Schroeder (1970) for simulation of early echoes by direct summation, using a standard reverberator such as shown in figure 34.3 or 34.4 for the late echoes.

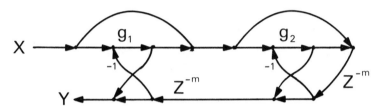

Figure 34.6
An oscillatory all-pass.

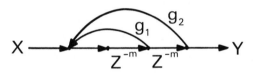

Figure 34.7
An oscillatory comb. The impulse response of the oscillatory units is a train of pulses whose amplitudes correspond to a decaying sinusoid.

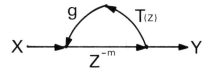

Figure 34.8
A comb filter with another filter inside the loop, identified by its transfer function $T(z)$.

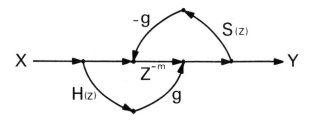

Figure 34.9
An all-pass with filters in the loops identified by their transfer functions: $H(z)$ in the feedforward path and $S(z)$ in the feedback path. For this to remain all-pass, these filters must be complex conjugates of each other.

which depend upon the frequency. For the nonoscillatory case, these are shown in general form in figure 34.9 for the all-pass and in figure 34.8 for the comb. There exist straightforward extensions to the oscillatory cases of comb and all-pass for these configurations also. What must be discussed now is what the general utility of these units is and when they should be used. In fact, the only really useful one is the comb form shown in figure 34.8, but I include a discussion of the others for completeness and to provide additional insight into the problems involved. These reverberators are all modifications of Schroeder's original designs (Schroeder 1961, 1962), and can all be described as various forms of recirculating delays since they all use delays with feedback and sometimes feedforward. These units were known as early as 1966, when Date and Tozuka simulated these units using analog filters and variable-speed multihead tape-recorder delay. Needless to say, the filter realizations were somewhat complex.

The reverberators in figures 34.3 and 34.4 have been used extensively at Stanford University, at IRCAM, and at many other sites around the world in varying configurations. With the all-pass reverberator of figure 34.3, problems have been noticed:

• The decay did not start with a dense sound and die out slowly in an exponential manner. In fact, the higher the order, the longer it took for the density to build up to a pleasing level. This produces the effect of a lag in the reverberation, as if the reverberation followed the sound by some hundreds of milliseconds.

• The smoothness of the decay seemed to be critically dependent on the choice of the parameters involved (the gains and delay lengths of the individual unit reverberators). Just changing one of the delay lengths from its prime-number length to the next larger prime number, which could be a change as small as 2 samples, has been noticed to occasionally make the difference between a smooth-sounding and a ragged-sounding decay.

• The tail of the decay showed an annoying ringing, typically related to the frequencies implied by some of the delays. This produced a somewhat metallic sound that was generally found objectionable.

It would be nice if we could somehow derive these subjective properties directly from the transfer functions of the filters. In this way, we would be able to lift the evaluation of these filters out of the domain of empirical study and to design high-quality reverberators entirely on paper. Unfortunately, there does not seem to be any way to do this at this time. Perception of the quality of a reverberator does not seem to be simply related to the quantities usually derived from transfer functions, such as group delay or root locus.

Although the reverberator of figure 34.4 did not show exactly these same problems, it did show other problems: Any attempt to reverberate very short, impulselike sounds, such as drum strokes, gave distinct patterns of echoes rather than smooth reverberant sounds. The sound was somewhat like flutter echo in rooms with parallel walls. Also, the decay continued to sound metallic, especially with longer reverberation times.

The first attempt to improve this situation was to try the oscillatory networks shown in figures 34.6 and 34.7. The transfer functions of these two unit reverberators are then

$$H(z) = \frac{g_1 + g_2(1 + g_1)z^{-m} + z^{-2m}}{1 + g_2(1 + g_1)z^{-m} + g_1 z^{-2m}} \qquad (3)$$

and

$$H(z) = \frac{z^{-2m}}{1 - g_1 z^{-m} - g_2 z^{-2m}}. \qquad (4)$$

Both these units can be described completely by the decay rate of the exponential envelope and the frequency of the oscillation. The decay rate r is the factor by which the amplitude is diminished every m samples (in the impulse response). The frequency θ is that of the sinusoidal part of the decay. In the case of the oscillatory comb, we can compute the coefficients g_1 and g_2 from the frequency and the decay rate as follows:

$$g_1 = 2r\cos(\theta/m), \tag{5}$$

$$g_2 = -r^2. \tag{6}$$

Negative decay rates can also be used, making each pulse of the impulse response alternate in sign. The condition for stability is that the magnitude of r must be less than 1. We can now design with the oscillatory comb just the way we have with the simple comb, with r taking the logical place of g and with one more parameter to choose. The frequency θ is divided by m because of the delay in m samples between each pulse in the impulse response.

We can likewise compute the coefficients of the oscillatory all-pass from the desired decay rate and frequency as follows:

$$g_1 = r^2, \tag{7}$$

$$g_2 = -2\frac{r}{1+r^2}\cos(\theta/m). \tag{8}$$

In the case of the *all-all-pass reverberator* [or *series-all-pass*—Ed.], such as is shown in figure 34.3, the use of the oscillatory all-pass made little or no perceptible difference, even when all units were so modified. There was a slight difference in the tail end of the decay in that the dominance of one pitch over another kept shifting so that the pitch of one delay was heard for a short while, then the pitch of another delay, and so on.

With the combination *comb-all-pass reverberator* (figure 34.4), the use of oscillatory combs did help the decay a bit in the same way as with the all-all-pass case, but it did not correct the principal problem, which was the response to short, impulselike sounds. The improvement is enough, however, to say that, short of placing a filter in the loop (which will be discussed subsequently), the comb-all-pass reverberator with oscillatory combs was the best-sounding reverberator up to this point.

Figures 34.8 and 34.9 show unit reverberators with filters in the loops.

Figure 34.8 shows a comb type, and figure 34.9 can be made an all-pass if the loop filters $H(z)$ and $S(z)$ are complex conjugates of each other. This implies that their impulse responses are the time reverse of each other. Since the feedforward filter $H(z)$ passes directly into the output, it should be unconditionally stable. This gives the entertaining result that either $H(z)$ and $S(z)$ must be FIR filters or $S(z)$ must be an unstable filter when viewed in isolation. Strangely enough, if the magnitude of $S(z)$ when evaluated on the unit circle is everywhere less than unity the unit reverberator as a whole will be stable. This notwithstanding, it is a somewhat bad idea to put an unstable filter in the loop because the delay of m samples prevents any annihilation of the response of $S(z)$ for a certain time, during which the response of $S(z)$ may well have exceeded the bounds of the computer on which it is being run. For this reason, it is more reasonable to use FIR filters for $H(z)$ and $S(z)$. To make the circuit realizable, we must insert—after the node where the feedforward path breaks from the original signal and before the node where the feedback path adds into the original signal—a delay equal to the total delay of the feedforward filter $H(z)$. Some additional efficiency can be obtained by the use of linear phase filters here.

The purpose of placing a filter in the loop is to simulate the effect of the attenuation of the higher frequencies by the air. This attenuation is due "partly to the effects of viscosity and heat conduction in the gas and partly from the effects of molecular absorption and dispersion in polyatomic gases involving an exchange of translational and vibrational energy between colliding molecules." (This description is lifted, with minor paraphrasing, from Beranek 1954.) Unfortunately, there is much disagreement in the literature as to exactly what these constants are. The reported values vary by as much as a factor of 5 in the decay rate. In any case, the intensity of the sound is generally thought to vary, for any given frequency, according to the formula

$$I(x) = \frac{1}{x^2} I_0 e^{-mx},$$

where I_0 is the intensity at the source, x is the distance from the source in meters, and m is the attenuation constant, which depends on frequency, humidity, pressure, and temperature. Table 34.1 was taken from Kuttruff 1973; Kuttruff claims to have taken it from Harris (1963) and Harris and Tempest (1964). The absorption seems to go up even higher at lower

Table 34.1
Dependence of absorption coefficients on humidity and frequency. Values represent attenuation constant m of air at 20°C and normal atmospheric pressure. Upper tabulation gives m in units of meter^{-1}, lower tabulation in dB per meter.

Relative humidity	Frequency in hertz			
	1,000	2,000	3,000	4,000
40	0.0013	0.0037	0.0069	0.0242
50	0.0013	0.0027	0.0060	0.0207
60	0.0013	0.0027	0.0055	0.0169
70	0.0013	0.0027	0.0050	0.0145
40	0.0056	0.0161	0.0300	0.1051
50	0.0056	0.0117	0.0261	0.0899
60	0.0056	0.0117	0.0239	0.0734
70	0.0056	0.0117	0.0217	0.0630

values of humidity and at higher frequencies. These absorption coefficients may not seem very high, but in a large space such as Boston's Symphony Hall the reverberation time of more than 1.7 sec implies that the sound has traveled more than 600 meters in being reflected between the various walls. This would mean (at 40 percent relative humidity, a typical figure in the Boston area during the concert season) that the 4-kHz signals would have been attenuated upwards of 60 dB more than the 1-kHz signals. This just shows that this process is significant and cannot help but have a substantial effect on the resulting spectrum of the late decay.

Now we can approach the question of modifying the unit reverberators to simulate this facet of sound transmission. We must keep in mind, however, certain perceptual relations in reverberation that have been noticed over the years. During the performance of a passage of music only the first 10–20 dB of the decay of the reverberation is typically audible, because of the changing nature of the music. Only in pauses or at ends of movements will the entire decay of the reverberant sound be audible. It is not clear what this fact implies, except perhaps that we must concentrate equally on the early decay and the late decay for a comprehensive simulation.

Since one problem that arises immediately with the new unit generators is that of the stability of the resulting unit when one inserts a filter into the feedback loop, it is important to take a closer look at the stability conditions for such filters. We can compute the stability of the comb by explicitly carrying along the transfer function of the filter that has been inserted in the loop, then separating it into its magnitude and phase functions as follows:

$$G(z) = \frac{z^{-m}}{1 - gT(z)z^{-m}}. \tag{9}$$

This then has as a magnitude function, evaluated on the unit circle, the following:

$$G(e^{j\omega P_s}) = \frac{1}{1 + g^2|T|^2 - 2g|T|\cos(\theta(\omega) - m\omega P_s)}, \tag{10}$$

where $|T|$ is the magnitude of $T(e^{j\omega P_s})$ and $\theta(\omega)$ is the angle of $T(e^{j\omega P_s})$. ω is the radian frequency around the unit circle, and P_s is the sampling period in seconds. Ignoring for a moment the angular term, we can see that $|T|$ follows g around at each point in the formula. This implies that we can consider separately the effect of the filter on the radii of the roots and the filter's effect on their angular placement. Without the filter, the roots are placed evenly at multiples of the frequency $(1/m)P_s$ and at a uniform radius of the mth root of g. With the filter, the radii have been changed to $g|T|$, which depends on the input frequency ω, and the angular position has been distorted to the following:

$$\omega_i = \frac{2\pi i + \theta(\omega)}{mP_s}, \qquad i = 0, 1, 2, \ldots. \tag{11}$$

For stability, all we need to do is ensure that the radius never reaches 1.0, so the condition for stability becomes

$$g < 1 / \max_{0 \leqslant \omega \leqslant 2\pi} |T|. \tag{12}$$

Thus, knowing the absolute maximum value of $|T|$, we can easily scale g to be unconditionally less than the reciprocal of this. This guarantees stability.

To test this idea, the filter shown in figure 34.10 was incorporated into a reverberator of the form shown in figure 34.4. The loop filter is a simple first-order filter. For stability, the magnitude of g_1 should be less than 1. If we insist that the loop filter be strictly low-pass, then g_1 should be positive, and the maximum of $|T|$ will occur at $\omega = 0$, as is shown by its transfer function

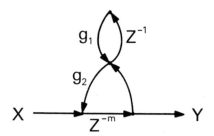

Figure 34.10
One form of the comb with a filter in the loop as shown in figure 34.8. Here we have chosen a simple one-pole filter. If g_1 is positive, it will be a low-pass filter. For stability, the magnitude of $g_2/(1 - g_1)$ must be less than 1. (If g_1 and g_2 are positive, this reduces to the condition that $g_1 + g_2 < 1$.)

$$T(z) = \frac{1}{1 - g_1 z^{-1}},$$ (13)

and its maximum value at $\omega = 0$ will be

$$T(1) = \frac{1}{1 - g_1}.$$ (14)

Thus, if we set g_2 to $g(1 - g_1)$, where g is now between 0 and 1 as before, the resulting filter is unconditionally stable and has the side benefit of giving us a parameter in the familiar 0 to 1 range.

Again, the idea of inserting such a filter in the loop is to simulate the absorption of the high frequencies by the air. The frequency response of such a simple low-pass filter as that shown in figure 34.10 can never conform to the spectral modification necessary to exactly simulate this property, but was chosen as a compromise with efficiency, since it adds only one multiplication. There is a question, however, of how to set the parameter g_1, which controls the rolloff of the filter. To this end, a series of optimizations were performed using the Marquardt algorithm (Marquardt 1963) to match the frequency response of this low-pass filter in a least-magnitude-squared manner to the actual data reported in the literature. The results are summarized in table 34.2. The resulting optimal values of g_1 are shown in figures 34.11–34.13. Unfortunately the values are strongly dependent on sampling frequency and somewhat dependent on humidity, temperature, and pressure. The figures given are for sampling rates of 10 kHz, 25 kHz, and 50 kHz at four different values of humidity.

Table 34.2
Examples of parameters for actual reverberators of the type shown in figure 34.4, using six comb filters with the low-pass filters in the loop, such as shown in figure 34.10, and one standard all-pass following, as shown in figure 34.1. In each of these cases, the all-pass should be set to a 6-msec delay with a gain of 0.7 or so.

	Delay (msec)	25 kHz g_1	50 kHz g_1
COMB 1	50	0.24	0.46
COMB 2	56	0.26	0.48
COMB 3	61	0.28	0.50
COMB 4	68	0.29	0.52
COMB 5	72	0.30	0.53
COMB 6	78	0.32	0.55

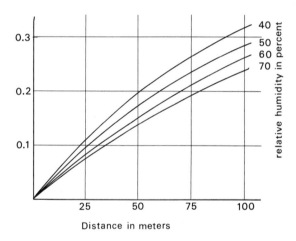

Distance in meters

Figure 34.11
This and the following two figures are graphs of the optimal gain, g_1, of the low-pass filter in the feedback loop of a comb filter as shown in figure 34.10 for simulating as well as possible the natural high-frequency attenuation of the air. The delay length must be converted to meters; then, for the appropriate humidity (higher on the east coast of North America), the value of the coefficient can be read off directly. For intermediate sampling rates or humidities, an interpolation must be done. Since this value is not highly critical, no special care is required in the interpolation. This graph is for a sampling rate of 10 kHz.

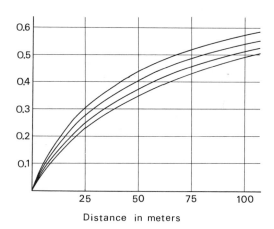

Figure 34.12
As figure 34.11, for sampling rate of 25 kHz.

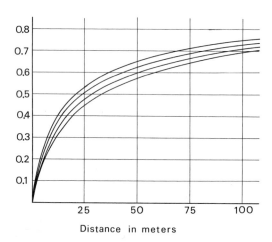

Figure 34.13
As figure 34.11, for sampling rate of 50 kHz.

Again, the weakness of the first-order filter as a low-pass means that these can be considered only very vague approximations of the actual sound absorption of air, so the exact value of this coefficient should not be taken too seriously. These should be considered only guideline values.

Following these guidelines, we can choose a value for the low-pass filter coefficient that represents the attenuation that a specific delay will produce. Whatever delay we choose for this comb, we can convert that delay into meters by multiplying by the speed of sound in air, which is generally taken to be 344.8 meters per second at 22°C and standard pressure of 751 mm of mercury. For the appropriate value of humidity and sampling rate we can read off directly the value of g_1 from figures 34.11–34.13. For intermediate sampling rates, an interpolation can be done. This procedure does in fact produce a reverberation such that the decay of the higher frequencies is somewhat faster than that of the lower frequencies, and the resulting sound is indeed somewhat more realistic. Several other benefits occur immediately, such as the loss of sensitivity to the exact delay length and a more robust treatment of short, impulse-like sounds. The configuration we have been favoring is six comb filters, each with low-pass filters in the loop, and a single all-pass filter.

Beranek (1962) reports that for "good" bass quality a concert hall should have a ratio of the reverberation time at 125 Hz and the middle-frequency reverberation time (average of the 500-Hz and 1,000-Hz reverberation times) somewhat greater than 1. The comb of figure 34.10 exhibits exactly this property for any positive value of g_1. Specifically, for the values of g_1 in figures 34.11–34.13, the ratio is around 1.02, which is designated by Beranek as customary in a "good" concert hall. This point is actually somewhat moot in the computer-music domain. The reason that bass is to be emphasized in concert halls is that string basses are somewhat weak (especially when one considers the ear's lack of sensitivity to lower frequencies) and must be amplified by the room if possible to balance properly with the orchestra.

We have found that in the use of the six-comb reverberator certain distributions of values make more sense than others. For instance, with more than six combs or more than one all-pass, the difference in sound quality is largely unnoticeable. The delays seem to work well when distributed linearly over a ratio of 1:1.5 with all the g_2 terms set to a constant number g times $(1 - g_1)$. The all-pass seems to work well at about a 6-millisecond delay and a gain of 0.7 or so. As a concrete example, table 34.2 shows the values of delays and low-pass filter gains for such a reverberator at 25-kHz sampling rate, and at 50 kHz. Again, the loop gains g_2 should be set to a number g times $(1 - g_1)$ for each comb. Each comb will have a different value of g_1, but all should have the same value for g. This number g determines the overall reverberation time. For example, values around 0.83 seem to give a reverberation time of about 2.0 seconds with these delays.

The distribution of these numbers g for the combs determines the dominance of one comb over another in the decay. If one notices that a particular comb's pitch is dominating the decay, the value of g for that comb can be reduced. With fewer than six combs, one can never arrive at a set of values of g that mask entirely the dominance of a particular comb.

Additionally, the all-pass seems to be a somewhat sensitive subject. Too short a delay for the all-pass gives an annoying "puff-puff" response to background noise. If there are any clicks or pops in the sound being reverberated, a short all-pass will surround each click with a "puff" consisting of its own impulse response, sounding not unlike a very quiet cymbal crash. To eliminate this kind of sensitivity, shorter delays should be avoided. A further complication, however, is that any delay longer than 6 msec seems to produce an audible repetition period; thus, the delay of the all-pass is pretty well limited to 6 msec.

We have tested this formulation with delays as short as 10–15 msec for the combs. The sound is still good, and long reverberation times can still be obtained with such short delays. The subjective impression of the simulated concert hall changes in this case such that, at the shorter delay values, one might well imagine that one were inside a garbage can rather than Symphony Hall. However, the density and "naturalness" are still good, although one might quarrel with the subjective impression of the timbre.

Indeed, this seems to be about as good as one can do with the recirculating-delay system of reverberation. Putting more complicated filters in the loop does not seem to add anything, except that one can then simulate other architectural decisions, such as the compositions of the walls or the absorption of an audience. The low-pass filter in the loop seems to help the response to short, impulsive sounds by smearing out the echoes. Each echo is no longer a discrete impulse but is lengthened by the simulated transmission characteristics of the air itself, so that, even in the early reverberation period with its correspondingly lower density, the discrete echoes seem to be effectively masked. It likewise did not seem to add anything to use the all-pass network with filters in the loop (figure 34.9); thus this unit does not appear useful.

It is not absolutely necessary to set the values of g_1 from the optimal values shown in figures 34.11–34.13. One can just set the values arbitrarily to produce different kinds of sounds that have little or no relation to physical reality. Larger values of g_1 produce a reverberation with a very bright beginning and a very muffled decay. Small values of g_1 tend toward the case where there is no filter in the loop. The use of different values of g_1 for different combs produces no particularly different sound, but can cause dominance of one comb over the others.

Normally, these reverberation schemes will be implemented either on special-purpose digital hardware or on general-purpose computers. In either case, one should pay special attention to the error characteristics of these reverberators, as this is important with all types of filters. Following the formulation of Oppenheim (Oppenheim and Weinstein 1972; Oppenheim and Schafer 1975), we can approximate the error amplification of the reverberator of figure 34.10 as $1/(1 - g)$. Likewise, the signal itself can be amplified by that same factor. For example, if $g = 0.75$, we can expect the quantization error of the input signal to be increased by about a factor of 4. This would imply that we should keep two or more extra low-order bits in the computation so that this error would be truncated at the output. Likewise, we would have to keep two extra high-order bits to ensure that the total dynamic range would not exceed the word length of the machine. This implies that, for instance, to get 12 good bits of output, one would have to do the intermediate computations with 14 to 16 bits, or more. Likewise, to get 16 good bits of output, one would need even more bits internally. This is improved a little when we consider that generally the reverberated signal will be attenuated before it is added into the output, but in any case one cannot afford to ignore the effects of finite register length in the implementation.

Yet another phenomenon that occurs with fixed-point implementation of digital filters is that of limit cycles. Depending on the type of arithmetic used (rounding, truncation, etc.), the output of the filter (reverberator) may not descend exactly to 0 even after the input has vanished. Output values of 1 in the last bit, or sequences of $+1$ and -1, are quite common in fixed-point implementation. This last case of alternating sign is espe-

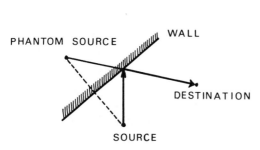

Figure 34.14
Diagram of a sound ray going from a sound source to a destination listener via a wall
reflection. Just as in the case of light, we can think of the reflected sound as originating
from a "phantom" source which is behind the wall, located on a line from the source that
is perpendicular to the wall.

cially annoying, because in twos-complement arithmetic truncating the
low-order bits does not cure the problem. Again, it is not a particularly
disastrous effect, but one should not be surprised when it happens.

But What About Real Rooms?

The only drawback of these systems of recirculating delays is that they
can never correspond to the reflection pattern in a real room. This is
because the reflections in a room, even a square one, do not typically
come in regular sequences separated by equal amounts of time. To see
why this should be so, we have to take a brief look at the science of room
acoustics. The interested and brave reader is referred to one of the many
introductory texts on the subject, such as Beranek 1954 and Kuttruff 1973;
I will only describe a small corner of what is called geometric acoustics.
This entire section is largely tutorial in nature and presents a somewhat
naive view of acoustics that will subsequently be shown to be useless for
simulating the sounds of real rooms. The more advanced or impatient
reader might want to skip to the conclusions in the next section.

   Much as in the study of light, we can keep track of the reflections in a
manner that depends only on the position of the source and not on the
position of the destination listener. To compute the actual impulse
response of the room we must specify the position of the destination
listener, but by using the method of phantom sources we can keep track
of the reflections independent of the position of the listener up until the
last moment. To see how this works, turn to figure 34.14, which illustrates

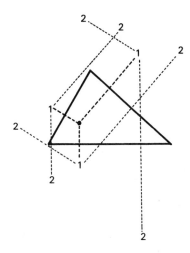

Figure 34.15
First-bounce and second-bounce phantom sources for a triangular room, with the
perpendiculars of construction shown.

a simplified case consisting of one wall, one source, and one destination. In the case shown, direct sound omitted, the wave reflects off the wall and strikes the destination. This is equivalent in effect to the case where the wall does not exist and there is another identical source that spoke at the same time as the true source. This "phantom" source is located on a line connecting the destination point and the reflection point. We may also locate the phantom source by drawing a line from the source that is perpendicular an equal distance on the other side of the wall. Thus, if we now consider a room with three walls, as shown in figure 34.15, we can trace the various phantom sources given only the position of the source and the room geometry. In doing this for a two-dimensional room, we are assuming that the floor and ceiling are infinitely absorbing and thus do not reflect. We see that the phantom sources are represented by their bounce number. Each first-bounce phantom source reflects off the other two walls to make six "second-bounce" sources. Figure 34.16 shows an ensemble of phantom sources up to the fifth bounce.

To get some slight additional insight into how these phantom sources work, we can consider the case of a corner in isolation such as shown in figure 34.17. In this case, all the phantom sources will be located on a circle whose radius is the distance from the source to the vertex. In a

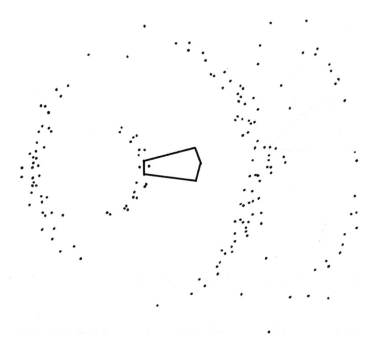

Figure 34.16
Pattern of phantoms up to fifth bounce for a different room. Although there are no parallel walls, the phantom sources show regular patterns.

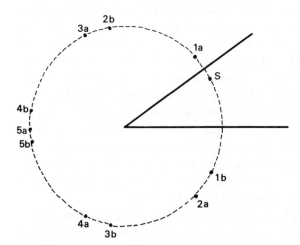

Figure 34.17
The phantom sources in a corner fall in a circle whose center is the vertex of the corner. In this diagram there are five phantoms that start with the first reflection off the upper wall; these are labeled 1a, 2a, 3a, 4a, and 5a. Likewise, there are five phantoms that start with an initial reflection off the bottom wall; these are labeled 1b, 2b, 3b, 4b, and 5b.

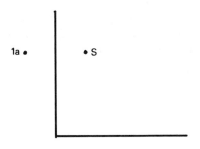

Figure 34.18
A rectangular corner, wherein the phantom sources number only three. One of them is a superposition of the two-bounce sources from each wall.

corner, there will be a finite number of reflections. A phantom source cannot reflect off a wall which it is behind (obviously). Thus, as we follow the reflections in figure 34.17, starting with the reflection off the upper wall, we find phantom sources at positions 1a, 2a, 3a, 4a, and 5a, the number corresponding to the number of bounces. Likewise, starting with the lower wall, we find the phantom sources 1b, 2b, 3b, 4b, and 5b, after which the phantom source is behind the wall it would reflect off of, thus terminating the sequence. Figure 34.18 illustrates the well-known case of a right angle where there are exactly three phantom sources, of which two are first-bounce sources and the third is a second-bounce source that receives contributions from both first-bounce sources. With any angle greater than 90°, any given corner will create only two phantom sources.

We can easily write a computer program to keep track of these phantom sources. To do so, at least for rooms that are convex polygons, we only need keep track of the locations of the phantom sources and be able to determine whether the phantom source is in front of or behind a given wall when we are computing new phantom sources. The normal form for a line in the Euclidian plane is

$$Y\cos(\theta) - X\sin(\theta) = \rho, \qquad (15)$$

where θ is the inclination of the line and ρ is the perpendicular distance from the line to the origin. Given the endpoints of a line as (X_0, Y_0) and (X_1, Y_1), we can determine the equation for the line as follows. Let

$$d = \sqrt{(Y_1 - Y_0)^2 + (X_1 - X_0)^2},$$

$$\sin(\theta) = \frac{Y_1 - Y_0}{d}, \tag{16}$$

$$\cos(\theta) = \frac{X_1 - X_0}{d}, \tag{17}$$

and

$$\rho = Y_0 \cos(\theta) - X_0 \sin(\theta)$$

$$= Y_1 \cos(\theta) - X_1 \sin(\theta)$$

$$\equiv \frac{Y_0 X_1 - X_0 Y_1}{d}. \tag{18}$$

Now that the line is in normal form, we can test any given point (X_t, Y_t) to determine which side of the line it is on. That is,

$$Y_t \cos(\theta) - X_t \sin(\theta) \geqslant \rho$$

means that (X_t, Y_t) is on one side of the line, whereas

$$Y_t \cos(\theta) - X_t \sin(\theta) < \rho$$

means that (X_t, Y_t) is on the other.

With the normal equations for a line, there is always an ambiguity. We can always add π to the angle and negate ρ, which gives a different equation for the same line. This is less an ambiguity than a fortunate extra degree of freedom, for we can use this to orient the wall equations in a standard way such that for any point (X_t, Y_t) that is inside the polygon (again, assuming convexity), with N walls whose equations are determined by θ_i and ρ_i, the following will be true:

$$Y_t \cos(\theta_i) - X_t \sin(\theta_i) > \rho_i, \qquad i = 1, 2, \ldots, N. \tag{19}$$

All we need to do to allow us to use this simple test is to go through the wall equations with any one point (X_d, Y_d) that is known to be inside the polygon and flip any equation for which the above does not hold. For a convex polygon, we can construct such an "internal" point by averaging (separately) the X and Y coordinates of all the vertices. Given the normal equations for the wall lines, we can now decide whether a given source will reflect off a given wall by verifying that the above condition is satisfied for the appropriate value of i.

Continuing in this manner, we can compute the position of the new phantom source by taking the equation of a line going through the originating source (phantom or not) that is perpendicular to the wall. If the equation of the wall is as shown in equation 15, then such a line is given by

$$Y\sin(\theta) + X\cos(\theta) = Y_s\sin(\theta) + X_s\cos(\theta) = \rho_s,$$

where (X_s, Y_s) are the coordinates of the originating source. If we then intersect this with the wall line, we can find the coordinates of the intersection (X_x, Y_x) as follows:

$$X_x = -\rho\sin(\theta) + \rho_s\cos(\theta),$$

$$Y_x = \rho\cos(\theta) + \rho_s\sin(\theta).$$

Thus, the differences in the coordinates are

$$\Delta X = X_x - X_s,$$

$$\Delta Y = Y_x - Y_s$$

and the coordinates of the new phantom source on the other side of the wall are

$$X_n = X_x + \Delta X = -2\rho\sin(\theta) + Y_s\sin(2\theta) + X_s\cos(2\theta),$$

$$Y_n = Y_x + \Delta Y = 2\rho\sin(\theta) - Y_s\cos(2\theta) + X_s\sin(2\theta).$$

Now that we know how to keep track of the sources, we must see how this affects the listener. There are three main sources of attenuation of the sound from a phantom source. The first is that each bounce presumably reduces the amplitude a bit. Wall reflection characteristics are actually very complex, depending on both the frequency and the angle of incidence of the wavefront. We will brush aside this nasty intrusion of nature and for the time being represent the attenuation of each wall by a single number: the reflection coefficient. Another source of attenuation is just the fact that any spherical wave is diminished over some distance at a rate proportional to the reciprocal of the distance it has traveled. (Note that we are working in amplitude here, and not intensity. For intensity, it is the reciprocal of the distance squared.) The last source of attenuation is that of the air itself, discussed in the previous section.

If we ignore for a moment the frequency dependence of everything, it should be quite straightforward to compute the contribution to the listener from each phantom source. We must only assure ourselves that the ray from the phantom source to the listener crosses the wall that produced the phantom source. Otherwise, the listener would not be able to "see" that phantom source. Thus, at each step we can compute the effect at the listener by adding up the contributions of all the phantom sources.

A program was written at IRCAM for examining two-dimensional convex polygonal rooms using this simplified phantom source model. The procedure was to first construct the impulse response of the room and then to convolve this directly with the desired signal to produce the effect of that sound in the ficticious room. When we started making trials with this program, we found that the pattern of echoes quickly got extremely dense, so that after a certain time every sample in the computed impulse response was nonzero. Visually, it greatly resembled white noise in the decay. One of many surprises was that, although the strength of each phantom source diminished exponentially with each bounce, the overall contribution of all the phantom sources did not diminish nearly as rapidly, because the number of phantom sources grows exponentially also, thus helping to counteract the decreasing strength. Thus, even though the strength of a given source was down by 120 dB, it might not be negligible because there happen to be 10,000 of them of roughly that same strength and same distance, thus raising the total contribution to only 40 dB down. This implies that the results of ray simulations of room reverberation (Schroeder 1970) should be carefully examined, since they cannot take this effect into account. With ray simulations, one arrives at a total reverberation time that can be somewhat shorter than those calculated by the phantom-source model described above.

Having written this program, we are now in a position to use it to gain some insight into how reverberation works. The first case we will discuss, however, is the classical example that needs no program: the rectangular room. This is one case where so many of the phantom sources

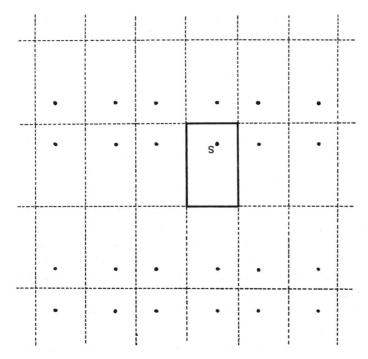

Figure 34.19
Phantom-source patterns for a rectangular room form perfectly regular patterns of rows and columns. Any room shape that tesselates a surface by reflecting across each of its edges will have such a repeating pattern of sources. Such shapes include equilateral triangles and regular hexagons.

fall on top of each other that they form a rectangular array, as is shown in figure 34.19. This is similar to the barbershop mirror phenomenon, where one sees an endless array of phantom sources stretching off to infinity in both directions, some facing forward and some facing backward. The point of discussing this case, however, is to show that no artificial reverberator based on recirculating delays can ever be identical to even this geometrically simple case. This is immediately clear from putting a listener into the room. The contributions from just the row that crosses the room are at distances that are related by the square root of the sum of the squares of the vertical and horizontal distances. If it is granted that the vertical distance increases in regular increments of multiples of the room's height, the resulting distances are not integer multiples of anything. In the limit as the sources get further and further away, the distances become almost equally spaced, implying that, although the early response could never be simulated exactly by recirculating delays, it may be possible to approximate the late response. This also gives us some insight as to why typical artificial reverberation is always easily distinguishable from natural reverberation. The case of the rectangular room is a very special one, and we choose it as an example here just to show that the echo pattern will be different from anything we can produce using any of the usual combinations of recirculating delays.

Following an idea reported by Schroeder (1970), we may directly simulate the early response by a finite impulse response filter, and simulate the late response with a standard reverberator such as is shown in figure 34.5. Here we choose to simulate the first n delays separately with separate gains, then to send the delayed signal into a standard reverberator $R(z)$ with its own gain of g. We must then ask what the design requirements of this reverberator are and how they differ from stand-alone reverberators. Our experience is, sadly enough, that they do not differ from stand-alone reverberators; they need all the usual complexity. Again the most pleasing and natural-sounding system we have tried is the comb–all-pass combination with six comb filters, low-pass in the feedback loops, and one all-pass. It is not necessary, however, to use the very long delays (for instance, 10–15 msec). All the design guides described in previous sections apply for these reverberators, including considerations of total reverberation time and ratio of minimum delay to maximum.

The rationale for simulating just the early echoes is based on the various perceptual phenomena that ensue with the spacing of echoes. With the case of two impulses spaced closely in time, the separation of these two impulses determines a wide range of perceptual effects. Certainly, if the two pulses are more than 30–50 msec apart they will be heard as two separate and distinct pulses. Between this figure and 1 or 2 msec, they will not be heard as distinct pulses, but the timbre of the combination will change (Green 1971). At a separation of less than 1 msec, the timbre of the ensemble does not change any further, but if the ensemble is presented binaurally, localization effects still occur down to a spacing of tens of microseconds. With this in mind, it is clear that if we simulate the discrete echoes down to a limit of 1 msec before switching to a recirculating-delay reverberator we can capture much of the effect of a specific concert hall, except possibly for localization effects.

One might criticize this approach for being two-dimensional. However, the formulas do not get terribly more complex when three-dimensional geometry is used, so one could write the simulation program entirely in three dimensions. The winged-edge polyhedra model of Baumgart (1972, 1974a, 1974b, 1975) seems almost ideally suited to this, because the faces are canonically ordered (which makes inside/outside determination simple) and because local connectedness is represented simply.

Another interesting result is that nonparallel walls do not necessarily imply uniform echo patterns. Figure 34.16, for instance, shows a simulated hall with nonparallel walls that exhibits a highly regular impulse response regardless of source placement. The phantom sources cluster in circles about the source of radii roughly twice the length of the hall. Likewise, the fact that the best-liked concert halls are exactly rectangular in shape (Vienna Grosser Musikvereinsaal, Boston Symphony Hall, Amsterdam Concertgebouw) leads one to wonder whether parallel walls really do have anything to do with the subjective characteristics of the halls. It would seem that the detailed structure and composition of the walls are perceptually more important than the overall shape.

So Now What's Wrong?

I have described several different approaches to simulating concert-hall reverberation. One approach is largely disconnected from physical reality; recirculating delays are used to simulate the echo patterns of concert halls. The other approach is a computer simulation of the actual reflection pattern of a concert hall based upon its geometry.

The only problem with simulating room reverberation by direct geometrical simulation of room acoustics is that it doesn't sound at all like real rooms. This somewhat startling fact means that one or more of our assumptions does not hold water. To follow this up further, we obtained copies of the responses of many natural concert halls which were taken by Schroeder et al. (1974) and Gottlob (1975). Careful examination of these impulse responses made it quite clear that a very important consideration that we have been ignoring is the effect of *diffusion*. This comes about when walls are not in fact flat but are irregular. This is, of course, true in all respected concert halls. Boston's Symphony Hall has fluted side walls and a box well ceiling, each of which furnishes a plethora of new phantom sources. Figure 34.20 shows the doublet response of the old New York Philharmonic Hall before reconstruction, obtained by placing a powerful

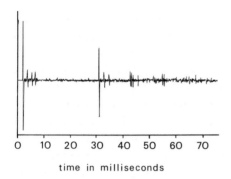

0   10   20   30   40   50   60   70

time in milliseconds

Figure 34.20
Doublet response (echogram) of Philharmonic Hall in New York before reconstruction, collected by D. Gottlob. Even though certain distance reflections are clear, there is a great deal of activity throughout the response.

spark-gap device on stage and an omnidirectional microphone in a particular seat in the audience. We notice immediately that some distinct echoes are visible, but a great confusion soon follows with virtually no silent portions. This confusion is clearly the result of the infinite multiplicity of diffused sources caused by every little irregularity in the hall. The rough surfaces completely wash out all but the first few images, making any use of geometric acoustical modeling, either with phantom sources or ray models, useless for determining the actual sound of a concert hall. These simulations may still be useful for determining reverberation time and other more gross qualities of a given room, but not for the detailed calculation of the impulse response. We can, of course, convolve our music directly with the recorded response (corrected for the spectrum of the spark gap itself) to produce the sound of that concert hall, but even with a 25-kHz sampling rate and a 2.0-sec reverberation time this comes out to 50,000 multiplications and additions per output sample. This is clearly only in the domain of very patient researchers with great quantities of computer time available. Even with fast Fourier transform techniques (Stockham 1966), we consumed about 6 minutes of PDP-10 computer time for every second of sound time thus processed. Is there any way to simulate at least some of these effects without such an obese expenditure of computer time? Indeed, it would appear that a modification of the Schroeder design of figure 34.5 can give somewhat improved results at only a moderate increase in computation time.

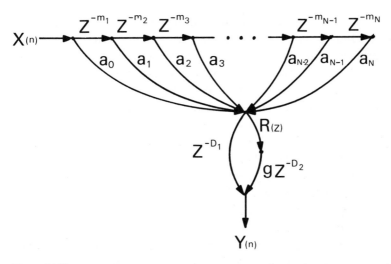

Figure 34.21
Signal-flow diagram of reverberator using an FIR portion to simulate early echoes and an IIR portion, denoted by $R(z)$, to simulate late echoes. Delays D_1 and D_2 are adjusted so that the last pulse from the FIR section corresponds roughly in time to the first pulse to exit from the IIR section. One or the other of D_1 and D_2 will be zero for any given diagram.

Figure 34.21 shows our new formulation. As before, we have N delays, which simulate the first N reflections plus the direct signal. This presumably takes care of the first 40–80 msec of the decay. This entire signal is now forwarded to the reverberator, $R(z)$, which is then added into the early decay with a gain of g. What this provides is that all the density of the first N reflections is then repeated many many times by the recirculating delays of the reverberator. The delays D_1 and D_2 are set such that the first echo from the reverberator coincides with the end of the last echo from the early response. This means that either D_1 or D_2 will be 0, depending on whether the total delay of the early echo is longer or shorter than the shortest delay in the reverberator. Adding this separate discrete early echo makes a substantial difference in the sound. In fact, if the actual room response is used for the early delays, the sound does begin to approach the sound of a real concert hall. Since using the first 80 msec of the actual room impulse response is still well beyond the bounds of sanity, except in certain restricted circumstances for research purposes, we may then ask how simple this early response can be and still give a rich, lifelike sound.

Various ways were tried to synthesize a suitable early response, from using the results of the geometric simulation of a real or fictitious room to choosing random numbers to determine the positions and amplitudes. Many problems quickly became clear. It would seem that one cannot just compute a bunch of impulses at random and expect the result to sound good, in that there is always the possibility that a very strong comb-filter effect will be formed. Even if the positions are chosen to be prime numbers of samples from the origin, the differences among them in time may well be highly composite. This is easy to see when one realizes that the sum or difference of two prime numbers is always divisible by 2. As a result, we cannot give at this time any general method for finding different early responses that will sound good. We have, essentially by trial and error, determined at least two that sound reasonable without too much coloration of the sound. These are given in table 34.3. There is a seven-tap section and a nineteen-tap section. The first tap is the direct signal and can be changed to provide more or less reverberation if desired.

Thus, we are now in a position to give a systematic technique for designing a reasonably good-sounding reverberator, albeit not one that corresponds to any particular concert hall in existence today. The formulation of figure 34.21 with the nineteen-tap model is preferred, although the seven-tap section can be used, or even a no-tap system if computer time is at a premium. The recirculating part, as mentioned before, should consist of six combs in parallel, each with a first-order low-pass filter in the loop. The outputs of the six combs should be summed and forwarded to a single all-pass network with a gain of 0.7 and a delay of about 6 msec. The gains of the low-pass filters in the feedback loops of the combs should be set to the values from figures 34.11–34.13 for the delay used. The delays should be distributed linearly over a ratio of 1:1.5, with the shortest delay about 50 msec. Again, if computer memory is at a premium, this can be reduced to as low as 10 msec without gross degradation. The delay lengths in samples should be set to the closest prime numbers to prevent exactly overlapping pulses, although with higher values of g_1 in the feedback filters the sensitivity to the exact length of the delay becomes negligible. The gains g_2 of each comb should be set to $g(1 - g_1)$, where g now determines the overall reverberation time. Figure 34.22 shows the total reverberation time as a function of g, computed at a sampling rate of 25 kHz.

We originally computed the reverberation time both as twice the time to fall from 5 to 35 dB and as the time to fall from 0 to 60 dB, but these numbers were quite similar (within 10%) at most values of g except very small or very large ones. The reverberation time of this system can be

Table 34.3
Tap times (in seconds) and gains for reasonable-sounding FIR sections for reverberation. Upper tabulation is for 7-tap FIR section; lower tabulation is for 19-tap FIR section (values taken from a highly idealized geometric simulation of Symphony Hall, Boston). Tap number corresponds to subscript of coefficient a_i and delay m_i in figure 34.21.

Tap	Time	Gain
0	0	1.00
1	0.0199	1.02
2	0.0354	0.818
3	0.0389	0.635
4	0.0414	0.719
5	0.0699	0.267
6	0.0796	0.242
0	0	1.00
1	0.0043	0.841
2	0.0215	0.504
3	0.0225	0.491
4	0.0268	0.379
5	0.0270	0.380
6	0.0298	0.346
7	0.0458	0.289
8	0.0485	0.272
9	0.0572	0.192
10	0.0587	0.193
11	0.0595	0.217
12	0.0612	0.181
13	0.0707	0.180
14	0.0708	0.181
15	0.0726	0.176
16	0.0741	0.142
17	0.0753	0.167
18	0.0797	0.134

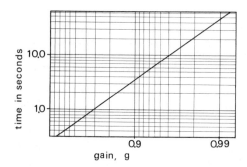

Figure 34.22
Reverberation time of the six-comb, one-all-pass reverberator when the low-pass filter gain g_1 is set according to figures 34.11–34.13 and the delays are set according to table 34.2. In this case, the gain g will determine the reverberation time. This curve can be approximated by the function $0.366/(1 - g)$. Conversely, g can be estimated as $1 - 0.366/T$, where T is the desired reverberation time in seconds.

estimated without use of figure 34.22 as $0.366/(1 - g)$ to an error of about 10%. Likewise, the gain can be computed for a given value of reverberation time as $1 - 0.366/T$, where T is the desired reverberation time in seconds. This will change with the sampling rate, but the deviation should not be too drastic. Likewise, this time will scale directly with the delay lengths, as long as the $1:1.5$ ratio between the shortest comb delay and the longest is maintained.

We made a somewhat striking discovery in simulating natural-sounding impulse responses. While digitizing the impulse responses from concert halls around the world, we kept noticing that the responses in the finest concert halls sounded remarkably similar to white noise with an exponential amplitude envelope. To test this observation, we generated synthetic impulse responses by shaping unit-variance Gaussian pseudorandom sequences with an exponential of the desired length. The direct sound was added by including an impulse at the beginning. The balance between the impulse height and the strength of the decay was determined empirically to be about $12:1$ for a natural sound. We then convolved this synthetic impulse response with a variety of unreverberated musical sources and compared the results with the sounds of actual concert halls. The results were astonishing. Although the synthetic impulse response did not produce a sound that could be identified with a specific concert hall, the sound was clearly a very natural-sounding response. With this method of creating synthetic impulse responses, one can "tailor" the characteristics to one's needs. By selectively filtering the impulse response before convolution, we can get any desired rolloff rates at various frequencies. It was the most natural-sounding of all the techniques we have tried, outside of using the measured impulse response of a concert hall. Stereo can then be produced by simply generating two synthetic impulse-response sequences and calculating the left and right ears separately. This gives perfectly uncorrelated binaural reverberation. Frequency dependence in the decay can easily be introduced by filtering the synthetic impulse response before doing the convolution. Again, the only problem is the enormous amount of computation involved for direct convolution. The fast Fourier transform can help ease the computational burden, but real-time operation is still more than a factor of 10 away for even the fastest commercially available signal processors. The impulse response decays fairly rapidly, such that fewer than 30% of the points need more than twelve bits of precision. Another 30% need between eight and eleven bits, and around 10% can be specified in four bits or less. (This all assumes a 16-bit sample width.)

Conclusions and Suggestions for Further Work

In the course of this work, it became quite clear that all the geometric simulations of concert-hall acoustics that have been done to date result in simulated room reverberation that does not sound at all like real rooms. This is probably due to the effect of diffusion of echos that results from irregularities in the reflecting surfaces, and to the fact that the spectrum of the echo is modified by the reflection in a manner that depends strongly on the angle of incidence.

Despite these facts, we have been able to achieve a good-sounding, smooth artificial reverberation system that, although it does not sound like actual concert halls, does sound good enough to be used everywhere that artificial reverberation is desired and does eliminate some of the problems that plagued earlier reverberation schemes (such as "fluttery" response to short, impulsive sounds and metallic-sounding decay). We also found a much larger number of nonuseful unit generators than useful new unit generators.

Several topics that were revealed in the course of this study would make excellent objectives of future work. These objectives include the following:

● Improve the computer modeling of concert halls by geometry. This would require a leap of insight to figure out a reasonable way of dealing with the effects of diffusion, or even a way of describing the diffusing properties of reflecting surfaces.

• Figure out what gives recirculating-delay reverberators their characteristic "sound." This would be an acoustic/psychoacoustic study in timbre. One would have to vary the physical characteristics of the impulse response and attempt to correlate this with the subjective perception, possibly involving the use of multidimensional scaling or factor analysis to help decompose the perceptual dimensions.

• Make up some new unit reverberators and see what they sound like. Try putting more complex filters in the loop and see if that has any substantial effect.

• Figure out some clever way to do all this with less computer time, possibly using the whatsit transform or the whoosit decomposition.

Acknowledgments

As usual, it would be out of the question to attempt to thank individually all the people and institutions that went into this research. My thanks, as always, go to my dear colleagues at Stanford: J. Chowning, J. Grey, G. Loy, L. Rush, and P. Wood. Thanks to D. Gottlob, who so patiently sat through two harrowing days of digitizing all these impulse responses with us at IRCAM. Thanks also to Jean Derechapt, my co-conspirator and programming aide in this work, who got my imagination going on this subject. Finally, of course, to the Institut de Recherche et Coordination Acoustique/Musique (commonly known as IRCAM) for providing one of the few places in the world where this kind of in-depth research can be done, and to my boss, Gerald Bennett, for letting me heed my notions in plowing through the maze of half-baked ideas.

Notes

1. W. C. Sabine published the first study of room reverberation in 1900; this was reprinted as Sabine 1972.

2. A quick word about the use of signal flow graphs to represent filter structures: In my formulation, X always represents the input to a filter and Y always represents the output. An arc of a graph that is not labeled is a unity gain arc. Sometimes I insert extra nodes for supposed clarity. If two or more arcs come together at a node, they are to be summed. When several arcs leave a node, the same signal is supplied to all of the arcs. An arc can be a gain (a multiply), a delay (denoted by Z, the unit advance operator, raised to a negative power), or another filter (usually represented by a capital letter as a function of z).

References

Baumgart, B. G. 1972. Winged Edge Polyhedron Representation. Memo AIM-179, Stanford University Artificial Intelligence Laboratory.

Baumgart, B. G. 1974a. GEOMED—A Geometric Editor. Memo AIM-232, Stanford University Artificial Intelligence Laboratory.

Baumgart, B. G. 1974b. Geometric Modeling for Computer Vision. Memo AIM-249, Stanford University Artificial Intelligence Laboratory.

Baumgart, B. G. 1975. "A polyhedron representation for computer vision." *AFIPS Conference Proceedings* 44: 589–596.

Beranek, L. L. 1954. *Acoustics*. New York: McGraw-Hill.

Beranek, L. L. 1962. *Music, Acoustics, and Architecture*. New York: Wiley.

Date, H., and Y. Tozuka. 1966. "An artificial reverberator whose amplitude and reverberation time-frequency characteristics can be controlled independently." *Acoustics* 17: 42–47.

Gottlob, D. 1975. Vergleich objektiver akustischer Parameter mit Ergebnissen subjektiver Untersuchungen an Konzertsälen. Ph.D. diss., Georg-August-Universität Göttingen. Translated by M. Barron as Comparison of Objective Acoustic Parameters in Concert Halls with Results of Subjective Experiments, publication LT 1985, Department of the Environment, Building Research Establishment, Garston, Watford, England.

Green, D. M. 1971. "Temporal auditory acuity." *Psychological Review* 78(6): 540–551.

Harris, C. M. 1963. "Absorption of sound in air in the audio-frequency range." *Journal of the Acoustical Society of America* 35:11.

Harris, C. M., and W. Tempest. 1964. "Absorption of sound in air below 1000 cps." *Journal of the Acoustical Society of America* 36:2390.

Kuttruff, H. 1973. *Room Acoustics*. London: Applied Science Publishers.

Marquardt, D. W. 1963. "An algorithm for least-squares estimation of non-linear parameters." *Journal of the Society for Industrial and Applied Control* 11(2):431–441.

Oppenheim, A. V., and C. J. Weinstein. 1972. "Effects of finite register length in digital filtering and the fast Fourier transform." *Proceedings of the IEEE* 60(8):957–976.

Oppenheim, A. V., and R. W. Schafer. 1975. *Digital Signal Processing*. Englewood Cliffs, N.J.: Prentice-Hall.

Sabine, W. C. 1972. "Reverberation." In *Acoustics: Historical and Philosophical Development*, ed. R. B. Lindsay. Stroudsburg, Pa.: Dowden, Hutchinson, and Ross.

Schroeder, M. R. 1961. "Improved quasi-stereophony and colorless artificial reverberation." *Journal of the Acoustical Society of America* 33:1061.

Schroeder, M. R. 1962. "Natural sounding artificial reverberation." *Journal of the Audio Engineering Society* 10(3): 219–223.

Schroeder, M. R. 1970. "Digital simulation of sound transmission in reverberant spaces (part 1)." *Journal of the Acoustical Society of America* 47(2): 424–431.

Schroeder, M. R., D. Gottlob, and K. F. Siebrasse. 1974. "Comparative study of European concert halls." *Journal of the Acoustical Society of America* 56:1195–1201.

Stockham, T. G., Jr. 1966. "High-speed convolution and correlation." *AFIPS Conference Proceedings* 28:229–233.

35 Timbre Space as a Musical Control Structure

DAVID L. WESSEL

Research on musical timbre typically seeks representations of the perceptual structure inherent in a set of sounds that have implications for expressive control over the sounds in composition and performance. With digital analysis-based sound synthesis and with experiments on tone-quality perception, we can obtain representations of sounds that suggest ways to provide low-dimensional control over their perceptually important properties.

In this article I describe a system for taking subjective measures of perceptual contrast between sound objects and inputting the data to some computer programs. The computer programs use multidimensional scaling algorithms to generate geometric representations from the input data. In the timbral spaces that result from the scaling programs the various tones can be represented as points, and a good statistical relationship can be sought between the distances in the space and the contrast judgments between the corresponding tones. The spatial representation is given a psychoacoustical interpretation by relating its dimensions to the acoustical properties of the tones. Controls are then applied directly to these properties in synthesis. The control schemes described are for additive synthesis and allow for the manipulation of the evolving spectral energy distribution and various temporal features of the tones.

Tests of the control schemes have been carried out in musical contexts. Particular emphasis is given here to the construction of melodic lines in which the timbre is manipulated on a note-to-note basis. Implications for the design of human control interfaces and of software for real-time digital sound synthesizers are discussed.

Musical Timbre

Timbre refers to the "color" or quality of sounds, and is typically divorced conceptually from pitch and loudness. Perceptual research on timbre has demonstrated that the spectral energy distribution and the temporal variation in this distribution provide the acoustical determinants of our perception of sound quality. (See Grey 1975 for a thorough review.) With the notable exception of Erickson (1975), music theorists have directed little

Originally published in *Computer Music Journal* 3(2):45–52, 1979.

attention toward the compositional control of timbre. The primary emphasis has been on harmony and counterpoint. The reason for this probably lies in the fact that most acoustical instruments provide for very accurate control over pitch but provide little in the way of compositionally specifiable manipulation of timbre. With the potential of electroacoustic instruments the situation is quite different. Indeed, one can now think in terms of providing accurate specifications for, by way of example, sequences of notes that change timbre one after another.

Synthesis Technology

Digital technology offers powerful, general, and flexible sound synthesizers. A number of such synthesis machines have already been constructed and are producing musical results. Notable examples include the digital synthesis and processing system designed by Samson (1980), now in operation at the Stanford Center for Computer Research in Music and Acoustics, the digital oscillator bank designed and constructed by diGiugno (1976) and the digital synthesizer of Alles and diGiugno (1977), the Alles synthesizer at Bell Labs (Alles 1977; Alles and diGiugno 1977), and the Dartmouth digital synthesizer (Alonso et al. 1976). Some of these devices offer the alluring possibility of a "brute force" additive approach to the synthesis of complex and musically rich time-variant spectra. In this article I concentrate on this form of additive synthesis, because of its generality, and on the accompanying problem of providing direct control over the perceptual properties of the synthesized sounds.

Before beginning a description of a procedure for developing controls that could facilitate the musically expressive manipulation of complex time-variant spectra, we will examine the nature of both the acoustical and perceptual data bases involved. Additive synthesis requires a considerable if not overwhelming amount of explicit information, and we shall explore ways to reduce this quantity of data without sacrificing richness in the sonic result. On the other hand, the data we can obtain about our perceptual experience of timbre have quite a different character from the physical data of acoustics, and so we shall also examine such notions as subjective scales, perceptual dimensions, and structural representations of subjective data. We shall then see the extent to which we can give an account of the subjective experience by examining the relationship between the acoustical and the perceptual data bases. We seek a psychoacoustics of timbre that has implications for timbral control in musical contexts.

Additive Synthesis and Possibilities for Data Reduction

In the additive model for sound synthesis, a tone is represented by the sum of sinusoidal components, each of which has time-varying amplitude and frequency. Moorer (1977) gives an excellent account of the details. To synthesize a sound, one specifies a number of software or hardware sinusoidal oscillators, each with its own amplitude and frequency-control envelopes. Additive synthesis of this form has two important advantages. First, it is general; that is, with a sufficient number of independently controllable oscillators a very large and highly varied class of signals can be generated. At some sacrifice in computational efficiency and with an increase in the quantity of data for specifying the envelopes, one can mimic FM synthesis (Chowning 1973) and other nonlinear techniques (Arfib 1979; Beauchamp 1975; LeBrun 1979; Moorer 1976). Of course, one can produce effects that are not possible with these techniques. Second, one can analyze existing sounds and obtain data that can be used to resynthesize exactly the signal that was analyzed. Moorer (1978) has described the application of the phase vocoder (Portnoff 1976) to the analysis and synthesis of musical sounds. The phase vocoder is an advance over methods like the heterodyne filter (Beauchamp 1969; Moorer 1973) in that the analysis does not have to be pitch-synchronous nor do the waveforms have to contain more or less harmonic components, thus permitting the analysis of tones with pitch variation as well as inharmonic tones like those produced by percussion instruments. The method also guarantees that when the analysis data are not modified the original signal is recovered exactly.

Let us say that we want to synthesize, using data from phase vocoder analysis, a musical-instrument timbre with 25 harmonics. In this case, 25 amplitude and 25 frequency envelopes will be required. Storing these functions in full detail demands considerable memory. If we are using a computer-controlled digital synthesizer like those mentioned at the start of this article, then transfer of the envelopes may exceed the bandwidth of the link between the computer and the synthesizer. Furthermore, if the shapes of the envelope functions are to be modified, the computation time required to rescale every point of the functions may easily exceed the capabilities of real-time manipulation. Clearly, some form of data reduction is required if one wants to work in real time.

A particularly attractive procedure that produces a significant reduction in the quantity of data involved is to approximate curvilinear envelope functions with functions composed of a series of straight line segments, such as those given in Moorer 1977. Such straight-line-segment approximations can be stored in terms of the coordinates of the break points of the function, thus greatly reducing memory demands. Furthermore, the digital synthesizers constructed by Alles, DiGiugno, and Samson provide digital oscillators that include straight-line ramp controls for both amplitude and frequency. In working with these oscillators, one provides as data the starting value for a ramp, its slope, and a terminating value or time that indicates when a new slope is required. The actual generation of the values along the specified line segments is provided within the oscillator itself. In supplying control data from the computer's memory to these synthesizers, the break points of the line-segment approximations can be passed directly from the computer to the synthesizer, thus greatly reducing the data-rate demands on the interface. Finally, the straight-line-segment approximations make possible rapid modification of the function shapes, as only the coordinates of the break points need be modified. But can we get away with such a drastic data reduction? If we approximate curvilinear functions with a small number of connected straight lines, will high audio quality and timbral richness be maintained?

Indications that the straight-line-segment approximations would provide satisfactory results have been obtained for brass tones described in Risset and Mathews 1969 and in Beauchamp 1969. Grey (1975) carried out a carefully controlled perceptual discrimination experiment to determine the extent to which the tones with completely detailed amplitude and frequency functions could be discriminated from those with line-segment approximations consisting of from five to seven segments per envelope. (See also Grey and Moorer 1977.) Grey used 16 different orchestral-instrument tones, and in general he found the discriminations extremely difficult. His findings strongly suggest that it is not necessary to retain the highly complex temporal microstructure of the amplitude and frequency functions in order to preserve timbral quality. It would appear that the line-segment approximations can be made with little harm. Besides the resulting data reduction, an important advantage of such approximations is that the resulting tones have more clearly defined acoustical properties. This will prove especially important when we wish to determine those physical properties that are especially important for perception.

Representation of Timbre Dissimilarities

From a quantitative point of view, data from subjective judgments have a peculiar if not uncertain status (Luce 1972). The notion of a unit of measurement such as the decibel or hertz is difficult if not impossible to establish for subjective scales. We can of course choose units for subjective scales, such as the "sone" and the "mel" (Stevens 1959); however, the so-called unit derived in one experimental context fails to remain fixed in other contexts. In fact, the "sone," the unit for subjective loudness, is not invariant across the two ears of individuals with normal hearing (Levelt et al. 1972). Such units are useful in that they provide a common language for discussing the auditory abilities of a population of listeners, but they cannot justifiably be treated with the algebra of dimensional analysis that underlies measurement in the physical sciences. I think it right to be pessimistic about the possibility of subjective scales being elevated to the same form of measurement as physical measurement, but subjective judgments, if collected over a sufficient number of objects (in this case, sounds), can have a representable structure, and this structure can in turn be related to various acoustical parameters.

Perceptual judgments tend to be relative. With few exceptions, we tend to judge an object in terms of the relationships it has with other objects. Relational judgments are of great interest in music, because music involves patterns composed of a variety of sounds, and the relational structure within and between the patterns is of primary importance. Judgments of the extent of perceptual similarity or dissimilarity between two sounds can be made in a very intuitive fashion. One can say that sound A is more similar to sound B than to sound C without having to name or otherwise identify explicitly the attributes that were involved in the judgment. Research groups at IRCAM, at Michigan State University, and at the Stanford Center for Computer Research in Music and Acoustics have been using perceptual dissimilarity judgments in a variety of musical and other-wise audio-related contexts. One of the general techniques is to represent the perceptual dissimilarities as distances in a spatial configuration. One begins with a set of dissimilarity judgments typically taken for all pairs of sounds that can be formed from the set. This matrix of dissimilarities is then processed by one of a variety of multidimensional scaling programs, such as KYST (Kruskal 1964a, b). The multidimensional scaling programs produce an n-dimensional spatial arrangement of points that represent the various sound objects. The programs operate to maximize a goodness-of-fit function relating the distances between the points to the corresponding dissimilarity ratings between the sounds.

Perhaps at this point it would be best to show how the multidimensional scaling experiments were carried out. At IRCAM we have recently developed a set of programs that greatly facilitate the design, execution, and interpretation of such experiments. In the following example we use the same set of sounds used by Grey (1975) and by Gordon and Grey (1978). This set consists of 16 synthetic orchestral-instrument timbres and a group of eight hybrid-instrument timbres produced by exchanging spectral envelopes between members of the original set. The goal of our experiment will be to provide a representation of these 24 timbres as points in a Euclidian space and an interpretation of this representation in terms of the acoustical properties of the tones.

General Method

The procedure that provides an interpreted representation of the sounds involves the following five steps: selection of materials for study, collection of the dissimilarity judgments, representation of the dissimilarity judgments with spatial and other schemes such as clusters and graphs, psychoacoustical interpretation of the structure, and verification of the interpretation in musical situations.

Selecting the Materials for Study

The Number of Sound Elements A meaningful representation requires a certain minimal number of sound elements in order that the dissimilarities impose a sufficient amount of constraint for fixing accurately the locations of the points in a space. Some of the multidimensional scaling programs, like KYST, operate with only qualitative or "ordinal" constraints on the distances in the space. These algorithms seek arrangements of the points such that the rank order of the interpoint distances in the space matches, in terms of a well-defined goodness-of-fit measure, the rank order of the dissimilarities between the corresponding stimuli. If we begin with interpoint distances from a known configuration of points, the programs provide a very accurate recovery of the positions of the points, even when the distances are subjected to radical monotonic transformations or perturbations due to random error (Shepard 1966). It is hard to set down a precise rule of thumb for determining the minimum number of elements to use. The choice depends on the number of dimensions and the distribution of the points in the space, an issue to which we shall return below. In most psychological research using multidimensional scaling, 10 points have seemed sufficient for two dimensions and 15 for three. In our recent research we have tended to encourage the use of between 20 to 30 points for spaces of two and three dimensions, respectively.

Equalizing the Tones with Respect to Extraneous Parameters If possible the tones should be equalized with respect to the properties that are not to influence the judgments. When studying timbre, the usual procedure is to equalize the pitch, subjective-duration, loudness, and room-information aspects of the tones. On the other hand, if we are studying room information (that is, reverberation structure) we probably want to use a standard source and manipulate only the reverberation parameters. Attention should also be paid to just what is being equalized. If we are equalizing with respect to loudness, for example, and the tones in the set have different spectral shapes and attack rates, then simply matching sound-pressure level (in terms of decibels) will not provide the appropriate equalization. In this case we are without a satisfactory model for the perception of the loudness of complex time-variant spectra (Moorer 1975) and we must resort to empirical matches. Grey (1975) provides a good example of such subjective matching procedures for pitch, duration, and loudness.

Controlling the Range of Variation within the Set The range of variation in the timbres of the sounds will certainly differ from one type of study to another. In some instances we will want to investigate a timbral domain having a broad range of variation (including, perhaps, inharmonic percussion sounds as well as sounds with more or less harmonic components). In other situations, more restrictions are imposed on the range of variation —as in the study to be described below, where we use only sounds derived from standard orchestral instruments played in a conventional manner. For even more refined investigations of timbral nuance one might use a very limited range of sounds.

Once a general range of variation has been determined, some attention must be paid to the homogeneity of variation within the set. Consider the following example. If we choose eight distinctively percussive timbres and eight distinctively nonpercussion timbres but provide no linking elements between the two domains, it is likely that all the subjective dissimilarities that are made for pairs that cut across the two classes of sounds are larger than all the intraclass dissimilarities. In situations like this, some of the multidimensional scaling programs give "degenerate" solutions and the intraclass structure is not fully displayed. Shepard 1974 provides a detailed discussion of this problem and the prospects for its solution. In addition, in such a situation I find that in making the judgments I have a difficult time concentrating on the relatively subtle differences for pairs within a class in the context of the much larger dissimilarities for the pairs spanning the two categories. Unfortunately, since we will deal most often with timbral domains about which we have little knowledge, clear rules for the preliminary selection of the variation in the material are hard to set down. Selection procedures depend ultimately on our specific interests and desires for control.

To facilitate the preliminary screening and selection of the sounds, we have developed an interactive random-access audio playback program on IRCAM's DEC-10 computer. This program is called KEYS and was written by Bennett Smith (Wessel and Smith 1977). One supplies KEYS with a list of the sounds written out as a list of the names of the files in which each of the sound elements is stored. Each sound file in the list is then related to a character that can be typed on the terminal keyboard. The relationships between the characters and the sounds are listed on the computer terminal's CRT display. When a character is typed, the corresponding sound file is played through the digital-to-analog converters and the playing action is indicated by an increase in the brightness of the character-file name entry in the table displayed on the CRT. This program permits rapid auditory comparisons among a large number of different sounds. Currently the limit is 100 files of arbitrary length.

Collecting the Timbre-Dissimilarity Judgments

Though there exist a variety of ways to collect perceptual dissimilarities, we have found simple ratings of the extent of dissimilarity to be the most efficient and least tedious way to make the judgments. At IRCAM we have been using direct estimates of the dissimilarity between two tones.

Our listening judge, using a program written by Bennett Smith called ESQUISSE, sits before a CRT display terminal and an audio system fed by the computer's DACs. The two sounds in a pair are related to the terminal keys m and n; this allows the listener to play the sounds at will. After listening, the judge enters a rating with one of the keys 0 through 9 on the terminal. Immediately after the judgment is entered, the next pair of tones is ready to be played from the keyboard. The sequencing of the judgment trials is random, and all of the $n(n - 1)/2$ pairs are used, where n is the number of sounds under study. After all the pairs have been judged, the random sequence is unscrambled and a matrix of dissimilarities is formed.

The data-collection program includes what we call a "coffee break" feature. This allows the judgment session to be interrupted by either machine failure or human fatigue. The listener can then return to the experiment at a later time and continue from the point in the sequence where the interruption occurred. With this program, one can listen to the sounds rapidly and freely and enter the judgments with ease.

A Two-Dimensional Representation of 24 Orchestral-Instrument Timbres

I served as a judge, using the dissimilarity-data-collection program on a set of 24 orchestral-instrument timbres obtained from John Grey. These sounds were synthesized using line-segment envelopes and were equalized subjectively for pitch, loudness, and duration. A two-dimensional representation of the sounds provided by the KYST program is shown in figure 35.1 along with an interpretation of the dimensions of this space. The vertical axis is related to the spectral energy distribution of the tones, and the horizontal to the nature of the onset transient. The sounds at the top of the plot are bright in character; as one moves toward the bottom the timbres become progressively more mellow. In a number of studies on timbre spaces (Wedin and Goude 1972; Wessel 1973; Grey 1975; Ehresman and Wessel 1978; Gordon and Grey 1978; Wessel and Grey 1978) this dimension related to the spectral energy distribution has appeared. A consistent, quantitative, acoustical interpretation has also been obtained by calculating an excitation pattern for the spectrum provided by Zwicker's model for loudness (Zwicker and Scharf 1965). This transformation on the acoustical spectrum compensates for certain

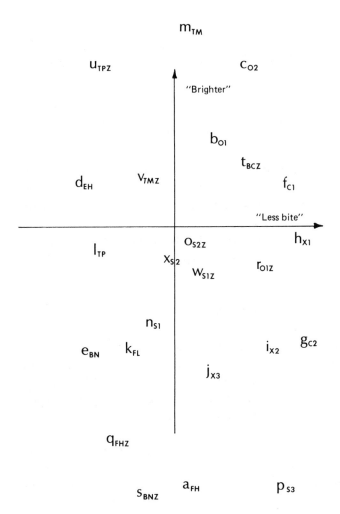

Figure 35.1
Two-dimensional timbre-space representation of 24 instrumentlike sounds obtained from Grey. The space was produced by the KYST multidimensional scaling program from dissimilarity judgments made by Wessel. The upper-case subscripts identify the tones as reported in Grey 1975 and 1977, Grey and Gordon 1978, and Gordon and Grey 1978. Abbreviations for stimulus points: O1, O2 = oboes, FH = French horn, BN = bassoon, C1 = E-flat clarinet, C2 = bass clarinet, FL = flute, X1, X2, X3 = saxophones, TP = trumpet, EH = English horn, S1 = cello played *sul ponticello*, S2 = cello played normally, S3 = cello played muted *sul tasto*, FHZ = modified FH with spectral envelope, BNZ = modified BN with FH spectral envelope, S1Z = modified S1 with S2 spectral envelope, S2Z = modified S2 with S1 spectral envelope, TMZ = modified TM with TP spectral envelope, BCZ = modified C2 with O1 spectral envelope, O1Z = modified O1 with C2 spectral envelope.

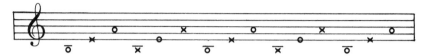

Figure 35.2
Ascending pitch patterns in "three" with two alternating timbres (o and ×). If the timbral difference between adjacent notes is large, then one tends to perceive interleaved descending lines formed by the notes of the same timbral type.

properties of the auditory system, such as critical bands and the asymmetric spread of masking from low to high frequencies. The centroid or mean of this compensated spectral energy distribution is then calculated and correlated with projections of the points on the axis assumed to be related to brightness. In all of the studies these correlations have been very high. The horizontal dimension is related to the quality of the "bite" in the attack.

Predictions about Timbre Patterns

To a large extent, music consists of syntactic patterns. The nature of the relationships among the elements of the patterns is of primary importance in their perception. In the next series of examples I would like to show that when note-to-note timbral changes are organized in terms of the timbre space, predictable perceptual organizations of timbre patterns can be obtained.

First we will examine some auditory effects that we can relate to the dimensions of the space and the distances spanned. In the following patterns the sequence of notes will alternate between two differing timbres, but otherwise the pitch sequence and the rhythmic timing will remain fixed. The pitch sequence is the simple, repeating, three-note ascending line shown in figure 35.2. The alternating timbre sequence is shown by the alternating notes marked respectively with o and ×. When the timbral distance between the adjacent notes is small, the repeating ascending pitch lines dominate our perception. However, when the timbre difference is enlarged along the "spectral energy distribution" axis the perceptual organization of the pattern is radically altered. The line now splits at the wide timbral intervals, and for many listeners two interwoven descending lines are formed, each with its own timbral identity. This type of effect is called *melodic fission* or *auditory stream segregation* in the psychoacoustic literature (Bregman and Campbell 1971; McAdams and Bregman 1979; van Noorden 1975) and is a consequence of the large spectral energy distribution between the alternating timbres.

A different effect is obtained by moving along the dimension we interpreted as relating to the onset characteristics of the sounds. When this is done we obtain a perceptually irregular rhythm, even though the acoustical onset times of the notes are the same. This observation has some important implications for the control of sound in synthesis. When we alter the properties of the attack of the tone, we are also likely to influence the temporal location of the perceived onset of the tone. This lack of accord between physical onset time·and subjective onset time has been observed with speech sounds by Morton et al. (1976). Morton's experimental procedure offers the possibility of determining the relative perceived onset times for a set of notes. The procedure uses a simple *ABAB ... AB* alternating sequence similar to those just described. The listener adjusts the shift in onset for all the *B*s in the sequence until the sequence is perceived as regular, and the temporal displacement in the physical onset is then noted. With the application of such a method to musical timbres and with the employment of a good model of auditory temporal integration of complex time-varying spectra, we may be able to predict more precisely where the perceived onsets of tones with differing spectral evolutions will occur. Nevertheless, both the fine tuning of rhythm in music and psychoacoustic research will benefit greatly if the control software of our synthesis systems allows easy and flexible adjustment of physical onset times in complex musical contexts.

The previous examples have further verified the interpretation of the timbre space and have demonstrated that to some extent the properties of the space retain their validity in richer musical situations. In the next section I hope to demonstrate that other properties of the geometry of the timbre space allow us to make predictions about pattern perception as well.

Timbral Analogies

Composers frequently make transpositions of pitch patterns. It seemed natural to ask if transpositions of timbral sequences work as well. To get some preliminary indications regarding this possibility, David Ehresman and I (Ehresman and Wessel 1978) tested a parallelogram model of

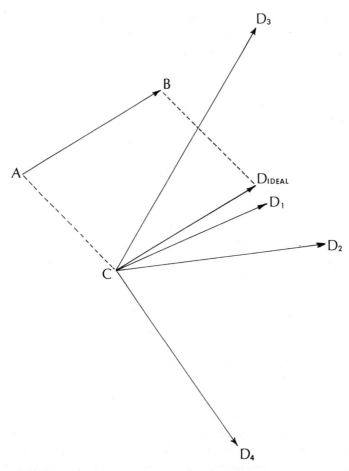

Figure 35.3
Parallelogram model of timbre analogies. $A \to B$ is a given change in timbre; $C \to D$ is a
desired timbral analogy, with C given. D is the ideal solution point. D_1, D_2, D_3, and D_4
are the actual solutions offered to the listeners.

Although these timbre changes have proved to be a consistent irritant to the experimenter pursuing the elusive "missing" fundamental, the implied relationships between timbral "brightness" and pitch "height" may prove interesting to investigate in terms of stream formation and to apply (both experimentally and compositionally) to the construction of melodic sequences. Grey (1977) has delineated a three-dimensional timbre space roughly defined by spectral distribution, spectral fluctuation and synchronicity of higher harmonic transients, and low-amplitude, high-frequency attack transients. How does the "distance" between events in this timbre space affect the temporal coherence and fission boundaries? Do the effects obtained vary differently along these different dimensions associated with timbre? Research by Wessel (1979) and Grey and Gordon (1978) has provided information that would allow the composer to deal with timbre as a compositional parameter. This information also allows a certain degree of prediction of the perceptual relationships between sounds resulting from such timbral variations.

Fusion, Timbre, and Frequency Streaming

The idea of competing perceptual organizations is an exciting one for music composition and theory. Bregman and Pinker (1978) investigated the competition between sequential (frequency) organizations and simultaneous (timbral) organizations in the formation of auditory streams. The stimulus used by Bregman and Pinker was a sine tone alternating with a two-tone complex. In figure 36.22, tones A and B would represent the sequential organization and tones B and C the simultaneous organization. The harmonicity and synchronicity of tones B and C in the complex were varied, as was the frequency separation between the sine tone A and the upper component B of the complex. The rationale for varying these two parameters was as follows: Tones with frequency relationships derived from simple ratios (i.e., those that exhibit "consonance") should tend to fuse more readily than combinations considered dissonant. The evidence for this was very weak in the Bregman-Pinker study, but work currently in progress in Bregman's laboratory strongly suggests that this is indeed the case. The new evidence further suggests that the effect of harmonicity itself is relatively weak and may be overridden by stronger factors, such as frequency contiguity and synchronicity of attack and decay. Tones with synchronous and identically shaped attack and decay

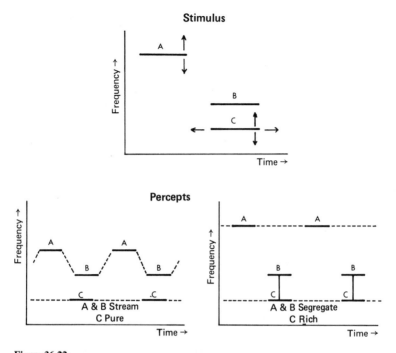

Figure 36.22
The competition between sequential and simultaneous organizations in the formation of
auditory streams is shown here. Tone *B* can belong either to the sequential organization
with tone *A* or to the simultaneous organization with tone *C*, but not to both at the same
time. Bregman and Pinker (1978) varied the frequency separations between tones *A* and *B*
and between tones *B* and *C*, and also varied the relative synchrony of onset of tones *B* and
C. The broken lines in the figure indicate the stream percepts, and the vertical solid lines
represent the fusion of tones *B* and *C*. (See taped illustration 15.)

ramps are more likely to fuse than those with asynchronous or dissimilar
attacks and decays (Bregman and Steiger 1978; Dannenbring and Bregman 1978). This may be a major cue in the parsing out of different instruments playing together in an orchestra, since they have substantially
different attack characteristics and since there is a very low probability
of several players precisely synchronizing their attacks.

In light of this work, one might make the following predictions for the
perception of the stimuli used by Bregman and Pinker: 1) Sequential
streaming is favored by the frequency proximity of tones *A* and *B* (as we
have illustrated in the earlier examples). 2) The simultaneous (or timbral)
fusion of tones *B* and *C* is favored by the synchrony of their attacks.

3) These two effects "compete" for tone B's membership in their respective perceptual organizations. 4) Finally, when tone B is "captured" by tone A, it is removed from the timbral structure and tone C sounds less rich. Thus, it is reasoned that if the two simultaneous sine tones B and C are perceived as belonging to separate streams they should be heard as sine tones, but if they are heard as one stream they should sound like one rich tone.

It is appropriate to introduce the notion of *belongingness* at this point, since we talk of tones belonging to streams and of frequency components and the timbre resulting from their interaction belonging to a perceived tonal event. Belongingness (a term used in the perceptual literature of Gestalt psychology) may be considered as a principle of sensory organization that serves to reconstruct physical "units" into perceptual events by grouping sensory attributes of those events into unified percepts. As Bregman (1978a) points out, "belongingness is a necessary outcome of any process which decomposes mixtures, since any sensory effect must be assigned to some particular source." In this case, when the simultaneous tones B and C are segregated, the timbre resulting from their interaction still exists and can be heard if one listens for it, but it is not perceptually assigned to either of the tones B or C and thus does not affect the perception of them. The nature of a stream is such that its qualities are due to the perceptual features assigned to it.

In taped illustration 15 one can hear a case in which A is close to B in frequency and C is asynchronous with B. Then a case is heard where A is further away from B in frequency and C is synchronous with B. Tones B and C have the same frequencies in both cases. Listen for both the $A-B$ stream and the richness of tone C. The listeners in the Bregman-Pinker study reported perceiving C as richer when B and C were synchronous. This judged richness dropped off with an increase in asynchrony, i.e., as C either preceded or followed B by 29 or 58 msec. As the frequency separation between A and B was increased, C was reportedly perceived as increasingly rich.

The Role of Context in Determining Timbre

These findings indicate that the perceived complexity of a moment of sound is context-dependent. (Grey 1978 is another example of the trend toward viewing timbre as depending on context.) Context may be supplied

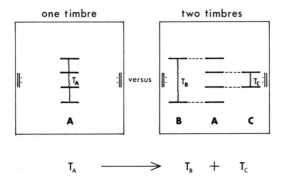

Figure 36.23
The left diagram shows a repeating tone (*A*) consisting of four harmonics. This tone would elicit a certain timbre percept, T_A. In the right diagram, this tone is preceded by tone *B* (consisting of the top and bottom harmonics) and succeeded by tone *C* (consisting of the two inner harmonics). Tone *B* elicits timbre T_B and tone *C* elicits timbre T_C. However, owing to the streaming of tone *A*'s components with those of tones *B* and *C*, timbre T_A disappears completely and is replaced by T_B and T_C. (See taped illustration 16.)

by a number of alternative organizations that compete for membership of elements not yet assigned. Timbre is a perceived property of a stream organization rather than the direct result of a particular waveform, and is thus context-dependent. In other words, two frequency components whose synchronous and harmonic relationships would cause them to fuse under isolated conditions may be perceived as separate sine tones if another organization presents stronger evidence that they belong to separate sequential streams.

A very compelling demonstration of the decomposition of a timbre organization by alternate frequency-streaming organizations is illustrated in figure 36.23. When tone *A* is presented by itself it elicits a timbre, denoted T_A. If this tone is preceded by tone *B* (eliciting timbre T_B) and succeeded by tone *C* (eliciting timbre T_C), one notices that timbre T_A disappears completely and is replaced by timbres T_B and T_C. Here the highest and lowest components of tone *A* are streamed with those of tone *B* and subsequently assume a timbre identical to that of tone *B*. Also, the inner components of tone *A* stream with those of tone *C* and assume a like timbre (taped illustration 16).

An important question concerning the assignment of timbre and pitch to a tonal event arises. Both timbre (Bregman and Pinker 1978) and pitch (Guilford and Nelson 1936) have been found to be context-dependent.

However, each may be determined by different ongoing contextual organizations; thus, they may be considered to be associated perceptual dimensions of a sound but may not be inextricably bound to one another. How relevant to music theory, then, are studies that deal with the perceived pitch and timbre of tones in isolation? This question is not meant to insinuate that sensory and psychophysical experimentation are useless. Far from it. If we think in terms of investigating the experience of music at different levels of processing (figure 36.24), we see how important all these areas of research are in building the whole picture. The raw physical input is modified by the limits of the sense organ, whose output is modified still further by cognitive processes. By studying steady-state (or at least relatively simple) signals, however, we can find the interactions of the sense organs and peripheral processes, such as temporal and spectral resolution, lateral inhibition, and masking, and their limits, which affect the final percept. Beyond these, the central perceptual processes, such as pitch extraction, timbre buildup, coherence, and fission, modify the initial neural result of stimulation of the sensory system. Further interactions in higher brain processes, such as attentional processes, memory and comparison of pitch, timbre and loudness, context extraction, and form and texture integration, sculpt the transduced information into meaningful percepts. It is felt that all of these levels of processing feed into each other in a sort of heterarchical (as opposed to hierarchical) system. The point being made is that in the framework of music, where all these complex interactions are of great importance, the context that is created may be the essential determinant of the musical result of a given sound. One sound can be perceived in a great number of ways, depending on its context.

Melody

This leads us to believe that the fundamental perceptual element in music may be the "melody" rather than the isolated tone, or (in the terminology of auditory perception) that the fundamental structure is the auditory stream. This is not, of course, a new notion, but an empirical approach may allow us to clarify and delimit the concept to the extent that we may predict the perceptual results. That, in the mind of the first author, is the primary concern of the composer. Let us, then, examine melody and its relation to attention.

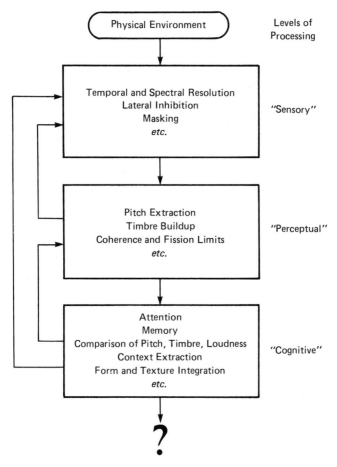

Figure 36.24
This block diagram suggests a possible arrangement of the processing of acoustic information at different interconnected levels of the auditory system.

For our purposes, we can think of melody as a connected and ordered succession of tones (van Noorden 1975). It follows, then, that temporal coherence is necessary for a sequence of tones to be perceived as a whole. On the other hand, a sequence of tones may segregate into two or more separate streams that are individually coherent. In this case, we would perceive several simultaneous melodies rather than one.

If such an operational definition of melody is tenable, how is it that some of the extensions of elements other than pitch for "melodic" material are valid perceptually? For example, when a composer uses timbre as thematic material do we still perceive the sequence as maintaining a temporal continuity? Sometimes coherence is maintained by sensitive performers, and sometimes it can be very difficult to perceive. Of course, we have not included other elements that affect the perception of melody, such as underlying harmonic structure, but we are only attempting to convey the notion that temporal coherence should be considered essential to melody formation. Conversely, one may use the principles of fission to develop rules for creating polyphony and counterpoint in sequences of acoustic events.

Attention and Musical Structure

It has become apparent to the first author that musical structure, as it is perceived in real time, is inextricably bound to attentional processes. A bit of introspection will reveal that there are at least two kinds of attentional processes, which we might call active or willful attention and passive or automatic attention. One might willfully direct one's attention to some object or sequence of events (such as particular events within a piece of music), or some unusual event might attract one's attention unexpectedly (such as the honking horn of an oncoming car). Both kinds of attention may participate in the process of listening to auditory streams. For instance, in figure 36.5, when a sequence of tones lies above the temporal coherence boundary, no amount of active attention can extract the percept of one coherent stream. Here perception is limited by passive attentional processes (van Noorden 1975). This has important consequences for composers who intend to use fast melodic sequences, since it suggests that there are tempi at which the listener may not be able to follow as a melody the sequence the composer has constructed, regardless of the attentional willpower invoked. An example of these effects may be found in the sequences presented at different rates in Charles Dodge's *Earth's Magnetic Fields*. It can be amusing to listen to the same sequence decompose and reintegrate itself during various tempo changes. In a multistream sequence one can relax attentional effort, with the result that attention might alternate randomly among the available streams. Or one might selectively focus attention on any one of them individually and even play them against one another.

Van Noorden reported that the temporal coherence boundary (the boundary below which all tones may belong to one stream) is not affected by previous knowledge of the sequence. He considered it a function of a passive attentional mechanism, given that the listener "wants to hear coherence." However, what happens between the boundaries of temporal coherence and fission depends upon a number of factors, such as context, and seems to be under the influence of attention. Dowling (1973) reported that if listeners knew beforehand which melodies were being interleaved, they could, with a bit of practice, extract the appropriate melody even at very small separations of the ranges traversed by each melody. It is currently assumed that this ability would degenerate at faster tempi. In addition, van Noorden found that at very fast tempi it was virtually impossible to hear sequences within a range of two or three semitones as other than temporally coherent. At very fast tempi (about 12.5 tones per second) the tones of such narrow patterns are not heard as separate members of a sequence but actually merge into a continuously rippling texture, as one can hear in taped illustration 17. There are thus attentional limits in the ability of the auditory system to track a sequence of events. When events occur too quickly in succession, the system uses the various organizational rules discussed in this article to reorganize the events into smaller groups. It may then track events within a particular group if the listener is paying attention to it, but this narrowing of focus causes a loss of information. One result is the inability to make fine temporal order judgments between streams. These organizational mechanisms reflect the tendency of the auditory system to simplify things in the face of excessive complexity. In the example where the fast sequence of tones merges into a continuous "ripple," the auditory system is unable to integrate all the incoming information into a temporal structure and simplifies the situation by interpreting it as texture. (See also Thurlow 1957.) Thus, the auditory system, beyond certain tempi, may interpret the sequence as a single event and assign to it the texture or timbre created by its spectral and temporal characteristics.

An understanding of (or an intuition about) these organizational processes can lead to new dimensions of control over musical structure. For example, one might construct contrapuntal sequences that play across various stream boundaries and through different borderline, regions between temporal coherence and fission. (It may be that composers such as Bach were already using perceptual ambiguity consciously in their work.) Any or all of the relevant musical parameters might be used to accomplish this. Then, an appropriate use of events that vie for or demand the listener's attention can be used by the composer to "sculpt" the attentional processes of the listener. Since some events seem more striking to some persons than to others, this attentional sculpture in time would lead different listeners through different paths of auditory experience. Further, perception is bound to vary from time to time within a single person, so the experience would be different with each listening. A composition of sufficient, controlled complexity might thus be perceptually infinite for a given listener.

Conclusion

An attempt has been made here to point out that composers and music theorists should thoroughly examine the relationship between the "musical" principles they use and espouse and the principles of sensory, perceptual, and cognitive organization that operate in the human auditory system. Many of the principles discussed in this article extend to higher-level perceptual analysis of musical context and structure and may well represent a scientific counterpart to some extant music-theoretical principles. In other cases, though, this group of phenomena suggests perceptual organizations that have little relation to methods currently used to construct or analyze musical structure. To ignore the evidence from the real-life system in developing a theory of music or a musical composition is to take the chance of relegating one's work to the realm of what might be termed "paper music."

Acknowledgments

This article is based on a workshop entitled "The Perceptual Factoring of Acoustic Sequences into Musical Streams" delivered at the 1978 International Computer Music Conference in Evanston, Illinois, and published in the proceedings of the conference. The authors would like to thank Leon van Noorden for his many helpful suggestions and valuable criticisms of the manuscript. Figures 36.5, 36.8, 36.9, 36.10, and 36.20 were redrawn, with permission, from Dr. van Noorden's thesis. The present version of this article was prepared while Mr. McAdams was a Graduate Fellow of the National Science Foundation. Dr. Bregman's research has been supported by grants from the National Research Council of Canada, the Quebec Ministry of Education, and the McGill University Faculty of Graduate Studies and Research. Much of the research used the facilities of the Computer-Based Laboratory of the McGill University Department of Psychology.

Appendix: Description of Taped Illustrations

1. A repeating sequence of three high tones (1,600, 2,000, and 2,500 Hz) is interspersed with three low tones (350, 430, and 550 Hz) used by Bregman and Campbell (1971). (a) At a tempo of 5 tones per second, the sequence is perceived as one stream of alternating high and low tones (figure 36.1a). (b) At a tempo of 10 tones per second, the sequence segregates perceptually into one stream of high tones and one stream of low tones (figure 36.1b).

2. Another repeating six-tone sequence is played at a tempo of 10 tones per second, but the higher triplet is closer in frequency to the lower. Tone F may be perceived as belonging to either the high stream or the low stream, depending on the listener's focus. Tone F cannot belong to both streams at once (figure 36.2).

3. A repeating six-tone sequence starts at a slow tempo. As the tempo is gradually increased, the sequence is progressively decomposed into smaller perceptual streams until it is no longer possible to follow the tonal events, which merge into the percept of timbre or texture (figure 36.3).

4. Using the same initial sequence as in taped illustration 3, the frequency separation between temporally adjacent tones is gradually increased. The same sort of decomposition into smaller streams occurs. The limits in this example are determined not by temporal resolution but by the audible frequency range (figure 36.3).

5. The tones of two familiar melodies are interleaved in the same frequency range. As the frequency range of one melody is shifted away from that of the other, the melodies become recognizable.

6. (a) Tones *A* and *B*, alternating in one frequency range, form a separate stream from tones *X* and *Y*, alternating in another frequency range (figure 36.4). (b) Tones *X* and *Y* are moved into the proximity of the frequencies of tones *A* and *B*, with a subsequent perceptual change. Now tones *A* and *X* stream, as do tones *B* and *Y*. The rhythms of the respective streams change between the two examples.

7. This example demonstrates the streaming potential of a sine wave used for frequency modulation of a sine tone. The progression heard is from a very slow, trackable modulation, through a point where the high and low peaks of the modulated sound segregate, and then to the point where a timbre is perceived. The example then returns to the initial modulation frequency.

8. Two sine waves are modulated exponentially in frequency. One ascends in frequency, the other descends in frequency, and they cross at one point. Most listeners report hearing high and low V-shaped contours rather than the full glissandi.

9. First, gated speech is heard. The message is difficult to discern. However, when the gaps are filled with white noise, the spoken message sounds continuous and a pulsing noise is heard in the background.

10. The same demonstration as in taped illustration 9 is used on musical material. It is difficult to induce the information lost in the gaps until those gaps are filled with white noise.

11. The first part of this example is a repeating four-tone pattern in which all the tones have the same timbre. This represents a pattern usually perceived as temporally coherent. However, when the third harmonic is added to the second and fourth tones of the pattern, thus changing their timbre, two streams of differing timbre may be heard. The frequencies of the fundamentals are not changed (figure 36.14).

12. Two glissandi with identical spectral structures moving in opposite directions are heard separately since none of their spectral components cross in frequency (figure 36.16).

13. Two glissandi with differing spectral structures moving in opposite directions are made to cross each other in frequency. Their differing timbres still allow the listener to segregate them perceptually (figure 36.17).

14. The same timbres used in taped illustration 13 are arranged such that their pitches cross but none of the frequency components cross. They are still heard as separate glissandi (figure 36.18).

15. In the first part of this example (see figure 36.22), tones *A* and *B* are close to each other in frequency while tones *B* and *C* are asynchronous (tone *C* leads tone *B* by 29 msec). Tones *A* and *B* form a sequential stream, and tone *C* is perceived as fairly pure. In the second part, tone *A*'s frequency is separated from that of tone *B* and tones *B* and *C* are synchronous in attack and decay. Tone *A* forms a stream by itself, and tones *B* and *C* fuse into a single, richer percept.

16. First, a repeating four-component tone is heard. Note the timbre of this tone (see figure 36.23). Then this tone *A* (at the same repetition rate) is preceded by a tone *B* consisting of the top and bottom components of tone *A* and is followed by a tone *C* consisting of the two inner components of tone *A*. Two streams are formed, and the components of *A* are split into separate streams with tones *B* and *C*. Accompanying this stream organization is a decomposition of tone *A*'s timbre into the timbres of tones *B* and *C*.

17. In this example a sequence of tones very close to each other in frequency is slowly accelerated in tempo until the percept of one continuous, rippling tone is achieved. Then the tempo is decelerated until the individual tones can be heard once again.

References

Bismarck, G. von. 1974. "Sharpness as an attribute of the timbre of steady sounds." *Acustica* 30: 159–172.

Bregman, A. S. 1978a. "Asking the 'what for' question in auditory perception." In M. Kubovy and J. Pomerantz, eds., *Perceptual Organization*. Hillsdale, N. J.: Erlbaum.

Bregman, A. S. 1978b. "Auditory streaming: Competition among alternative organizations." *Perception and Psychophysics* 23: 391–398.

Bregman, A. S. 1978c. "Auditory streaming is cumulative." *Journal of Experimental Psychology/Human Perception and Performance* 4: 380–387.

Bregman, A. S. 1978d. "The formation of auditory streams." In J. Requin, ed., *Attention and Performance VII*. Hillsdale, N. J.: Erlbaum.

Bregman, A. S., and J. Campbell. 1971. "Primary auditory stream segregation and the perception of order in rapid sequences of tones." *Journal of Experimental Psychology* 89: 244–249.

Bregman, A. S., and G. L. Dannenbring. 1973. "The effect of continuity on auditory stream segregation." *Perception and Psychophysics* 13: 308–312.

Bregman, A. S., and G. L. Dannenbring. 1977. "Auditory continuity and amplitude edges." *Canadian Journal of Psychology* 31: 151–159.

Bregman, A. S., and S. Pinker. 1978. "Auditory streaming and the building of timbre." *Canadian Journal of Psychology* 32: 19–31.

Bregman, A. S., and S. I. Rudnicky. 1975. "Auditory segregation: Stream or streams?" *Journal of Experimental Psychology/Human Perception and Performance* 1:263–267.

Bregman, A. S., and H. Steiger. 1978. Auditory Streaming and Vertical Localization: Interdependence of "What" and "Where" Decisions in Audition. Unpublished manuscript, Department of Psychology, McGill University.

Dannenbring, G. L., and A. S. Bregman. 1976a. "Effect of silence between tones on auditory stream segregation." *Journal of the Acoustical Society of America* 59: 987–989.

Dannenbring, G. L., and A. S. Bregman. 1976b. "Stream segregation and the illusion of overlap." *Journal of Experimental Psychology/Human Perception and Performance* 2:544–555.

Dannenbring, G. L., and A. S. Bregman. 1978. "Streaming vs. fusion of sinusoidal components of complex tones." *Perception and Psychophysics* 24:369–376.

Deutsch, D. 1975. "Two-channel listening to musical scales." *Journal of the Acoustical Society of America* 57:1156–1160.

Dowling, W. J. 1973. "The perception of interleaved melodies." *Cognitive Psychology* 5:322–337.

Grey, J. M. 1977. "Multidimensional perceptual scaling of musical timbres." *Journal of the Acoustical Society of America* 61:1270–1277.

Grey, J. M. 1978. "Timbre discrimination in musical patterns." *Journal of the Acoustical Society of America* 64:467–472.

Grey, J. M., and J. W. Gordon. 1978. "Perceptual effects of spectral modifications on musical timbres." *Journal of the Acoustical Society of America* 63:1493–1500.

Guilford, J. M., and H. M. Nelson. 1936. "Changes in the pitch of tones when melodies are repeated." *Journal of Experimental Psychology* 19:193–202.

Halpern, L. D. 1977. The Effect of Harmonic Ratio Relationships on Auditory Stream Segregation. Undergraduate research report, Department of Psychology, McGill University.

Heise, G. A., and G. A. Miller. 1951. "An experimental study of auditory patterns." *American Journal of Psychology* 64:68–77.

Houtgast, T. 1972. "Psychophysical evidence for lateral inhibition in hearing." *Journal of the Acoustical Society of America* 51:1885–1894.

McAdams, S. E. 1977. The Effect of Tone Quality on Auditory Stream Segregation. Honours thesis, Department of Psychology, McGill University.

Miller, G. A., and G. A. Heise. 1950. "The thrill threshold." *Journal of the Acoustical Society of America* 22:637–638.

Miller, G. A., and J. C. R. Licklider. 1950. "Intelligibility of interrupted speech." *Journal of the Acoustical Society of America* 22:167–173.

Ritsma, R. J. 1962. "Existence region of the tonal residue. Part I." *Journal of the Acoustical Society of America* 34:1224–1229.

Schouten, J. F. 1962. "On the perception of sound and speech: Subjective time analysis." In *Reports* of Fourth International Congress on Acoustics, Copenhagen, vol. 2, pp. 201–203.

Steck, L., and P. Machotka. 1975. "Preference for musical complexity: Effects of context." *Journal of Experimental Psychology/Human Perception and Performance* 104:170–174.

Thurlow, W. R. 1957. "An auditory figure-ground effect." *American Journal of Psychology* 70:653–654.

van Noorden, L. P. A. S. 1975. *Temporal Coherence in the Perception of Tone Sequences.* Eindhoven, Netherlands: Institute of Perception Research.

Verschuure, J. 1978. Auditory Excitation Patterns: The Significance of the Pulsation Threshold Method for the Measurement of Auditory Nonlinearity. Doctoral diss., Erasmus University, Rotterdam.

Warren, R. M., C. J. Obusek, and J. M. Ackroff. 1972. "Auditory induction: Perceptual synthesis of absent sounds." *Science* 176:1149–1151.

Wessel, D. 1979. "Timbre space as a musical control structure." *Computer Music Journal* 3(2):45–52. Article 35 in this volume.

Name Index

Subject Index

Italic page numbers indicate illustrations.

Software (*cont.*)
  graphic input, 537
  hierarchical data structure to represent music, 368
  menu-driven, 199, 380–383, 385–386, 389, 392–393
  orchestration, 384
  parallel processes model, 372
  piano-roll notation, 379
  process-model based, 368
  scope, 393, 395, 397–398
  score-editing, 376–402
  score format, 480–485
  use of high-level languages in, 371
  user interface, 368–369, 372, 376–380, 384, 387, 390–391, 397
Software, sound synthesis, 467–511. *See also* Hardware; Microcode; Microprogramming
  access to low-level hardware, 274
  combined with real-time inputs, 484
  expression evaluation, 370
  incorporating real-time control information, 370
  instrument definition, 238, 483
  interconnection, 486
  I-time code, 238
  note list, 30, 483
  orchestra, 238
  structured programming in note list, 485
  unit generator, defined, 370
  vs. hardware synthesis, 200
Sone, 644
S-100 bus, 202
Sonic Landscape No. 4 (Truax), 81
Sonology, 421
Sound synthesis. *See also* Hardware; Software
  analog, 577–578
  circumventing multiplication in, 192
  digital, 577–578
  hardware vs. software, 200
  hybrid, 194, 577
  of natural sound, 1, 6, 27, 28, 30
  off-line, 194
  on mainframes, 191–192
  real-time, 160
  subtractive, 4
Spectra-Strip, 349
Spectrum evolution matching, 95–98. *See also* Waveshaping
Spectrum, sound, 2. *See also* Timbre
  analysis of, 2, 136. *See also* Fourier transform
  center of gravity, 650, 682

envelope of, 123–124, 126, 645–646, 649, 655, 676
  related to tuning system, 193
  time-varying, 6, 426, 642–643, 651
Speech, 116–124
  formant, 123, 125–126
  mixed voiced, 119
  noise driving function, 121
  pulse train driving function, 121–122
  synthesis of, 3, 125–133, 571, 604
  unvoiced, 119, 121
  vocal tract, 116–124
  voiced, 119, 121
  vowels, 119–120
  whispering, 118
  whistling, 118
Sprechstimme, synthesis of, 114
SSML, 581
SSP, 573
SSSP. *See* Computer music studios
Stanford Applied Engineering (SAE), 361
Stochastic Music Language (SML), 581
Stria (Chowning), 193
Streaming, auditory, 659–664
  coherence, 660, 665, 668–669, 691–692
  continuity effect, 671–672, 674–675
  frequency and tempo effects, 662, 667–669
  loudness effects, 670–676
  pulsation threshold, 672, 675–676
  roll effect, 671–672
  timbre effects, 676–689
String, 409
String instruments, simulated 62–64. *See also names of instruments*
String Quartet No. 4 (Bartók), *446*
Studie II (Stockhausen), 156
Studies for Trumpet & Computer (Morrill), 31
Summation formulas, 3, 318, 642
sview, 400
Symbol, 406
Symbol table, 495
Symphony Hall, Boston, 614, 631
Synclavier, 201, 206, 209, 212, 536–537, 641
SYN4B, 449, 467–490
Syntax, musical, 406–407, 423, 431, 558–561, 564–566, 650
Synthesis. *See* Sound synthesis
Synthesis by instruction, 4, 160–187, 201, 369, 572–573
Synthesis technique (digital), xii, 1, 161. *See also names of techniques*
Synthesizers. *See also* Hardware; Keyboard